VENDETTA

Also by Bryan Burrough

Barbarians at the Gate (with John Helyar)

BRYAN BURROUGH

VENDETTA

AMERICAN EXPRESS AND THE SMEARING OF EDMOND SAFRA

HarperCollins*Publishers*

Photographs follow page 144. Their credits are as follows: page 1: Safra—Karsh/Woodfin Camp; pages 4 and 5: Robinson—Larry Barns/Black Star; Smith and Cohen—Wide World; page 9: Sutherland and Palladino—Max Ramirez/California Lawyer; page 16: Freeman—John S. Abbott.

HarperCollins*Publishers*
77–85 Fulham Palace Road
Hammersmith, London W6 8JB

Published in Great Britain
by HarperCollins*Publishers* 1992
9 8 7 6 5 4 3 2 1

A catalogue record for this book
is available from the British Library

ISBN 0 00 215957 0

Set in New Caledonia

Printed by Haddon Craftsmen Inc., Scranton, PA

To Marla

*A lie can travel
halfway around the world
while the truth is putting
on its shoes.*

—MARK TWAIN

Author's Note

In these pages can be found an array of published allegations that a man named Edmond Safra, the international financier at the heart of the narrative, has been involved in illegal activities ranging from murder-for-hire to, most commonly, drug-money laundering. As far as I've been able to determine, none of these charges have ever been substantiated. Neither Safra nor his banks, including his flagship, the Republic National Bank of New York, one of the twenty-five largest banks in America, have been implicated in or charged with, much less convicted of, any major violation of law. In fact, many of the allegations aired against Safra during a concentrated period of negative publicity in 1988 and 1989 have proven to be false.

What remain are wispy rumors of drug money, arms dealings and covert bank accounts, many of them peddled by Safra's enemies, anti-Semitic fringe groups and the odd conspiracy theorist, which nothing short of a major international law-enforcement investigation could clear him of, if then. To be fair, not all of these rumors can be attributed exclusively to the American Express Company, which went to great lengths to spread the darkest stories about Safra in the late 1980s. As noted in Chapters One and Two, vague suspicions have long clung to the Safra family for any number of reasons, including its unusual mix of businesses, professional jealousy, anti-Semitism and the family's obsession with secrecy. To this day, there are businessmen and journalists who swear Safra must be involved in criminal endeavors; all that's lacking, they acknowledge, is proof.

"There's always been chatter, raw intelligence stuff, about Safra, but nothing concrete," notes Jeff Leen, a *Miami Herald* reporter who has written extensively on money laundering. That chatter can still be overheard in certain quarters of U.S. law enforcement. "There's been tidbits about them from time to time," notes a top money-laundering expert in the U.S. Attorney's Office in Miami. "Some investigators have traced large quantities of seized currency back to Republic of New York. There have been [drug] cases where money has been traced back to bills they issued. But of itself it means nothing, absolutely nothing. I know of nothing that suggests they're dirty."

Much of Edmond Safra's image problem, if it can be called that, can be traced to his family's historical involvement in two businesses that, for many Western observers, have long had shady overtones: Swiss banking and the gold trade. But the real complications have come in recent years with the rise in public awareness of drug money, and the financial crimes known collectively as money laundering.

Money laundering can be defined as the hiding and processing of illicit proceeds, through banks, otherwise legitimate businesses or complicated networks of offshore shell companies, into untraceable investments. Narcotics is a cash business, and the first step of every money-laundering scheme involves disposing of the cash, typically by depositing it into bank accounts. Once into a bank, drug proceeds can be moved electronically to other banks, and it is here, for the international banking system, that money laundering takes on its truly insidious nature. It's easy enough for a bank to refuse large cash deposits that are the telltale sign of drug money. What's far more difficult is recognizing already-laundered money that has moved through dozens of reputable banks, legitimate businesses, and offshore corporations. To truly defeat money launderers, banks must know not only their own customers—by no means an easy task—but their customers' customers, and in many cases their customers' customers' customers. When a bank has thousands of accounts, this checking process becomes a herculean task.

Thus experts say that every major bank in the world probably unknowingly hides some amount of drug-connected money. That supposition was borne out in 1990 when the U.S. government froze $400 million in drug-related deposits at 173 different banks, including the Safra-owned Republic of New York and almost every other major American bank. Republic, along with Citibank, American Express Bank and the now-infamous Bank of Credit and Commerce International, was also among nine major banks forced to disgorge drug-related deposits in one of the largest crackdowns ever, Operation Polar Cap in 1989.

After talking with money-laundering experts in both the public and private sectors, I can find scant evidence that Safra or his banks have been any less vigilant about fighting money laundering than any other major bank. In 1991, in an effort to stem rumors of its involvement in dirty money, Republic officials brought in a respected money-laundering expert named Charles Morley to assess their internal controls. A consultant to large banks and law-enforcement agencies, Morley had previously been an investigator for the U.S. Senate for five years, and before that, a treasury agent for eleven more; he has created training tapes on money laundering for the U.S. Drug Enforcement Administration and Interpol. Morley is adamant about Republic's controls.

"I found their procedures to be far more effective and extensive than any I had ever heard of," he says. "Most banks do as much as the law requires—they do what they have to do—but they don't go any further. The thing that impressed me about Republic was they had gone far beyond what the law requires. The time and effort they have put into [their anti-money-laundering] system may well be unprecedented. I would put it up as a model for the entire banking system."

Other experts say they know of nothing that would implicate Republic in money-laundering activities.° Charles Intriago, editor of the Miami-based *Money Laundering News*, says he's never heard suspicions about Safra or Republic. A spokesman for Senator John Kerry's subcommittee on narcotics and terrorism, which held lengthy hearings on money laundering in 1988, told *New York* magazine: "There was no mention of Republic or Safra in any way in the hearings." A spokesman for the Federal Reserve, which oversees U.S. bank holding companies, says: "We have done no public or private enforcement actions against [Republic]." In 1988, the American ambassador to Italy, reacting to press allegations against Safra in Europe, wrote an official letter stating: "I have asked the Drug Enforcement Administration to check into this matter. They have

°One of Safra's smallest holdings, SafraBank (California) of Encino, California, has been the subject of more than a dozen lawsuits alleging that it promoted and lent critical financial help to commodities dealers who used high-pressure sales tactics to swindle consumers out of $60 million or more in risky precious-metals trades. People involved in the litigation say the suits have spawned at least one grand jury investigating the collapse of a currency broker, in Denver. A SafraBank executive involved in the allegations has reportedly been tied to a money-laundering scheme at a previous job, and lawyers involved in the litigation, while offering no direct evidence, coyly suggest that SafraBank might also somehow be involved in money laundering. In January 1992 SafraBank settled the suits out of court and said it would cease all involvement with the commodities dealers.

advised that there is no adverse information concerning Mr. Safra in their files."

The clearinghouse for tips and intelligence in the U.S. government's war on money laundering is a little-known unit of the Treasury Department called the Financial Crimes Enforcement Network, known as Fincen. Manned by veterans of the Customs and Internal Revenue Service intelligence divisions, Fincen uses computers to track the international flows of drug money and works closely with law-enforcement agencies worldwide. In August 1991 I visited its headquarters in an unassuming office building in Arlington, Virginia, and asked one of its top officials about Safra and Republic. A twenty-five-year veteran of investigating financial crimes, this man wrinkled his brow in thought.

"I don't remember Republic ever having been anything to worry about," he said finally. He shook his head. "It just doesn't ring any warning bells with me." We had been talking for about fifteen minutes when the official suddenly pointed a finger in the air. "Now I remember something," he said. "In recent years, Republic of New York has actually come forward to do positive things with the government." Safra's bank, in fact, has hosted a series of gatherings with law-enforcement agencies to volunteer its help in the fight against money laundering. Those meetings, the official added, had resulted in Republic making some solid suggestions about new ways the government could track dirty money.

"We have had, I think, a very good relationship with Republic," the chief of the DEA's financial operations section, Greg Passic, told a Republic-sponsored money-laundering conference in 1991, "and one of the things that first impressed me in dealing with [its] leadership was their earnest and very legitimate concern that the bank not be made available to money launderers."

Whether it's Edmond Safra or anyone else, proving beyond a doubt that a person or a bank has never broken a law is an impossible chore. I certainly can't do it. Much to Safra's frustration, law-enforcement agencies won't even try. But due to the efforts of lawyers on three continents, Safra has managed to effectively clear his name in specific situations ranging from the Iran-Contra affair to hazy, thirty-five-year-old allegations of narcotics involvement. He has received crucial help from government officials, most notably from the DEA and the office of the Iran-Contra prosecutor, Lawrence Walsh. In fact, at the urging of his lawyers, DEA authorities have come to Safra's aid on several occasions, writing letters to news organizations in Germany and the United States to correct reports in which its documents or spokesmen were wrongly cited as implicating Safra and his banks in money-laundering activities.

Another persuasive endorser of Safra's ethics is the man who was for years his fiercest competitor, the former chairman of American Express International Banking Corporation, Robert F. Smith, who had occasion to inspect Safra's centerpiece bank at the time, Trade Development Bank of Geneva, after it was purchased by American Express in 1983. "I'm sure they weren't" involved in money laundering, Smith told me. "Believe me, we used to investigate it. We made damn sure we knew his depositors. There was no dirty money there." Smith's comments are echoed by American Express Bank's top auditor at the time, Frank Johnson. "Nothing ever swirled around them that I ever heard, as far as money laundering," Johnson says. "I never saw it. I never heard it."

For every reporter or competitor who peddles innuendo about Edmond Safra, there is an old friend or ally who insists he is among the most honest bankers in the business. Theodore Kheel, the prominent Manhattan labor lawyer who served as Republic's chairman for nine years, says he investigated Safra's background thoroughly before joining his operations in 1966. "You bet I checked him out," Kheel recalled. "He's Lebanese, he's swarthy, he's Jewish, you think he's gotta be a wheeler-dealer. He looks like an Arab money-changer. You're prepared to believe the worst about a man like Edmond Safra." Nine years at Republic convinced Kheel of Safra's integrity. "He was so conservative, so worried about his reputation and his image, he would have never got involved in anything criminal," he says. "He is honest to a fault. I have absolutely no doubt about his honesty and integrity, no doubt at all."

Another close friend of Safra's who testifies to his integrity is Elie Wiesel, the noted Holocaust historian and Nobel laureate. "For me, Edmond is like the brother I never had," Wiesel has said. "What has been said [about him] is inconceivable to me. That's not the friend I know....It is impossible that Edmond Safra is a man such as has been described in some newspapers. Edmond Safra is a gentle person. He is always alert to the sufferings of others."

At least some of Safra's problems can be laid to mistaken identity. Republic of New York, a favorite of Wall Street analysts and one of the strongest financial institutions in America, is sometimes confused with the smaller Republic National Bank of Miami, whose president was indicted (and later acquitted) on money-laundering charges in December 1988. On occasion the Safra-owned Republic of New York has been forced to issue statements denying any link to Republic of Miami.

Apparently the mixup has confused some in law enforcement. I once asked a longtime IRS investigator if he knew of any criminal activities at Republic of New York. "Are you kidding?" he told me. "One of the dirtiest banks around." He proceeded to relate a litany of money laundering and other scams Republic had supposedly backed throughout the Caribbean. After a while I stopped and asked him if perhaps he meant Republic of Miami. "Well, yeah," he said. "Gotta be the same bank, right?"

Perhaps one day someone will unearth evidence of serious wrongdoing among the hazy rumors that plague Edmond Safra and his family. To date, no one has. Until they do, he remains an innocent man.

Almost two years after I began reporting the *Wall Street Journal* story that grew into this book, I am the first to acknowledge that there remain unanswered questions about Edmond Safra and the campaign to ruin his reputation. To this day, I have not been granted unfettered access to the inner sanctums of either Safra or American Express, and while representatives of several law-enforcement agencies have been helpful, I cannot claim to be familiar with all the information in the files of the DEA, the FBI, or the CIA on participants in this book. There are those to this day who believe the effort to smear Edmond Safra was some form of CIA plot; if so, no one will be more interested than I to read the book on that conspiracy.

I have done my best to get at the facts, but my efforts have been hindered by any number of people, including a few who, to my dismay, lied repeatedly to me, changing their stories only as I returned to them with new, more damning facts. The most insistent roadblock in my search has been American Express itself, which to this day refuses to discuss the events of this book. Its representatives have stonewalled me at every turn, sought to prevent current and former employees from speaking with me, and threatened me with lawsuits.

Still, I attribute no particular animus to the company as a result of these actions; these days, whether investigating Wall Street criminals or

corporate polluters, every journalist is confronted with intimidation tactics. I finish this book as I started it: with an image of American Express
as a stalwart company, like so many others neither perfect nor rotten at
its core. On many fronts—merchandising, marketing, quality control—
American Express is almost unparalleled among modern corporations.
Its reputation for civic responsibility and philanthropy is well docu-
mented, as are its profits and returns to shareholders. And that is why, to
me, this story remains so compelling: how something so unseemly, so
sordid, could happen at a company with an ethical track record like that
of American Express. Only after almost two years of sometimes frustrating digging do I believe I have begun to understand.

Bryan Burrough
New York City
February 1992

NOTE: Four investigators who have worked undercover—two in private practice, two at the IRS—have asked that their names be changed. The altered
names in the text are: James Delgado, Dan Avanti, Matthew Wolinsky, and Jennifer Taylor.

PART
ONE

1

The French Riviera, August 1988

High above the Riviera it rose, gazing down on the luxurious estates of Cap Ferrat and the twisting byways of the fabled roadway known as the Moyenne Corniche. Far below, from out on the quiet yachts rocking at anchor in the blue waters of the harbor at Villefranche, it must have appeared amid the surrounding forest like some distant palace, a shrouded glen of hidden fortune. La Leopolda the great villa had been named, after the estate's first owner, Leopold II, King of the Belgians, who at the turn of the century swept the peasantry off eighteen surrounding properties to make way for the summer palace he envisioned—and at which, it was whispered in Monte Carlo, he intended to keep his mistress.

On this steamy August evening, as air-conditioned black limousines carrying the *crème* of the Riviera's summer royalty fell into line at the foot of the hill, the King of the Belgians would have felt snugly at home in the grand, laurel-shrouded villa he had never lived to see built. Upon his death in 1909, Leopold's plans for the estate were abandoned, and his successor, King Albert I, donated much of the land and its scattered peasant cottages as a convalescent home for Belgian soldiers wounded during the Great War. Over time Domaine La Leopolda, as it was called, had fallen into disrepair, passing through the hands of several owners until purchased by Mme. la Comtesse Robert de Beauchamp, who paid gardeners to prune the magnificent Chaliapin rose trees and camelias the King had planted, as well as the twelve hundred old olive, orange, lemon, and mandarin trees that blanketed the estate.

Not until a wealthy English architect named Ogden Codman was shown the grounds in 1929 were King Leopold's visions to be given life. The Englishman bought the land and set about building his own great villa, inspired by the palatial Château Borelli in Marseilles and by the works of the nineteenth-century Italian architect Giocondo Albertolli, who designed the magnificent Villa Belgiojoso at Milan. Stone for the portico's monolithic columns was carted in from a quarry at La Turbie, a massive marble mantelpiece was found in a château near Avignon, curtains were woven in Lyon. A great oval dining table of San Domingo mahogany was found, and laurel trees were planted to give the grounds the proper air of nobility. On its completion, La Leopolda was one of the Riviera's grandest estates, complete with orange groves, the finest of rose gardens, flowered terraces, tennis courts, chauffeurs' quarters, and rooms for eleven servants—in the basement, of course.

Now, on a sweltering night half a century later, the Riviera fairly buzzed with anticipation of the goings-on high atop the villa's forested hill. All week, from St. Tropez to Cannes to sleepy Menton on the Italian border, haute society could talk of little else but the extraordinary party La Leopolda's new owners were throwing. It was said that one of the privileged guests, the heiress Isabelle d'Ornano, had instructed her designer to weave a special taffeta dress to complement the mansion's tones of green and ocher. The last-minute preparations had been feverish. Leapfrogging from yacht to yacht, ducking into Cap Ferrat estates, society hairdresser Laurent Gaudefroy could be glimpsed scurrying to ready ladies for the evening's event. And how many beautiful heads there were to coif! The American broadcaster Barbara Walters would be there, as would Amyn Aga Kahn, Betsy Bloomingdale, and a raft of other society stalwarts. Rumors flew that Liza Minnelli and Frank Sinatra were flying in as well.

Down in the harbor, the Niarchos clan readied themselves aboard their massive yacht, the *Atlantis II*, its private helicopter perched regally atop. Nearby the designer Valentino, who had dreamed up so many of the dresses to be worn that evening, had moored his own spanking new yacht, the *TM Blue*, where Mikhail Baryshnikov was said to be staying. The sight of the designer's $20 million ship prompted a round of catty comments from rivals like Karl Lagerfeld. "How can he sell so many dresses?" one was overheard to snipe.

They came at sunset, three hundred in all, pausing at the high gates at the foot of the hill to flash their invitations at Israeli security guards who peered deep into the darkened rear of each limousine. Up the winding drive the chauffeurs brought them, past the gently sloping lawn dotted with clusters of gnarled olive trees, all the way up to the villa's great stone façade, its brooding towers and gables rearing over a long lagoon from which geysers of water burst dozens of feet into the moist twilight.

Stepping from the graveled courtyard into the front vestibule, they plucked up glasses of Dom Perignon before gliding over the marbled frescoes of the grand Italian ballroom and down to gaze on the pool their hosts had enlarged, no doubt to make way for the swarms of grandchildren they so adored. Texas oilman Oscar Wyatt strode by with his wife, Lynn, elegant as always in one of Valentino's black, white, and pink satin ensembles. The Princess Firyal was there, wearing a Chanel taffeta, as were the Gutfreunds, John and Susan, he the powerful chairman of the Wall Street trading colossus Salomon Brothers, she a former Pan Am stewardess in an understated white mousseline Chanel. As the glittering crowd assembled there was a trill when Monaco's Prince Rainier and his daughter Princess Caroline entered.

At the fence lines, French security men brandishing machine guns prowled the gardens and green hillsides and swept the curious off the nearby Corniche. Inside, the guests sipped their champagne and politely *ooh*ed and *aah*ed at the mansion's latest remodeling, especially the second floor so elegantly redone by Mica Ertegun, the wife of the Turkish record mogul Ahmet Ertegun. All told, everyone agreed, it had the makings of a wondrous evening, the kind found only on the Riviera at the height of summer, when the trading floors and cutting rooms and thrones seemed so very far away.

Amid the welcoming murmur and the gentle whoosh of air kisses, talk inevitably turned to the host of the evening. The short, bald financier greeting his guests near the villa's front portal was one of the world's wealthiest men and, no doubt, one of the strangest. They had all heard the stories. The small blue gemstones he carried to ward off the evil eye. The fear of curses. The superstition about the number five; his New York limousine, they said, bore the license number EJS 555. Far more fascinating to the sprinkling of Wall Streeters in the crowd was their host's secretive banking empire, which for years had generated tremendous profits in the most unorthodox ways, a performance few could fathom and even fewer could duplicate.

His name was Edmond J. Safra, and he was a Middle Eastern Jew, what they called a Sephardi, and in some respects that was all you needed to know. For decades, whether doing business in his native Lebanon, his adopted home of Brazil, his headquarters in Switzerland, or at the site of his newest challenges, the United States, Safra had surrounded himself with clannish, publicity-shy Sephardim who had little use for outsiders save for their millions of dollars in deposits. They were devout men from the Levant whose fathers and grandfathers had made their fortunes financing the camel caravans that crisscrossed the Fertile Crescent. Though they now did business all over the world, only grudgingly had Safra and his brethren, many of whom he had known since childhood, opened themselves to modern ways. More than one competitor remarked that Safra's people would feel more at home in the 1880s than the 1980s.

All of which only heightened the suspicion that always seemed to trail Safra and his banks, rumors often born of ignorance and bigotry and fanned by jealousy. The Swiss had whispered about the Safras when they first came to Geneva in the 1950s; to this day, though a pillar of the Brazilian economy, Banco Safra remained in some sense an outsider, known in winking asides as Banco Judeo, the Jewish bank. Much of it, Safra and his kinsmen knew, was simply anti-Semitism, and if it forced them to close ranks and deal more with their old friends and relatives, so be it. They had survived insults and pogroms and wars and had proven time and again they could fend for themselves.

As he stood in the foyer greeting his guests, Safra himself seemed older than his years. He was fifty-five now. In conversation his quiet voice channeled effortlessly from Arabic to French to Portuguese to English, the last spoken with a distinct Middle Eastern lilt. His slight frame was topped by a large, bald head, thrust forward and ringed with a halo of white and steel-gray hair, the eyes placid and heavy-lidded. His movements were achingly slow and smooth, almost tortoise-like, the sliding steps the walk of a postsurgical patient making a first, painful trip down the corridor. Only when he smiled his wide immigrant's smile was Safra transformed, the great pelican's throat trembling, the face a symphony of merry wrinkles, dimples and rosy cheeks. In neither guise, though, was there any sign of the visionary genius nor the lightning-fast mind his more fawning admirers saw in him. Snatch away the tuxedo and Edmond Safra could have been a greengrocer.

Socializing, at least outside Sephardic circles, had never come easily for him. The Western press called him reclusive, though it was more accurate to say he was most comfortable with his own kind. His social incarnation was largely a creation of his wife, Lily, a wealthy Brazilian widow who loved the finer things and who made sure her husband got them. Lily, as usual, had overseen the evening's every detail, down to the cotton tablecloths the servants had made by hand. "Chérie, what is happening?" Safra had asked a week before. "Darling," his wife replied, "you're going to a party."

Under Lily's guidance the Safras had cut a vigorous social profile in recent years, attending balls and benefits in Paris, London, and New York, though Safra, with American tax laws in mind, was always mindful not to spend too much time in the United States. No less a social arbiter than John Fairchild, publisher of haute society's best-read publications, *W* and *Women's Wear Daily*, had trumpeted what he called "the Safras' meteoric rise to social power. They have taken the Riviera, Southampton, New York, the Metropolitan Opera, Geneva—all in a space of five years. What's next?"

What was next, indeed. Tonight, after all, was a night for Safra and his family to celebrate a rebirth of sorts, a victory over men he thought had been his friends. Misjudging them had cost him one of his children, he sometimes said, and the fight to break free, to start over once more, had consumed him—had consumed them all—for so long now. Could it really have been five years? Five years of pure, unadulterated grief. Still, as he circulated among the sundry princes and billionaires, Safra seemed genuinely relaxed. For the first time in months, maybe years, he seemed more or less at peace. Finally the long nightmare of American Express seemed over.

Everyone, including the man standing beside him in the receiving line, his handsome, English-educated brother Joseph, who ran the family's Brazilian banking operations, had warned him against selling one of his beloved banks—one of his *children*—to a vast, impersonal conglomerate like American Express. But at the time, it had seemed the right thing to do. The American company's chairman, the well-mannered southerner Jim Robinson, had seemed like a man he could trust. But then came the lies, the broken promises. The corporate marriage had lasted less than two years, and the divorce had fast grown bitter. The charges, the countercharges; Safra had grown sick of it all. Eventually things had gotten personal. Edmond Safra was a man, it was said, who could curse in eleven languages, and no doubt he had tried all those and more in his denunciations of the man who headed American Express. To hear Safra talk, aides would have thought Robinson's first name was "That-son-of-a-bitch Jim."

Severing his ties with American Express, his centerpiece Swiss bank abandoned to a corporation he had grown to loathe, Safra had promised to stay out of Swiss banking for three years, and he had, though it hadn't stopped the sniping with American Express from mushrooming into a full-blown feud. Jim Robinson's men, he knew, were convinced that Safra's people had been secretly stealing back their old clients and depositors for months. It had just gotten nastier and nastier; they had even taken him to court.

Now, Safra hoped, the worst was over. After three long years he had finally returned to the world of Swiss banking that spring, reopening the doors of his squat green-glass headquarters on the shores of Lake Geneva for hundreds of millions of dollars in new deposits. The skirmishing with American Express continued, of course, but now at least it was all aboveboard, a clear, clean fight for deposits, the type of intercontinental rumble any banker worth his salt would relish. In a way, all the glittering people whirling beneath La Leopolda's walls that evening—there was Felix Rohatyn, the American investment banker, and Alfred Taubman, the Detroit shopping mall king—were weapons in Safra's fight. All the hobnobbing, all the power circles milling about the pool, the food, the music, the tulips airlifted in from Holland—they were Safra's way of showing he was back on the scene, safe and solid as ever, ready to take on deposits as never before.

As dinner approached, the guests crowded beneath a tent blanketing the rear terrace, dominated by a giant painted canvas draped over the villa's entire rear façade to make Leopolda resemble an ancient Pompeiian temple. While Safra held court with Prince Rainier, Walter Weiner found himself seated beside a dark-haired young woman with a large diamond heaving in the cleavage of her low-cut dress. Weiner, a New York lawyer who was chairman of Safra's largest bank, Republic National

Bank of New York, resembled the American actor George Kennedy; intimates knew he acted as Safra's globetrotting chief of staff, always ready to jet off to a foreign capital at his boss's whim. Weiner noticed the woman beside him perspiring heavily, and draining glass after glass of Coca-Cola. Her face was familiar, and he realized he had seen it before: she was Christina Onassis, daughter of the late billionaire Aristotle Onassis.

The banker and the heiress introduced themselves and began polite dinner chat. As the evening wore on, Christina, who seemed nervous and somewhat depressed, poured out her troubles in what Weiner realized was a classic "poor little rich girl" tale: how all her money hadn't bought her happiness, how her financial advisers' conflicting advice had left her hopelessly confused.

"What kind of bank do you have?" Weiner asked.

"Citibank is one," she replied. "American Express is the other."

"I'd love to have a chance to call on you, and see what we could do for you."

Christina mentioned that she was aware of the bad feelings between Safra and the international banking arm of American Express. "You know," she said, "they keep pushing me to take loans."

Weiner smiled. "We don't like to make loans. We prefer to take deposits."

As disingenuous as the statement sounded, it was true. Edmond Safra's people didn't do banking the old-fashioned way, they did it the ancient way. For more than a century the Safra family had run its banks far differently from their Western counterparts: Safra bankers emphasized accumulating deposits rather than making loans. It was safer that way, and Safra, who like so many of his depositors had fled the Middle East during the tumult of 1948, was consumed with a passion for safety. Besides, his banks had more unusual ways to make money, as attested by the hundreds of gold bars quietly stacked in massive vaults beneath his buildings in Geneva, London, and New York.

As they chatted, Weiner and Onassis dined on artfully displayed servings of *soupe de poisson,* *feuilletée aux asperges* and *saumon aux truffes,* all arranged by famed chef Roger Vergé of the Moulin de Mougins. One of Safra's favorite musicians, the Brazilian band leader Sergio Mendes, had been flown in for the evening from California along with his entire orchestra, and as dinner was cleared, the crowd was anxious to begin dancing. No one was to rise from dinner, however, before Prince Rainier, and to everyone's consternation, the prince was staying put. Eventually someone roused him, and Safra and his guests danced until the early hours.

There was spaghetti and more food at 4:00 A.M., and some guests, mostly the Safras' Brazilian grandchildren and their friends, literally danced until dawn. As they left, each of the women was slipped a beautiful enamel box depicting La Leopolda to commemorate the evening. Two nights later they did it all again. The Safras' guest list was so vast they had been forced to throw two parties, one Saturday and another Monday, a more relaxed "B-list" affair for business associates, lawyers and the like.

Again and again, as they passed their firm handshakes and patted their guests' broad tuxedoed backs, Safra's aides were struck by how relaxed their billionaire boss seemed. Maybe the worst *was* over. At one point, Safra took a microphone and, accompanied by an aging French crooner named Guy Beart, actually began singing an old French love song. "I'm not seeing straight," Walter Weiner said with a chuckle. "Is that Edmond up there?" Weiner couldn't tell which was more shocking, that Safra would sing in public, or his voice, which wasn't that bad. One thing, at least, was certain. After the last five years, it was a wonderful thing to worry about.

August was a time for all the Continent's weary denizens, especially the French, to flee to the tranquil green countrysides and sunbaked beaches for rest and relaxation. In Paris and Geneva the financial centers all but emptied as the wealthiest players escaped to their hideaways along the Riviera. As they recovered from the memorable evenings at La Leopolda, Edmond Safra and his aides were no exception. While the Safras and their grandchildren rested at their estate, Walter Weiner and his wife, Nina, slipped away to a fishing village on the Italian coast. They interrupted their getaway only to accept a surprise invitation to a party thrown by their new friend Christina Onassis, where they felt decidedly out of place in a strobe-lit crowd of pouty Parisian models and sleek men wearing odd combinations like bow ties and T-shirts.

For three weeks there was peace. Then, as September neared, thoughts inevitably returned to more profitable pursuits than sunbathing, and many of the tourists headed back to the cities. All along the

Côte d'Azur, the crowded clubs and beaches began to thin. The Safras began thinking of the return to Geneva. The Weiners dragged themselves onto a plane for the long flight back to New York. There was much to be done that fall, banks to run, a massive new European stock offering to launch, not to mention the continued sniping with American Express. And then it happened.

There was no hint of the gathering storm that Wednesday morning, August 31. Slipping out of bed around seven, Safra worked the phones in his second-floor bedroom at La Leopolda for two hours or so, touching base with executives throughout his European operations before stepping into a hot shower, where many mornings one of his loyal valets continued to hand him calls. At a bathroom mirror he shaved, lathering up and slicing off the black beads of beard not once but twice, as was his habit; Safra's stubble was so heavy he sometimes shaved a third time for evening affairs. Afterward he stepped into a casual warm-up suit and headed downstairs to his gym, where he lightly worked the treadmill and exercise cycle. It was the only forty-five minutes of his day when Safra was not to be disturbed.

Returning alone to his bedroom, he dressed and prepared for the morning blessings known as *Birkhot HaShahar*. When in New York or Geneva, these prayers were Safra's final task before heading to his office. Just as he had every weekday morning since he was a boy in Beirut, he quietly took out his *siddur*, the prayer book that contained the blessings the devout Jew needed for both weekday and Sabbath services. As he wrapped his shoulders in the fringed, blue-and-white prayer shawl called the *tallit* he intoned the first of a series of Hebrew prayers: *Barukh atah Adonai eloheinu melekh ha-olam, asher kidshanu b'mitzvotav, v'tzivanu l'hitatef b'tzitzit* (Blessed be Thou, Lord our God, King of the universe, who sanctified us with His commandments, and commanded us to wrap ourselves in the *tzitzit*.)

Murmuring prayers quietly to himself, he took out the leather straps of the *tefillin*, placed its small black box against his left bicep and wrapped the straps seven times around his forearm, making certain the final knot in his palm faced outward, as dictated by Sephardic tradition. As an adult male Jew, Safra wore *tefillin* for weekday morning prayers as a reminder of the commandments. *Barukh atah Adonai eloheinu melekh ha-olam ...*

Next he took out the head *tefillin*, the *shel rosh,* and, carefully placing the tiny box above his broad forehead, knotted it securely at the base of his skull, allowing the leather straps to dangle loosely. Finally he unwrapped the strap in his palm and wound it around his middle finger three times, tightly, before taking the last inches of leather into his palm once more. He remained there alone, softly breathing his prayers, for a long time.

As the sun rose toward noon, Safra emerged once more and padded downstairs to his office, where he returned to the phones, eluding the younger grandchildren scampering about just long enough to check the markets and touch base with Geneva and the early risers in New York. When the call came in from Paris, he wasn't especially worried. The message was troubling, if not cataclysmic: one of the very worst of the Parisian scandal sheets, *Minute*, a newspaper renowned for its hostility toward Jews and Communists, had published an article that day mentioning Safra. Details were scant, but it sounded ugly. Safra's antennae rose immediately; two weeks earlier they had seen another strange article, in an obscure French newspaper, and had already directed the lawyers to complain about it. Instinctively mistrusting the phone lines to his office telefax machine, Safra ordered a messenger onto the next plane out of Paris with a copy of *Minute*'s latest issue.

For Edmond Safra, a warm Riviera summer ended suddenly and prematurely, as if a guillotine blade had dropped, when the messenger arrived at La Leopolda that afternoon. At first glance, a casual reader might not have shared Safra's dismay as he gaped at the two articles on an inside page. He wasn't mentioned in the main headline, which read: "The Playboy Knew Too Much." Beside it, however, was a smaller headline: "The Death of Glenn Souham."

Most Parisians had heard of the Souham case. Glenn Souham was a thirty-four-year-old French-American security consultant—his company supplied bodyguards for wealthy Europeans—who had been shot dead by an unknown assailant while walking with his girlfriend in a Parisian suburb two years before. Now *Minute* was purporting to have solved the case, a claim few skeptics would waste time believing. Beneath the lurid headline, the paper narrated a story straight out of Robert Ludlum: how Glenn Souham had been murdered while pursuing a secret investigation of the Iran-Contra scandal in which he uncovered the fact that certain Swiss banks were laundering drug money—"especially," *Minute* noted in its conspiratorial tone, "one banker who has two villas on the Riviera and whose ties with Irangate are evident." These discoveries, the paper reported breathlessly, were so scandalous that it became "absolutely necessary that the principal author of the revelations, Glenn Souham, be silenced."

To learn the identity of the mysterious Swiss banker "at the center of the spider web Souham, to his misfortune, discovered," *Minute*'s readers had to look no further than a second, adjacent article, its tabloid headline heavy with druggy innuendo: "Millionaire of the White Stuff."

It was Edmond Safra.

Safra's amazement grew as he waded through *Minute*'s tangled verbiage. The article amounted to a litany of outrageous insinuations: that he was behind Glenn Souham's murder, that he was the financial mastermind of the Iran-Contra scandal, that he was a consort of any number of unsavory figures, including arms dealers, drug traffickers, and mafiosi—here Safra could only stare in disbelief—"one of whom is the well-known silversmith of the Mafia, Meyer Lansky." It was a stunningly confused mishmash of the vaguest allegations, not a hard fact in sight—except his Brazilian passport number—and no clue at all as to what sources, if any, the reporter, one Jean Roberto, was drawing upon.

Safra's eye was drawn to an official-looking letter printed alongside the article. It was dated 29 January 1988, just seven months before, and addressed to "Interpol, Vienna." The letter had a typed letterhead and an official seal identifying it as correspondence from the U.S. Embassy in the Swiss capital of Bern. Only the first page was reproduced, so no signer's name was evident, but it clearly came from someone in the U.S. government investigating the two-year-old Iran-Contra scandal.

RE: Oliver NORTH
     Albert HAKIM

Dear Sir:

The captioned investigation being conducted by the Office of the Independent Counsel (OIC) has determined that Willard I. ZUCKER, aka Bill, doing business as Compagnie de Services Fiduciaires of Geneva, Switzerland, was primarily responsible for managing approximately $45 million in revenues taken in by General Richard SECORD and Albert HAKIM during the course of the Iran/Contra affair.

A source of our Miami office has reported that ZUCKER is an associate of Edmund J. SAFRA, a Lebanese Jew, who is a Brazilian citizen. According to news media accounts, SAFRA is one of the wealthiest private citizens in the world. SAFRA owned the Trade Development Bank of Switzerland (sold to American Express in 1983) along with Republic National Bank of New York; SAFRA Banks (Florida, New York and California); Banque de Crédit Nationale, S.A.I. (Beirut, Lebanon); Banco SAFRA, S.A. of Brazil; Sabon S.A. of Panama; Concord Trust Ltd., in London; and numerous other banks throughout the world.

The Miami source has also advised that Republic National Bank of New York was issuing duplicate letters of credit in a scheme to defraud banks in Switzerland and Austria. The source said the letter of credit was worth $40 million and was confirmed by a teletype sent from a telex other than Republic National Bank of New York.

And that was it. There was no second page, no signature. To Safra it was mind-boggling. The idea of a letter-of-credit "scheme" was ridiculous. And he knew full well he wasn't under investigation by Iran-Contra prosecutors; his people had actually been helping the Americans for months now. None of it made any sense. Of course he knew Willard Zucker, one of the bank's Swiss customers; Zucker's problems with the Americans had inconvenienced Safra for more than a year now. But murdering some Parisian playboy? Drugs? The Mafia? *Meyer Lansky?* Where on earth could anyone have gotten these kinds of vindictive accusations? Where?

And in the blink of an eye, Edmond Safra knew. He knew, with a certainty that sank to the marrow of his bones. He knew, and five years of pain and anger came rushing back to him all at once. Oh, yes: he knew.

"Oh, shit."

Fax copies of the two *Minute* articles were lying on Walter Weiner's desk when he walked into his office six floors above Fifth Avenue that Wednesday morning. Weiner cursed as he read the accompanying translations, not because he couldn't read the French—here was an international banker who couldn't get through the menu at Le Cirque—but because he knew Safra was probably going ballistic over the articles. What with the new bank having opened that spring and the stock offering only two weeks away, the last thing he needed now was for Safra to be distracted.

As awful as *Minute's* allegations were, Weiner found he couldn't get himself worked up over them. He felt a sense of déjà vu. Several years earlier they had seen similarly crazy stories in journals backed by the American extremist Lyndon LaRouche; LaRouche's people had thrown Safra's name into one of their articles about Jewish conspiracies to control the world. Those had disappeared after a while, and Weiner's reaction was to ignore *Minute* as well. It, too, would go away. He suspected, though, that Safra wouldn't feel the same. When the call came in from La Leopolda later that morning, Weiner realized Safra was livid, but not at the French newspaper. He was mad at American Express.

"You know it's them, Walter," Safra said. "They're trying to hurt me. Something is going on."

To Weiner's surprise Safra had come to the conclusion that Jim Robinson's people were behind the *Minute* articles. It was what they had feared all along, wasn't it? That American Express would crucify him in the press? To Safra, nothing about Robinson's company was more threatening than its vaunted public relations machine: "Don't leave home without it," it admonished consumers. "Do you know me?" its pitchmen asked, and both lines passed into American consciousness. In the corporate world, Jim Robinson's ability to manipulate information and images was second to none; his wife was even one of New York's top corporate flacks.

Safra reminded Weiner of the strange article they had seen out of Rome that January. Out of the blue a top Italian news magazine, *L'Espresso*, during the course of an article on an indicted money-launderer, had listed Safra as one of the man's associates. To Safra's amazement, the magazine had then mentioned a U.S. narcotics report from 1957 that supposedly detailed the Safra family's involvement in the morphine trade. Safra lawyers had strongly protested, and *L'Espresso* had quickly printed a letter of retraction. Everyone had dismissed the incident as a freak occurrence.

Now Safra, citing its mention in *Minute*, brought up the Italian article as evidence that someone—and he was convinced it was American Express—was systematically spreading rumors about him, and had obviously been doing it for months. Weiner too considered American Express a blood enemy. But he found the idea of some international press conspiracy against Safra a bit farfetched, and gently tried to say so. "Edmond, this is another LaRouche thing," Weiner said. "The thing with *L'Espresso* happened seven months ago. Forget it. There's no connection between the two."

But Safra wasn't listening. He was particularly incensed by the letter *Minute* had printed from the U.S. Embassy in Bern, Switzerland, which seemed to give credence to the newspaper's charges.

"Edmond, that letter is just a forgery," Weiner said. "Just look at it. It's a typed letterhead. Someone has just cut out the seal of the United States and created a Xeroxed forgery."

"Well, I don't know..."

"I'll call Arthur Liman." Liman was regarded by many as the top corporate lawyer in New York. His work as counsel to the Senate Select Committee investigating the Iran-Contra scandal had made him a familiar face during the committee's televised hearings the previous summer. Surely Liman would know if the letter was a fake.

"That's a good idea," Safra said.

Weiner hung up, relieved for the chance to calm Safra, even for a moment. Soon he had Liman on the line. He described the letter in detail.

"It's a phony," Liman said. An embassy official, the lawyer explained, would never use a term like "Lebanese Jew" to describe someone. "The whole thing is a crude phony," Liman said.

"All right," Weiner said. "I agree with you. I think it's phony as hell." Weiner faxed Liman a copy, and the lawyer repeated his judgment: the letter was faked. Weiner redialed Safra in Geneva and assured him they had nothing to worry about. Arthur Liman couldn't be wrong.

But if Weiner thought that was the end of the matter, he was mistaken. Across the Atlantic, Safra couldn't take his eyes off the strange articles in a Parisian newspaper. And the more he stewed, the angrier he became. He decided to convene an emergency meeting at La Leopolda that Saturday. Weiner sighed; he knew he would be expected to attend. What he didn't yet suspect was the depth of the bitterness toward Jim Robinson and American Express the strange articles had dredged up within Edmond Safra. "Joe, I promise you," Safra called and told his brother in Brazil, "I'm going to fight this until the last drop of my blood."

As Weiner packed his things at his spacious Park Avenue apartment, he could tell his wife wasn't happy, not happy at all. Nina Weiner had thirty of their closest friends due at their country home in East Hampton that Sunday for a clambake to celebrate Weiner's 57th birthday. Thirty people. What was she supposed to do now?

"I'll be back in time for the party, dear," Weiner said. "I promise."

His wife looked skeptical. She had been through this too many times.

"No, look," Weiner said, "I'm only taking two suits."

"You'll be exhausted."

"No, no, I'll be back in plenty of time."

Weiner kissed her as he left. They both knew he was lying. Weiner's friends ended up singing "Happy Birthday" to him over a transatlantic phone line.

For the overnight trip to Nice, Weiner brought along a diminutive Safra attorney named Alan Levine, who was as confused by the strange articles as he. The two men reached Monte Carlo shortly after dawn Saturday and checked into the elegant Hôtel de Paris, on the main plaza across from the casino. They had time for only a quick nap before a car picked them up for the short drive to La Leopolda. Passing through the villa's gates and up the sloping drive, they stepped from the car and were escorted by a white-uniformed butler through the public salons into a small rear dining room looking onto the rear terrace. Beyond, the view of Cap Ferrat and the blue waters of the Mediterranean was panoramic.

The celebratory air of the grand parties three weeks before was forgotten as Safra welcomed the two Americans. Charles-André Junod, his tall, crisp Swiss attorney, was already there, as was J. F. Pratt, their Parisian counsel. As he gathered them all around the dining room table, Safra was all business. His normal, placid demeanor gave no indication of the turmoil he hid inside. Of those around the table that day, only Weiner knew how greatly any kind of publicity truly unnerved Safra.

On the table an aide had laid out manila folders containing the day's agenda for each man. Inside, Weiner found the two *Minute* articles, a suggested reply the lawyers had drafted, and, to his surprise, two more articles Safra's people had discovered, both from a French newspaper named *La Dépêche du Midi*, based in the southwestern city of Toulouse. The more recent of the two was dated August 13.

"Drugs and Money from Drugs," the headline read, and Weiner saw that the accompanying article was just as jumbled and confused—and venomous—as the two in *Minute*. Safra, it charged, "is at the head of an immense banking empire with links, according to *The New York Times*, to the Mafia [and which] the Italian press asserts was involved in trafficking morphine base.... [A] Drug Enforcement Administration inquiry [into Safra], which was stopped for a while on orders from above, is alleged to have established that Safra had been an ally of the CIA, which solicited him to play the role of financial agent in the Iran-Contra operation."

There was more, each passage more convoluted than the last: Safra and the CIA, Safra and drugs, Safra and Willard Zucker and Iran-Contra. To Weiner, it was absurd, but he knew there was nothing funny about the effect this kind of press could have on their businesses. The wealthy, publicity-shy depositors drawn to Swiss banks, particularly Safra's banks, wouldn't take kindly to being associated with drug traffickers and spies. Perhaps most worrisome, *La Dépêche* mentioned that newspapers in Peru and Mexico had published similar articles about Safra: Latin America, along with the Middle East, held the largest concentration of their depositors.

Weiner turned to the second *La Dépêche* article, which had been published five months earlier, on March 11, 1988. It was even more confusing. The first several paragraphs discussed French efforts to stem drug trafficking, then swerved off into another section under the subtitle "Gangsters in White Collars."

"The Americans have understood for a long time that gangsters of the period of Al Capone have exchanged soft hats and pale shoes for the respectable three-piece suit. The new generations have arranged for financial institutions to launder the monies coming from gaming, prostitution and the drug business," the article read. Then the reporter homed in on Safra, hinting that he was among those "persons in white collars who call on professional killers for the elimination of nuisances. Themselves, they do not touch murder; to each his specialty. During five years in Turino, twenty-five people have been killed [by one organization.] According to an official source, a certain Edmond Safra is among the leaders of this organization...."

For Weiner, the two articles in *La Dépêche* changed everything. If possible, the new stories were even crazier than the ones in *Minute*: Edmond Safra, the leader of some kind of Italian Murder Incorporated? For the first time, Weiner realized their dilemma was far greater than he had feared. Even if Lyndon LaRouche's conspiratorial followers were behind the articles, this was the kind of publicity that could kill a bank.

Putting aside the obvious question—where the bizarre articles were coming from—Safra and his lawyers spent much of the afternoon mulling their damage-control options. The fine points of French libel law were reviewed in detail, as were the merits of less aggressive options, such as writing angry letters to the newspaper's publishers or ignoring the articles altogether. To everyone watching Safra that day, it was clear there was little possibility of letting the articles pass without rebuttal.

"My honor is at stake," he said more than once. "Even if there were only one article, I can't leave something like this without responding. It's utterly false."

As they spoke, white-coated butlers glided in and out, serving tall, thin glasses of iced Evian water. Safra was especially angered by the suggestion that he was somehow involved in the Iran-Contra scandal. Of the bank accounts Oliver North and his people had used to divert money to the Nicaraguan Contra fighters, several had been at Republic, and Weiner and his people had spent long hours helping the Americans track North's circuitous money trail. To refute *Minute's* accusations, Safra wanted an official letter clearing him of any involvement in the scandal. After all his people had done, he thought it should be easy to get. The American lawyer, Alan Levine, wasn't so sure.

"Edmond, it could be days, and then they may not give me a letter like that," said Levine, who had been Safra's point man with the Iran-Contra prosecutors. "The government very, very rarely gives a letter that someone isn't under investigation. As ridiculous as it sounds, they just don't do that."

Eventually the talk turned to the articles' substance, but there the questions far outnumbered any answers. What was this about a DEA investigation? No one knew. Who was the strange Miami source mentioned in the Bern letter to Interpol? They could only guess. And who had killed this Glenn Souham, the dead playboy? No one had the faintest idea. They had been caucusing for most of the afternoon when, during a break, Alan Levine motioned to Weiner and Safra to join him on the veranda. The day was poised for a striking sunset over the Mediterranean, and Levine was struck with the beauty of the view. He spoke softly, not wanting to be overheard.

"Look, there's a possibility that this is American Express," the lawyer said. Both Safra and Weiner had kept their suspicions to themselves. "They could be behind all of this. We ought to try and find out," Levine said. "We ought to think about hiring detectives. Maybe someone working undercover could interview a journalist or two and find out who the sources were for the papers' articles."

Weiner seemed to agree, at least in theory. "I don't want to take that step right now," he said. "But that's something to think about." To one side, Safra was impassive.

The meeting broke up before nightfall. Levine returned to Monte Carlo, and the other lawyers hustled back to their respective cities. Not until everyone had left and the sun had set did Safra reiterate to Weiner his true thoughts. "It has to be American Express," he said. "It has to be. Who else would do this? Who else would have an interest other than American Express?"

"Yeah," Weiner replied, "but how are we going to prove that? These guys are too smart to get their hands dirty. There's got to be layers of people between them and this."

The two men plotted strategy all the next day, and by Monday Safra had laid out several paths of attack. In the United States, his American lawyers would head to Washington to visit authorities investigating the Iran-Contra affair, deduce whether they had any interest in him and, if not, secure an official letter saying so. In Geneva, his Swiss lawyers would approach the national police to see what, if anything, their files held. In Milan, his Italian lawyers would pursue the source of the strange magazine story that January. In Paris, his French lawyers would meet with libel counsel to explore the possibilities of suing the French newspapers. Walter Weiner's first stop, meanwhile, was to be Rome, where he hoped an old friend might help trace the one piece of solid evidence they had, the strange letter from the U.S. Embassy in Bern.

Maxwell Rabb, the American ambassador to Italy, was nearing his eightieth birthday, but as he bounded across his large office to shake Weiner's hand, he evidenced all the energy of a man in his prime. Weiner stepped to one side as he entered, and with Rabb at his shoulder, smiled as a photographer commemorated his visit to the ambassador's office.

Max Rabb was an old-line conservative politician, a crony of Dwight Eisenhower and Henry Cabot Lodge, passing his twilight years in another vital overseas posting. Weiner knew him best as a onetime neighbor in his Fifth Avenue apartment building, but the ambassador was also friendly with Safra. Both Weiner and his boss had thought of him as they pored over ways to investigate the strange missive that would come to be known as the "Bern letter." After a quick call, the ambassador had promised to check into it.

"It'll be all right, it'll be all right," Rabb now told Weiner in his quick, peppery style. "There is some kind of letter. We may have some problems here, but it'll be all right, it'll be all right."

Weiner stopped him. "You mean it's real?"

"Well, I think you ought to go up and talk to the guy in Switzerland," Rabb rattled on. "He'll treat you nice. I talked to him. Everything will be all right. Everything will be all right."

Weiner left Rabb's office stunned to learn of the Bern letter's authenticity. On the flight back to Paris, he wondered whether it could be true. Maybe the ambassador had made a mistake. He decided to find out as fast as possible.

His office hadn't been able to reach the American ambassador in Bern, but the next morning Weiner flew there anyway. At the embassy, he was greeted by the ambassador's tall, handsome number two, Frederick H. Hassett, who seemed embarrassed when Weiner brought up the letter. Yes, Hassett said, the letter was authentic. It had come from the embassy's "legat office," the legal attaché.

"That's strange," Weiner remarked, "because the letterhead is typed." Hassett explained that the legal attaché was embassy-speak for the handful of FBI men stationed in Bern. The bureau's operations were so distinct from the embassy's that the FBI men didn't have their own stationery; they simply typed a letterhead onto each piece of embassy stationery they used.

Weiner was still puzzling over that as Hassett led him down to see the legal attaché, whose name was Robert Fanning. Fanning stood in a well-appointed office with another FBI man. In minutes Weiner sized up the two as typical police functionaries, laconic, "just-doing-our-job" types.

Yes, Fanning confirmed, the letter had come from his office. But it was simply restating an inquiry from FBI stateside. "All we did was rewrite a telex from the U.S.," he said. "We did what we were told. It's the usual course of business."

"Why did you write to Interpol?" Weiner asked, trying to disguise his irritation.

"That's the normal thing to do."

"How did the letter leak out?"

"We don't know."

Weiner asked to see the letter's second page, and Fanning handed it to him. There were just two paragraphs, one formally requesting Interpol's help on the alleged letter of credit scheme, the other a closing. The letter was signed by Fanning.

"May I have a copy?" Weiner asked.

"I'm sorry," Fanning said, taking back the letter. "It's a government document."

Weiner began to get angry. "I can't believe this," he said with a sarcastic laugh. "Here is the chairman of a large, well-regarded American bank, asking for help, and you won't give me a copy of what's in my hand? When you caused it to leak out in the first place? This document is floating all over the world, circulating in newspapers. You let me see it. But you won't give it to me? Isn't that a little ridiculous?"

"I'm sorry," the FBI man said, "but you'll have to file a Freedom of Information request."

Weiner was getting hotter by the minute. Fanning grew defensive. "You don't think we circulated this letter, do you?" the FBI man asked.

"Of course we do," Weiner said.

"Why would we do that?"

"For money."

The FBI man looked aghast.

"I'm not saying you did it," Weiner said. "But somebody did, maybe some clerk."

Weiner wasn't through. "And I am personally offended," he continued, "by the description here of Edmond Safra as a Lebanese Jew."

"We were just using Washington's wording," Fanning protested.

"You mean you would describe someone as an English Episcopalian? I doubt that."

Fanning tried to calm Weiner, emphasizing that the letter was routine, that it did no harm. But Weiner was having none of it. "It may be routine," he said. "But somebody's got to realize the consequences when things like this are put on paper."

Weiner telephoned Safra the minute he reached the Bern airport. Safra was openly disappointed at the FBI's explanation, and pressed Weiner to push the embassy harder. "I would," Weiner said, "but it's like talking to a wall."

It took Safra's lawyers months to obtain a copy of the full letter, and when they did, the FBI had blacked out most of the names on it—a wholly unnecessary precaution, since thousands of *Minute* readers had already read it. In any case, it was purely a formality. Before leaving the embassy, Walter Weiner had committed the entire letter to memory.

Even as Weiner sought the origins of the strange Bern letter, two new bombshells exploded in the Safra camp. One of the French articles had referred to similar stories in Mexico and Peru, and by midweek items from two Latin American newspapers reached Safra's office at La Leopolda. The first, from a Peruvian paper named *Hoy*, was dated July 4, two months before. Beneath the headline, "Mafioso Bankers Turn Their Eyes to the South," a full-page article traced Safra's career from Beirut to Brazil and Switzerland, but told it through a prism of criminal dealings, including the now-familiar litany of arms dealers, CIA men, and money laundering. A chart showed drug routes between North and South America.

"Safra made his first fortune putting his bank at the disposal of drug traffickers," *Hoy* reported. "This would be the reason why years later, the CIA would look to him for the Iran-Contra operation. It is said that Safra banks devote themselves to laundering local money that drug traffickers obtain for their illegal operations.... Everything seems to indicate now that the Drug Enforcement Agency, the U.S. government agency in charge of fighting drug traffic, has placed all eyes and ears on Safra and his banks.... All roads lead to Safra."

The second article, in a Mexico City paper named *Uno Mas Uno*, was almost an exact duplicate of the Peruvian article, and printed just five days afterward, on July 9. Both pieces carried the same byline, which Weiner took note of: Pedro Cardozo. A lawyer by training, Weiner didn't ordinarily traffic in wild theories, but there was only one word to describe the half-dozen articles they had now found: conspiracy. Edmond Safra was the target of some kind of bizarre, worldwide press conspiracy. As improbable as it sounded, there was no other explanation. Italy. France. Peru. Mexico. True, the publications weren't widely read.

But as that traumatic first week of September 1988 wore on, Safra grew petrified that a larger newspaper—Britain's *Financial Times* or, God forbid, *The Wall Street Journal*—would pick up on *Minute* or the other articles and give them wider readership. As the initial furor died down, Safra and his aides held their breaths, praying that no one would follow them up. For the most part, their prayers were answered. All week only one media inquiry of note came in, from, of all places, *Women's Wear Daily*, which had made the Safras a regular feature of its energetic society reportage.

A Madison Avenue public relations firm, Kekst & Company, had handled Safra's press contacts for several years, and one of its veterans, an elfin p.r. man named Robert Siegfried, returned the reporter's call. It was a quick conversation. Siegfried tried to stress that *Minute* was an anti-Semitic fringe publication, and the reporter seemed to agree. But if Safra thought that was all it took to squelch a journalist's interest, he was in for the first of many rude surprises. That Friday *Women's Wear* carried a vague, one-paragraph squib alluding to the *Minute* allegations.

"The lunchtime gossip in Paris social circles this week once again concerns Edmond and Lily Safra, the ball-giving couple," *Women's Wear* reported. "Safra, an international banker, is the subject of an unsigned article in *Minute*, a right-wing scandal sheet. The newspaper makes all sorts of serious allegations, none of which it substantiated, about Safra's banking business. Safra could not be reached for comment on *Minute*'s charges but a spokesman for Republic Bank in New York, of which Safra is honorary chairman, issued the following statement: 'We will not comment on such an untrue, contemptible, preposterous and defamatory article.'"

Robert Siegfried read the article and realized they had survived a close call. For now, at least, their luck was holding.

Safra sat in the parlor of his palatial London apartment the following Sunday, elegantly swathed in silk pajamas and bathrobe, morose. Only the most veteran Safra observers arrayed before him that afternoon could read his mood, but the signs were there. They weren't in his round, bald man's face, which was still, never smiling or frowning. Nor were they in his arms, which lay flat on the armrests, becalmed. The giveaway was his right leg, draped over the left and shaking, slow at times, faster at others. It was a pose his aides would come to know well in the weeks and months to come, as the worst of Safra's nightmares came true.

They had all assembled in London, coming in on flights from Geneva, Paris, and New York, for the kickoff of Safra's new European stock offering, to be announced at a major press conference the next morning. The two American p.r. men, Robert Siegfried and his boss Gershon Kekst, were there to coordinate media coverage. But as his aides gathered to talk strategy for the next day's events, Safra remained transfixed by the bizarre news stories. He found no solace whatsoever in the harmlessness of the *Women's Wear* item; now, Safra was convinced, the articles would begin appearing in America.

"They're trying to ruin me," he said ominously. "They are threatening my life."

A furious Lily Safra stood at her husband's side. "You've got to help him," she pleaded. "This stuff is terrible, just terrible."

It was up to Kekst, the wizened p.r. guru from New York, to try to calm Safra and bring his attention to matters at hand. "Look, I want you to relax," Kekst told Safra. "Stop worrying. We'll take care of it. I promise, we'll take care of it."

But Safra was stricken, obsessed by a campaign mounted by unknown forces to destroy the reputation he had painstakingly built over forty years in international banking. It was an obsession that would come to dominate his life for years to come. Gershon Kekst sensed the wounds in his client's troubled mind, and did everything he could to soothe them for the moment.

"Edmond, we'll get to the bottom of this," Kekst swore. "I promise you. We'll get to the bottom of this...."

And they did. What Edmond Safra and his aides would discover over the course of the following year was in fact a conspiracy, a conspiracy so strange they could never have imagined it. The investigation they launched would range across three continents, from modern press offices in Rome to the grimy back alleys of Peru, from plush suites on Manhattan's Fifth Avenue to the sidewalk bistros of Paris, from Washington's embassy row to the gilded corridors of Geneva's private banks. Ultimately they would find many of the answers they sought exactly where they suspected, in the upper reaches of a gleaming skyscraper in lower Manhattan, the American Express Tower.

It was there, had they known, just six months earlier, that four top officers of the American Express Company gathered in the chairman's corner office overlooking the Hudson River to once again review their options in dealing with Edmond Safra. The four had been commiserating about Safra for almost five years by then, and to a man they considered him among the company's most dangerous enemies. Still, the evidence would later suggest, only two of the men in the room that day, Jim Robinson himself and his savvy idea man Harry Freeman, were aware of the extent of their developing counterattack against Safra.

The meeting ended like so many others, with much discussed and little decided. Afterward, as the men in the chairman's office rose to leave, Harry Freeman paused and took aside the chief of American Express's international banking subsidiary, Bob Smith, the hatchet-faced former auditor who led the day-to-day fight against Safra. Many at American Express felt Bob Smith despised Safra with every fiber of his being. Freeman, a secretive type by nature, didn't say what was on his mind, but suggested that perhaps they should have dinner. There was something they needed to talk about.

That night the two men dined at a dimly lit Chinese restaurant near Rockefeller Center named Pearl's. As they ate, Harry Freeman began to tell Bob Smith a strange story. He mentioned a news item they had picked up out of Rome. Deep within an article on money laundering, an Italian magazine named *L'Espresso* had suggested that the Safra family might have a hidden past—in narcotics. There was, Freeman said as Smith listened in growing amazement, more than a little evidence that Safra might still be involved in drugs.

And then Harry Freeman described the plan they had set in motion a year before, a covert operation using a woman with very special talents. If everything went as planned, Freeman pledged, their problems with Safra would soon be over.

Bob Smith was surprised. The plan sounded daring. "Does Robinson know what you're doing?" he asked.

Freeman looked at Smith as if it were the silliest question he had ever heard.

"You don't think I'm stupid, do you?"*

---

*Freeman and Smith, as will be seen, differ on the content of their conversation that evening. This version is based largely on Smith's recollection.

2

On a series of limestone hills thirty miles from the Turkish frontier and the threshold to Europe known as the Gate of Winds stands the bustling Syrian city of Aleppo. Though details of its founding are lost in prehistory, local tradition traces the city's naming to the patriarch Abraham, who was said to have milked his cows in nearby fields, thence the city's Arab name, Halab, the word for "milked" in both Hebrew and Arabic. Seventy miles inland from the blue Mediterranean, the city's ancient walls stand astride trade routes crossed and conquered over the centuries by Hittites, Hurrians, Egyptians, Assyrians, Persians, Romans, Byzantines, Crusaders, Turks, and the Macedonian armies of Alexander the Great.

In the thirteenth century it was the Mongols' turn, and their orgy of raping, pillaging and burning left wide areas of Aleppo in ruins. In their wake the city's inhabitants were forced to rebuild, and over the years their toil produced a classic monument of roiling, screaming, yelling, sweating Middle Eastern commerce: the souks of Aleppo. Across fifteen square miles of the city's oldest quarters sprawl some of the most famous covered bazaars in all the Middle East, mile upon mile of dusty, winding warrens lined by merchant houses and stalls of every stripe. The souks have changed little over time, their vaulted stone roofs and archways still spanning the streets and Saracen gateways just as they have for five hundred years, producing a gloom pierced only by random beams of sunlight.

It was here that men from across the Levant came for centuries to trade, descending from camelback to shake the sand from their robes:

musty shepherds from the Turkish mountains, stolid craftsmen from Baghdad and Damascus, wheedling traders from Beirut and Alexandria, and, beginning in the fifteenth century, from England and France. They all came to buy Aleppo's specialties, barley and cotton and the city's famous pistachios, but also for the more exotic wares that found their way to the souks in caravans from the faraway kingdoms of China and India and Europe.

Visitors were often led through the steaming, noisome alleys by a *dalal*, one of the ubiquitous middlemen who brought together buyers and sellers for a fee. The *dalal* was expert at threading his way through the archipelago of interconnected *khans*, groupings of offices and warehouses, each surrounding a central courtyard and devoted to a single craft or trade: from the *souk il-ittereen* wafted the subtle smells of Eastern herbs and spices; from the *souk il ni'heh seen* the clammer of coppersmiths. Inside each courtyard Muslim porters splayed about on hay bales waiting for work, as the merchants harangued each other. Everything—*everything*—ended up as a *bazraah*, a negotiation.

Deep inside the souks of nineteenth-century Aleppo one could find not only the finest in spices and cloth and precious metals but also the finest in businessmen, many of them members of one of the most renowned mercantile classes of the Middle East: the Jews of Aleppo, the Halabim. Unlike their cousins in Damascus, a heady, irresponsible lot who melted into Syria's French-colonial culture, the restrained, serious-minded Halabim persistently clung to the old Jewish traditions, building a tight, clannish community of tradesmen and businessmen centered on their famed souks. Many served as bookkeepers to the Arab merchants, but many more were merchants themselves, especially in textiles and fabrics of all kinds, silk weaving and cotton printing, as well as wool, hides, dried fruits and nuts. Their offices and warehouses lined the huge Khan il Gimrog—the "customhouse khan"—as well as the equally massive Khan il Qassabiyet, the Khan of the Golden Threads.

The Halabim had been in Aleppo since biblical times, and for centuries had lived in harmony with their Turkish and Arab rulers, escaping the pogroms and massacres that from time to time inflicted Damascus. Though aggressive in commerce, in day-to-day life they found it best to remain inconspicuous, often yielding the right of way to a Muslim on the sidewalk. A Jewish money lender could make loans to Arab businessmen, but he was forced to await repayment at the Muslim's whim; he could not demand anything. The lives of the Halabim revolved around the souks and Aleppo's two famed temples, the Great Synagogue in the ancient Bahsita quarter, and the smaller Bet Nassi in the Sa-ha quarter. For circumcisions in the morning, weddings in the afternoon, and always on Shabbat, the men and their obedient wives, adorned in the thin cloth covering known as a *habbaraat*, came from throughout the city, from the Jewish districts of Djaloum, the Illeh, and from Hari-il-Yahood (the "area of the Jews") to worship.

In the wider world, the Halabim belonged to the class of Jews known as Sephardic, a term initially applied to those Jews expelled from Spain in 1492, but which came to loosely describe all Jewish communities in the Islamic countries of North Africa and the Levant. Though they worshiped using the same Torah, the traditions of the Sephardim bore little resemblance to the Jews of Europe, the Ashkenazim, for whom they had little use. The Ashkenazim, in turn, generally more educated, cosmopolitan, and enlightened than their Middle Eastern cousins, considered the Sephardim the great unwashed, "conservative, Puritan, observant, extremely hierarchical and family-oriented, and, to some extent, chauvinistic, militaristic and xenophobic," as an Israeli novelist once put it.

In truth many Sephardim were poor and uneducated, raised as second-class citizens in backwaters like Yemen and Bukhara, the most destitute living in caves in the Atlas Mountains of Algeria. But many were urban dwellers, subordinate perhaps to their Arab brethren, but no less sophisticated in Middle Eastern ways than the Ashkenazim were in the more cultured climes of London and Paris. The clannish, inbred world of the Sephardim revolved not around art or education but around commerce and the family; the way Sephardic children worshiped their industrious fathers bewildered many an outsider. Well into the twentieth century many Halabim, like many Sephardic Jews, remained illiterate and intensely superstitious. Some wore magical amulets and talismans to ward off evil spirits; many believed in the evil eye. With no tradition of higher learning—only the wealthiest received Western educations at the French-speaking Alliance Israelite schools sprinkled across the Middle East—most Halabi sons left school at thirteen for the souks. Daughters were fit only to be wives.

In the first years of the twentieth century another young Halabi found his way into the souks. Born in 1891, Jacob Safra was still a boy when his father, one of the city's *sir-eh-feen*, or money changers, died of a burst appendix. More fortunate than most, young Jacob was taken in by his uncle Ezra, who like all the Safra cousins spent his days striding between shops jangling with the gold coins that oiled the thrumming commercial machine of the Halabi merchants. In fact Ezra Safra and his cousins were a step above simple money changers, for their grandfathers had founded a respected firm of their own in the mid-nineteenth century, Safra Frères & Cie., a *maison du banc*, or banking house, with branch offices run by cousins in Alexandria and Istanbul.

Their business, like the souks where they spent their days, had changed little over the years. In a region whose residents had little or no faith in the Ottoman Empire's paper money, the Safras benefited from a brisk traffic in gold and silver pieces. They exchanged coins for the almost worthless paper money, then sent the bills in bundles—sometimes smuggled by their wives and sisters—to the banks in Istanbul, where they fetched full value and could be exchanged once more for gold. Safra Frères traded with firms across the Ottoman Empire, from Istanbul to as far away as the Persian Gulf. It also did a bustling business financing the caravans to Egypt and Iraq, as well as the Turkish *ghanaameh*, or cattle dealers, who brought down to Aleppo their massive herds of cattle and sheep, sometimes 400,000 head or more, where the Safras and other bankers would issue them checks on their Istanbul connections.

As a teenager Jacob Safra took his place at Safra Frères, though he was always to be known as "the poor cousin." In time he adopted the style of the elite Jewish bankers who had shed their traditional cotton robes to don Western-style suits, though Jacob always wore the red Aleppan fez, which was taller by several inches than the squat fezes worn in Alexandria or Tangiers. He was said to be a dedicated young man, a pillar of the temple, far more interested in pursuing his fortune than dallying with gambling or women.

In better days Jacob Safra could have looked forward to living the life of his father and grandfather before him, but it was not to be. For Aleppo was a city in decline as young Jacob and his cousins struggled to make a living in the years before World War I. Since the opening of the Suez Canal in 1869 the days of the great caravans had been waning, though the Safras would continue funding the desert treks to Iraq as late as World War II. Depressions swept northern Syria in 1903 and 1907, and scores of businesses went under. Matters only grew worse during the war itself, when the Turks closed down the Alliance school and disease swept the city's poorer districts. Worst of all, the Ottoman Empire, humiliated by defeats in a number of small wars, began to conscript Jews into the army. When Muslim recruiting officers appeared in the souks with lists of young Halabim, many of Jacob Safra's friends quietly melted into the countryside, finding their way illegally *wahra il barda-yeh*, "behind the curtain," to Beirut and from there to Cairo, Istanbul, or faraway London or New York.

In 1914, at the age of twenty-three, Jacob Safra followed the well-worn track to Beirut, though he was fortunate enough to go legally, with authorizations from his cousins to open a new branch office there for Safra Frères. He arrived in the vanguard of what became a flood of Jewish refugees. As conditions grew worse in Aleppo, the Halabim left in droves, until by the end of World War I only six thousand Jews remained. When Jacob returned home after the war there was nothing left for him: with the Jewish community a shadow of its former self, and the Ottoman Empire being sliced up by the victorious Allies, Jacob and his cousins voted to dissolve Safra Frères. Each of the cousins —Ezra in Aleppo, Jacques in Alexandria, Jacob in Beirut, and David, who emigrated to Istanbul—would go it alone in their respective cities.

Returning to Beirut in 1920, Jacob Safra opened his new bank, which he named Jacob E. Safra Maison de Banque. By far his largest source of customers, like his son Edmond's forty years later, were the Jewish refugees of Aleppo, who were pouring into Beirut, doubling its Jewish population by 1929 and reshaping the seaside city's Jewish quarter. In Beirut the families of the Halabim, the Dweks and Suttons and Shammahs and Tawils, affirmed their prowess as merchants by resuming the textile and money-lending businesses they had left behind in Aleppo. "Before they even found themselves a home," a Beirut Halabi once explained, "they hurried to the commercial center, *khan-il-shoonah,* to establish a business place." In the 1920s Jacob Safra's bank prospered from deposits taken not only from his Jewish brethren but from Druse and especially Arabs, with whom he established strong connections. In later years Jacob helped build an entire mosque for Beirut's Moslems, though the gesture was not without self-interest: he built it across the street from his bank.

Then as now, the basic difference in the Safras' brand of banking was what they did with the money their depositors gave them. While in the West much of a bank's capital is parceled out in the form of loans, in Jacob Safra's banks, and later in his son Edmond's, loan-making, while important, was deemphasized in favor of trading. The Safras traded everything—all manner of foreign currencies, commodities, and, especially, gold. (The family's very name, Safra, means yellow in Arabic.) Jacob Safra and many other Halabim thrived in Beirut's gold business after World War I, as each new wave of refugees turned in their worthless paper money for gold coins. The Safras imported gold from London and Zurich, sold it to the Kuwaitis and Saudis, and laughed at the suckers who paid their big markups. "Why [didn't] our customers buy from our sources?" a Safra cousin once asked. "They didn't know! They weren't sophisticated. *Hamoreem!*"—jackasses in Hebrew.

It was a good life for the Jews. In the 1920s and 1930s Beirut was the jewel of the Middle East, serene, French-accented, and cosmopolitan. The Jews were tolerated, the richest, like the Safras, buying summer homes in the mountains outside town, and quietly channeling money to other Syrian Jews trying to immigrate to Palestine. Jacob Safra became a leader in Beirut's Jewish community, often called upon to settle disputes and contribute to charities. In 1918 he had taken a wife, marrying one of his cousins, who after accepting his hand became Esther Safra Safra. In time she joined the wealthy Halabi wives at the Jewish Club, where they played cards most afternoons until their husbands joined them after work for a buffet supper.

In 1922 Esther Safra bore Jacob their first son whom, according to Sephardic tradition, they named Elie, after Jacob's father. Ten years later, a second son arrived, whom they named Edmond. Elie and Edmond soon had younger brothers, Joseph and Moise, who in later years would run the family operations in South America. Four sisters were born as well: Evelyn, who would marry a doctor and join her sister Ughette in São Paolo; Gabi, who would marry a Safra cousin, and settle in Buenos Aires; and the warm-hearted Arlette, who in later years would scandalize the family by marrying an Ashkenazi in Brussels. All the children worshiped their father. One of Edmond's fondest childhood memories was of his father making him eggs the Sephardic way, swimming in butter. "He did it with love," Edmond said. "The one thing we got with the eggs was love."

In time each of the children was enrolled at the Alliance school where, by all accounts, Jacob and Esther Safra's second son was a truly abysmal student. From his earliest years Edmond seemed far more interested in his father's business than schoolwork. At the age of seven he was accompanying Jacob into the souks of Beirut to call on depositors among the shopkeepers and tradesmen. There Jacob Safra taught his second son that the essence of money-lending was a borrower's character, and he drilled young Edmond in the ways to deduce character by reading a man's face. "Look him in the eye," he would say, for eyes tell more than balance sheets. Notice everything. Was the man's wife wearing silk? Or threadbare? Feel the merchandise. Was it as rich as advertised? How much was the man *really* giving to the synagogue? These were the intangible ways Edmond Safra's father judged a man, and they were the ways his sons would do it for decades thereafter.

Ducking into shop after shop, young Edmond became his father's faithful eyes and ears. While Jacob chatted with the merchant, Edmond would count the bolts of cloth in the man's shop. Outside, he would dutifully report his findings to his father. "He had seventy-five bolts," Edmond might say, and his father would sagely nod his head. "That's very good, Edmond," he would reply, "because the man told me he had one hundred and twenty."

By the age of ten it was obvious that not only did Edmond harbor a special relationship with his father, but that the child was a born banker. A visitor to the Safra household in 1940 was captivated with the precocious, eight-year-old Edmond, who was full of chatter about banking, gold, and the long walks he and his father took into the souks. Already Jacob Safra knew his second son was special. "When I'm walking with Edmond," Jacob told the visitor, a newlywed bride from the Arabian Sea country of Aden, "I don't have to speak. There is an electricity between us. He understands what I'm thinking, and I understand what he's thinking."

However heartwarming, Edmond's relationship with his father was to cause the Safra family suffering, for Sephardic tradition emphatically holds that the eldest son inherits the family business. In the Safra household that tradition would be broken, as Edmond, rather than his older brother, Elie, was recognized early on as the natural inheritor of their father's mantle. "Edmond's brother Elie was totally destroyed by their father's decision," one of Edmond's investment bankers, Lee Kimmel, noted years later. "These are people so mired in history and tradition that even though Edmond was a prodigy, he was still to go to work in his older brother's business. The passing of the mantle over Elie to Edmond was unprecedented. Elie never recovered. For the rest of his life he lived a quiet, secluded life in Switzerland. It's a burden that Edmond wears on his shoulder every day of his life."

By the age of thirteen Edmond, so hopeless a student that his father had to hire special tutors for him, was racing from school each day to his father's offices, where he pestered bank officers about gold-trading strategies and calculating discount rates. Like his father and many other Sephardim, he never gave a thought to college. "Ya Sidi," went the Halabi saying, "a hundred universities cannot teach you trading, such as you learn by doing. The market teaches better than a university."

With his own personal valet, and summers in the mountain resort town of Aley, Edmond lived a pampered childhood; he was named captain of the Alliance soccer team, it was said, because he owned the best pair of shoes. Then came World War II. As the German tide crested to the west, at Rhodes and El Alamein, fear arrived on the Safras' doorstep. During the war Lebanon was overseen by a Vichy government, and young Edmond and his brothers watched as their father and other Jewish leaders returned from meetings with the Vichy High Commissioner, deeply worried that the government would carry out its warnings to crack down on Jewish merchants and professionals.

For the most part, Beirut's Jews escaped the war unscathed, and with the arrival of British soldiers the Safras celebrated. But their peace wasn't to last. To the south, Jewish refugees and Zionists were already pouring into Palestine, inflaming the region's budding Arab nationalism. As guerrilla war flared, acts of random violence replaced the goodwill that had endured toward Jewish communities across the Middle East, from Damascus and Baghdad to Algiers and Alexandria. In 1947 rabid Arab crowds burned the synagogues in Aleppo, along with many of the remaining Jewish businesses; among the buildings to go up in flames were the old offices of Safra Frères, still operated by members of the Safra family. Eventually the waves of anti-Jewish hatred began lapping at the once-placid shores of Beirut. Arabs picketed Jacob Safra and his bank. From roving cars they chanted on loudspeakers: "Don't believe Jacob Safra is Lebanese! He is Jewish! He is a Jew!"

Jacob Safra knew then that the Safra family's days in Beirut were numbered. He decided to split up the family, sending his two youngest boys, Joseph and Moise, off to private school in England. The family's future he entrusted to Edmond, then sixteen. Brimming with curiosity about banking and finance, Edmond, like his father in 1914, was to go away, to Italy, and establish a European foothold from which the Safras could look for a new home. "Do not worry, my son," Jacob Safra told him. "Traveling is a good thing."

And so, at an age when most Western children were preoccupied with drive-in movies and sock hops, Edmond Safra boarded a plane for the first time and flew west, to Rome. Accompanied by his valet and one of his father's young bankers, a Halabi named Jacques Tawil, young Edmond checked into an Italian hotel, where he and Tawil stayed for nearly a week, giving both men time to discreetly acquaint themselves with Western mores and table manners. From Rome they pushed on to the Italian financial capital of Milan, where they were thrilled to find crowds of young Sephardic refugees like themselves milling around the Hotel Continental, sharing their dreams of new wealth in the cold, strange countries of Europe.

Settling into a suite of three cramped offices in Milan, sixteen-year-old Edmond Safra and four of his father's trusted Halabim set up a small trading operation that bartered all manner of precious metals and commodities across Europe and the Middle East. Much of Safra's business was deceptively simple: Austrian gold pieces, for instance, were widely accepted as currency across the Arab world, but because of what one writer would term "the patriarchal nature of Arab society," there was little demand for the coins bearing Empress Marie Therese's likeness. Safra and his father's traders bought up Marie Thereses and shipped them to Vienna, where they were exchanged for fully valued Franz Josefs, an arbitrage no more complicated than the paper-for-gold trades the Halabim had been doing in Istanbul for decades.

Every three months Safra walked down to a Milanese police station to get his visa stamped, an experience that not only intensified his gnawing insecurities about living in the West but endowed him with a lifelong aversion to publicity and gossip. For his first appointment he was worried, not for any particular reason, but because he was a natural worrier. He sought a friend's advice on the best way to handle the situation. "If they ask you how you came into the country—was it through the window?—your answer is 'No,'" the friend said. "Just no. Not, 'I came in through the door.'" The story became one of the fables Safra would regale his aides with in years to come. The lesson, at least for young Safra: the less said about oneself the better.

For five years Edmond crisscrossed Europe, cutting deals for gold and silver with Halabim and other Sephardic Jews in every major city. In Amsterdam on a gold-buying expedition, he encountered one of his father's friends, an Egyptian banker, and explained he was on a business trip. The older man was amazed: "A business trip? You're seventeen years old!" Everywhere, Safra looked for a suitable country his family could call home, but most he ruled out because of the difficulty in becoming citizens. His father would demand that they become citizens. During the Korean War Edmond even took his search to America for the first time, returning from a trip to Manhattan sadly disappointed at the crime and filth and, worst of all, the steep banking competition.

It wasn't until 1952, on a trip to inspect a customer's paper mill, that Safra finally found the safe haven his father sought: Brazil. Its jungles brimming with timber, its river flowing with gold, its cities filling with Jewish immigrants from across Europe and the Middle East, Brazil was near the height of a postwar economic boom, and Safra knew immediately that its wide-open frontier and stable government would be perfect for his family. He mailed his father a rare ten-page letter, extolling its virtues and urging that they make the move from Beirut soon.

And so, in 1953, at the age of sixty-two, Jacob Safra left the Middle East forever and resettled his family in Rio de Janeiro, though within months he ordained a second move, to São Paolo, finding Rio and its carnival atmosphere too frivolous an outpost for serious financial dealings. Edmond pulled up stakes in Milan, moved to São Paolo and, reunited with his brothers and sisters, began to learn Portuguese by listening to the radio. His Lebanese bank Jacob Safra left in the hands of trusted employees, and through civil wars and terrorist attacks—and the demolition of its original building in a 1976 artillery duel—the bank has remained in the Safra family to this day, in his children's minds a living monument to their father's greatness.

In Brazil the Safras thrived. They found themselves in the vanguard of a wave of Sephardic immigrants fleeing the Middle East for havens in Argentina, Brazil, Mexico, and Venezuela; by 1984, a study would find the cities of Latin America held 50,000 of the 800,000 Sephardic Jews outside Israel, the second largest concentration outside France. Few of the Halabim, the Safras included, mixed with the Ashkenazim they found there, especially after Ashkenazi rabbis in Buenos Aires haughtily refused to approve the sanctity of the new immigrants' kosher butchering. Instead, as in Aleppo and Beirut, they kept to themselves and built their own synagogues and Hebrew schools, around which they clustered their homes. Even among the other Sephardim, Aleppan Jews were notoriously clannish and suspicious of outsiders. "Although many Halabim emigrated to the New World," author Daniel J. Elazar noted in his 1989 study, *The Other Jews: The Sephardim Today,* "they have been notably tenacious in retaining traditional ways generations after leaving their city of origin."

In many countries approval to form a bank is bestowed only after applicants have shown success in other businesses, typically trading companies. Until they could plunge into banking full time, Edmond and his father busied themselves trading all manner of goods—mostly industrial equipment, tobacco and coffee—as well as pursuing traditional finance activities such as buying and selling Brazilian cruzeiros. The Safras were eventually so successful trading Brazilian corporate paper that it became known as "Safra paper."

In the years to come all the family became Brazilian citizens. But even as the Safras put down new roots, Edmond was restless. Brazil was fine, the family would prosper there, but this was the 1950s, and every banker in the world knew where the action was. Switzerland was the place to be, an idea that appealed to his father even more as the family accumulated greater wealth—wealth they, like many of the other Halabi refugees, wanted in a safe place. And so, with seed money from friends and a group of Brazilian businessmen, Jacob Safra's second son once more left his family, establishing his first Swiss trading company in 1956, in that most fabled of international banking havens, Geneva.

The vaults of Geneva have safeguarded the riches of Europe's wealthy for nearly three centuries, since French Protestant financiers first flocked to Switzerland to escape persecution from King Louis XIV in 1685. Huddled on a pair of hills guarding the River Rhone's exit from the southernmost point of Lake Geneva, the old city was a perfect haven for the fleeing Huguenot bankers, who saw in its long tradition of neutrality and commerce, and above all its position just across the French border, the potential for a great European financial center. Forgiving their oppressor, the Huguenots pursued this dream by stepping forward to bankroll Louis's European wars, supplying the French king with badly needed cash and transporting it to all corners of the continent.

It wasn't until the French Revolution a century later, though, that Geneva came into its own as a center for what is now known as flight capital. As peasant mobs stormed the Bastille and guillotine blades flashed in Paris, the wealthiest French families scrambled to hide their money, and many of them found safety just across the border in Geneva. Almost completely surrounded by France—only a narrow corridor along the lake leads to the rest of Switzerland—Geneva was more French than anything else. City fathers had gone out of their way to underscore their own discretion, passing the first bank secrecy law in 1713. Ever since, it has been an article of faith that every wealthy French family maintains at least one Swiss account. "If you see a Geneva banker jump out of the window," said Voltaire, a loyal client of Swiss banks, "follow him, for there is sure to be money where he lands."

The great private banking families of Geneva, names like Hentsch and Lombard and Pictet, all trace their origins to those first hectic years after the Revolution, if not earlier. They weren't bankers then, really, but portfolio managers who skillfully guarded the great French fortunes, using a few tried and true methods to ensure discretion. Letters to depositors were mailed from just across the border in France, thereby avoiding a telltale Swiss postmark; and rarely if ever sent to business or home addresses, the better to keep nosey spouses and coworkers in the dark. When traveling, a Geneva financier's passport never identified its holder as a banker, but as a businessman or lawyer. And of course, for the ultimate in discretion, all accounts were numbered, with the owners known only to a handful of trusted bank managers.

For generations the proud, secretive descendants of these Huguenot families formed the core of Geneva's private banking community, their eighteenth-century mansions lining the grand Rue des Granges, their understated townhouse offices clustered around the Rue de la Corraterie, just steps above the Rhone. Protestants to a man, they kept to themselves, married among themselves, and excluded all Catholics and Jews from their clubs amid the steep cobblestoned streets of the old city. Through revolutions and world wars and currency devaluations the continent's richest families trod quietly to their unmarked townhouses, noted only by the most discreet of brass plates: "H et Cie." for the Hentsches, "LO et Cie." for Lombard Odier. More often the bankers left

Geneva to visit their customers—to this day far more Swiss banking is done in hotel rooms and private villas than banks—but those who preferred to visit Geneva were led to special "consulting" rooms to do their business; when finished, they might be led out one of the secret entrances the Genevois loved to whisper about.

Into the twentieth century Geneva's genteel private banks prospered, though as the years went by they were overshadowed by the growth of huge commercial banks that offered an array of modern financial services, most notably the Big Three of Swiss banking: Swiss Bank Corporation, Swiss Credit Bank, and the mightiest of them all, the Union Bank of Switzerland, led for so many years by its stiff-backed, pince-nez-wearing chairman, Alfred Schaefer. These gargantuan cousins, gorged by frightened depositors from all over Europe during World War I, crowded to the forefront of Swiss banking in the years after World War II, a time of unprecedented growth and stability for the Alpine financial centers.

Non-Europeans had always come to Switzerland to hide their wealth, but it wasn't until the 1950s, as revolutions swept Africa and South America, oil kingdoms sprouted up along the Persian Gulf, and a number of major countries relaxed restrictions on moving wealth overseas, that the trickle of foreign money became a torrent. Landed Argentines worried about Juan Perón's politics, Guatemalans frightened by the 1954 coup, Venezuela's new oil barons—they all came and joined the French and the Saudis in Switzerland, stuffing fortunes new and old into banks sprouting not only in Geneva, but in Basel and Bern and along Zurich's burgeoning bank row, the Bahnhofstrasse. In the south, the Italians poured the fruits of their postwar economic recovery into the border town of Lugano, whose 25,000 citizens by the mid-1960s were surrounded by thirty major banks. By 1976 the assets controlled by Switzerland's top five hundred banks had grown from $5 billion after the war to $139 billion.

The sudden onrush of foreigners was a decidedly mixed blessing for the clubby Genevois. Fun-loving Arab sheiks adored Geneva, where nightclubs like the Moulin Rouge and the Pussy Cat Saloon stayed open until 4 A.M., unlike prudish Zurich, which closed down by midnight. The Pictets and Lullins and Lombards took their share of the new money, but took pains not to advertise it. Handed a competitor's pamphlet written in Arabic, one Swiss banker sniffed to a writer, "We assume that the

Arab customers we want will already know English." Another, shown the same pamphlet, went even further. "We publish nothing," he noted, "in any language."

The problem, as far as the Swiss were concerned, was that the newcomers were exactly like the Huguenots three centuries before: they preferred to deal with their own kind. And to Switzerland's dismay they did, founding dozens of new, foreign-owned banks. By one count, more than two-thirds of the new banks formed in the postwar years were owned by outside interests: Germans, Italians, Israelis, British, Scandinavians, Arabs, Americans—everyone, it seemed, wanted his own Swiss bank. American conglomerates soon got into the act as well. Dow Chemical started a Swiss bank in Zurich in 1965, followed shortly after by Firestone, with Bank Firestone Ltd., then by Cummins Engine and others. A group of businessmen from Gary, Indiana, even founded something called the Banque Indiana Suisse. "It's easier to open a bank than a barber shop," the Swiss were overheard grumbling.

Thirty years later the results can be seen along the Geneva skyline, the great neon names looming high above the graceful swans of the Rhone: Banque Indosuez, Kleinwort Benson of Britain, Citibank, the British Bank of the Middle East. As time went by, the older private banks quietly moved up the hill deeper into the old city, to quarters far removed from their noisy new foreign neighbors. The newcomers, after all, cared nothing for the gentleman's agreements that had served the Swiss for so long. They cut rates and raided depositors and, worst of all, they went bankrupt, and in large numbers. By the end of the 1960s, nearly a third of the banks opened between 1960 and 1967 had gone under. The worst became virtual synonyms for scandal: Bernie Cornfeld, IOS, Robert Vesco.

Of all the world's worried wealthy who flocked to Geneva after the war, perhaps the single largest contingent was composed of Sephardic Jews, who fled their Middle East homes in the late 1940s and early 1950s by the tens of thousands, driven by newly hostile Arab neighbors intoxicated by revolution and vowing jihads against the Zionists who had driven their brothers from their Palestinian homeland. Like the Safras, many moved from country to country as they sought a permanent home, preferring to keep their money in a single safe place, often Switzerland. For many of the clannish Sephardim, the Swiss bank of choice became the bank of their fathers, the bank of the Safras.

As in Brazil, Edmond Safra laid the foundation for a bank in Geneva by forming a trading company in 1956. Not until 1960 did Safra begin formally accepting deposits as a bank, which he named Trade Development Bank, referred to by its initials, TDB. Safra shuttled between Geneva and São Paolo until 1962, when he sold his Brazilian interests to his brothers Joseph and Moise, who ran Brazil on their own when their father died a year later, a wrenching moment his sons commemorate every year by spending a night in temple.

In Geneva the backbone of Safra's depositors became the scattered Jews of Aleppo. By the early 1950s many of the remaining Halabim, the Dweks and Shammahs and Sassons and Tawils and Hedayas, had left the Middle East, taking their reputations as merchants extraordinaire to new homes in Milan and Buenos Aires and Rio and Brooklyn. Everywhere they prospered, opening textile mills and importing firms and trading houses from Yokohama to Haiti. And as they did, in back offices and synagogues and Jewish country clubs, the representatives of Edmond Safra's TDB sought them out, offering the safest of shelters for their hard-earned money.

The Safra pitch was always the same, a soothing elixir of discretion, safety, and tradition, all uttered in the language of old Aleppo. "We let you sleep at night," he and his aides told their fellow Halabim, and the message struck a chord. "Safra banking means one thing," they said. "When you give Safra your money, you get your money back, plus interest. Guaranteed." To the old, distrustful Halabi families with fond memories of Jacob Safra in Beirut and Aleppo, TDB offered an irresistible appeal. The fact that Jacob's son paid modest returns mattered far less to his clients than the fact that he was one of them.

In style Safra, though prone to occasional outbursts of temper, adopted the studied calm of his father; "he was just this quiet little man," as one American executive put it. But in those early days Safra surrounded himself with aggressive aides and traders—his "Tigers," Safra called them—who cared hugely about money and little about civility, a reputation that did nothing to endear TDB to other Geneva bankers. Safra didn't care what the Genevois thought; his customers weren't Swiss. A surprising number, in fact, were Arab, many of them money changers who had banked with his father. To them, and to any loan-seeker, Safra's banks remained unabashedly old-fashioned; a man's visage was still as important as his balance sheet. "What did you think of his face?" Safra asked aides. "I didn't like his face." Or: "I didn't like his eyes. He wasn't telling the truth. He couldn't look us in the eye."

Over the years Safra's base of Sephardic depositors grew as satisfied customers brought in more business. TDB rarely advertised; its appeal was almost strictly word-of-mouth. Safra spread the gospel by traveling regularly to Sephardic enclaves in Buenos Aires, São Paolo, London and elsewhere, seeming to make an appearance at every wedding, every bar mitzvah, every bris. In time he became a living legend in the Sephardic community, dispensing his growing wealth to aid needy rabbis, to build and refurbish synagogues in Madrid, Cannes, Cairo and Manhattan, to construct yeshivas and kibbutzim in Israel. At temples and social centers the people pressed in close to shake his hand, the children strained to touch him.

Safra's Sephardic customers rarely bothered to come to Geneva, which though fashionable by Swiss standards remained a small, dreary city to those accustomed to the finest salons of Rome or Paris. It was with his wealthiest customers in mind that Safra opened a TDB branch on Paris's elegant Place Vendôme, not because he had many French depositors, but because so many of the wealthy Sephardic wives flew in to pay calls on Parisian couturiers; now the wives had a place to cash their checks.

For the rare occasion when a customer wished to visit Geneva, the routine varied little over the years. At Safra's boxy little headquarters on the Place du Lac, security was paramount; only the best-known TDB customers could gain entry without flashing a passport to prove their identity. The appearance of a stranger in the small, ficus-lined banking hall was a cause for genuine alarm. Walk-in traffic was almost unheard of; as a rule, no one who appeared at TDB without an appointment would ever be allowed to open an account. It was considered suspicious.

Those with appointments were greeted at the white-marble lobby dais by two blue-coated *huissiers*, who after checking passports telephoned upstairs to verify the appointment. To one side, a pair of little-used teller windows were set up almost as a formality. After confirming the appointment, the *huissier*, who usually spoke three or four languages, escorted the customer to one of three tiny elevators, whose ascent was controlled by a hidden button at the dais. Upstairs, the visitor was welcomed by one of TDB's three dozen or so account officers, called *garants*, and led into one of the small customer rooms, where the *garant* would pull out a loose-leaf binder to review the customer's investments. Once under way, the *garant* pressed a small switch to light a red button in the hallway outside, signaling that the room was in use.

Far more typical was the customer who handled his banking from afar. Safra's *garants* worked most often by phone, but were strictly cautioned against doing so unless they knew the voice on the other line; several account officers demanded special code words before beginning a conversation. Once their money was deposited at TDB, Safra's customers often preferred to speak only in numbers instead of names. Even in their correspondence, Safra's clients could substitute a number for their signature, writing out, say, six nine eight three two four, which in Geneva would be compared against the same "numbered" signature card prepared in advance. TDB's return correspondence came only in unmarked envelopes. Numbered accounts were especially important to customers in the Sephardic communities of Brazil and Argentina, where many of TDB's customers were evading tight foreign-exchange controls that almost always outlawed the movement of money offshore. For TDB there was nothing illegal about taking deposits from residents of these countries; only the actual removal of money was against the law and, as Safra's men said with a wry smile, *that* was a matter left to the customer.

For the most sensitive of customers TDB maintained so-called hold-mail accounts, which strictly prohibited all correspondence to the depositor. The rules on hold-mail accounts were considered sacrosanct, since a single errant letter could well get a depositor thrown into prison. By their nature, hold-mail accounts often sat for years without any communication with the depositor whatsoever, until the day the depositor telephoned or appeared without warning in Geneva. Not surprisingly, these accounts were by far the most prone to internal fraud, and TDB constantly audited its accounts to prevent this.

For Safra's depositors, there was nothing shady or suspicious about any of this. Numbered accounts and discreet banking had long been the rule for the world's wealthy in almost every country outside America, whose heritage of political stability—a blessing few Americans truly appreciated—made such practices unnecessary. Safra's depositors felt safe at TDB, and it was safety, caution, and conservatism that Safra pounded into the minds of his bankers every day of the year. TDB wasn't a bank for the 1960s, or even the twentieth century, he told them; it was a bank for the millennium. "To be conservative in banking is to be in banking for one thousand years," he said. "The day you are not conservative you cannot survive. This is what I learned from my father."

As the popularity of Swiss banks rose in the 1960s, their reputation, perhaps inevitably, began to erode. It was a problem of image. During London's great sterling crisis of 1964, Europe's newspapers speculated about shadowy cabals of international financiers manipulating the silver and stock markets from bases in Switzerland. Most famous were the so-called Gnomes of Zurich, a phrase first tied to a mysterious league of private bankers said to operate in Central and Western Europe but which came to be loosely applied to all Swiss bankers. For outsiders, Americans especially, the image of Swiss banking changed forever in 1967. That year *Life* magazine, in a famous series of articles, reported how Mafia couriers for the legendary gangster Meyer Lansky were using Swiss banks to launder millions of dollars skimmed from Las Vegas casinos. Accompanying one article was a single, grainy photo of a mob courier trudging toward a Swiss-bound jet, weighed down by two leather bags brimming with cash. "This image stuck in the memory of all who saw it," one historian of Swiss banks observed. "For millions of Americans it symbolized an automatic mental connection between the Gnomes of Zurich and criminals of every description, from fraudsters and stock market manipulators down to, and most glamorously including, the Mafia."

In the wake of the *Life* articles, Congress held lively hearings in which Swiss bankers were held up to be the shady financiers of all manner of dirty deeds, their institutions havens for every tax dodger, tyrant, and criminal in the world. A crusading American prosecutor, Robert Morgenthau, charged that "a substantial percentage of our citizens are evading the payment of taxes and violating other laws through the use of Swiss and other foreign banks." A series of sensationalistic books—*The Swiss Bank Connection, Dirty Money*—appeared, regaling readers in lurid detail with accounts of how the world's worst dictators were storing their plundered millions in Swiss banks, where they were converted into gold. "The Swiss like gold," went the cover of one such book. "It doesn't tell tales. And the blood washes right off." In the wake of such accounts the phrase "Swiss banking" took on new, scandalous overtones. It was taken for granted that anyone who had money in a Swiss bank had a reason to hide it; any transaction channeled through Alpine banks was assumed to be shady. The financial columnist Adam Smith, having invested in a Swiss bank himself, told of teasing his banker: "I bet we must have one Mafioso. What's a Swiss bank without at least one Mafia account?"

In hindsight, it probably wasn't the best time for a secretive, Middle Eastern–born Swiss banker named Edmond Safra to burst onto the international scene. But Safra had ambitious plans. Over time he had expanded, opening TDB branches in Chiasso, a thriving banking center on the Swiss-Italian border; in Nassau; and in London, where TDB traders quickly become powers in the City's lucrative bank-note business. As he surveyed the world in the years after his father's death in 1963, Safra saw where the real power lay, where he would need to succeed to reach the true apex of international banking. There was, in truth, only one major market where the family hadn't yet tested its mettle, and it was with renewed determination that Edmond Safra laid plans to conquer it: America.

Any New Yorker walking down Fifth Avenue past the grand old Knox Hat Company building that chilly morning in January 1966 might have been surprised to see the crowd of photographers and gray-suited men milling about on the sidewalk outside. At the center of the assemblage, posed before a long yellow ribbon draped across the front entrance, stood the familiar figure of New York's junior senator, Robert F. Kennedy. Polite applause sounded as the senator bent and snipped the ribbon with a pair of scissors, then exchanged congratulations with the owners and officers of New York's newest bank. Few of those passing by noticed the short, cherubic man peering past the senator's left shoulder—in a pose captured by a *New York Times* photographer in the next morning's editions—and even fewer would have recognized his name, or known that he was the happiest Lebanese banker in the crowd that day.

Here in the heart of Fifth Avenue, Edmond Safra had finally established his beachhead in America. The headquarters of his newly formed bank, Republic National Bank of New York, stood shoulder to shoulder with the massive stone edifice of the New York Public Library. Safra had spent $2 million remodeling his building in the style of a grand European bank. Its walls were covered in the same fine pine paneling as TDB in Geneva, the furniture tending toward the Louis XIV antiques Safra favored, the languages lilting through the executive suite dominated by

French and Arabic. Safra even had the washrooms equipped with a distinctly European accoutrement whose presence never ceased to amuse his new chairman, a New York lawyer named Theodore Kheel. "Jesus, Edmond," Kheel chuckled, "we've got to be the only bank in the United States with a bidet."

It hadn't been easy starting a bank in America. American executives wouldn't work for Safra until his banking license was approved, and federal regulators wouldn't approve his banking license until he had a staff in place. Eventually Safra hired Kheel, a prominent Manhattan labor lawyer, to act as Republic's chairman, though his authority was nominal at best. With American tax laws in mind, Safra himself took the title of honorary chairman, though there was nothing honorary about the total control he exercised over the new bank's operations.

As at other banks, loans were approved by committee, but everyone around the table knew it was a committee of one. As at other banks, loans were made on the basis of an individual's net worth, but at Republic there were seldom financial documents for officers to peruse, for the simple reason that many of the bank's clients—Arab sheiks, Nigerian businessmen, Argentine cattlemen—refused to quantify their wealth on paper. In their volatile countries, where governments changed with the season, it could be a dangerous, even fatal, thing to do.

"So how do we know if this guy's good for the loan?" Ted Kheel would ask.

"He's okay," Safra would say, and all discussion would end. Either Safra had the information he needed in his head, or some other intangible entered the picture; often Jacob Safra had known the man's father. "My father told me it was all right to bank with that family," Safra once noted of a certain Saudi clan. Many customers, in fact, had been banking with the Safra family since before anyone on the loan committee had been born. Whatever the case, no one questioned Safra's decision. He was the undisputed ruler of his realm, a banker on duty twenty-four hours a day. "He was one thousand percent business," Ted Kheel remembers. "I don't think there was anything else he was conscious of."

So total was Safra's obsession with his new American bank that when in New York he saw no reason to leave the building. On the ninth floor architects had tucked away a small apartment for him, as well as another small room for his valet Francisco; in Republic's early days Safra would fly in from Europe or Brazil, take a limousine to the bank, and stay there until the limo returned weeks later to take him back to the airport for his outbound flight. A telephone was installed in his bathroom, and when aides would visit early in the morning, Safra would stand at the wash basin, shouting orders over the phone and at them while shaving.

From the outset Republic, like TDB, was an institution notoriously insulated from outsiders and non-Jewish influences. At first its depositors and borrowers were almost exclusively foreign, many of them Sephardic clients of TDB who needed the services of a bank in New York. Ted Kheel's assistant, Charles Wardell, was one of the few Christians anywhere near its executive suite, and he felt the cool distance of Safra's men, who while scrupulously polite never consulted any non-Jew on matters of import. "I never felt like I knew what was going on; they wouldn't give me an ounce of authority," Wardell recalled years later. When the time came to make a decision, Safra would summon his circle of Sephardic aides behind closed doors and then issue their marching orders. Not even Peter White, a Manufacturers Hanover man Safra brought in as president to satisfy federal banking authorities, was allowed in.

"Rare was the non-Jew they would deal with," Wardell recalled. "Their world consists of the Jewish world, and they are unwilling to risk any relations with non-Jewish people. They keep to themselves, and deal only with each other." Only after considerable nagging was Wardell able to drag Safra down to Citibank to meet one of his old Princeton pals. "I thought it was important for him to get to know the WASP community," Wardell recalled, "but Edmond was just so suspicious of the whole thing."

By American banking standards, Republic was a throwback to the nineteenth century. When in 1969 a young Wall Street investment banker named Jeffrey Keil strolled into its lobby to meet a college chum for lunch, he almost laughed upon finding a stack of prospectuses laid out for customers' perusal. The papers covered an offering of a few million dollars in bonds, so small Keil could have sold it all in an afternoon on the telephone; Safra, though, was selling it over the counter in lots of $1,000, no real surprise for a man whose only sales aid for Republic's public offering in 1966 was a single advertisement in *Time* magazine's international edition.

In time Jeff Keil met Safra and impressed him with dozens of ideas to spur Republic's growth. In 1971, having persuaded him to float a stock offering for Republic, Keil took his gently eccentric client on a swing through California to generate interest at the West Coast brokerages. For the first time he had long, private discussions with Safra about his strange little bank, whose steady growth had brought it to $17 million in capital from the $11 million Safra had used to start it five years before. Keil had all but memorized Republic's pristine balance sheets, had fallen in love with their strength and dependability, and saw no reason why, with the minuscule returns Safra paid his depositors, the bank couldn't be a major player in American financial circles.

"Edmond, there's no reason you can't take this to $100 million in a matter of years," Keil said, and he was surprised by Safra's answer. "To really be in the right league," Edmond Safra said, "you need $250 million in capital."

"Two-fifty? Why two-fifty?"

"Because that's how much Irving Trust has." Irving Trust, as everyone knew, was the smallest of the elite New York banks. That Safra was shooting so high so fast should have been laughable. But Keil, who soon came to work for Safra full time, was slowly beginning to understand this sly Lebanese. "Edmond, we can do it in five years," promised Keil.

It took four, but it wasn't easy. Safra's first step toward expansion was nearly disastrous, and would lead to a brush with the criminal world whose echoes would still be heard in the odd, unexplained newspaper articles seventeen years later. In 1971, having bought a ten percent block of its stock from the investor Saul Steinberg, Safra began quietly building a stake in a small Brooklyn-based bank named Kings Lafayette. The problem, as soon became embarrassingly evident, was that Kings Lafayette, its seventeen branches strewn through working-class neighborhoods in Brooklyn and Queens, had equally close ties with far less desirable customers.

Safra approached Kings Lafayette stealthily, employing a little-used securities-law loophole that allowed him to maintain secrecy by buying his shares as an individual rather than as a corporation. Then suddenly, even as he pondered his next move, federal agents arrested eight purported members of New York organized crime families for giving false information to gain thousands of dollars in loans from Kings Lafayette. One of those apprehended was a suspect in the previous year's bloody shooting of mob chieftain Joseph Colombo. "Kings Lafayette," one investigator said, "is what we call a 'family bank,'" and it was clear he didn't mean the nuclear kind.

Safra eventually won out in a nasty takeover battle, sending Jeff Keil to buy up stock from the bank's largest holders, a group of lawyers and small businessmen along Brooklyn's Court Street. But the takeover brought Safra his first taste of American-style publicity, as well as a healthy dollop of suspicion. His use of the secrecy loophole, bypassing traditional American takeover tactics, only made things worse. "If Al Capone came back with $100 million and bought control of Chase Manhattan, he wouldn't have to account to anybody," fumed one New York banker to *Business Week*, which described Safra as a "respected but little known Lebanese-born Sephardic Jew."

Still, Safra was thrilled and followed up his triumph a month later by announcing plans to take TDB public in a European stock offering underwritten by the Rothschilds, a partnership with Ashkenazi royalty that Safra felt brought his banks to the threshold of international acceptance. "I'm now competing with the big boys," he preened in an interview with *The New York Times* that fall. "I must say, the Americans have been very kind to me. Doing business in America is beautiful."

The next step in Safra's expansion proved far more creative. TDB had always attracted deposits by virtue of its status as the Sephardic community's Swiss bank; Republic, though growing rapidly, had nothing so unique to offer. And so in 1969 it came up with something new: free color television sets. Safra offered sixteen-inch Zenith sets, and Singer sewing machines, for every three-year deposit of $10,000 or more, evading federal regulations on gift-giving by bestowing them on the person who brought in, or "sponsored," the depositor. It was a gimmick, but a spectacularly successful one. Shareholders arriving at Republic headquarters for the annual meeting in the spring of 1972 had to pick their way through crowds milling in the lobby. Several shareholders pleaded with Safra to throw off his clinging veil of corporate secrecy and let the world know how well Republic was doing. "As it is," one complained, "all anyone knows about us is that we sell more TV sets than anyone else in New York."

It was true. By one count, Republic was doing more television business than Macy's. Safra's competitors snickered, calling Republic "the TV bank," but it was Safra who had the last laugh. A color television was a small price to pay for long-term deposits with low interest rates; if the crowds thronging Republic's lobby had thought it through, they would have realized that they could have bought several televisions, plus a toaster and a second-hand refrigerator, by putting their money in better-yielding investments. Safra could only watch the crowds and smile. "Thanks God," he said one day, rapping his knuckles on one of the bank's fine antique desks. "People are so stupid."

The TV gimmick gave Republic a base of low-cost deposits any competitor would envy, but the real engine of the bank's profits lay deep in the sub-basement of its Fifth Avenue headquarters. There, in specially constructed vaults patrolled by armed guards, Safra hid vast quantities of products considered so volatile, so risky, that no other major American bank dared deal in them: gold and silver, row upon row of shining metal bars, bought and sold by a cadre of Republic traders in countries around the world. (When completed in 1982, Republic's new vaults were said to be the most modern precious metals warehouse in North America, their interior loading bay capable of handling four armored trucks and two tractor-trailers at once.)

Before individual Americans were allowed to own gold in 1975, Safra's traders haunted the markets for gold coins and industrial gold, at one point controlling up to a third of the U.S. market for gold used by dentists and other businesses. By 1980 Republic had become the largest distributor of gold coins and gold bullion in the United States, and it was the only American bank daring enough to dive into widespread international trading. Safra's family, of course, had been trading gold and silver across the Middle East since Abraham Lincoln sat in the White House. It was a natural complement to a banking business centered on refugees and the worried wealthy.

But gold, like Swiss banking, could be a dirty business, a fact that did nothing to quell the murmurs spreading even then about Safra. Before the advent of airport security machines, fully half of all the gold bars bought and sold in the world were transported by Middle Eastern smugglers, often wearing specially designed "gold jackets," in which up to fifty pounds of gold bars could be secreted. No one knew where Safra's banks got their gold supplies—Nigeria and South Africa were the best guesses—but gold jackets weren't unknown at TDB. "Gold has no smell and no nationality," *Forbes* noted in a rare 1975 profile of Safra. "Neither does it have any morals. It is a world where gangsters and dictators and tax dodgers—and the sincerely worried wealthy—are all alike. Don't ask and don't expect to be asked questions is a Safra credo. It has served the Safras well, as it has served bankers since time immemorial."

To Safra, who knew the gold markets like he knew the Talmud, there was nothing risky or speculative about gold. "I could have made $20 million in gold last year, but I chose to make maybe $8 million," he explained to the reporter from *Forbes*, motioning to the portrait of his father hanging behind his desk. "That's what my father always taught me: take the sure thing."

But in truth he worried; worrying, after all, was what Edmond Safra did best. "It's the Jew in me," he said, and his aides knew it was true. The prism of suspicion through which Safra viewed the world, they noted, was a classic Jewish mind-set; his own virulent brand of fretting was uniquely Sephardic, the birthright of an immigrant people who had lived under an Islamic yoke for centuries before finally being chased from their homes a generation before. "You have thousands of vultures who are always trying to eat you," Safra liked to say. "If you're not strong, they'll eat you up." It was the hymn of refugees everywhere. For despite his wealth, the mansions and yachts and palatial apartments, Safra was still a refugee at heart. Everything about his businesses—the secrecy, the Swiss accounts, gold hoarding—belonged to the cult of the refugee. Everywhere, among his competitors, in the press—which he zealously shunned—he saw vague enemies, challenges to his safety. He hired bodyguards and, it was rumored, tucked away his own caches of gold should Armageddon approach.

A few of his American aides, whom he peppered with phone calls at all hours of the day, thought he was neurotic, but he was simply a tireless worrier, a chief executive who managed his minions by talking them to death. He didn't believe in memos, nor was he adept at delegating authority. Both TDB and Republic ran less like modern corporations than medieval merchant families, every decision personally reviewed by Safra, whose style was to talk over the tiniest details for days on end. His wife, Lily, would wake at all hours of the night to find him whispering on the telephone; it was, she complained, like trying to sleep in a board meeting.

Safra thought nothing of keeping his men cooped up for hours in a telephone booth on a sizzling summer day, poring over some interest rate move by the German Bundesbank or details of an upcoming gold auction. When aides grew impatient Safra calmed them with a soothing endearment, either the Arab *habibi*, or the French *mon chéri*, terms he bestowed on men and women alike, a habit that prompted more than one male associate to emerge from his office and exclaim happily, "Edmond called me 'dear'!"

Safra's marriage to the wealthy Lily Monteverde in 1976 had a soothing effect on him. Edmond, who had dated over the years, had always been wary of gold-diggers; friends suspected he was attracted to Lily in part because she didn't need his money. Their marriage ceremony in Geneva was presided over by Haham Ovadia Yossef, the chief rabbi of worldwide Sephardim. Though his lawyers denied it, the prenuptial agreement was rumored to run to six hundred pages. "Congratulations on your upcoming merger—I mean marriage," quipped Ted Kheel. In Lily, Edmond discovered a new world. He delighted in her grandchildren, whom he called *mes amours*, my loves. In later years the two increased their social profile, but their idea of a relaxing evening remained playing backgammon at home with the grandchildren, eating TV dinners washed down with a good claret.

By 1980 Safra, approaching the age of fifty and the height of his power, had grown to be a man of ritual. Whether in Europe or America, he rarely arrived at his office before noon, preferring to work the phones from his bedroom all morning. He always wore an identical, navy blue, three-piece suit, usually with a dark polka-dot tie; he called it his "uniform." The closets at his sprawling apartments—in Geneva, Paris, London, and New York—held rack upon rack of these suits, as well as identical sets of other clothes, allowing Safra to travel without luggage. Each morning he donned his uniform with the help of one of his valets, a different man at each apartment; all had been with him for years.

The same could be said for many in Safra's inner circle. Cyril Dwek, a wisecracking Lebanese playboy who tooled around Manhattan in a chauffeured Porsche 928, had been among the trusted Halabim who founded Republic in 1966; Dwek's family had known the Safras longer than many Westerners could trace their ancestry. Jacques Tawil, the banker who had escorted the teenage Edmond to Rome in 1948, was still at his side in Geneva three decades later. Walter Weiner, a Manhattan lawyer who had represented Lily Safra over the years, became one of the few Americans advising Safra in the late 1970s; Safra was so impressed with Weiner, a hard-driving control addict, that he named him Republic's president, and later chairman. In 1978 Jeff Keil brought on board one of his closest friends, a promising young Wall Streeter named Peter Cohen, but Cohen remained at Republic only a year before returning to his post as assistant to the chairman of the Shearson Loeb Rhoades brokerage firm.

Safra rewarded those who stayed lavishly; the two Americans, Keil and Weiner, who by the late 1980s would be Safra's most trusted aides, became multimillionaires and built vast, cathedral-like vacation homes in the Hamptons. In return, Safra demanded a degree of subservience and loyalty few American executives could fathom. At least one of his top men hung Safra's portrait behind his desk; in winter Walter Weiner, though chairman of one of the United States's twenty-five largest banks, could be seen helping Safra on with his coat. In meetings Safra could scarcely begin rubbing his eyes before a secretary would snatch up one of his half-dozen pairs of glasses and hand them to him. And always, when talking with depositors and financial analysts, Weiner and the others spoke in awed tones of the Safra legend, regaling listeners with tales of Safra's extraordinary instincts and insight, which they portrayed as bordering on the metaphysical. "The only time I can truly understand Edmond," Weiner liked to say, "is when I sit back and believe in ghosts and witches."

Rarely glimpsed was the dark side of his personality, Safra's rumored ruthlessness. Though never a screamer, he could be quietly brutal when aides let him down. After learning that one of his longtime investment bankers had been fired from his job in disgrace, the first words from Safra's mouth weren't about the man's mental state or his future, but about the loan Republic had extended on his New York apartment. "How much exposure do we have?" Safra wondered. A longtime associate confides: "No one ever sees it, but we all believe Edmond would cut your balls off if he had to."

By the late 1970s his dark side was just one of the stories rival bankers were whispering about the enigmatic Middle Eastern-cum-Swiss banker with the strange vaults beneath Fifth Avenue. As TDB and Republic grew, the only thing more notable than their success was the mystery that enshrouded it, a fact noted in a ground-breaking *Institutional Investor* cover story on Safra in 1979. The first full-fledged profile of Safra ever published outside Brazil, it was this single, lengthy article more than any other that alerted much of the financial community to his stunning successes.

"The Secret World of Edmond Safra," the headline read. "He may well be the richest and most successful banker in the world. He is also one of the least known. Until now." Writer Cary Reich termed Safra "perhaps the most successful banking entrepreneur of the postwar era" and likened his fortune to that of David Rockefeller and Guy and Edmund de Rothschild. Reich also delved into the Safra mystique. "Inevitably, Safra's incredible track record, unusual business mix and passion for secrecy has spawned considerable speculation and innuendo about what he is *really* up to," he noted. "A loan syndication officer at a major American bank remarks that 'whenever you mention Safra's banks in a meeting, everyone sort of grins. It's assumed they have shady connections.' With his heavy involvement in the gold market and his Middle Eastern origins, some outsiders surmised that he was a heavy speculator whose banks stockpiled smuggled gold."

Safra, in an interview, shrugged off the rumors, as did the magazine. "First my competition says, 'Safra has no heart,'" Safra complained. "Then they say, 'He has no hair.' They tell you everything. But I usually say, 'Thanks God, I would like to always have my competition jealous of me.'" The only thing that mattered to him, Safra indicated, was his reputation for honesty and thrift: a man's honor, he always said, was the only thing that outlived him. "My father used to tell me there are three things you need to succeed in banking," Safra told the magazine. "They are honesty, reputation and hard work. Of course reputation is very important to me—that is my Oriental side."

In New York as in Brazil and in Switzerland the Jewish flavor of all the Safra banks remained undiluted. In the early days Republic's dining room served only kosher food, until Ted Kheel complained it was inedible. From time to time rabbis were still called in to settle customer disputes. In Republic's executive suite, Jeff Keil opened his conference room Thursdays at noon to allow the more devout bank officers and customers to hold Talmudic reading sessions. And like prominent Jewish businessmen the world over, Safra knew and conferred often with the leaders of Israel, including Golda Meir and Chaim Herzog. He was a large and frequent contributor to Israeli causes, leading to the inevitable rumors that his banks were hospitable nests of Israeli spies.

Safra's adherence to Jewish tradition caused dilemmas seldom faced by other major banks. After breaking ground on the green-glass skyscraper that would tower over Republic's old Fifth Avenue headquarters when opened in 1984, the question arose: how to secure the all-important mezuzahs—tiny cylinders holding bits of the Torah—to granite pillars at the entrance? Architects first planned to attach them with no outer protection, until Walter Weiner pointed out they would become the target of every vandal with a sledgehammer. A new design was drawn up in which the mezuzahs were planted inside the granite and covered by windows of bulletproof glass. But that gave rise to a thornier question. Tradition called for those passing the mezuzah to kiss it, or touch it and kiss one's hand: would rabbinical law allow Safra's customers to kiss bulletproof glass instead? A rabbi was summoned, and with his official thumbs-up, construction was allowed to proceed.

As the 1980s dawned, Edmond Safra found himself facing far thornier problems than bulletproof mezuzahs. His banks were rock-solid performers, among the strongest in their countries. In later years Goldman Sachs & Co. would term Republic the "closest to perfection" of the "peerless three American banks," one step above even the vaunted J.P. Morgan. But outside, the world was changing. Years before it became fashionable, Republic and TDB had both lent tens of millions of dollars to Latin American governments like those of Venezuela and Mexico, and there were ominous signs that these countries might not be able to repay their debts. By 1980 angry talk was beginning to course through the Third World about imperialist bankers who were suffocating developing countries. One of Safra's men had returned from Mexico City with news that Mexico might actually default on its debt. Wide anxiety over Latin American debt wouldn't intensify for several years, but Safra saw it coming, and it worried him.

Later, many of his friends would look back on this period and try to analyze where Safra went astray. Yes, there had been problems on the horizon, but the banks were strong, incredibly so; for all the troublesome Latin American loans, there had been no reason to do anything drastic. The changes, it seemed, were in Safra the man, not Safra the business. From Geneva he looked out at the harsh new realities of his world, then glanced back into his living room, where Lily and the grandchildren sat so adoringly, so calm, so unlike the unruly Argentinas and Mexicos. His brother Joseph and his closest aides noticed a change in him then, a mellowing, a yearning for something simpler, a break from the manic, twenty-four-hour-a-day, phone-in-the-bathroom pace he had set over the last three decades. For the first time they heard him talk of slowing down, taking it easy.

But for all the subtle differences, no one was prepared for the dramatic new course Safra veered onto during the winter of 1982. One morning that December he called in Walter Weiner and broke the stunning news. The time, Edmond Safra said, had come to make some changes.

He was selling the children.

3

For the trim, perfectly coifed young man in the corner office forty stories above Wall Street, the glowing headlines changed everything. Hands down, the best had to be *The New York Times*. "All Agog Over Jim and Sandy," the *Times* had gushed. For Jim Robinson the accolades were long overdue. At forty-five he had endured four years of sniping about his stewardship of the American Express Company, four years of digs about his baby face, his rich Atlanta drawl, and, more pointedly, his string of badly botched acquisition attempts. Behind his back catty Wall Streeters even made fun of the Roman numeral after his name, calling him "Jimmy Three-Sticks," a nickname he despised.

But now, in the spring of 1981, in a single stroke of genius, he was Jimmy Three-Sticks no more. The financial press had crowned him James D. Robinson III, the visionary corporate chieftain who was pioneering the bold new concept of "financial supermarkets" by shelling out nearly $1 billion to buy the Wall Street brokerage firm Shearson Loeb Rhoades. "Era of Finance Conglomerate May Dawn on Wall Street," *The Wall Street Journal* trumpeted. Forgotten overnight were the awkward overtures to Philadelphia Life; to Book-of-the-Month Club; to Walt Disney; worst of all the wrenching, scandal-tinged mugging of McGraw-Hill. Around the Xerox machines at headquarters they whispered that Robinson even looked a little older, the hairline a tad higher, a statesmanlike streak or two of gray in the precision-combed hair.

Looking back a decade later, it was all a perfect coming-out for the new Jim Robinson, the corporate leader for the 1980s, the executive of vision one mentor after another had seen beneath the bourbon-smooth façade ever since his graduation from Harvard Business School twenty years earlier. That Tuesday morning in April he and Sanford I. "Sandy" Weill, Shearson's Brooklyn-raised chief, had emerged from their long, emotional negotiations—Weill had actually broken into tears when they were finally concluded—and been escorted by Robinson's public relations people into a perfectly planned press conference, choreographed down to the American Express ties both men donned for the occasion.

It was the beginning of a new era for Jim Robinson's American Express, a period of unbridled expansion that over the next decade would take both the man and the company to the pinnacle of the business world. By the time Robinson's personal merger mania ran its course, the acquisitions he oversaw would make American Express one of the few companies that could legitimately be called a financial superpower. It would be the largest American service company of all, flexing its muscles in insurance, banking, credit cards, and on Wall Street. Its revenues by decade's end would top $25 billion, on a par with the economies of Ireland and North Korea. It would hand out paychecks to 108,000 employees in 2,673 offices in over 130 countries, and manage $200 million in funds. Thirty-four million people used its charge cards. Robinson himself would become one of the best-known corporate leaders in the world, rubbing elbows with presidents and kings, floating plans to solve the world debt crisis and helping to open up Japanese markets for American products.

It was rare in the annals of American business to find a chief executive so perfectly matched to his empire as Jim Robinson was to American Express. Both conveyed an image of clubby exclusivity, Old World prestige, and square-jawed integrity, an aura Robinson, with his monogrammed cufflinks, gold tie clasps, and boarding-school reserve, wore like the finest cologne. It was an image, artfully promoted and manipulated, incessantly beamed around the world via television, radio, newspaper, magazine, billboard, hot-air balloon, corporate sponsorships, lobbyists, and practically every other means of communication known to man short of tribal drums.

At American Express the proper corporate image wasn't an afterthought, a throwaway ad on the Sunday-morning issue shows alongside those of General Electric and Archer-Daniels-Midland. To Robinson, and to American Express chairmen going back a century, it was the heart and soul of the business, not only to the millions who used the

American Express Card, but to the hordes of tourists from Paris to Penang who bought American Express travelers cheques each year expecting repayment, no matter what. Without public confidence in their products, the men of American Express had long known, they were out of business. "Integrity," Jim Robinson liked to say, "is fundamental to every business we're in."

In Robinson's early years as chairman the financial embodiment of this commitment was the company's unbroken streak of thirty straight years of annual profit increases. In the halls of American Express they called it "The Record." Robinson's predecessor Howard Clark had guarded it with an ardor bordering on obsession, making sure that each year the company's profits inched up at least a little, even if it meant a sprinkle of accounting magic. Through scandal and wars and economic hardships The Record symbolized American Express's tradition of solidity, both to financial analysts and Main Street consumers. Above all else, American Express executives were pledged to preserving it.

Image, too, consumed the man who ran the company. Early in his career Robinson had turned to speech coaches to smooth his boardroom delivery, which over time, colleagues felt, became second to none. His top consultants included Roger Ailes, the savvy Republican kingmaker. Even the tall, thin second wife he was to take in 1984, Linda Gosden, was president of her own influential public relations firm; friends could only roll their eyes when Linda Robinson cast adoring looks at her husband or urged a reporter to caress his bulging pecs. With her coaching, and with the energies of legions of attentive American Express p.r. people, by the height of his fame in the late 1980s Jim Robinson would have been among the least likely choices to pose for one of his own company's commercials: "Do you know me?"

Everyone knew Jim Robinson. At the height of his fame Robinson's life was packaged into easily digestible factoids that slid seamlessly into an unending series of adoring corporate profiles. Readers of *Business Week* and *Fortune* and *The Wall Street Journal* all knew of his passion for weightlifting, how he got started with barbells after a bully beat him up in college. Robinson's morning routine had been published so often that members of the financial press could recite it by memory: Up at 5:40 A.M., onto the rug for three hundred sit-ups and leg-lifts, followed by strenuous aerobics to his favorite exercise video, "Buns of Steel."

Sometimes forgotten in all the adulatory profiles, all the hype of the eighties, was that there had once been a smaller American Express, headed by a smaller Jim Robinson, a young, tentative chief executive with big ideas and one or two stalwart businesses to build them on. Back before the turn of the decade, few knew of Jim Robinson and fewer still paid serious attention to the machinations of the sluggish old company he ran. American Express was just one more American company trying to shake off its musty history and emerge into a newer, tougher, more aggressive age of business.

From its headquarters on lower Wall Street, the budding multinational corporation Jim Robinson oversaw in the 1980s bore no resemblance to the tiny company his corporate forefathers had founded in 1850 in Buffalo, New York.° The American Express Company had emerged fully formed from the truce ending a furious struggle between rival express-messenger companies over the rights to transport freight through upstate New York. In what went down in company annals as the Treaty of Buffalo, members of three warring companies sat down at Mansion House, the main financial building in downtown Buffalo, and over the course of eight days in the spring of 1850 agreed to merge. They called the new company American Express.

The oldest of the three firms, Wells & Company, was headed by a flamboyant former Erie Canal ticket agent named Henry "Stuttering" Wells; its chief rival was led by a former stagecoach driver named John Butterfield, who already dominated the stage traffic west of Albany. When the two realized that neither would win a price war, they agreed to form an uneasy alliance, taking in a third concern, Livingston Fargo & Company, which handled courier service into the frontier areas west of Buffalo as well.

The business of the newly formed American Express Company was a forerunner of express services like Federal Express today, except that messengers in those days carried packages and money on railroad cars, steamships, and stagecoaches. Before the advent of the parcel post and an efficient nationwide postal service, American Express was one of a handful of firms that dominated the courier trade, with each company handling

---

° Since 1874 American Express has occupied three headquarters buildings in the Wall Street area. Until 1975, it remained at 65 Broadway, when it moved for a decade to a new skyscraper near the southern tip of Manhattan. In 1985 it moved to the new World Financial Center development on the Hudson River across from the World Trade Center.

the right to packages aboard each of the major railroads. The men who ran American Express in those early days—and it was only men; no women were hired until the twentieth century—were solid, unspectacular executives who wasted much of their energies in endless squabbling among themselves. Visionaries they weren't. After the board defeated a proposal to extend courier service to California in the early years, two of the founders sat down at the Astor Hotel in New York and formed a company of their own to do it anyway. The new firm took its founders' names as its own, and for Wells Fargo & Company, the rest was history.

For much of the next century, American Express remained a largish, little-publicized cousin to the titans of U.S. industry, its nondescript headquarters on lower Broadway in the heart of Wall Street overseen by a series of colorless, autocratic chairmen. In its early years the company stuck to the express business, a teeming little niche of profits that first exploded during the American Civil War. From the frontlines at Gettysburg, Antietam, and Vicksburg, Yankee soldiers sent home a flood of letters, money, and souvenirs, all in the hands of express agents who swarmed around Union armies like flies.

"Around bivouac fires in the stillness of Southern forests [the agents] were found waiting for the homeward-bound messages that were hastily scribbled on the torn fly-leaves of prayer books, or even on scraps of newspapers," *Harper's* magazine noted in 1875. "Many a time in the thick of battle a faint voice called them to the side of a fallen soldier, with blood oozing from a death-wound in his breast, and entreated them to remain a moment while he transferred to their care a letter or a locket addressed to a girl in the North." Often, *Harper's* noted, a fallen soldier would die before finishing his letter, though for American Express a death merely substituted one profit center for another. The company made even more money shipping home corpses.

Though little known, the leaders of American Express were ruthless competitors. In the early days the board once authorized "criminal means" if necessary to recover money stolen by a company agent in Utica. After the war, a new competitor tried to hone in on the company's courier routes, launching a series of scathing advertisements and planting newspaper articles charging American Express with price-gouging. The company and its allies fought back with ads and articles of their own, forming a committee "to controll [sic] the public press upon Express matters"; even then the men of American Express were notoriously sensitive to their image and dedicated to shaping the media's perception of it. The long, nasty fight ended only when American Express bought out the upstart, as it would several others in the years to come.

The first of the innovations that would transform American Express was the money order, championed at headquarters by a persistent little man in a straw boater named Marcellus Fleming Berry. The U.S. postal service had introduced money orders in 1864, cutting into the express companies' monopoly on transporting small sums of cash, but it wasn't until 1882 that Berry persuaded his cautious bosses that American Express should try it as well. To everyone's surprise the new product was an instant hit, especially with the Italian and Irish immigrants thronging Ellis Island, who discovered money orders were the safest way to send cash back to the old country. The burgeoning immigrant business forced American Express to open offices overseas, in Ireland and Italy, and soon it struck a deal with a British bank to cash its new product at offices across Europe. Almost overnight, American Express money orders could be cashed at thirty-nine locations in ten countries.

In 1890 the company's imperious chairman, J. C. Fargo, traveled to Europe to review the new arrangements, and found not only that money orders were difficult to cash, but that the letters of credit he carried were even more problematic. Wealthy travelers had always carried such letters from their home bank to pay expenses, simply presenting them for cash at foreign banks, where a teller would mark off the sum remaining under the letter's terms. J. C. Fargo, however, steamed as bank after bank forced him to wait for hours to get his money. Surely, the chairman huffed to M. F. Berry upon his return to New York, there must be a better way for travelers to carry money.

And so was born the American Express travelers cheque, to this day the only major invention the company has ever spawned. Introduced in 1891, the cheque was a slow seller before gradually gaining acceptance, eventually becoming the engine of American Express's profits for the next century. Over the years any number of competitors would try to duplicate it, but none would ever be as popular. What few outside the company knew was that profits on the cheque came not from the skimpy sales charge, but from investments of the tremendous "float," that is, the sum of all money the company took in, and which it promised to repay upon demand at offices from Tokyo to Tucson. For American Express the sale of a single cheque was essentially a short-term, no-interest loan;

as long as tourists carried them uncashed in their wallets, the company was free to invest, and profit, from the idle funds.

For American Express this diversification couldn't have come at a better time, for by the opening years of the twentieth century the express industry was swiftly approaching extinction. For fifty years the company and four other expresses had operated as a vast, unregulated monopoly, raising rates at a whim and fighting off legislative encroachment, it was rumored, with bribes to state and local politicians. American Express had grown so rich that an in-house summary, comparing its $28 million in capital to that of major banks, ranked it second only to the giant National City Bank of New York.

But by 1900 times were changing; populists and muckraking journalists were crusading against monopolies in industries ranging from beef to oil to grain, and in time they turned on the express industry. Scathing articles appeared in the *Atlantic Monthly* and elsewhere, prompting Congress to bring the expresses under tight regulation. A series of government investigations unveiled the system of rate-gouging, causing the industry to lose all credibility with the public and laying the groundwork for the government to introduce the parcel post in 1914, the industry's death-knell. By World War I, when Congress finally took over the express business, most of the major expresses had already gone under.

But not American Express, which, buoyed by the growing popularity of travelers cheques, had deftly sidestepped into the travel and tourism business. It hadn't been planned that way, of course. J. C. Fargo, whose reign ended in 1914, had fought the move into travel at every turn; tourists, he said, were "rabble" and "loafers." Fortunately, the company's man in Europe, a onetime Idaho gold-mine superintendent named William Swift Dalliba, was a veteran of American Express's western division, where disobedience to the edicts of headquarters was not only condoned but encouraged. From his office in Paris, Dalliba, seeing firsthand how dependent American tourists were becoming on travelers cheques, developed his own vision for American Express: the company for people who traveled.

Alternately ignoring and fighting the men at headquarters who opposed him, William Swift Dalliba almost single-handedly made his dream come true. Against all orders, he began selling steamship tickets and arranging sight-seeing tours out of American Express offices in London, Paris, and Berlin; when J. C. Fargo found out, he was furious. But

Dalliba wouldn't be stopped. He won a tumultuous fight with Fargo to open a vast new office in a superb location on the Rue Scribe in Paris; to this day the office remains a mecca for American tourists. While headquarters fumed, travelers and his European hosts alike sang Dalliba's praises; the French awarded him the Legion of Honor in 1906. Dalliba's legend was complete when, in the opening days of World War I, he kept the Paris office open day and night to arrange safe passage home for 150,000 stranded American tourists; as panicky crowds thronged the Rue Scribe office, raising fears the office would run out of cash, a pistol-waving Dalliba personally escorted in workers carrying strongboxes of gold. The resulting outpouring of good feeling and favorable press changed forever the image of American Express. In the span of a few years, it became what Dalliba had wanted it to be: the company for Americans who traveled.

Upon Fargo's retirement in 1914 and the demise of the express business, a crew of young turks at headquarters attempted to capitalize on Dalliba's heralded successes by outlining a new vision for the company. They foresaw what they called a "round-the-world" organization, a global power in investments, finance, trading, travel, and tourism, exploiting niches the company's overseas offices had already opened in such areas as freight forwarding and banking. It was a farsighted plan, a glimpse of what American Express would ultimately become, and it led to new offices in Manila, Hong Kong, and Buenos Aires, and a skein of new businesses run out of headquarters, including a foreign-exchange operation and a trading desk.

But it was the right idea at the worst of times. Before the new ventures were given a chance to blossom, World War I and German U-boats torpedoed the tourist business. Soon after, a series of disasters in the company's trading operations, followed by steep losses in foreign exchange, left many of the young turks in disfavor. The board, backed by a new chief executive named George Taylor, held up the ambitious expansion plans. Instead they promoted a taciturn New Englander, Frederick P. Small, who vowed to ensure that American Express "stuck to its knitting."

F. P. Small, named chief executive in 1923 when Taylor keeled over dead from overwork, wasted no time in weaning American Express from what he called "fancy things" and "adventures," eliminating most of the trading, placing tight restrictions on banking experiments in Europe and

China, and clearing out the elements who he felt had led the company astray. He concentrated instead on the company's one consistently profitable business, travelers cheques. Under Small the company actually shrank—business was so slack half of headquarters was rented out—and American Express quietly and uneventfully stagnated through the rest of the 1920s.

No one realized it until it was too late, but F. P. Small's American Express, bland, stale, and marginally profitable, was an ideal candidate for a hostile takeover. In 1929 the unthinkable happened: the hungrily acquisitive Chase Manhattan Bank, eyeing American Express's network of European offices as a quick and easy way to expand overseas, snapped up the company's stock in a bear hug of a takeover that F. P. Small endorsed only after realizing he had no hope of fending it off. It was a jarring, humiliating loss—and probably the best thing ever to happen to American Express. Under the sheltering arm of Chase's financial reserves the company quietly rode out the Depression, gaining its freedom after five short years when Chase's top executives were forced to resign in the banking scandals of the early 1930s.

In the spring of 1934 American Express was the booby prize handed out as severance to Chase's fallen chairman, Albert H. Wiggin, in his day one of the titans of Wall Street. Wiggin demoted the hapless F. P. Small after Small made the inexplicable mistake of asking the board for a raise at the depth of the Depression. To replace him, Wiggin's aides groomed the company's young comptroller, an up-from-the-streets "green-eye-shade" type named Ralph Reed, to take over. Reed was pulled in from his middle-class home in Queens, installed in an apartment at the Park Lane Hotel, and given memberships to the right golf and social clubs; before long Wiggin's men felt he was sufficiently groomed to make him chief executive. In the years before World War II, Reed asserted his control at headquarters by tightening controls and cutting costs with the help of three loyal bean-counters. Together they were known as the Four Horsemen of the Apocalypse.

Once again, a war changed American Express's fortunes. Emerging from twenty years of lethargic management in which its core businesses had remained frozen as if in amber, Ralph Reed's men were prepared for World War II when it came and ready to capitalize when it ended. The American GI was the perfect American Express customer, and the company went all out to woo him. The company advertised its travelers cheques as "torpedo-proof," and the GIs responded. Sales not only didn't fall; they grew. For American Express the war years produced a string of fantastic stories. Its man in Berlin kept the office there open until June 1941 with the help of spies inside the German government. In the Far East company managers weren't so lucky; several were swept up in the Japanese advance on Manila and Singapore and spent the war in concentration camps.

It was after the war that American Express hit its stride. Ralph Reed remembered the travel boom that followed World War I after American doughboys had first seen Europe and bet that a similar boom was in the offing after World War II. "Now You Can Go Places," Reed headlined his self-penned article in *American* magazine in 1946, even before war-era travel restrictions had been lifted. But even Reed was stunned by the postwar explosion in travel, as millions of Americans took advantage of new transatlantic air services to see Europe for the first time. And in every wallet and purse they carried American Express travelers cheques. Cheque sales doubled between 1946 and 1952, with the company recognizing commensurate gains in quietly investing the float. American Express offices around the world became magnets for these first-time tourists; on a busy day twelve thousand people would cram into the Rue Scribe offices in Paris. Worldwide, Reed more than doubled American Express offices in the postwar years, to 139.

The 1950s were a golden era for American Express, as they were for much of American business, a time when more and more wealthy suburbanites discovered travel and came to identify American Express as the company to help them do it. Cheque sales topped a billion dollars a year as Ralph Reed continued his ceaseless efforts to promote tourism, harvesting all manner of medals from thankful European governments and leaping onto the cover of *Time* magazine in 1956 as "The Grand Poohbah of Travel." Two years later, as Americans continued to flex their new economic muscles, the company joined a tide of new charge cards by introducing one of its own, the American Express Card, in its early days a frightfully ugly little rectangle of purplish paperboard. Overcoming steep initial losses and a series of accounting nightmares, the Card ultimately became a mainstay of the company's profits, overtaking the travelers cheque itself as a symbol of the company in the public's mind.

In 1960 Ralph Reed retired and was replaced by Howard Clark, a gray-flanneled, stoutly ethical lawyer and accountant dedicated to introducing the company to modern management techniques. In his last years, Reed had run American Express as his personal kingdom, lining up aides outside his office door each morning for lectures and expecting them to appear at his desk within minutes at the first sound of the special buzzers he kept in their offices. Under Howard Clark, American Express was computerized, reorganized, and slowly decentralized; planning and marketing departments were formed, making way for the company's first slick, national advertising campaign, which identified American Express as "the company for people who travel." It was the best of times, with the Card gaining popularity each season, cheque sales surging, and dozens of new overseas offices opening every year.

Things were humming along beautifully, in fact, when American Express suddenly stumbled into the darkest scandal in its history. One of the company's smallest subsidiaries was involved in an esoteric branch of finance known as field warehousing, in which American Express guaranteed a small company's inventories for bank loans. By far the unit's largest customer was Allied Crude Vegetable Oil Refining Corporation, one of two client companies run by a gregarious character named Anthony "Tino" DeAngelis, whose stated goal in life was to become the "Salad Oil King." Tino DeAngelis's oils were stored at a sprawling tank farm across the Hudson River in Bayonne, New Jersey, and in the early 1960s American Express had made possible much of his growth, vouching for his inventory to major banks.

But in November 1963, in the days immediately following the assassination of President John F. Kennedy, Tino DeAngelis suddenly filed for bankruptcy, and American Express inspectors returned from the Bayonne tank farm with startling news: Allied Crude's oil reserves, which would normally be sold to pay off its debts, were less than estimated — far less. Allied's receipts had shown reserves of 1.4 billion pounds; only 80 million could be found.

It was, Howard Clark said, as if a bomb had gone off in his office. Allied's potential liabilities, which its lenders and creditors would no doubt seek from American Express, were over $150 million, and while American Express was a thriving company, it didn't have anywhere near $150 million in spare change. As the enormity of the fraud sank in, rumors of American Express's own bankruptcy swept Wall Street, and Clark watched his stock fall by half. Doomsday loomed.

But then an incredible thing happened. At the worst moment in the company's 113-year history, Howard Clark engineered its finest hour. Setting the ethical tone, he overruled a contingent of board members who wanted to disown the little warehousing unit and fight its creditors. Instead Clark issued a public statement proclaiming that American Express felt "morally bound to do everything it can" to satisfy the creditors and banks. By all accounts Clark didn't have to take responsibility—many shareholders certainly wished he hadn't—but he felt American Express was duty-bound to do the right thing. It was more than Clark's personal morals, of course. He knew American Express's products were uniquely dependent on public confidence, and without the certainty that American Express would stand behind its commitments, no matter how small, Clark knew the company had no future at all.

Howard Clark's bold decision led to years of legal wrangling—the final lawsuits wouldn't be settled until the 1970s—and an ultimate settlement with creditors of $60 million. American Express emerged from the salad oil scandal stronger than ever. Morale soared. Confidence in the company's products not only didn't drop, it rose sharply; in 1964, during the scandal's darkest moments, cheque sales alone were up nearly twelve percent. Howard Clark was hailed, in one rapturous admirer's words, as a "demigod."

Clark's obsession with personally righting wrongs also led to a fundamental change in the way the company was run; in his absence, his lieutenants for the first time took on real responsibility, and in the process American Express management grew more decentralized, leading to a looser environment and more independence for the company's far-flung divisions. When Clark acquired the San Francisco-based Fireman's Fund insurance company in 1968, Fireman's Fund executives kept their corporate culture, resisting all efforts to integrate it into the larger company. In the years to come a series of new American Express units would follow suit, exercising great autonomy from headquarters.

For all its creeping diversity, Howard Clark's American Express remained at heart the Ozzie and Harriet of the corporate world well into the late 1960s, a rock-solid, family-oriented company whose words and deeds were wrapped snugly in the American Dream. The rioting and demonstrations of a new generation scarcely touched the men of American Express: their idea of a nonconformist was someone who wore a pink shirt. "We were God-fearing family men," recalls one of Clark's top aides, a Dartmouth man named Dick Blanchard. "At the company, there was definitely a family feeling—very decent people acting decently."

It was a family, all right, but an exclusive family of white, Anglo-Saxon Protestants among whom Jewish executives were about as welcome as the flu. One of the company's board members was a southern businessman said to be so prosegregation, so anti-Semitic, people joked that he believed in slavery. In truth, American Express had never been especially sensitive to Jewish interests: Ralph Reed had traveled around Europe in deluxe train cars built for Hermann Goering. In 1956 Reed had kicked up a storm by closing the company's Tel Aviv office, a move that appeared to give in to the Arab boycott of Israel. After denunciations by Jewish leaders, the office was reopened. "We were all a bunch of WASPs; you'd almost have to say we were anti-Semitic," recalls Dick Blanchard. "There wasn't a shred of evidence that we ever used anyone or hired anyone Jewish. They just weren't around. I don't recall this ever even being talked about."*

Into this clannish group in 1970 stepped Jim Robinson, then a young Georgia WASP nine years out of Harvard Business School by way of Morgan Guaranty Bank. Robinson was the ideal up-and-comer for a lily-white American Express, a son of southern wealth, bright, hard-working, happily married to his college sweetheart, with two children. So comfortable was Jim Robinson in the halls of corporate power, so polished and at ease with the older men who guided his career, that colleagues joked it was as if he had slipped from his mother's womb into pin-striped diapers. He had been born into a line of corporate chieftains in the world of Atlanta aristocracy, enjoying an upbringing of debutante balls and white gloves, golf at the exclusive, whites-only Augusta Country Club, prepping at Virginia's Woodberry Forest and pressure, intense, unyielding pressure, to be the kind of man his father demanded.

As president of Atlanta's First National Bank, "Big Jim" Robinson was, like his father before him, a powerful southern banker, a towering man who wrapped his six-four, 220-pound frame into a commanding presence. The Robinsons were rich, but as rich people go they were unpretentious, and it was assumed that young Jim would follow in his father's footsteps. In his undergraduate years at Georgia Tech, Robinson,

---

* Earlier American Express executives had been even more openly anti-Semitic. "Do not like the name Cohn," J. C. Fargo had written of a prospective employee in the 1890s. "Sounds somewhat Jewish and should therefore advise your looking into his character and business reputation very closely."

at 125 pounds a skinny kid, suffered a thrashing by an obnoxious Alabama football fan, and afterward returned to Atlanta to literally transform himself into an image of his father, pumping barbells for up to three hours a day until, by graduation, he was a rock-solid 205 pounds.

In later years many of Jim Robinson's friends, observing with awe his insatiable drive, twenty-hour workdays, and incredible zeal for solving business problems, would nod knowingly and observe that the son had never stopped trying to live up to his father's expectations. Those who didn't know him assumed Robinson's fast-track career had come with the silver spoon, but it simply wasn't true. Thanks to his father's friends, Robinson did manage to attract a glittering constellation of establishment mentors, but it was hard work and natural leadership that shot him through the doors they opened. At Harvard he wasn't the smartest, but he was the one to whom other students looked to guide their study groups. At post-graduation jobs at two of Wall Street's WASPiest firms, Morgan Guaranty and the investment bank White, Weld & Co., his demanding work ethic was the envy of his peers. "I've never, ever seen anyone work so hard," one of his early bosses told *Business Week*.

After rising to be assistant to the chairman at Morgan and, after his father's death in 1968, a brief stop at White, Weld, Jim Robinson was drawn into the American Express fold by one of his most powerful mentors, Eugene Black, a family friend who had headed the World Bank and who sat on Howard Clark's board. Even then, scarcely into his thirties, there was a buzz in East Coast boardrooms about Robinson, the consummate young man going places, and Howard Clark managed to ensnare him with the promise that, within ten years, he could be chairman of the company.

Howard Clark's old guard, many of whom had been with the company since the war, found young Jim Robinson to be one-hundred percent business. The words they used to describe him were always the same. Gentlemanly. Congenial. Gracious. Controlled. Measured. In his personal style there was never a rift or a ruffle, not in his perfectly pressed white shirts or in the flawless boarding-school manners. Few could say they really knew him, and few who worked alongside him would claim to be his friend. Around the office he was the last man anyone thought to ask out for a beer after work, though he was always affable if coolly and correctly formal. Only on the rarest of occasions would a crack appear in the façade, as in the time he was seen dancing close with a secretary at the Christmas party.

Aside from a brusque assistant his colleagues loathed—and with whom it was rumored Robinson was having an affair—there were no black marks on Robinson's slate, and after seven short years, mostly spent running the company's main Travel Related Services (TRS) unit, Howard Clark retired and made him the new chairman of American Express at the annual meeting in the spring of 1977. The man who lost out on the race for the chairmanship, another bright young newcomer named Roger Morley, was named president; at least initially, the two ran their new empire as a team.

Under Robinson, the changes came quickly. Where Clark had run a tightly knit, familial-style executive suite, Jim Robinson's American Express, like the man himself, was very polished, very professional, and, some noticed, a bit cold. Robinson wasn't out to build the collegial atmosphere of an Apple Computer, certainly not the boys'-club raunchiness of his buddy Ross Johnson's Standard Brands. His gurus were the professors of Harvard Business School and the mainstream consultants at McKinsey & Co. Jim Robinson ran the kind of big, impersonal American company where employees were called "head count"; his style was business by textbook, business by the numbers. One executive remembers Louis Gerstner, a former McKinsey man who became Robinson's No. 2 in the mid-1980s, asking during one meeting how many "units" would need to be cut under a cost-containment plan. "It finally dawned on me," the executive recalled, "that the 'units' he was talking about were people."

At the lower Wall Street headquarters of American Express every presentation was a slide show, and every slide show was faultless, with pie charts and line graphs and yards and yards of analysis, all done according to the latest Harvard and McKinsey concepts. Though he endured as many face-to-face meetings as the next CEO, it was no secret Robinson preferred short, punchy memos he could stuff in a briefcase and peruse in the quiet of his limousine or on the corporate jet; on business trips he would have aides bring him briefcases packed with new work at each stop.

His youthful look had landed him the moniker "Boy Scout," but in fact Robinson deserved the nickname for another reason: He was *always* prepared. In many ways it was the secret to his success. He was a demon for the most detailed budgets imaginable, and every division compiled yearly and monthly cost estimates that they were expected to meet—or else. Robinson hated nothing more than being unprepared, and every year he forced his executives to assemble lists of any possible questions that might arise at the annual meeting. "The book," Robinson's loose-leaf binder of these lists was called; by one count, he had been stumped only once by a shareholder question in his entire career.

Everything was done properly, down to the helpful hints for "good telephone practices" in the company telephone directory. "Answer your phone promptly on the first ring," the guide instructed. "Be efficient by keeping pad and pencil handy. A friendly and sincere voice demonstrates a pleasing personality and reflects a positive attitude." Noted a former American Express marketing executive: "When you see a corporate environment on some old training tape, that's American Express."

But Robinson's by-the-book management style masked his desire to inject new blood into American Express. To his credit Robinson realized that the company's WASPy homogeneity was limiting, and he vowed to bring in talented people with different voices, different backgrounds, and give them freedom to thrive; it was, his supporters felt, his single greatest talent. The changes could be seen in Robinson's new executive team, which included two Jewish executives, the general counsel Gary Beller, and the quick-thinking Washington lobbyist who would later become Robinson's right-hand man, Harry Freeman.

He didn't stop there. From the outset Robinson and Roger Morley focused on ways to expand the franchise they had inherited. A secret McKinsey study had concluded that new challenges being mounted by Visa and others would soon make inroads on their dominant position in travelers cheques, a finding that fueled the argument to diversify the company's earnings. American Express hadn't made a major acquisition since Fireman's Fund in 1968, and there was the feeling in some quarters that the company was stagnating.

Together Robinson and Morley moved quickly to make sure that did not happen. Morley formed a small squad of executives to hash through acquisition candidates, and by the end of their first summer at the helm, the two had a target in their sights. In the opening days of September 1977 American Express surprised Howard Clark's old guard by lobbing in an unsolicited $230 million bid for Philadelphia Life Insurance Company, already the object of a takeover bid from its largest shareholder, the big Houston-based conglomerate, Tenneco. It was a short, sharp fight, and it left American Express's young management team flat on their rears: Tenneco simply upped its bid, sweeping aside Robinson's offer and winning over Philadelphia Life's board. Among the old guard there were snickers, and more than a few raised eyebrows. American Express simply didn't pick fights. And when it did, it didn't lose.

Things only got worse. Two months later Robinson and Morley, accompanied by Howard Clark, flew to Los Angeles on the American Express corporate jet and marched boldly into the headquarters of Walt Disney Productions. It was hardly a subtle approach, and as word of it floated through Disney's halls that afternoon, Disney stock began rising on suspicions of a merger. In a humiliating move, Robinson and Disney executives were forced to issue a joint press statement denying a takeover was in the works; it was only a get-acquainted session, they said. Members of the old guard shook their heads in disgust, even more so after still another overture, this one to the Book-of-the-Month Club, was rejected out of hand.

But Robinson and Morley were not to be deterred. In January 1979 they took aim at their biggest target yet: McGraw-Hill, owner of *Business Week* magazine and the Standard & Poor's rating agency, among other holdings. Roger Morley sat on McGraw-Hill's board, and he and Robinson agreed that the company's mix of publishing and financial-data services were a perfect match for American Express. The problem, it soon became painfully clear, was that McGraw-Hill's combative chairman, Harold W. McGraw, Jr., didn't agree, a message that Robinson and Morley, in a face-to-face meeting with McGraw, inexplicably failed to fathom before they launched an $830 million tender offer they insisted was "friendly."

There was nothing friendly about the ensuing takeover fight, a bruising, two-month affair in which McGraw-Hill, charging that Morley was "a Trojan Horse" on its own board, fought American Express with every weapon in its arsenal, including a series of outraged newspaper advertisements and letters to shareholders, even a libel suit, charging that the American Express offer was illegal, improper, and unethical. Caught flat-footed by the vehement counterattack, Robinson refused to fight back, and continued to insist that American Express wasn't a hostile attacker. The outcome was never really in doubt; after more than a month of non-stop criticism, Robinson and Morley dropped their bid.

It was the low mark of Robinson's career, a devastating defeat that threatened to permanently stain the company's white-shoe reputation. With American Express stock sagging near record lows, headquarters was awash in rumors that both Robinson and Morley would lose their jobs. But of course only one did, and after their performances in the heat of battle, the board's choice was clear. "After it turned negative in McGraw-Hill, there was a small group of us, eight or ten or twelve of us, lawyers and finance guys, just living in the office," recalls a former American Express executive. "Jim's attitude, his demeanor, everything, never changed. He was the steady statesman: let's not lose our heads, let's not get caught up in the emotions. It was a textbook performance. I've never seen anybody better in my life. He was absolutely textbook. Roger, on the other hand, some days he was on the ceiling, some days he was on the floor, some days exuberant, some days quiet."

Seven months later Roger Morley disappeared into his last American Express board meeting. Everyone knew someone had to pay the price for McGraw-Hill, and Morley, as the focus of public criticism, was the obvious scapegoat. Morley resigned that October, pledging to obtain a chief executive's job elsewhere. His quest, alas, was not to have a happy ending. After the poisoned atmosphere of McGraw-Hill, Morley was unable to find a major company to head. Ultimately he withdrew to a small village in France, where friends say he lives to this day.

In the wake of Roger Morley's resignation a feeling spread at American Express that it wasn't good for one's health to get too close to Jim Robinson. It was a tangible fear that grew stronger in the years to come as Robinson went through a series of presidents: a former GE man named Alva Way, who resigned in 1983; Shearson's Sandy Weill, who resigned in 1985; Louis Gerstner, who resigned in 1989. "The feeling was, if things weren't going well, don't be the messenger of bad news, because Jim will cut off your head, without a moment's notice, without any second thoughts at all," recalled a former executive vice president.

While Robinson's management style hardly promoted collegiality, it was this fear more than anything else that explained why he appeared to inspire little personal loyalty among his executives; of his top aides, only Harry Freeman and the general counsel Gary Beller were considered tried-and-true Robinson men. "Jim was less like a father figure than the general manager of a hockey team," recalled one of his former aides. "The atmosphere he fostered was 'every man for himself.'"

Instead, Robinson was given to occasional fits of idolatry. As a chief executive committed to attracting new and innovative talent, he regularly "fell in love," as associates put it, with a succession of swashbuckling corporate partners. The first, to the old guard's dismay, was Steve Ross, the glitzy chairman of Warner Communications, which agreed to sell American Express half its cable operations in 1979. At the time Ross was under criminal investigation in the scandal surrounding gangland's Westchester Premier Theatre, and rumors were flying that he was soon to be indicted, though he never was; Warner-Amex, as the joint venture was known, was created only after American Express attorneys thoroughly investigated Ross. In later years Robinson lavished his attentions on a series of men like Ross: Wall Street buccaneers like Sandy Weill and Peter Cohen of Shearson and his pal Ross Johnson of RJR Nabisco, among them. All were men who appealed to Robinson's need, as one longtime friend put it, "to walk on the wild side."

In the wake of the McGraw-Hill debacle, Robinson continued his search for major acquisitions. Study upon study was undertaken internally, one of the best by Harry Freeman in Washington, and all seemed to point to the most promising hunting ground as Wall Street. Robinson looked long and hard at Merrill Lynch, Bache, E. F. Hutton, almost every name in the brokerage business, before finally settling on Shearson. The merger, when it became final in 1981, was Robinson's crowning glory, the first step in what *Business Week* would in 1986 term "what is widely considered the most successful financial services diversification drive of the 1980s."

Together with his new partners Sandy Weill and Peter Cohen at Shearson, Jim Robinson outlined a vision of a financial empire that would offer all things to all people: charge cards, insurance, brokerage services, money management, private banking. It would be unlike any other company ever formed, offering cradle-to-grave financial care for anyone in the world, anywhere in the world. The potential synergies were awe-inspiring: Shearson mutual funds and Fireman's Fund insurance offered to American Express card holders; American Express travel planning offered to Shearson's Wall Street clients. The combinations seemed endless. "The financial supermarket," the press called Robinson's vision, convinced to a man it was the wave of the future. Inside American Express they called it "One Enterprise," the cross-pollination of goods and services to millions of American consumers.

They were heady times. That spring of 1981, no one knew of the acquisitions Jim Robinson and his crowd of boisterous newcomers would embark upon: regional brokerages Foster & Marshall and Robinson-Humphries by early 1982; Investors Diversified Services, a Minneapolis financial consulting concern, in 1983; Lehman Brothers Kuhn Loeb, the venerable Wall Street brokerage, in 1984, and E.F. Hutton in 1987. Nor, in those early days, could anyone have predicted the consequences of Robinson's merger mania: an executive suite torn by jealousy, recriminations, and some of the most virulent corporate politics in memory; Sandy Weill's resignation in 1985; the 1983 Fireman's Fund disaster that wrecked Howard Clark's vaunted earnings record; the fiasco over the $25 billion leveraged buyout of RJR Nabisco, the Atlanta tobacco giant run by Robinson's friend Ross Johnson; the costly 1990 bailout of Shearson followed by Peter Cohen's resignation. No one knew then that the travails of Jim Robinson and American Express would become one of Wall Street's favorite running soap operas in the late 1980s.

Over time the influx of new people and ideas would change the culture of American Express until it became almost unrecognizable. Ralph Lauren remained the designer of choice, and the hottest young bucks still came from Ivy League schools. But the old, white-bread American Express culture—"decent people acting decently"—was relegated to the company's oldest, core businesses, the stodgy men of travelers cheques, the crafty marketers of the Card. Bulging with 100,000 employees by the late 1980s, American Express had no more corporate culture than the federal government. Each operating unit had its own feel, its own rules: go-go Shearson, standoffish Fireman's Fund, the raffish expatriates of the overseas banking offices. As their nominal leader Jim Robinson could strike poses of quality and integrity, but in truth he had no more control over much of his empire than Ronald Reagan did over the squabbling bureaucracies of Washington, D.C.

Still, as Robinson gazed out his office window in the spring of 1981, the future looked bright. Certainly, there were doubters, mostly professional ones. In their Sunday features the beat reporters all speculated how long it would take a canny operator like Sandy Weill to push him out of the chairman's seat. But that didn't bother him. He had weathered stiffer challenges before, and he was confident in the underlying premise of the Shearson merger. From Robinson's vantage point, he was entering a bold new era where the lines between banking, insurance, and the securities business were increasingly blurred, and his company—his empire—sat triumphantly astride all three.

The only nagging problem—it was always the only nagging problem—was the bank, the little hangnail of an overseas subsidiary whose name that year was American Express International Banking Corporation. At American Express, it was known simply as "the bank." The goddamned, godforsaken bank.*

First you heard the sex stories.

The incident at an American Express villa in Manila was practically legend. A half-dozen executives from American Express Bank, accompanied by a like number of Filipino prostitutes, had gathered for a night of merrymaking at the bank's barbed-wire-ringed estate. There was plenty of alcohol, some pinching, lots of grabbing, and before they knew it, the bankers had been enticed from their business suits into the pool, naked but for their smiles of anticipation. All were waiting eagerly for the girls to leap in when someone noticed things had suddenly gotten quiet. When one of the bankers got up the courage to tiptoe back into the villa, he found, of course, that not only were the girls gone, but so were the bankers' wallets and passports. The best part came when a bank representative had to explain it all to the American embassy.

Then there was the one about the American Express Bank executive in Hong Kong who paid a local prostitute with an American Express travelers cheque. The next morning the girl, skirt up to here, blouse down to there, sashayed into the bank to cash it, only to be told she couldn't do so without an account. "Ask that man," the prostitute yelled, pointing at the bank executive standing frozen across the way. "That man over there. He gave it to me."

The bank's rowdy culture during the 1970s could aptly be summed up not only by these oft-told, off-color tales, which may or may not have been apocryphal, but by a joke of the times. The eight-year-old son of a wealthy Arab sheik asks his father for an airplane. Father buys him a 747. Next the son asks for some toys. Father buys him Disneyland. Finally the son asks for a cowboy outfit. Father buys him American Express Bank.

---

*For readability, the subsidiary will be referred to hereinafter by its current name, American Express Bank.

It was a bank, Jim Robinson once said, "without an identity or a history," at least none that the buttoned-down men of American Express wanted to acknowledge. Having accumulated by World War I a mélange of banking licenses necessary to do travelers cheque business in places like Hong Kong, American Express executives had long debated whether to consolidate these pieces into a formal bank. Every few years a different set of executives would take up the debate, and each time it was tabled. American Express, it was always decided, was a travel company, maybe a financial services company, but it was not, and never would be, a bank.

Not until 1964 had Howard Clark asked one of his top men, Dick Blanchard, to investigate the possibility of formally establishing an overseas banking unit. Others had championed banking over the years, and their groundwork persuaded Blanchard that the notion was eminently feasible. The new unit, when formed in 1968, was an odd duck: though headquartered in New York, because of American Express's substantial domestic holdings the bank's charter prevented it from operating in the United States. As its first president in 1968, Blanchard built the bank around its strongest franchises, in Pakistan, where American Express was the only American bank operating in the city of Karachi, and in India and Greece, paying special attention to its single most valuable asset, American Express's long-term contract to provide banking services to American soldiers at bases in West Germany, Japan, and Okinawa. None of it was easy.

"For starters, we didn't have any bankers," recalled Blanchard, who retired from American Express in 1981. "We had to build up a staff of American Express retreads and younger guys from outside, a lot of them mediocre at best. I mean, if a guy had a strong background, why would he come to American Express Bank?"

It was the very question that would dog the bank for the next two decades. Still, by the end of 1970 Blanchard had succeeded in forming something that resembled a small, profitable international bank, at which point he handed off responsibility for its second phase of growth to the young newcomer, Jim Robinson. In two short years as the bank's chairman, Robinson brought in a raft of talented bankers. But the ambitious Robinson by several accounts viewed the bank as the bureaucratic swamp that it later became, and quickly moved on to greater things, hiring a Bankers Trust veteran named Richard Bliss to take his place.

During the 1970s Dick Bliss steered American Express Bank through a period of outstanding growth, doubling its assets in his first four years, though outsiders were often at a loss to fathom what was fueling the helter-skelter expansion. Only after Bliss opened his third office in Bangladesh did anyone think to ask how wise it was to be banking in the world's poorest country. Many thought the bank had no real sense of direction; every other year there seemed to be a new strategic plan. The joke went around that whenever American Express Bank changed directions, it was usually a 360-degree turn. Financially, the bank wasn't a poor performer. Its return on equity could generally be found between twelve and fifteen percent—not bad for a bank, but less than spectacular by American Express standards, which were set by the mushrooming growth of travelers cheques and charge cards. Country heads, acting almost independently, made money where they could, dabbling in commercial lending, trade credits, and foreign exchange.

Some of the bank's other profit centers weren't as orthodox, former executives recall. As the black sheep of American Express, Bliss's men weren't above squeezing profits out of other subsidiaries. Assured they were getting a "special rate," American Express's European charge card managers had been depositing funds in the bank for years, until a sharp-eyed auditor pointed out that the rate was special all right—less than half what competitive banks offered. In Tokyo the bank's practices were even more questionable; for years, a former company auditor says, it had been lending large sums to Japanese loan sharks. "The bank was just this bunch of strange gypsies," recalls a former American Express international treasurer. "No one at headquarters ever really knew what they were doing."

Never actually rising above its charter group of "retreads," Dick Bliss's odd little bank became the unofficial dumping ground for those who couldn't or wouldn't cut it at American Express. The overseas office network was overseen by a cantankerous type named Bill Beam, who preferred bolo ties and was known for throwing grand parties at his Greenwich Village apartment. Another of Bliss's top aides, who would last considerably longer, was Bob Savage, a tiny, combative Cockney who boasted of having been thrown out of the Royal Air Force for braining a drill sergeant with a rifle butt. At five feet, Savage was known around the bank as "The Dwarf," though to mention it in his presence risked a punch from the prickly little Brit.

It was, by all accounts, one hell of a place to work. American Express Bank, it was said, was the kind of company where the secretaries wore running shoes, less for commuting comfort than for the speed they needed to outrun their randy bosses. Country heads, it was rumored, earned their stripes by throwing the best parties and providing the best-looking escorts for visiting headquarters executives. "Fooling around with secretaries and trainees was not an infrequent thing by any means," one former banker recalls. "It was almost encouraged."

In the late 1970s Jim Robinson's new executive team hauled out its own set of strategic plans for the bank, which amounted to tearing down parts of what Dick Bliss had spent the decade building. After pushing aggressively into European markets earlier in the 1970s, Bliss reluctantly began backing out, shutting down operations in Belgium, Heidelberg, and Lausanne. Demoralized, Bliss pushed to buy the bank himself in a leveraged buyout, and assembled a motley crew of Far Eastern investors to help him do so. One thing led to another, and the bank was put up for sale, for what seemed like the umpteenth time, in the summer of 1981. It was widely shopped, and a number of substantial offers came in, but in the end Robinson decided not to sell. One Friday in late August 1981, Bliss disappeared into a meeting of American Express's board. For a number of subordinates, it was the last they ever saw of him. The bank's general counsel, a soft-spoken lawyer named Mark Ewald, found Bliss on the following Monday, packing his belongings into boxes. "It's probably for the best," Bliss said quietly.

What doomed Dick Bliss and his LBO, and what kept his odd little bank in the American Express fold, was Jim Robinson's new "One Enterprise" theory of financial synergies. A worldwide network of banking offices capable of offering Shearson investment products was obviously of enormous value, if someone could only whip the place into shape. And to do it Robinson had found just the right man, a fast-rising newcomer named Robert F. Smith, a man with the face of a Dick Tracy villain and the bedside manner to match. In the months and years to come, Bob Smith, first as vice chairman, later as chief executive, would do more than any other individual to mold American Express Bank's future.

"Gentlemen," he announced in his first days on the job. "I'm here to run a bank, not a country club."

As a young man Bob Smith combined the mind of a mathematician with the manners of an auto mechanic, which, in fact, he had once been. Born in Staten Island, Smith had grown up the son of a factory worker in a gray milltown twenty miles north of Boston. During high school he worked as a mechanic's helper at the local Oldsmobile dealership, a job he loved. He was a hustler, volunteering to undercoat cars during the winter and running down to Boston to pick up parts and cars when needed. College didn't interest him; no one in his family had made it past high school.

What Bob Smith wanted to do was race stock cars, and he pursued his dream on dirt tracks all over New England practically every weekend. At eighteen he was good enough to try the big-money circuit down in Florida, but after a few months he returned north, victories few and cash scarce. He went to work at his father's textile mill for six months, but soon saw that, too, as a dead end.

Looking for something better, young Bob Smith made up his mind to give college a try, and used his savings to enroll at Bentley College, a two-year school in Boston. At nights and on weekends he scraped by, working at his old garage, until the day his boss pointed out a rusty green Olds 98 that needed fixing up. Smith bought it for practically nothing, spent forty hours restoring it, then sold it for $1,000. For Smith it was an epiphany. Working part-time in the garage in order to get spare parts at cost, he fixed up twenty two more cars in the next two years, enough to get him through Bentley with a degree in accounting and launch a career that would lead him far, far from his father's milltown.

A recruiter from General Electric spotted the earnest young mechanic during a recruiting trip, and after graduation Smith joined GE's audit staff. For eight years he inched up the corporate ladder, making stops at places like Bridgeport, Connecticut; Lowell, Massachusetts; and Schenectady, New York. He traveled widely, supervising three-month audits at GE operations all over the world, and was eventually named audit administrator. By 1966 he had been promoted to finance manager at GE's $100 million radio receiver business. Over the next decade he made steady if unspectacular progress through a series of finance positions until, after heading the analyst team on GE's $2 billion acquisition of Utah International in 1976, he was named planning chief for all of GE's international businesses.

It was a good, solid job for Bob Smith, the former milltown mechanic, then almost fifty years old. His wife, Miriam, and their two children were proud. Still, when one of Jim Robinson's top men, a former buddy at GE, offered him the attractive job of corporate treasurer at American Express, Smith instinctively made the jump, leaving behind the only company he had ever known.

At American Express Bob Smith was an instant smash. Long accustomed to living on its cash reserves, the company had begun borrowing from its Chase Manhattan-led bank group to fund Jim Robinson's acquisitive ambitions. Smith's predecessor, an amiable former FBI agent, had done little more than take an occasional lunch with the banks, and the result could be seen in the high interest rates the company was paying. Two weeks after joining American Express, Smith phoned Robinson and requested an immediate meeting of the board's executive committee. He wanted to change the company's master loan agreement before it renewed itself; Robinson gave the go-ahead on his own. Smith then selected the most eager member of American Express's bank group, Security Pacific, and invited its man out to lunch. He dangled before him the prospect of replacing Chase as lead bank, if only Security Pacific could offer better rates. It could, it turned out, and Smith's divide-and-conquer strategy saved American Express an estimated $9 million.

Impressed, Jim Robinson sent Smith to try the same tactic at the company's Warner-Amex joint venture. When its lead bank, the First National of Boston, balked at offering lower rates, Smith got up and walked out of the meeting. "To hell with you guys," he told the Boston bankers. "We'll get someone else." But before he could, First of Boston saw the light, cut its rates, and the savings came out to $50 million or more.

Suddenly, after scarcely six months of hardball, Bob Smith was the new golden boy at American Express. Robinson was thrilled with him. When offered the shot at a line position—his first ever—at American Express Bank, Smith jumped at it. The only problem, of course, was that in nearly thirty years of business Smith hadn't picked up a scintilla of banking experience. It was his inexperience, in fact, that saved the jobs of several of Dick Bliss's colorful aides, including Bob Savage. A number of American Express executives wanted to clear out the bank's entire executive suite, but Smith, knowing he needed guidance, blocked the moves. "Why fire 'em now?" he reasoned. "We can always fire 'em later if we want to."

Bob Smith's arrival created a stir among the fast international crowd at American Express Bank in more ways than one. His speeches were wooden, though they would improve in the years to come, thanks to Dale Carnegie courses. In a business of natty blue and gray pinstripes, Smith's ties were garish and short, his suits shiny and ill-fitting; one bright green model is remembered by subordinates to this day with a shudder. "He looked like he should have been a supervisor on the factory floor instead of a banker," one executive recalls. At first Smith moved cautiously, aware of his inexperience. In his initial weeks few at the bank got a close look at the real Bob Smith, though the general counsel, Mark Ewald, came close. "I'm here for one reason and one reason only," Smith told Ewald, taking out his wallet and slapping it three times, hard. "To make money."

Though his mathematical dexterity was apparent to all, after barely a week even Smith's nimble mind was growing clogged with unfamiliar banking terms. "LDCs and BAs and FDICs—what the hell are you guys talking about?" Smith half-jokingly beseeched a meeting one day. "Speak in English." It was the little Cockney, Bob Savage, who took Smith aside afterward.

"Banking is very easy, Bob," he said. "Good bankers make loans. Excellent bankers collect them back."

That fall teams of young McKinsey MBAs were brought in to assist Smith in his review of bank operations. At Savage's suggestion, the two men and their wives embarked on a whirlwind tour of the bank's empire in November, stopping first in Zurich. There, on a bitterly cold Sunday morning, Smith and Savage took a long walk through the snow, thinking aloud of changes to come if the bank were to survive its current predicament. Then it was on to Germany, Egypt, and Bahrain, where they chartered a Lear jet for a flight to Athens, before ending the trip with a swing through London.

A former Chase Manhattan banker named Derick Richardson was brought in to perform a more thorough analysis, and after touring the empire himself, Richardson brought back to New York the message Smith already expected: American Express Bank was a mess, its European offices wallowing in overhead, with no strategic focus or planning whatsoever. But Richardson, like his superiors, glimpsed a silver lining. If costs could be slashed, he reported, the American Express name alone practically ensured profitability.

They had crackerjack offices in Bahrain and Dubai. The operation in Greece was marginal at best—it seemed to generate more bombings than profits—but Richardson reasoned it was nothing a healthy Greek economy wouldn't overcome. Italy was in the process of selling most of its businesses and consolidating the remainder into a smaller operation. Switzerland, the only bank office catering primarily to wealthy individuals, was the best managed of the bank's European offices, a tight little operation run by an Austrian named Heinz Zimmer. Germany was a constant headache: the Frankfurt-based country head ran it as his personal fiefdom, and no amount of haranguing would make the man take orders from headquarters. The bank's oldest outpost, Paris, with three offices paying titanic downtown rents, was drowning in its own overhead. But the biggest mess was in London. Its basic business, lending money to British firms, was healthy enough. But the sheer cost of running the business was strangling them. The place seemed to function as a country club. White-coated butlers served wine and cigars after lunch. At five o'clock, Richardson reported, he could have shot a rifle through the executive suite and not hit a single man.

Waves of anxiety swept American Express Bank as Smith's study neared its end in March 1982, its findings to be unveiled in several gatherings of bank executives. Invitations to the meetings were sent out weeks in advance. Bank executives scratched their heads, though, at the odd nature of the guest list: branch heads, from, say, Hong Kong, but not those from Singapore or Thailand. Paris was summoned, but not Zurich. There seemed to be no rhyme or reason to who got asked. Was a new pecking order being built? What did it mean?

More than sixty bank executives, some of them still jet-lagged from long international flights, assembled that Monday to hear a Smith aide named George W. Carmany sketch the bank's new direction. As the lights dimmed for the first slides of Carmany's presentation, Smith was nowhere to be seen. "Back to basics" turned out to be the none-too-earthshaking theme of the speech, but before long the bankers were distracted by something else altogether. One of Smith's assistants had padded through a rear door and tapped a gray-suited executive on the shoulder.

"Mr. Smith wants to see you," the aide whispered. Within minutes the aide had returned and tapped another executive on the shoulder, then another, and another. Some of the seated bankers traded anxious glances. Others exchanged curious whispers: "What's going on?" Soon it became clear that none of the executives called from the meeting were returning. As Carmany's presentation flashed from slide to slide, fear replaced his listeners' curiosity. No, more than one whispered, this can't be what it seems. But it was. One by one, each of the branch heads and overseas executives was being summoned from the room, escorted in to see Bob Smith or another executive, and fired. Each was handed a non-negotiable severance package. By the time Carmany finished his presentation, the only executives left in the room were those from headquarters.

Bank executives repeated the same scene at American Express venues across Manhattan; the worst of the slaughterhouses, it was said, was the conference room in the midtown offices of *Travel & Leisure* magazine. Not one of the American Express men who kept appointments in that room were ever seen again. Before the day was over, twenty-one executives with the rank of assistant vice president and above had been sacked. For years afterward, the mass firings would be known within the bank as "Bloody Monday." Most of those who survived the slaughter were too shell-shocked from the day's events to comprehend the new direction mandated by Smith's study: the future of American Express Bank, they had decided, was in private banking, catering in specialized service to the world's wealthiest individuals.

It seemed like a good idea—after all, they had tried everything else—and Bob Smith began assembling a team to bring the new plan to life. To no one's surprise, Bill Beam didn't make the cut; Smith fired him personally. Bob Savage, the fighting Cockney, was brought aboard, as were several newcomers, including Robert Budenbender, a commonsensical Morgan Guaranty finance man who came despite misgivings about the more lurid aspects of the bank's culture. Budenbender became the bank's fourth chief financial officer in five years.

The untidiness of Bloody Monday behind, Smith capitalized on his ties to the American Express executive suite to consolidate his control of the bank. He made quick work of his only rival, the bank's stolid president, Jim Greene, who was elbowed from the command-control loop despite a directive from headquarters that Smith and Greene confer daily. "If I felt like it, I talked to him, if not, I didn't," Smith recalled of Greene. "I did pretty much what I wanted. [Greene] never resisted me.

He knew I had a line to the top he didn't have." Many afternoons, while Smith masterminded the bank's new direction, Greene could be found on the tennis court.

As the last challenges to his power ebbed, Smith instituted what can only be described as a corporate reign of terror. His personal style, never warm to begin with, grew icy and demanding. His treatment of subordinates was brutal. On one occasion, when an overseas telex was misplaced, Smith ripped into a secretary so hard the woman was reduced to tears. Only when she produced the name of the offending telex operator did Smith brighten; he wanted to call the man and fire him personally.

At staff meetings Smith would chastise any executive who arrived seconds late. "I don't pay you to be a minute late!" he would bark. Smith was in his office each morning by seven-thirty, and wouldn't tolerate any banker who arrived a minute past eight. Otherwise, "they got their ass chewed out," he noted proudly. Bob Budenbender recalled, "He would rip into you right in front of your subordinates, which would embarrass the hell out of you."

The tiniest errors could set Smith off. He was forever upbraiding one executive vice president for misspellings in memos and letters. "Can't you spell?" Smith would demand at meetings. "Do I have to do it for you?" These observations inevitably led to Smith's favorite line: "If I have to do it for you," he would say, "then I don't need you here, do I?" Budenbender was among the few to regularly escape Smith's wrath, a fact he half-jokingly attributed to his excellent spelling. Budenbender was so good, in fact, that Smith took to having him write his letters, too.

Sometimes it seemed Smith didn't realize how he terrorized underlings. When an internal study suggested his bank executives suffered the worst morale in the American Express empire, he demanded an explanation. "God damn it," he announced at a staff meeting, "why is our morale so shitty?" When no one answered, Smith turned on one forlorn executive, practically cowering in a corner. "You," Smith jabbed, "your morale is okay, isn't it?" No one said a word.

At other times it was clear Smith knew exactly what effect his tirades were having. Sloppy documentation often left the bank responsible when loans went bad, and that fall Smith ordered that each of the bank's thirty-four country heads hire an outside attorney to review the documentation of every loan in their portfolios. Smith made it clear that he wouldn't tolerate any slipups. When Germany's thorny chief suffered a loan loss shortly afterward and poor documentation was blamed, Smith summoned the man to Zurich and fired him on the spot. "It was kind of a symbolic firing," Smith recalled years later. "It said that if you didn't do what Bob Smith said, you got your head cut off."

There was, of course, method to Smith's madness. American Express Bank was an outfit badly in need of discipline. And under Smith's puritanical sway, it began to get some. On overseas trips Smith finished dinner and headed to his hotel room for paperwork and an early bedtime. Subordinates knew they had to follow his example, or else. The parties, needless to say, ended. "In those early days Smith's behavior bordered on the irrational. It was just constant screaming fits," a longtime Smith aide recalls. "But it was all necessary, you see, to counter the laziness he found all over."

Smith put the British consultant, Derick Richardson, in charge of the bank's European offices, though cleaning them up was a struggle. The London office was so disorganized Richardson realized he couldn't even get an accurate count on the number of employees he had. Every time he asked, the number kept changing. Finally he was forced to pad down the corridor of every American Express location in London and physically count the number of occupied desks. In the end he had thirty more desks than paychecks. "Chaos," Richardson muttered. "Absolute chaos."

The move toward private banking progressed slowly. A number of new investment products for individual investors were discussed, and that summer Smith's team came close to buying a small Swiss bank in Lugano to enlarge its base of wealthy depositors. Still, by that winter, the road ahead finally seemed clear, and no one doubted that Bob Smith was firmly in charge. But unknown to all but a few, Smith's vision would never be realized, at least not in any way he could have foreseen. A week before Christmas, he was summoned upstairs to Jim Robinson's executive suite and given some incredible news. He managed to keep it secret for a week, while events hurtled past unseen. Then, the day after Christmas, he called in his two top aides, Savage and Budenbender, and closed the door behind them.

Smith's reputation had grown so fearsome that for a moment Budenbender thought they were to be fired. If so, he wouldn't have been any less startled than he was by Bob Smith's first words. "Listen," he said, "we've got a great opportunity. You're never going to believe this, but Robinson is thinking about buying TDB."

4

Out at Montauk, on the far eastern tip of Long Island, the bluefish and striped bass run past the lighthouse by the hundreds on cool summer nights. On the best evenings dozens of fishermen come out, some all the way from the city, to stand on the beach and cast their long, snaking lines into the surf. For harried businessmen like Peter Cohen, the young president of American Express's newest business unit, Shearson, it was a soothing tonic to the office, a quiet place to stand and talk with a neighbor or debate the future with an old friend.

Many nights that long, lazy summer of 1982, Cohen and his best buddy, Republic National Bank's young treasurer Jeff Keil, piled into Keil's battered Range Rover at sunset and drove out to Montauk to surf-cast for stripers until well past midnight. Mostly they caught weakfish, but it didn't bother them. Fish, after all, were only the excuse to relax, to decompress. In their mid-thirties, both men were already richer than they had any right to be. As brash young Wall Streeters a decade before, they had met fresh out of business school; now, just over the Fourth of July weekend, Cohen had moved into a vast, modern home in the Hamptons, so grand his friends joked it looked like the TWA terminal at Kennedy.

Both men had their hands full at the office. Keil, a laid-back sort who loved puttering in his gardens, was deeply involved in an analysis for Safra about somehow combining Republic and TDB. Cohen, in turn, was still getting the feel of his new surroundings at American Express, looking for ways to build and exploit the synergies of the financial supermarket Jim Robinson was assembling. He was particularly fascinated by the unfulfilled potential of Bob Smith's odd little American Express Bank. Keil, who had examined Smith's bank for Republic when it came onto the auction block the previous summer, could only agree with Cohen's downbeat assessment. "You're right," he said. "That bank's a mess."

The idea, when it hit them, was simplicity itself. Why not salvage American Express Bank by combining it with Safra's banks? Bob Smith's people were already trying to mimic the private bank model of TDB. Why not buy TDB itself, and transform the entire operation? Keil mulled the idea through September, and the more he thought about it, the better it sounded: like Robinson and Cohen, he too was convinced that the financial world was heading to consolidation, toward a select few financial supermarkets. If so, what better name to be associated with than American Express? He noodled through the financials for six weeks before springing the idea on Safra during a trip to Geneva in October.

To Keil's surprise, Safra listened patiently through his presentation and admitted he had thought of the benefits of a merger as well. The rising threat of Third World loan defaults, the promise of a safe harbor for his "children," the unparalleled reputation of the American Express name—Safra mulled over them all in the coming weeks and found himself warming to the idea of some kind of partnership with American Express. A global conglomerate like Jim Robinson's would give his banks unrivaled clout all over the world. The fact that his other aides disdained the idea of combining with American Express Bank didn't faze Safra. "It's a shit bank," Walter Weiner harrumphed.

Later, analyzing Safra's decision to sell would become a regular parlor game for his aides and associates. Most agreed that the biggest factor in his thinking was his growing fear of Third World debt problems. "The sale of TDB," theorized his investment banker Lee Kimmel, "was the ultimate expression of Edmond Safra's paranoia. He sold out of a fear of the future. His decision to sell would be akin to getting castrated because of a feeling that people with testicles would somehow get in trouble in the years to come."

The courting of Safra began that fall, when Cohen and Keil flew to Paris on November 7 and met him at his apartment. There the three spent the better part of two days talking about the world, about the future of banking and financial services, about the wonderful benefits of the American Express name. Safra had always liked Cohen, was sorry, in fact, that he had returned to Shearson four years before. To Safra, American Express sounded like an elite organization, its board of directors studded with stars like former President Gerald Ford, and if he were going to sell, he wanted his banks in good, strong hands: safety, for himself and his depositors, remained uppermost in his mind.

Cohen, too, was encouraged; he had always regarded Safra as a genius, a living legend. Returning to New York, he briefed Jim Robinson. Robinson was already thinking about attending a trade conference in Geneva at Thanksgiving, and Cohen suggested he use the trip as a cover to meet Safra. The two men did meet in Geneva, and in an unremarkable first encounter, agreed it made sense to explore the idea of a business combination. For Robinson TDB appeared to be a sparkling new aisle to add to his financial supermarket, a collection of exclusive Swiss services to be offered to Shearson and American Express clients, plus a glittering constellation of Safra's wealthy customers to snap up Shearson mutual funds and American Express Gold Cards. The "synergies" were thrilling.

From there things moved swiftly. Safra was paralyzed with fear that word of the discussions would leak, so code words were assigned to all parties. TDB was "Copper." American Express was "Tiger." Safra insisted the acquisition plan itself be code-named Mazel Tov, Yiddish for "good luck." Over New Year's Bob Smith led a team of executives through a whirlwind due diligence tour of Safra's Geneva headquarters, and though they found nothing alarming, it was agreed that because of American Express Bank's prohibition to operate in the United States, American Express would buy only TDB, and would find a way to buy Republic's international operations at some later date.

By the second week of January 1983 Safra was comfortable enough to begin negotiating a price. Montreal's Four Seasons Hotel was chosen as a neutral site for the talks. Publicly the participants would say they chose the Canadian city for secrecy, but in truth it had more to do with Safra's concern with staying too many days in the United States. When Robinson, Cohen, and Bob Smith assembled their team in suite 2908 one Sunday afternoon, they found Safra and his aides already waiting a floor above, in suite 3014. Cohen was the natural intermediary; someone called him "little Kissinger" as he shuttled back and forth between the two groups. By that night, it was clear not only that they were heading for a price around $500 million, but that finishing details would take several more days.

They adjourned for the week, with Robinson flying to Florida, where he joined an outing on Malcolm Forbes's yacht. Safra, meanwhile, boarded an American Express jet and flew to São Paolo to join his brothers Joseph and Moise at a family gathering, where he took time for a trip to talk things over with his father's grave. In New York, Peter Cohen and Jeff Keil convened top-secret meetings every night at a midtown law firm to pound out details. Swarms of lawyers hovered over every decision; at one conclave, Keil counted thirty-two different American Express lawyers. Still, by the weekend everything seemed in place for a final round of talks in Montreal.

There was only one glitch. John Gutfreund, the powerful chairman of Safra's investment banking firm, Salomon Brothers, had gotten wind of the deal and thought it a horrible idea. Gutfreund, who had known and respected the Safras for years, felt Edmond would never fit into the dense American Express bureaucracy and urgently sought an audience to tell him so. Informed that Safra was away in Brazil, Gutfreund felt so strongly he flew to São Paolo; finding Safra at a bar mitzvah all day, he made his case during Safra's long return flight to Montreal aboard an American Express jet—a development that outraged Peter Cohen.

For all Gutfreund's protestations, Safra remained staunchly in favor of the deal when he arrived back in Montreal. A large part of his peace of mind came from a special clause his lawyers had managed to force upon American Express. Walter Weiner had been pondering ways to ensure that Safra remained powerful once inside the American Express fold. "If they don't go along with Edmond's way of running things, he should be able to get out," he observed.

"He should be able to call for a vote of confidence, like Margaret Thatcher," Jeff Keil agreed. And that was what they called it, the Margaret Thatcher clause. Under terms of his five-year employment agreement with American Express, Safra could resign if for any reason his management decisions were overruled. It was an astounding concession for American Express to make, but it reflected the zeal with which Cohen and Robinson pursued Safra.

That Sunday Robinson convened the American Express board in a special meeting at the Helmsley Palace Hotel in Manhattan to vote on the acquisition of TDB. By several accounts, there was some grumbling among board members when details of Safra's employment agreement were aired. But both Robinson and Peter Cohen urged restraint. "You've got to have faith," Cohen assured the directors, as one listener remembers. "Edmond is a great man."

Afterward Robinson, Cohen and a half-dozen other American Express men flew to Montreal, where they arrived around midnight. The concluding negotiations at the Four Seasons stretched past dawn, and as noon approached the next day, everything seemed set. The final price was to be $550 million; a compromise had made a portion of the purchase price in warrants convertible to American Express stock. All told, the shares would make Safra American Express's single largest shareholder, with about three percent of the stock. Leaving last-minute details for the lawyers, Robinson shook hands with Safra and boarded a jet for the return flight to New York.

Shortly after, the negotiators were surprised to see Edmond's trim brother Joseph arrive in the suite. There were smiles and handshakes all around as Joseph Safra introduced himself to the American Express men, but Robinson's people wouldn't have been so cordial had they known the reason for Joseph's surprise trip: he had flown all the way from Brazil for one reason, to kill the deal.

That weekend Joseph had telephoned Walter Weiner in New York and confided his growing doubts about selling TDB. "I just don't know what to do," he told Weiner. "Edmond thinks he's going to sell a bank and take it easy. But he's really going to be buying a bank. They're going to want him to run their bank, which isn't in great shape, you know." Weiner had listened and given the only counsel he could. "Joe, regardless of what you think," he told the younger Safra, "you should be at his side."

And so Joseph Safra had raced to Montreal. By two o'clock Monday afternoon he was closeted in a bedroom with his brother and their advisers. Inside, Joseph made a strong appeal against the sale. "Edmond," he pleaded, "you don't even know these people."

As lawyers from both sides continued work on the fine print, the brothers spoke alone and with Edmond's bald, pink-cheeked New York lawyer, Peter Mansbach, for hours. Edmond patiently explained to his brother the virtues of American Express and the intricacies of the Margaret Thatcher clause, which guaranteed he would stay at American Express only so long as his wishes were followed. But the strongest argument against killing the sale was simply timing. The deal was all but done, Edmond told his brother. "The lawyers are just finishing up, that's all," he said.

In fact, the deal wasn't yet concluded, as Safra was stunned to learn while the talks with Joseph continued that evening. Peter Cohen took Safra aside and informed him that it would be necessary for him to take Bob Smith aboard as his No. 2, as president and chief operating officer of the combined TDB-American Express Bank.

"What are you talking about?" said Safra, who believed he would have the power to name the executive team. Safra barely hid his contempt for Smith, a man with virtually no banking experience who at that moment was sprawled lazily on a hotel couch across the room. To Safra, Smith was a glorified clerk atop a two-bit bank. But Cohen made it clear: no Smith, no deal.

The Safra brothers retreated to their bedroom. "You see?" Joseph told his brother. "You can't live with these people." Edmond was shaken. He had no wish to share his power with Bob Smith or anyone else: this was to be his bank, a Safra bank, run independently as part of the great American Express empire. Still, he telephoned and woke his longtime second-in-command Albert Benezra from a sound sleep in Geneva and broke the news that Smith would have to be president. Benezra, who had been promised the job, burst into a rage. Safra managed to placate his aide by promising him more money and the slightly less prestigious title of vice chairman.

But even as Safra did his best to close the deal, Joseph kept hammering at him: these people were strangers, he said, they couldn't be trusted, they would make him an employee for the first time in his life. The hour grew late, but still the two remained behind closed doors in discussion. Shortly before midnight Edmond and Joseph, having emerged to consult with Peter Mansbach, retreated one last time into the bedroom. Mansbach, left outside, studied the door carefully. He sensed this was it: if the deal was to die, it would die now.

Outside, the tension was electric. After several minutes the door opened and Joseph Safra emerged, leaving his brother with his thoughts. He had made one last appeal, his strongest yet. Now only Edmond Safra, alone in the bedroom of a Montreal hotel, knew the fate of his empire.

Finally, a little before midnight, Safra opened the bedroom door and stepped out. He walked over to Peter Cohen and they shook hands.

"Let's sign," Edmond Safra said.

They could have closed the deal then, but Safra insisted they wait until shortly past midnight. He wanted the deal struck on Tuesday, January 18 because eighteen, as every good Halabi knew, was good luck.

The next morning in New York, reporters hustled into American Express's lower Wall Street headquarters to hear Jim Robinson, Sandy Weill and Bob Smith unveil their latest stunning acquisition, Trade Development Bank of Geneva. "We are ecstatic at having pulled this off," Robinson told the assembled press. "This clearly was a moon shot for us." Yes, the rosy-cheeked chairman acknowledged with camera-ready graciousness, their track record in banking wasn't the best. But now, Robinson promised, chuckling about Bob Smith's bank, "We have changed an ugly duckling into a swan."

The smiling trio fairly tripped over themselves piling tribute upon tribute to Edmond Safra's brilliance, and to their own brilliance at having snared his services. "We identified TDB as a jewel in the banking world," Robinson said. "Edmond is the man who energized and built that jewel. We went at it and won it." The best line was saved for Weill, who later told a magazine writer, "I feel smarter every time I see Edmond."

So where, several reporters wondered, was the jeweler himself? Where was Edmond Safra? As the press craned their heads in search of Jim Robinson's new genius partner, the genius was fast asleep on a jet back to Geneva, having refused to have anything to do with reporters or publicity. All that the press knew, as Robinson basked before the flashing cameras, was that his newest partner was nowhere to be seen. A superstitious person might have called it an omen.

In fact, there was a good deal of doubt about Safra's deal with American Express from the start. As London's *Financial Times* noted, "Rival bankers are skeptical as to whether Safra's liaison with American Express will survive over the long term." Other skeptics, at both American Express and Republic, questioned how much attention Safra would pay to TDB when he still had the task of running Republic. Safra's attorney, Peter Mansbach, thought American Express's failure to buy Republic was a terrible mistake, and told Jim Robinson so.

"How can you do this?" Mansbach had asked a group of American Express men, including Robinson, in Montreal. "You're not going to own Edmond Safra if he keeps Republic. The only way you can 'capture' Edmond is to keep hold of his only way to be a banker. Leave him an outside interest like Republic, and I know he'll never stay on board."

But Robinson, seemingly in awe of Safra's reputation, didn't seem to be listening. "Jim was just enamored, absolutely enamored of Safra," says a former American Express vice president. "He was just on cloud nine, buoyant about the whole thing. It was good textbook thinking, synergistic. He used to say he would get better advice from Edmond than from Paul Volcker," the Federal Reserve chairman.

In London, Derick Richardson, one of the few American Express executives familiar with TDB, cautioned the men at headquarters that working with Safra's Sephardic "tigers" wouldn't be easy. "I hope you realize this is going to be an extremely difficult culture to deal with," Richardson told Sandy Weill. "It's totally alien to everything that is American Express." Richardson listened in amazement as Robinson and the company's publicity people hailed Safra as the world's premier banking mind. "Everyone," Richardson recalls, "was just mesmerized by Edmond."

For his part Safra welcomed the lavish attention—he certainly didn't mind being lauded as a genius—though he might not have appreciated the line Robinson began throwing around at company luncheons. "You know," the chairman of American Express took to saying, "I've never had a billionaire report to me before."

Of all the grandiose ideas swirling around Edmond Safra's entry into American Express, the first to die was the notion that Safra, along with Jim Robinson and Sandy Weill, would form a governing triumvirate to rule their new corporate empire.

No sooner had TDB's sale closed than Safra's tax lawyers ruled that the only way to ensure that the Internal Revenue Service wouldn't lay claim to his gargantuan profits on the deal was for Safra to stay out of the United States altogether—for the entire year of 1983, a development that all but killed any chance Safra had of smoothly insinuating himself into the upper reaches of American Express. In addition, because Safra remained honorary chairman of Republic, the lawyers had also ruled he would need a special waiver from the Comptroller of the Currency to become chairman of American Express Bank, a process that would take months.

And so, in the spring of 1983, Safra found himself exactly where he had been in the spring of 1982, sitting in his Geneva office overlooking the Rhone, running TDB. As one British magazine later put it: "The newly married couple slept in separate beds almost from the start."

After all but deifying Safra in their press statements, Harry Freeman and American Express's p.r. people had deftly tiptoed around the issue of their new partner's "complications," noting in a press release that Safra would become chairman of American Express Bank "as soon as he is able to do so." Because Safra himself refused to have any contact with reporters, Freeman drafted Jeff Keil to help explain the situation. But before Keil was allowed to answer a single question, he was put through a lengthy tutorial in the ways American Express handled the media. For Keil, whose only experience with a publicity person of any kind at Republic had been firing one, it was an eye-opening experience.

On a tour of American Express's p.r. department, he was shown the studio where the company produced its own internal programs and groomed executives for television appearances. He sat in on strategy sessions where Freeman's people spent hours debating the exact wording of a press release and plotting the best way to "spin" individual reporters. Freeman's aides coached him in ways to talk to the press, how to get his message across by repeating key phrases, how to go "off the record" and "on background." To make sure he understood, he acted out interviews with American Express staffers who portrayed reporters and zinged him with tough questions.

Keil had never seen anything like it; he had no idea major companies even did these things. "You mean you let your own people talk to the press?" he asked upon discovering that Bob Smith and other executives routinely spoke with reporters. Republic, which disdained all publicity, didn't even have a full-time p.r. person. To Keil, American Express was a veritable publicity *machine*.

During the blitzkrieg of interviews and articles that spring, Keil could only marvel at how deftly Robinson, Freeman, and the company's other spokesmen managed to spin coverage of the purchase—playing up Safra's intellect, playing down American Express Bank's problems—exactly as they had planned. Freeman especially fascinated Keil; on the surface an affable, harmless bumbler, Jim Robinson's top p.r. strategist concealed the clearest thinking on manipulating the press that Keil had ever witnessed.

Only one thing bothered Keil. In several articles he noticed unattributed speculation that Safra's ways might not mesh with those of a modern corporation like American Express; it was the first time he had read such doubts about his boss, and it made him suspect that Freeman's people were hedging, discreetly inventing possible problems in case the merger didn't work out. When he mentioned it to Bob Smith, Smith scoffed.

Keil's leeriness of the American Express p.r. machine intensified after an incident involving *Fortune* magazine. In time he had grown confident enough with reporters American Express had sent his way that he acceded to the persistent requests of *Fortune*'s Gwen Kinkead to interview Safra. But when he ran the idea past Freeman, he was surprised to find him opposed. "What's wrong with her?" Keil asked. He had checked Kinkead's background and found nothing that suggested she would do a hatchet job. When Freeman continued to deny his requests, Keil began to get angry. "How come you don't like my reporters?" he asked. "You only like your own reporters." It seemed to Keil that American Express wouldn't help any journalist it couldn't control. He argued with Freeman about the matter for weeks, his frustration coming to a head when he heard a rumor at American Express that he was sleeping with the reporter. It stunned him. How nasty, Keil thought, was American Express willing to go to get its way?

For all Jeff Keil's concerns, the honeymoon between Safra and American Express continued into the spring as the two sides began gingerly melding their disparate operations. The decision had been made not to fully integrate TDB into American Express Bank, at least not at first; the two were so different in structure and style that an immediate merger could well result in chaos. At first only the obvious areas of overlap would be combined, chiefly the United Kingdom, France, and Uruguay.

Everyone was on his best behavior. Bob Smith's top two aides, Savage and Budenbender, enrolled in French courses. Throughout American Express's white-bread executive suite people began buying and reading books on Judaism; *Our Crowd*, Stephen Birmingham's history of the great Jewish families of New York, was a particular favorite. Bob Smith even hired a Sephardic banking consultant in hopes of understanding Safra's people. Safra, too, did his best to build bridges, surprising Smith with a small paperweight commemorating the lucky date and time of the merger, 2:12 A.M., January 18, 1983. Robinson and Cohen flew to Geneva for the official closing March 1, and Safra threw them a lavish dinner party, complete with gold Bulgari watches honoring the occasion.

Many at American Express got their first glimpse of their fabled new partner that spring. For all the backslapping in the boardroom, the rumors that had swept the middle levels of American Express about Safra weren't kind: an Arab-Jewish-Lebanese mystery man, frozen by fears of the evil eye, so cheap he had sold his yacht, the story went, because the toilet paper was overpriced. In groups of four and five Bob Smith's men were brought to luncheons in London and Geneva to see the real item. They listened patiently as Safra spoke loftily of his private talks with President Reagan and Paul Volcker. As aides looked on, savoring every pearl of his wisdom, Safra would interrupt his oratories to pluck up a telephone and, as the American Express bankers swapped quizzical glances, quietly chat with callers in French and Arabic and Portuguese. Everyone was so deferential the American Express executives half expected Safra to hold out his knuckles to be lightly kissed. "They weren't lunches," one of Bob Smith's men recalls. "They were Edmond holding court."

Safra's imperial demeanor raised eyebrows at American Express headquarters as well. A story made the rounds that one of Robinson's aides, arranging lodgings for a European board gathering Safra was expected to attend, had been taken aback by the haughty reception he received from Safra's secretary. "You don't understand," the Safra man supposedly replied, "Mr. and Mrs. Safra will be staying at their home. They are the new aristocracy of Europe." A former American Express vice president remembers: "That one went through headquarters like a bullet. People were just rolling their eyes."

Things only got worse as the American Express men familiarized themselves with Safra's operations. What they found wouldn't have surprised anyone who knew Safra well, but Bob Smith's people had done no more than a week of due diligence. "Everyone was just aghast," recalls one of Robinson's strategists. "TDB ran like nothing we'd ever seen. It ran like an extended family. The management style was just Edmond, who knew everyone. It was very loose, there was no documentation, only Edmond knew the structure. If someone wanted to talk to him, they simply picked up a phone and called him. It was about as different from a McKinsey model as you could find. Our attitude was, well, we'll show these guys how to run a company."

The first signs of conflict came in Paris, where, rather than merge peacefully, the resident TDB and American Express Bank executives went after one another like Hatfields and McCoys. Safra finally ended the squabbling by summoning the warring parties to London and negotiating a peace. In Britain Bob Smith wanted to sell TDB's new building, but Safra protested, and got his way. The real headache came at the new, combined loan committee in New York, where Safra's second-in-command Albert Benezra was placed in charge of processing loan requests from throughout the empire. Steeped in Safra's ultraconservative lending tenets and wholly unfamiliar with American Express businesses in far-off places like India and Pakistan, Benezra coped by rejecting most every application that came across his desk. "I don't like it," he would say, and Bob Smith's men would simmer in frustration. Before long, it became clear, Benezra wasn't approving loans for entire areas of the world. Panicked American Express officers in places like Bahrain, faced with a near-total stoppage in their loan business, howled to Derick Richardson in London to do something about the man they called "Dr. No." "My guys," Richardson recalled, "were just going crazy."

Everywhere they looked the American Express men found things to dislike about the TDB people. Safra's men were polite enough, but they had the irritating habit of speaking French among themselves, to the exclusion of anyone else in a meeting. Their condescending attitude toward American Express Bank was thinly disguised. "They always acted like they bought us," one former American Express banker recalled. "They always acted superior, so superior."

For the most part, Safra's aides simply failed to acknowledge they had been bought. At American Express, budgets were a division's bible, their annual compilation a process almost holy. But Safra's top financial officer, a thorny Frenchman named Michel Cartillier, not only refused to finish a 1984 budget by December, he refused to assemble one at all. "We don't do budgets that way at TDB," he sniffed to Bob Budenbender. There then ensued a soon-to-be familiar routine: Cartillier complained to Safra, Safra complained to Robinson, and Robinson phoned Smith, who glumly told Budenbender: "Robinson says they just won't have a budget this year."

The handful of American Express men given offices at TDB's Geneva headquarters fared no better. Several were quietly shuttled into out-of-the-way offices and ignored. A few fared even worse. When Bob Budenbender paid a visit to one of the transplanted Amex men, he was surprised to see his friend put a finger to his lips. "Shh, Bob," he whispered, then led Budenbender to an elevator, down to the lobby and across the street to a sidewalk café. "I think my office is bugged," the man explained.

For all the petty infighting, neither Bob Smith, in New York, nor Safra, in the TDB penthouse in Geneva, let it distract them from far greater issues. Where Safra was concerned, Smith had to tread carefully. Privately, aides knew there was no way Smith was giving up control to Safra; but because Safra's arrival was heartily endorsed by Robinson, he couldn't do anything overt to thwart him. In his executive suite, Smith turned to Bob Savage to devise the best way to handle Safra.

"You can never take Edmond head-on," Savage counseled. "You'll lose." They had to find a way to work around Safra, isolate him, take over his bank before he took over theirs. For now Safra, stuck in Europe, was making the job easy. He showed little interest in American Express Bank, and seemed more than willing to let Smith carry on as before. Left alone, Smith and Savage were free to calculate the best way to assert control over TDB, and it didn't take long to identify the most promising opening: Albert Benezra. Over the next several months Bob Smith became one of Benezra's best friends, making sure he was invited to luncheons with Robinson and other luminaries, arranging limousines for him and generally granting his every wish. In time Benezra, who had spent his entire career in Safra's shadow, began to warm to the attention.

Marooned in Europe, Safra realized he was losing his top aide to the come-hither tactics of the American Express executives. But Safra was more worried by another, more ominous gulf—the one growing between his office and Jim Robinson's. It mystified him. As soon as the government approvals were out of the way, Safra's contract called for him to become an American Express vice chairman and a member of the board. Robinson had promised he would be consulted on all decisions, major and minor, and Safra was eager to plunge into every nook and cranny of American Express operations. But the phone simply wasn't ringing. He and Robinson seldom spoke, and when they did, it was rarely about much more than TDB. Safra considered the chairman of American Express an equal, but as the weeks stretched on it was clear that, however deferential Robinson was in person, he regarded Safra as a subordinate.

Communications were no better at the bank. Aside from Peter

Cohen, the only American Express executive Safra talked to with any regularity was Bob Smith, who had given standing orders that none of his people could talk to Safra without his approval. Smith himself pointedly told Safra as little as possible. After he complained to Robinson, special red phones for Safra's exclusive use were installed in the offices of Smith's top aides. Smith's men spent hours eyeing the phones, waiting for them to ring. When Bob Budenbender's red phone finally rang, he was so startled he froze. He stared as it rang and rang, until he mustered enough courage to pick up the receiver to hear the great man's voice—only to feel ridiculous when the call turned out to be a wrong number.

The tension came to a head that July when Safra was handed a dispatch hot off the Dow Jones news wire: American Express was announcing plans to pay $1 billion for a Minneapolis-based financial services company named IDS. Safra was stunned. No one had given him the first hint of such a move: one billion dollars, and Jim Robinson hadn't bothered to tell his largest stockholder, the man who was supposedly part of a governing triumvirate? That Robinson would make such an announcement without consulting Safra mocked the very idea of Safra's supposed influence at American Express.

"What kind of people are these?" Safra asked his aides. "I ask you, what kind of people are these?" Safra called Peter Cohen and fumed about the IDS deal for weeks. Matters only grew worse when the drastically overpriced deal had to be renegotiated, and recriminations among American Express executives surfaced in the press. That type of public spectacle deeply disturbed Safra, who for the first time began to have doubts about the family to which he had entrusted TDB. The whole affair—the high price, the politics, the public spectacle, the dilution of his stock—made his stomach turn.

When Robinson failed to respond to his concerns, Safra became even angrier. By September he began circulating a draft letter threatening his resignation under the Margaret Thatcher clause. "I have expressed my substantial dissatisfaction and concern relative to the proposed acquisition" of IDS, Safra wrote Robinson. "Although you have tried to assuage these concerns, they are profound and they are continuing." Eventually Robinson talked Safra off the limb, promising he would be kept better informed. But the damage was done.

Safra's disillusionment deepened with each passing week. The smallest things unnerved him. When Robinson granted him a $500,000 bonus for completing the sale of TDB that spring, Safra had been genuinely flattered. But having decided to donate the money to the Red Cross, Safra was flummoxed when one of Robinson's men called to ask that he give the money to another charity; American Express, it seemed, had already given enough to the Red Cross that year. Safra, a man who had never in his life taken a paycheck from another man, simply couldn't fathom anyone exerting such control over him.

Equally bothersome was the jarring difference in style between Safra's Swiss-honed discretion and American Express's mass-marketing psyche. By that fall the easy work of merging London, Paris, and Uruguay had been done, and American Express executives began looking for ways to realize the "synergies" Robinson foresaw at TDB. Bob Smith had assembled an entire group to cobble together product tie-ins: Shearson and IDS brochures to be sent to TDB clients; an American Express Gold Card for TDB customers, complete with Broadway tickets and limousines when they came to New York. But all their plans encountered a roadblock in Safra. The idea of handing over a mailing list of TDB clients made him cringe; it went against every tenet of banking he knew. Safra promised he would think about tie-ins, but in truth he thought only of ways to avoid them. He hadn't sold his oldest bank to see it turned into K mart.

Still, by late fall, executives in both camps were bravely maintaining that success was just around the corner. "We cut the diamond," Smith told *The Wall Street Journal*. "Now we have to polish it." When the American Express board toured TDB offices in London, Paris, and Geneva after Thanksgiving, Safra was his usual generous host. The directors' hotel rooms overflowed with flowers and chocolates. Safra's friend Edmund de Rothschild hosted a banquet. In Geneva, Safra's personal assistant Terry Weiner—Walter Weiner's niece—put together a memorable luncheon for the board members' wives, complete with a gold ingot hidden in a pink suede pouch by each of their plates.

But by December the government approvals for Safra to become chairman still hadn't come through, and rumors began circulating that he might never come aboard. The situation was so awkward that even *Fortune* magazine, in an article that December—"The Mystery Man American Express is Banking On"—speculated that the marriage might not last. "Cultural differences could shorten Safra's tenure. His approach to business is dramatically different from theirs," the magazine wrote, noting of Safra, "a more unlikely team player can scarcely be imagined.... Some of Safra's friends say that if he indeed becomes [the bank's] chairman he will feel choked by American Express's corporate tendrils and will quit before long."

The nettlesome publicity was nothing compared to the bombshell that exploded just days before Christmas. In a surprise announcement, Robinson stunned the investment community—and Safra—by disclosing that the company's California-based insurance company, Fireman's Fund, had been waylaid by a sudden jump in claims and would post a $242 million pretax loss for the year, dragging American Express's overall earnings to barely $30 million and bringing an ignominious end to the company's hallowed record of thirty-six straight annual earnings gains. A rescue squad from headquarters was rushing to the West Coast to contain the damage. But with no virtually no warning, the myth of American Express's financial supremacy had ended.

In Geneva, Safra was dumbstruck. Once again, he had been blindsided; Robinson had given him no indication of the impending disaster. "I can't understand how this could happen!" Safra repeated over and over. "Where was the management? Where was Jim Robinson?" Peter Mansbach had never seen his client so mad. His disillusionment with Jim Robinson was total. Now, once and for all, he realized that all the promises were lies. Robinson had said he would be part of a governing triumvirate; he wasn't. He had said he would be consulted on matters great and small; he hadn't been. After IDS he had been promised greater communication; nothing changed. His bank, Safra railed, was in the hands of liars and cheats.

To Safra, Fireman's Fund was the final straw, exposing Jim Robinson once and for all as a creature of his own publicity machine, a man with no control over his company, an emperor with no clothes. This was it. It was over. He wanted out; but of course he couldn't just leave. He couldn't abandon TDB and his customers to a company like American Express; that would be unthinkable. First TDB had to be strengthened; write-offs were needed, Safra felt, more of them, and faster, if the bank's troubling Latin American loans were to be dealt with. Capital would have to be infused, and quickly. Two billion dollars struck Safra as a good number. Only then, once TDB had been set right, could he think about departing. That winter he urged the moves on Robinson, but in the middle of the furor over Fireman's Fund, nothing was done. Safra was so furious he considered suing.

Just as the Fireman's Fund problem broke, the long-awaited government approval for Safra to assume the chairmanship of TDB-American Express came through. Safra wasn't at all sure he wanted the job. "Why should I take it?" he fretted to aides. For weeks he wavered, until finally Robinson took notice. The two men held a series of one-on-one talks in which Robinson did his best to explain what had gone wrong, and how important it was for Safra to stay on board. "Jim," recalled Peter Mansbach, "tries to sweet-talk Edmond. It was crucial to them that Edmond not resign right after the disaster with Fireman's Fund. It would look horrible. They pleaded with him to work one more year. Edmond was only dragged in kicking and screaming."

Before a decision was reached on his employment, however, Safra delivered to Robinson a distinctly European-style vote of no-confidence, dumping almost all his American Express stock. He sold into the teeth of the stock plunge following the Fireman's Fund disaster, and his losses were huge; by some counts, they topped $100 million. Safra wanted to dump even more, including all his stock warrants, but to do so, he had to formally register with the Securities and Exchange Commission, and American Express, to his consternation, delayed delivering a registration statement to him. News that Safra was selling out, of course, would look every bit as bad as his resignation. Even when Safra finally put his hands on a registration statement, American Express lawyers objected to its filing, claiming that Safra was privy to inside information that made it impossible for him to sell his stock. Safra thought it was the ultimate irony. "What confidential information do I have?" he asked his aides in amazement. "They don't tell me anything!"

Eventually Robinson persuaded Safra to assume his post as chairman of TDB-American Express, but no one was fooled into believing the arrangement was permanent. Too much damage had been done. In exchange for a pledge that he wouldn't exercise the Margaret Thatcher clause for trivial reasons, Safra signed a new, one-year employment agreement, valid only through the following March. Peter Mansbach had pointed out the catch-22 that forced his client's hand. If Safra wanted to resign, the only way to do so was by exercising the Margaret Thatcher clause in his employment agreement. And the only way to exercise the clause was by becoming an employee. To get out, he had to get in.

When Edmond Safra ascended to the chairmanship of American Express Bank on February 16, 1984, the outside world saw it as evidence that the grand scheme of merging the two banks was going forward as planned. Nothing could have been further from the truth. To Safra, and to many at the top levels of American Express, it was glaringly apparent that it was only a matter of time before the disillusioned billionaire fled the American Express fold.

Everywhere he looked Safra perceived slights, and Jim Robinson, perhaps growing weary of Safra's demands, made little effort to assuage him. Instead of an office in Robinson's executive suite, Safra was given a small office near Bob Smith's on the lower floors of American Express Bank. To Safra it was a personal insult, and during his trips to New York, Safra's visits to American Express began to drop off. Everything about Jim Robinson's company seemed strange and forbidding, the worst possible feeling for a man who liked to do business in his "home." In time Safra quit coming altogether, preferring to work out of his Fifth Avenue apartment or his office at Republic.

No one was hit harder by Safra's ascension to the chairmanship than Bob Smith. Smith had all but convinced himself that Safra would never take over, that he would sit in Geneva and let Smith run American Express Bank as he pleased. Laid up with pneumonia caught during a ski trip, Smith summoned Bob Savage to his Connecticut home for a summit meeting. Between coughs and sniffles, Smith complained endlessly about how senseless it was for Safra to run the banks. "There's no integration," Smith continued. "I can do anything I want. He could care less what I'm doing. He doesn't know, and he doesn't care. Why the hell should he be allowed to be chairman?"

To Smith, it was clear that the mysterious Lebanese was up to something. Somewhere, he suspected, Safra had a hidden agenda, and it didn't include him or American Express Bank. "We've simply got to crack this Safra situation because he's going to end up eating our lunch," Smith told Savage. "What do you think he's going to do?" As Bob Smith listened, Savage laid out a number of "what if" scenarios, the two most prominent being these: Safra could allow TDB to decay to the point where American Express no longer wanted it, then try and buy it back. Or he could resign, open a new bank and try and steal back his old customers. Neither option was attractive from American Express's viewpoint.

By March Smith was ready to act. One Sunday afternoon he dropped by Jim Robinson's apartment high above the Museum of Modern Art and threw a startling idea onto the table: Safra should be fired. To Robinson, who had done his utmost to keep Safra on board, it must have seemed like lunacy. "Bob," he cracked, "it looks like you got sunstroke along with your pneumonia." Robinson waved the idea aside, but in the weeks to come Smith continued to fixate on it, endlessly musing upon ways to force Safra's departure.

For all Smith's fears, nothing really changed when Safra became chairman. Safra still showed no real interest in running American Express Bank; he remained far more involved with TDB. He refused to accept the realities of American Express's bureaucracy. He foreswore memos. He delegated little authority. He liked to work in his bedroom until late each morning. And to the frustration of the American Express men, the finer points of modern business rules eluded him. At the first meeting he chaired of the American Express Bank board that spring, Safra had to be reminded to call the meeting to order and review the previous meeting's minutes. "He looked up at me like a child, just totally lost," recalls a former American Express attorney who helped Safra convene the meeting. In short order Bob Smith took over the session, efficiently reviewing operations while Safra assumed a more comfortable role, posing questions and suggesting solutions.

By late spring Safra could take it no longer; he wanted his old life back. To make matters worse, Jim Robinson had finally begun talking to him, but he was saying exactly the things Safra didn't want to hear. Robinson had taken to complaining to Safra about Sandy Weill, a split in the family unity Safra found profoundly depressing. The great American Express empire he had envisioned joining was nothing more than a bird cage packed with squabbling parakeets. "This whole place is about politics," Safra groused. "You kiss the ass of Jim Robinson all day—that is the business here."

The solution hit him at an American Express Bank board meeting in New York. "Bob, I'm very unhappy," he was telling one of the directors, a Swiss executive named Robert Genillard. "I don't like the way we work. I don't like anything about this place."

"Why don't you buy the bank back?" Genillard asked.

Yes. As Safra pondered the idea, he decided it was exactly what he wanted to do: reacquire TDB, turn the clock back, erase the last year's nightmare as if it had never happened. In the weeks to come he discussed the concept with his aides, and found them in agreement. By early summer he had decided to make his move.

Bob Smith had just arrived in Frankfurt on the way to a tour of a Mercedes factory when Robinson reached him with news of Safra's decision. Smith scrambled back onto the private jet, dropped Bob Savage off in Stuttgart to keep their appointment, then flew on to Geneva, where he met Peter Cohen, who had flown in from New York.

The two met with Safra in the banker's penthouse office. "I'm not happy," Safra repeated. "We should structure some type of separation agreement."

"Can't we make it work?" Cohen asked. "Isn't there any way?"

"No, Peter, I don't think so," Safra said.

They went through it again and again, but Safra would not be moved. It was Cohen who reminded his old boss that, should he leave American Express without buying TDB, he wouldn't be able to start another Swiss bank, until the spring of 1988, when the last of his employment agreements expired.

"I have a legal right to compete," Safra said at first. His agreement only precluded him from opening a bank in Geneva, he suggested, not anywhere in Switzerland.

"Edmond, you can't go into business for yourself, you just can't," Cohen said.

Bob Smith, who had to suppress an impulse to stand up and applaud Safra's plans to resign, saw the need for a little hardball. "Edmond," he said, "if you think we paid $500 million for this bank to see you open a bank in Zurich, you're crazy. Do you think we would allow that to happen? Let me tell you, we could do a lot of things to make sure that didn't happen. We could destroy you. Have you ever heard of trial by newspaper? You start seeing your picture on the front page of *The Wall Street Journal* or *The New York Times* as a no-good so-and-so, you'll know trouble."

Safra froze; it was the one thing he simply couldn't abide. Years later Bob Smith would smile—and Safra would cringe—at the memory of his threats that day. "Edmond's face just turned grayer than that wall," Smith recalled. "He got up and left the room, then he came back, and basically what he said was, 'I won't compete.'"

It didn't end there, of course. For weeks Safra endured the same solicitous conversations with almost everyone at American Express: Why do you want to leave? Can't we work this out? Isn't there anything we can do? "You're unhappy?" Jim Robinson's wife, Linda, asked Safra at a society affair at the Plaza Hotel in New York.

"Not only am I unhappy, Linda, I am disgusted," Safra said. "I feel like I have quicksand under my feet. I'm not on cement here. I built the bank on cement and steel. But with you, I feel I'm sitting on quicksand."

"Why won't you stay?" Linda Robinson asked. "Why can't we work something out?"

"I don't feel at ease with you, Linda," Safra said. "I just don't. It's quicksand here."

If Safra had second thoughts about leaving the American Express fold, they vanished in the wake of petty contretemps like an episode that summer involving one of the company's corporate jets. Robinson had asked Safra to introduce him to the president of Brazil, and not long after the face-off in Geneva, he and Smith flew there to meet Edmond and his brother Joseph for a number of engagements, including a private audience the Safras had arranged with the president.

The fireworks started before they reached Brazil. Robinson was to fly south on one of American Express's Gulfstream III private jets, and Safra was offered another Gulfstream III for the long flight from Geneva. But for some reason Sandy Weill, who normally used the second Gulfstream, needed it, and refused to relinquish it to Safra. The company had an older Gulfstream II that Robinson offered to send to Geneva, but Safra, irritated, waved it off and flew commercial. When the story made the rounds at American Express headquarters, the Safra-haters had a field day.

Later, after flying to Brasilia to caucus with the country's president, Robinson held out hope that Safra might be kept in the fold. "Maybe we'll keep it together," he suggested to Smith on the flight back.

"I doubt it," Smith said. "Things have gone too far."

They had. That summer, with Safra still insisting on leaving, teams of investment bankers were brought in to negotiate TDB's sale back to him, and both sides sat through endless sessions of briefings and flow charts and slide shows that stretched through August. Aware that without him TDB would be at best damaged goods, Safra felt he was in a strong bargaining position; he offered barely $450 million, $100 million less than he had sold it for eighteen months earlier. Furthermore, he wanted to exclude from the sale TDB's troubled Latin American loan portfolio, a demand that drove Bob Smith up the wall; at one point, Smith got so mad he heaved a pile of papers across the room at Jeff Keil.

The talks dragged past Labor Day and into the first days of October, with American Express insisting on at least $500 million and Safra refusing to pay it. Finally, with the two sides only $20 million apart, Bob Smith had enough. He took his calculations to Jim Robinson's corner office and laid out the situation.

"Look at the price they want to pay," he said. "Now look at the return we'll get at that price. Jim, if I can't do twice that by myself, I'll eat my shorts."

"Do you feel comfortable running TDB yourself?" Robinson asked.

"Sure I do," Smith said. "We'll run it. Screw Safra."

And so the negotiations ended, with Robinson and Smith deciding to take the risk of running a Safra-less TDB. Years later, Smith remembered their negotiating posture. "Basically, Safra was trying to steal the bank back," he said. "They figured there was no way we'd ever keep the bank and run it ourselves without Safra. But we did. We said, 'Screw you, Edmond. We're keeping it.'"

It was clearly not what Safra wanted to hear. When in frustation some of his people made noises about establishing a new Swiss bank to compete with TDB, Smith became enraged. Safra's employment agreements simply wouldn't allow that, he reiterated, and he brought in lawyers to hammer the fact home. The low point came when one of them, Ken Bialkin, took off the gloves in a discussion with Peter Mansbach. If Safra didn't go along with the noncompete agreement, Bialkin suggested, American Express was prepared to take drastic action. The IRS, he hinted, might be curious to know some facts about Safra's American tax situation.

"Kenny, you're out of your fucking mind," Mansbach retorted.

"Edmond is not a U.S. citizen. He's got opinions coming out of the ear saying so. You don't have a leg to stand on."

When Mansbach relayed the conversation to Safra, he erupted. For months he had avoided grouping Bialkin with the other American Express men he so loathed, largely because of the lawyer's prominence in the U.S. Jewish community. Bialkin was so active in Jewish charities he had been given the informal moniker, "King of the Jews." But this kind of threat was simply too much. In a barely concealed rage, Safra telephoned Bialkin and leveled perhaps his ultimate insult: "What kind of a Jew are you?"

It was over. With Safra's promise not to compete against TDB—and with a similar promise extracted from his brother Joseph—the buyback negotiations quickly gave way to severance negotiations. As difficult as the earlier talks had been, Safra's men were surprised by a subtle change in tone in the new set of discussions; suddenly Robinson's men seemed genuinely eager to please Safra. The explanation was simple. Robinson badly wanted their parting to appear amicable. The truth was simply too painful for public consumption: American Express had paid $550 million not for TDB, but for Edmond Safra, and now Safra was jumping ship.

"Their main concern was always, always the public relations; all they cared about was how things looked," Peter Mansbach recalled. "We caught on to this early on. Anytime we threatened anything, we got so much good feeling back from them, they just caved in again and again in order to maintain good p.r. We had this enormous power over them. I've never seen anything like this before, where the threat of public embarrassment was such a useful negotiating tool, as with American Express."

In several days of talks, Jim Robinson gave Safra almost everything he wanted: his old TDB headquarters building on Geneva's Place du Lac, TDB-France, and his London bank-note operation. In return Safra promised not to open a competing Swiss bank until March 1988 and accepted a seat on American Express's board, allowing Robinson to claim publicly he was still a loyal member and adviser to the American Express team.

Pleased with what he had wrung from Robinson, Safra had only one remaining concern: the announcement. He vividly remembered Bob Smith's threats about a "trial by newspaper." The idea that American

Express would somehow "spin" the press coverage against him paralyzed him. "You like working for me, don't you?" he called and asked Jeff Keil early one morning that October.

"Yes, Edmond."

"You've done a good job for me."

"Thank you, Edmond."

"But Jeff, if you don't find a p.r. firm to defend my honor in twenty-four hours, you're fired."

"Fired? Edmond..."

"I'm serious," Safra said. "I can't take this anymore. These people control the newspapers. They're crazy. They'll do anything."

And so Keil began casting around for a p.r. firm. He nearly despaired when several turned him down, citing existing relationships with American Express. Not until his investment banker, Lee Kimmel, suggested Kekst & Company, a small outfit known for its aggressive work in takeovers, did Keil see a solution.

From its tidy offices on Madison Avenue, Kekst had been a power on Wall Street for a decade, dishing dirt on its clients' adversaries while mastering the weaponry of major takeover contests, including "attack" ads, shareholder letters, and "spinning" reporters at *The Wall Street Journal* and *The New York Times*. Kekst's founder, Gershon Kekst, a health nut who quietly advised a plethora of Wall Street titans like Henry Kravis, had solidified his reputation with the famous "Jewish Dentist Defense." Representing a dental-supply company named Sterndent against a group that included the government of Kuwait, Kekst had used pointed advertisements and public letters to threaten that Sterndent's clientele of Jewish dentists would flee the company if it was taken over by Arab investors. As crazy as it sounded, it worked, and Kekst and his boutique of two dozen or so spin doctors had been riding high ever since.

One evening that fall Jeff Keil and Cyril Dwek arrived at Kekst's midtown offices and met with Robert Siegfried, a small, slender p.r. man who had been with Kekst since 1971, handling clients like Carter Hawley Hale and Colgate-Palmolive. "Edmond," Keil began, trying to explain the situation, "is very unhappy with American Express. He's a man who's used to running everything. He feels himself put into a structure. He has to respond to memoranda. He has to be at certain places at certain times. The minute after he sold, he felt it was a mistake."

"So what's the issue?" Siegfried asked, not grasping why his firm was needed. It seemed like a simple severance agreement.

"What they have threatened him with is publicity," Keil said.

"What do you mean?" Siegfried countered. "He's gotten terrific publicity." The few articles Siegfried had seen on Safra described him as a financial genius.

"Yes, but that was the first real publicity he's ever participated in. Edmond has always shied away from the press. When American Express bought TDB, they wanted to make a big deal out of Edmond. They persuaded him to sit down with reporters."

Siegfried nodded.

"They've threatened Edmond with this publicity machine," Keil continued, "which, as you may know, is extremely powerful. They believe that the one thing Edmond fears is negative publicity, which would affect him with his depositors. This is something Edmond could not tolerate."

"So why are you hiring us?" Siegfried asked.

"I have to have someone to show them, when we're negotiating Edmond's separation, that we have our own publicity machine. That we're prepared to do battle with them on the p.r. front."

Siegfried was skeptical. Keil's worries seemed to verge on paranoia. Edmond Safra was one of the world's richest men. What did he have to fear from American Express?

When Gershon Kekst joined the meeting, Keil repeated his concerns. As he finished, Kekst turned to Cyril Dwek, who had remained silent. "And Cyril, do you feel the same way?"

"Absolutely," Dwek said. He was deadly serious. "Edmond's reputation is *the* most important thing to us."

Fine, Kekst said. They would take the assignment. Siegfried wasn't too sure what to expect, but open combat didn't seem out of the question. In anticipation of a fight, he made sure he understood exactly why Safra was leaving American Express—and exactly what skeletons Safra could expose if things got nasty. Jeff Keil briefed him in detail about American Express's disaster with Fireman's Fund as well as American Express Bank's unpublicized problems with Third World debt. "Do you think *The Wall Street Journal* would be interested in things like that?" Keil asked.

"Sure," Siegfried said.

On a Friday afternoon several days later, Siegfried took his first orders from Keil, who called him down to Republic's Fifth Avenue offices. "I'll tell you what's going on in the car," the banker said. A half hour later Siegfried was in a limo with Safra's aide, speeding downtown to American Express headquarters. "Look, I'm in the process of negotiating the separation," Keil explained. "By physically presenting a Kekst guy, I think it'll be helpful. I hear they have a press release they want to show us."

As Siegfried listened, Keil embarked on a tirade about how American Express was mistreating Safra, and how its "publicity machine" posed a threat to Safra's reputation. "Their p.r. machine is incredible, and the guy who runs it is very powerful, incredibly devious."

"Who's that?" Siegfried asked. As far as he knew, the American Express "machine" was its p.r. man Walter Montgomery, whom he knew well. Montgomery, a former teacher at Brown University, had been the first partner to ever leave Kekst. Siegfried, in fact, had been the one to recruit Montgomery many years before. His departure had strained their relationship.

"You know, Harry Freeman."

"Who?"

"He's Jim's right-hand guy."

"Oh."

Downtown, the two men waited in a conference room before an American Express lawyer came in and handed them a copy of a release the company was set to issue on Safra's impending departure. "What do you think?" Keil asked Siegfried.

"Jeff, I mean, it's totally unacceptable."

A quick glance showed Siegfried that the release treated Safra as a wayward employee who was to be fired. There was no sense that Safra himself had initiated the move. After Keil relayed their displeasure, Siegfried decided to prepare for the worst. Left alone in the conference room, he placed a call to David Hilder, the *Wall Street Journal* reporter who covered American Express.

"I can't tell you why I'm asking," Siegfried probed. "But do you think you would be interested in some stuff on American Express?"

"Could be," Hilder replied. "It depends." Hilder knew whom

Siegfried represented; he could guess there was top-quality dirt being offered. Siegfried let the matter lie for the moment. They could follow through if things got out of hand.

A few minutes later Jim Robinson and Harry Freeman returned to the conference room to discuss the press release. They volunteered to rework it in accordance with Safra's wishes, and everyone was quite civil. Siegfried noticed that Freeman's hands seemed to shake as he read from the release. For some reason, Siegfried got the impression he was intimidated. This was the p.r. genius who struck fear into Edmond Safra's heart?

Final negotiations continued through the weekend. By Sunday afternoon most of Safra's inner circle had gathered in a conference room at Kekst to look over a draft of the press announcement, which was to be released the next morning. It had been a grueling weekend; at one low point in the talks, Siegfried had touched base with the *Journal* reporter, Hilder, but had held off leaking anything damaging about American Express until talks fell through. To everyone's relief, that hadn't happened.

At five o'clock, Siegfried stepped out of the crowded conference room into the lobby to take a call. It was Hilder. "I understand that Edmond Safra is leaving American Express," the *Journal* reporter ventured.

"What?" Somewhere there had been a leak.

Hilder repeated himself.

"Where'd you get that from?" Siegfried asked. Hilder didn't have to say; Siegfried already knew the answer. Putting the reporter off, he returned to the conference room and broke the news. Keil and the others erupted. "The bastards leaked it!" Walter Weiner exclaimed.

Within minutes Siegfried was on the phone to the American Express p.r. man, Walter Montgomery.

"What's going on here?" Siegfried demanded.

"Look, events are moving quickly," Montgomery replied. "Robert, I know how you guys operate. Our belief is, you were going to do something preemptive. I told my people that we had to do something preemptive to avoid that."

"How could you do something like that?" Siegfried said. "I thought we were going to put out a joint release."

"We are," Montgomery said, and the next morning they did. But by then the damage was done. Siegfried had been around long enough to know that reporters tended to print the "spin" of the first leak they received; it was one reason Kekst's people leaked so often. And indeed, the *Journal's* article on Safra's departure, and much of the subsequent press coverage, was spun Jim Robinson's way. There was no suggestion of Safra's disillusionment, no hint of the betrayal he felt. Rather, the departure was portrayed as amicable, the result, perhaps, of Safra's inability to get along in a modern bureaucracy. That theme, in fact, was woven through many of the dispatches that analyzed Safra's resignation in the days to come.

American Express, it was clear, had won round one of the public relations battle. No one knew, of course, that the war was only beginning.

5

Y ou don't threaten me!"
Bob Smith's angular face was red and trembling as he tore into the
Safra man across the table. "Nobody threatens me!"

It was July 1985, seven months since Edmond Safra had formally
resigned his executive positions at American Express, and relations
between the two camps were deteriorating fast. In a conference room on
the Geneva waterfront, negotiations on the sale of TDB's Place du Lac
headquarters back to Safra had degenerated into another shouting
match. In the latest altercation Safra's American attorney, Peter Mansbach, was threatening Smith with a defamation suit over comments by
American Express officials in yet another news article, this one in the
Los Angeles Times, the latest in a series of press notices on the American
Express–Safra breakup to infuriate Safra.

"We learned a lot from Edmond," Smith was quoted as telling the
reporter. "But I think we're a lot better off without him." Jim Robinson
had told the reporter, "Edmond couldn't make the cultural and mental
jump from being his own boss to being part of a big organization." An
outraged Safra, after forcing the reporter to submit his questions in writing, had fired back a statement charging that Robinson's comments were
"dangerously misleading."

All that winter and into the spring similar incidents of petty sniping had
thrown gasoline on the smoking ruins of what remained of the relationship

between Edmond Safra and American Express. There was the magazine article in which an American Express man, explaining Safra's seeming lack of interest in working at the company, had quipped, "How do you motivate a billionaire?" Or the one where the American Express executive had sniped anonymously, "Dealing with billionaires just isn't like dealing with ordinary folks. He just wasn't meant to be a corporate chairman."

Jeff Keil flipped through the clippings in disgust, pointing out the little catch-phrases he suspected American Express spokesmen had planted. "'Safra couldn't adjust to bureaucracy,'" Keil read from one of the articles. "That means he's stupid."

"'Resigned to pursue other matters,'" he read from another. "That means he was fired."

"'Wanted to be an American Express director,'" Keil read again. "That means he was begging."

Behind every line, every hint of criticism, Keil saw the guiding hand of Harry Freeman's p.r. people. "It's Freeman, it's all Freeman," Keil said. "They're doing this. I tell you, Edmond, they can get the papers to write anything they want."

"I am very concerned about American Express," Safra began one meeting with the Kekst people that winter, heaving a huge sigh. "I do not trust these people. They have not dealt with me fairly. They have tried to humiliate me. And I am fearful they will try to destroy me with publicity."

It was a notion the two Americans, Gershon Kekst and Robert Siegfried, found odd. Though they could dish out negative publicity as fast and effectively as anyone, the idea that American Express would somehow attempt to *destroy* a man like Safra seemed farfetched, even paranoid. Siegfried was already complaining to American Express about every minor business story that even mentioned Safra. Each time Kekst's Madison Avenue offices were called for comment by another obscure European business publication, Siegfried would phone Walter Montgomery at American Express. "Do you know anything about this one?" he asked Montgomery about one article.

"I just hear that Edmond Safra is up to his old tricks."

"What old tricks are those?"

"You know, trying to get publicity."

If it was a joke, Siegfried didn't get it. "Well, I know we're not doing anything. You must be doing something."

"We're not."

"Walter, you keep telling me you're not doing anything. What's really going on?"

"Look, public relations is a big operation here, Robert. There are all types of p.r. guys here. I've told all these guys they shouldn't be doing anything. But they don't always listen. Sometimes it's hard to control them."

If Safra could have waved a magic wand and made American Express go away, he would have. But even now, months after mentally washing his hands of Jim Robinson, Safra remained inextricably bound to the company he had grown to loathe. The cost of his freedom had been a seat on the American Express board, from which, Robinson and Safra had pledged in ridiculous canned statements, he would continue to offer the chairman advice. The truth was, Safra spent far more hours looking for excuses to resign than fulfilling his duties as a director. All year he hadn't attended more than a handful of board meetings, which he considered a complete waste of time. No one listened when he urged writeoffs of the bank's Latin American loans. None of the other directors, not Henry Kissinger or Gerald Ford or especially Jim Robinson, gave him the respect he felt he was due.

Safra had conceived scenario after scenario in which he would quit the board, perhaps citing his concerns about Third World loans, but each time his aides persuaded him to stay. Better to serve out his term on the board quietly, they advised, than resign in a huff and give Robinson's people the chance to poison the inevitable articles explaining it all.

Even after the breakup, however, Safra, as a board member, was unable to escape the unslackable thirst of American Express's publicity needs. Heinz Zimmer of American Express's Zurich office had pestered him all winter to give an interview to a Swiss magazine, and the requests so unnerved Safra he took the unusual step, for him, of writing a letter to Jim Robinson to complain.

"Another article at this time would, in my view, increase the damage already done to the TDB employee-depositor community," Safra protested to Robinson in December 1984. "As a result of my long relationships with them, many employees and depositors identify with me. When I was attacked, they felt attacked. They regard insults to me as insults to them. All of this was discussed between us, yet it was then ignored or forgotten. Great ill feeling was created by the media effort, which has been exacerbated by [American Express] management's approach to the [TDB] staff—now great bridges must be built. And I tell you, Jim, they must be built quickly. Jim, I am not sure what you can do to reverse the damage."

Much to his irritation, Safra remained tied to American Express not just by his seat on its board of directors, but by the office buildings in Geneva and London and on Paris's Place Vendôme that Robinson had agreed to sell back to him. American Express had pledged to relocate its people as soon as possible, but the process would take months, and Safra wanted them out, and out now. Deadlines had been set for vacating each building; in Geneva Safra had insisted on firm dates for clearing each floor. But as the months wore on, he suspected the first deadlines that fall wouldn't be met—not the worst thing in the world, Peter Mansbach kept reminding him, since their agreements with American Express could be declared null and void if even the tiniest portions weren't followed to the letter. "We were sitting back dumb and happy, saying, 'Okay, don't leave,'" Mansbach recalled.

But Safra, of course, found no solace in the murmurings of counsel. From his office window in Geneva he could watch the hated American Express men file in and out of the building—*his* building, the headquarters where he had built and would someday rebuild his Swiss banking business. He and a cadre of secretaries remained upstairs alone, marooned in the seventh-floor executive suite, while below the men who now worked for Bob Smith took their time vacating the premises.

Of all the things he was forced to share, Safra drew the line at the executive dining room. He had had to go to Smith on bended knee just to keep his kitchen staff. One of his oldest waitresses, Madame Crispini, had come to him in tears after the breakup, pleading for him to keep her, a request he was able to grant only after seeking Smith's permission. But when Smith's men asked to use the seventh-floor dining room, Safra wouldn't budge. Breaking bread with turncoats like Albert Benezra, who had stayed at American Express rather than join Safra in exile, was more than he could bear.

By that summer, with the American Express men still showing no signs of leaving, Safra grew worried that they would stay and ultimately try to filibuster him out of reopening his bank in three years. He had his Swiss lawyers look long and hard at ways to evict them, but because Geneva was so overcrowded, eviction proceedings seldom succeeded. Safra could only count the days till they would be gone and the building would be his again. But of course it wouldn't truly be his again until the last of the noncompete agreements with American Express expired in the spring of 1988. Until then Jim Robinson's lawyers had wrapped him in every restriction imaginable, down to the size of the Republic sign Safra could display on the building. Under the agreements, he could mount no sign at all until American Express had vacated the premises, and then only plaques four inches high or less, and those only in the elevators, on the building directory, and in other selected spots. It was humiliating.

On other fronts, at least, there had been progress. Talks on buying back the London bank-note business and TDB-France had gone on through the spring without incident, though each side had picked at every comma and missed few chances to one-up the other. Only the calming presence of American Express Bank's general counsel, Mark Ewald, who was liked and admired by the Safra men, prevented a major falling-out.

Restrictions on his work in Switzerland, meanwhile, had hardly kept Safra from busying himself in the rest of the world. No sooner had he left American Express than he began laying the groundwork for the Swiss reopening. In quick succession Safra beefed up Republic's London office and opened new Republic subsidiaries in Milan, Luxembourg, Gibraltar, Guernsey, and Paris. The move into Luxembourg, which provided many of the same tax and disclosure advantages as Switzerland, was key, allowing Safra to take in wealthy depositors who didn't need the full benefits of Swiss secrecy. Republic even launched a fancy new European advertising campaign, designed to keep the Safra name in the minds of his former depositors. One ad showed a well-tanned millionaire, phone in hand, lounging aboard a yacht: "If you knew Republic had been called, 'Possibly the safest bank in the United States,'" the caption read, "you'd be calling them, too."

What no one suspected was the sheer scope of the bank Safra intended to open in Geneva. If everything went according to plan, the new bank, to be called Safra Republic, would have one of the biggest debuts ever: $1 billion in capital, with a goal of $10 billion in deposits in five years. Neither Switzerland, nor American Express, had ever seen anything like it.

• • •

Jim Robinson read the press coverage of the breakup and got almost as incensed about it as Safra. For Robinson, Safra's departure had been an acute personal and professional insult. After all, it was he who had pushed the TDB acquisition on his board, it was he who had assured worried directors that Safra could be smoothly brought into the American Express fold. By itself, the breakup wasn't personal. Though they had never become close friends, Robinson genuinely liked Safra; the two had never exchanged a harsh word.

Now, though, Robinson felt Safra was piling insult upon injury by sniping at American Express in the press. Though the initial coverage had toed the American Express line—most everyone, from *The Wall Street Journal* on down, had attributed it to Safra's anachronistic methods—as time went by, more and more articles appeared in which Safra's aides were lobbing back volleys of their own. Bit by bit, the story of Safra's disillusionment was creeping into the press: Fireman's Fund, IDS, Robinson's management style. When Harry Freeman, who had helped spin much of the initial coverage, came to Robinson's office to complain about the criticism emanating from the Safra camp, Robinson authorized him to sharpen their own comments on Safra, though he cautioned Freeman to keep it on a "not-for-attribution" basis.

Many of the most stinging anonymous comments about Safra in the press that winter had thus come from Freeman, often cloaked by reporters as a "source" or as "one American Express executive." Freeman's strategy was subtle, sniping at Safra in off-the-record comments while publicly maintaining a diplomatic, "above-it-all" posture. In the anonymous barbs Freeman parceled out to reporters, Safra was invariably the one out of step with modern business, Robinson the patient chief executive who had brooked his shortcomings as long as he could. When Freeman went on the record, it was to downplay the breakup and suggest that Safra's departure would have little effect on the company's banking operations. "Two months is a long time at our company," he told one reporter that winter, in a comment whose irony wouldn't be apparent for years. "The deal is pretty much history."

While Freeman handled the press, the task of leading the day-to-day jousting with Safra fell to the hyperaggressive Bob Smith. As Republic kicked off its expansion that winter, Smith watched it all with blood in his eyes. In the wake of the breakup, he and his aides had embarked on a single mission of overriding importance: to stop Safra from rebuilding his empire at their expense. Even before Safra resigned, Smith was having Republic watched closely. He had no doubt that long before he reopened his doors in Geneva, Safra would begin building an infrastructure for his new bank by stealing back as many TDB employees and depositors as he could—efforts specifically restricted in Safra's agreements with American Express. Bob Smith was determined not to lose a single man, not a single deposit, without one hell of a fight.

Already that spring, Smith's people had tracked $24 million of TDB deposits lost to Republic, half of it from a handful of wealthy Brazilians jumping ship. At board meetings, Smith gave Robinson and the bank's other directors detailed briefings listing every account he believed had deserted to Republic. One report, for instance, had crossed Smith's desk claiming that Safra's old comrade Jack Tawil was courting TDB clients in Belgium, and had stolen away a $500,000 deposit. In the Far East, a couple of Asian clients were defecting as well, a development in which Smith saw the guiding hand of Republic's Hong Kong office.

"I am bringing these facts to your attention in the expectation that you will wish to take prompt remedial action," Smith wrote Walter Weiner in May 1985, reminding Weiner that "this kind of activity violates" Safra's severance agreement. Forwarded Smith's letter at London's Dorchester Hotel where he was negotiating the repurchase of TDB-France, Weiner could only smile at the notion of worrying about $24 million in deposits, a minuscule sum for a $10 billion bank. He would always claim Republic hadn't solicited any TDB deposits, and in fact, a good many defections were only to be expected, given the loyalty Safra commanded among both depositors and employees. "[This] hardly seems worth either your attention or mine," Weiner responded to Smith in a Memorial Day brush-off letter.

But Bob Smith would not be deterred. He simply wouldn't stand losing a nickel of TDB money to Safra. "Such solicitation violates the spirit of our agreement," he wrote Weiner again in June, "and we trust that you will act upon the information we have provided to ensure that this kind of activity ceases forthwith." Though careful to tread gently where an American Express board member was involved, Smith sent copies of the correspondence to Safra himself. "I am certain," he wrote Safra, "you would not wish [this] kind of activity to continue." One of the American Express attorneys, Ken Bialkin, emphasized the seriousness of

Smith's warnings in a visit to Weiner, an old Michigan fraternity brother. "Walter, they're really going to sue you if you don't stop this," Bialkin warned. "Bob is really angry. I'm telling you, they're really going to sue you."

Bob Smith's hounding of Republic coincided with the birth of a theory that in the years to come would receive wide airing among American Express executives disgruntled at the breakup. Safra, this theory held, had planned the whole thing from the start—the sale of TDB, his subsequent resignation, his planned reopening in Geneva—to "cleanse" his empire of its troubled Latin American loans, and start anew. "In my grave I'll believe it was all a conscious effort to fleece American Express," a former aide to Jim Robinson recalled. "If you look at what happened, Edmond got every significant thing he could have wanted—his profits, his bank headquarters, his Latin American loans paid off. It was the perception we all had. We had been screwed. And it was the ultimate humiliation that after having caved on everything, to have beaten us so thoroughly, it was just the absolute humiliation for Edmond, in his same headquarters, to come and get back his old customers."

For that reason, negotiations over the sale-back of Safra's headquarters that summer of 1985 were especially galling for Bob Smith. Only after the signing of Safra's severance agreement had it dawned on him what a blunder agreeing to sell the Geneva building had been. To Safra's depositors and to the entire Swiss banking community, the squat, green-glass building *was* Edmond Safra. It was a living monument to his longevity, an unspoken message to every would-be depositor that Safra was still Safra, no matter the unfortunate dalliance with a cold American conglomerate. If American Express feared losing a duel over TDB depositors, Bob Smith faced the realization that they had handed their opponent an elephant gun. "Selling back the headquarters," he said years later, in a sentiment widely echoed inside American Express, "was the single stupidest fucking thing we ever did."

Safra's people thought so, too, and would regale each other for many years with tales of how they had faked Jim Robinson out of his pants. Of course, the official American Express line, always accentuating the positive, took the exact opposite tack. "Jim Robinson did a masterful job of negotiating that one," one American Express executive, almost certainly Freeman, had bragged anonymously that spring to *Institutional Investor* magazine. "They sold [Safra] a few pieces of dreck and got it over with."

But Bob Smith knew the truth, he knew they had been outmaneuvered, and he single-handedly made sure negotiations were hell for all involved. That summer, in a Geneva conference room, Smith and Safra's attorneys came up with a wide array of issues to argue about. They argued over the building's price. They argued over real estate valuations. They argued over independent appraisers brought in to make more valuations. They would have argued about the weather if they hadn't been so busy pelting each other with threats. After Peter Mansbach thrust with the prospect of a suit over the *Los Angeles Times* article, Smith parried with a threat to cancel the sale of Safra's headquarters altogether, a prospect that left even his own aides shaking their heads. "Bob, we agreed to do this," one, a newly hired Swiss finance expert named Jean-Robert Terrier, pleaded with Smith. "We have to go through with it."

Adding to Smith's frustration was his inability to exert any real control over TDB and the longtime Safra aides jostling to fill the vacuum left by their mentor's absence. In the weeks after the announcement of the breakup the previous October, Smith had all but moved to Geneva to supervise the emergency damage-control effort. All winter he worked overtime soothing and placating the bruised egos of Safra's aides and the worried minds of so many of TDB's Sephardic depositors.

To ensure the *garants'* loyalty, the most valued of Safra's men were slipped raises and blocks of American Express stock worth up to $250,000, as well as other special favors. Smith lavished special attention, including a chauffeur-driven limousine, on the man he hoped could replace Safra, Albert Benezra. But though Benezra was a capable banker with strong ties to the Sephardic community, he wasn't Safra, nor would he ever be. "We are a very chauvinistic bunch, and we don't necessarily trust Benezra," a prominent Beirut Sephardi griped to a reporter that spring. "He's from Turkey, and his first language is Ladino, not Arabic or Hebrew. Under him, the Turkish Jews will rise at TDB over those from Aleppo and Beirut." Another Sephardic depositor warned: "Our tribe, if you will, followed Edmond Safra, not Albert Benezra." Still another put into words the very fear spreading through American Express: "If you buy my thesis that TDB *was* Edmond Safra, then you'll realize that Amex is sitting on a half-billion dollar investment that is worth [nothing]."

Bob Smith soon realized that he couldn't spend all his time in

Geneva. He needed someone there he could trust, a loyal set of eyes and ears to ride herd over Safra's disgruntled *garants*. That summer of 1985 Smith found the man he needed, Jean-Robert Terrier, whom everyone called Bob, a level-headed numbers man hired away from the international finance area at General Electric the previous year. Terrier was dispatched to Geneva as assistant chief administrative officer, and began the difficult job of insinuating himself into the bank hierarchy. But while Terrier was Swiss, which put him closer to the TDB men than Smith, he wasn't Jewish, much less a Sephardi, and that all but precluded socializing with the Safra men. "Friday night is out; Saturday is a day of celebration, when everyone was at the synagogue," Terrier recalled. "That pretty much eliminates all the social opportunities."

It didn't take long for Bob Terrier to see how badly Smith needed him at TDB. With Safra's departure, his former aides had begun bickering among themselves as they jostled for control of the bank. TDB splintered into a number of feuding factions, the strongest led by the Frenchman Michel Cartillier and by Albert Benezra, who commanded the loyalty of many of the bank's account officers. Behind closed doors at TDB headquarters, Cartillier and Benezra were practically at each other's throats over any number of petty turf squabbles, into which Terrier inevitably found himself drawn as referee.

The only thing the squabbling TDB men seemed to agree on was their open defiance of New York; to a man they refused to recognize Bob Smith's authority over them. On Smith's visits to Geneva, he found it almost impossible to deduce how the bank, now his single largest base of operations, was doing. "They simply wouldn't tell Smith what was going on," Terrier recalled. "I remember meetings where Smith was starving for information and they wouldn't give it to him. They launched into these empty, long talks, just bullshit." Smith remembers them, too. "It was probably the most frustrating experience of my entire professional life," he said. One excuse the TDB men gave for stonewalling Smith and his aides was that they weren't Swiss. When Bob Budenbender came to Geneva to help prepare TDB's budgets, he found it an impossible task, since the TDB men wouldn't let him examine records of any customer accounts, asserting that Swiss law allowed only Swiss residents to do so.

For Smith the first ray of hope shone that fall, when negotiations on the headquarters sale were wrapped up, forcing TDB to finally move its headquarters, and two of Safra's veteran aides, Michel Cartillier and the marketing chief, Sem Almaleh, announced their resignations. Bob Terrier managed to procure a lease on a new building for TDB several hundred yards down the lakefront, but the new location was so cramped that much of the bank's administrative and technical staff ended up farmed out to new quarters near Geneva's airport. The evacuation of their longtime headquarters was tough on the oldest TDB veterans; Albert Benezra, it was said, didn't stop wringing his hands until he had managed to construct an exact duplicate of his former office in their new premises.

Cartillier and Almaleh, meanwhile, dutifully attended a strained going-away party Bob Terrier threw at the elegant Hotel Metropol, then signed pledges not to go to work for Safra. But despite the pledges, Bob Smith remained wary. All year he had waited for disaffected TDB executives to begin resigning. He had always been wary of Cartillier in particular, and he was certain that if an exodus of TDB talent were to begin, it would begin now. In the wake of Cartillier's resignation, Smith ordered a strict watch on Republic. Every resignation from TDB, anywhere in the world, was to be scrutinized. "Anyone that leaves, we want to know where they're going," he told his aides. "We have to track the exits, where they go, and do they stay there. Are they going to UBS [Union Bank of Switzerland] and staying? Or are they using it as a stepping-stone to Safra?"

And when Bob Smith said he wanted every resignation watched, no matter how small, he was serious. Just how serious, an unsuspecting Edmond Safra would soon be stunned to learn.

On Thursday morning, November 21, 1985, less than a month after Michel Cartillier's resignation, one of Republic National Bank's newest loan officers, a shy young Lebanese named Yasha Dwek, emerged from his flat in a quiet London neighborhood and led his little daughter to their car for the morning ride to her school. A Sephardic Jew raised in Beirut, Dwek was a distant cousin of Safra's aide Cyril Dwek, and had been thrilled to rejoin his cousin's bank after five months of unemployment following his resignation that June from an American Express Bank office in London.

As Dwek helped his daughter into the car, he noticed a man standing on the sidewalk down the street. The man's presence might not have registered but for an odd telephone conversation Dwek's Israeli wife had had with an overly inquisitive messenger. Yasha Dwek was a cautious man, and as he slid into his car and pulled away from the curb, he found himself eyeing his rearview mirror more than usual. That morning, as always, the young banker's route to his daughter's school was circuitous, cutting across main avenues and zigzagging down back streets. Even an amateur could have spied the blue Ford Sierra keeping a discreet distance behind.

His years in Beirut had taught Yasha Dwek not to take chances, and the moment he was sure the Sierra was following him, he veered from his appointed route and circled back to his flat. Growing more fearful by the minute, he ducked inside, herded his wife into the car and, wasting no time, drove his frightened family straight to the nearby Paddington Green police station.

There a police detective listened politely as the badly shaken young banker, convinced he was being followed by kidnappers or terrorists or worse, told his story. Before long Yasha Dwek grew irritated, convinced that the British detective wasn't taking him seriously. He collected his family and left, driving straight to his new office at Republic, where he hurried in to see his boss, an executive vice president named Adrian Fletcher. Fletcher was well accustomed to dealing with the security concerns of Edmond Safra's rich Middle Eastern clients, and immediately called a security agency he sometimes used, Lynx Security Services.

That afternoon Lynx dispatched an investigator named John Weatherall to Republic, where Fletcher explained Yasha Dwek's brush with an unidentified pursuer. Neither man could figure out why Dwek, a quiet family man with no obvious vices, might attract surveillance. "He's the least likely man I can think of to have this happen to," Fletcher told the detective.

Yasha Dwek was brought in and Weatherall saw that he was scared out of his wits, all jitters and quick, nervous gestures. No, Dwek said, he wasn't politically active; there was no reason for extremists to take an interest in him. His father owned a property concern in Paris, as did his brother in Monte Carlo. But no one in his family had ever been kidnapped or even threatened. His former employer, American Express, might conceivably be worried about his approaching his former clients, but that seemed unlikely. His only enemy, Dwek speculated, was a man against whom he had testified in a fraud trial at the Old Bailey some years before. Yasha Dwek's wife later revealed a family secret that might also explain the surveillance: during the Yom Kippur War, she had briefly worked for Israeli intelligence.

All told, John Weatherall could see, he had little to go on. He told Dwek to calm down and urged him not to worry; the surveillance was probably just the preamble for the serving of some type of writ, possibly a subpoena. Still, that night, after getting the go-ahead from Republic, Weatherall had his men sweep the area around the Dwek family's building. They found no sign of the blue Sierra. But Dwek had managed to get the Sierra's license number, and the next morning John Weatherall had its registration in hand. The car belonged to Carratu International, a London detective agency. Just whom Carratu was working for was anybody's guess.

That afternoon Weatherall visited Scotland Yard and briefed a detective there on Carratu's surveillance of the Dweks. He was worried, Weatherall said, because Carratu might be unwittingly laying the groundwork for someone who wished to harm the young couple; stranger things had happened. The Scotland Yard man obligingly telephoned Carratu's offices and ordered one of its men down to explain its actions. Soon a Carratu representative appeared at the station, but refused to say much about the surveillance, explaining only that his client was involved in a "commercial dispute of a non-political nature." When he left, leaving both investigators unsatisfied, the Scotland Yard man agreed to put the Dweks under round-the-clock surveillance.

The next morning members of an elite antiterrorist squad swept the Dweks' neighborhood, as did John Weatherall's men. In no time they realized the family was still being watched. A red Sierra was spotted parked outside the Dwek flat's front door. A bearded man sat behind the wheel for most of the morning and through the lunch hour. When one of Weatherall's men challenged him the man drove off. The same morning a slight, balding man in his forties was seen loitering on a nearby corner; when Weatherall approached, the man walked away. Another of Weatherall's men saw a man with a clipboard who seemed to be following Mrs. Dwek and her daughter on an errand.

John Weatherall had one last card up his sleeve. He had friends among the Carratu people, one in particular who might be able to help out. He put in a call and, inside a day, the source came through. The Carratu client was an American company, the source said, though the request for surveillance on Yasha Dwek had come through its British subsidiary. The U.S. company, it was said, wanted "all the info they [could] get" on Dwek because of a fraud of some kind. When Weatherall pressed for the client's identity, the source suggested the client might be "the card people." Weatherall pressed harder, and the source acknowledged it was American Express.

Irritated, Weatherall drove straight to Carratu's offices in Worcester Park and confronted two of the agency's executives. It must have been a busy morning at Carratu; when Weatherall arrived, he learned that members of Scotland Yard's antiterrorist squad had been there all morning asking their own questions. In their wake, the Carratu men seemed genuinely abashed and promised to stop their surveillance. Periodic checks showed they were as good as their word. Surveillance of the Dwek family ended.

When Safra was finally briefed on the episode, he couldn't believe it: American Express following innocuous little Yasha Dwek? "Yasha Dwek?" he asked in amazement. "Yasha Dwek? Those bastards, what are they doing?" Against his lawyers' wishes, he telephoned Jim Robinson to complain. "Jim, what are your people doing?" he asked in exasperation. "Let's be gentlemen, let's act as gentlemen. Don't do this!" Peter Mansbach, meanwhile, pushed protests through legal channels. "This is disgraceful, Mark," Mansbach lectured American Express Bank's general counsel, Mark Ewald. "The guy was fearful for his life. He thought it was the PLO. What did you hope to find? Can't you control your crazies?"

Rumors of the Yasha Dwek episode made the rounds at American Express, though in wildly twisted form. According to the version accepted as gospel by many, an American Express investigator had been staking out the Dwek flat when a pair of Israeli intelligence agents stuck a gun in his ear and brusquely asked why he was following their former operative, Mrs. Dwek. Exactly how the investigator would have known they were Israeli agents isn't clear, but the story was told time and again as American Express men shook their heads knowingly. Edmond Safra, that shady Lebanese, had sicced the Mossad on them.

Though it outraged Safra and deepened his aides' distrust of American Express, the Dwek episode had little practical impact on the wintry relations with American Express. By that fall Bob Smith and Walter Weiner had forged a truce of sorts to work out all manner of minor outstanding issues, from Republic's possible purchase of TDB's Tokyo office to American Express's request to extend its occupancy of TDB buildings in Geneva and London. Eventually it was all hammered out in one final amendment to Safra's employment agreement that January of 1986. In a series of holiday-season phone calls and lunches, Weiner and Smith agreed to a swap: American Express was granted six-month extensions of its leases in Geneva and Paris in return for granting Safra the right to hire Michel Cartillier. On Smith's insistence, the two men also worked out an impossibly detailed formula under which Republic was to pay TDB a fee for all deposits it took beyond $300 million.

It was to be Safra's final agreement with American Express, a last, small footnote to one more of the brief, failed mergers so common in business circles during the acquisitive eighties. A month later, with no more than a one-line mention in *The Wall Street Journal*, Safra quietly allowed his term on American Express's board to run out. The long, bitter marriage was finally, irrevocably over.

The severing of his last ties to American Express not only liberated Safra; it also set Bob Smith free. Off came the kid gloves Smith had been obliged to don in dealing with an American Express director; with Safra off the board, he was free to pursue his aggressive defense against Republic with a vengeance, and he wasted no time doing so. Since the Yasha Dwek episode, Smith had counted three more departed TDB officers in Safra's employ, a Geneva *garant* and an executive in Luxembourg, both seen at Republic offices in Luxembourg. Worse, the man in charge of TDB's branch at Chiasso on the Swiss-Italian border, Luc Marschall, had quit in a huff and joined the Republic office in Milan. At the end of March 1986 Smith cited all three examples in a sharply worded letter of protest he fired off to Walter Weiner.

"Such action constitutes a systematic disruption of our business," Smith wrote. "We hereby demand that you and Edmond immediately cease and desist from such activities, including your hiring of Mr. Marschall, and that you refrain from any other conduct which might violate the letter or spirit of our agreements. We hereby advise you that we intend to enforce our rights in an appropriate manner."

Weiner, fast growing weary of Smith's complaints, brushed him off once more. "I have found that your assertions are substantially incorrect," he replied, adding sweetly: "We sympathize with your distress over the many recent departures of your personnel, but we are not the cause of those departures."

For all Smith's complaints, no real exodus of TDB executives had followed in the wake of Michel Cartillier's resignation the previous fall; only one of Cartillier's assistants and a secretary had followed the Frenchman out the door. Still, Smith's fears were kept alive by his continued inability to get his arms around TDB, and by the plummeting morale among Safra's disaffected veterans.

Smith had only himself to blame, of course, for American Express was doing its best to shake up a corporate environment that hadn't seen significant change in twenty years. As Smith laid plans for a new, post-Safra TDB, he had in mind nothing less than the total revamping of the system that Safra had used to bring the bank to prominence. No longer would the bank's Sephardic clients swap Safra's skimpy returns for near-total safety. Instead American Express, hoping to capitalize on the synergy Jim Robinson sought between its different units, would transform TDB into a vital cog in the financial services machine Robinson envisioned. Smith and his men inaugurated a full-fledged program of asset management, promising TDB depositors greater returns, albeit at greater risk. As Safra's *garants* looked on with undisguised disdain, a host of outside experts were brought in to oversee a whole new system of investing. A wide range of investment "products" were to be offered, including Shearson Lehman mutual funds, junk bond funds, and other foreign-exchange vehicles.

It was all doomed, of course. Safra's stodgy *garants* were the key to the new strategy: if they didn't urge the new products on their wealthy Brazilian and Argentinian clients, no amount of financial alchemy would make TDB a docile member of the American Express family. And, as became abundantly clear, the *garants* weren't inclined to cooperate, certainly not for a bunch of pushy Americans like Bob Smith. Smith hoped to buy their loyalty, but for the most part the *garants* took the money and ignored the new items.

A veteran banker named Amos Bergner was hired to oversee the changes, but Bergner inspired no more loyalty than Smith. Though Jewish, Bergner was Ashkenazi, and his pleas to peddle American Express products succeeded only in further antagonizing the Sephardic account officers. Still, Bergner was better than the man who ultimately replaced him, the flinty Austrian Heinz Zimmer. The former head of American Express Bank's Zurich office, Zimmer was first named vice chairman of private banking. He was a talented banker, but among TDB's harried Jewish *garants* no amount of savvy could disguise his Teutonic bearing nor his Austrian roots. Already beaten down by two years of American Express management, the inevitable cries of alarm spread among the *garants*. "He's a Nazi!" more than one exclaimed. "They've brought in a Nazi!"

Again and again, American Express's WASPish management would prove woefully insensitive in its wooing of Safra's veterans. The merging of American Express and TDB in London left several of Safra's oldest Israeli clients reporting to one of American Express Bank's Palestinian account officers, which sparked a predictable hue and cry among the customers, who were certain the man was a PLO spy. All of which generated little sympathy among Safra's men for Bob Smith's nagging letters of complaint about defecting clients and loan officers. "What the fuck do you want us to do?" Peter Mansbach harangued an American Express lawyer after another earful of recriminations. "You're putting a Palestinian on the Israeli desk! Why do you think everyone's leaving?"

Still, by the spring of 1986, Smith and his men had some reason to hope their transformation might ultimately succeed. Despite the complaints to Republic, TDB's deposit base hadn't eroded; it had, in fact, shown modest growth. With any luck, Bob Terrier reported, they might actually make headway in 1986 toward the difficult task of assimilating TDB into the American Express family. No one had to remind Smith or any of his aides that Safra was reopening his doors on the Place du Lac in two years, and that they had to be ready if they hoped to beat back the inevitable onslaught.

But as wary and hopeful as Bob Smith's men remained, no one was fully prepared for the jarring events of that spring. It all began innocently enough one day in March, when two of Bob Terrier's top men walked quietly into his seventh-floor office at TDB's new downtown Geneva headquarters, a grave look on their faces. Hans Hofer, the bank's slim director of data processing and administration, was among the most important men in the bank's operations. Hofer oversaw TDB's computer systems; he knew the ins and outs of every technical system the bank owned. Claude Frossard was TDB's accounting director and looked the part. "We need to talk to you," one of them said, and Terrier motioned for them to take seats.

The two men announced that they were resigning to form their own consulting business. Terrier stopped them before they went further, suggesting they split up the meeting and allow him to meet with each man separately. They did so, and Terrier wasn't surprised to find their stories were identical: both professed to be bored at TDB and claimed to harbor a secret longing to be entrepreneurs, to form their computer and accounting consulting firm.

Bob Terrier smelled a rat. Both men reported directly to him, and this was the first he had heard of desires to be consultants. He suspected they were leaving to join Safra, but both men denied it. Terrier thought it over for several days, talked to Bob Smith, then decided to lay a simple trap. He called the two in, congratulated them on their decision to form their own firm, then sprang his surprise: he wanted TDB to be the consulting firm's first client. Would they agree to continue working with their old employer? When the two men graciously declined, Terrier knew for certain their story was a fabrication.

In the weeks to come the departure of Hans Hofer and Claude Frossard sparked an exodus of TDB executives that virtually emptied the bank's entire administrative group. Costakis Plastiras, director of management controls, left at the end of April, as did his assistant Ariane Reymond. Jean-Christian Chevallier, one of Terrier's top computer technicians, left the same day. Claire Favre, assistant director of taxes and publicity, left in May, as did another pair of top computer specialists. By mid-summer nearly all Terrier's top aides—his "direct reports"—were gone, along with many of their assistants, secretaries, and technicians, eventually more than twenty people in all.

To Bob Terrier it was obvious what was going on. Administrative staff—computer specialists, controllers, accountants, auditors—formed the heart of what made a bank run. You couldn't operate a bank without them—or start one. Somewhere, Terrier suspected, Michel Cartillier was reforming the core of his old administrative group for Safra with an eye toward their reentry into Swiss banking. If Safra was to begin banking two years hence, he needed to start early. It would require mountains of preparatory work, and Safra now had the nucleus of key staff members to do it.

Gradually Terrier's fear gave way to anger. He was prepared to compete fairly with Safra, but not this way, not by stealing and raiding each other's employees in violation of Safra's severance agreements. Something had to be done. Terrier called in one of his Swiss lawyers, and the two men agreed: before they could complain to Safra, before they could do anything at all, they had to establish the facts. That meant one thing, an investigation. And an investigation, Terrier knew, meant bringing in private detectives, a notion with which he wasn't entirely comfortable. "We have to do something," he told Bob Smith in a call that spring. "Give me the mandate and the means to investigate this, and I will do it."

Terrier had given the matter some thought, and had decided to throw in a kicker, something he knew would make his plan irresistible to Smith. There was, he said, a slim chance of finding a silver lining amid their growing problems with Safra. In order to formally return to Swiss banking on March 1, 1988, Safra would need a new banking license. Under Switzerland's banking regulations, licenses could be granted only to those with reputations that were "above reproach," that is, who exhibited qualities of honesty, integrity, trustworthiness, and what one Swiss judge termed "character strength." If American Express could establish that Safra had stolen its employees in a breach of contract, they might be able to build a case that his scheme was so reprehensible the federal banking commission should block his request for a new banking license. It was a long shot, Terrier knew, but the prospect of stopping the flow of refugees while at the same time waylaying Safra was simply too tempting to pass up.

Bob Smith loved the idea.

"Do it," he told Terrier. "But make sure you do it right. Call in security." Smith, in turn, briefed Jim Robinson on their plans, and emphasized the need to maintain total secrecy. No one could be trusted. "We can't afford a leak," he told Robinson, who swiftly approved Smith's plan.

To begin his investigation Bob Terrier needed help. One night that spring, he opened the door of his suburban Geneva home and welcomed in Paul Knight, American Express's London-based security chief for Europe and the Middle East. Knight, the former head of the DEA in Europe, was an expatriate New Englander with a knowing smile who many inside American Express believed to be friendly with the CIA. Terrier didn't care; he just wanted a job done. He knew Bob Smith valued Knight's services highly. More than once, Smith had summoned Knight or his men down to Geneva to sweep his hotel room for electronic recording devices.

That evening in his living room Bob Terrier laid out his problem for

Knight, and the two men talked over the best way to pursue an investigation. The job seemed simple enough: find out whether the bank's missing employees were working for Safra in violation of Safra's severance agreements. It was just a question of following each man to find where he was employed, simple tail jobs. Knight suggested that three detectives could do the work, and he knew a trio of former Geneva policemen who would be willing to handle it. As they spoke of the investigators, both Terrier and Knight used the term favored at American Express headquarters. The men weren't to be called private detectives—they were "consultants."

Once Paul Knight made the arrangements, he came to Terrier's office and slipped him the name of a downtown Geneva bistro where they would meet Terrier's contact, the ex-Swiss cop—the "consultant"— who would supervise the other "consultants." That night Terrier arrived at the bright little restaurant, just blocks behind Safra's headquarters, and took a seat beside Paul Knight. Slowly, a bit dramatically, Knight raised his arm and pointed to a man sitting at a table across the room. Terrier stared. The man across the room turned and nodded. Their eyes met. That, Knight murmured, is your contact man. Terrier suppressed an impulse to laugh. It was like something out of *Day of the Jackal*.

Before their probe began, there was one more favor Bob Terrier asked of Paul Knight. Terrier wasn't overreacting; he feared that someone—Safra, Cartillier, one of their former aides—might have planted recording devices in TDB's new offices. He wanted the building swept for bugs. And so, one night that spring, when headquarters had emptied for the day, Terrier crept down from his office, unlocked the front doors and let in a pair of British electronics experts Knight had sent. Terrier guided the pair through the building as they waved electronic sensing devices over desks and behind paintings and unscrewed phone receivers to check inside.

Everything was going smoothly until they reached the basement switchboard, of which Terrier was especially suspicious; there had been several unexplained calls made on the one remaining "tie line" to Safra's Place du Lac headquarters, and Terrier wanted to see what the experts might find when they inspected it. But as they bent over the console, one of the bug men somehow touched a live wire. Suddenly, to their dismay, alarms clanged throughout the building. Minutes later, as a mortified Terrier scrambled to turn them off, he was stunned to see a squad of

Geneva policemen rushing the building, pistols drawn. Only when he assured the officers he was the bank's top administrator did they withdraw—as did the embarrassed British bug men, who never found a thing.

Within days Terrier's three Swiss detectives, armed with photographs of Michel Cartillier and the other TDB refugees, began a stakeout of Safra's headquarters. It was boring work made more difficult by the fact that within days, Safra's plainclothes security men spotted the surveillance and began shooing off the American Express detectives. Soon Terrier's men threw in the towel at Republic, having seen no sign of Cartillier or the others. It didn't surprise Terrier: if Safra had stolen his people, he was too cagey to display them at headquarters. No, Terrier reasoned, if the refugees were working for Safra, they were hidden away from prying eyes.

Security was tight as Terrier's three detectives began the next phase of their investigation in the summer of 1986, finding the refugees' homes and following them to work each day. Terrier trusted no one. At TDB only one other officer, the audit manager Jean-Louis Hoehen, knew of the bank's investigation. Even Terrier's secretary was kept in the dark; she, too, had worked for Safra. Terrier refused to let any of the detectives be seen around TDB. Instead, when there was information to be passed, he met them discreetly in public parks or darkened bistros around downtown Geneva. Terrier was careful never to leave the investigators' reports lying on his desk; each night he slipped them into his office safe or took them home, where he hid them in a second safe.

It didn't take long for Bob Terrier's men to track down the key TDB refugees, and what they found was revealing. Three of the former TDB computer scientists were followed to an office building on the corner of the busy Rue de Stand, less than a half mile down the lakefront from Safra's headquarters. They seemed to work together, for a firm named Prochimex S.A. The name meant nothing to Terrier.

Not so the location to which they tracked the single largest contingent of TDB refugees, including Michel Cartillier. Five of them—including Hofer, the computer chief; Frossard, the accountant; Plastiras, the systems man; and Favre, the tax expert—were trailed to a grand, mansionlike office building on the Rue François Billot, a quiet side street half a mile above the lake through Geneva's winding cobblestone streets. Terrier knew the address well. It was the same building where Jean-

Pierre Jacquemoud, a lawyer frequently used by Safra, housed his offices.

In New York, Bob Smith was delighted as each piece of Terrier's puzzle fell into place. Where Safra was concerned, Smith was more than ready to play hardball. Following through on their early threats, he had ordered the bank's general counsel, Mark Ewald, to look for weaknesses in Safra's most vulnerable line of defense, his American tax position. "If the son of a bitch competes with us," Smith growled, "we'll turn him into the IRS." Smith even told Ewald to look into the possibility of somehow grabbing a copy of the log kept aboard Safra's private jet. Not only did he suspect Safra was using the plane for personal uses—more ammunition for the IRS—but they might learn whether any of the TDB refugees were flying with him.

Seemingly alone among those swept up in the Safra probe, Mark Ewald found the whole affair a tad unseemly. He cringed at the idea of tracking down dirt on Safra's taxes and gently tried to tell Smith it was overkill. Why couldn't they simply fight aboveboard? If they did their best to make TDB's employees and depositors happy, how many would really jump to Safra? But Smith wasn't listening; he wanted Safra's head, and by all accounts, he had Jim Robinson's full backing to get it. Ewald shared his doubts with American Express's general counsel, Gary Beller, but Beller seemed as gung-ho as the rest. Upon Ewald's resignation in 1986 to enter private business, the last known voice against American Express's aggressive investigation of Edmond Safra was silenced.

Bob Smith, meanwhile, stayed abreast of every detail of Terrier's Swiss investigation, waiting for the day he could slap the smile off Safra's face. One evening in Geneva, he was walking across the Pont du Mont Blanc, the lake bridge leading to his hotel. Smith stopped, turned around, and took a moment to ponder Safra's hunched green-glass head-quarters at the lakeside, its blank panes glaring malevolently down at him. "You know," he told an aide standing at his side, "if we had a bazooka, we could take him out right now."

As is so often the case in tangled corporate fights, the seeds of the grow-ing dispute between American Express and Edmond Safra lay in the fine print—specifically, two seemingly contradictory sections of Safra's 1983 employment agreement with American Express.

It was the five-year expiration of this contract, the central document governing Safra's obligations to American Express, that pegged Republic's reentry to Swiss banking at March 1, 1988. In the contract, as Mark Ewald reminded Safra lawyers in yet another nagging letter that July of 1986, Safra had agreed not to "knowingly, directly or indirectly, employ, solicit for employment, or advise or recommend to any other person that they employ or solicit for employment, any person employed at the time by [American Express Bank] or American Express or any of their respective subsidiaries or affiliates."

To American Express, it couldn't have been clearer: Safra, and by extension all the banks he controlled, was forbidden from luring away his former employees. But as a Republic lawyer pointed out in Safra's reply to Ewald a key loophole specifically omitted executives of Republic from any such restrictions. "Nothing in this agreement," Safra's contract read, "shall impose any restriction on the conduct of the business and affairs of Republic...or any of [its] subsidiaries...." Not even, Republic insisted, hiring TDB executives.

It was this loophole that Republic's two top officers, Walter Weiner and Jeff Keil, were using to secretly pluck up some of Bob Smith's best people. Safra's two aides had been at it from the start, drawing up informal lists of TDB executives they wanted to hire, then quietly approaching them one by one, often after hearing a rumor of the executive's disillusionment with American Express. Jeff Keil had flown to Montreux, Switzerland, in October 1985 to meet secretly with one of the first TDB refugees, Claude Frossard, and map out Frossard and his partner Hans Hofer's return to the Safra fold. Keil had quietly corresponded with several other TDB executives as well, making clear that jobs awaited them at Republic should they become dissatisfied with American Express management.

Republic's lawyers would later argue, somewhat disingenuously, that the prohibitions against Safra soliciting TDB employees didn't apply to these efforts, since Safra wasn't personally involved in them—and that in any case, they had created a "Chinese Wall" of secrecy around their solicitations to ensure that Safra stayed in compliance.

Who was right was a matter for the courtroom, but on the surface it appeared that American Express had left itself vulnerable with some sloppy lawyering. In later correspondence its attorneys would take to arguing that whatever the loopholes, Safra's hiring of TDB employees violated the "spirit" of their contracts. And clearly, it did. But Safra was playing hardball; he and his aides had little use for the spirit of anything where it pertained to American Express. They were holding Jim Robinson's people to the letter of the law, and as the fine print made clear, the law seemed to be on their side. For Edmond Safra this would prove to be a dangerous tactic, because, as events would later show, the men at American Express did not take kindly to being outmaneuvered.

Into the fall of 1986 Bob Terrier and his trio of Geneva detectives quietly pieced together a portrait of the TDB refugees' new lives. Through long hours and a dollop of luck, they managed to assemble a picture of a web of companies where the executives were working. All, no one was surprised to find, could be linked to Safra. Michel Cartillier's former secretary and three others, for instance, were tracked to a Geneva firm named Rasmal Finance S.A. that had been formed the previous fall. One of Rasmal's administrators was Jean-Pierre Jacquemoud, the lawyer who did work for Cartillier and Safra.

Rasmal, in turn, seemed to be paying the rent for the Prochimex firm where TDB's former computer scientists had congregated. It was also making payments on behalf of the shell company where Cartillier and the others worked. Perhaps most worrisome, Rasmal appeared to be taking in deposits from Republic's Luxembourg office—accounts, Bob Terrier firmly believed, that had been stolen from TDB. For all the hours his detectives put in, one of Terrier's biggest breaks came when a package was mistakenly delivered for one of the refugee executives to his former office at TDB. Inside, one of Terrier's men found a collection of confidential vouchers that afforded an invaluable glimpse at the network of payments linking Rasmal and the other Safra shell companies.

Incriminating vouchers were far from the only thing the American Express detectives unearthed on the refugees. Terrier was embarrassed to learn that one of them, a married man, was carrying on a secret homosexual affair. A proper Swiss, Terrier squirmed over how to handle the information, which was potentially quite useful. He realized blackmail was a real possibility: if they confronted the man with the affair, he might become an informer and lay bare Safra's entire refugee network. The idea made Terrier's skin crawl; it was a moral line he simply couldn't make himself cross. He didn't dare tell Bob Smith, who, he suspected, might push for blackmail—Smith might actually *enjoy* it—and Terrier didn't want to have to refuse him. In the end, after confiding only in Paul Knight, Terrier did nothing.

Bit by bit, Terrier and his detectives assembled the case against Safra, which they planned to file with the Swiss banking commission sometime in 1987. Their work remained a tightly guarded secret and in fact, during all the months his detectives were on the job, Terrier discussed his work with only one other person from American Express headquarters, Jim Robinson's right-hand man Harry Freeman, whom he unexpectedly encountered at a conference in Lausanne, forty miles up the lake from Geneva. Terrier had invited Freeman down to Geneva and briefed him on his investigation. He had been disappointed, though, by Freeman's tepid reaction. The man from headquarters listened politely but said nothing, nothing at all. "He just wasn't interested," Bob Terrier would recall.

American Express's probe was still moving quietly along in January 1987 when Terrier took a disturbing call from a TDB internal auditor. One of the bank's IBIS files was missing. To Terrier it was startling news. Each of the IBIS files—the name stood for Internal Bank Information System—was a detailed blueprint of TDB's computer and communications systems. Their contents were considered so sensitive that no more than a half-dozen of the files—actually bulky binders—were assembled for the bank's senior officers. Each officer's copy was numbered.

The missing file, Terrier was told, had belonged to Hans Hofer, the systems chief who had left the previous spring. When Terrier had Hofer's old office searched, only the empty IBIS binder was found—the documents themselves were gone. This was a crisis of the first order, not so much because of what American Express and TDB had lost but because of what Edmond Safra had gained. If Hans Hofer had handed a complete IBIS file to Safra, it would represent a dollar savings that could run into the millions, money that Safra would have spent designing and assembling a new bank's entire administrative system.

"Are any of the other files missing?" Terrier asked. Days later the bad news came back. Three other IBIS files were also gone. "Whose were they?" Terrier asked, already knowing the answer. The missing files had belonged to Michel Cartillier, his assistant and the accounting chief Frossard, all now working for Safra.

For Bob Terrier, it was the final indignity. He called in his Swiss lawyers, and they agreed: they were looking at a case of theft. There was only one thing to do. Again Terrier took his plan to Bob Smith, who swiftly approved it after running it past Jim Robinson. The Swiss lawyers went to work, and by March 23 they were ready to move. That day, in papers delivered to Geneva's main courthouse, Trade Development Bank filed a criminal complaint against "unknown persons" who had stolen the four IBIS files.

A state prosecutor, a woman, was assigned to the case, and Terrier was assured the matter would be investigated. Though neither Safra nor any of the refugees were officially named as defendants in the complaint, TDB's filing made clear where its suspicions lay. Briefed on a daily basis, and wary of Safra's renowned political clout, Bob Smith had just one concern as they moved forward. "What's the chance this lady d.a.'ll get bought off?" he asked Terrier.

"This is Switzerland, Bob," Terrier said, as if it were the silliest idea he had ever heard.

"Well," Smith said, "with guys like we're dealing with, anything is possible."

Swiss criminal investigations are so secret that Edmond Safra might never have learned of the American Express complaint except for a Republic officer's ruined date. The Republic man was dating the secretary of one of TDB's Swiss lawyers, and one Saturday night she was forced to cancel an outing, explaining in a pique that she had been ordered to stay late at her office to type up a hundred-page briefing on the criminal case against Safra.

Word of the remark shot straight to Safra, who was immediately and predictably furious. Now they were calling him a criminal, a thief! His American aides at first weren't sure whether to believe the flimsy report. "Come on, Edmond, this is bullshit," Walter Weiner advised. "What on earth could they be complaining about?" But though his Swiss lawyers were unable to confirm the filing for weeks, Safra was certain it existed. "What kind of people are these?" he complained, cursing Jim Robinson again and again. "How could they do this?"

The usual whirlwind series of strategy meetings ensued, with Safra repeatedly telephoning Gershon Kekst's home in suburban New York to demand his presence in Geneva. Kekst counseled restraint and resisted going, though an increasingly despondent Safra clearly wanted him at his side. "Does this mean you can't help me?" the billionaire moaned to Kekst's wife on an occasion when Kekst couldn't come to the phone.

Ultimately Robert Siegfried was dispatched to Geneva, but the scene there was chaotic. Republic's Swiss lawyers were counseling restraint, and in truth there was little Safra could do from a legal or public relations standpoint. A public defense of a private charge made no sense. The best approach, everyone advised Safra, was no approach at all. "If we do anything to precipitate attention," Kekst advised, "we're just doing American Express's job for them. Remember, the more controversial Edmond Safra is, the less comfortable the Swiss bank board will be." Peter Mansbach took the same view. "Edmond, they're just making fools of themselves," he said. "They're just going to piss the Swiss off. This won't go anywhere."

But Safra was inconsolable. Despite all the soothing words, he was convinced word of the American Express charges would leak out, to the newspapers, to his major depositors, to the Sephardic community. He remembered Bob Smith's threat about destroying him via "trial by newspaper" and knew it was only a matter of time until the whole world knew he was being called a thief. And while other men might have dismissed the entire affair as a nuisance, Safra, a man for whom honor and respect remained paramount, was consumed with anxiety and, ultimately, paranoia. Gradually the stress took itself out on his body. For months Safra was plagued with headaches and stomach disorders. He couldn't eat. He couldn't sleep. Doctors were no use.

In such a supercharged atmosphere, every tremor, every rumor, every hint of something negative about Republic, Safra and Keil attributed to American Express. A magazine article took a swipe at Republic's earnings? Somehow American Express must be behind it. When two customers telephoned him with concerns about the safety of their money, Safra was convinced that an American Express plot to discredit him was behind the calls. "There's a campaign going on," he complained to Gershon Kekst. "I know there is."

All through the summer of 1987 the tension mounted. In May, two months after the criminal complaint was filed, Safra's lawyers formally lodged their application with the Swiss bank board to open Safra Republic's Geneva offices for deposits the following March. Meanwhile, at

TDB, Bob Terrier and a number of his aides disappeared into a Swiss courtroom to give secret testimony on the missing IBIS files. Defections from TDB's executive suite continued. Two more computer specialists resigned to join the mysterious Prochimex firm on the Rue de Stand. Both the director of TDB's exchange office and its assistant budget chief left to join Rasmal, though Terrier later tracked one of them to Republic's Paris office. One of TDB's top *garants* left to work for Safra in Luxembourg, where Terrier heard he was soliciting TDB's wealthy Brazilian clients.

Then, on August 31, American Express's Swiss lawyers filed the company's long-awaited opposition to Republic's new license. Laying out the results of Terrier's investigation—naming Rasmal, Prochimex, and the other firms where the TDB refugees had gathered—their twenty-one-page filing described in detail the company's grievances against Safra, whom it charged with "serious violations" of his noncompete agreements. Not only did American Express ask the federal banking commission to turn down Safra's request for a new license, it requested an administrative inquiry into their charges that Republic was stealing TDB employees. For good measure, the lawyers asked the Swiss commission to delay its ruling until the company's criminal complaint could be ruled on.

Republic fired right back, saying the bank was "outraged" by American Express's complaint. "You certainly will not fail to notice," Jeff Keil wrote the Swiss bank board that summer, "that the only aim of the American Express group is to delay, as much as possible, the opening of our bank."

Their best shots fired, everyone sat back to wait.

Anyone watching American Express during those turbulent days of 1987 would have assumed Jim Robinson's company was willing to go to almost any length to save its banking subsidiary—and indeed, as would later be revealed, some employees were already going to extreme lengths. And so there was a deep irony in a set of secret talks that took place through much of that summer at American Express headquarters in lower Manhattan. Even as the company's lawyers fought to block Edmond Safra's banking license in Switzerland, even as Bob Smith whipped his troops into fighting trim for Safra's expected attack, Robinson was seriously considering selling the American Express Bank/TDB combination. The proposed buyer was none other than a management group led by Bob Smith.

The latest in sixty years of plans to unload the company's banking operations had its roots in the board's decision to take a massive write-off of the bank's Latin American loans that June. That summer Robinson, disillusioned by the bank's continuing problems, had broached the idea of selling American Express Bank and keeping TDB. Bob Smith thought about it for a while and came back to Robinson with a different idea: unload the whole thing, and sell it to the bank's executives in a leveraged buy-out.

According to Smith and others, Robinson offered to sell both banks to a group led by Smith, Bob Savage, Bob Budenbender, and Smith's friend Sheldon Gordon for book value, roughly $600 million. Smith got permission from Robinson to approach some of the banks' largest clients for funding, and within weeks he had enough commitments to convince him they could swing the deal. Smith was so confident of success he directed that a press release be written up.

But when he reported back to Robinson, Smith was stunned to find the chairman had inexplicably changed his mind: the bank wasn't for sale. Variants on the buy-out idea sputtered along all that summer; as late as August, Smith sat with Robinson's No. 2, Lou Gerstner, at a bank soirée in Monte Carlo hashing through ways to make an LBO work. But it never did. Smith talked with at least one potential outside buyer for the bank, the New York–based American International Group, but nothing came of that idea, either.

And so that fall, they all returned their attention to Edmond Safra, and to fighting like hell to save a bank no one seemed to want in the first place.

By September workmen were crawling over the first floor of Safra's Geneva headquarters, installing the lavish customer-service facilities that were expected to greet clients new and old when Safra reopened for business in the spring. Michel Cartillier oversaw the remodeling, making sure no trace of American Express was left behind. Upstairs, nearly one hundred executives, including most all the TDB refugees, readied computer and control systems.

Jacob Safra (inset) fled Beirut for Brazil, where, after his death in 1963, his sons built on his legacy of Middle Eastern contacts to form an international financial empire. His son Edmond (above), perhaps the world's most successful banking entrepreneur of the post-World War II era, gambled his oldest bank on a grand alliance with the American Express Company, only to see his plans crumble in a series of recriminations that would eventually lead to one of the world's most bitter corporate feuds.

Edmond Safra's world: His centerpiece banks located on Manhattan's Fifth Avenue (left) and fronting the River Rhone in Geneva (right), Safra surrounded himself with a cadre of intensely loyal aides, including (beside him at bottom right) Jeffrey Keil and Albert Benezra and (bottom left) the chairman of his ultraconservative Republic National Bank of New York, Walter Weiner, who served as Safra's chief of staff and global troubleshooter.

Jim Robinson: The gentlemanly, Atlanta-born chairman of American Express bet that Safra's bank would become a thriving new aisle of the financial supermarket he foresaw; later, his plan in shambles, Robinson authorized aides to launch a vigorous investigation of Safra that evolved into a covert smear campaign, leaving in its wake questions about the chairman's personal involvement.

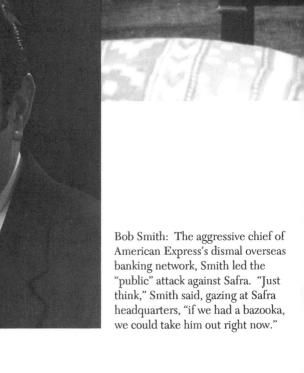

Bob Smith: The aggressive chief of American Express's dismal overseas banking network, Smith led the "public" attack against Safra. "Just think," Smith said, gazing at Safra headquarters, "if we had a bazooka, we could take him out right now."

Peter Cohen: Having once served at Safra's side, the bright young Shearson chairman initiated one of the most ill-fated acquisitions in American Express's 140-year history.

אדמונד
כספי סמים

בליק', הטייק לספרא, כתחנת־המעבר
וקדה בספרא, או בבנק שבבעלותו

minute

Chardon

Du 26 octobre au 1er novembre 1988 · 13 F · N° 1386

1 500 000 VICTIMES
ESCROQUERIE AUX H.L.M.

60 milliards détournés

Pages 4, 5

DANS SA PROPRIÉTÉ DE MILLIARDAIRE
SUR LA CÔTE D'AZUR

Nos reporters ont retrouvé le banquier qui blanchit la drogue

Pages 6, 7, 8

▲ LOCAL

Banqueros mafiosos

DANS SA VILLA DE BEAULIEU
IL VIT DANS LA PANIQUE

Le milliardaire condamné à mort

On l'accuse d'avoir blanchi l'argent de la drogue

un des hommes les plus riches du monde erre dans la luxueuse riete de Beaulieu (Al-Maritimes) comme une forteresse gardée ie véritable petite
Des hommes en patrouillent dans les sisinantes. D'au-Libanais, armes dents, roulent en e dans le parc motocyclettes.
milliardaire, de avons parlé otre numéro Edmond J. l'une dynas s du Liban a com-emettre voilà au temps ncait le avanes

Edmond J. Safra : l'argent ne fait pas le bonheur...

eu-
.un Safra. Au-jourd'hui, bien qu'ils soient toujours richissimes, la si-tuation est nettement moins brillante. Edmond Safra est l'objet d'une enquête du Sénat américain. On le soupçonne d'avoir blanchi les millions de dollars du rafic de la drogue et no-'amment la moitié de la fortune du général No-riega, l'homme fort de Panama qui est l'un des plus redoutables hommes à État gangsters de ce siè-cle
Rappelons à ce propos que le général Saulnier, ancien chef d'état-major de Mitterrand, lui a, le 10 février dernier, remis au Cercle interallié les in-signes de commandeur de la Légion d'honneur, en vertu d'un décret signé par Mitterrand lui-même.
Tanton a d'étranges amis et tient à honorer de la plus prestigieuse décora-tion française certains des hommes les plus méprisa-bles, les plus nuisibles et les plus corrompus du globe.
C'est la moitié de la fortune de Noriega, soit quatre cents millions de dollars, que Safra aurait, dit-on, « lavé » grâce aux rouages innombrables de sa chaîne de banques qui a des succursales ou des filiales à Genève, New York, Panama, Monte Carlo, Rio de Janeiro, Luxembourg, Miami, Paris (la Republic Bank of New York, avenue Montaigne), etc
Mais ce ne sont pas Noriega et ses amis qui

font trembler Safra, ce sont d'autres adversaires au moins aussi redoutables, ces trafiquants de drogue colombiens archimillir-daires connus sous le nom de « cartel de Medellin ».
Il leur a en effet joué un sale tour et, dans ce milieu, on a le pardon rare et difficile...
Il y a quelques années, deux gros parrains colom-biens de la drogue appar-tenant au cartel sont en effet venus déposer cent millions de dollars dans la banque de Safra à ru-nama. Étrange coïnci-dence : les deux hommes ont été assassinés quelques semaines plus tard et d'au-tres membres du cartel se sont présentés à la banque pour retirer les fonds.
« Ils ne vous appartien-nent pas ! nous ne vous connaissons pas ! » a pro-teste le directeur.
Le cartel est intervenu auprès de Safra et lui a fait savoir que si la banque ne leur donnait pas les cent millions de dollars, son directeur serait kidnappé et exécuté.

Safra a fait répondre qu'il ne saurait s'en soucier moins. Le malheureux di-recteur a donc été enlevé et embarqué de force sur un yacht. Safra a encore refusé de payer... On a retrouvé le corps du mal-heureux à Guayaquil, en Équateur.
Safra n'a toujours pas payé.
Mais il n'a plus un poil de sec... Et c'est tout juste s'il ose sortir de sa splen-dide villa de la Côte d'Azur.

Discret

Edmond Safra, qui est non seulement l'un des dix hommes les plus riches du monde mais aussi l'un des plus secrets, vient de sortir de sa retraite pour donner, évé-nement rarissime ! une inter-view à quatre journalistes. Il veut, en effet, faire appel à des investisseurs privés pour réunir 350 millions de dollars destinés à une nouvelle ex-pansion de son déjà formi-dable empire.
Il n'a bien entendu pas prononcé le nom du général Noriega ni celui du cartel de Medellin.

ic
es

d o en Pi
s sudam
en en dól
nar la in
de arige
ciós legal

epublic P
de los han
roa que
lo en los
algunos
americán
s relaci
cios de
nes venid
vieron la
continua
que le p
os menc
te.
rero todo
abora, la D
Administratin,
del gobierno n
da de combati
poesto todos s
Safra y sus ho
Todo empe
recieron 40 mi
producto de l
a Irán y su
"Contras de N
Safra, antig
CIA en e! lo
habría sido

Zona franca fin serviría para la

Por: PEDRO CARDOZO

ZAFRA. Para la mayoría de países de América Latina donde se produce caña de azúcar, significa la época de cosecha y el acto en sí de recoger ese dulce producto.
En algunos países de Europa y en determinados círculos fi-nancieros y oficiales de Estados Unidos, Safra significa otra cosa, porque Edmond Safra, el propie-tario del Republic National Bank y bancos en todo el mundo está siendo investigado por la desa-parición de 40 millones de dóla-res del recordado tráfico de ar-mas conocido como "Irán Contra", destinado a proporcio-nar armas al Ayatollah Khomei-ni y de las utilidades de esas ventas, dar ayuda a los "Contras" en Nicaragua.
Edmond Safra es hombre hábil en los negocios, empezó de la nada, hace casi 40 años llegó al Brasil y fundó el Banco Safra, venía del Líbano y en Brasil amasó una gran fortuna.
Según fuentes bien informa-das, y ha sido publicado en el prestigioso semanario Expresso de Italia y en el diario "La Depeche" de París, Safra hizo su

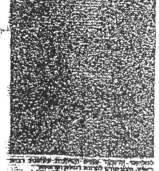

The secret campaign and its aftershocks:
Beginning in the summer of 1988, a stunned
Safra found himself engulfed in a blizzard of
stinging international press reports, many
alleging he and his banks had secret ties to
drug traffickers, organized crime, the
Central Intelligence Agency and the Iran-
Contra scandal.

PFPBPAZG   RPT ZG
PL LIMA 559
TOD/
NARCOTRAFICO-CACERIA   2 FINAL
    ES EN ESOS PAISES DONDE LA DEA PRESUME QUE PUEDA APARECER
LA FORTUNA DEL BANQUERO LIBANES, EN QUIEN CONFIESA QUE SE
COMENZO A FIJAR A PARTIR DE LA DESAPARICION DE 40 MILLONES
DE DOLARES DEL JUG...

CELEBRE TENIENTE C   EL REPUBLIC NATIONAL BANK, DE PROPIEDAD DEL BANQUERO LIBANES
HAKIM Y WILLARD ZL   NACIONALIZADO BRASILERO, EDMOND J. SAFRA, ES UNO DE LOS
    LA DEA ALERTA A   BANCOS NUEVOS DE MAYOR AUGE EN ESTADOS UNIDOS. SU PROSPERIDAD
MEZCLARSE CON SAFF   FUE OBTENIDA AL FUNGIR DE INTERMEDIARIO EN LA ADQUISCION
REPUBLIC NATIONAL   ILEGAL DE ARMAS. PRECISAMENTE HA SIDO DETERMINADA SU RESPONSA-
TRANSITO CONOCIDO   BILIDAD EN EL EXTRAVIO DE 40 MILLONES DE DOLARES QUE ESTABAN
    QUIZAS EL INFOI   DESTINADOS AL SUMINISTRO DE ARMAS A LOS CONTRAS NICARAGUENSES.
DEL ESCANDALO SURK
LA MINISTRA DE JU: SEGUN TRASCENDIO EL REPUBLIC BANK E DMOND SAFRA HABRIAN ORIEN-
OBLIGADA A RENUNC   TADO SUS ACTIVIDADES A LA CAPTACION DE DOLARES PROCEDENTES
NARCOTRAFICO.   DE PERU,ARGENTINA,BRASIL,VENEZUELA, DEL FLORESCIENTE NEGOCIO
    EL DOCUMENTO   DEL NARCOTRAFICO.
ESTAFADOR, REFIER
HARIDO DE LA KOPP   PARA LA DEA LO QUE BUSCA EL REPUBLIC BANK Y SAFRA ES APODERARSE
FUE PROPIETARIO D   DE LAS RUTAS DE LOS DOLARES LAVADOS QUE INGRESAN A BANCOS DE
LN/FIN/OPR JC 010   MIAMI, LOS ANGELES, NEW YORK, LUXENBURGO, FRANCIA Y SUIZA.
                      LOS DOLARES DE ESTE ILEGAL NEGOCIO PUEDEN ASI INGRESAR LEGAL-
                      ,MENTE AL CIRCUITO FINANCIERO INTERNACIONAL DEJANDO GRANDES
                      UTILIDADES PARA LOS AGENTES COMPROMETIDOS EN LA OPERACIN.

                      LA INTERPOL, EN BASE AL INFORME DE LA DEA, HA ADVERTIDO A LAS
                      INSTITUCIONES BANCARIAS DE LOS 4 PAISES SUDAMERICANOS INVOLU-
                      CRADOS PARA QUE ESTEN ALERTAS SOBRE LAS OPERACIONES DEL
                      REPUBLIC NATIONAL BANK Y SUS SUBSIDIARIAS EN LAS CUALES EL
                      CIUDADANO LIBANES EDMOND J. SAFRA, EJERCE CONTROL.

                      AP/11:35 AM.
                      JMP.RAZ-068/432

The counterattack: A hard-charging bundle of creative energy, Stanley Arkin (upper left) was the colorful New York lawyer Safra selected to lead an investigation of the bizarre newspaper articles; Arkin used a squadron of private detectives to locate the first major break in a Staten Island trash can. Joe Mullen (lower left) was the grizzled head of an entire family of New York private eyes who broke open the case during a frantic pursuit through the streets of lower Manhattan.

Jack Palladino and Sandra Sutherland (lower right), a San Francisco–based husband-and-wife team, masqueraded as journalists to track a mysterious newspaper "source" across Europe. Safra's Madison Avenue media guru, Gershon Kekst (upper right), was convinced the press campaign was motivated by anti-Semitism and successfully pushed for a confrontation with American Express.

NAME
GRECO, ANTONIO

N

| SEX | RACE | BIRTH DATE | | HA |
| M | W | 12/16/39 | | BR |

FINGERPRINT CLASS   SO   NE
03 TT SR 21 04
AA 02 16 23 06

OCCUPATION

AKA
GRECO, GUISEPPE
GRECO, GIUSEPPE ANTONI
GRECO, ANTONIO GIUSEPP

ARREST- 1   10/06/8
    ARREST AGENCY-METRO
        AGENCY CASE-15611   OF
        CHARGE 001-STOLEN
    JUDICIAL-
        AGENCY-MIAMI SPRI
        CHARGE 001 -COURT   CO
            COURT DATA-   C
                STATUTE   LE
                DISP DA   DI
                PROVISI

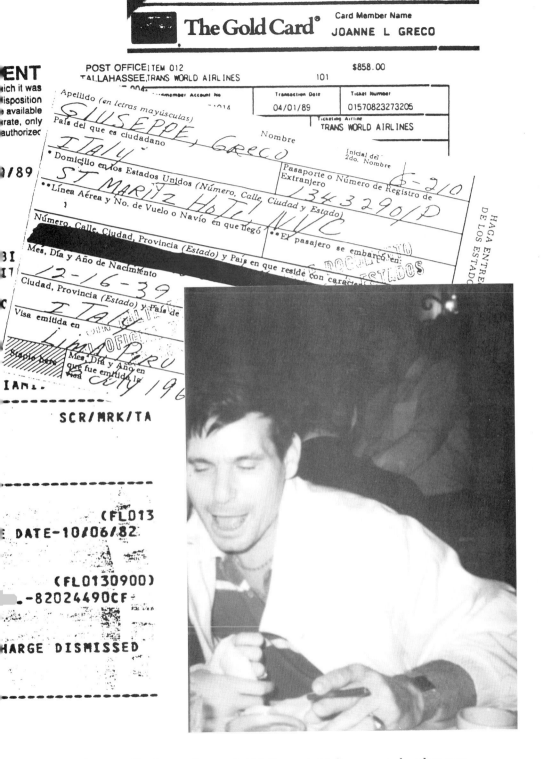

The Gold Card® Card Member Name JOANNE L GRECO

POST OFFICE ITEM 012 $858.00
TALLAHASSEE, TRANS WORLD AIRLINES 101

Transaction Date 04/01/89   Ticket Number 01570823273205

Ticketing Airline TRANS WORLD AIRLINES

Apellido (en letras mayúsculas) GIUSEPPE, GRECO

País del que es ciudadano ITALY

Nombre

Inicial del 2do. Nombre

• Domicilio en los Estados Unidos (Número, Calle, Ciudad y Estado) ST MARITZ HOTEL NYC

Pasaporte o Número de Registro de Extranjero 1343290/P

•• Línea Aérea y No. de Vuelo o Navío en que llegó

•• El pasajero se embarcó en:

Número, Calle, Ciudad, Provincia (Estado) y País en que reside con carácter

Mes, Día y Año de Nacimiento 12-16-39

Ciudad, Provincia (Estado) y País de ITALY

Visa emitida en LIMA PERU

Mes, Día y Año en que fue emitida JULY 196

SCR/MRK/TA

(FL013
DATE-10/06/82

(FL0130900)
-82024490CF

HARGE DISMISSED

The shadowy world of Tony Greco: Paid informant, Mafia-connected undercover detective, accused drug trafficker, the globe-trotting Italian had seen the inside of jail cells in at least five countries before accepting a $1 million assignment from American Express for a special covert operation.

The stakeout: Safra detectives watched as Greco sat in his car outside American Express headquarters just minutes before a key moment in the case.

Susan Cantor: Secretly photographed here by Safra detectives at the climactic moment of their surveillance, the onetime ABC News reporter spearheaded the American Express investigation of Safra as it careened toward scandal.

Harry Freeman: As Jim Robinson's right-hand man, the loyal Freeman (right), shown here with Robinson, resigned after acknowledging that the Safra affair occurred "on my watch," but later grew embittered. "What happened," he says today, "was a game common in corporate America called 'Protect the CEO.'"

Safra triumphant: The vengeful billionaire, trailed by p.r. man Robert Siegfried as he left a Swiss courtroom in November 1991, having heard testimony in his fourth successful libel suit against European journalists who had unwittingly printed American Express's disinformation. "After all," Safra's friend, the Nobel laureate Elie Wiesel, told the court, "what remains of a man after death? It is his name, his reputation, his honor."

As they waited for the banking license to come through, Safra and his men remained incensed over the filing of the six-month-old criminal complaint, which, despite all their efforts, they still had been unable to review. Peter Mansbach fumed when he learned American Express had filed a copy of the complaint with the Swiss bank board, in his view a clear violation of Swiss criminal-secrecy laws. In Manhattan he marched down to American Express headquarters and confronted Jim Robinson's general counsel, Gary Beller.

"Look, Gary, this is all bullshit," he said. "You're not going to block us. You know it, and I know it. Your guys are just making asses out of themselves in Geneva. They're not going to stop anything. They're just embarrassing themselves. Now let's stop this whole nonsense."

To Mansbach's dismay, Beller denied any knowledge of the criminal complaint. As Beller explained it, the various American Express subsidiaries were given wide autonomy, and it wasn't surprising that headquarters wouldn't be aware of every last lawsuit they filed. Mansbach didn't know whether to believe him, but toned down his anger when Beller promised to consider withdrawing the complaint if it could be done without humiliating Bob Smith and the Swiss lawyers who had filed it.

Getting no satisfaction from American Express, Safra was powerless to do anything but wait for the license. All his lawyers said its approval was a certainty, but by late fall it still hadn't come through, and Safra was growing increasingly anxious. Where was it? What was the holdup? The Swiss would give no explanation. Safra was convinced that American Express was behind the delay.

By Christmas the license still hadn't come through, and Safra was beside himself. As the days ticked by with no word from the bank board, Safra railed and railed at Jim Robinson's dirty tactics. Not until January 26, 1988, scarcely a month before their planned reopening, did the word come: the license was theirs.

"*Mabrouk!*" Walter Weiner exclaimed when Safra passed him the news, uttering the Arab phrase for blessing. For the first time in months, Safra allowed himself to believe the reopening was actually going to happen. In Geneva, as his top aides exhaled giant sighs of relief, Safra triumphantly ordered a huge Republic sign erected over headquarters, though in deference to American Express the sign was draped with a tarpaulin until the official reopening March 1. Another surprise came several days later, when Jim Robinson telephoned. Robinson proved nothing if not gracious in defeat. "Congratulations," he told Safra. "I hope you do well."

That winter, in fact, Jim Robinson gave every indication of giving up the fight to block Safra's opening. The criminal complaint was allowed to lapse, and that spring it would be quietly dismissed by a Geneva judge. After a briefing from Bob Smith, Robinson personally ordered an end to the investigation of the TDB refugees, details of which, by all accounts, he hadn't kept up on. In Geneva, Bob Terrier got the news in a strange call from American Express Bank's new general counsel, John Junek. "Bob," Junek said, "I just want you to know that Jim Robinson said if anybody, I mean anybody, says that Mr. Safra won't get his banking license, he won't be with this bank much longer."

"What do you mean?" Terrier asked.

"You heard what I said," Junek said.

Terrier was stunned. The lawyer's words were ambiguous, but the message wasn't. "The tone was, 'Terrier, lay off,'" he recalled. "It was a subtle way to tell me to stop all my efforts and stay quiet."

For weeks Bob Terrier brooded in his Geneva office, trying to make sense of what had happened. He simply couldn't figure it out. The case against Safra was strong. Everyone thought they had a chance of winning on appeal. Now they were simply quitting? It didn't add up. As far as Terrier could see, there was only one possible explanation. In the weeks and months to come, he thought it through again and again until he was sure of it. Headquarters wouldn't simply give up. Not Bob Smith, not Jim Robinson, not Harry Freeman. Somewhere, somehow, he knew, there had to be another plan to stop Edmond Safra.

*Just because you're
paranoid doesn't mean
they're not out to get you.*

—ANONYMOUS

6

There's been another article."

The tone of Gershon Kekst's voice told Siegfried he was in for another sudden European trip, and he was correct. The right-wing Parisian newspaper, *Minute*, had struck again, and its third article looked every bit as bad as the first pair in August. "Walter Weiner wants you to go over with him to London tonight," Kekst told Siegfried, "and Edmond wants to have a meeting on what to do."

And so, early on the evening of October 13, Siegfried found himself edging down the aisle of Pan Am's overnight flight to London and settled beside an obviously distracted Walter Weiner. The little p.r. man didn't really know Weiner; for four years he had worked mostly with Jeff Keil. But as Weiner hauled out his briefcase shortly after takeoff, it dawned on Siegfried that Weiner was taking over Safra's investigation of the bizarre articles they had seen in Italy, France, and Latin America.

Together the two examined the latest *Minute* article, whose only illustration was the photograph of a smiling Edmond Safra.

"In His Villa in Beaulieu He Lives in Panic," the headline read. "The Millionaire Sentenced to Death."

One of the richest men in the world lives in terror on his luxurious property in Beaulieu, which is like a fortress guarded by a small army. Men in cars patrol the surrounding streets. Other guards, Lebanese, armed to the teeth, are patrolling the park on motorcycles around-the-clock.

The millionaire is Edmond J. Safra, the head of a dynasty of Lebanese bankers whose fortune started to build up five generations ago, when his family financed caravans during the time of the Ottoman Empire....

Those were the happy days of the Safra clan. Today, even though they continue to be very rich, the situation is clearly not as great. Edmond Safra is the object of an investigation by the American Senate. He is suspected of laundering millions of dollars of drug money and notably half of the fortune of General Noriega, the strong man of Panama who is one of the most fearsome statesmen/gangsters of this century....

But it is not Noriega and his friends that make Safra tremble; it is other adversaries at least as fearsome: Colombian multimillionaire drug traffickers known by the name of the Medellin Cartel. He dealt them a dirty hand and, in this circle, one is hardly ever forgiven.

Some years ago, two big Colombian "godfathers" of the drug world belonging to the Cartel came, in fact, to deposit $100 million in Safra's bank in Panama. Strange coincidence: the two men were assassinated some weeks later and other members of the Cartel appeared in the Bank to withdraw the funds.

"It does not belong to you! We do not know you!" protested the director.

The Cartel pressured Safra and made him understand that if the Bank would not give them the $100 million, his Director would be kidnapped and executed.

Safra answered that he [couldn't] care less. The unlucky Director was therefore kidnapped and forced to embark on a yacht. Safra still refused to pay. The body of the unlucky man was found in Guayaquil, Ecuador.

Safra still has not paid.

He is perspiring in fear. He barely dares to leave his splendid villa on the French Riviera.

When he finished, all Siegfried could say was, "Wow." Weiner's expression of disgust spoke for itself. Both men could only marvel at the story and wonder: where was this stuff coming from? The only grain of truth in the entire article was that accounts at Republic had, in fact, held some of the Noriega regime's funds, as had accounts at banks like Marine Midland and Bankers Trust. When the Panamanian opposition sought to freeze Noriega's millions, all the banks had transferred the money into escrow.

Weiner took out the other French articles they had found, two in *Minute*, two in *La Dépêche du Midi*, as well as the articles in the Peruvian newspaper *Hoy* and the Mexican paper *Uno Mas Uno*. If the articles themselves weren't bad enough, Weiner said, there were rumors American Express was copying them and mailing them to Republic clients, which generated even more rumors. A story was even making the rounds that Safra was dead.

As far as Weiner had been able to determine, there were no obvious links among the four papers, no wire services, correspondents, or sponsors they had in common. At first glance, the four also had little in common politically. *Minute,* by far the most extreme, had been denounced by the Anti-Defamation League for regularly carrying anti-Semitic articles. According to the ADL, *Minute* was closely aligned with the leading voice of the French right, Jean-Marie Le Pen, whom the ADL labeled as "deeply racist and anti-Semitic." In Paris *Minute* was generally dismissed as a cross between the *National Review* and the *National Enquirer,* though it was noted for the occasional scoop embarrassing to the Communists.

La Dépêche, based in Toulouse near the Spanish border, was a little-known regional newspaper with no history of anti-Semitism or extremism. *Hoy* was the semiofficial organ of Peru's ruling APRA party and its president, the charismatic young Alan García. The ADL considered *Hoy* to have what it called a "Third-World orientation," and noted that, like *Minute,* it "has carried anti-Israel, anti-Zionist, and anti-Semitic articles." *Uno Mas Uno,* meanwhile, was a credible left-wing newspaper in Mexico City, known for solid investigative reporting. It had no history of anti-Semitism.

The trail from paper to paper, at least, was clear: Safra had first been mentioned briefly in the Italian magazine *L'Espresso* that January. Two months later in France, *La Dépêche* had invoked the Italian account in its own jumbled article. Three months after that, *Hoy* published a still longer article in Peru, crediting both the French and Italian publications while adding charges of its own. *Hoy's* article had then been reprinted almost word for word five days later in Mexico's *Uno Mas Uno.* A month after that, *La Dépêche's* second article had commented favorably on both Latin American stories. There was no clue as to how *Minute* fit into the pattern.

Weiner handed translations of all the articles to Siegfried, and together the two began poring over them, seeking to identify parallels and patterns, anything that might make sense of what was happening to Safra. Aside from the allegations of drug involvement, the most obvious thread running through all the articles was Safra's supposed involvement in the Iran-Contra affair. And alongside every reference to Safra and Iran-Contra was the name of a Geneva attorney named Willard Zucker.

Minute, August: A rich man Willard Zucker, seems to be closely associated with Safra. He has one of the largest bank accounts in one of his banks, Republic National Bank of New York. Zucker, who has the reputation of being a financial wizard expert in dissimulating funds, has brought a plane, a Falcon Fan Jet 20M429, registered in Switzerland, which flies regularly to Geneva to take to a private airport in the south of Paris suitcases full of documents which are afterwards brought by car to a warehouse. A certain source says that these documents are pertaining to the most secret deals for the sales of arms to Iran.

Uno Mas Uno, July: According to two officials of the DEA in Miami, William Zucket [sic] is a close associate of Edmond Safra, whom they described as a Lebanese Jew. According to sources, the $40 million that disappeared from the Contra operation were spotted for the last time at the Republic National Bank in New York.

Weiner sometimes wished he had never set eyes on Willard Zucker or that stupid plane. As Safra's people knew him—and they knew him well—Zucker was a talented American lawyer in Geneva, a former partner at a top New York firm who had come to Switzerland in the early 1970s and married a Frenchwoman. Weiner had known and trusted Zucker since their days as young attorneys in New York, and often sought his advice on Swiss legal matters.

Zucker's firm was what the Swiss called a *fiduciaire*; that is, he was one of the multitude of lawyers who formed the shell companies that capitalized on Swiss secrecy laws to do business. Much as his legal brethren did in tax havens like the Cayman Islands, Zucker created companies for his clients, named himself or his assistants as their officials, and ran the company's financial affairs. For any number of reasons, the Swiss had been doing business this way for years. Safra had turned to Zucker at least twice over the years to form companies. One incorporated a home Lily Safra owned in France; Zucker's shell company paid the villa's upkeep and taxes. The other, Republic Air Transport Services, incorporated a small jet, an eight-seat Falcon, that Safra bought in 1985 after years of flying commercial.

To Edmond Safra's everlasting regret, he was far from Willard Zucker's only prominent client. Another was an international businessman named Albert Hakim, the same Albert Hakim who would gain fame as a figure in the Iran-Contra scandal. Though he lived on a California hilltop, the Iranian-born Hakim was an experienced international middleman who had long-standing contacts with the Iranian military. It was Hakim, and his partner, retired U.S. Air Force General Richard Secord, who with Oliver North formed "The Enterprise," the maze of Swiss and Panamanian shell companies that served as conduits for moneys used in the Iran-Contra scandal. And it was Zucker who handled Hakim's money.

"Zucker was a discreet, efficient, and rapid channel for moving money," concluded a report produced by congressional committees probing Iran-Contra in April 1987. "By merely telephoning Zucker in Switzerland, Hakim, and later Secord, could order the movement of funds from Swiss bank accounts to the destination of their choice without a paper trace to either of them."

Willard Zucker, who had chosen to cooperate with American prosecutors in exchange for immunity, would go down in history as a bit player on the periphery of the Iran-Contra scandal, meriting no more than one or two mentions in the various books later published on the affair. But his involvement was to have severe repercussions for Safra. Walter Weiner remembered well the moment Zucker's name had first pulled Safra into the news. It was in the first days after U.S. Attorney General Edwin Meese told a crowded Washington briefing room in late November 1986 the initial details of what came to be known as the Iran-Contra scandal.

In the wake of Meese's stunning announcement, Zucker's name had been among the first of the scandal's figures to surface publicly. Reporters from all over the world combed through Zucker's public filings at the Geneva commercial registry and interviewed Swiss officials cooperating with the U.S. probe. Quickly they learned that at least one plane purchased by the Contras had been paid for by a Zucker-formed company in Bermuda. The money had allegedly come from a Zucker account at Republic National Bank of New York.

For Republic it was the beginning of a long, recurring headache. No sooner had its name been mentioned publicly than on December 3, 1986, the Swiss newspaper *Tages-Anzeiger* reported the surprising news that Safra's private jet had been used to fly Robert McFarlane, the former national security adviser, to Iran for secret talks. Reporter Maya

Jurt, quoting unnamed sources, revealed how Zucker had incorporated the plane for Republic a year earlier.

The Swiss report flashed out over the Reuters international news wire that afternoon, prompting a flustered denial from Walter Weiner. "These reports are absolutely untrue," Weiner told Reuters. "Our corporate plane has never been used at any time by the United States or any other government or by any individual acting officially or unofficially on behalf of any government, including Mr. McFarlane."*

As he sat on the Pan Am flight a year and a half later, Weiner still had only the vaguest idea how Republic's plane had been pulled into the fringes of the scandal. He had told reporters time and again that the little Falcon, which was housed and maintained for Republic by a Swiss company, wasn't even big enough to make the flight from Geneva to Teheran. Still, Safra's name had continued to occasionally appear in press coverage of the scandal, usually to identify him as Republic's owner. Now someone—and Weiner had his own ideas who—was using Willard Zucker's travails in an attempt to portray Safra as a major figure in Iran-Contra.

Aboard the Pan Am jet, Weiner and Siegfried turned to the first *Minute* article from August, which hinted at Safra's involvement in the murder of the French-American playboy, Glenn Souham. "Are you sure Edmond didn't know this guy?" Siegfried asked

"No," Weiner said. "Never heard of him."

The killing of Glenn Souham had been a source of international curiosity since an unknown assassin pumped six bullets into his body on a quiet Paris street two years before, on the evening of September 24, 1986. Three months afterward the *Washington Times* broke the news that Souham had performed some unexplained favors for Oliver North

---

*From all indications, it wasn't. Willard Zucker's Washington attorney, Sherwin Markman, who worked closely with Iran-Contra prosecutors, confirmed that the government inquired about Safra's plane but concluded that neither it nor Safra had any involvement in Iran-Contra dealings. "They asked us about the Safra plane," he said. "The result was there was no connection in any respect. All their returns came back negative." Former Iran-Contra prosecutors privately confirm this as well.

The Swiss reporter Maya Jurt, who would play her own role in the events enveloping Edmond Safra, later came to doubt her own article. She acknowledges that no single source confirmed that Safra's plane had been used in Iran-Contra matters; rather, she says she pieced her story together from inferences and hints made by a number of people. "I never said the plane *was* used, I said it might have been used," Jurt says today. "There's a big difference. I knew my case was pretty weak, but it was a possibility."

and that the French police, seeking links to his killing, had interviewed two Reagan administration officials. Both had denied that Souham worked for the U.S. government.

The mystery thickened when *The Washingtonian* magazine, in a lengthy profile of North, wrote that Souham had helped the dashing lieutenant colonel in a scheme to divert a Polish arms shipment to the Nicaraguan Contra fighters. Souham knew people in the outlawed Polish labor movement Solidarity, the magazine reported, and had helped North open a channel to its underground network. With Solidarity's help, North was able to divert an entire trainload of Soviet arms intended for the Polish army, including assault rifles and SA-7 missiles, to the Contras.

None of which shed the first ray of light on why anyone would try to link Safra to Glenn Souham's killing. Flummoxed, Weiner and Siegfried turned to the other *Minute* article, with its strange letter from the U.S. Embassy in Bern, Switzerland. Weiner remained transfixed by the so-called Bern letter. To him it was the single most vexing piece of evidence they had uncovered. With its seamy invocation of Safra as a "Lebanese Jew," it appeared to be a bald attempt to connect Safra with Willard Zucker's Iran-Contra dealings. According to the letter, the tip had come from a confidential source of the FBI's Miami office.

Tracing that source, Weiner felt, was of paramount importance. Three weeks earlier, he had sent two Republic attorneys to Washington to meet with a young Iran-Contra prosecutor named David Zarnow and a pair of FBI agents. Over the course of two long meetings, Weiner's men managed to secure what Safra so badly wanted, an official letter clearing him of allegations in the Bern letter.* They also learned a few things about the mysterious Miami source. The FBI men were cagey, but when pressed had acknowledged that the source was a former bureau informant, no longer active. They described him as a businessman who traveled abroad on a regular basis. The source had simply

---

*The October 5, 1988, letter to Republic's general counsel from the special Iran-Contra prosecutor, Lawrence Walsh, read in full: "Please be advised that the Office of Independent Counsel has requested the Federal Bureau of Investigation to forward a teletype to its legal attaché at the United States Embassy in Bern, Switzerland, requesting the legal attaché to send a communication to Interpol, Vienna, as a follow-up to his January 29, 1988, letter, advising Interpol that the Office of Independent Counsel has been unable to confirm either of the allegations referred to in the January 29 letter and that the Independent Counsel's investigation of those allegations is closed."

brought tips on Safra to his former handlers, who had forwarded the information to Iran-Contra prosecutors. The resulting inquiry to Interpol, the FBI men said, was routine, and hadn't turned up anything.

The FBI did mention one thing that piqued Weiner's interest. The Miami source, they said, had described a surveillance of Willard Zucker at a Paris airport. During that stakeout—and it wasn't clear who was doing the watching—Zucker had been observed carrying boxes to a limousine. The limo's license plate, the source claimed, had identified it as a car leased by Safra. The anecdote was meaningless to Safra's men, except for one detail: precisely the same story had surfaced in *Minute*. Could the FBI and *Minute* have had the same source? Or worse: could one person have fed information on Safra to the FBI, taken the resulting Interpol inquiry, and then fed it to *Minute*?

Old FBI hands were familiar with just such a tactic, known as "salting" government records. It was a uniquely devious way to smear an enemy. Make up spurious allegations about Mr. X, leak them to a law-enforcement agency, then, when the agency investigates, use its probe as evidence that police are interested in Mr. X's activities. It was practically foolproof and, given the way the FBI zealously guarded the identity of its informants, almost impossible to detect. Was Safra the victim of this sort of scheme?

Over the darkened North Atlantic, Weiner and Siegfried turned their attention to perhaps the most worrisome of all the allegations against Safra: that a 1957 U.S. narcotics report implicated him in the morphine trade. Weiner had laughed off the suggestion when it surfaced in the Italian magazine *L'Espresso* nine months earlier. But after the story was picked up by *Minute* and others, he had sent attorneys scrambling across Europe to find out exactly what U.S. government files contained about Safra's past.

It hadn't been easy, but over the previous three weeks attorneys in Italy and Switzerland had begun to unravel the mystery of what had happened thirty-one years before. What they discovered, though it cleared Safra's name, was nevertheless deeply unsettling. A Safra lawyer in Milan had identified the source of the allegation as an Italian police report on an indicted money launderer named Albert Shammah, the man profiled in *L'Espresso*. The report recounted Shammah's life and included intelligence from police in Geneva, where Shammah, who came from a family of Syrian Jews, had once lived. Geneva police had ticked off the names of several people Shammah had cited as references over the years, including Safra and other Republic officials. Safra insisted he had never met the man, though it was hardly surprising to find his name used as a reference by one of his Halabi brethren.

After listing Safra's businesses and addresses, the Geneva police had mentioned—and here was the bombshell—a 1957 "Report of the U.S. Bureau of Narcotics" indicating that Safra was involved in the traffic of morphine base. Almost as an afterthought, the Geneva police stressed that the reliability of this information had not been confirmed. To no one's surprise, Safra's man in Milan memoed Weiner that Italian police had no reason to suspect Safra of any wrongdoing.

Another Safra attorney, the taciturn Charles-André Junod, had taken it from there, contacting Geneva police to inquire about the 1957 report. The next day police officials confirmed the existence of the long-ago report, but said their files didn't contain a copy. Junod next contacted Rudolf Wyss, chief of the Swiss national police, and asked Wyss to check his files. A week later Wyss came through. What he found was alarming. Swiss police clerks had discovered a letter, dated August 21, 1957, in which an American narcotics agent in Rome had asked a half-dozen agencies, including Swiss police and Interpol offices in Rome, Rio de Janeiro, and Beirut, for information on a suspected morphine trafficker named "Edmond Y. Safra." From the letter's text it was clear that some-one had indeed suspected Safra of being involved in drugs.

"We [have] received information that Edmond Y. SAFRA, from Beirut, was associated in the narcotics traffic with his brother Joseph SAFRA, and they are suspected of smuggling large quantities of morphine base from Beirut, Lebanon, to Milano, Italy, " the agent, Andrew C. Tartaglino wrote. Noting that Edmond was believed to be traveling to the United States soon, he added: "It is requested that the Central National Interpol Bureaus alert their frontiers and that the activities of this individual be closely watched. It is also requested that District 2, New York City, have the name of this suspect placed on the Customs suspect list."

The letter's assertion was overwhelmingly damning, if true. But as the Swiss police pointed out, they weren't correct. On October 9, 1957, less than two months later, "the Bureau informed us that there was no basis to continue the investigations against Edmond J. Safra."* In fact, Chief Rudolf Wyss wrote, Safra had been mistaken for a certain David Safra, about whom Swiss files contained no information. Inexplicably, the mix-up had never been communicated to Geneva police, who had kept the first letter in their files unchallenged for thirty-one years. "I consider this omission as regrettable," Wyss wrote, in what Safra considered a massive understatement.†

Weiner and Siegfried continued poring over the six—now seven—articles all night and arrived at London's Heathrow Airport the next morning bleary-eyed and dry-mouthed. Dragging themselves from their seats, they strode down airport corridors to a pay phone.

"What are we going to do?" Siegfried asked.

"I'm going to call Edmond," Weiner said, placing coins into the phone slot.

Siegfried listened when Weiner reached Safra.

"I can do that," he heard Weiner say. "I don't know." A long pause as Safra spoke. "I'll have to see." Long pause. "I'll have to see." Pause. "I'll see." Pause. "Yes." Long pause. "When I land I'll tell you."

Weiner hung up. "What are we doing?" Siegfried asked.

"You're going to Edmond's."

"Where are you going?"

---

* It took Weiner three years of pestering the American and Swiss governments before he finally laid his hands on the elusive October 9, 1957, letter. Heavily redacted by government censors, it nevertheless clearly showed that Safra had been mistaken for another man, perhaps one of his relatives. "Edmond Y. SAFRA is a young man, whereas [___] is much older," concluded the letter, which was written on stationery of the U.S. Bureau of Narcotics' Rome office. "I do not believe there is any criminal connection between these two men, consequently, no further investigation is being made of Edmond Y. SAFRA."

Taking no chances, Weiner also tracked down the original letter's signer, a long-retired narcotics agent named Andrew Tartaglino, who confirmed that the original letter had been an unfortunate mistake. Despite all Weiner's efforts, the 1957 letter and the *L'Espresso* story may never be completely expunged from the files of Italian law enforcement. On January 11, 1989, the Italian Guardia di Finanza, in an internal report analyzing a suspicious account at Trade Development Bank, once again related what seemed to be echoes of the earlier correspondence. "Safra...is suspected by the American authorities of being involved in various traffics: from that of morphine to those of gold and currencies."

† It hadn't been the Americans' last inquiry about Edmond Safra, Wyss continued. "On the 24th of June 1966," he wrote Junod, "the United States Bureau of Narcotics made a new request regarding your client, to which we responded the 12th of September 1966, that nothing was known to his detriment and that we were not in possession of any information that would confirm suspicions raised at that time concerning any implications that Mr. Edmond J. Safra was involved in drug traffic." Whether the 1966 inquiry was new, or simply an echo of the earlier 1957 letter, is unknown.

"I'm going to Italy."

"Italy? What are you going to do in Italy?"

"I'm going to see the ambassador, Max Rabb."

After helping them track down the Bern letter a month earlier, Rabb had volunteered to go a step further. He was putting together an official letter exonerating Safra of any involvement in drug trafficking and expressly denying the existence of any such information in the files of the DEA. An eager Safra wanted the letter as a defense against more stories.

As Weiner picked up his bags and trudged off for the flight to Rome, Siegfried took a limousine to Safra's apartment. There, a butler escorted Siegfried into a sitting room, where he found Safra as he had left him a month before, slumped in a wing chair in his silk pajamas and bathrobe, morose. Safra thanked Siegfried for coming. The p.r. man sensed his client badly needed someone to talk to.

Taking a seat, Siegfried began going over the new *Minute* article.

"What about this Panama stuff?" Siegfried asked, referring to the supposed assassination of a Safra bank manager there.

"We closed our office in Panama years ago. I don't even know who these people are."

"What about this director being kidnapped and executed?"

"It's all nonsense." Safra heaved a great sigh. "All my life I've tried to build a reputation," he said. "Now it's being ruined."

"Who do you think it is?" Siegfried asked, already knowing the answer.

"American Express," Safra said. "No question."

They waited three hours before Weiner called. He had arrived in Rome safely, and was waiting to see Max Rabb. Safra's spirits seemed to lift a bit. Just the fact that Weiner was on the scene seemed to calm him. As they waited for further word, Safra sipped from tall glasses of iced Evian, which a butler brought in on silver trays, and picked at a bowl of macadamia nuts. Finally, around five-thirty, Weiner called. "Yes," Safra said. "Good....yes...okay." All at once Safra smiled. His entire body seemed to go limp with an almost palpable sense of relief. "Good news," he said. "Walter has a letter from the ambassador."

Siegfried took the receiver and listened as Weiner read the letter. "Dear Mr. Weiner," it began. "Pursuant to your request on the occasion of your recent visit to Rome regarding certain allegations concerning

Edmond Safra appearing in newspapers in France, I have asked the Drug Enforcement Administration to check into this matter. They have advised that there is no adverse information concerning Mr. Safra in their files. I have also checked the files in this embassy and there is absolutely no information concerning improper activities by Mr. Safra in our files. Very truly yours, Maxwell M. Rabb, ambassador."

The next day everyone moved on to Paris, where Siegfried and Weiner closeted themselves in a hotel all weekend to prepare a "white paper" summarizing the articles to date. Sunday at five, Safra telephoned and summoned both men to his apartment for a strategy meeting. When they arrived, they found him once again in low spirits. A new problem had arisen: the Safras hadn't received an invitation to a reception being thrown by French President François Mitterrand, and Edmond was certain the *Minute* stories were to blame.

Heading the agenda that evening was the decision whether to sue *Minute*. Gershon Kekst and others had argued against it; a libel suit, they felt, would only draw more publicity to the articles and wouldn't answer their main question: where were the stories coming from? Financially troubled *Minute* was rumored to be up for sale, and Peter Mansbach, the American lawyer, had actually argued in favor of buying the entire newspaper. "We're billionaires—let's buy the damn thing," he urged Safra, only half-jokingly. "We'll own the reporters. We'll own all the files. We'll know exactly what happened." There was little likelihood, though, of Safra's acquiring an anti-Semitic newspaper.

That Sunday evening Siegfried spied a new face in Safra's apartment, a leading French libel lawyer named Georges Kiejman. They hadn't been discussing their options long before the self-assured Kiejman began a stirring speech, pacing the room as he spoke—at least Siegfried and Weiner thought it was a stirring speech. They couldn't tell, since Kiejman refused to speak English. As his voice rose, the two Americans exchanged bemused looks. The lawyer clearly had a Frenchman's flair for the dramatic. Suddenly, reaching the climax of his argument, Kiejman broke into English: "If somebody called you Hitler, would you allow it to stand?"

Edmond Safra, noted patron of worldwide Jewry, was not backing away from any Hitler analogies. Barring opposition from his aides, it was clear he was ready to sue. "Do you have any objections?" he asked Weiner.

"Look, I have to go with Georges," Weiner said. "He says do it, you want to do it, my objections are not that big. Let's go."

The next day, Monday, October 17, Georges Kiejman filed Safra's first suit against *Minute* in a Paris court. French libel law is quite different from American libel law; while a similar suit in the United States might drag on for years, Kiejman told Safra they could expect a resolution by year's end. The process was simplicity itself: both plaintiff—in this case Safra—and defendant—in this case, *Minute*—made a single argument to a panel of judges, each offering whatever documentary evidence it had to advance its case. Damages were generally small—rarely more than a few thousand dollars—but if it lost, *Minute* could be forced to print the court's condemnation of its article. That, after all, was all Safra wanted.

But if Safra hoped a lawsuit would intimidate *Minute*, he was mistaken. That Wednesday the weekly issue of *Minute* hit the newsstands, and to Safra's dismay, it contained another article. There, on page ten, the self-congratulatory headline read *"Minute*, the First to Reveal the Traffic of Bankers in Drugs." Though it again carried Safra's picture, the article only mentioned him in passing, to remind readers that it was *Minute* that had "unveiled" Safra's role in money laundering. The remainder of the article detailed, in *Minute*'s tangled prose, the U.S. government's investigation of a big Luxembourg-based bank, the Bank of Credit and Commerce International, known as BCCI.

"Watch out!" reporter Jean Roberto concluded. "The struggle against bankers' laundering drug money has just begun. We will soon know of new episodes. In our territory. And one other bank in the district of the Champs-Élysées which will be implicated...."

Georges Kiejman hardly noticed the article. That day he filed Safra's second suit against *Minute*, detailing the lies in the article that had Safra "perspiring in fear" of Colombian drug assassins. On Friday he filed his third suit, against *Minute*'s most recent article.

By the following week, it was clear that Kiejman's suits had caught *Minute*'s attention. On Wednesday, October 26, the *Minute* reporter, Jean Roberto, weighed in with his strongest attack yet. "A Parisian Bank Launders Drug Money," the headline announced. "Its president begins proceedings against *Minute* to try to keep us quiet." Below that, a second headline read "Our reporters have traced the banker who launders drug money to his multimillionaire villa on the Côte d'Azur."

Edmond J. Safra, one of the ten wealthiest men in the world—this powerful Lebanese banker is guarded by a small army in his villa at Villefranche—has started proceedings against us. He is asking for 1 million francs.

Why? Because we revealed that he is highly suspected of laundering, via his banks, money from the world's biggest drug traffickers, namely the money of General Noriega and some of the Colombian cocaine multimillionaires. We were the first to supply these revelations to our readers, as well as the extraordinary operation launched by the American Customs and the FBI against several banks. And this doesn't please Mr. Safra.

Does he hope to win his case? No, certainly not. The charges against his banks are numerous but he hopes to intimidate other newspapers worldwide and—if unable to stop them—at least to delay the scandal in which he is directly involved. It will be a difficult job.

The article then shifted into high gear, linking Safra to Panama's General Noriega, asserting that Republic was the target of an American racketeering probe, and offering more details about Willard Zucker and Safra's private jet. Then it took an even stranger tack. Quoting at length from a 1987 *Life* magazine article, Roberto launched into a sixteen-paragraph tangent about an array of obscure con men and offshore corporations supposedly connected to the late Mafia kingpin Meyer Lansky. Most had Jewish-sounding surnames like Sigelbaum and Rosenbaum, and one or two had colorful nicknames like Niggy. "Dozens of companies and people were cited in this [*Life*] article," *Minute* reported. "They almost all belonged to Mr. Safra's direct or indirect circles."

It was too much for Safra. "They're killing me! They're killing me!" he moaned to Weiner as he read the articles in his Paris apartment. "Walter, they want my blood."

In truth Safra was as confused as he was furious. Not only weren't any of the purported mobsters mentioned by *Minute* part of his "circles"; he barely knew their names. Several were past figures of controversy from Swiss banking; others, Meyer Lansky certainly, he had read about. More perplexing still, Weiner had *Life* magazine's New York offices checked and rechecked but found no article in 1987 that vaguely matched the facts *Minute* laid out. Where the gangsters had come from, and how in the world *Minute* had linked them to Safra, was for the moment a mystery.

Then, even as they attempted to make sense of the latest article, Safra picked up a rumor that *Minute* was planning yet another piece in its next issue, scheduled for the following Wednesday, November 2. Learning of the tip, Georges Kiejman pointed out a useful facet of French law: if they could prove that the upcoming article's libel was serious enough, they might be able to persuade a court to enter an instant judgment against *Minute*, complete with damages and a court-ordered retraction. It was possible, though rare, and they would have to move fast to do it.

By Tuesday everything was in place. That night Safra had men poised outside *Minute's* printing plant in a Parisian suburb, hoping to snare an early copy of the next morning's issue. Weiner was all for charging into a judge's home that very night and asking for an injunction stopping the paper's delivery. "No, no, in France we can't do that," Kiejman told Weiner. "Judges sleep here."

As expected, the next morning Safra's smiling face again graced the pages of *Minute*. In a complex article spread over two inside pages, reporter Jean Roberto alleged that Safra was part of a group of financiers buying shares in a large European company, Société Générale, then offered more background on the paper's previous allegations. "New Charges About the Banker Safra," one of several headlines read. "The Four Questions Safra Will Not Answer.

"We stirred up a big fuss with our revelations last week about the banker Edmond Safra, one of the ten richest men in the world, who is suspected of laundering millions of dollars made from drug trafficking," Roberto wrote. "And yet we have raised issues that call for clear-cut answers." The article restated many of *Minute's* allegations in the form of questions, from the tale of the murdered bank manager to Noriega's missing millions. "Safra had better watch out!" it concluded. "His silence tends to give complete credence to what has only been up till now a strong presumption of the truth."

The next morning Georges Kiejman strode into a Parisian courtroom and shoved that "strong presumption" down *Minute's* throat. Over the objections of the paper's lawyer, Kiejman argued that the latest article had libeled Safra and that an immediate judgment should be granted against the newspaper. The court agreed. The next day *Minute* was ordered to pay Safra ninety thousand francs in damages and print a notice of the libel judgment in its next editions. Weiner was jubilant. "Ha!" he exclaimed. "In your face!"

• • •

For three weeks the French legal process ground on. Safra now had four separate suits pending against *Minute*, one for each article. Apparently it was enough. For the moment, Jean Roberto seemed to have sheathed his poison pen.

Returning to New York, Weiner tried to focus on other matters, but found himself distracted. He spent long hours reviewing Republic's procedures to spot drug money, realizing that any slip-ups would inevitably contribute to *Minute*'s arguments that the bank was some kind of playground for drug traffickers. One of Robert Siegfried's French p.r. friends, meanwhile, looked into Jean Roberto's background and found little to speak of. The reporter was described as *Minute*'s senior writer, in his forties, intelligent and, as might be expected, possessing strongly conservative political views.

As yet there wasn't a shred of proof to buttress Safra's belief that American Express was behind the articles. But Safra felt it in his bones. As dawn broke November 23, the day before the American holiday of Thanksgiving, the last thing he and his aides expected was for the proof to literally be handed to them.

For the thousands of tourists who stream across the Seine River bridges to Paris's Ile de la Cité each week, the island's primary attraction is the ancient gray cathedral of Notre Dame, its grand Gothic interior topped by a cluster of gargoyles made famous by the frolickings of Victor Hugo's Quasimodo. Fewer venture past the high spiked gates of the nearby Palais de Justice to view the magnificent stained glass of Sainte-Chappelle. Fewer still wander through the Palais's stone corridors to its massive inner sanctum, the Grande Salle du Palais, beneath whose great arched ceilings the daily work of the Parisian courts is still pursued.

It was through the sunlit aeries of this historic hall on the afternoon of November 23 that Georges Kiejman and his young assistant Olivier Laude, draped in the black robes of French jurists, strode toward a three o'clock hearing in the First Chamber of Paris's principal court, the Tribunal de Grande Instance de Paris. It was to be the second of two hearings in which Kiejman was arguing that the *Minute* articles had libeled Safra. So far, the newspaper's defense was predictably weak, and revealed no hint whatsoever of the articles' sources. Kiejman had beaten *Minute* before, and was confident he would do so again.

Inside, the courtroom had the feel of a small chapel, the three black-robed judges arrayed in a low arc at its front, autumn sunlight pouring through a set of high windows. As Kiejman readied his presentation, his assistant, the dark, model-handsome, twenty-five-year-old Laude, sat by on one of the pewlike wooden benches, ready to feed him various pleadings and papers. When his time came, Kiejman's presentation was simple and forceful, disposing of each of *Minute's* contentions in businesslike fashion. It lasted no more than ninety minutes. None of the three magistrates asked questions afterward, a good sign.

Soon after *Minute's* two young attorneys began their rebuttals, Olivier Laude realized neither had much experience. As proof of Jean Roberto's assertions, they began presenting the court, and the Safra attorneys, with a number of exhibits. Laude was particularly pleased when he was handed the *Life* article Safra's people had waited so long to see. He glanced at it only long enough to make sure it was authentic before dropping it on the growing pile of papers at his side. Not until half an hour later, as the *Minute* presentation droned on, did Laude take a moment to peruse the article. It was long, he saw, more than twenty pages. "The Mob," read the large bold headline. It appeared to be an exposé on the American Mafia.

Laude saw what he had been given was actually a faxed copy of the *Life* article. It took him a moment to realize that something else was written on the faxed pages. It took another moment to decipher the strange code. When he did, the young lawyer could only stare in amazement.

The fax he held, Laude realized in an instant, was the key to the entire case, maybe to all the articles they had seen. Apparently *Minute's* young lawyers hadn't realized what they had handed over. Laude glanced at Kiejman sitting beside him, but the elder lawyer was absorbed in his opponents' arguments. Laude forced himself to stay calm: he couldn't let on what he had seen, not while there was the slightest chance *Minute's* lawyers could yank the document back.

Not until the hearing had adjourned and they were walking into the great arched hall outside did Laude pull Kiejman aside and hand him the *Life* article. "Look at this," he said. "I think they've given us a very important document without being aware of it."

Kiejman looked at the article, but at first didn't see what his young associate was so excited about.

"This, this," Laude said, pointing.

As he started to explain Kiejman saw it. Laude could only smile as he watched the look of surprise spread over Georges Kiejman's face.

The two lawyers, black robes trailing in their wake, wasted little time scrambling to their Rue de Tournon offices and alerting Safra in Geneva. "I knew it," Safra said emphatically. In no time the news flashed to New York. On Madison Avenue, Gershon Kekst called Siegfried into his corner office and told him, "It looks like we've got the smoking gun."

"What?...*Life* magazine?...I don't understand...Outside the courtroom?"

Weiner, a phone to his ear in his Fifth Avenue office, couldn't grasp what his niece Terry was so excited about. *Life* magazine—courtroom— American Express—telltale—it was too much for him to digest at once. Not until the *Life* article began inching across his fax machine did Weiner fathom what had happened.

There, at the top of several pages of the article *Minute*'s lawyers had handed over, was a clear fax "telltale," the data automatically printed during transmission by many telefax machines. It read: "FEB 25 '88 21:25 AMEX CORP COMM • NYC." Translation: nine months before, at nine-twenty-five on the evening of February 25, 1988, the article had been faxed by someone using a machine in the corporate communications department of American Express headquarters in New York. It was concrete evidence linking American Express to the *Minute* articles.

Weiner couldn't believe it. It was too good to be true. Why on earth would *Minute*'s lawyers let this out? He called Olivier Laude in Paris.

"How could they be so stupid?" Weiner asked. In the back of his mind he feared a setup.

"Oh, I don't think the guy even knew what he was handing me."

"Wait, wait. Start all over again. Why did they give it to you?"

"To show they did their journalistic due diligence." What was strange, the French lawyer pointed out, was that the article didn't even mention Safra or Republic. Even stranger, he said, was the date. Weiner flipped to the article's first page and found it.

1967. The article had been printed in September 1967.

"Wait a minute," Weiner said. "Nineteen sixty-seven?" *Minute* had said 1987.* In the court hearing, Laude explained, *Minute*'s lawyer had

---

* It was, had Weiner known it, the famous article that had changed the image of Swiss banking for millions of *Life*'s American readers.

dismissed the date issue as a mix-up, but Weiner could see what might have happened. Jean Roberto had likely misstated the date to camouflage the fact he was recycling twenty-year-old information; it was exactly the kind of ridiculous subterfuge Weiner expected *Minute* to pull. Neither man, though, could figure out what the *Life* article had to do with Safra.

Not until the day after Thanksgiving did Weiner's questions begin to be answered. Working alone in his Fifth Avenue office, he first identified a faint second telltale on several of the article's pages. It appeared to be a British telephone number. Weiner sent for a British fax directory. He found the American Express listings and went through them line by line. There. He peered down the line and made sure: the number was for a fax machine in American Express's London legal department. Two telltales, two phone numbers, both American Express.

His excitement grew when a pouch containing the rest of the *Minute* exhibits arrived from Paris. The bulkiest item, a sheaf of documents several inches thick, turned out to be a stack of TRW credit reports. They were standard corporate credit reports on Republic, much of them publicly available financial data, nothing of any great importance.

What fascinated Weiner was a second exhibit. It was some kind of report, seven pages long, untitled and already translated from its French original, and nominally about Edmond Safra's supposed criminal connections. No author was given; in fact, the document carried no identifying marks of any kind. At a glance Weiner saw it contained many of the same elements they had seen in all the newspaper articles: Willard Zucker, Iran-Contra, drug money. The report came complete with appendices and a bizarre, hand-drawn graph purporting to link Safra to everyone from Meyer Lansky to Adnan Khashoggi. The report itself was divided into seven sections, lettered "A" through "G," preceded by an introduction:

The objective of this report of enquiry is to present with as much logic and as concisely as possible, concrete results pertaining to the lawful or unlawful character of Safra Bank. The diagram of interconnections given in the appendix will illustrate the many direct or indirect associations with Safra Bank, reconstituted with the help of attached documents.

We shall try in this report to explain the various associations, and to give a detailed description of the persons mentioned. Also, we shall present certain allegations as to the incorrect or illegal activities of Safra Bank or its branch as well as of RNB (Republic National Bank) or of its branches. It is not possible to guarantee the exclusivity of these allegations as these questions are being investigated by the FBI in the U.S. Such investigations are highly confidential.

Weiner scanned the text.

Section A identified Republic National Bank and several of its officers, including Safra.

Section B detailed Willard Zucker's connections to Republic and to figures in the Iran-Contra scandal.

Section C described Republic Air Transport Service, the company Zucker had formed to incorporate the bank's jet.

Section D listed and described nine other companies Zucker had created over the years for other clients, none of them apparently related to Safra or Republic.

Section E described one such company, named Golodetz/Primary Industries, and listed its president as Republic's chief counsel, Ernest Ginsberg. That was ridiculous; Weiner knew Ginsberg wasn't the president of anything.

Section F described another Zucker-created company that also had no apparent links to Safra. In an accompanying appendix a dozen different names, the company's current and former officers, were listed, beginning with one Sylvain Ferdman in 1976—and here, Weiner saw, was where *Life* magazine entered the picture.

In *Life's* 1967 exposé on the Mafia and Swiss banking—and in *Minute*—the magazine had listed a lawyer named Sylvain Ferdman as a courier for the gangster Meyer Lansky; Ferdman, in fact, was the man carrying satchels of cash in the magazine's famous grainy photo. Weiner saw that whoever had assembled the anonymous report was using this Sylvain Ferdman—a long-ago name on one of Willard Zucker's multitude of shell companies—to draw the astounding conclusion that there were links between Meyer Lansky and another, totally separate Zucker client years later, Republic Air Transport Service.

"This link could also go further to [Republic] and to Mr. Edmond Safra," the report noted. Like *Minute*, it then proceeded to quote at length from the *Life* article about an assortment of crime figures, with the inference that Safra was linked to them as well.

The whole convoluted series of entanglements was laid out in the accompanying chart: there sat Edmond Safra and Republic at the center of a web of official-looking circles and boxes populated by *Life* magazine's 1967 Mafia men, various arms dealers and obscure Willard Zucker shell companies. The graph looked like the type American drug agents used to chart illegal relationships, and it made Weiner wonder whether its author—no doubt the person spreading these stories about Safra—might have links to law enforcement.

The mention of drugs came in the report's final three paragraphs, Section G. There the anonymous author noted information from a "confidential and reliable source" that Safra Bank, the little Miami bank Safra had bought in 1978, had been under FBI investigation since 1984. "Well-known U.S. drug dealers were using these to launder money," the report said. "This source was unable to say where this story stands at the present time." °

Weiner spent hours going over the seven-page report. It was all so strange it bordered on the surreal. Someone with evident knowledge of American law enforcement and obvious links to American Express was drawing up reports and charts purporting to tie Safra to a smorgasbord of criminal activity. It was the only conclusion to draw. Whoever it was had already gone to one newspaper, *Minute*, and, Weiner was willing to bet, had also paid visits to papers in Peru and Mexico.

For the moment, identifying the report's author almost didn't matter

---

° On first reading, Walter Weiner all but ignored the odd mention of drugs, writing it off as more of the anonymous author's distortions. Only later would he realize that Safra Bank had in fact been ensnared in a money-laundering investigation. In November 1987, prosecutors in South Florida had unsealed an eighty-one-count indictment against a group of marijuana smugglers headed by a champion powerboat racer named Ben Kramer; the indictment detailed how the ring had laundered its profits through banks in Miami, Los Angeles, the British Virgin Islands, and the European principality of Liechtenstein. Among the final stops on the Kramer ring's international laundering circuit was Safra Bank, where two of the smugglers kept accounts and which had loaned two of the ring's money men $2.8 million to build a marina. Federal agents working on the case had asked some pointed questions about the bank, but had found no evidence that it was anything other than an unknowing stopover for the Kramer ring's funds.

"We don't really have anything at all against [Safra] or his banks; it was just one of the banks being used," confirms Jim Shedd, a DEA agent in Miami acting as his office's official spokesman. He adds: "I did money-laundering cases here for three years before taking over this job [as spokesman]. We never had any money deposited in [Safra] accounts. We never had anything to do with their accounts. The dopers were not going in that direction."

This account is also confirmed by Jeff Leen, an award-winning investigative reporter for the *Miami Herald*, who wrote in detail about the Kramer probe. "I talked with the federal agents a lot about that case," recalls Leen, "and I don't remember the agents having anything at all against [Safra's] bank."

to Weiner. What mattered was the proof, in the form of the fax telltale, that American Express was behind the scheme. That night, as he retired to his Park Avenue apartment, Weiner was so excited he couldn't sleep. All day Safra had kept asking, "Can we sue? Can we sue?" Visions of damages danced in Weiner's head. It was a lawyer's dream: American Express smearing a renowned Jewish banker in an anti-Semitic newspaper. A jury would love it. How high could the damages go? Millions? Billions? Weiner hadn't been so excited in years.

But then, as abruptly as the excitement had flared, it cooled. In the following days lawyers in Europe and the United States informed Safra and Weiner what they should have known all along. No, they couldn't sue—not now, at least. There were a dozen explanations of how *Minute* might have come into possession of a document once faxed by American Express. And what did it prove, anyway? That someone at the company had sent a French reporter a magazine article on organized crime? The piece didn't even mention Safra. No, the lawyers ruled, while the case against American Express was compelling, it had far too many holes to seriously consider litigating.

Nor, to Weiner's discouragement, did the remaining *Minute* exhibits offer much in the way of clues to follow. The seven-page report was anonymously written, and its appendices were all public records of Zucker-related companies, most available to anyone who requested them at the commercial registry in Geneva. Their best shot, Weiner felt, was to identify whoever had ordered up the TRW credit reports. But TRW refused to help, citing company policy. Republic's credit department glumly informed Weiner there was almost no way to pressure TRW into breaking its policy.

Still, both Safra and Weiner smelled blood. Late every afternoon in New York, as he would do regularly over the next six months, Safra called as he prepared for bed in Geneva and, often with Kekst and Siegfried on extensions, exhorted his aides to rehash everything they knew, everything they could do, to root out the source of the articles and prove once and for all that American Express was behind them. Slowly at first, then more quickly in the days to come, the emphasis of their talks shifted. For weeks they had simply wanted to stop the *Minute* articles. Now that they had been halted, Safra was left with nothing but a bitter taste in his mouth and a handful of tantalizing loose ends, all of which pointed to American Express. Though no one put it into words, it was clear that retribution would now motivate their efforts.

For Safra, it was time to strike back at American Express for what it had done to him, and show the world the depths to which Jim Robinson's company was capable of stooping. He would turn this crisis to his advantage, and maybe, just maybe, soil Robinson's reputation as his American Express minions had soiled his own.

But how?

"We've got to get detectives," Weiner told Safra repeatedly as their discussions stretched into December. To which Safra would reply, "Yes, Walter, we do," and then nothing would happen, nothing at all. They talked and talked until they talked it to death, and still they hadn't done anything. It was so typical of Republic, Weiner mused. If words were bullets, American Express would be fifty-one stories of Swiss cheese.

The problem was, Safra didn't trust private eyes. He had heard too many tales of detectives betraying their clients. Still, Weiner interviewed a pair of detective outfits, one French, the other Israeli. Neither was too impressive.

They were still debating what to do when, one morning that December, Weiner picked up the phone in his New York office and heard a strange tone in Safra's voice. He was calling from Geneva. "Anyone in the room with you?" Safra asked.

No, Weiner said, his curiosity piqued.

"I've got a name," Safra said. "Write it down."

"I think it's Greco," he said, pronouncing it Greek-o.

"How do you spell it?" Weiner asked. Safra spelled it.

"And the first name?"

"I think it's Tony," Safra said.

This Tony Greco, Safra went on, was a name apparently being bandied around the offices of *Minute* in connection with the stories on Safra. He had picked it up through a circuitous route: a bank secretary's Parisian boyfriend had heard it from a friend at the paper. Safra speculated that this Greco might work for American Express, perhaps in security.

"And what did he supposedly do?" Weiner asked.

"He's the guy who was feeding stories to *Minute*, they say."

"Who'd he meet with?"

"I don't know."

"Did he meet with Roberto?"

"I think so. I can't be sure."

After hanging up Weiner called in Vince Chisari, Republic's security chief, and gave him the name. "Find out who this guy is, see if he works for American Express," Weiner said. "He might be an independent security guy. Check that, too."

Several days later Chisari returned with a name, Michael Creague, in American Express security. He handed Creague's business card to Weiner and said, "This is the closest I can get" to the name "Greco."

Weiner called Safra with the new name, Creague.

"Who is he?" Safra asked.

"He works for American Express."

"No, that's not the name."

"Well, the way you pronounced it..."

"No, I think it's Greco," Safra said, pronouncing it correctly, Greck-o.

"Well, this is as close as we come."

Later Weiner told Vince Chisari to run the Greco name through available listings of private investigators, but Chisari again came up with nothing. At that point Weiner dropped the matter. It seemed like another frustrating dead end.

As a Parisian court moved toward a decision on the remaining *Minute* suits, Safra nervously watched the unfolding of a major political scandal in Switzerland. On December 12, Elisabeth Kopp, the country's justice minister and the only woman to serve on its ruling Federal Council, stepped to a microphone in the Swiss capital of Bern and announced to a jammed press briefing that she was resigning. The fifty-two-year-old Kopp's fall couldn't have been bigger news in the Alps: under Swiss law, each of the council's seven members regularly rotate to serve one-year terms as the country's president. Named vice president–elect just five days before her resignation, Kopp would probably have become president of Switzerland in 1990.

Her resignation wasn't a total surprise. Several days before, in an emotional session of the Federal Council, Kopp had admitted tipping off her husband, Hans, to the existence of a federal investigation into a company upon whose board he sat: Shakarchi Trading Company of

Zurich. A prominent Swiss lawyer, Hans Kopp had resigned from Shakarchi's board just days before prosecutors disclosed their investigation, allowing both him and his wife to escape some measure of scandal, or so they thought. Weeks later, a newspaper's scoop of Elisabeth Kopp's tip-off wrecked the couple's careers and threw Swiss politics into turmoil.

The Kopp affair, as it was dubbed, generated massive coverage in the Swiss press of the Shakarchi Trading probe, which centered on allegations that the currency-trading firm was being used by Turkish drug traffickers to launder money. Safra followed the news with concern, for the Shakarchi family had been a Safra client for years. With *Minute's* allegations still fresh in the air, he was beset with worries that Republic might somehow be dragged into the developing Shakarchi scandal.

A week after the Kopp announcement, a Paris court handed down the decision Weiner and Safra knew it would, the first of a series of decisions citing *Minute* for libeling Safra.° "The Court for its part can only acknowledge the inadequacy of the research which led *Minute* to level against Mr. Safra the very serious and defamatory accusation of heading a banking network handling shady business," the court wrote. "In no way could it be imagined that a few traces, presumed to be suspicious but incapable of genuinely supporting the insinuations and affirmations made, should be used in the most categorical way and in an often peremptory manner, to the exclusion of the most elementary prudence. The offense of public libel of an individual is [therefore] perfectly established."

The decision was gratifying news, but as the holiday season passed and the new year dawned, the larger problem remained: what to do about American Express? "We can talk and talk and talk," Gershon Kekst told Safra. "But we can't go on like this forever. You have to decide. Is it time to engage them? Do you want to go to war?"

While Safra stewed, Weiner continued casting around for a detective he could trust. In early January Jeff Keil came up with a new name, a former FBI man named Tom Sheer. "Where'd you hear that from?" Weiner asked.

"Peter Cohen."

"Come on, Jeff," Weiner said in exasperation. He could see it now:

° Safra would later win similar decisions in suits against *La Dépêche du Midi.*

Edmond Safra hiring a detective suggested by one of Jim Robinson's top men.

"No, I mean it," Keil insisted. "Meet the guy."

Weiner did. And to his surprise, he liked the man. Tom Sheer was a straight arrow, a former top administrator in the FBI's New York office, now working on his own while looking for a permanent job in corporate security. The real surprise, though, came as Weiner briefed Sheer on their suspicions about American Express. Weiner stopped cold when the former FBI agent mentioned he might know the man rumored to have fed the stories to *Minute*, Tony Greco.

"You what?"

Yes, Sheer said, not only did he know a Tony Greco, but he had been introduced to him by a onetime American Express security man. Greco, he said, was some kind of private detective.

Weiner was floored. As Sheer told the story, he had only recently left the FBI when the former head of American Express security had mentioned Greco's name to him as a possible partner in some overseas investigative work. When Sheer met this Tony Greco, the man hadn't been very forthcoming about who he was or how he made his living. Sheer hadn't thought much of the encounter, and that was that. Among the few things Sheer knew about him was that Greco had an address in the New York borough of Staten Island.

Weiner fought back his excitement. After all, the name Tony Greco was not uncommon. He gave Sheer the go-ahead to check out the Greco in Staten Island, and perform a morning's surveillance of his home, which Sheer did on January 23. But in those cautious first days of what would grow into a months-long investigation, Tom Sheer came up with almost nothing on Tony Greco save a December 1939 birthdate, making Greco almost fifty years old. Still, Weiner told himself, it was a first step.

A friend once mused that Gershon Kekst could smell anti-Semitism a mile away, and to Kekst there was no mistaking the stench rising from the press campaign against Edmond Safra. As long as he had worked on Wall Street, Kekst and his Jewish friends had whispered darkly about Jim Robinson and American Express, how clean and white and WASPish they were. Ten years before, fears of anti-Semitism had spurred on Kekst and several other Jewish Wall Streeters who formulated McGraw-Hill's devastating counterattack against American Express in 1979; the thought of Robinson's company getting its hands on a major news outlet like *Business Week* had made Kekst shudder.

There wasn't anything concrete he could point to, of course. Kekst liked to tell the story of a sailing trip he and another Jewish Wall Streeter had taken one summer off the coast of Maine. Running low on supplies, they had docked at a WASPy old New England yachting club and wandered up its immaculately kept green lawn to a deserted clubhouse, where vacant rocking chairs lined the porches like something out of Norman Rockwell. "Where is everybody?" the friend had asked, to which Kekst had shrugged and joked, "They must be hiding." But to Kekst the feeling of exclusion was all-pervasive: as New York Jews, they simply didn't belong in a world of L.L. Bean and men with Roman numerals trailing their names. "We were on enemy territory," he liked to joke.

To Kekst, American Express was like that yacht club, enemy territory. It was just a feeling, of course, but sometimes that was all he had, a feeling. "One of the things about being Jewish is you can't afford to wait and find out," he sometimes said. American Express and James D. Robinson III, raised from the cradle of the Southern establishment, were a powerful part of that other world, the world to which Kekst as a Jew felt he could never belong. To him the anti-Semitism of that world, whether conveyed by winks or curses or sophisticated defamation campaigns, was as real and vivid as graffiti on a synagogue.

Raised in a devout Jewish family in Massachusetts, as an adult Kekst had become a major contributor to Jewish causes, the kind of Jewish man who took his children on pilgrimages to Israel to play with the offspring of Soviet and Ethiopian Jews resettling there. A Conservative Jew, he enjoyed needling Reform Jews like Robert Siegfried who assimilated their culture to the point of putting stained glass in their synagogues. "You really ought to learn about Judaism," he often teased Siegfried, to which the younger man always responded: "I *am* Jewish." Kekst would scowl and say, "No you're not." Kekst was amused by Jews like Gary Beller, American Express's general counsel, whose rumored pursuit of perhaps the ultimate WASP sport prompted Kekst to dub him "the Jewish polo player."

Siegfried, though not as devout as his boss, had also experienced the ugliness of anti-Semitism. As the only two Jewish boys in their grade at a tweedy Connecticut boarding school, he and a classmate had suffered the stinging taunts of other children, a hazing that culminated on the day that Siegfried raced to rescue his friend from a pack of boys who were holding him down and beating him. By the time Siegfried broke the group up by bashing one of the attackers with a chair, it was too late. He found his roommate covered with blood, a Star of David carved into his chest. A year later, at the age of fourteen, the boy committed suicide.

To both Siegfried and Kekst, what was happening to Safra was more than just another assignment. It was a fight against the most detestable form of anti-Semitism, plain and simple, and they were determined to have it exposed. Over the years Kekst had grown to care for Safra as he had few clients. He and Siegfried relished walking into Republic's headquarters, its outer doors proudly displaying the mezuzah, and feeling this was *their* bank, a Jewish bank, a bank where they didn't have to genuflect or apologize for their beliefs. What made what American Express was doing even more despicable, in Kekst's view, was that Safra was Sephardic, from the class of Jews so maligned even other Jews discriminated against them. That Jim Robinson's company would set his minions on a man like Safra struck Gershon Kekst as obscene.

In his airy corner office nineteen floors above Madison Avenue, Kekst thought long and hard of ways to force a confrontation with American Express. Left to his own devices, Safra might never do anything. Kekst wanted to press the issue, and press hard. What Safra needed, he saw, was a catalyst, someone who could strike fear into Jim Robinson's heart. During the struggle against *Minute* that fall, they had used William Rogers, the former secretary of state, to put out fires in Washington. But Bill Rogers was a nice man—too nice, in Kekst's view. What they needed was a ballbuster.

"What would you think if I recommended Stanley Arkin?" Kekst asked Siegfried one day that January. Known for his crusading defenses of figures in Wall Street's insider scandals, Arkin was as aggressive as any major attorney Kekst knew. "We need someone who's a street fighter," Kekst said, "who'll really go for the jugular, who'll really go after Jim Robinson if there's something there."

Siegfried thought a moment. "Great idea," he said, "but you'll never get Walter to buy into it. Because Walter will perceive Stanley as a threat. Walter's reporting right to Edmond on this. You know Stanley." Kekst nodded; both men knew well the side of Arkin others politely called "controversial." Siegfried continued. "He has his own personality, his own mind. Is Walter going to want to be subjected to all that?"

"I don't know," Kekst said, smiling. "But one thing's for sure. Stanley would scare the shit out of Jim Robinson."

In truth, Stanley Arkin scared a lot of people, particularly those on the opposite side of the high-profile cases he craved. A hard-charging bundle of sharp intellect and gnawing insecurities, Arkin was a legal maverick known for aggressive and unorthodox tactics. Representing the wife of financier Ronald O. Perelman in the early 1980s, he had grown frustrated that Perelman wasn't treating the divorce proceedings seriously enough. To jolt him into paying attention, Arkin audaciously filed a form with the Securities and Exchange Commission, claiming partial ownership of Perelman's largest company on behalf of his wife. Arkin even issued press releases about the filing, just to make sure reporters didn't miss it, all of which snapped Perelman to attention posthaste. Before he knew it, Arkin had wrapped up the proceedings, and the former Mrs. Perelman walked off with a handsome settlement.

Raised in Los Angeles, Arkin had sold Fuller Brushes to get through USC and later attended Harvard Law on scholarship, apprenticing himself after graduation to a busy criminal attorney in Manhattan. Opening his own practice in 1969, he spent the 1970s defending a series of militants, muggers, and drug dealers before stumbling onto a client who would change his life, a Wall Street financial printer named Vincent Chiarella, the first person prosecuted on federal insider-trading charges. Arkin's success in the Chiarella case, which he argued all the way to the Supreme Court, placed him in an ideal position to capitalize on the insider-trading scandals that engulfed Wall Street in the 1980s.

Brash, streetwise, an outsider who loved tilting at the establishment, Arkin by the age of fifty had become one of the most prominent of a cadre of Manhattan lawyers who made millions defending a long line of Yuppie investment bankers accused of insider trading and other securities crimes. He reveled in the publicity the cases brought him, topped off by a front-page profile in *The Wall Street Journal*. He cultivated an image as a big-money gunslinger, tooling around Manhattan in a gnarled little cowboy hat, briefly managing the personal affairs of singer Debbie Harry and vacationing at California's Golden Door, a spa, Arkin liked to say, "where high-powered people hang out to chill out."

In Gershon Kekst's mind Arkin would pose a special threat to Jim Robinson. Everyone knew Arkin was representing Robinson's friend, the

Wall Street arbitrager Sandy Lewis, who was under indictment for allegedly manipulating the price of a stock offering for American Express's Fireman's Fund unit. Though Robinson himself wasn't the target of the investigation, federal investigators were looking at whether any American Express officials had been involved in the manipulation. Arkin, as Lewis's attorney, was obviously privy to the trader's secrets, and thus, at least theoretically, in a unique position to put the screws to American Express.

Arkin arrived in Kekst's corner office late one Monday afternoon in the first days of February. As Kekst and Siegfried briefed him on the situation—the articles in France and Latin America, the legal victory in Paris—they were pleased to see how fast he grasped the essentials of the case. But it was when Arkin used the word "campaign" to describe the scathing articles that both p.r. men knew they had the right man for the job.

Stanley Arkin's eyes brightened as he sketched how he would approach the case. He would use detectives, he said, in Europe, and in Latin America to interrogate the articles' authors and seek the confidential sources lurking behind them. But it was when he spoke of the pressure this would apply to Jim Robinson that Arkin really came to life. *Jim Robinson*. The thought of bagging a trophy that size clearly excited him more than any legal brief. It would be any attorney's finest hour.

"Well, all right, go solve this thing," a smiling Kekst told Arkin after a second meeting with Jeff Keil. "I don't want to hear, 'Maybe yes, maybe no.' Do it. I don't want to hear it's not possible."

Both men laughed, but Arkin could see there was something else on his friend's mind. He listened as Kekst explained how important he felt Safra's plight was, how he thought it represented the very worst of the corporate anti-Semitism he saw. Arkin, too, had experienced anti-Semitism firsthand. As a child he had been called a "Hebe"; selling Fuller Brushes he had heard the taunt of "Get away, Jew Boy." To Arkin a taint of anti-Semitism was just one more reason to attack American Express with everything he could muster.

And so, pending Safra's approval, Stanley Arkin joined the team. It seemed like perfect timing, now that there appeared to be a lull in the skirmishing with American Express. No one knew it at the time, of course, but it was the calm before a new, far more violent storm, a fresh gust of intrigue that would begin with an odd phone call just two days later.

Winter winds were blowing hard along the Geneva lakefront as Weiner strained to get off the telephone in Safra's crowded top-floor office. A half-dozen bank officers were in for a meeting, but Weiner was on a transatlantic call with his younger son. There was some kind of problem back in the States, and Weiner was trying to pay attention to what it was. But he was already late for the Friday afternoon flight to London, and if he didn't hurry, he would miss the last Concorde out of Heathrow to New York.

Finally Weiner extricated himself from his phone conversation, only to be confronted with one last call. Ernest Ginsberg, Republic's general counsel, was on the line, and it sounded urgent. One eye on the door, Weiner took the call, hoping it would be fast.

Even over the transatlantic line, the excitement in Ginsberg's voice was palpable. "I just got a call and I can't believe my ears," the lawyer said. A man who gave his name as Victor Tirado had telephoned Republic's office in Miami and asked to speak to someone in authority. This Tirado, Ginsberg said, claimed to have information on a man named Tony Greco who was planting defamatory articles about Safra in newspapers around the world.

Aware of the milling crowd in Safra's office, none of whom knew the first thing about the brewing counteroffensive against American Express, Weiner tried to remain calm. But it was difficult, especially when Ginsberg told him the rest of the mysterious Victor Tirado's message.

"And Walter," the lawyer said, "this guy Greco says he's working directly for Jim Robinson."

7

Any thoughts of catching the last Concorde evaporated in the split-second it took Weiner to digest the lawyer's news. "Hold on, Ernie," Weiner said. "Let me call you back in five minutes." Hanging up, Weiner motioned to Safra to clear the room.

"I have to talk to Walter," he announced, and within moments the office had emptied.

Quickly Weiner briefed Safra on the call; then the two telephoned Ginsberg and heard again the extraordinary message from the man called Victor Tirado. No, Ginsberg said, no one knew who this Tirado was. He had left a telephone number somewhere in south Florida. But there was no mistaking his message: a man named Tony Greco was behind the articles, and Greco claimed to be working directly for Jim Robinson.

"It's a trap," Safra said. "Somebody's trying to see how much we know. We have to be very careful."

"I absolutely agree," Weiner said. "It's gotta be a trap."

They debated the best approach to take. "If we see this Tirado," Safra said, "we don't want a Republic person meeting with him."

"No," Weiner said. He already had someone in mind, the ex-FBI man Tom Sheer. Safra wasn't so sure. "Edmond, trust me on this,"

Weiner said. "Sometimes you've just got to go on a gut feeling. This guy Sheer isn't going to sell us out."

"All right," Safra said. "Use your best judgment."

Later Weiner called Sheer and had the former FBI man make an appointment with the mysterious Victor Tirado. Several days later, Sheer reported back that a rendezvous had been set. He was to meet with Tirado at a restaurant in Washington, D.C., on Thursday, February 23.

The meeting with Victor Tirado was still a week away when a ringing phone jarred Weiner and his wife, Nina, from a deep sleep in their downtown Geneva hotel room. Picking up the receiver, Weiner took a moment to realize it was Safra on the line. He had never heard his boss cry, but the sounds of a gentle sobbing were unmistakable. "Edmond, what's wrong?" Weiner asked. It took Safra several moments to get the words out. Finally, he said, "Claudio and his son are not with us any more."

Claudio Cohen was the eldest of Lily Safra's four children. The day before, he and his four-year-old son, Raphael, had been killed in Brazil, their car crushed in a head-on collision with an out-of-control pickup truck while driving to the family's weekend home outside Rio de Janeiro. It took most of the day for the Safras to find a plane for the flight to South America, though finally Sandy Weill, the former American Express president, graciously made his available. In many ways Claudio was the closest of her children to Lily, and Safra spent long hours in the days that followed comforting his wife over her loss. In his time of need, Safra's aides went out of their way to ease his workload.

And so the curious fax Weiner received shortly after returning to New York couldn't have come at a worse time. He fired off a call to Robert Siegfried. "They're at it again," Weiner said. "I've got to speak to Gershon."

"Who's at it?"

"American Express."

"I thought we stopped this during litigation."

"No, they're at it again. I know they are."

In his hand Weiner held a faxed copy of a new article, the first since *Minute's* final barrage three months before. This one had surfaced in

Switzerland. There on February 20 a tiny, Geneva-based newsletter named *Noticiero* had printed a seven-paragraph article on Edmond Safra's alleged links to narcotics traffickers and the Iran-Contra affair titled "The Swiss Drug Connection." The newsletter was printed in Spanish, and many of its five-thousand or so subscribers were Spanish or Latin American expatriates.

LIMA—The U.S. Drug Enforcement Agency (DEA) is behind a man who seemingly pinched 40 million U.S. dollars from the U.S. government in the Iran-Contra affair.

In its attempt to catch the banker Edmond Safra, identified as a Lebanese Jew with Brazilian nationality, the DEA has been circulating a detailed report which reveals another chapter in the scandal of secretly financing the Nicaraguan counterrevolution, also called Irangate.

Despite the risk of appearing to contradict the Central Intelligence Agency (CIA), to which the DEA indicated, as usual, the services rendered by Safra, perhaps with the aim of improving his image by following a suspected partner in his illegal dealings, the DEA has launched a warning against any dealings with Safra, who is described as a dangerous person.

Who, actually, is Edmond Safra? Where does he live, with whom is he connected, where has he invested his money, who are his friends or associates? All these questions may be answered correctly, some of them incorrectly, with the explosion of a new scandal in Argentina, Venezuela, or Brazil.

It is in those countries that the DEA suspects finding the fortune of the Lebanese banker, on whom it confesses it began concentrating since the disappearance of $40 million from the juicy Irangate deal which the famous Colonel Oliver North handled, together with Richard Secord, Hakim, and Willard Zucker.

The DEA alerted private banks in South America not to become involved with Safra who is said to be the owner of Republic National Bank of New York, the last-known transit point of the lost 40 million....

To Safra, still in mourning, the new article was a devastating déjà vu, a replay of the fall nightmare in Paris. Everyone rushed to downplay its significance; the lawyers would get a retraction, they said, and they could forget about it. "Let's not go crazy again," Weiner counseled. "It's only five thousand people. Come on, Edmond, let's calm down and go back to work."

"It's spillover," Siegfried decided, just an echo of the *Minute* articles. Surely, Safra's advisers agreed, *Noticiero* was simply a nasty aftershock from the *Minute* affair, a case of a newsletter appropriating something from a foreign paper. Who, after all, would go to the bother of exposing himself by planting an article in such a marginal newsletter?

But Safra wasn't convinced. Alone in Geneva he brooded, and the more he brooded, the more he feared the events of the previous fall were repeating themselves. No matter how much Weiner and the others assured him it was an aberration, the *Noticiero* article nagged at his troubled mind. "It's starting again," he warned his aides. "It's starting all over again."

And, as usual, Edmond Safra was right.

The restaurant at the Holiday Inn near Washington's Embassy Row, Herb's, is one of those perky fern bars where the walls are adorned with autographed photos of not-so-prominent song-and-dance men and comedians. It was an odd setting for such a rendezvous, but Herb's was the place the man called Victor Tirado had chosen for his meeting.

As Tom Sheer took a seat to wait for the mysterious caller, his orders were to play things by the book. Weiner and Safra had debated whether to secretly photograph the meeting, but had judged it too risky. Everything had to be aboveboard; Sheer was to listen to Tirado, and report back to Weiner. There could be no hint that Safra would pay money for information, or anything else that carried even the whiff of illegality. If they were walking into a trap, they knew they had better be on the right side of the law.

When Victor Tirado ambled into Herb's that afternoon, he was a surprise—a very big surprise. The man easily weighed three-hundred pounds. Far more noteworthy to Sheer, though, was his identity, which explained his selection of a Washington fern bar as their meeting place. After easing his bulk into a seat opposite Sheer, Tirado explained that he was a deputy press attaché at the Peruvian Embassy, just around the corner from the Holiday Inn. He was Peruvian himself, and had only recently arrived in the United States, having previously served in the capital city of Lima as press secretary to his country's president, Alan Garcia.

Whatever else Victor Tirado was, that day he appeared nervous. As Sheer listened, he repeated what he had said on the phone, that he knew Tony Greco well, and he knew exactly how Greco was planting stories for American Express. Greco had come to Lima six months before, he said, shown him several European news articles about Safra, and assured him that Safra was a notorious money launderer. Then, or so it was rumored, Greco had paid to have an article on Safra printed in the Peruvian newspaper *Hoy*. And yes, Tirado repeated, Greco claimed he was working directly for Jim Robinson. In fact it was almost all Greco talked about, the big Peruvian said: Jim Robinson this, Jim Robinson that.

Victor Tirado knew more, of course, much more, tantalizing Sheer with the names of four or five other Peruvians Greco might have contacted. But he made it clear he wasn't prepared to tell his whole story, not yet anyway. No matter how much Tom Sheer pressed, Tirado wouldn't budge. Not, at least, until the moment arrived that Sheer had been half-expecting all along.

He might, Tirado acknowledged, be persuaded to tell his story, under certain circumstances. Perhaps, he said, for a small "honorarium." Sheer knew what that meant.

"How much?"

"In Peru, they say, Greco paid ten thousand dollars," Victor Tirado explained. "That would be fine with me."

Tom Sheer's meeting with Victor Tirado sparked a week of intense debate among Safra and his circle of aides. Though the big Peruvian diplomat seemed to hold at least part of the solution to the strange articles they had seen, everything about him filled Safra's men with revulsion—and suspicion. "I think you're being set up," Stanley Arkin advised. Arkin wasn't the only one who suspected the guiding hand of American Express somewhere in the murk from which Tirado had emerged. "It may be something," he said, "where they're trying to trap us into doing something illegal."

Safra and Weiner didn't rule out paying Tirado his ten thousand dollars, not until their lawyers told them that paying a foreign official on American soil was at the very least a gray area of the law. Tom Sheer was dispatched to have one final meeting with Tirado, this one in New York, but the Peruvian still insisted on being paid "an honorarium" for his information. In the end Safra and Weiner felt they simply had no choice but to turn their backs on Tirado. Now, it was clear, they would have to do things the hard way.

• • •

"You're never going to believe this," one of Safra's men, Cyril Dwek, was saying on the phone. "But we're all over the radio in Argentina."

"What do you mean, all over," Siegfried said. "What kind of stuff?"

"It's more of the same stuff," Dwek said. "The same stuff as in *Minute*. Do you have a way to get a copy of what was said?"

That day, Wednesday, March 1, as Safra and his aides continued their debate on Victor Tirado, a leading Buenos Aires radio program called "El Mundo" ("The World"), had broadcast a news item that the DEA was supposedly warning Latin American banks against doing business with Edmond Safra. Safra, the radio reported, was attempting to corner the South American market in money laundering. No one at Republic had actually heard the report, but a number of worried Argentine depositors had. Already the bank's Buenos Aires switchboard was lighting up with their anxious calls.

Cyril Dwek had good reason to be concerned. All along Safra had been worried about South America. The wary, close-knit Sephardic communities there formed the core of Safra's depositors. Accustomed to periodic outbursts of anti-Semitism, they picked up the latest rumors and relayed it through networks of social clubs and synagogues quickly and more efficiently than any newswire. If stories about Safra's involvement in drugs spread, they could be disastrous.

For twenty-five years Safra's lawyer in Buenos Aires had been a courtly Argentine named Carlos Basilico, a third-generation Italian immigrant who when not up to his elbows in Republic's legal work was an ardent Los Angeles Dodgers fan. "Lalo" Basilico had worked as a staff counsel at TDB until shortly after its sale, then formed his own law firm. From an elegant second-floor office looking out into the lazy jacaranda trees of a downtown park, he still spent much of his time looking after Safra interests.

As he pondered the "El Mundo" report, Basilico was perplexed. A corporate lawyer by trade, his experience with journalism stopped at the North American box scores. He had once picked up the autobiography of Al Neuharth, the founder of *USA Today*, and found it bewildering. Still, he was Safra's representative in Argentina; it was him or no one else. So Basilico did what any corporate lawyer would do. He called the station's owner, a Buenos Aires advertising man, who agreed to meet Basilico the next day.

Much to the lawyer's surprise, getting a retraction was easy. Once at the station, he and the owner ran into a pair of pleasant commentators who, though they professed to know nothing of the Safra item, agreed to air an immediate correction, no questions asked. No one, including Basilico, seemed entirely sure who was responsible for the previous day's story, and in the scramble to obtain a retraction, the lawyer never found out. He simply handed the radio men a copy of the suggested correction he had brought, then sat by in a sound booth while an announcer ad-libbed it on the air.

"We have to make an important clarification," the announcer read. "The production team handed to us yesterday a dossier containing bulky information on money laundering and bank business. Today the production team, having submitted to a check-up on the information related to Republic National Bank..."

Afterward Basilico returned to his office, pleased at how easily his first, and he hoped last, venture into journalism had gone. No sooner had he returned, though, than he took a worried call from a major Republic client. Had he heard the news on Radio Argentina? Was it true? About Edmond Safra and the DEA warning?

Surprised and annoyed to find the rumors had spread to a second station, Basilico hung up and phoned Mayer Attie, the smiling, white-haired Halabi who had run the Safra family's Buenos Aires offices for twenty-five years. Attie, too, was worried. Scores of anxious Republic depositors were milling about in Republic's hushed thirteenth-floor lobby, anxious to know whether the news was true. Was Edmond Safra, the same Safra who held their millions in far-off Swiss accounts, really a drug lord? Meyer Attie and his people were busy calming and explaining, photocopying the *Minute* articles and judgments, handing them out as fast as possible. In twenty-five years, he told Basilico, nothing like this had ever happened.

Now Lalo Basilico became alarmed. He arrived at Radio Argentina's downtown offices the next morning at six o'clock sharp, determined to get a retraction on the air as soon as possible. Finding no one to handle his complaint, he was standing on the sidewalk outside the station entrance when one of Radio Argentina's best-known anchormen ambled up. "Hello," Basilico began, "you don't know me, but..."

The anchorman listened politely as the lawyer explained his plight. "I'd like to help," he said, "but I'm not the right guy to talk to. You need to talk to Cinnamon." Cinnamon, Basilico realized as the anchorman hurried into the station, was the on-air nickname of Radio Argentina's breezy women's affairs correspondent. What, he wondered, was a woman named Cinnamon doing accusing Edmond Safra of drug dealing?

He was still standing on the sidewalk when Cinnamon herself scurried up, apparently late for work. "No, I don't know Mr. Safra," she hurriedly told the lawyer. "It came from a dossier someone passed to me. I just put it on the air." And with that, she was gone.

Basilico followed her into the station and, after a brief search, located a general manager who agreed to help with the retraction. By nine-thirty Basilico was again sitting in a sound booth, listening while a pair of announcers chatted their way through the correction.

"Do you have any news from abroad?" one asked.

"Something concerning Republic?"

"*Sí*, correct."

The retraction was read. "I believe that this must be a war between companies," the announcer noted, more accurately than he could have known, "making up news like this." Satisfied, Basilico picked up a cassette tape of the retraction, returned to his office, and mailed it to Safra in New York. Then he crossed his fingers, hoping it was the last he had heard of the odd drug stories.

It wasn't. Monday morning Republic's small suite of offices high above the trendy shops of Florida Street was again deluged with calls from worried depositors. Over the weekend one of Buenos Aires's major government-owned television stations, Channel 7, had aired the same strange story of a DEA warning on one of its news updates. "What am I going to do?" Basilico pleaded with Cyril Dwek. "I don't know anything about television."

Eventually, Basilico got through to a secretary at the station, who agreed to do her best to get a retraction aired. That Monday night, as a dozen lawyers and associates clustered around a television at Basilico's firm, the correction was aired. Everyone breathed a collective sigh of relief. So did the depositors phoning Republic, though only after Safra personally authorized the overnight payment of full cash refunds to anyone who wished to close their accounts. Only a handful did.

Arriving in New York at the height of the Argentine controversy, Edmond Safra remained cloistered in his Fifth Avenue apartment, obsessed with the man he was convinced was behind the stories: Tony

Greco. It was during the siege in Buenos Aires that Safra began repeating the phrase his aides would hear over and over in the weeks to come. "Tony is working," he took to saying. "Tony is working."

Returning from a two-week business trip in California, Stanley Arkin finally turned his full attention to Safra's growing troubles in the first days of March. He was pleased with the decision to stiff-arm Victor Tirado, in part because it cleared the decks for the plan he had in mind.

Arkin had conceived an ambitious, two-pronged investigation. For the routine surveillance and digging—"the dog work," he called it—he had chosen a former FBI man named Hank Flynn, a big, ruddy-faced Irishman who worked out of a neat condominium in the Connecticut woods an hour north of Manhattan. A twenty-two-year veteran of the bureau, Flynn had ferreted out espionage in Baltimore, handled stakeouts in Brooklyn, and probed the Dixie Mafia in New Orleans. He had been a special investigator with the Iran-Contra committees before setting out on his own.

From an earlier assignment Arkin knew Flynn's style was straight-on and conservative, exactly what he sought. "I don't need anyone with imagination," Arkin told Tom Sheer, who was bowing out of the case, and Sheer agreed that Flynn would be fine. On Wednesday afternoon, March 1, as Lalo Basilico scrambled to deal with the first of the Argentinian radio reports, Arkin sat down with Flynn and sketched out his assignment, which was simply to find out everything he could on Tony Greco. "Run a DMV, do all the normal background checks," Arkin said, handing Flynn the address in Staten Island. "And start a surveillance. I want you to pick this guy up in the morning and put him to bed at night."

At first glance, the man who followed the stolid Hank Flynn into Arkin's office later that afternoon might have been a well-dressed carnival barker, maybe a Soho art dealer. Jack Palladino draped his barrel chest in a flashy Italian double-breasted suit and a bright blue Perry Ellis tie swarming with parrots. Bald down the middle, he wore shiny Italian loafers and a massive pair of maroon Gianni Versace glasses that seemed to swallow his face. Most people didn't have to be told that Jack Palladino lived in California.

In fact, his twelve-year-old detective agency, Palladino & Sutherland, was headquartered in the heart of San Francisco's Haight-Ashbury district, in a rambling old Victorian mansion decorated with an eclectic mix of Sam Spade memorabilia, primitive tribal art, and Art Deco knick-knacks. A fast talker from a mean Boston neighborhood, Palladino had gone to Berkeley as a Ford Fellow and left with a law degree; he became a private investigator after growing bored working for the famed San Francisco attorney Melvin Belli. His top operative was his wife, Sandra Sutherland, an attractive blond Australian who had drifted into detective work in the early 1970s after exploring Bay Area radical circles, writing poetry and trying her hand at investigative journalism at the muckraking *Mother Jones* magazine.

They had met in 1971 as neophyte undercover operatives for a San Francisco detective agency; their mutual assignment had them masquerading as prisoners—Palladino as a Mafioso, Sutherland as a drug courier—to investigate corruption at a Long Island, New York, county jail. They formed their own agency in 1977, got married soon after, and began reeling in a string of local radical clients like Black Panther Huey Newton and members of the Symbionese Liberation Army before slowly going national, chasing down leads for defendants like John Z. DeLorean and cultists involved in the 1978 Jonestown Massacre in Guyana. Palladino and Sutherland got good word-of-mouth among the California lawyers who retained them, and eventually attracted some publicity, garnering favorable mentions over the years in *Newsweek*, *People,* and *Harper's Bazaar*.

They made a good team. The garrulous Palladino was always the front man, the bossy organizer, the client-handler, the one who kept abreast of corporate issues like computer crime and product liability. Sutherland, reserved and artsy, did much of the investigative work, charging eight-hundred dollars a day working undercover as a factory worker, a journalist, or, in one case, a prostitute. The couple's staff of detectives, a hodgepodge of onetime journalists and student radicals— not a former cop among them—was made up of a dozen or so full- and part-timers much like themselves, California dreamers who found detective work an exciting diversion.

Over the years Jack Palladino had had his share of odd cases—tracing stolen musical instruments for the Grateful Dead, probing the owner of a Nevada whorehouse—but never had he heard anything like what Stanley Arkin outlined that afternoon in his Third Avenue office. "This is kind of ludicrous," Palladino said, laughing. "Don't Safra's people realize the best thing they can do is let this thing run its course? Can't they see these are publications that nobody reads? I mean, why bother?"

"No," Arkin said, shaking his head. "It can't be done that way, Jack. It's too personal. It's gone too far."

Arkin described his leading suspect, Tony Greco. "I'm guessing, but Greco is probably someone with governmental connections," he said. "I've got him in Staten Island. But he travels all over the world, I think. France, Peru, all over. But I don't want to get stuck on him. He could be just a lure. We've got to go at this another way." This, Palladino could see, was where he came in. "I'm not giving you the domestic work," Arkin went on. "You're going to do the foreign side. We have to deal with these publications. Your mission is not to go after Greco. It's to go after the publications."

Both men realized it wouldn't be an easy task. Journalists the world over are notoriously secretive about their sources: why would one simply hand over something that sensitive to a detective? "They're going to pull this journalistic shit," as Arkin put it. The solution, and Palladino & Sutherland's assignment, was to go undercover as perhaps the only people in the world who could get information out of journalists: other journalists.

The cover, as Arkin imagined it, would be simplicity itself. They would pose as reporters digging into the secret world of Edmond Safra. The idea had a certain ironic beauty: not only could they hope to root out information about who was spreading the stories about Safra, but maybe, just maybe, they might attract the attention of whoever was behind the campaign. In the best of all scenarios, maybe the source would contact *them*.

"I love it," Palladino said, warming to the idea. "This is a natural for Sandra. She'll be great." The more they talked, the more excited he became. Odd cases appealed to Palladino; he hated mundane detective chores like surveillance. Watching a house for hours on end was unbelievably boring; he would flip the radio to "All Things Considered," get lost in a book, and never notice a suspect leaving the front door. His wife was only a little better. She used stakeouts to memorize poetry.

Later that night Palladino returned to his room at the Pierre Hotel, a satchel of documents and articles on the Safra case under one arm. He found his wife already in bed. Quickly he sketched out the case. He wasn't surprised to find she didn't share his enthusiasm.

In fact, Sandra Sutherland was downright skeptical.

"American Express?" Sutherland exclaimed, her voice betraying only the slightest trace of her Australian birth. "Jack, if there's a conspiracy against Safra, it's by somebody tawdry and seamy, not a great company like American Express. A large company wouldn't do anything that stupid. This sounds like this Safra guy's paranoid fantasy."

Palladino took out the articles and offered them to her. She passed. "I'll read it in the morning," she said, then fell fast asleep. Palladino stayed up until three, poring over everything he had been given.

As he read, Palladino knew the operation they foresaw already faced a far deeper problem than his wife's skepticism. It was her health. For obvious reasons he hadn't mentioned this to Arkin. But for more than a year Sutherland had suffered from an unexplained chronic fatigue. She slept ten or twelve hours every night, and still never felt rested. She had lost twenty-five pounds. Doctor after doctor had failed to diagnose her malady, though one suggested she might have an intestinal parasite. As far as Palladino was concerned, the bottom line was that his wife hadn't worked in over a year. She was simply too tired. Palladino badly wanted this case, and he badly wanted his wife to handle it. He secretly hoped that an exciting assignment like the one Arkin was offering might help her pull out of whatever she was fighting.

"It's only three interviews, baby," Palladino cooed when his wife woke the next morning. One journalist at *L'Espresso* in Milan, one at *Minute* in Paris, one at *La Dépêche du Midi* in Toulouse. "You're going to love this. It's perfect for you."

"Jack, why is Safra, this incredibly wealthy, powerful person, bothering with these little mice? These gnats?" Sutherland asked. "These articles seem so slanderous as to be ludicrous. Even if it's true that American Express has done all this, so what? Does it really harm anything?"

"Baby, the client doesn't feel that way," Palladino said. "He has his family honor at stake. You have to understand, this is a Sephardic Jew, dealing with other Sephardic Jews. Much of his business is based on trust, not balance sheets. His personal word, his reputation, means everything."

Palladino, confident his wife would come around, pondered a plan of action all that day before ducking into Arkin's offices early Saturday morning, where he typed a four-page plan of action and left it with Arkin's assistant, Jeffrey Kaplan. They could start work in Europe, he promised, in three weeks.

• • •

After securing approval from each rung of the Republic ladder, Arkin was finally cleared to meet Safra himself the following Monday. That afternoon, he hustled up to his client's Fifth Avenue apartment, where Safra waited with Weiner. As they shook hands in the study, Arkin took in the rich English pines, the antique French furniture, the photo of a smiling Safra with Ronald Reagan. On the wall he spied an extraordinary Modigliani.

Suitably impressed, Arkin took a seat facing the windows overlooking Central Park, Safra beside him on a couch, a telephone always within reach. It was to be the first in a series of meetings in which Arkin tried to soothe Safra's concerns about the investigation he planned. As wrenching as he found the publicity onslaught, Safra remained leery of the less palatable aspects of detective work, and he repeatedly sought Arkin's assurances that neither he nor his investigators would do anything illegal, nothing that, should it backfire, might further sully the good name of Edmond Safra or Republic National Bank. Weiner, too, made it clear: there must be no funny business. No phone taps. No break-ins. No bribes.

Arkin played his part well. "My reputation to me is the most precious thing I own," he said. "I'm not going to sacrifice my reputation, my life, for anything, for any client. There is no client in the world I would break the law for. You have my word on that." Their conversations were interrupted as Safra took telephone calls. As Arkin and Weiner waited, he would murmur softly in French, sometimes Arabic, once or twice in English. When Safra gave him his full attention, Arkin made it clear this was to be his investigation, not the bank's.

"Look, I've got to have some freedom to do this, and my people need freedom," he explained. "I can't have you breathing down my neck every five minutes. I'll give you conclusions, not facts. One of the ways I shield you is to keep you away from the details. When you are up on that witness stand, I want you to be able to say, honestly, 'I don't know what happened.'"

From a legal standpoint, Arkin explained, this approach had an added benefit. When they sued American Express—and that, after all, was everyone's goal—Arkin could refuse to hand over their investigative reports only if the papers could be classified as a lawyers' work product, an exception to the rigorous rules of discovery. By meeting's end, Arkin thought Safra seemed more comfortable with the idea of an investigation, but of course it was only a guess. Reading Safra's feelings was a full-time occupation for some men, and Arkin had neither the time nor the energy for it.

By midweek Arkin could see things were falling into place. He had met again with Hank Flynn, who was poised to start surveillance of Tony Greco's Staten Island home. In San Francisco, Palladino and Sutherland were busy crafting a cover story for their trip to Europe, and one of Palladino's men was being readied for a trip to Peru. If everything went smoothly, Arkin saw, they would begin turning up the heat on American Express very soon.

Whatever peace of mind Safra took from his talks with Arkin collapsed the following Thursday morning, March 9. That day the largest tabloid newspaper in Buenos Aires, *Cronica*, published a short article that once again tied Safra and Republic to money laundering, echoing the charges that the DEA was warning South American banks against Safra. It also added the surprising allegation that Safra was a fugitive from American justice.

"According to the DEA," *Cronica* reported, "what Republic Bank and Safra are looking for is the total control of the ways to launder dollars that come to banks in Miami, Los Angeles, New York, Luxembourg, France, and Switzerland. The dollar proceeds from this illegal business could enter legally to the international finance circuit, giving big profits to the agents. Interpol, acting on confidential information from the DEA, has advised the banking institutions of Argentina, Peru, Brazil, and Venezuela to be alert with respect to the operation of Republic National Bank."

Unremarkable in itself, the new Argentine article threatened to throw an unforeseen kink into plans for Arkin's investigation. That afternoon he and Weiner were again summoned to Safra's Fifth Avenue study, where they found him distraught. This time Weiner, always attuned to Safra's moods, discerned something new in the air. He had reached some kind of decision.

For Safra, it wasn't just that the articles were starting again—that alone was enough to infuriate him—it was where they were appearing. South America, even more than Switzerland, was the family's bread and butter. Peru he could ignore—the country simply wasn't that vital to

Republic's interests—but Argentina was another thing altogether. The family's ties to the Sephardic community there were too deep. And Argentina was just one step from the motherland, Brazil.

"This is it," Safra announced. "I'm calling Jim."

Weiner had been afraid of this. They had been through the debate too many times. "No, Edmond," Weiner pleaded, motioning to Arkin. "Give these guys a chance to work. We're just getting started."

"No, maybe I can stop it. Let's remember our objective here. If I can talk to Jim, I think we can stop it. I really think we can."

Weiner laid out the same old arguments. "Edmond, if you do talk to Jim, what are you going to say to him? Are you going to tell him about Tony Greco? We don't have anything on this guy. It's all supposition."

"I'll tell him the facts."

"But the facts don't say anything. What have we got? Someone faxing a *Life* magazine article to someone? This guy Tirado? What does that tell us about Tony Greco?"

"Maybe I can stop him."

Arkin, too, opposed an approach to Robinson.

"In going to him," the lawyer said, "what you may end up doing is forcing them to ground. If they go to ground, I may not be able to do anything for you here. It could make any investigation almost impossible. Secondly, you're going to show them you're being hurt. You're showing them your pain. They may like that."

But Safra was resolute. "Why is anything else important if we can stop it?" he repeated. "That's our primary objective."

"Maybe it'll stop," Weiner countered. "But then it could start again. And we'll never be able to prove it was them."

"I'm going to do it," Safra said, and the tone in his voice ended all debate. Later he told Weiner a meeting with Robinson had been arranged. The chairman of American Express had promised to drop by Safra's apartment the following Sunday afternoon, March 12.

Staten Island is the forgotten borough of New York City, a neglected child cast off at the foot of New York harbor. Its most famous landmark, and its lifeline to Manhattan, is the Staten Island Ferry, which still floats legions of working people past the Statue of Liberty to lower Manhattan each morning for only fifty cents. These days Staten Island may be as well-known for the massive garbage dumps that sprawl over much of its far shore, where flocks of angry seagulls hover over mountains of trash from all five New York boroughs. When the wind blows the wrong way, many of Staten Island's working-class neighborhoods smell like the inside of a month-old milk carton.

German and Irish families settled the island in the 1800s, and dominated its commerce and politics well into the twentieth century. But with the completion of the Verrazano-Narrows Bridge to Brooklyn in 1964, Italian families from the teeming streets of Bensonhurst and Bay Ridge flooded into Staten Island, eager for easier lives amid its leafy suburban hills. By the 1980s fully sixty percent of the borough's registered voters were Italian, most of them firmly middle-class.

In 1980 an Italian man named Paul Castellano made the move as well, buying a sumptuous home in Staten Island's most prestigious section, Todt Hill. "Big Paul," the American Mafia's secretive Boss of Bosses, was followed by many of his mob cronies, who proceeded to buy up some of the choicest properties on Staten Island's South Shore. Suddenly city cops noticed many of Gotham's best-known wiseguys disappearing from Brooklyn and popping up cruising down Hylan Avenue, marking the near side of Staten Island as a hot spot for upwardly mobile mobsters.

At first Big Paul's Todt Hill neighbors loathed his presence—the godfather never could get into the country club—but eventually they came to appreciate him, for an obvious reason. Almost overnight burglaries in the area dropped off. Street crime of all types disappeared. The reason was the influx of clean-cut men in dark glasses, members of more than a dozen law-enforcement agencies who kept Big Paul and his associates under constant surveillance. At any given moment, cars registered to the FBI, the DEA, New York's Organized Crime Task Force, Staten Island police, or the Brooklyn, Manhattan, or Staten Island district attorney's offices could be seen parked on Todt Hill. It became the safest neighborhood in the borough, at least until Big Paul was gunned down outside a Manhattan steakhouse in 1985, making way for a man named John Gotti to take his place.

Until the spring of 1989, Staten Island's Emerson Hill neighborhood, two hilltops over from Todt Hill, had been largely free of surveillance cars. Originally a center of the borough's German community—for years its most notable resident was an elderly survivor of the 1937 *Hindenburg* disaster—Emerson Hill rose like a gentle sentry over the approaches to the Verrazano Bridge. Its wooded eastern face was honey-combed with narrow, twisting roads no wider than private driveways, most flanked by low, ivy-covered stone walls. High above the entrance gate on Richmond Road, spacious split-level homes could be glimpsed through the trees, their walnut decks affording sweeping vistas of New York Harbor. In all of Staten Island only Todt Hill was a more prestigious address; by the late 1980s most homes in the area sold for at least half a million dollars, many for well over a million. The majority of Emerson Hill's residents were quiet professionals and businessmen. Over the years police had never identified more than two or three mobsters on the entire hill, and thus no one had any real reason for intensive surveil-lance. That was about to change.

On Thursday morning, March 9, as Safra read an Argentinian news-paper in dismay, Hank Flynn and a partner drove across the Verrazano Bridge in a rented car and sped onto the Staten Island Expressway. Min-utes after paying the bridge toll, Flynn pulled off at the second exit, then turned left under the freeway onto busy Richmond Road. Douglas Road, where Tony Greco was supposed to live, was the first right off Rich-mond, a stone's throw from the freeway. Flynn turned onto Douglas and his heart sank. A pair of aging stone pillars flanked the steep, winding lane. Beside them, on a high concrete wall running along Richmond, a small plaque read "Emerson Hill."

Even before he saw the Greco home, Flynn knew the surveillance would be problematic. As he edged his car up the hill, he saw that the fence-lined street was almost too narrow to pull over, much less park; a stakeout team would be as inconspicuous as a fire engine. Twenty Dou-glas Road was the third house on the left as Flynn passed, a heavy white stucco sunk down the slope behind an eight-foot wall; only its top floor could be seen from the street. The front door was no more than six feet from the road, behind a gate flanked by an intercom. "Jesus, to put a guy up here would be inviting all kinds of problems," Flynn groused. "Cops would be on us in a minute."

Flynn circled back down to Richmond Road. Above, through a tan-gle of vines and trees, he could just make out the Greco home. Then he saw it: the Achilles heel. Behind and below the house stood a two-story garage; beside the garage, a driveway opened through a pair of wrought-iron gates onto Richmond. The surveillance cars, Flynn realized, would need to sit out on Richmond beyond the Emerson Hill pillars, watching their man come and go via his driveway. Flynn decided two cars would be needed, one to keep an eye on the driveway, the other to watch the entrance to Douglas Road, in case a cab ducked in to the front curb. It was far from an ideal stakeout, but it would have to do. That night Stanley Arkin okayed the plan.

Friday morning Flynn had two cars parked on Richmond across from Greco's driveway. Inside each was a pair of private investigators Flynn had subcontracted the actual surveillance to, mostly former New York cops armed with walkie-talkies. Charged only with keeping tabs on Greco's movements, they knew nothing of American Express or Safra. Their cars, which Flynn rotated every few days, were anonymous and littered with the detritus of stakeout teams everywhere: coffee cups and empty Dunkin' Donuts containers.

By nine-thirty that morning there was no sign of Tony Greco or anyone else, and the stakeout teams were growing restless. Was Greco sick? Was it his day off work? Before long the watchers were confronted with the age-old question confronting all surveillance teams: was the man even home? At ten one of them called Flynn, who remained behind at his Connecticut condo to supervise the investigation, and told him of their dilemma.

Flynn moved fast. Within minutes he called a woman friend who had worked in law enforcement. At ten-thirty the woman called the Greco home in Staten Island and asked for "Mary." It was a simple subterfuge, but it worked. A man picked up the phone and, in a deep, accented voice, said no, there was no Mary there. Flynn's friend apologized. "That's okay," the man in Staten Island said. "It's no problem." He sounded pleasant and, the woman told Flynn, very Italian. Flynn was willing to bet it was Tony Greco.

The rest of the day passed with no sighting of Greco or any family members, and the next morning, a Saturday, the surveillance teams were again in place by six forty-five. At ten-fifteen they got their first sighting of the man they believed to be Greco. From a distance, the detectives could tell he was on the small side, maybe five eight, paunchy, with dark hair parted down the side. The man climbed into a large white Lincoln and eased the car out of the driveway onto Richmond Road. The detectives noticed a girl in the passenger seat, most likely a daughter. One of the surveillance cars followed the car several blocks to a Citibank branch on nearby Hylan Avenue, then across the street to a dry cleaners.

When Tony Greco and his daughter emerged from the cleaners, their followers got the first fuzzy photographs of the man Edmond Safra so badly wanted to find.

That same weekend, as Hank Flynn's men began their surveillance of a Staten Island home, Switzerland's spreading Shakarchi Trading scandal crept slowly toward the nervous Safra camp. In Brooklyn that Friday, March 10, a federal judge quietly approved a government request to freeze one of Shakarchi's accounts at Republic in New York. No explanation was given publicly, but U.S. investigators clearly believed the account was brimming with drug money.

A white-coated butler guided Jim Robinson into the study where Safra waited Sunday afternoon. The two men shook hands, but there was little warmth exchanged in their greetings.

On a table Safra had placed a folder that held a copy of the *Life* fax with the damning American Express "telltale." Safra gestured to the unopened file as he began to talk of the strange articles he had seen in newspapers around the world. He explained all that had happened with *Minute*, with *La Dépêche*, and his fear that it was starting once more in Argentina and Switzerland. "I'm concerned, Jim," Safra concluded simply, "that your people are conducting a defamation campaign against me."

The surprise registered clearly on Robinson's face. "Edmond," he said in his gentle southern accent, "I'd be dumbfounded if that were true."

"Jim, I have proof. I have papers here I can't show you. This is the file. I know everything your people are doing."

Robinson pled ignorance. "Edmond," he said several times, "I just don't know what you're talking about. I don't."

As the chairman of American Express piled denial upon denial, Safra realized how much he had come to hate Robinson's southern drawl. "Jim, I have this lawyer, Stanley Arkin," he said finally. "He is very aggressive, and he is willing to start biting. And he will bite hard. Jim, don't make me set my dogs on you. Let us stop this campaign. Let us end this like gentlemen."

But nothing was to be resolved that day. Later, as he left, Robinson promised he would look into Safra's complaints and get back to him. They shook hands again, and once more Safra had occasion to look deeply into Jim Robinson's eyes. He felt then what he had felt all along. As he told Walter Weiner shortly after Robinson's departure, "I know Jim is lying."

The first photos of Tony Greco crossed Stanley Arkin's desk the next morning. They were only fair in quality, but clearly showed Greco's face in profile, the dark hair, the slight paunch. Arkin sized up the face, the Lincoln, and the area, and came to a New Yorker's snap conclusion. "Guy looks like a two-bit guinea hoodlum," he told Flynn.

The stakeout was continuing after an uneventful weekend. That Sunday, as Robinson and Safra met on Fifth Avenue, Flynn's men had followed a woman, who appeared to be Mrs. Greco, and four children to nearby St. Sylvester's Church for services. At two forty-five the whole family, including Greco, emerged in the white Lincoln and drove down Richmond Road to rendezvous with another car, filled with what appeared to be another family. The surveillance team snapped pictures of the second car, making sure to get the license plate, but didn't follow. It appeared to be a family outing, nothing more. At five the Greco family returned home.

Flynn, meanwhile, had been busy on his own. He had all but ransacked the Staten Island Borough Hall looking for official records on Greco, anything at all, at the very least confirmation that the man living at 20 Douglas Road was, in fact, the Antonio Greco he had been assigned to investigate. It wouldn't be the first time he was put on the wrong man's tail. First Flynn checked the list of registered voters, but found no Antonio Greco. Next he pored over the trade name index, to see if an Antonio Greco had opened a business on Staten Island. Again he found nothing. He checked the index of civil suits, hoping Greco had been sued, divorced, or married in Staten Island. Nothing. In fact, the only trace Flynn could find of Greco was the deed to his house: the man who had bought the home at 20 Douglas Road on June 10, 1983, was, in fact, Antonio Greco. His wife's name, Flynn noted, was Joanne. The deed carried no other information that might be remotely of use to Safra. Strange, Flynn thought. The man seemed to leave no footprints.

After passing the surveillance photos to Arkin, Flynn checked to see whether Greco had a New York driver's license. He used a Manhattan record-searching agency to obtain the license, and what the agency found was revealing. The Antonio Greco who lived at 20 Douglas Road had no New York driver's license. But a Giuseppe A. Greco on Bay Street in Staten Island did; Flynn consulted a map and found Greco's address less than a mile from Douglas Road. The clincher was the birth date: December 16, 1939, the same birthdate Tom Sheer had come up with. Later Flynn had the address on Bay Street checked out and found a mattress shop on the first floor, an apartment on the second, and no one named Greco in sight. Flynn decided Greco probably used the address as a mail drop.

Flynn next asked his agency contact to research Giuseppe A. Greco's driving record, which he knew would take several days. In the meantime, he spread his net for Greco wider and wider. Through a contact at Citibank he learned that Greco held a Citibank Visa card. But the primary card holder was Joanne L. Greco; Greco himself held what was called a secondary card, which required no biographical information. Again, no footprints. Through another buddy, Flynn was able to check Consolidated Edison records for the house at 20 Douglas Road. The records showed uninterrupted electrical service dating back to 1983 under the name Antonio Gag. Flynn pondered the name for a while before he saw it: Gag, or G.A.G., Giuseppe Antonio Greco. "This guy's being cute," Flynn muttered.

Clearly Tony Greco was a man who not only didn't want personal information in the public domain, but knew how to prevent its release. Interesting enough, Flynn saw, but it told him little about who Greco was, or how he made his living. Arkin was breathing down his neck on a daily basis to come up with something to show the Safra people. The fact was, Flynn was drawing blank after blank. And worst of all, Greco had disappeared.

On Monday, March 13, the day after watching his wife and children attend church, Flynn's men had seen no sign of their man. Nor the next day, nor the day after. There was little to do but wait: one day a car followed the Greco children's bus to an exclusive day school. They watched the wife go shopping. But by Friday there was still no sign of Greco himself.

Waiting for news in his Third Avenue office, Arkin fumed. Apparently Greco had slipped away before the surveillance cars arrived at six-forty-five Monday morning. He was willing to bet the Italian had left town, probably flown overseas, and he racked his brains trying to find a way to learn where. "This fucker did not take the Train to the Plane," Arkin mused aloud to his assistant Jeffrey Kaplan, referring to the express subway to JFK. "We should've had him."

Arkin and Flynn discussed checking with the airlines for some sign of Greco's flight plan, but decided against it. The lawyer kicked himself for not having men stationed at airports in Paris and Geneva to watch for him. "He's out roaming somewhere," Arkin told Walter Weiner. "Next time it won't happen. Next time, we'll have people in Geneva and all over, waiting for him. We'll have him covered."

As Hank Flynn's men kept the Staten Island home under surveillance, the European arm of Stanley Arkin's investigation was swinging into action. On Monday night, March 20, Jack Palladino and Sandra Sutherland arrived, exhausted, in Milan, Italy, after a grueling trip from San Francisco.

As Arkin saw it, the press campaign against Safra had probably begun with the *L'Espresso* article a year earlier, and he had approved Palladino's plan to begin their work at the magazine's offices in Milan. At an airport newsstand Palladino picked up a copy of *L'Espresso's* latest issue, checked to make sure the January 1988 article's two authors still worked there—they did—and taxied to the Grand Hotel Duomo, where they had reserved a suite. After a day recovering from jet lag, Sutherland went to *L'Espresso's* offices in a downtown high-rise, where a security guard curtly informed her that both men she sought worked out of the magazine's Rome offices. "Shit, Jack," Sutherland told her husband upon her return, "we've got to get to Rome."

It was an ignominious beginning, and things got worse before they got better. The two quickly checked out of the hotel and grabbed a cab to the Milan airport. But the airport was swamped with preholiday travelers—that Sunday was Easter—and all flights to Rome were booked. Hurriedly Palladino rented a car and sped out of Milan to Florence, where they stayed overnight. The next morning Sutherland took a train to Rome, while Palladino returned to a friend's cottage in Tuscany to await her return.

In Rome Sutherland went straight to *L'Espresso's* offices on the Via Po. One reporter was not expected until after five, a receptionist told her. Another, Roberto Chiodi, had arrived, but was now out, and also wouldn't return until after five. When she returned at ten past five, laden with Italian breads and Easter presents, Chiodi agreed to see her, and she was escorted into his spacious corner office.

Roberto Chiodi's brown mustache was flecked with gray, and Sutherland noticed the elegant cut of his slacks and tweed jacket. By way of introduction she began explaining her cover. To Chiodi, and to others she met in coming weeks, Sutherland presented herself as a free-lance writer from Australia. She explained she was investigating the infamous Australian bank Nugan Hand, whose ties to senior U.S. military and intelligence officials had made it the subject of intense press coverage. The name of another shady international banker, Edmond Safra, had come up, Sutherland explained, and she was in Europe probing his links to the bank.

To Sutherland's relief, Chiodi accepted the story without question. He was, in fact, exceedingly cordial, especially considering that the magazine was approaching deadline. Sutherland tested her Italian—she had taken four semesters at San Francisco State—while Chiodi shuttled between tasks necessary to complete the edition. She saw him flush at the mention of Safra's name. The January 1988 article's passage on Safra was brief, Chiodi emphasized, only *"una riga,"* a line, and the paper had published his letter of complaint. As far as he was concerned, the matter was history.

Where, Sutherland asked, had they gotten the tip on Safra's 1957 drug ties? In a *"cenno,"* a secret document, Chiodi replied, provided by the Italian police to the Rome magistrate's office. Had the document come from a confidential source?, Sutherland asked. Yes, Chiodi said, he had gotten the document from a source with connections to the Rome magistrate's office. He spent ten minutes rummaging through two file folders in a vain attempt to find it.

All told, Sutherland saw, it was a fairly useless interview—until she asked if anyone had visited *L'Espresso* to inquire about the article. No one important, Chiodi said, just an "Italo-American investigator" whose name he couldn't remember.

Sutherland stopped cold, then smiled to herself. She was willing to bet the visitor's name was Tony Greco.

"There's no question, this asshole Greco's been down there," Arkin told Walter Weiner when he received Sutherland's report. "No question. It fits. It smells right. He was there."

"What can we do?"

Nothing at this point, Arkin said. "It just means we're getting closer, Walter. It means we're getting warm."

That week Jim Robinson got back to Safra. His reply to Safra's charges was predictably disappointing. After checking with a half dozen of his top people—Robinson mentioned his top aide Harry Freeman and the bank's Bob Smith by name—he said he hadn't been able to discover any effort by anyone at American Express to spread rumors or news articles about Safra or Republic.

"I don't believe it," Safra told Robinson. "Your people aren't telling you the full story."

"I've challenged them personally," Robinson replied. "Edmond, if you have any information that can pinpoint what it is that concerns you, help me. Tell me what is being done wrong."

But Safra, of course, couldn't do that. Stanley Arkin had warned him repeatedly not to divulge any details of their investigation. Now angrier than ever, Safra could see that his only hope now lay with Arkin and the detectives.

Tony Greco resurfaced in Staten Island on Sunday, March 26, but it was hardly an occasion for Arkin to rejoice. That afternoon Flynn's men followed the entire Greco family in the white Lincoln to the circus at Madison Square Garden. Arkin was more than a little irked. At Flynn's suggestion, he had pulled the surveillance teams off the Greco home for several days. Stakeouts weren't cheap, and Safra wasn't paying to watch Greco's kids go to school. But as a result, when Greco reappeared, Flynn's men had no idea when he had returned. Nor, Flynn had to admit, did anyone have the first clue where he had been.

All Arkin had to show for two weeks of expensive surveillance were some hazy photos of a Staten Island Italian whose only failing seemed to be sloth. No suspicious behavior. No proof of international travels. And no discernible ties to American Express. Nothing. The next day Arkin told Flynn to cancel any further stakeouts. They would need more to go on before wasting any more time lurking in the streets of Staten Island.

After a relaxing weekend in Tuscany, Jack Palladino and Sandra Sutherland flew to Paris on Tuesday morning, March 28, to approach the

Minute reporter, Jean Roberto. Through their hotel concierge, they were put in touch with a translator, a charming woman named Sophie Hardy.

Hardy, who would come to play her own small role in the events of coming weeks, was no ordinary translator. In her salad days, in the 1960s, she had been a promising Parisian starlet, appearing on French television and in films, and had even edged into British cinema, appearing opposite Stewart Granger in a long-forgotten movie, *The Trygon Factor*. But then had come a tragic high-speed car accident, followed by a flurry of sympathetic press notices and, as time went by, a long, steady career decline, ending in some little-noticed foreign films and, by the 1980s, a life in obscurity. By the time Sandra Sutherland got her name in early 1989, Sophie Hardy was living in a suburb of Paris, working as a translator, albeit one whose résumé came with an old picture of its owner posing gaily with the Beatles.

It took most of a long afternoon, but after checking several wrong addresses, Sutherland and Hardy finally found *Minute*'s offices in a distant arrondissement. Entering through a central courtyard, they stepped inside a clean, modern office, where a receptionist told them Roberto would return in ten minutes. The Frenchman, when he appeared, was in his forties, dressed neatly in a sport jacket, with thick brown hair combed straight back. He graciously led Sutherland and her translator into a neat office, where Sutherland promptly offered her cover story.

"It's quite likely your sources would know about Nugan Hand," she began. "If I could talk to them, it might be quite valuable. Maybe we could be valuable to one another." She smiled and tried to establish eye contact.

Showing no signs of skepticism, Roberto insisted his enthusiasm for Safra had died, killed by the billionaire's successful libel suits. But there was someone else who might be interested in Safra, he noted, a Swiss reporter named Jean-Claude Buffle, who was working on an article for a Swiss magazine. To Sutherland's surprise, he telephoned Buffle in Switzerland, but got no answer.

Sutherland steered the conversation back to the matter of Roberto's sources. "This is all so incredibly brave of you," she said, hoping flattery would work. "This man Safra is so powerful. Yet you've continued in the face of all of his threats? You must have considerable faith in your sources."

"Oh yes," Roberto said. "My source is an American, and I have great faith in him." Sutherland noted the singular tense: source, not sources.

"Why is this person going to so much trouble to give you this information?" she wondered. "What's in it for him?" Hardy translated.

"He is doing it out of a great personal resentment for Safra because Safra swindled him out of much—millions—of dollars."

Sutherland nodded. "How long have you been investigating the story?"

"Six months. But my source has been investigating him for two years."

Roberto took some papers out of his desk drawer. Sutherland, not knowing it had already surfaced the previous fall, got excited when Roberto pulled out a copy of the strange graph linking Safra to Meyer Lansky and other gangsters. She was certain the writing on the chart was American. "Where did you get this?" she asked.

"I got it from the source."

"Could I have a copy?"

Roberto obliged. He took several minutes putting some papers together for her. Later, as they rose to leave, he promised he would attempt to reach his American source, and arrange a meeting. Sutherland thanked him and left, confident she had taken the first steps toward meeting whoever was spreading stories about Edmond Safra.

For the moment, it was as far as Arkin's European investigation would go. Palladino returned to San Francisco, while his wife flew to Australia for ten days to visit her ailing mother. Arkin wasn't happy with the delay, but Palladino had warned him about it before their hiring. For the time being, they would simply have to wait. Palladino promised to resume operations in France and Switzerland as soon as his wife returned.

On the day that Sandra Sutherland played up to an unsuspecting Jean Roberto, a rare media inquiry came into Republic's Fifth Avenue switchboard. The caller identified himself as Peter Samuel, a Washington-based reporter for the *New York City Tribune*, a small newspaper published by the Unification Church of the Reverend Sun Myung Moon. Though Republic was one of the nation's twenty-five largest banks, it didn't employ a full-time public relations person, reflecting Safra's visceral disdain for publicity. Samuel's call was routed instead to an administrative assistant named Sharon Connor; when asked for comment about something to do with Shakarchi Trading, Connor declined to be drawn into a discussion, citing bank policy against commenting on clients.

It was a mistake, as Connor later realized. She called Robert Siegfried at Kekst, who was immediately curious about the call. "What did you tell this Samuel?" he asked.

"I told him we don't comment on customer situations."

Siegfried rolled his eyes and took a breath. "What's his number?"

As irritated as he was, Siegfried knew they had only themselves to blame. Safra was insisting on secrecy so intense even his own press spokesmen didn't know about the strange articles appearing in overseas publications. Siegfried called Peter Samuel in Washington, but didn't reach him in time. The reporter's article came out the next day, and Siegfried and all of Safra's other aides were stunned when they saw it.

On its face, the piece wasn't about Republic or Safra, but about the involvement of Bulgarian government officials in drug trafficking. "Senior Bulgarian Aides Linked to a Booming Trade in Heroin," the headline read. "Trading Firm Seen as a Front for Secret Police." The Bulgarian "front" firm, the paper charged, was none other than Shakarchi Trading. Shakarchi, the paper quoted a DEA report as saying, was "in reality an agency of the Bulgarian government operated by the secret police."

The Shakarchi Trading Co. of Zurich operates as a currency exchange company but, according to the DEA, is "utilized by some of the world's largest drug trafficking organizations to launder the proceeds of their drug trafficking activities...."

The DEA report says that the founder of the Shakarchi Trading Co., the late Mahmoud Shakarchi, "maintained a close relationship" with Edmond Safra, owner of the Safra Bank and the owner of 38 percent of the stocks issued by the Republic National Bank of New York....The DEA report says that "all of those banks surfaced in Mahmoud Shakarchi's alleged drug money laundering activities."

Safra and Weiner were beside themselves. They were convinced the DEA report was a fake, no doubt planted by American Express like the odd report they found in Paris. When Stanley Arkin arrived at Republic's Fifth Avenue offices for a meeting that morning, Weiner thrust a copy of the *Tribune* article into his hands. "Why can't we stop this stuff?" he demanded. "Why can't we stop it?"

Arkin scanned the *Tribune* article, and immediately understood Weiner's feelings. But Arkin's legal eye spied something else, an opportunity. "Walter, I know this is unpleasant," he said. "But this is a marginal newspaper. You've got a reporter here who's clearly not top of the mark. Here's a guy we can really get in on." After a minute Weiner caught on. If American Express or Tony Greco had leaked documents to this Peter Samuel, Arkin's detectives were far more likely to pressure it out of the little *New York City Tribune* than from a more powerful paper like *The New York Times*.

"What'll you do?" Weiner asked.

Arkin thought it best if Weiner not know the details. "I'll have someone deal with the reporter," he said.

A plan was forming in Arkin's mind. Later that day he called Jack Palladino in San Francisco and had Palladino dispatch a new operative to New York. If Arkin's idea was to have any chance at success, they had to move fast.

Leaving Weiner's office, Arkin hustled downtown to the Doral Hotel for lunch with, of all people, Ken Bialkin, the lawyer who often represented American Express. Bialkin had called the day before and asked to meet; it had sounded important, and both Arkin and Weiner wondered if it was about the Safra articles.

But during lunch Bialkin was all smiles, asking about mutual clients, Arkin's family and career, nothing at all about Safra.

"Well, is there something else you wanted to talk to me about?" Arkin probed. "Something specific?"

"Oh, no, no, no."

"Is there any other reason you wanted to see me?"

"No, you're a good friend, Stanley. I hadn't seen you in a while."

Arkin didn't buy it for a minute. Bialkin, he decided, had wanted to talk about the Safra articles, but had canceled his plans, perhaps at American Express's insistence. That afternoon Arkin returned to Weiner's office and told him so.

"What do you think it means?" Weiner wondered.

"My sense is," Arkin said, "there are some very nervous people over there."

• • •

Even as Safra's aides reeled from the article in the *New York City Trib-une*, Republic was being drawn into another, larger money-laundering controversy, albeit one in which federal authorities never suspected it of wrongdoing. At a crowded press conference the next day in Washington, U.S. Attorney General Richard Thornburgh announced the culmination of the largest money-laundering crackdown in history, Operation Polar Cap, which exposed an international scheme by Colombian cocaine traf-fickers to move drug profits out of the United States to banks in South America. More than 125 people were indicted, half a ton of cocaine and $45 million in cash were seized and, in an unusual twist, the U.S. govern-ment filed suit against nine major U.S. banks, seeking the return of $433 million of the drug cartel's profits. The banks included Citibank, the Bank of New York, the soon-to-be-infamous BCCI, and both Republic National Bank of New York and American Express Bank. "Federal pros-ecutors stressed that the civil suit does not charge that the banks know-ingly handled drug money," the *Washington Post* reported.

Weiner and other Republic officials, who had cooperated with pros-ecutors in the probe, braced themselves for an onslaught of negative publicity. For the most part, it didn't come; the nation's press accepted the explanation that the banks were unknowing dupes of Colombian drug lords. Weiner was almost ready to exhale when a call came in the next afternoon. Another Washington-based reporter, Knut Royce of *New York Newsday*, had questions about Republic and Operation Polar Cap, and it seemed clear he was homing in on the bank for a major piece. Siegfried returned the call from Weiner's office that Friday morning.

"Why are you focusing on Republic?" Siegfried asked Royce as Weiner sat by and listened. "As you know there are other banks men-tioned in this thing."

"Well, I think there's more there than meets the eye with Republic," the reporter replied.

"What do you mean, specifically?"

"Well, there's some information floating around."

"What kind of information could possibly be floating around?" Siegfried, the DEA report on Shakarchi Trading still weighing on his mind, tried hard to sound annoyed at the mere suggestion of wrong-doing at Republic.

"Well, no, it's the Shakarchi matter."

"Shakarchi happened to be a client of ours," Siegfried said evenly. "We don't comment on clients, but the Shakarchi account is going to be closed. Anyway, we're not Shakarchi, we're Republic."

"I have some very specific information."

"What?"

"There's a report being passed around."

Siegfried flinched. Passed around? "What kind of report?" It crossed his mind that the *Newsday* reporter might have the same report Peter Samuel had published. If not, Siegfried certainly wasn't about to point it out to him.

"A government report."

"A government report?" Siegfried saw Weiner's eyes widen. "We're not aware of any government report." A lie.

"Well, I've got it right in front of me."

Knut Royce wouldn't provide any details of the report, nor was Siegfried willing to give any ground. They went a few more rounds before Siegfried realized it was useless. "We've got to get this report," an agitated Weiner said when he hung up. "It's got to be a phony." They discussed it for several minutes, until Weiner instructed Siegfried to phone Royce once more to try to learn more about the report: was it an authentic DEA report, or something like the anonymous seven-page document they had unearthed at *Minute*? But it was useless; Royce was playing his cards close to the vest.

"It's them," Weiner said when Siegfried hung up a second time. American Express.

"No, Walter, this is a legitimate reporter," Siegfried said. "This is a guy who checks out. Guys like this don't get bought."

"No, I'm sure of it, they're at it again. They're passing this report around."

As the weekend dawned, Weiner and Siegfried realized they were powerless to stop Knut Royce's piece, whatever it might say. All they could do was wait. All told, it had been a terrible week. First the *New York City Tribune*, then Operation Polar Cap, now the possibility of an article in *New York Newsday*. Safra's men tried to rest that weekend, but were stunned by the appearance of Royce's article Sunday morning. From Republic's point of view, it was worse than anyone could have feared.

"Dirty Money," the tabloid's cover story blared. Inside, Knut Royce broke the surprising news that Operation Polar Cap overlapped with the Swiss-American probe of Shakarchi Trading. "The junction of two major narcotics money-laundering investigations spanning four continents," Royce reported, was a single Shakarchi Trading bank account, No. 606347712, at Republic. It was the very account U.S. authorities had frozen three weeks before. Into the Republic account, as well as accounts at Citibank and Chase Manhattan Bank, a Los Angeles jeweler indicted in the Polar Cap case had allegedly wired drug-related proceeds.

"Federal authorities and a bank spokeswoman say Republic National Bank is not a target of the investigation," Royce noted late in the story. But for Safra's aides, that caveat did nothing to reverse the impression formed by the juxtaposition on the second page of Royce's article, with its headline "Drugs Turn into Gold," and, beneath it, a sidebar profiling Republic and illustrated with a picture of Safra.

Resting at his rented country home in upstate New York, Siegfried was ordered to the bank Sunday morning by Jeff Keil, who read the article at his Brooklyn Heights apartment. Keil was every bit as convinced as Weiner that American Express was behind the *Newsday* story. "This shows you they know how to get at these people in Washington," he told Siegfried.

"Who?"

"Harry." Harry Freeman. "Harry could do something like this."

"Come on..." As always, Siegfried was the skeptic.

"No, they could do it. They're experts at manipulating the media."

At his home in East Hampton, Weiner spent the entire day reading and rereading the *Newsday* story to Safra, who had returned to Geneva. Siegfried and the others worked late into the night preparing a reply for press inquiries that never came. Royce's story stung, but at least no other papers showed signs of following it up.

Newsday's dispatch was, however, reprinted by at least one other newspaper. One convoluted version surfaced the next day in a large Israeli newspaper, the Hebrew-language *Yediot Aharonot*. "The Jewish Billionaire, Edmond J. Safra, Linked to the Laundering of Drug Money," read the headline, which vastly overstated the facts contained in the accompanying article. The Israeli story summarized the *Newsday* piece, focusing on Safra's supposed involvement with drugs. Not until the fourth paragraph did the paper note: "Federal investigators state, however, that neither Edmond J. Safra nor his bank is under investigation..."

In the stories' wake, something approaching hysteria gripped Safra and his inner circle. Weiner hit the phones, calling a number of DEA officials in efforts to find a copy of the agency's report—which he was beginning to suspect might be authentic—and learn how it had leaked to the press. Ultimately he would visit DEA headquarters in Washington three times, never gaining a complete copy of the report and never coming close to identifying the leaker. For the moment, it seemed, their best hope at cracking this latest mystery lay in a hastily arranged scheme freshly sprung from the fertile minds of Stanley Arkin and Jack Palladino.

Washington, D.C.'s power brokers were winding down for the day as Jennifer Taylor strode into the Sheraton Carlton's elegant lobby a few minutes past five o'clock that Friday afternoon. Taylor was petite, thirtyish and, as she glanced about the lobby, the last person anyone would tag as a private detective.

If American Express had gotten to Peter Samuel and the *New York City Tribune*, Arkin and Palladino had agreed that feminine wiles might help them prove it. Taylor's cover, though assembled almost overnight, seemed strong enough. When she passed through New York on the way to Washington, Arkin had laid it out: She was to present herself to Samuel as a free-lance filmmaker, preparing an hourlong documentary on money laundering for the Home Box Office cable network. Both Arkin and Palladino had contacts at HBO—Palladino & Sutherland had provided technical advice to its "America Undercover" series—and a few calls had ensured the necessary backup in case Taylor's story came under scrutiny. When she had telephoned Samuel's home in suburban Maryland, the reporter had eagerly accepted a dinner invitation to discuss her project.

Among the crowds in the Sheraton's busy lobby, Taylor spied Samuel hunched over a small table reading, sprawled amid a pile of his things, umbrella, trenchcoat, satchel. She walked over, introduced herself and led him into the hotel bar, where the reporter ordered a gin and tonic. As Samuel sipped his drink, Taylor regarded him closely. An Australian, he appeared to be in his late forties, with the disheveled air of a harried academic, thinning gray hair, a salt-and-pepper beard and glasses. He wore wine-red polyester pants, a beaten-up leather jacket, and a horrendous madras tie. That Peter Samuel was the weak link in this chain couldn't have been more obvious if the words had been painted on his forehead.

Taylor got right to business. Unveiling her cover story with a flourish, she described her documentary as a "60 Minutes"–style look at drug money entitled "Global Money Laundering and the Halls of Power." Samuel seemed impressed, though he admitted he didn't watch much television and wasn't familiar with HBO. What seemed to get his attention was Taylor's estimate of her budget: $700,000. If Samuel agreed to help on the documentary, she continued, her production company would want to hire him as a consultant. And of course, they would insist on compensating him for his time. She wondered aloud: would one-hundred dollars an hour be enough?

"Yes," Samuel said quickly, though often, he added, he worked for less. Of that Taylor had no doubt.

After listening to Samuel pontificate a bit on drug trafficking, the detective gently steered him toward the real object of her interest: the source of his story a week before, and the DEA report on Shakarchi Trading at its core. "How did you even think to start writing about money laundering, Safra, and the Bulgarian connection?" she asked.

"I can't tell you my source," Samuel said. "I don't even tell my wife my source. But yeah, the DEA report came from my source. Let's just say I got interested because stories are leaked. They get out when disagreements break out between different agencies on how to handle things."

Taylor was trying to delve further into the dynamics of this bureaucratic squabbling when Samuel stopped her. Once again, he expressed his fear at revealing his source's name. "People could get killed," he said.

"Why?"

"Portions of the report reveal the names of cops, of undercover agents, of middlemen informers. I promised my source I would destroy the report. And I did. He should have given me a report with some names whited out, but he didn't."

Samuel hauled out his briefcase and took from it several papers. One by one, he handed them across the table to Taylor. First was a page of the DEA report; it was numbered "Page 6 of 12." There was no mention of Safra. "I don't understand half of this myself," Samuel muttered as he shuffled through more papers. He handed Taylor copies of some DEA cable traffic on the Bulgarians. But Taylor needed more. Over dinner she pumped Samuel again: where could she get a complete version of the DEA report? "There may be more than one way of getting it," the reporter noted between mouthfuls of pepper steak and corn chowder. "But I can't go into that here."

Taylor asked whether Safra was mentioned in the report.

"Yeah, he's in it a lot. He appears to be associated with things through the bank. I was very interested in what the feds have on Safra. I think he's a suspect. I went to some lengths to try and check this out. My strong impression is that he's a suspect, but they have told me there are no charges against him at this time. But they're looking at him. From the report, I can say the feds think he's a crook, but they can't prove it."

After a plate of raspberries and cream and a cup of cappuccino, Samuel repeated his eagerness to help Taylor on her HBO documentary, and they agreed to talk again soon. Before leaving he also offered a cautionary word on prejudging Edmond Safra. "True, Safra and the Shakarchi family have close ties," the Aussie journalist noted. "But this country has a strong ethic. They don't judge people guilty by association here."*

All that spring stories in the Swiss press tracked the investigation of Shakarchi Trading. Republic was mentioned in several, prompting weeks of sleepless nights for Safra and endless hours of useless strategizing for his aides. Lost in the media scramble was the fact that neither Shakarchi nor any of its principals had been charged with any crime. Nor, after the day Jennifer Taylor met with Peter Samuel, was Shakarchi subject to any regulatory action with U.S. or Swiss authorities.

Two days earlier, attorneys for both Shakarchi and Republic, after tallying the moneys flowing through the account frozen at the bank, presented a New York judge with a report showing that four times more money had been imported into the account than out of it, a strong argument that the account wasn't being used for the export of drug money.

---

*During dinner, Peter Samuel says, he grew suspicious of Jennifer Taylor's credentials. "She acted like no other journalist I'd been around in 25 years in the business; no one has ever pumped me that hard for a source," he says, adding that he never got a hint she worked for Safra. "I suspected that she worked for the Bulgarians or the Colombians or the money launderers." Samuel says he was concerned enough that he wrote a letter to the Department of Justice alerting them to Taylor's approach.

The new findings, in fact, were almost exactly the opposite of numbers presented by U.S. Customs, leading Shakarchi lawyers to question whether Customs had somehow reversed their own figures, an ignominious mix-up if true.

Whatever the case, government prosecutors didn't dispute the new figures. On April 6 prosecutors representing the U.S. Attorney's office in Brooklyn quietly dropped their forfeiture action against the Shakarchi account at Republic, unfreezing the account with nary a peep of explanation.

At his condominium in the Connecticut woods, Hank Flynn had stayed busy. He hadn't been thrilled when Arkin cut off his surveillance. But he was still pursuing other leads on Greco, and the following Monday one finally paid off.

Several days earlier, Flynn's search for Giuseppe A. Greco's driving record had revealed a string of tickets and at least one minor accident. Among those records, the only new piece of information Flynn found was a Florida address Greco had once given on an accident form: 19261 Royal Birkdale, in the Miami suburb of Hialeah. Flynn had called a friend in Florida and asked him to check whether Antonio Greco had a criminal record in the state.

That Monday Flynn's friend called back. They were in luck: a check with the Florida Department of Law Enforcement had produced a brief rap sheet, with just a single arrest, no conviction.

"Fedex it to me," Flynn said.

He had the one-page report in Arkin's hands the next day. It read:

DATE REQUESTED
4/10/89

NAME
GRECO, ANTONIO

SEX	RACE	BIRTH DATE	HEIGHT	WEIGHT	EYES	HAIR	BIRTHPLACE
M	W	12/16/39	5'07"	145	BRO	BRO	IT

FINGERPRINT CLASS NO.SCR/MRK/TAT	SOCIAL SECURITY NO.	MISCELLANEOUS
03 TT SR 21 O4	——	SC R FGR
AA 02 16 23 06		

OCCUPATION   ADDRESS   CITY/STATE
————   19261 ROYAL BIRKDALE   MIAMI, FL

AKA   DOB   SOC   SCR/MRK/TAT
GRECO, GIUSEPPE
GRECO, GIUSEPPE ANTONIO
GRECO, ANTONIO GIUSEPPE

ARREST– 1   10/06/82   OBTS NO.–
  ARREST AGENCY-METRO DADE POLICE DEPARTMENT
    AGENCY CASE–156117   OFFENSE DATE-10-06-82
    CHARGE 001-STOLEN PROP-BUY CONCEAL RECEIVE
  JUDICIAL-
    AGENCY-MIAMI SPRINGS POLICE DEPARTMENT
    CHARGE 001-COURT SEQ
      COURT DATA   STOLEN PROP-TRAFFIC
        STATUTE/ORDINANCE-FL812-0191 LEVEL
        DISP DATE-10/28-82   DISP-CHARGE DISMISSED
      PROVISIONS-
          NO INFORMATION FILED

THIS CONTAINS FLORIDA RECORD ONLY. UNKNOWN AS TO
NATIONAL RECORD STATUS.

•••• END OF REPORT ••••

Antonio Greco—no occupation, no Social Security number—had been arrested in Miami in October 1982 for receiving stolen property. The charge, Arkin saw, had been dismissed three weeks after being brought, without any explanation.

It was the first piece of solid evidence they had found on Greco's identity in a month. Excited, Arkin called Weiner with the news, and a question. "What kind of scumbag," he asked the banker, "is American Express using?"

8

M atthew Wolinsky stepped to the window, pulled back the layers of gauze and blackout curtains, and opened it. He leaned far out. Forty feet below, traffic streamed noisily through the Plaza San Martín. Beyond, out in the middle of the great square, rearing above the puttering Volkswagen taxis, the soot and the grime, stood the statue of the nineteenth-century freedom fighter José de San Martín, who along with Simon Bolívar liberated much of South America from Spanish rule in the early 1800s.

The smell hit Wolinsky first, thick and sour, a pungent aroma more like a gas than an atmosphere. He recognized it at once: the smell of rotting fruit on a filthy sidewalk, truck and bus exhaust, hemp and wet newsprint. It was the smell of the Third World, and for Wolinsky it brought back a flood of images from long-ago journeys to places like Bangkok and Upper Volta. It was the smell of Lima, Peru, and Matthew Wolinsky knew, in a strange way, that he was home again.

Wolinsky pulled a chair to the window and brought out his sketch pad. It was more than an hour until his first interview, and he would spend the time sketching the Plaza San Martín into a corner of a small notebook page. One of Jack Palladino's most reliable investigators, Wolinsky had come to Peru on behalf of a man he had never met, Edmond

Safra. The detective had a carrot-red Viking beard and deep creases around his eyes, the legacy of his years as a river guide in the American West. Fifteen years earlier he had enjoyed a short, successful career in New York publishing before chucking it to run rivers and, in off seasons, tour the world as a free-lance travel writer. His articles had appeared in the *Village Voice, Geo,* and *Connoisseur*, among other publications. Fleeing a broken marriage, he had joined Palladino & Sutherland three years earlier and found he had a natural affinity for investigative work.

His first sight of Lima had reminded Wolinsky of all the other first times, in obscure corners of Africa, Asia, and the Middle East. The day before, Monday, April 10, he had flown from Los Angeles to Mexico City and on to Lima. Emerging from the terminal, Wolinsky had hailed an aging taxi, a black-and-white Pontiac LeMans, which drove him into the city through neighborhoods that reminded him of the poorer sections of his native Los Angeles.

Lima, Wolinsky found, spread over a sunbaked plain beside the Pacific, the Andes rising out of sight far beyond the bare brown suburban foothills. As the cab bore him into the city, the people Wolinsky saw were dark-haired and olive-skinned, making him conscious of his red beard and freckles. On every corner, sometimes thronging entire intersections, swarmed Lima's ubiquitous *gambistas*, the black market money-changers who waved down passing cars with a pocket calculator and a tight fist of Inti notes. Beyond the sidewalks, clouds of dust enveloped dark-skinned youths as they deftly maneuvered soccer balls through dirty roadside lots. The sound of bells was in the air, or what sounded at first like bells; it was actually ragged children sitting in the dust, running bottle openers across their wares, warm bottles of Pepsi, Inca Kola and sweet red Kola Inglés.

His hotel, the Gran Hotel Bolívar, sat near the heart of a dense, grimy downtown, several miles inland on the muddy River Rimac. The Bolívar was a grand old pink-and-white colonial, recommended by a friend who had worked in Lima for the Peace Corps twenty-five years before. The lobby had been empty and depressing when Wolinsky dragged himself in that morning, but the staff was bilingual and tolerated the fact that he wasn't. His suite, two rooms for seventy-five dollars a night, was filled with an eclectic mixture of ersatz Louis XIV furniture; the walls sported engravings of homely European women.

The Peru Matthew Wolinsky confronted was a land near collapse, wracked by a growing cocaine trade and brutal Maoist guerrillas, the Shining Path, who had taken to bombing power stations and regularly plunging Lima and its seven million residents into darkness. The country remained achingly poor, its per-capita income only half of Mexico's. Four years earlier a charismatic, thirty-six-year-old European-educated lawyer named Alan García had swept to power, raising hopes that the country's long decline might be reversed. García was the protégé of his ruling APRA party's legendary founder and guiding light, Victor Raul Haya de la Torre, who had died in 1979 at the age of eighty-four without realizing his lifelong dream to see one of his "Aprista" brethren assume power in Lima's ornate Government Palace.

For a time, García had seemed a model Latin American president, imposing strict new economic measures, battling drug traffickers, and refusing to repay Peru's massive international debt on any terms but its own. But in time the country's problems had proven too much for the young ruler. By 1989 García was on the defensive, his Aprista government under attack from all sides. The Lima newspapers Wolinsky saw were brimming with news of García's latest challenge, a bitter power struggle with his chief rival inside the APRA party, the former finance minister Luis Alva Castro.

As he sketched the plaza below, Wolinsky let his mind wander onto the case at hand. He and Palladino had argued again: his boss wanted him to pose as a journalist, and Wolinsky had objected, for he simply didn't like lying. In the end, the two had negotiated a tortured cover that, to Wolinsky's surprise, wouldn't be seriously questioned during the coming days in Lima. He would tell people he was a part-time journalist (true), investigating the source of stories on the banker Edmond Safra (true), for a client interested in doing business with Safra (well, not so true). His task seemed easy enough: to find the source of an article on Safra in a government-sponsored newspaper named *Hoy*. If along the way, he learned anything about the former presidential press secretary Victor Tirado—or, better yet, Tony Greco—so much the better.

Wolinsky had approached the case the way he usually did, phoning friends and friends of friends who had passed through Lima over the years, and inquiring about useful contacts. The notebook in his lap held the resulting six-digit phone numbers of more than a dozen people in Lima, but so far a full day of calls had produced only one hit, a Michael E. Shifter, a Ford Foundation executive who tracked human rights and justice issues throughout South America.

As the time to meet Shifter approached, Wolinsky put down his pen and stood, readying himself for the walk to the Ford Foundation offices. Again he inhaled the thick Peruvian air, and realized, almost sadly, that it seemed neither as pungent nor unpleasant as it had an hour earlier. His nose, Wolinsky decided, was going Peruvian. He only hoped the rest of him would have it so easy.

"Ah, you know your reputation has preceded you," Jonathan Cavanaugh said, extending his hand. "Everyone in Lima is talking about this shady character who is in town, looking to speak with journalists!"

Wolinsky waved for two more Cristal beers. It was the following afternoon, and he had invited Cavanaugh to his hotel's bar after getting his name from a helpful Michael Shifter. A cheery Briton, Cavanaugh published a respected newsletter, the *Peru Report*, and wrote for a number of foreign publications, including *The Wall Street Journal*. He dressed in a black suit and black tie, and carried a stack of papers he put down with great relief.

When the beers came, Wolinsky repeated his cover story and showed Cavanaugh a copy of the article in Mexico City's *Uno Mas Uno* that had cited the Peruvian newspaper *Hoy* as its source. Cavanaugh sipped his beer as he scanned the article, asking a question or two as he read.° Just as he finished, the two were joined by Wolinsky's second guest, Michael Reid, a colleague of Cavanaugh's at the *Peru Report* who also wrote for *The Guardian* of Britain.

"I think this is a red herring," Reid said after reading the article. "I cannot imagine your average Peruvian journalist writing this. We would certainly know any Peruvian journalist who wrote like this, this detailed. It may have been planted by the government—if it did originate here."

Wolinsky asked about *Hoy*'s reputation. "Hardly anyone reads it," Cavanaugh said. The paper had been founded in 1984 to support Alan

---

° Parts of Edmond Safra's hasty investigative effort were a bit slapdash. Wolinsky, for instance, journeyed to Peru never having seen a copy of the July 1988 *Hoy* article, which Safra had possessed for seven months; all he carried was its near-identical reprint from *Uno Mas Uno* in Mexico City.

García's run for the presidency, and its influence had declined with García's popularity. Among Lima's dozen or so major newspapers, *Hoy*, by reputation and circulation, was lodged securely in the lower half. No more than ten thousand people subscribed.

Both journalists chuckled when Wolinsky asked about Victor Tirado. "He's a García fawner," Cavanaugh said. "A big man, fat, would do anything García asked. He used to have a column in *Hoy* until not too long ago. If someone at *Hoy* were asked to write the story, he would be the one. He has the talent; he's the only one at *Hoy* who could wield a pen like that."

A thought crossed Wolinsky's mind. Before leaving San Francisco, Palladino had mentioned the possibility of a second article on Safra in a Peruvian magazine named *Oiga*. Reid vaguely remembered the piece, adding that *Oiga* had a decent enough reputation. As they wound up, Cavanaugh struck a skeptical note about Wolinsky's cover. "You know, none of this sounds very true," he said. "Why would a businessman interested in knowing whether he should continue doing business with Safra or not have someone looking into a two-bit paper like *Hoy*, instead of spending the money to look into Safra himself?" Wolinsky confessed his ignorance and beat his retreat, pleased at his introduction to this strange new world.

Fog was rolling through the streets of Lima the next morning when Wolinsky hailed a Volkswagen cab for the ride to the offices of the magazine named *Oiga*. The cab took him out of the city's pedestrian-choked downtown into a quiet residential section called San Isidro, where the tree-lined streets were dappled in soft light amid the spreading fog. Accompanying him was an interpreter, an English theology student named Rosemary Underhay.

Wolinsky had decided to visit *Oiga* after failing to locate a copy of the *Hoy* article at *Hoy*'s offices. When the cab stopped, he found himself before *Oiga*'s headquarters in a modern, two-story home. Behind a tall iron fence a pistol-toting guard stood in a well-landscaped garden of red, pink, and yellow geraniums. Inside, a clerk quickly found a copy of the article Wolinsky sought. It had been printed just three months before, on January 30, 1989. Wolinsky saw from the accompanying photographs of Safra that he had hit pay dirt. Excitedly he had Underhay begin translating the article right there; as she spoke, Wolinsky scribbled her translation into his notebook.

The first mention of Safra's name came deep into the story; it took Underhay a few minutes to reach it. "Dirty War in the APRA: The File That Did Not Circulate," the headline read. "On Tuesday the 17th [of January], representatives from the Government Palace visited a dozen foreign press correspondents, offering a large sum of money in exchange for the international publication or dissemination of a news item that was given credence by a series of official-looking documents, about the activities of an individual who is a stranger to Peruvian political life. Thus began a new chapter in the sordid battle that President Alan García and the Secretary General of APRA, Luis Alva Castro, have been carrying on for supremacy over the party."

Foreign reporters, *Oiga* asserted, had been offered 200 million Intis—roughly four hundred dollars—to print details from the file. One suspicious correspondent, the magazine said, had questioned the U.S. Embassy about the authenticity of certain documents the file contained. Warned of the inquiry, President García's men had pleaded with the correspondents to return the file, offering an extra 200 million Intis for the files *not* to be published. When the furor died down, none of the information contained from the file was published, but one of the dossiers had fallen into *Oiga's* hands.

Finally the translator came to Safra's name.

"What did the Palace file contain?" the article asked. "The file delivered to the correspondents contained a report on the supposed illegal activities of Edmond Safra, a Lebanese individual who—according to the photocopies submitted by the Palace—acquired Brazilian citizenship and owns a vast financial empire dedicated to the laundering of drug dollars; he also is involved in armaments traffic. It also contained a number of documents on the letterheads of the DEA and the U.S. Embassy in Switzerland to prove Safra's participation in drug traffic and make him responsible for the handling of $45 million, profits from the 'Iran-Contra' operation in which, it is said, Safra participated because he was an old partner of the CIA."

It was familiar terrain, Wolinsky saw, the same charges aired in many of the articles he had read. But why on earth would the government of Peru spread lies about Edmond Safra? *Oiga* had its own theory, suggesting that the scheme was the first of a two-step operation to smear García's opponent, Alva Castro. At a later date, the magazine said, a second dossier was to have been circulated. In it, Alva Castro would be somehow linked to Safra, and thus to a "known" money launderer.

Matthew Wolinsky looked at the photos accompanying the article, and saw they were a collage of articles contained in the Safra dossier. Wolinsky recognized several immediately. Two *Minute* headlines loomed large, as did a copy of the Bern letter. Somehow, Wolinsky understood, the government of Alan García was using bogus material about Safra in an attempt to smear a political opponent, Luis Alva Castro. But why Safra? And why Peru? Excitedly, the detective closed his notebook and headed for the door. This was getting good.*

"It was a pretty amateurish thing," Mike Smith was saying. "The idea was to undermine Alva Castro."

Returning to his hotel, Wolinsky had telephoned Smith, the Lima stringer for the *Washington Post* and *Newsweek*, whose name he had gotten from Michael Shifter. "I don't know how high up the thing went, but probably not too high," Smith said. "It seems that they were aiming for Peruvian writers who worked for the wire services."

The Safra dossier, he continued, "was superficial. The idea was to get it out on the wire and start a chain reaction. I discussed this with colleagues. As far as we know, it was the first attempt to plant a story in the foreign press that was based on dirty politics. We decided to alert members of the Foreign Press Association not to use it, or investigate it thoroughly. And number two, to send a message to the Palace to complain." In time the matter had blown over with little fallout.

Afterward, Wolinsky pondered what he had found. First, in July 1988, an article on Safra appears in the government-backed newspaper *Hoy*. Six months later, in January 1989, government aides reportedly distribute dossiers on Safra to the foreign press. Somehow, Wolinsky saw, the incidents had to be linked. Maybe both episodes were aimed only at embarrassing the political opponent, Alva Castro. Maybe not. At this point, he could only speculate.

The fog was clearing that afternoon as a taxi brought Wolinsky and

* The *Oiga* article wasn't entirely new to Safra's people. Walter Weiner had been faxed the piece, then put it aside, finding it simply too confusing to investigate. Like the *Hoy* article, the *Oiga* piece had never made it into Wolinsky's hands.

his interpreter to the home office of the reporter who had complained to the American embassy about the Safra dossiers, Alberto Ku King, the head of Lima's Foreign Press Association. A smiling Ku King, who headed the local office of the Italian news agency ANSA, met Wolinsky in a small office leading out into a garden. "You are entering a mined area, something very, very dangerous," Ku King said dramatically when Wolinsky explained his mission. "You are carrying cyanide tablets, maybe?" Melodrama appealed to the man, Wolinsky decided, though Ku King otherwise appeared sincere.

"The documents came to me and four other journalists on January 17, 1989, in a secret fashion," Ku King acknowledged. "It came in an envelope, delivered to my door. There was nothing to identify where they had come from. This was the same method with the others as well. The first thing I did was to send these materials to my source at the U.S. Embassy. I asked them whether any of it was true. Within twenty-four hours they assured me they had no such information [on Safra]; they even showed me the reply which they had faxed and which said that Safra was not under investigation. In my opinion, the documents given to me had no substance to them."

The key document, Ku King said, ran four pages and detailed how Safra was ready "to invest $50 million in Peru, to open a bank and have a presence in Peru." It appeared as a cover letter to the other documents, many of them European newspaper articles. "The four-page document was the most important thing in the package," Ku King said. "It was a classified report from the U.S., translated into Spanish. I'd give you the document if I still had it. It was clearly an intelligence document. I recognize that kind of work. It was typical American intelligence, not at all from here."

Wolinsky asked about Victor Tirado.

"You are getting the puzzle together when you mention that name," Ku King said.

And Tony Greco? "Now this name Greco," Ku King said after a moment. "Perhaps one might think this great man, this big, big noise in the financial world, paid for these pieces?"

Wolinsky fought back his excitement. But when he pressed for more on Greco, Ku King declined to elaborate. "It's a high-level fight," he concluded, waving his hand over his head, "and I'm low level. This does not interest me."

It sure as hell interested Wolinsky. Returning to his hotel room, he quickly redialed Mike Smith, the *Washington Post* stringer. Ku King had strongly implied that Smith too had received a Safra file. Smith denied it, but mentioned the name of a low-level government p.r. man who might have been involved in the scheme.

"Who would have been pulling the p.r. man's strings?" Wolinsky asked.

"That would be Carlos Morales, at least back then. But now he is president of Aero Peru, since early this year."

Wolinsky instantly recognized the name: Carlos Morales was one of the men Victor Tirado had named as cohorts of Tony Greco.

The next morning Wolinsky returned to *Hoy*'s offices, in search of the paper's managing editor, who he hoped had higher standards than the other journalists he was meeting at *Hoy*. "Here we do not practice such exhaustive research as you do in the United States," one editor had lectured Wolinsky. "We do not scrutinize as you do. There are no laws here that protect people from press damage. It's practically a custom here to defame people in the press. And if you try to take them to court, the person who does is accused of being against the freedom of the press. Articles which insult people are the most normal thing here. They are like balloons in the air, they just float away."

That morning the managing editor was again out. Instead Wolinsky was introduced to a man named Juan Carlos Reyes, who identified himself as the paper's director of editorial information. Reyes was a short, dark-skinned man "with the narrow, bony and articulated features often associated with various species of rodents," as Wolinsky noted in his report to Stanley Arkin. "Yes, I remember this story," Reyes said, upon seeing the article with the "Pedro Cardozo" byline.* Several people had told Wolinsky the name was almost certainly a pseudonym. "My opinion as a journalist," Reyes continued, "is that someone paid someone here to publish this, because this is not the kind of thing we publish. I am going to start an investigation into this."

Wolinsky wanted to believe the little man was serious, but found something suspicious about his promises. Before leaving Wolinsky

---

* Wolinsky had finally managed to locate a copy of the original *Hoy* article, but only after three hours of digging through Lima's National Archives.

slipped him a hundred-dollar bill to cover his "expenses." "Think we can trust this guy?" Wolinsky asked his translator as they left the office.

"Trust him, I think," Underhay ventured. "Peruvians love this sort of thing, this kind of mystery and the ferreting out of the truth. It's entirely likely that he is sincere, that he does wish to clean up past mistakes or corruption. Wait and see what he comes up with."

Wolinsky was less confident. That day, and all day Sunday, he continued phoning the home and office of *Hoy's* managing editor, but to no avail. Not until the next evening did he hear from Juan Carlos Reyes, when the newspaperman showed up at his hotel. He was buoyant and asked for a beer; Wolinsky ordered some from room service.

His investigation, Reyes announced, was finished. An informant had told him the story of the Safra article. "It was nine o'clock when we were going to put [the paper] to bed, and Pedro Cardozo arrived," Reyes began, recounting his informant's tale. He described Cardozo as an international blackmailer. "He's Mexican. A traveling correspondent.... His method is to find high-level people, all over the world, the super-rich. He likes to find competitive industrialists, confront them with what he knows, and work for the one who pays him the most."

Pedro Cardozo, Reyes continued, paid an editor at *Hoy* fifteen-hundred dollars to print the Safra article. Wolinsky asked him to describe Cardozo. This all seemed too pat. "I remember him. I've seen him two or three times," he said. "He spends a lot of money on drugs and alcohol, dealing with journalists, trying to find out who he can work with." Then Reyes unveiled his proof: a tape recording of his interview with the informant. He inserted it into a recorder, and for the next hour and fifteen minutes, Wolinsky scribbled Underhay's translation of the tape into his notebook.

On the tape, Reyes asked the informant, "Do you remember Cardozo?"

"Who?"

"Cardozo."

"Yeah, I remember him. He looked like a sleuth, a secret policeman. I think he bought some news...."

After the tape had rolled awhile, Reyes disappeared into the bathroom for a moment. Wolinsky and Underhay exchanged skeptical looks. "I think it's a setup," the translator whispered.

Wolinsky politely listened to the rest of the tape, but had already made up his mind he was being conned. By the time he escorted Juan Carlos Reyes from the room, he was laughing at himself for being so easily fooled. Standing with the man on the sidewalk outside his hotel, Wolinsky turned to his translator for one last question. The detective had been reading the works of the Latin American novelist Gabriel García Márquez, and felt swept up in a bit of the "magic realism" of which García Márquez writes.

"Señor Reyes, I have just one final question for you. Do you swear upon your mother's breast that you suckled as an infant that everything you have told us is the truth?"

Reyes looked down, into the gutter.

"Yes," he said, "I would swear on it."

Writing off Juan Carlos Reyes as a would-be con man in search of a quick payoff, Wolinsky returned upstairs and phoned *Hoy*'s offices one more time, attempting to find its elusive editor, a man named Luis Guerrero. To his surprise, Guerrero came to the phone, and invited Wolinsky over. Wasting no time, the detective grabbed his interpreter, hopped into a cab, and was at *Hoy*'s offices within minutes.

Luis Guerrero turned out to be everything Reyes was not: straightforward, well-dressed, sincere. Ushering Wolinsky and his translator into his office, Guerrero explained that he had been named editor of *Hoy* only six months earlier, in October 1988. He knew nothing about the Safra article the previous July, but asked for a day to look into its origins. Wolinsky happily consented, hopeful he was finally on the right trail.

The next evening Wolinsky returned to hear what Guerrero had found. They sat in the editor's office, ignoring a soccer game aglow on the television behind his desk. First, Guerrero said, no one named Pedro Cardozo had ever worked or written for *Hoy*; the name was clearly a pseudonym. The most likely culprit, he said, was a man named Francisco Landa, a close adviser to President Alan García who had run *Hoy* for a time the previous year.

"As far as I can tell," Guerrero said, "this article came from Landa. It was edited by an editor close to Landa. I spoke with this man today, and he said he had no recollection of the article. I find this quite suspicious. What I am trying to find out is how Landa got the article to begin with. I imagine that if the article came from people around Landa, it originated from people in political spheres."

For the first time Wolinsky mentioned that the *Hoy* article had been reprinted in Mexico City's *Uno Mas Uno*. Guerrero's eyes lit up. "Señor Landa has close connections with *Uno Mas*," he said emphatically. "He has often managed to publish articles in both newspapers almost at the same time. I did not know about this in *Uno Mas*, but it definitely leads me to believe that Pedro Cardozo is Francisco Landa. It's his style, this kind of manipulation."

Wolinsky left *Hoy*'s offices in high spirits, wanting to believe he was homing in on the article's source. Guerrero had wanted another day to ask questions, and had invited Wolinsky back the following evening. The next morning Wolinsky tracked down Guerrero's predecessor, a man named Pablo Truel, who had edited *Hoy* at the time the Safra article appeared. Truel, now a functionary at Peru's banking and insurance agency, greeted Wolinsky at his downtown office. A hunched, balding man in a cheap suit, he nodded when Wolinsky handed him the *Hoy* article and said, yes, he knew Pedro Cardozo.

"Señor Cardozo is a contributor to the newspaper," he said. "He is not a journalist, but he contributed articles from time to time. As it says here, this was put together from articles which had appeared in France and Italy. When he brought the article to me, he gave me the originals and then his summary."

Wolinsky was skeptical. Pablo Truel was the first person to assert that Pedro Cardozo was a real person. He asked whether Truel had personally accepted the article for printing. "Yes," he replied, "I accepted the article from Cardozo."

This makes no sense, Wolinsky thought. He asked: wasn't "Pedro Cardozo" a pseudonym?

"No," Truel said, "he is a real person. Pedro Cardozo has been the mayor of the La Victoria section of Lima. If you do not find his name at *Hoy*, then certainly you would find it at the Hall of Records." Wolinsky later tried exactly that, but found that the Pedro Cardozo who had been La Victoria's mayor spelled his name "Cardoso." Pablo Truel, Wolinsky decided, was lying. Disgusted, he rose and cut off the interview after barely fifteen minutes.

That afternoon Wolinsky finally reached Carlos Morales, the chairman of the state-owned airline, Aero Peru. Like Victor Tirado, Morales had served as Alan García's press secretary, and in addition to being named a friend of Tony Greco's, had been identified as the man likely to have "pulled the strings" of government p.r. men passing out dossiers on Safra. Wolinsky sat in the bathroom of his hotel room, cradling an extension, while his translator handled the interview in Spanish. Wolinsky listened as she introduced herself and asked Morales if he was familiar with a man named Antonio Greco.

Morales quickly said, "No."

Underhay pressed. Morales started to say "No" a second time, then stopped. "Well," he said, "I remember the existence of some person with that name, from twenty years ago, connected with the government." Underhay prodded him to say more. "Get in touch with Victor Tirado in Washington," Morales said.

The translator tried again: would anyone in Lima know Greco?

"No, Tirado," Morales snapped. "That's the only one."

Wolinsky wasn't satisfied with his translator's performance—he would have been far more tenacious—but realized it was a moot point. She was all he had. Wolinsky decided that Carlos Morales, too, was hiding something.

That night the detective returned to *Hoy* for a final visit with Luis Guerrero. "There is no Pedro Cardozo," Guerrero repeated when he heard about Wolinsky's latest encounters. "He is absolutely an invention of Señor Landa, and, apparently, he uses this name regularly for articles of this sort. There is no doubt in my mind—after speaking with ten different people—that Landa was responsible for this." Most likely, Guerrero concluded, the article had been printed on orders from the palace. "Either it was a direct order from the government—in which no one would have dared to charge any money—or a third party would have paid Landa to publish it. This, with the corruption we have here and elsewhere in South America, would not be unusual."

All roads, Wolinsky could see, led to the palace. But they were roads the detective would not travel. The next day Wolinsky received orders to pull out of Lima. Stanley Arkin made the decision. As interesting as his information was, Wolinsky's inquiries weren't getting them any closer to American Express or Tony Greco. Arkin was also worried that Wolinsky's questions might be attracting attention in the wrong places. The last thing he wanted while working for Edmond Safra was to have one of his private detectives thrown into some dank Latin American jail.

• • •

Robert Siegfried was in his Park Avenue apartment one Saturday morning when he took a call from an obviously shaken Walter Weiner. "We've got a big problem," Weiner said, speaking quickly, as he did when excited. "We need to get hold of Gershon fast."

Siegfried had never heard Weiner so agitated. "What's the problem?"

"There was something last night on Swiss TV. The nightly evening news. It was some kind of report on money laundering. They don't mention Edmond, but Republic is all over the report. Edmond is in New York. He's having the tape sent over on the Concorde. We're all meeting at Edmond's tonight. Gershon has to be there."

That night Siegfried was the first to arrive at Safra's apartment. Ushered into the living room, he was surprised to see Safra in what passed for casual clothing: gray slacks and an unbuttoned collar, tie loosened. Siegfried realized he had never seen his client in anything other than dark suits and silk pajamas.

Safra, standing quietly with Lily at his side, appeared grave.

"I don't know what we're going to do," he said. To Terry Weiner, who hovered nearby, he said, "Put on the tape."

The first images of the Swiss broadcast flickered on the screen. It was in French, which Siegfried had trouble following. The Washington bureau chief for a Swiss television network, a reporter named Philippe Mottaz, delivered the report, a compendium of much they had seen in previous weeks: Republic and Shakarchi Trading, carefully couched allegations of money laundering, suggestions that both the U.S. and Swiss governments were investigating Republic. When the tape ended, no one spoke. Lily heaved a heavy, prolonged sigh. If it was possible, Safra looked more grave than before. "It's American Express," he intoned. "They've gotten to this reporter Mottaz."

"Look, Edmond, before I say anything, can we run the tape again?" Siegfried asked. "As you know, I don't speak French fluently."

Weiner arrived as the tape was being rewound. Greetings were funereal. "This is terrible," Lily said to Weiner.

"Yes, Walter," Safra said. "What are we going to do about this?"

"Hold on, Walter, we're just about to see the tape again," Siegfried said. As they waited, Safra mentioned that the reporter, Mottaz, occasionally wrote for the *Journal de Genève*, a Geneva paper. An article similar to the broadcast had appeared there that morning. But it would have none of the impact that a broadcast on the evening news promised. The tape finished rewinding, and began again. They watched in silence. When it finished, Weiner agreed with his boss. "They've gotten to this Mottaz."[*]

Minutes later Kekst arrived and was briefed. Lily Safra was growing more upset by the minute. "They're trying to destroy my husband," she said. "You people must do something. You can't let this continue."

"Look, let's not overreact," Siegfried said. "After all, what does the tape show? It addresses a subject—drugs and money laundering and Switzerland. It shows a bunch of thugs. Operation Polar Cap. It shows a bunch of banks, Citibank, everyone. What we shouldn't do, I think, is to assume that this is more of the same."

"No, this is more of the same," Weiner said emphatically. "It's them. They obviously have some kind of operation going on. This could be the tip of the iceberg in Switzerland. They've never really focused on Switzerland, and that bothers me."

"Don't you think we ought to find out where they got their information?" Kekst said. Maybe Mottaz had gotten his facts through government channels that could be pinned down. "We've got to find out what's going on in the DEA," Weiner said. "We've got to get something to show there's no investigation going on here."

But how? The rumors Safra faced were so flimsy they were next to impossible to pin down. Everyone knew how hard it was to prove a negative—that Safra wasn't a drug kingpin—but bureaucracies like the DEA were notoriously tough to budge, especially on such an unusual request.

What Safra needed, it was clear, was for Stanley Arkin and his detectives to force a breakthrough, something that would set the stage for a massive lawsuit against American Express that would end the stinging publicity once and for all. But Arkin's operatives were having little luck. No one knew it better than Arkin himself. Down at his Third Avenue office, the lawyer had decided it was time to quit clowning around and wheel in the heavy artillery.

In certain quarters Joe Mullen is known as "the Love Dick."

An awful moniker, to be sure, but one that accurately portrayed the J.T. Mullen Company's position as one of the country's premier matrimonial detective agencies. In his thirty-five years as a private investigator

---

[*]Later they would realize they were mistaken.

the gruff, white-haired Mullen had been called into the divorce cases of Johnny Carson, Mike Tyson, and Donald Trump, to name a few. His half-dozen young operatives, including his brawny son Tommy and his married daughter Bonnie, specialized in the down-and-dirty tasks that characterized divorce work, especially surveillance and document searches. When Mullen heard that Stanley Arkin wanted him to replace the dogged Hank Flynn on a sensitive case, he could only chuckle. "I eat these ex-FBI guys for lunch," he said.

Joe Mullen was a private eye from the old school, rarely leaving his cluttered, unmarked office in a midtown skyscraper without sticking a snub-nosed revolver in his belt. A Bronx-born Irishman, he had apprenticed himself to a trio of detectives by the time he was eighteen. For years he worked for others, doing it all, bodyguard work, subpoena service and stakeouts, lots and lots of stakeouts, every last one a boring mélange of discarded coffee cups, candy wrappers, and legal pads. He finally started his own agency in 1971 and, charging rates up to $150 an hour, he prospered, bringing each of his five children into the business at various times.

Much of the Mullens' practice was run-of-the-mill divorce work, but from time to time they stumbled onto something interesting, like the case of the two insider traders at a major Manhattan law firm; Mullen had his son Tommy follow the suspects around the city on a motorcycle and pose as a drug dealer to listen in on their sidewalk conversations. Though Joe Mullen was always in touch with the gossip columnists at the *Post* and *Daily News*, the papers never learned of his biggest coups, like the time his men somehow managed to photograph the shoes of a major industrialist and his mistress outside their hotel bedroom—a break that made his client on the case, Stanley Arkin, very happy, and led to a stream of assignments from the lawyer's office.

By the time Arkin called with his latest assignment, Joe Mullen's hair had gone snow white, his kids did most of the street work, and he spent much of his time behind his paper-strewn glass desk, mulling ways to get his colorful life turned into a television pilot or a book. His office walls were lined with form letters from Presidents Bush and Reagan, and he counted G. Gordon Liddy among his best friends. Still, Joe Mullen jumped on Arkin's new case personally. It smelled like something even the Love Dick would enjoy.

As Arkin laid it out, Tony Greco was the key, and they needed more, much more, on the mysterious Italian than Hank Flynn had discovered in over a month of work. Mullen was in Florida when he got the call, taking a few days off at his Key Biscayne condo, and decided to first track down Greco's old address, on Royal Birkdale in Hialeah. Using a reverse directory to pinpoint occupants of surrounding homes, he sent a flurry of calls into the neighborhood. Masquerading as a confused freight forwarder, he asked whoever answered the phone for the address of his neighbor Mr. Greco. Wasn't it 19261 Royal Birkdale? No, came each puzzled response, no one named Greco lived anywhere nearby.

Curious, Mullen snared one of his drinking buddies, a sea captain named O'Neill, and drove over to Hialeah to find the house, which turned out to be in a well-to-do private development called The Country Club of Miami. Mullen was waved through the entrance gate by a security guard. Beyond the guard box, the road crossed the green fairway of a golf course before snaking into a web of streets lined by expensive homes. Greco's address was a Spanish-style ranch house with a meager palm tree out front. A Dodge Aries was parked in the driveway, alongside a white convertible. Children's toys littered the yard. Mullen got out and walked up to the front door and listened. From inside he could hear children playing. More important, he saw that the name on the door wasn't Greco.

Mullen had another trick up his sleeve. He slipped back behind the wheel and drove back to the guard box. Once there, his buddy O'Neill got out and began inspecting the tires, as if he had a flat. Seeing their predicament, the guard came over to help out. As O'Neill pulled the guard over to the far side of the car to inspect the tire, Mullen ducked into the guard box and opened a ledger inside. Sure enough, it held an alphabetical listing of every homeowner in the development. Mullen flipped through it quickly. There was no one named Greco.

A dead end. If Tony Greco had lived in the house, he didn't any longer. Joe Mullen wasn't worried. He had seen dead ends before. And before this case was over, he would see plenty more.

"Be patient, just be patient," Jack Palladino was saying. "Peru, no, we didn't score big. But we learned an awful lot. Eventually when we unmask this whole thing, that stuff'll be valuable. Just be patient. Don't get excited."

Arkin wasn't being paid to be patient. He was getting daily calls from a worried Walter Weiner demanding to know when they would crack this case and end the onslaught of stinging press reports. And every last bit of heat Arkin was taking he passed on to Palladino. When the detective passed through New York on his way to Amsterdam for the second leg of their European investigation, Arkin let him know his patience was running thin.

"True, you couldn't expect too much out of Peru," Arkin told the detective over dinner. "But you know, Jack, a lot of what you gave me is this huge amount of just bullshit. What I need is more focused, much more about what we're after, about what they're doing. I don't need the whole fucking history of the War of the Roses, all the local color, the political shit. I need concrete facts. I need names. I need to know how this guy got to all these reporters."

Palladino was well aware of Arkin's demands. He had purposely scheduled Matthew Wolinsky's Peruvian excursion to coincide with his wife's trip to Australia in order to keep a steady flow of information to Arkin. He was flying to Europe the next day to meet Sutherland, and together, he promised, they would push the Safra case, and push it hard. "Stanley, don't worry, we're going to do it," Palladino assured. "This is like making a cake. It takes time. You don't want to rush it. We'll get the job done, I promise you."

Had Arkin known the truth, he might not have believed Palladino's assurances. What the detective didn't say was that his wife's fragile health was deteriorating. She had called from Australia in tears and begged to be taken off the case. "Jack, I can't do this," Sutherland pleaded. "I want to go home. I want to go to the hospital and find out what's wrong with me!" Even so, Palladino hadn't grasped the gravity of his wife's plight. He was, Sutherland realized, like so many people who never got ill and considered it a character defect in those who did.

Not until Palladino stepped off the flight in Amsterdam did he comprehend how frail his wife had become. "Why are you so thin?" he asked. When they hugged, Palladino's arms embraced skin and bones. Sutherland's clothes were hanging. Her skin was haggard and yellow, and she looked at least ten years older.

"Oh, I can wear anything now," Sutherland joked feebly, but Palladino wasn't laughing. There were deep shadows under his wife's eyes, and the rings were loose on her fingers. They drove to the home of Sutherland's sister, and in a quiet moment, Palladino and his sister-in-law compared notes on Sutherland's health. Both weren't sure she was up to the investigation ahead. Eventually Palladino asked his wife the obvious question. "How in the world are you going to do this case?" he asked. "You look like hell."

"We'll just do it slowly," Sutherland answered. "Piece by piece. But we're going to do it." Palladino wasn't sure, but his wife now seemed determined to follow through. In fact, she had grown mildly excited about the case, and looked forward to seeing Jean Roberto again. If the truth were known, it was the only thing taking her mind off how miserable she felt.

The next morning, Friday, April 21, the two hopped a short flight to Paris. Sutherland had telephoned her translator, Sophie Hardy, from Australia and arranged a dinner with Roberto that evening. They found the French reporter at his desk just as they had left him, smiling and glad to see them. Her cover, Sutherland was pleased to realize, was holding fast. "Well, did you get in touch with your source?" Sutherland asked.

"The source was willing to meet," Roberto said, "but I've had a very difficult time getting through to him." He was traveling constantly, Roberto said, in Europe, the United States, and South America. Sutherland made a note at the mention of South America: it fit the profile they were developing, of a single provocateur—Tony Greco, perhaps—traveling the world, spreading stories.

Leaving *Minute*'s offices, the three strode into a nearby brasserie for dinner. Sutherland was impressed with the degree of subservience Roberto showed his source, unlike many reporters, who privately denigrated their sources. It was as if Roberto were in awe of the person. Sutherland asked whether he planned any more stories on Safra, and Roberto said probably not—not after losing so many libel cases. "I hope Safra goes to jail soon because then I won't have to pay him," he said.

They spent nearly three more hours talking, but learned nothing more about the mystery source. "What the hell is this guy up to?" Palladino asked when Sutherland returned to the hotel room. "I think he's just jerking us around."

"No, Jack, I don't think he's jerking us around," Sutherland averred. "He's awed by this source. I think he's being genuine. This is just one of those cases where it takes some time to get to the source."

The next morning Palladino and Sutherland headed to the southwestern French city of Toulouse, where they hoped to interview the other French reporter who had written about Safra, Jacques Bertrand of *La Dépêche du Midi*. The four-hundred-mile train trip was uneventful, and they took Sunday off, enjoying the sights and sounds of the town the French call "La Ville Rose" for its red-brick buildings. There wasn't much to see: Toulouse, France's fourth-largest city, is draped around a wide bend in the River Garonne, and known more for industry and technology than wine and roses. Plunked down halfway between the Riviera and the wine country around Bordeaux, the best slogan city fathers have come up with to attract tourists is "Gateway to the Pyrenees."

Monday morning Sutherland and a new translator hopped into a cab for the long ride out to *La Dépêche*'s suburban offices. After several minutes, a hunched, bald man stepped out of a nearby elevator and walked over to where Sutherland and her translator waited in the lobby. Jacques Bertrand was around sixty, Sutherland guessed. As she had in Paris and Rome, Sutherland explained her cover in detail, and asked for a few moments to discuss Safra. Bertrand paused and seemed to study her. He pointed at her purse, to a British Airways tag still dangling from it.

"You've been traveling," he said via the translator. Sutherland got the impression Bertrand was skeptical of her story.

"Yes, I've come in from Australia."

Bertrand considered that for a moment, then said he wouldn't be able to meet with Sutherland right away. "I'm going to have to decide whether to talk to you or not," he said. She pressed for an appointment, and after several minutes of hemming and hawing, managed to secure a lunch date for the following day.

"This guy's totally weird—he looks like George C. Scott playing Mussolini," Sutherland told Palladino when she returned to the hotel. "I've got bad vibes about him, Jack."

Palladino decided to take no chances on lunch the next day. His wife had agreed to meet Bertrand at their hotel's brasserie, and Palladino was there thirty minutes early, alert to any other diners who might come in to observe their meeting. Palladino still had no idea what they were up against, and until he did he wasn't taking any chances. At one o'clock, Sutherland walked in with her translator and took a table. She saw her husband off in a corner, but didn't acknowledge him. The bistro was nice and large, with big windows looking out over the picturesque River

Garonne. By one-thirty Bertrand hadn't appeared, and Sutherland was growing impatient. Fifteen minutes later she told the translator they had been stood up.

When Bertrand walked in a few minutes later, a surprised Sutherland had to suppress a wry smile. Wearing a battered trenchcoat, the old reporter took a seat for only a few seconds before rising and walking out of the restaurant. "I'll be back in a moment," he said. Sutherland watched Bertrand make a phone call outside. After a short while, he hung up, stepped back, craned his neck around, and returned to the table. Clearly someone was outside, or at least Bertrand wanted to leave that impression. Fascinating, she thought.

When he returned, Sutherland again explained her cover, though it was clear Bertrand had no interest in her Nugan Hand cover story or anything else Australian. Their conversation was stilted, flowing as it did through the translator. Awkwardly they discussed the *Minute* articles for a few minutes before Sutherland brought the conversation around to her interest in Safra.

"Have you ever talked to American Express?" she asked cheerily. "There seems to be some history there with Safra." It was a natural question: one reporter asking another where to dig for dirt on a common target.

"No, definitely not," Bertrand replied, a bit too emphatically, Sutherland thought. "I have had no contact at all with American Express."

"What should I do in the U.S.?" Sutherland wondered aloud. "Maybe I should go to see American Express." The ditzy blond asking for help from the big, strong French reporter: maybe that would work.

"I don't know," Bertrand repeated. "I have had no contact with American Express."

Sutherland tried another tack. "Do you know anyone with business with Safra that might cooperate with me?"

"No, no one." Bertrand, it was clear, was no one's idea of a conversationalist: why had he agreed to see her?

"Not even an ex-wife?" She smiled.

"No."

"Well, perhaps I'd better stick with journalists awhile. That'll be more profitable than knocking on Safra's door." A little joke. She smiled. He didn't.

"Do you think these allegations will go away?" she asked. "Is Safra in serious trouble? Is his career over?"

"Yes," Bertrand replied gravely. "I think so."

Bertrand produced a folder of articles on Safra. Sutherland was surprised to see a copy of the recent *New York City Tribune* article, which had been published just three weeks before. Reporters in outlying French cities, she thought, don't typically subscribe to obscure American papers.

"How did you get these articles from American papers?" she asked. "Do you have a source there?"

"Yes."

Bingo. Sutherland saw her opening.

"Well, in that case, I'd very much like to talk to him, because he might have information I could use." It wasn't the cleverest of approaches, but she was getting desperate.

"I'd have to contact him to ask," Bertrand replied. "You understand I just can't give you his name."

"Of course I understand. It's one of the basic rules of journalism. How soon could you get in contact with him?"

"I would need two weeks. My correspondents are all over. They move around."

Oh, Sutherland noticed, so now he has correspondents.

Bertrand seemed to be coming out of his shell a bit. He mentioned Safra's corporate jet, something Sutherland had heard about at every stop.

"What does he have that for?" she asked.

"To smuggle money and agents into Lebanon."

This was a new one. "Why do you think Safra would be doing this? Because of his political beliefs?"

"No," Bertrand said scornfully. He rubbed thumb and finger together. Money.

The Frenchman continued. "Safra, you know, is a heavy contributor to the Dukakis campaign." My God, Sutherland thought, nodding in mock reverence, not only is Safra a smuggler and a drug trafficker, he's a Democrat. The interview was moving rapidly from the sublime to the ridiculous.

The lunch hadn't been terribly productive, Sutherland told Palladino when she returned to their hotel room, except for one thing. She pulled out a copy of a familiar-looking graph she had been given in Bertrand's folder. "Look what I've found," she said. It was the same chart they had gotten from Jean Roberto in Paris.

Palladino was satisfied. Here, at least, was proof that the reporters at *Minute* and *La Dépêche* were linked, almost certainly by a single source. The bad news was that Bertrand, unlike Roberto, had been smart enough to clip off the fax telltales from his papers. Even so, if they could somehow identify the person whose slender writing snaked across that chart, Palladino felt sure, they would have the person behind the campaign to ruin Edmond Safra.

Leaving Toulouse the next day, Jack Palladino made a mistake. They were hustling for a train when he asked a receptionist to confirm their hotel reservations in Geneva. It was a small matter, but within hours Palladino realized they had left a trail—a trail someone else could easily follow.

That night they arrived in Geneva late, and didn't check into their hotel, the Ramada Renaissance, until nearly eleven. Sutherland collapsed onto the bed and quickly fell asleep. All told, Palladino thought, she was holding up fairly well.

Palladino was doing some paperwork when the phone rang. He picked it up. "A call for you from the U.S.A.," the operator said.

Palladino waited for someone to come on the line.

Suddenly a male voice said, "Do you know who this is?"

"No," Palladino said.

"This is a friend," the voice said. "Do you speak Italian?"

"No."

"I'll call you back," the voice said.

The line went dead.

Palladino chewed his lip for a moment, then smiled. He sat on the bed and woke Sutherland up. "Well, we got a very suspicious call," he told his groggy wife, recounting the conversation. She, too, broke into a smile.

To both it was clear what had happened. Someone—Palladino was willing to bet it was the mysterious source—wanted them to know they had been discovered. But to Palladino, it wasn't they who had been sighted, but the anonymous caller.

He got more excited the more he talked it through.

"Oh yeah, baby, we've got this guy," he crowed. "We've got him. He can't leave us alone. He's worried. He's got to come out now. Oh, yeah, baby, he's hooked!"

They spent a half hour puzzling through how the caller had found them before Palladino remembered giving their Geneva address to the clerk in Toulouse. No doubt Bertrand had learned their forwarding address, and passed it on to...to whom? Tony Greco? That the caller spoke Italian certainly suggested Greco.

The downside, of course, was that Palladino realized they were now in a race. If Greco, or whoever the anonymous source/caller was, realized who they were, surely he would begin a counterattack. Palladino put himself in the caller's shoes. If he were Greco, he would begin contacting his sources and warning them, in effect, not to talk to strangers, especially a fragile-looking Australian named Sandra Sutherland.

The next morning, Wednesday, April 26, Sutherland dragged herself from bed feeling dreadful. She had no interviews set up, and badly needed to do so before someone beat her to the punch. First she checked in with Sophie Hardy in Paris to see if Jean Roberto had heard from his source. Nothing.

Picking up a new translator, Sutherland made her first stop that morning at the office of *Le Courier*, a medium-sized paper that, along with many of the Geneva papers, had been picking up the stories on Republic's links to Shakarchi Trading. The *Le Courier* reporter was out, so Sutherland headed for the nearby office of *Tribune de Genève*, another paper that had printed Shakarchi stories. There she was given the name of a reporter named Pascal Auchlin, whom she phoned and arranged an appointment with the next day. The day's third strike was at *Noticiero*, the tiny Spanish-language newsletter that had published a story on Safra's alleged drug ties in February. Sutherland taxied deep into Geneva's suburbs to find its address, which turned out to be a bleak housing complex. She tramped up to the ninth floor, walked down a corridor smelling of urine, and knocked at an apartment. No answer.

The day was a waste. Sutherland had just returned to her hotel room and collapsed on the bed when the *Tribune* reporter, Pascal Auchlin, telephoned to change their appointment. Auchlin suggested having lunch on Friday with a reporter named Maya Jurt, who, he said, knew a great deal about Safra; Jurt, in fact, had been the reporter to break the story of Safra's private jet and its supposed use in the Iran-Contra scandal. Then, abruptly, Auchlin changed tack, asking Sutherland whether she knew any other American reporters in Geneva.

"No," she said. "None."

"Did you travel from Australia alone?"

"Yes." Sutherland realized her cover was coming under scrutiny.

"I've received information," Auchlin said carefully, "that some American journalists are coming to Geneva. Are you traveling with them?"

"No."

"I've heard they may not be journalists at all. But maybe agents. With the CIA."

"Oh, well, that's quite possible," Sutherland said, feigning ennui. "I've heard the CIA often uses journalists as cover. It's quite common." She tried to twist the conversation around onto itself. "You know, I've talked to two journalists who've used an American source on this story, who may be a journalist or a pseudo-journalist. Do you know who that might be?"

"No," Auchlin said. "My source is different."

Neither Palladino nor Sutherland gave the conversation too much thought. Bone tired, Sutherland ordered room service and settled in for the night. A bit later, the phone rang again. Sutherland picked it up.

A deep male voice said, "I don't speak English. May we speak Italian?"

"Yes," Sutherland said, switching languages. She realized it must be the caller Palladino had heard from the night before.

"I'd like to meet you," the voice said. "I'm a friend."

"Oh, I'd be delighted," Sutherland said cheerily. "Where are you?"

"I'm not very far away. Can we meet tonight?"

"No, we just got in. I'm very tired. Can we meet tomorrow?"

The voice said he would telephone at nine the following morning and hung up.

"I bet it's Greco!" Palladino exclaimed when she put down the receiver. He began pacing up and down the room. "I think the guy's desperate. He's on the hook. I think he's reckless. This is the way he's gotta be! He's unraveling. We're getting close, we're getting close! He's stepping out from behind his cover!"

Palladino put his weary wife to bed and headed down to the lobby to walk off his excess energy. Once there, he began to choreograph how they would meet the caller the next morning. Janitors were buffing the lobby floor as Palladino nervously paced its length, working out where Sandra would sit, where Greco would sit, where he could stand and secretly photograph them together. He would pose as a tourist, Palladino decided, and photograph the two as they sat at a small café area at one end of the lobby. The area seemed to have good acoustics, for Sutherland would have to wear a hidden recording device, something Palladino never traveled without.

Well after midnight, he left the hotel and walked out along the deserted lakeside. Only after some time did he ask himself the obvious question: what if it wasn't Tony Greco? What if it was someone else entirely, or if Greco sent an intermediary? What would they do then?

All the next morning Palladino anxiously brushed off calls from his San Francisco office, trying to leave the phone line open for a call from the source. By a quarter to ten Sutherland was getting angry. By ten she had given up; she could have kicked herself for turning down the invitation to meet the night before. Whoever had called was playing with them, pure and simple, and it left both of them irritable.

In New York, Stanley Arkin followed Palladino and Sutherland's misadventures with some bemusement. The anonymous calls clearly indicated they were applying pressure to Greco, or to whoever was spreading the stories about Safra. "The more we pick on this fucker," Arkin told his assistant Jeffrey Kaplan, "the more nervous they get in New York. And that filters upward."

However annoyed, Sutherland kept an appointment later that morning to call Jean-Claude Buffle, the reporter for the Swiss magazine L'Hebdo, whose name they had received from Jean Roberto in Paris. To her surprise, Buffle sounded warm, charming, and responsible, not at all what she had expected. She mentioned Roberto, and Buffle acknowledged having gotten material from the French reporter. "He and I are on opposite ends of the political spectrum, though," he cautioned. A bit boldly, Sutherland brought up American Express. "American Express hates Safra," Buffle said. "High officials there will tell you awful things about him." Sutherland didn't press, but realized she would want more time to talk with Buffle. They set a meeting at the United Nations press gallery the next day.

Friday morning Sutherland woke in tears, her fatigue so complete she could barely drag herself from the bed. "Oh, Jack," she said, "I can't do this anymore." Palladino could see it was true, but gently encouraged his wife to try and make it one final time. Friday promised to be the busiest day of the investigation so far. Just once more, Palladino urged. One more day, and they would have the weekend to relax. Sutherland pulled herself from the bed, dressed, and tried to concentrate on the work at hand.

At eleven-thirty she met the *Tribune* reporter, Pascal Auchlin, in the lobby for the drive to Maya Jurt's home, which was hidden down a narrow lane beside green pastures on the outskirts of Geneva. Jurt, fortyish, with shoulder-length brown hair and a brisk, acidic manner, welcomed the pair at the door, and sat them at a sunlit table in her kitchen. Though the atmosphere was cordial, Sutherland immediately sensed suspicion in the air.

Her instincts were dead-on. Before she could explain her cover, Maya Jurt brought up the question of her identity. "I've received a call from a source I trust," she said, "who has advised me not to meet with you. The source wouldn't say why, but was extremely angry that I planned this lunch. I don't take kindly to being told whom I should or should not see. I told the source I was determined to see you and see what you had to say."

Pascal Auchlin wondered if Sutherland had traveled from Australia alone. Yes, she responded, she had flown to Europe on Qantas April 14. Auchlin then surprised her by asking if she knew anyone named Palladino. "I do," Sutherland said, feigning anger. "But that's personal." Maya Jurt, clearly suspicious, weighed in again. Was she, Jurt asked, working for American Express, the CIA, or Edmond Safra?

"No," Sutherland said emphatically, realizing she needed to get the interview on track before it collapsed under the weight of the two reporters' interrogation. Mustering some anger, she turned to Jurt and mentioned the two strange calls she had received. "There is no doubt that the source you are protecting is the person who is threatening me with anonymous calls," she said. "I think I have a right to know, at least, how concerned for my own safety I should be." But Jurt wouldn't rise to the bait; she insisted that Sutherland had nothing to fear from her source.

Sutherland parried, asking whether Jurt's source worked for a government. "Not for a government," the reporter replied, "but for something that could be likened to a government." Sutherland wondered if the description could be applied to American Express. She tried for more, asking what languages the source spoke, but Jurt cut her off. "One protects a source come what may," she snapped, "however sympathetic you may feel to someone else."

Sutherland tried a different approach, mentioning Jean Roberto's story that his American source had been swindled out of millions by Safra. Jurt snorted derisively. "I can tell you something," she said emphatically. "That is invented. He does not exist." Sutherland thought: How could she be so sure?

Later, after a strained lunch spent evading more questions, Sutherland told the pair she believed all the Safra materials circulating among European journalists had come from a single source—an American source of suspect motivation. Jurt pondered the statement. "I don't know," she said. "I am going to get to the bottom of all this. If that is true it is very, very serious."

But Maya Jurt did know. Sandra Sutherland wouldn't realize it for months, but she had just come as close to solving the mystery of the campaign against Edmond Safra as she ever would.

"I'm convinced Maya didn't believe me, Jack," Sutherland told her husband when she returned to the hotel. "This could be all over. Our cover is in deep trouble. She'll tell everyone. She's sharp. She knows."

"No, no, she believed you," Palladino assured his distraught wife. "You're a decent person who's absolutely credible. You've done this before. You'll make it. You always make it. It'll work out. It always does."

To himself, though, Palladino wasn't nearly so certain. Maya Jurt obviously had profound doubts about Sutherland's identity. And given the speed at which information ricocheted through the informal network of European journalists, it was only a matter of time before Jurt's doubts spread. His wife's cover, it was clear, was crumbling, and with it, Palladino realized, their whole investigation was slipping away.

"God, I wish I could just throw this whole cover story off and tell this Maya Jurt the truth," Palladino seethed. "The most powerful weapon we have here is the truth, and we can't use it. I want to go, 'Listen, bitch, this is what's happening. Here's twenty-seven facts to go ask your fucking source. You want to be Woodward and Bernstein? *Here's* your story.'"

But of course they couldn't do that. Their only course of action was to stick to the cover story until it was in shreds. At mid-afternoon Sutherland took what was left of it to the United Nations, where she had arranged to see the husband-and-wife publishers of *Noticiero*, the Spanish-language newsletter, at four. When she finally met Alberto and Louise Dufuy, Sutherland saw immediately that the two were way out of their depth. Alberto was young and plump, with a wispy mustache and little English; Louise was short and vivacious, spoke English, and, as they took seats in a bar area, was the last person Sutherland would expect to have published lies about Safra.

The Dufuys' publication, *Noticiero*, aimed at Switzerland's Spanish community, had published a retraction after Safra's lawyers had complained about the story. "Our information is essentially the same as what *Minute* had," Louise Dufuy said. "But we're very afraid of being sued."

"The *Minute* and *La Dépêche* stuff is also very similar," Sutherland noted. "They've told me things that make me believe their sources are the same person. If you're being accused of providing the same information, maybe you've got the same source."

Louise Dufuy turned to her husband and spoke for several moments in Spanish. Sutherland knew a word or two of the language, but couldn't follow their conversation. "Our source is a Latin American journalist," Louise Dufuy said after a moment. "Perhaps his source is the same as theirs. I'll ask him."

The Dufuys spoke for a bit longer in Spanish. Then, at one point, Sutherland clearly heard the name "Victor."

Victor? Victor Tirado?

A blitz of ideas raced across Sutherland's mind: Were Tirado and Tony Greco working as a team? Was Tirado working as some kind of bizarre triple agent?

She was still mulling the possibilities when Jean-Claude Buffle walked up. The Dufuys' tardiness had run the interview up to the five o'clock appointment Sutherland had set with the reporter from *L'Hebdo*. The couple excused themselves and left, explaining they had little else to say, but assuring Sutherland they would get back to her on the question of their source's information. They never did, however, and Sutherland would never follow up on the lead.

Sutherland's disappointment deepened with Buffle's first words. "I'm sorry," he began, taking a seat, "but I won't talk to you. I was not honest with you yesterday," he said. "Someone had called me and warned me not to talk. And someone else called me today. I trust both of them. I'm sorry, I would love to meet you socially, but I won't talk to you about this matter. I don't know you."

"Well, then," Sutherland said, playing her "threatened female" card, "can I ask, just for my peace of mind, whether I have anything to fear physically from this person?"

"I'm sorry," Buffle said. "I won't talk."

Afterward Sutherland was left deeply frustrated. Buffle's rejection meant their worst fears were coming true. The time they had left on the case could well be measured in days, if not hours.

Sutherland returned to the hotel to find the one upbeat piece of information she received all day. At seven-thirty Sophie Hardy had called from Paris to say that Jean Roberto's source was due there on Monday and wanted to meet. It was at least the third time they had heard a similar promise, however, and neither Sutherland nor Palladino was terribly enthused by the news. Palladino's spirits were also low; he had spent the day wandering through downtown Geneva, waiting for a photo shop to make copies of surveillance photos of Tony Greco sent from New York. At this rate, it appeared, they wouldn't need them.

"This guy Greco has stuff going that is killing us," Palladino fretted. "He never turns up. He teases us with phone calls. He knows we can't tell people the truth, so he spreads this CIA bullshit. We're being hoisted by our own petard. We really are. And I'm helpless to do anything."

That night, as the two hashed through the situation, Sutherland was surprised to take a call from Maya Jurt, who apologized for the brusque interrogation at lunch. She had talked again with her source, she said, who had repeated the claim that Palladino and Sutherland were members of a team of three CIA agents who had come to Geneva after a stop in London. But, Jurt went on, she simply couldn't believe Sutherland worked for the CIA. "My source is a media person," Jurt explained. "He has been working so hard and so long on Irangate. Now they are all getting paranoid. I'm the only one who's not."

Media person? Irangate? Sutherland knew that the bulk of Jurt's reporting had centered on Safra's connections to the Iran-Contra scandal. But this was the first suggestion that a "media person" working on "Irangate" might be spreading the stories about Safra. "I could be wrong about you," Jurt said, "but I have been a journalist for twenty years and I don't think so. If I am, it would be the best cover the CIA ever had."

When Sutherland hung up, she was relieved that her cover wasn't totally blown, but startled at the mention of "three" CIA agents disguised as reporters. "And Jack, they knew I stopped in England," she said. "What the hell is going on?"

Palladino saw it, too. How had the source known of his identity, or far more worrisome, about three detectives? Mentioning three detectives clearly suggested the source knew about Jennifer Taylor's brief mission to Washington, or possibly about Matthew Wolinsky's work in Peru. There was only one place that held so much information.

"Holy shit, Jack," Sutherland said. "There's got to be a source inside Republic."

Palladino saw it, too. It wouldn't be the first time someone inside a client firm had leaked information about their activities. "We're close, but we're in trouble here," Palladino told Arkin's assistant Jeffrey Kaplan in a midnight phone call to New York. "There is a real possibility there is a leak out of your organization. It sounds like someone who had a glance at our plans, but who doesn't know the whole story. Jeffrey, we have to entertain the idea that someone high up in the organization is leaking. You've got to get to the client right away. This is something that imperils our whole situation, maybe even our safety."

Kaplan was skeptical. "Jack, I really, really doubt that. This is strictly on a need-to-know basis. This is Stanley talking to Safra personally. The reports aren't being handed around."

"Well, something's going on," Palladino retorted. "Someone overheard something, or saw something."

When Jeff Kaplan brought the matter to his boss's attention, Arkin had to laugh. "Jeffrey, don't you see, this is terrific," he said. "Who gives a shit if there's a leak? Is there one? Probably. Was it deliberate, malicious? No. They talk too much over there. And I don't mind one bit."

At this point, Arkin reasoned, it might actually help if Jim Robinson knew Safra had detectives crawling all over Europe. He had taken to telling Jeff Keil how well the investigation was going, and how often Robinson's name was coming up. He knew Keil and Peter Cohen were best friends, and he hoped Keil might unwittingly pass on their suspicions. With any luck, the message would get back to Robinson and scare the hell out of him. When the time came to confront American Express with their findings, it would only make Arkin's job easier.

The following evening, having flown on to Rome for a second run at *L'Espresso*, Palladino again phoned Jeff Kaplan. He was sick of being toyed with by Tony Greco or whoever it was, and he was overdue to see a client in Copenhagen on a money-laundering case. "What do you want us to do, Jeffrey?" Palladino asked. "We can wait a week. But I don't know. We could be wasting our time. I say there's no more than a one-in-ten chance this source shows up in Paris."

"I agree. I think he's just playing games with you," Kaplan said. "Could Sandra stop in Paris on the way back, though, and try and make contact?"

"Yeah," Palladino said. "That'll work."

And so Palladino flew on to Copenhagen, leaving Sutherland to sleep most of the day in a vain attempt to gather her energy for another day of work. Monday morning she went to *L'Espresso*'s offices, where, trying to pry information out of one of the magazine's reporters, she received nothing more than a lecture on Italian "standards" of journalism. "You should relax—who cares if these things about Safra are true or not?" a reporter told her. "Here in Italy, you know, we don't take things so seriously."

Fatigued and depressed, Sutherland returned in defeat to Paris, where she checked in with Sophie Hardy and found, as expected, that Jean Roberto's source again hadn't shown. Afterward she boarded the long flight back to San Francisco, convinced her investigation was a shambles. She had no way of knowing, of course, that three thousand miles away, in the streets of New York, the odd case of Edmond Safra was about to be cracked.

9

Wﾗe've got some stuff," the Garbage Man was saying. "And I think
we've finally got a base hit."

In those few words Hank Flynn sensed that he might at last have
something solid on Tony Greco. Flynn had been disappointed when his
surveillance duties ended, but he still had a few leads to follow. Unfortunately, they were all garbage—literally.

At Stanley Arkin's direction, Flynn's operatives had swooped into
Staten Island on three occasions and grabbed bags of the Greco family's
trash. Among the discarded Kleenex and cereal boxes they were looking
for something—anything—that would tie Greco to the Safra articles or
American Express. On two previous attempts Flynn's men had found
nothing of use in Greco's trash. But now the Garbage Man, the former
New York cop Flynn had running the detail, said he had hit pay dirt on a
third try.

An hour later, Flynn eased his gray Saab off the West Side Highway
onto Manhattan's Riverside Drive and saw his man standing on the corner they had established as a rendezvous. Flynn pulled into a gentle
U-turn and parked behind the man's car. After talking shop for a minute
or two the Garbage Man walked to his car trunk, unlocked it and triumphantly lifted out two large yellow trash bags brimming with the
Greco household refuse.

Flynn understood the man's pride, however comic. Stealing garbage not only wasn't a pleasant job, it was legally tricky as well. Under New York law, Flynn's men couldn't walk onto the Greco property to snatch trash; that was trespassing. Nor could they pay off a garbage man. That was probably illegal, and it risked exposure. The Greco family's trash cans, to Flynn's irritation, were usually located in their driveway, on the property, where garbage men picked it up. Given those impediments, Flynn would later say he didn't know exactly how his people had gotten their hands on Greco's garbage. In truth, he probably didn't want to know.

Returning to his Connecticut condominium with the trash bags, Flynn went right to work. He took out a clear plastic drop cloth and spread it over the living room's beige pile carpeting. Then he dumped the contents of the garbage bags onto the drop cloth. Snapping on a pair of rubber gloves, Flynn switched on his stereo—he favored jazz and classical music for garbage work—got down on his hands and knees amid the trash, and began the difficult, smelly work of sorting through it all. At least his men had taken out the grapefruit rinds and coffee grounds and allowed what remained to dry. There was nothing worse than working with wet trash.

Flynn first sifted out some postcards, the biggest pieces of paper in the batch. Immediately he could see his man had been right about hitting pay dirt. At a glance, Flynn could see all the postcards had been sent from foreign venues. Tony Greco, his garbage said, was a seasoned international traveler. Flynn shook free a postcard Greco had sent to someone in Italy, apparently a family member, from Kowloon, Hong Kong. It was in Italian, which he couldn't read, but he noticed the postmark: April 4, 1975. Curious. Why were the Grecos throwing out old mail? Maybe Mrs. Greco was cleaning house.

There were two other postcards, one of Times Square, the other of Momotombo Volcano in Nicaragua, each of which Greco had written in Italian to people in Italy; neither, apparently, had been sent. A fourth postcard, in illegible Italian, had been sent to a friend in Italy from Bangkok. Flynn noticed the date again: October 20, 1975.

Flynn fished out an envelope. It was addressed to "Mr. Antonio Greco, 28 Langley Dr., Wan Stead E11, London, England," sent by an Amy Greco in North Miami Beach, Florida. It carried a 1979 postmark. So Greco had lived in Europe in the late 1970s. Flynn figured Amy Greco for a daughter, maybe a sister.

Next the detective took out the checks: personal checks and deposit slips, all of them blank, many of them ripped in two. One by one, Flynn pieced them together, and the results told him even more about Greco's life. There was half a blank check under the name Antonio G. Greco from McLachlen National Bank in Washington, D.C., dated December 7, 1977. Had Greco lived in Washington, too? Another half check under Greco's name, undated, from Valley Bank and Trust Company, Springfield, Massachusetts. Another from the Bank of Hallandale in Hallandale, Florida. And two from New York City, one with an address on East Fifty-sixth Street, the other on East Sixty-sixth Street. Flynn noticed that both addresses were in expensive Manhattan neighborhoods. Again he wondered how Greco made his money.

Flynn counted a total of twenty-one business cards amid the trash littering his living room carpet. Many were from the New York area—a Brooklyn gunsmith, a Manhattan art gallery, a New Jersey electronics store—but several were from south Florida. Another half-dozen cards came from Barcelona, Spain, and a smattering of others from all around Europe. A restaurant in Düsseldorf. A lawyer in Rome. Some type of corporate card from Milan. A restaurant in Nice. Flynn's head fairly spun at all the locations.

As interesting as the cards were, the detective could tell the most valuable information would come from the credit card receipts. They were ripped up, sometimes in tiny scraps, and it took awhile for Flynn to piece them together. But what he found was golden.

Tony Greco had been in Lima, Peru, just two months before. Flynn gently taped together a receipt that showed Greco had used an American Express card to pay a bill at Cesar's Hotel in the Miraflores section of Lima on March 3, 1989. On February 3, a month earlier, he had used the same card to pay a bill at the Restaurant Valentino in Lima, and at the Restaurant Costa Verde in Lima for February 27 and 28.

There were other restaurant receipts from Staten Island and Manhattan as well as records of two airline tickets Greco had bought from New York's JFK airport to Barcelona. Most interesting of the rest was a partial receipt from "Rodier Airport Hall, Orly Aerospace," which might refer to the Paris airport. Flynn couldn't make out a date.

There were other things in the trash that might have interested Hank Flynn, including what appeared to be a wedding picture of Greco and his wife. But Flynn didn't waste time on them for the moment.

Jumping to his feet, the detective strode to the kitchen to call Stanley Arkin's office. For once, he had good news.

In the fifty-six years since his birth in Beirut, Edmond Safra will probably remember the first week of May 1989 as one of the lower points in his life. On Monday, May 1, a Lebanese magazine named *Alkifah Alarabi* published an article on the downfall of Adnan Khashoggi, whom it linked to money-laundering activities. In an aside, it noted that Khashoggi was friendly with both Edmond Safra and Mohammed Shakarchi, then concluded: "It is expected that the U.S. Justice Department will issue a warrant to arrest these two partners of Khashoggi's momentarily."

Two days later Robert Siegfried stepped out of his office and took a call from a Republic executive in Florida. A newspaper in Fort Lauderdale had printed a strange article on Safra, the banker said, and he wanted to fax it up to New York. When a secretary handed Siegfried the article from the *Fort Lauderdale Sun-Sentinel*, he could see it was more of the same *Minute*-style disinformation.

Under the headline "Congress Has Barely Begun to Scratch Criminality in the Iran-Contra Mess," a syndicated columnist named Cody Shearer had written about the murdered French playboy Glenn Souham in an article that bore all the hallmarks of the anti-Safra campaign. Attributed to "members of French intelligence," Shearer's column repeated many of *Minute*'s charges: Safra and the CIA, money laundering, Mafia; Shearer covered all the bases. "Now they're starting to move into the United States!" Walter Weiner fumed when passed the article.

All night and into the next day Siegfried scrambled to gain a retraction before Shearer's column could be picked up by other newspapers. But the Fort Lauderdale paper wouldn't print a retraction unless Shearer's Washington-based syndicate did so first. It took hours to locate the syndicate and track down Shearer, who was unaccountably hostile. A conference call of Safra's advisers was convened the next day, and Bill Rogers calmed everyone, promising he would get the retraction in a day or two and they could forget the whole matter. And he did. The correction, published the following Tuesday, noted that any inference that Safra was involved in money laundering was "unjustified and false and Cody Shearer regrets making those inferences." Safra, for once, was pleased.

But before Safra's men could get the first inkling of where the Shearer article had come from, they were faced with the loudest broadside yet in Switzerland. That Friday, May 5, Jean-Claude Buffle, the reporter they knew had been in contact with *Minute's* Jean Roberto, weighed in with a long piece mentioning Safra in the magazine *L'Hebdo*. There, beside still another reprinting of the Bern letter, Safra and Weiner focused on five key paragraphs:

The controversy around Safra rests on the following facts. On January 17, 1988, *L'Espresso*—citing the Italian financial authorities—alerts that the banker was suspected, in 1957, of being involved in morphine-base traffic. But on January 31, in the same weekly, an aide to Edmond Safra formally denies the accusation. According to [Safra's lawyer] Jean-Pierre Jacquemoud, the real suspect was a namesake of the banker.

Two days earlier, on January 29, 1988, the American embassy in Bern sent to Vienna a letter suspecting a link between Edmond Safra and the Irangate scandal. We reproduce this letter above.

On July 4, 1988, the Peruvian daily *Hoy* reported, in an article about Safra, that: "Everything seems to indicate" that the American Drug Enforcement Administration "has opened eyes and ears on Safra and his banks." Jean-Pierre Jacquemoud answers that Edmond Safra is not the object of any inquiry from anybody.

On January 17, 1989, several press agencies announced from Lima that a warning against Republic National Bank of New York and against Safra was addressed by Interpol to the Peruvian authorities. According to this warning, the bank and its chairman would try to take control of drug money passing in transit from Latin America to the U.S. and Europe.

Finally, on May 2, Cornelius Dougherty—spokesman for the DEA in Washington—confirmed to *L'Hebdo* the existence of the warning—underlining that it came from Interpol and not from the DEA itself...

An outraged Walter Weiner fired off a call to the American embassy in Bern, demanding to know how, in another section of the article, they could say Safra's purported involvement with the Iran-Contra scandal was not a closed issue; he had an official letter saying so. An embarrassed embassy spokesman insisted he had been misquoted. The real problem, though, was *L'Hebdo's* claim that a DEA spokesman had confirmed the existence of a warning about Safra cornering the South American money-laundering trade. Irate, Weiner sent Bill Rogers to DEA headquarters in Washington, and in a week he managed to secure an official letter denying that any such confirmation had been issued. "Please be advised that the DEA knows of no warning by Interpol such as described by *L'Hebdo*," a deputy DEA administrator, Thomas Kelly, wrote Rogers.

The letters, however, had little effect on *L'Hebdo*. No matter how much Safra insisted, the Swiss magazine wouldn't grant a retraction. Worse, as the dust settled on one of the most tumultuous weeks of the spring, Safra and his people still hadn't the first clue where any of the latest three articles had come from.

In New York Joe Mullen's detectives were getting nowhere fast.

They had checked and rechecked every address they had for Tony Greco going back twenty years, in both Florida and New York, then mailed requests for forwarding addresses. Taking those addresses, they used reverse directories to locate phone numbers of nearby addresses, then sent ruse delivery calls raining down on those and every other home in the surrounding neighborhoods. They obtained copies of Florida driver's licenses for both Greco and his wife, as well as his wife's learner's permit in New York. They ran checks to see if Greco had been arrested in New York, and found nothing. None of it led anywhere.

Mullen took Hank Flynn's trash bonanza and followed up every blank check the former FBI man had found. Ruse calls were placed to each of the banks, and in every case Greco's accounts were long closed. Mullen even had a handwriting expert examine the writing on all the Greco documents in their possession; all the expert could say was they had all, in fact, been written by the same person.

Frustrated by the scant paper trail, Mullen was itching to restart a surveillance of Greco's home. He could see that the easiest—maybe the only—way to break the case was to follow the leading suspect, wherever he went, anywhere in the world. "We do an awful lot of surveillance, Stanley," Mullen told Arkin. "I mean, it's what we do. My guys aren't going into the neighborhood with suits and ties. My guys go in baseball caps, jeans, and sweaters. They can look like construction workers, any-thing."

But for the time being, Arkin wasn't biting. He had been embar-rassed by Hank Flynn's earlier frustrations, and wasn't at all ready to have it happen again.

• • •

On Monday morning, May 8, a week after her return from Europe, Sandra Sutherland was puttering amid the Italian pottery of her San Francisco kitchen, glad for the time to rest her aching body. Around ten she was surprised to take a call from her sister Heather in Amsterdam. "I think you should know, something's happened," her sister said.

"What?"

"Your translator Sophie called. The source was in Paris last night. Sophie said, 'Where's Sandra? We're about to go to dinner.' Then she actually put the source on the phone."

"Oh, my God. What did he sound like?"

Heather thought for a moment.

"Pretty sleazy. He sounded like someone out of a bad movie. He spoke English with a fairly strong accent."

"Did it sound more Italian or Spanish?"

Hispanic, Heather thought, but she couldn't be sure.

The next morning Sutherland got through to Sophie Hardy in Paris. Yes, the translator excitedly confirmed, she had met Jean Roberto's source Sunday evening. The man had introduced himself only as "Jaime," and said he was a journalist from Santiago, Chile, though he said he lived some of the time in the United States. He would give no other information.

Sophie Hardy described "Jaime" as medium height, stocky but not obese—not Victor Tirado, Sutherland thought—with medium brown hair, about forty years old. She said there was something seedy about him. "He was kind of an Al Capone-y man," Hardy said, by which Sutherland understood that "Jaime" came across like a gangster. "Jaime" had taken her to dinner at a Chinese restaurant on the Champs-Élysées, where he had intently questioned her about Sandra Sutherland. But the translator, who didn't know Sutherland was a detective, had insisted she knew nothing. Eventually, "Jaime" had become so upset by Hardy's denials that he left the table and stormed from the restaurant.

Sutherland wouldn't make it to Paris to fully debrief her translator for nearly a month. Once there, she laid before Hardy, one by one, photographs of several Latin American men.

Could she identify Jaime?

When Sutherland flipped down a photo of Victor Tirado, Sutherland shook her head. "No, not him," the translator said. "He's much too fat."

Then Sutherland laid out a surveillance photo of Antonio Greco. Hardy's reaction was immediate.

"Yes!" she squealed. "Yes! That's him!"

Far from waning, European media interest and rumors about Safra intensified in the wake of the story in *L'Hebdo*. Within days Robert Siegfried took a call from a Swiss journalist named Yves Lasseur, who explained that he was making a documentary about money laundering for a television news magazine named *Le Temps Présent*. Lasseur, Siegfried learned, was a colleague of Jean-Claude Buffle's at *L'Hebdo*, and from his queries, Siegfried discerned that Lasseur's interest in Safra was broad and deep.

In the days to come the two hashed over what Siegfried was now regarding as well-worn territory: the Bern letter, Shakarchi Trading, and Operation Polar Cap were all explained in detail. To those topics Siegfried now added the 1957 letter and the still-unexplained assertions from *Hoy* and elsewhere that U.S. drug agents were warning South American banks about Safra. It was wearisome, time-consuming work, and Safra and Weiner nervously monitored the goings-on with their usual worried eyes. Any day now, they were convinced, *The Wall Street Journal* or *The New York Times* would weigh in with a story of their own.

As Safra's anxiety grew, new gossip making the rounds threatened to totally unnerve him. Safra himself heard it first, from an old friend in London banking circles. "There are rumors I'm in jail," Safra said in an amazed tone as the inner circle ran through a day's events. "Can you believe it? Those bastards are spreading rumors I've been arrested!"

Within days Siegfried heard the same story from a far stranger source. Weiner called and said he had taken a message from the Swiss reporter Maya Jurt, and Siegfried returned the call.

"Now, you know how the press works, right?" Jurt asked.

"Yes."

"Normally we don't give out a source."

"That I understand."

"But, in this case, I tell you very frankly, I think something is very wrong here."

"Yes."

"And that's why I'll tell you. I was called up two days ago from somebody, one who has very close contact to brokers' circles in London, who told me that Mr. Safra was arrested. And I said, 'Forget it.' I didn't believe it, and I didn't do anything."

"Yes."

"And then, I got a second call yesterday from a guy, from Ticino—you know, in the south, the Italian part of Switzerland."

"He said the same thing, that Safra was arrested?"

"Right. But he didn't tell me the source."

"Yes."

"And then today I was called up by a guy in Lausanne who told me the same thing." A fourth and final caller, Jurt said, was a photographer for a Swiss paper looking for a photograph of Safra since he had heard Safra was to be arrested the next morning. "After this I felt that, well, the best thing would be to call Republic."

"Well, I can't tell you how much we appreciate it. As I said, this has been a nightmare for us to try to deal with. And, of course, we're hearing reports which are just nonsense all over the place."

"I guess so. Well, if it's true, then you'd better come out with it."

"No, it's not true. I can assure you."

Siegfried hung up, gratified that a reporter had been offended enough by the false rumors to notify the bank. But the momentary warmth he felt was soon quashed by the cold realization that there wasn't a damn thing they could do about it.

By mid-May Safra and his aides were fairly certain of two things: that a Staten Island man named Tony Greco was somehow behind the spreading of stories about Safra, and that barring a miracle, there was little hope of connecting Greco to American Express. After two solid months of digging, they had little more than a single fax telltale linking Jim Robinson's company to what they perceived to be a global press campaign against Safra.

That alone made the success of a lawsuit against American Express unlikely. "We simply don't have enough," Walter Weiner said as Arkin and the inner circle gathered to review their options at Republic one evening. The more they talked it over, in fact, the less everyone wanted to sue, which would cause an avalanche of publicity. They needed to end this now, and they needed to end it quietly.

"We need a shot across their bow, a warning to Jim," Weiner said again and again, something that would tell Robinson they were onto him, but that fell short of a messy public allegation. Gershon Kekst mulled a way to package what was happening to Safra and offer it to *The Wall Street Journal* or *The New York Times*. No doubt it was a page-one story, and there was a certain irony to fighting fire with fire. But whether it was a jury or a journalist, the same problem confronted them. They had no proof it was American Express.

On its face, Stanley Arkin could see, he had an alluring circumstantial case. A fax telltale linked American Express to *Minute*. A Parisian translator could link *Minute* to Greco. Tom Sheer could give an affidavit that he had been introduced to Greco by a former American Express security man. Certainly it would be enough to embarrass Robinson and his people. But, Arkin had to admit, it wasn't enough to win in court. They simply needed more proof. And as much as he hated to do it, Arkin knew there was only one way to get it. He picked up the phone and called Joe Mullen.

Friday morning, May 19, Siegfried stepped out of his office after a long phone call and sorted through a short stack of white message slips on his secretary's desk. One immediately jumped out at him: Philippe Mottaz, the Swiss television correspondent, had called. Few names worried Siegfried more. Ever since his broadcast a month before, Safra's aides had been picking up rumors that Mottaz and his network were planning a major investigative effort into Safra and Republic. Siegfried took the message and stepped back into his office. Within minutes, he had Safra and Weiner on the phone.

"They're going to start playing with me again, I know it," Safra said.

"I'll call you back as soon as I know more," Siegfried promised. He hung up and dialed Mottaz at his Washington office. When the Swiss reporter came on the line, his mood was cheerful, almost collegial.

"There's a rumor going around that Edmond Safra's in jail," Mottaz said. "Is it true?"

Siegfried wasn't laughing. "No."

"Where is he now?"

"I don't know." A lie. Siegfried had visions of a film crew ambushing Safra outside Republic to comment on the rumors of his jailing.

"Did you see the *L'Hebdo* article?" Mottaz asked.

"Yes."

"What about all that stuff in there?"

"The *L'Hebdo* article is misleading. It contains absurd innuendo that has no basis in fact."

"When is Mr. Safra coming to the States?" Mottaz asked.

"I don't know."

Afterward Siegfried faxed Mottaz a round of pro-Safra letters—from the DEA, from the Iran-Contra prosecutors—that he hoped would dampen the Swiss reporter's interest. But the new inquiry, combined with swirling rumors of Safra's arrest and the brewing *Le Temps Présent* documentary, drove Safra toward new heights of anxiety. That afternoon he summoned Weiner, Kekst, and Siegfried to a crisis meeting at his Fifth Avenue apartment. Over and over they talked through ways to get at Greco. Over and over Siegfried recounted his conversations with Mottaz. Over and over they debated how to quash the new Swiss documentary. But after nine months dueling with reporters in a half-dozen countries, everyone realized attempts at cornering these will-o'-the-wisp rumors were fruitless.

"Edmond, you have to decide," Kekst said. "Do you want to go to war?" To those watching Safra's face that afternoon, it had never been more clear how strongly he had personalized this vendetta. His reputation, his character, the only things that would outlive him on this earth, were being assassinated, as if by slow-acting poison, with each new article and broadcast. If these things he held so dear were to be destroyed, Safra was not above vengeance.

"I want to get that son-of-a-bitch Jim Robinson," Safra said slowly, without raising his voice. "I want to get him back for what he has done to me. But if we go to war, we can't lose. If we go to war, we're going to need ammunition."

Edmond Safra didn't know it, but after nine long months under attack, after six years of anguish, he was about to get his wish.

Mike Kohut pulled his gray Nissan to the curb a hundred yards beyond the gates of Tony Greco's Staten Island driveway and turned off the engine. Here, well down from the steep entrance to the Emerson Hill neighborhood, Richmond Road was lined with neat, cookie-cutter homes with shallow, Astroturf-green lawns. Through the Nissan's rearview mirror, Kohut regarded the entrance to the Greco driveway behind him. Earlier drive-bys had persuaded him, as they had Hank Flynn two months before, of the stakeout's difficulties. The streets surrounding

20 Douglas Road were either too narrow or too busy for a full-time stakeout.

But Mike Kohut wasn't Joe Mullen's best tail man for nothing. He had been following errant husbands and bail jumpers through the streets of New York for Mullen since 1976; the two met when Kohut, just out of the navy, was dating the detective's daughter. Like his boss, Kohut had never been in law enforcement, and would never pass for a cop. His close-set eyes, messy hair, and slight paunch gave him the look of a drunken millworker. But he had made surveillance a science. Tommy Mullen always said Kohut was the best "foot tail" he'd ever seen. Once he had followed a man to California and back, sitting a few plane seats away without ever being noticed.

Kohut loved a challenge, and with one eye on the Greco driveway, he set to surmounting this one. He took out a large mirror he had brought and fastened it to the Nissan's rearview. Once in place, the new setup enlarged Kohut's mirror to three times its normal size, making possible the long-distance surveillance he had in mind. Adjusting it for the best view through the Nissan's back window, Kohut eased his seat all the way back, almost flat, until he could see Greco's driveway while lying on his back. The car's windows were tinted, so neighbors and the occasional jogger couldn't peer in. With his head well below dashboard level, Kohut hoped no one would have a reason to. His hiding place complete, he took out a newspaper, turned the radio to a rock and roll station, and waited for Tony Greco to show himself.

Kohut passed the afternoon without a single glimpse of his subject. Toward evening, as he prepared to call it a day, he got out of the car, opened his trunk, and took out a dog leash. It was an old detective's trick: as Kohut ambled up toward the gates to Greco's driveway, anyone watching would assume he was looking for his dog. Reaching the gates, he quickly jammed a book of matches between them. If by morning it had dropped to the ground, he would at least know whether Greco had returned.

The next afternoon, Saturday, Kohut caught the first sight of his man. A large white Lincoln—"as big as a boat," Kohut would recall— whizzed by his car window, heading south down Richmond Road. When the detective glanced at the license plate, he realized the car was Greco's. He hadn't seen it emerge from the driveway. Kohut revved his Nissan into traffic, well behind the Lincoln. He followed as Greco drove fifteen minutes to another Staten Island home, where he and two women—his wife and mother-in-law, Kohut guessed—emerged and appeared to attend a yard party. Five hours later the three returned to the car with a young boy Kohut took to be Greco's son and drove back to the house on Douglas Road, oblivious to their tail.

Sunday was a washout. The green lawns lining Richmond Road, quiet for two days, were suddenly covered with laughing children, lawn-mowing fathers, and perspiring joggers. Kohut realized the Nissan and its smoked-glass windows were attracting too much attention, jeopardizing future surveillance. There was no sign of Greco, so by midday the detective called it quits.

Kohut returned to his surveillance Monday morning, when he followed Greco to the dry cleaners and a travel agency. Twice—once Monday, and again the next day—Kohut saw Hefty bags brimming with garbage perched tantalizingly on the curb outside the Greco home. Each time he radioed Mullen to send someone out to snatch them, but garbage collectors beat them to the prize on both occasions.

Tuesday Kohut tailed Greco to a dentist's office, where he remained for more than two hours. Afterward the detective watched Greco drive to a pharmacy to get a prescription filled, all the while clutching his jaw in obvious pain. By six-thirty he had returned home, and Kohut radioed Joe Mullen to call it a day. "He doesn't look like he's going anywhere tonight," Kohut said.

After five days of renewed surveillance, both men knew they had little to show. But Stanley Arkin gave the go-ahead to continue the stakeout Tuesday night. Who knew? Maybe they would get lucky.

Wednesday, May 24, was a miserable day. An unseasonably cold north wind was blowing, and a thin mist coated the city with enough wetness to break up the street oils and turn the pavement greasy and slick. By seven o'clock Kohut's Nissan was in place on Richmond Road, well past Greco's driveway. That morning he was joined by Joe Mullen's son Tommy, who had parked his black Maxima four blocks back to watch the entrance to the Greco home on Douglas Road. The two kept in touch on their mobile phones.

By ten-thirty there was no sign of Greco, and both men were growing restless. Kohut grabbed his leash, walked by the driveway, and noticed his latest matchbook was down, suggesting Greco had been out, either that morning or the night before. "Let me go look for this guy, Tommy," Kohut radioed his partner, and Mullen agreed.

Kohut started up the Nissan and headed south, away from the house, planning to drop by the travel agency Greco had visited in hopes of spotting him. Kohut hadn't gone far when, to his surprise, Greco's big white Lincoln passed him going the other way. "Holy shit, Tommy," the detective radioed his partner, "I've got him!"

Kohut braked hard, swerved into a U-turn and went in pursuit of the Lincoln. He had noticed Greco was wearing a sport coat and a tie, as if he had business; for the first time, Kohut smelled something interesting afoot. Far ahead, he lost sight of the Lincoln for a minute, and accelerated the Nissan well past seventy miles an hour to catch up. Braking at a stop light, Kohut spotted Greco emerging from his car in the parking lot of a Citibank branch across the way. They were in luck.

By the time Greco came out of the bank eleven minutes later, at 11:05, both Kohut and Mullen had their cars in place. The Lincoln pulled out of the parking lot and headed north, toward the freeway, with the two detectives well behind, careful of Arkin's warning not to be spotted. They were almost too careful: gliding through the mist onto an access road, Kohut was startled to see the Lincoln heading onto the freeway via an exit ramp he had just passed. For the second time Kohut slammed on his brakes. Looking over his shoulder, he reversed the Nissan back toward the exit, then accelerated onto the freeway in pursuit of the Lincoln.

As Greco's car passed over the windswept arches of the Verrazano-Narrows Bridge into Brooklyn, both investigators found themselves growing excited. At no time during their surveillance or Hank Flynn's had Greco left Staten Island, much less in a coat and tie. Something was brewing, and Kohut phoned Joe Mullen to tell him so. After a week of inactivity, the thrill of the hunt was so strong that, when Mullen came on the line, Kohut was actually singing: "Co-ming over the bri-idge...co-ming over the bri-idge."

"What?"

"We're on the Verrazano, and he's heading toward Manhattan," Kohut said. "I'm not kidding. I'll bet you he's going into lower Manhattan."

None of Mullen's men knew the full details of the case, but all were aware of the importance of linking Greco to American Express. And everyone knew the company's headquarters was in lower Manhattan, hard by the Hudson River in the shadow of the World Trade Center. "Holy Christ," Joe Mullen repeated. "He's coming to Manhattan." Keeping Kohut on the line, he phoned and briefed Arkin's assistant Jeffrey Kaplan.

Passing into Brooklyn, Greco's white Lincoln followed the pockmarked Gowanus Expressway along New York Harbor and eased into a line of traffic at the Brooklyn Battery Tunnel. Kohut and Tommy Mullen stayed well back. The tunnel led into the southern tip of lower Manhattan, less than a mile from American Express headquarters. "It's definitely Manhattan, all right," Kohut radioed.

Joe Mullen sensed something big was happening. "Shane! Shane!" he yelled.

Another of Mullen's young operatives, Shane Williams, stuck his head into his boss's cluttered office. Williams was dark-haired and good-looking, in his twenties, a would-be New York cop who had gone to work for Mullen a few years earlier while dating one of the firm's secretaries.

"Get down to American Express as quick as you can!" Mullen hollered, and within minutes the young detective had dashed out the office's ugly steel door and down to a waiting cab. Mullen grabbed another phone and dialed Don Biggs, a musclebound black weightlifter, who was sitting out a separate Manhattan surveillance.

"Dump what you're on," Mullen barked, "and get down to American Express." Within minutes Biggs, too, was heading at top speed toward lower Manhattan.

Now things began happening fast. As the four detectives converged on the gleaming towers of American Express, Tony Greco's white Lincoln pulled out of the Battery Tunnel into the crowded streets of lower Manhattan, cruised up through noontime traffic on West Street and, as Mike Kohut watched with glee, turned left, toward the front of American Express headquarters on Vesey Street.

"He's circling American Express! He's circling American Express!" Kohut excitedly radioed Joe Mullen. "It looks like he's looking for a parking spot!"

The elder Mullen, now juggling two phone lines and a pair of mobile phones, got Jeffrey Kaplan back on the line. "You're never going to believe this," he told the attorney, "but right now Tony Greco is circling American Express headquarters."

The normally reserved Kaplan let out a massive whoop. "Oh, my God!" the lawyer breathed. "Jesus, Stanley will never believe this."

Seconds later, Arkin came on the line.

"What's happening? What's going on?"

Mullen smiled. "Well, Stanley," he said, "it looks like we're all going to a party at American Express."

"For Chrissake," Arkin said. "Don't lose him."

"I got four people down there," Mullen said, chuckling. "Half the neighborhood'll be our guys."

As they spoke, Greco's Lincoln pulled away from American Express, recrossed West Street's six lanes of traffic, and nosed into the narrow streets behind the World Trade Center. Several car lengths back, Mike Kohut was growing nervous. He knew he couldn't keep following Greco for long without being spotted. Greco appeared to be looking for a parking space, but for all Kohut knew, he was trying to spot a tail. He was constantly looking in his mirrors. "We're gonna get made if we keep this up," Kohut radioed his boss.

Instinctively Kohut eased off, letting the Lincoln out of his sight for several minutes. Tommy Mullen had pulled his black Maxima up in front of the glittering gold façade of American Express's main entrance, and at three minutes past noon he saw Greco coast to a stop across the way. The Lincoln pulled up directly in front of the building's revolving-door entrance.

"I've got him," Mullen radioed his father. "He's right in front of American Express."

The younger Mullen pulled out his Minolta and hurriedly screwed on a zoom lens. Peering through the camera's viewfinder, the gold letters of "AMERICAN EXPRESS TOWER" were framed right above Greco's car. Furiously Tommy Mullen began snapping pictures.

Two miles north, Joe Mullen and the two lawyers, Arkin and Kaplan, were fairly leaping out of their seats in their respective midtown offices. Mike Kohut, meanwhile, found a parking space, pleased to let his partner take over the surveillance for a moment.

Minutes later, the cab carrying the third Mullen operative, Shane Williams, arrived in front of American Express. Williams, the office's snazziest dresser, was wearing a coat and tie and carrying a briefcase as he stepped from the cab onto Vesey Street. Fifty feet ahead, through the misty rain, he saw Greco's white Lincoln. Across the way, he spied Tommy Mullen discreetly taking pictures through his passenger side window.

As his cab pulled away, Williams walked past a row of idling black limousines and livery cars toward the rear of Greco's car. Ahead, through the Lincoln's rear windshield, he could just make out Greco sitting in the driver's seat. Reaching the car's rear bumper, Williams side-stepped past the trunk and noticed Greco reading a newspaper with the engine running. He seemed to be waiting for someone.

Boldly Shane Williams pushed through the revolving doors of American Express headquarters and took up a position in the marbled lobby. Above, atop a pair of silvery escalators, Williams could see a huddle of American Express security men. They hadn't noticed him, at least not yet. A nicely dressed young man with a briefcase and mobile phone wasn't at all out of place in the lobby, which was normally aswarm with all manner of colorfully clad messengers.

Moments later, Williams saw the fourth Mullen operative, Don Biggs, pull his gray Cadillac in front of the building. "I'm here, I don't see anybody," Biggs radioed Joe Mullen. "Where is he?"

Tommy Mullen's voice crackled over the mobile phone in his father's office. "Would you tell Don to get out of the fucking way?" he asked. "The guy is right behind him. Right behind him! I'm trying to take his picture!"

"Don, move," the elder Mullen radioed Biggs. "The guy is right, like, two feet behind you." Biggs, in fact, had pulled his car right next to Greco's Lincoln. Quickly he moved it away.

Within minutes, all four Mullen detectives were arrayed around the entrance to American Express headquarters, waiting for something to happen. Time crawled by as they watched Greco shift in his seat, browsing through a paper, by now obviously waiting to meet someone. In the lobby, Shane Williams glanced nervously at the milling security men, certain they would question him at any moment. Suddenly, through the lobby windows, he saw a security man in a blue baseball cap and yellow rain slicker approach Greco's car. Williams pushed through the revolving doors and onto the sidewalk to hear what the man was saying.

"You're going to have to move your car, no, move it," the raincoat was telling Greco. Greco seemed to be objecting, and the raincoat was giving him a hard time. The two talked for several moments, as Williams silently prayed Greco wouldn't drive off without keeping his appointment. "Please, buddy," the detective breathed to himself, "get busy hassling someone else." Finally Greco pulled his car up, double-parking beside an air-conditioning repair van, placating the raincoat. Williams returned to his post inside to wait. For what, no one was exactly sure.

Minutes ticked by.

Fifty floors below Jim Robinson's corner office, four pairs of eyes were riveted to every gray and blue suit emerging from the American Express lobby, anxiously waiting for one to break for Greco's car. Uptown, Mullen and the lawyers hunched over their speaker phones, waiting in agony for word of Greco's next move.

It happened in a split-second. At twelve-thirty-five, a woman brushed past Shane Williams's right shoulder and pushed through the lobby doors onto the rain-slickened sidewalk. She was around forty, wearing an expensive tan skirt, white blouse, and a well-cut black jacket and carrying a white handbag. All at once Williams realized she was angling for Greco's car. "He's got somebody, he's got somebody," the detective whispered urgently into his phone.

They all saw her at once. Greco emerged from the driver's side door, circled around the car, and opened the Lincoln's door for the woman, who tucked herself into the passenger seat. Pandemonium broke out among the detectives. All four were calling and yelling in Joe Mullen's ear at once: "It's a woman! It's a woman! We've got her! We've got her!"

As the detectives watched, stunned at their luck, Greco returned to the wheel and eased the car away from the curb. Mike Kohut's Nissan was right behind him, followed by the others. All three cars followed the Lincoln onto West Street, then, almost immediately, onto a side street. Again the Lincoln began circling, looking for a parking place. When it found one, Mike Kohut saw Greco get out of the car and swivel his head to and fro, looking around. He had seen the same movement before; apparently Greco was accustomed to watching for surveillance. More interesting, at least to Kohut, was the large manila envelope Greco held under his arm.

As the detectives looked on, Greco, carrying the envelope, escorted the woman across the street and through a massive wooden door into a restaurant named Bouley. None of the four was familiar with the place, but Joe Mullen was. It was a newly opened, four-star French restaurant, just growing popular with the Wall Street expense-account crowd. It was also small and crowded. "Don't go in," Mullen told his men. "You'll be spotted in a minute."

They waited.

Uptown, Arkin was already sorting through how he could use the day's events in court. "Look, I need pictures," he told Mullen. "She could be anybody. Make sure you get good pictures. Make sure you get Greco and the license plate in there, too." Arkin was already relishing the moment he would throw the pictures in Jim Robinson's face.

After an hour, everyone was growing impatient. Reluctantly Mullen gave the go-ahead, and Shane Williams walked into Bouley's darkened foyer. Sticking his head into a dining room, he saw no sign of Greco or the woman.

"May I help you?" the maître d' asked.

"No," Williams said, "I'm just looking for my party." The detective retreated, mindful of not being spotted or creating a scene. He told Joe Mullen the two must be in a rear dining area.

Apparently he was right. At two-forty-five Greco and the woman came out through the thick wooden door; the detectives immediately noticed that the woman was now carrying the manila envelope Greco had brought. All four had taken up positions around Greco's car, though at good distances. From his post atop a loading platform, Shane Williams watched Greco and the woman cross the street and step into the white Lincoln. By now, the day had grown so overcast that Tommy Mullen told his father he would need special film to get more photographs; that, or move in closer. The elder Mullen killed both suggestions, and his men followed the Lincoln back to American Express headquarters without incident.

"Follow the woman," Arkin told Joe Mullen, and Mullen relayed the orders to his men.

When the woman stepped from the Lincoln onto the sidewalk outside American Express, Shane Williams and Tommy Mullen were right behind her. Into the lobby she went, up the escalators toward a bank of elevators, the detectives barely twenty feet behind, nervously eyeing the security men all around. Mullen and Williams stopped as the woman passed through a security checkpoint, then watched as she nodded hello to a pair of well-dressed executives before disappearing into an elevator. "Seems like she knows her way around this place," Mullen noted.

At Arkin's direction, two of the detectives followed Greco back to

Staten Island, then returned to American Express. By five o'clock all four were again in position around the headquarters entrance. Arkin badly wanted to know who Tony Greco's female friend was, and the only way to find out was to follow her home.

At seven-fifteen the woman obliged, once more walking out and ducking into a cab. The detectives' cars effortlessly followed it north through midtown Manhattan, to an apartment building on Central Park West at Sixty-fourth Street. There the woman stepped from the cab and disappeared inside.

Arkin was thrilled. Now they needed her name. A number of major companies, including Merrill Lynch and Dow Jones, were headquartered in the same block of buildings as American Express, and there was always the possibility, however remote, that the woman worked for one of the other firms. They had to make sure she worked for American Express.

"Now you're in your element, Joe," Arkin told Joe Mullen that evening. "This is a simple doorman job, just like your garden-variety matrimonial, one of your 'who-fucks-who' jobs."

"I'll have one of my guys go up and—"

"No, Joe, you do it. I want this done right."

The "doorman job" was a hardy perennial for any New York detective. Mullen had done hundreds in his time, though these days he usually left such chores to his son Tommy and the others. There were a million ways to get information out of a doorman. Sometimes Mullen could simply put on a trenchcoat, say he was "up from Washington," and fire off a quick question or two. With any luck, the doorman would think he was FBI.

Sometimes flattery worked. One of Mullen's favorite tactics, used on shorter doormen of a certain age, was to chat up the man and remark about the years he must have spent "on the job," meaning, with the New York police department. What precinct? Mullen would ask. No, the smiling doorman invariably said, he hadn't been on the force, though he had wanted to. "Gee," Mullen would say, "I could have sworn you had the look of a New York cop." Of course Mullen had a card up his sleeve: for years New York police had enforced a minimum-height requirement, and he could be fairly sure the doorman wasn't an ex-cop. But his intentional mistake made the poor doorman feel ten feet tall—ten feet of putty in Mullen's eager hands.

Thursday morning Mullen opted for a different tactic, a twist on a scam he had played dozens of times in Manhattan apartment buildings. He took a package left in his office, marked "American Express" on one side, and set out on foot for the building on Central Park West, eleven blocks north.

Once there, Mullen strode into the lobby and instantly realized he was in luck. A uniformed doorman—the best were alert and protective of their residents—was nowhere in sight. Instead a man who appeared to be the elevator operator was alone on duty. Even better, when the fellow greeted Mullen it was clear he could barely speak English.

"I'm supposed to meet someone in the building," Mullen said, pointing to the package under his arm. "Uh, for a doctor, or something, I think."

"Who is it?" the man asked in a heavy Spanish accent. "What's the name?"

"I don't know. I think they're affiliated with American Express, American something."

The doorman opened the door to a small closet. Inside, on a chair, sat a book. He picked it up and leafed through it for a second or two. "Miss Cantor," he said. "Miss Cantor works for American Express."

Mullen peered into the book. On an upper floor there lived a Susan Cantor. A second occupant was listed as Alan Kahn, whom Mullen figured for a boyfriend or husband. He thanked the doorman and left with his package.

Minutes later Joe Mullen was back behind his paper-strewn glass desk, punching in the phone number for American Express headquarters. He asked for "Susan Cantor" and was passed through.

A secretary answered, "Miss Cantor's office."

He hung up.

It was time to go to war.

—— PART ——
THREE

*Integrity is
fundamental to every
business we're in.*

—JAMES D. ROBINSON III

10

For as long as she could remember, Maureen Duffy had wanted to be a journalist. In the 1970s, with a messy divorce behind her and two kids in school, she had finally given it a shot, trying her hand at local newspapers near the bedroom community of Edison, New Jersey. As a single mother, she was forced to take other jobs to make ends meet—for the longest time she was a "blood custodian" at New Jersey Blood Services—but always she yearned to return to writing. She was skeptical of authority and persistent the Irish way, and loved nothing better than digging into a good story.

By the time her kids were in high school, Maureen Duffy had decided to take the plunge. She enrolled in journalism classes at nearby Rutgers University and eventually got a degree. She took free-lancing jobs for several trade journals in New York City, and for a time worked at short-lived *Edison* magazine. By the early 1980s she was working regularly for a computer trade journal called *MIS Week* and loving every minute. It could be difficult, technical, sometimes boring work, but it beat the hell out of night shifts at the blood bank.

Maureen Duffy did her grocery shopping at the Food Town in nearby Highland Park, and as she trundled from aisle to aisle, she would often run into one of her neighbors, a bearded Stanford Ph.D. named John Crothers Pollack. Pollack ran his own opinion research company, which published corporate-subsidized pseudo-journalism like "The Miller Lite Report on American Attitudes Toward Sports" and "Small Business Speaks: The Chemical Bank Report." They had met when the fast-talking Pollack spoke at Rutgers, and every time Duffy saw him at the Food Town, Pollack would hold out the prospect of hiring her to do some writing.

In 1985 their grocery store chats turned serious. Pollack and his wife, Marilyn, an anthropologist, were starting an independent market research newsletter on the credit card industry, to be called the *Bank Credit Card Observer*. The newsletter would provide a forum for Pollack's computer-generated statistics on interest rates charged by the big banks' Visas and MasterCards, whose rise was already alarming consumer groups nationwide. The *Observer*, Pollack said, would serve as a much-needed watchdog for the industry, and Duffy, as associate editor, could be its principal reporter. Eager to aggressively report the truth about a controversial industry, Maureen Duffy accepted.

Its comfortable offices set up at the Hilton Hotel in nearby Iselin, the *Bank Credit Card Observer* debuted with a six-page issue in April 1986. It was an immediate hit. Pollack was soon in demand as a media expert on lofty Visa and MasterCard rates, quoted in newspapers like *The New York Times* and seen regularly on television. The *Observer* began staging seminars at hotels around the country in which consumer advocates were given a forum to blast high bank-card rates. In January 1987 *The Wall Street Journal* began regularly publishing data from Pollack's rate survey.

Maureen Duffy was thrilled with her new job. Stories were so plentiful they seemed to fall into her lap, and she produced a steady stream of articles on legislative efforts to curb bank card rates and other topics. It was good, solid work, the kind that had drawn her into journalism in the first place.

One question, though, sometimes puzzled her: where was the *Observer*'s money coming from? The newsletter was slickly published and professionally organized, its conferences smoothly run with long buffets piled high with rare roast beef and soft drinks. But neither they nor Pollack's computer surveys came cheap. Annual subscriptions were $290, and Duffy was certain that the subscriber base didn't bring in enough money to pay for all the costs the Pollacks were amassing. Bankers under attack in the newsletter would come up to her at conferences and ask slyly, "Who do you think is paying for all this?" Duffy would shrug and reply honestly, "I have no idea."

When she asked John Pollack, he explained, somewhat vaguely, that his backers were aging radicals from the 1960s, angry at high rates and willing to put their money behind their beliefs.* At first Duffy took Pollack at his word, but eventually the bankers' pointed questions made her wonder. She went to Marilyn Pollack and asked, point blank, who was funding the *Bank Credit Card Observer*. "You really don't need to know," she recalls Pollack saying. "If it was anything that would embarrass you, I'd tell you. But it's not. It's really not."

For a time Marilyn Pollack's answer placated Duffy. But soon her curiosity was up again. Dire possibilities ran through her mind. New Jersey had a reputation as a haven for organized crime: could the *Observer* be a money-laundering operation? The idea was ridiculous, she knew. But nothing else seemed to make sense.

Already uneasy, Maureen Duffy's nagging worries turned to disillusionment in early 1987 when the Pollacks decided not to publish her biggest scoop yet. Just hours before going to press with the February issue, Duffy learned from a trusted source that Visa and MasterCard's fiercest competitor, American Express, was poised to join battle by introducing a bank-type card of its own. To be called Optima, the new card would allow users to "roll over" payments from month to month just like Visa and MasterCard. Even better, from a consumer point of view, American Express expected to charge only 13.5 percent interest, as opposed to bank rates that ranged as high as 22 percent.

It was a story that promised to reshape the entire debate over interest rates, but the Pollacks refused to run it. Crushed, Duffy rationalized that her bosses were statisticians first and journalists second, and simply didn't appreciate a good scoop. Still, it was exasperating. The edition in question wasn't anything special, just another series of polemics against the bank cards. "Credit Cards Under Attack: A Nation Fights High Interest Rates," the cover story's headline blared. "And none too soon, say consumers," read a subhead.

And so Maureen Duffy wanted to scream when, soon after, American Express officially unveiled Optima, and the news made headlines across the country. "Charge of the Plastic Brigade: American Express starts a new credit-card war with Optima," read the *Time* magazine headline. John Pollack and the *Observer* seemed to be in every article and on every television screen, predicting how consumers would flock to the lower rates offered by American Express. *Time* magazine quoted

*John Pollack denies telling Duffy this.

Pollack forecasting a "Boston Tea Party of consumers dumping expensive cards and moving to cards with lower rates."

Maureen Duffy's despondency grew with her doubts about the Pollacks' journalistic instincts. She thought about quitting. For months she simmered, gradually withdrawing from many of her duties. Then, that August, another *Observer* staffer quietly came to her with news that rocked her to the core. She was handed a sheaf of documents, and as she read them, she found all her questions, all her concerns, suddenly, incredibly, answered: the *Bank Credit Card Observer* was being secretly funded by American Express.

And it wasn't just nickels and dimes. American Express, the documents showed, had covertly bankrolled the newsletter's launch and thereafter funneled it $20,000 a month to fund operations. The $240,000 annual subsidy dwarfed the $100,000 or more that the Pollacks took in on subscriptions.

To Maureen Duffy everything was instantly, achingly clear: the *Observer's* incessant attacks against high bank-card rates, the lush conferences, the spiking of her American Express scoop, most of all the Pollacks' refusal to reveal their funding source. Optima had been in the works for more than a year, Duffy knew. American Express must have started the *Observer* with the idea of fanning the flames against Visa and MasterCard and setting the stage for a lower-cost alternative. With the "impartial" *Observer's* enthusiastic help, it had all worked marvelously. Optima had been greeted by everyone as a savior against high bank rates.

Duffy was outraged. She felt used. "My Irish was up," she would recall. "I wanted blood." As a journalist, Duffy saw the obvious thing to do was leak the incriminating documents to a newspaper. She thought about *The Wall Street Journal* and *The New York Times*, but wasn't sure they would grasp the subtleties of what American Express had done. Then she thought of the *American Banker*, a top trade newspaper where she had free-lanced over the years. Within days she found herself at a banking industry conference in Manhattan, slipping into an empty office for a discreet rendezvous with a *Banker* reporter named Jeffrey Kutler.

Kutler was flabbergasted by Duffy's revelation. "If this checks out," he told her, "this is incredible. I can't believe a company like American Express would do something like this."

It *was* incredible. Perhaps no company in America possessed a better reputation for quality and integrity than American Express. But as Kutler investigated Duffy's allegations, he not only substantiated them, he added discoveries of his own. American Express, he found, hadn't paid Pollack directly. It had channeled its payments through an American Express consultant named Dorothy Gregg, an economist who had also supervised a public relations campaign to raise Pollack's profile and attract press coverage of his data.

But when Kutler confronted American Express, he was surprised to find its officials brazenly unapologetic. "We think Dr. Pollack has become the single best source of interest rate information in the United States," an executive named Meredith M. Fernstrom told him. Fernstrom headed American Express's office of public responsibility, which funded a number of not-for-profit consumer programs in addition to the Pollacks' newsletter. "We would not have done this unless the data had absolute integrity and objectivity," Fernstrom said. "It has become a great public service."

When Jeffrey Kutler printed his story about American Express and the Pollacks that fall, a minor scandal of the type not uncommon in Corporate America ensued. Ethics experts and bankers emerged to denounce as morally questionable the covert nature of American Express's relationship with the newsletter. *The Wall Street Journal* stopped printing the *Observer*'s rate survey. Almost overnight, demand for John Pollack's "watchdog" observations evaporated. Maureen Duffy and a number of coworkers moved on to other jobs. The *Observer* ultimately folded.

Like most such contretemps, it all blew over in a few days. And as it did, almost no one noticed that the man who had approved and overseen the secret funding, the man who supervised the ironically named office of public responsibility, was an unorthodox, slightly eccentric American Express executive named Harry L. Freeman.

Years later, when assessments were made of the damage to Edmond Safra's reputation, it grew clear that the whole unseemly mess had started with Harry, strange, exasperating Harry, a man who combined the air of an absentminded Harvard professor with the instincts of a Cold War spymaster.

No one ever doubted the intellectual wattage of Jim Robinson's right-hand man. Harry Freeman was a cum laude graduate of Harvard

Law School and a successful San Francisco tax lawyer long before he came to American Express in 1975; even his harshest critics described him as brilliant. What got people talking were the unusual ways Freeman's mind worked. The kindest words colleagues use to describe him were unconventional, unorthodox, daring. Others picked up on the more Machiavellian undertones of his character: scheming, manipulative, and secretive.

On one thing they all agreed. Harry Freeman was everything his buttoned-down peers at American Express were not: unkempt, intellectual, liberal, Jewish, a thinker energized by public policy and international affairs in a company obsessed with the bottom line. "Harry was a bloody enigma," recalls Hasbrouck "Hob" Miller, the corporate secretary who retired in 1984. "Able as he might be, he was a misfit. No one, to my knowledge, except for Jim Robinson, thought differently. Yet, as time went by, I can remember people commenting, 'Jesus, he is a misfit genius, an inventive oddball.' Everyone's attitude was, 'I can't believe he's even here. I can't believe he has the influence, the constant access to the chairman.' It was odd."

In the exalted reaches of American Express's fifty-first-floor executive suite, Freeman cut a colorful, if eccentric, profile, traipsing about with a beat-up Land's End bag as he shuttled between his family and an office in Washington and an apartment near Manhattan's Gramercy Park. He cared little about his personal appearance, wearing heavy flannel suits at the height of summer, jarringly juxtaposing the wildest colors and patterns. The need for combs eluded him—his most frequent hair stylist seemed to be the wind—as did conventional table manners. He couldn't eat a muffin without its ending up all over his sweater. "You ever eat with Harry? The most atrocious table manners you've ever seen," recalls one former colleague. "Always talking, food dribbling all over the place. It was awful. It got so people didn't want to eat with him."

Many of those who worked alongside Freeman found his eccentricities endearing. To aides he was a popular, benevolent figure, cracking jokes during even the worst crises, always up on colleagues' wives and families, never too busy to listen to a subordinate's complaints or concerns. It was in large part due to Freeman's liberal Democratic values, friends say, that American Express pulled out of South Africa, and he was a demon for putting only the most accurate facts in the speeches and congressional testimony he was forever making on the company's behalf.

"Harry was extremely bright, dedicated to issues, a terrifically moral person, very good, very sound values," says Matthew Stover, a former American Express public relations executive who worked for Freeman between 1987 and 1989. "He was terrific with his people, encouraging them, motivating them, collegial, very unstuffy, down to earth, not at all the type of guy you'd expect to be executive vice president of a major corporation."

Always around Freeman there swirled an air of preoccupation, as if he were juggling several thoughts at once. When speaking, every word seemed punctuated with a constant, informal chuckle. "You know [chortle] how [laugh] Robinson can be [breathy chuckle]," he would say. There also was a hint of mystery. Freeman's schedule was notoriously erratic: he seemed to come and go at all hours, gliding in and out on unexplained missions for Jim Robinson, the man to whom he was single-mindedly devoted. "The impression was that he was always off on special projects for Jim," Hob Miller said. "Clearly Harry would say that. But the nature of the projects was always a mystery to me."

On paper, Freeman's slice of the American Express empire covered the "soft" staff functions: government relations and lobbying, public and community relations, and a variety of fund-raising and philanthropic activities. In a company preoccupied with its public image, Freeman, along with Robinson's wife, Linda, was one of its most influential image-makers, especially among reporters in the business press, many of whom he had expertly "spun" for years. His highest value, though, was as Robinson's idea man and muse, and as the architect of many of the chairman's personal projects—from chairing Business Roundtable committees to the United Way—that had brought Robinson global stature as a corporate leader.

Fully half his average workday, Freeman always said, was spent in "crisis of the day" work with Robinson. One of five American Express executives to share the top floors of headquarters with the chairman—the others included president Louis Gerstner, general counsel Gary Beller, and chief financial officer Howard Clark, Jr.—Freeman shuttled into Robinson's corner office at all hours, hashing through the day's crisis, of which there were many at American Express during the 1980s, offering views that Robinson could count on to be unconventional. When the company was trying to isolate the issues that would define American consumerism in the 1980s, it was Freeman, an energetic Anglophile, who hired a clutch of Oxford dons to offer a true outsider's analysis.

Given his background, it was hardly surprising that Harry Freeman stuck out at American Express. Born in Depression-era Omaha, his family the owner of a company that sold dry-cleaning equipment across the upper Midwest, he went off to the University of Michigan and then Harvard Law, where upon graduation the dean secured him a clerkship on the U.S. Court of Appeals in San Francisco. Afterward he joined a Bay Area law firm, forged a successful tax practice, specializing in big shareholder derivative suits. In 1966, after nine years, he quit; newly married and a little bored, he and his wife traveled the world for eight months before landing in Washington, where they inquired about running a country program for the Peace Corps. Instead Freeman ended up running an obscure division of the Agency for International Development, authorizing insurance and loans for U.S. companies investing throughout the undeveloped world.

During five years of government work he became an internationalist, traveling widely through the poorest areas of sub-Saharan Africa, South America, and Asia, sometimes popping into global hot spots like Vietnam. AID had long been rumored to be a common hiding ground for CIA agents, a reputation that might explain rumors in later years that Freeman had a background in intelligence; he denies it, as do several of his former government colleagues. In 1972, Freeman left the government to join Bechtel, the big San Francisco construction conglomerate, where as director of project financing he helped oversee construction of Saudi Arabia's massive desert city of El Jubail; later he went on to supervise elements of projects in Russia, Indonesia, and Vietnam. Lured back to his old government job in 1974, he had barely readjusted to life on the Potomac before taking a call from Larry Ricciardi, a Washington friend who had joined the American Express Company. When Ricciardi's bosses dangled before him the prospect of starting a Washington office for American Express, the peripatetic Harry Freeman changed course once more.

From the beginning he displayed an ingenuity and an ability to get things done that attracted notice at headquarters. In the halls of American Express Jim Robinson's men shook their heads and grinned when they spoke of how Freeman had almost single-handedly defeated a government effort to revoke the deductibility of the three-martini lunch, a prospect met with horror at American Express, whose card was used by millions to pay for business lunches. He did so with an old "inside-the-Beltway" tactic, forging an unusual alliance with the Washington office of the bartender's and waiter's union. American Express and the unionists formed a "grass-roots" coalition of hoteliers and working people who, egged on by a glitzy public relations campaign, deluged Capitol Hill with complaints that the move would cost thousands of bartenders and waiters their jobs. It worked like a charm. The measure was defeated, not once but twice, and amid all the hoopla, no one really noticed that, with Freeman quietly working behind the scenes, it was American Express that stood to gain the most. "It was all," a former Freeman aide notes, "very CIA-like."

It was the first of several similar coalitions Freeman helped assemble over the years on American Express's behalf. Watching from New York, Jim Robinson was impressed. A man who by his mid-forties had little international experience—Freeman wasn't sure his young boss had ever left the country—Robinson took a shining to the worldly new chief of his surprisingly productive Washington office. Because many of the acquisitions American Express was considering in the late 1970s—Merrill Lynch and McGraw-Hill, among others—presented antitrust problems, Freeman and his Washington savvy were for the first time drawn into the company's strategic planning. At first so inexperienced a planner that he hired an outside tutor to teach him methodology, Freeman soon became an invaluable voice in Jim Robinson's executive suite.

The two men barely knew each other when, in 1979, Freeman authored a forward-looking internal analysis of the financial-service industry—some would later claim Freeman had coined the term "financial services"—that urged American Express to exploit its "obvious synergies" with the brokerage business by forging ahead into cutting-edge technologies like automatic-teller machines and home computer systems. Freeman's report, and its cry for synergy with other financial businesses, became an essential building block in Robinson's plan to make American Express the world's first financial supermarket.

Over time Robinson turned again and again to Freeman to brainstorm big-picture questions: when the Japanese steadfastly refused to allow wide distribution of the Card, Freeman was put to work on a ten-year plan to open Japan for American Express as well as U.S. business in general. Freeman's solution was as innovative as it was effective. Joan Spero, a Columbia University political science professor who had been

U.S. ambassador to the United Nations Economic and Social Council, was hired and sent on regular trips to Japan, where American Express ceaselessly promoted her as a leading pro-American voice. Eventually Spero grew so renowned she became an occasional commentator on Tokyo television, helping, along with regular visits by Robinson himself, to open Japanese markets.

It was Freeman who helped introduce Jim Robinson to the glitter and power of Washington and persuaded him that, as their defeat of the three-martini lunch bill had shown, the future of American Express depended on strong, decisive efforts to shape public policy. During the eighties the pair became a common sight around the capital, Robinson striding along to one hearing or another, Freeman ambling alongside, often trailing a retinue of aides. As the leaders of America's premier "service" company, Robinson and Freeman successfully lobbied for a variety of arcane issues, opening up European telecommunications and pushing for "services" to be included on the agenda at the international trade talks in Geneva. Their most ambitious project was assembling a coalition of American companies in favor of a U.S.-Canadian free-trade agreement; with Robinson as its nominal head, Freeman ran the coalition out of headquarters, with his staff doing much of the legwork.

As he rose within American Express, gaining assignment to the office of the chairman after only four years, Freeman became known for the same brand of subtle corporate gamesmanship he had perfected in Washington. It was a reputation he cemented after a promotion in the late 1970s. At the time, a rival for the job, a Howard Clark man, had been carrying on an affair with one of Freeman's young Washington staffers, a situation that came to a head when the woman was brought to New York and named a vice president though still in her twenties. As Freeman tells the story, the executive's resignation was obtained in a meeting the two men had with Jim Robinson in the chairman's office. Other former staffers, however, suggest that Freeman's role in the man's downfall was far more proactive, that if the affair had become widely known, it was because Freeman helped make it so.

It was a side to Harry Freeman's personality that over the years several associates found disquieting. He was in some ways an old-fashioned office gossip, except that Freeman's gossip sometimes had a bitter edge. He once told a reporter that an out-of-favor colleague was taking payoffs; when he disliked a rival, he collected unflattering anecdotes about him. "Harry can be the ultimate ambitious maneuverer and manipulator," says Jack Moorman, who as a government executive came to know Freeman well in the 1970s. "Harry was always scheming, around the clock. He's always thinking, always moving, always inhaling information. And he had the killer instinct. There was no quarter asked, and none given. To me he was totally glib in what he did. There wasn't an ounce of conviction. It was the game for the game's sake, and the only point was to win."

It was Freeman's penchant for intrigue, some colleagues felt, that led American Express into the *Bank Credit Card Observer* scandal in 1987. The newsletter scheme, after all, was little different from the behind-the-scenes roles he had orchestrated for American Express with consumer coalitions in Washington; in Freeman's eyes, American Express had simply identified a group with common interests, in this case a newsletter, and funded it.

Others, notably American Express's straight-arrow president Louis Gerstner, found the idea of American Express hiding behind the veil of a supposedly "objective" newsletter grossly unethical. When Gerstner stumbled onto Freeman's covert funding of the newsletter, he was outraged. What amazed him was that Freeman hadn't bothered to alert anyone working on Optima, which Gerstner oversaw, to the secret "help" he was giving them. "Harry, how could you do this?" he demanded. "I mean, it just doesn't pass the smell test." To Gerstner's dismay, his outburst rolled off Freeman's back like so many drops of rain. "Oh, don't worry," he said. "It'll never come out."*

But, of course, thanks to Maureen Duffy it did, leaving Lou Gerstner and his aides shaking their heads in bewilderment, not only at how misguided the scheme had been—"What did you hope to gain?" Gerstner kept asking—but that Freeman was able to escape with his job. American Express's second-ranking lawyer, a bearded Gerstner confidant named Larry Ricciardi—the same Ricciardi who had enticed Freeman to American Express in 1975—began wondering aloud how Robinson could justify keeping a "loose cannon" like Freeman in the highest reaches of the executive suite. "We gotta stop this guy," Ricciardi fretted

---

*Freeman said his memory is vague about this incident. "I don't recall discussing it with Gerstner," he said. "I may have."

to both Gerstner and his friend the general counsel Gary Beller. "One day he's going to destroy us."

Despite the criticism generated by the newsletter episode, Freeman was never in danger of losing his job, and everyone in the executive suite knew it was because Robinson found him indispensable. Freeman, after all, was not a company man; he was a Jim Robinson man. His mornings often began with coffee in Robinson's office, and much of his day was spent behind closed doors with Robinson, traveling for Robinson's pet projects, slipping Robinson little typewritten notes. The chairman returned his loyalty in spades, brooking little criticism of Freeman, as Lou Gerstner learned. Well before the newsletter scandal broke publicly, Gerstner took his fears about Freeman's little scheme to Robinson, but nothing had resulted, nothing at all. Robinson seemed no more worried by the covert funding than had Freeman.

Though colleagues spent years scratching their heads over the bond between Freeman and Robinson, there was nothing mysterious about it. The two weren't social friends; Freeman joked that Jim and Linda Robinson's black-tie social whirl was a lot of "crap" and said so. But Robinson had been there for Freeman in times of need, pushing him onto his private jet for the long flight to Phoenix when his father died. What bound them was nothing more than Robinson's zeal for creative thinking and, as time went by, by Freeman's key role overseeing the chairman's growing collection of outside projects.

By the late 1980s, in fact, the focus of Freeman's work had shifted away from his Washington base toward supervising Robinson's interests. When he wasn't pushing for a Canadian trade agreement, urging new ways to open Japan, or brainstorming solutions to the international debt crisis, Robinson served as chairman of the U.S. Trade Representative's private-sector committee, to which he was appointed by President Reagan; chairman of United Way; and chairman of the New York City Partnership, a group of leading executives seeking ways to energize the city. Over time Robinson and Freeman assembled a retinue of more than a dozen staffers to help out and keep track of the chairman's activities.

As Robinson's outside interests multiplied, critics inside and outside the company began to question how much time he was actually spending running American Express. To Lou Gerstner, to whom Robinson increasingly looked to run the company's operations, the projects were a tad pretentious—everyone speculated Robinson was angling to be Secretary of the Treasury someday—but it was what the chairman wanted. Gerstner often harangued Freeman to stay within his budgets, but it was no use. "It's all for Jim," Freeman repeated again and again. "Tell Robinson to cut back these projects, and I'll cut back my budgets."

As supervisor of Robinson's retinue, Freeman was a paradox, often up on his people's personal and business lives, but relaxed in his supervision of their work. Though American Express's line divisions were notorious for the density of their bureaucracy—the memos, the reports, the strict reporting requirements—the atmosphere in Freeman's group was sharply different, far more informal and goal-oriented. "You have never seen as unbureaucratic a place as the top levels of American Express—it was almost exhilarating how much freedom Robinson and Freeman gave us," recalls a member of Freeman's staff. "No one spent a lot of time on details. The place was loosely run, you just got the job done."

Freeman, in fact, had the freedom to free-lance solutions to any of the "crisis of the day" problems vexing Robinson, a role that made him an active participant in discussions about Edmond Safra. As the man closest to the chairman's ear, Freeman had always been a sounding board for those trying to pass messages to Robinson. Since the first hopeful days of the TDB acquisition, Bob Smith and others had stuck their heads into Freeman's office to commiserate, first about Safra's idiosyncrasies, later about their mounting fears that he would launch an all-out attack on TDB. As he listened to the tales of stolen employees, lost depositors, and missing computer files, Freeman couldn't help but agree that Safra had become Corporate Enemy No. 1.

"It was a very, very scary situation developing," he recalled years later. "One of [Safra's] real-life goals was to destroy TDB, and if he could get American Express, get them, too. [Bank executives] painted a portrait of him as a lifetime hater. Everyone at the bank was getting pretty paranoid. They felt Safra was not one of those 'forgive and forget' people. He was one of those who would spend his life trying to do you in."

Though he had no direct responsibilities in the struggle, Freeman proved a useful ally for Smith and others intent on taking a hard line against Safra. He was keenly aware of the personal embarrassment Robinson felt over Safra's planned reopening in Geneva, and as he noo-

dled through possible solutions, Freeman became a leading internal pro-
ponent of the effort to block Republic's license. He also took to collecting rumors and unflattering anecdotes about Safra. Among his favorites
was the story of Safra's supposed snit over the corporate jet, which he
relished telling again and again, to associates and reporters alike.

"Harry had the same attitude toward Safra [we all] did: he hated
him," Bob Smith recalled. "He thought Safra was a no-good person out
to do us in." Adds another former executive: "The impression you got
[from Harry] was that Edmond would do almost anything to achieve his
business objectives, that to protect the company, you had to do something aggressive and preemptive."

In Geneva, Bob Terrier's investigation of the TDB refugees had
been under way for six months when, in the waning weeks of 1986, with
anti-Safra paranoia inside headquarters mounting, Freeman saw two
things that would forever alter the course of American Express's feud
with Safra. The first came the morning of December 3. Freeman was in
his office flipping through *The New York Times* when the article leapt
out at him. "Small Quiet Building in Geneva Had Wide Use," the headline read. The story sketched the involvement of Willard Zucker's Swiss
finance company in the budding Iran-Contra scandal, and included the
story from the Swiss newspaper *Tages Anzeiger* about the purported use
of Safra's jet to fly U.S officials to Teheran for hostage negotiations. The
Times story, detailed enough that it carried the registration number of
Safra's jet, also reported that money for Contra aircraft had come from
Zucker-controlled accounts at Republic.

Astounded, Harry Freeman realized the *Times* article was, in his
words, "a gift from heaven." He hustled into Jim Robinson's corner suite
overlooking the Hudson, where Robinson, too, had his nose in the
Times. "We looked at each other and said, 'Good grief, if this guy is really
involved in Iran-Contra, our problems with him may be way behind us
fast,'" Freeman recalls. Here, both men could see, was a vulnerability
dying to be exploited. If American Express could somehow prove Safra
was involved in Iran-Contra, well, the possibilities for the creative use of
corporate dirt were endless.

"Jim said, 'Check this out in depth,'" Freeman remembers. "He
called the legal department and told them to figure out how they could
stop [Safra's] banking license on the grounds of moral turpitude, or the
Swiss equivalent. Then he told me, 'I want an investigation started as

soon as possible to determine what role [Safra] played in Iran-Contra. Get with it...Don't worry about the money. Go do it.'"

Freeman was still pondering the best way to pursue Robinson's idea when he saw the résumé. It had been sent over by Robinson himself, with a note explaining that he had received it from the chief of the company's main TRS subsidiary, Aldo Papone. Freeman studied the résumé carefully. It belonged to a thirty-nine-year-old woman named Susan Cantor, a former staffer at ABC News looking to make the move into the cushy world of corporate public relations.

As résumés went, Cantor's was impressive. Work for the Ford Foundation. Something called the North American Congress for Latin America. A master's from Yale in political science. An internship at CBS News. Five years at ABC. Personal assistant to correspondent Richard Threlkeld. Reporter on an award-winning documentary on the international debt crisis. Advance work for Peter Jennings himself. Member of a special investigative team. Stories on espionage, drug-money laundering, Salvadoran death squads.

If life were a cartoon, someone might have drawn a light bulb over Harry Freeman's head. Just think of it: their very own investigative reporter. And did American Express have someone it needed investigated. But the best of it, and also the worst of it, was that in Susan Cantor, a woman he would come to call his "secret weapon," Harry Freeman had found a true kindred spirit.

Ten years after she first walked into his office at ABC News, an aging radical looking for a new career in journalism, Lowell Bergman still groans at the mention of Susan Cantor's name. Back then, in the fall of 1981, Bergman had badly needed someone with credible left-wing credentials in Latin America—liberal, radical, hell, he didn't care, Communist—to fill out the team of investigative reporters and researchers he was assembling for the network. A veteran reporter and producer himself, Bergman's lineup sorely needed a left-leaning Spanish speaker who could circulate among Latin America's multitude of liberal groups to unearth the occasional story on south-of-the-border death squads, sundry atrocities, coups, and drug runners.

At thirty-four, Susan Cantor appeared to have real potential. Though she had no real experience in network-level journalism, she came recommended by Bergman's friend Dave Marash, who had used her as an intern that summer on a local magazine show at CBS in New York. A Yale-educated Latin American specialist with an avid interest in Cuba, she had radical ties going back to her days as a student protester in the 1960s. In her interview that day Cantor came off as a vivacious, outgoing intellectual with a Jimmy Carter smile, sharp and sympathetic—she was, after all, making a late career change. Best of all, she seemed to know everyone who was anyone in East Coast liberal circles. Bergman hired her as a researcher for a ninety-day tryout, and regretted the decision for years afterward.

"She completely snowed me," Bergman recalled years later. "As soon as I hired her, I started getting calls, saying, 'What have you done?' I was blamed by everybody at ABC for everything that woman did wrong. Every few months I'd get a call from someone, you know, saying, 'Why the hell did you hire this [woman]?'"

Lowell Bergman was neither the first nor the last to be taken—her critics might say taken in—by Susan Cantor's ample charm and gilt-edged résumé. Longtime acquaintances, colleagues, and former bosses uniformly describe Cantor as a hard-working, intensely ambitious career woman with an awesome knack for New York–style name-dropping. A walking encyclopedia of Manhattan's radical chic, she was capable of blinding dinner partners as well as potential employers with a blizzard of liberal names, places, and faces. She might start with the Columbia demonstrations, then Havana in the summer of 1969, Bess Myerson, Sy Hersh, Peter Jennings, David Aaron, Mort Halperin, the Ford Foundation, the "Missing" case. Combined with her obvious intellect and a dollop of self-deprecating humor, the effect could be spellbinding. "I've seen people, highly paid professional people, who would meet Susan Cantor, and after their first or second meeting, would just be gaga over her," says an acquaintance of twenty years. "She has an incredible knack of getting in good with people."

Raised in Manhattan, the daughter of a fashion industry executive, Cantor was radicalized as a young Barnard College coed in the wake of the Columbia demonstrations of 1968, friends say. She joined a crowd of angry student radicals that included members of the Weather Underground, where she took pride in being an extremist. "Susan always wanted you to think she was on the furthest edge of the left, that she was more radical than anyone," recalls one longtime Manhattan radical. At demonstrations she was the one who spotted undercover members of the Red Squad, the police unit that kept tabs on radical groups. "Every movement," says a friend, "needs a Susan."

In those years the chic thing to do was join Cuba's Venceremos Brigade, bands of American students who volunteered to chop sugar cane shoulder to shoulder with their proletariat brethren in the fields outside Havana. Susan Cantor made the trip and in the years afterward developed a fascination with Cuba and Latin America, visiting Havana and ultimately going to work for one of the most doctrinaire of American pro-Castro groups, the North American Congress for Latin America, known as NACLA.

NACLA worked out of a communal-style headquarters on Manhattan's Upper West Side, and from its offices Cantor wrote articles in the early 1970s on liberation struggles in Uruguay, Chile, and other Latin American countries for the NACLA newsletter, whose unofficial slogan was "Kick the Ass of the Ruling Class." At NACLA, former colleagues say, Cantor, who spoke Spanish with a pronounced New York accent, was always the one who knew the latest gossip, the latest intrigues in Washington and Santiago and Caracas.

"She was a conspiracy junkie," recalls an acquaintance from those days. "At NACLA she kept the files. She had thousands of files. She was always very secretive, very conspiratorial. It seemed to be very important to her that people think she was doing more than she was doing, that she knew more than she knew."

Among the events Cantor monitored was the overthrow of Chilean leader Salvador Allende in 1973; NACLA's intelligence was so thorough she became a source for a number of journalists, including famed *New York Times* reporter Seymour Hersh. But by the mid-1970s, Cantor's radical flames had cooled with age, and she reentered the academic world at Yale, processing Cuban-related grants at the Ford Foundation before earning a master's in 1981. That year, with an eye toward a new career in journalism, she secured an internship at CBS. "The biggest thing I remember about Sue was how unsure she was, how insecure she was," remembers Neil Cunningham, then a CBS producer. "She always had to be reassured, told that she was doing okay, which in turn made me nervous. You really don't expect somebody with that kind of background to be that insecure, which in turn makes you wonder about the information she was giving you."

By the time she walked into ABC's Upper West Side offices, Susan

Cantor was many things, but she was not a journalist. A number of colleagues who came to know her in her years at ABC considered her an ambitious idealogue for whom the boundaries between fact and rumor were sometimes fuzzy. From her first days at the network Cantor was disliked by many coworkers, who found her mix of ambition, radical theories, and journalistic inexperience disquieting. "She didn't know how to be a journalist; she was playing at it," recalls one of her first office partners, an associate producer named Richard O'Regan.

Secretive, a fount of rumors and gossip, Cantor is remembered by former colleagues as almost a caricature of an investigative journalist, forever spinning fantastic conspiracy theories that never made it onto broadcasts. "Susan had this constant habit, which drove Lowell [Bergman] and others crazy, of coming to you and promising that she had this great story—this arms dealer, a diplomatic contretemps," recalled Robert Ross, a former ABC colleague who worked with Cantor in her early years at the network. "But when you asked for proof, looked at the documents, it just kind of dissolved. It happened again and again. Her stories just evaporated."

But if her story ideas passed quickly into the night, Susan Cantor never quite followed. For five years she stayed at ABC, eventually coming to work briefly for anchorman Peter Jennings. Her first step forward came when Lowell Bergman's unit quickly broke up and she landed as an associate producer in ABC's award-winning documentary unit, "CloseUp," where, since she was still largely unknown at the network, her arrival caused a minor stir. "There was a buzz about her; she had a certain amount of mystique when she came," a former ABC producer named Tom Lennon remembers. "Her time at NACLA was known admiringly. The sense was, this woman really knows Latin America, she's really plugged in."

At "CloseUp" Cantor befriended a young staffer named Fabienne Marsh, and the two women resolved to further their broadcast careers by tutoring each other in languages, Cantor offering an informal course in Spanish, Marsh in French. During their breakfast sessions Marsh was struck by how Cantor kept close track of how many minutes she tutored in Spanish, making sure she received at least as many in French. Marsh and others were even more struck by the nakedness of Cantor's ambition.

"She was so open about it, it was just shocking," Marsh recalls. "It was constant, chronic. Yes, chronic—that's the word. She was obsessed, always plotting, like an Italian at the Medici court, with ways to get ahead. You know, 'I've got to get Lowell to get me in to see David Burke [an ABC vice president].' She was obsessed with getting ahead. Don't let anyone tell you she didn't have an endearing, humorous side, because she did. She wanted to hang out with the girls. But she *violently* wanted to be at the center of power, where the men were, where she would be taken seriously."

Among Cantor's early assignments at "CloseUp" was a documentary on the Third World debt crisis. The program was being assembled by a veteran director named Richard Gerdeau, working closely with correspondent Bill Sherman, a crusty ex-newspaper reporter who had won a Pulitzer Prize at the *New York Daily News*. Higher-ups suggested that Cantor's Latin American experience might be useful, and though neither man knew her, they agreed to take Cantor on. Looking for chores to busy her with, Gerdeau suggested she prepare a reading list on international debt. When Cantor returned with an armful of seven or eight books and pamphlets, the two newsmen were surprised by her selections.

"We didn't recognize any of the titles or authors, so we began looking at the overleafs," Sherman recalled. "It was all this Marxist stuff. It was all like North American Marxist, all left-wing Marxist or Communist groups. It was incredible. We just started laughing."

But if the newsmen were wary of her leftist leanings, Cantor seemed proud of them. To anyone who would listen she bragged of her extensive left-wing contacts throughout Latin America. "She would talk for so long about herself that you kind of tuned her out after a few minutes," Richard Gerdeau recalled. "The themes that came out were of how she was this real conscious Communist. We always joked about her living on Central Park West and passing herself off as Che Guevara." Adds Bill Sherman: "I would kid her that she didn't even do her own grocery shopping. If she was such a devout socialist, why didn't she do her own grocery shopping? She just said she had some maid do it."

It shouldn't have come as a surprise, then, that when the team began exploring the origins of the debt crisis, Cantor rooted out some particularly creative ones. "She started coming in with these wild—I mean, truly wild—stories about Citibank and Manufacturers Hanover, how they were trying to control governments, and unseat presidents, just wild, schemelike things," recalls Bill Sherman. Sherman wouldn't have cared about Cantor's conspiracies, except that his bosses insisted he spend hours attempting to confirm them. "Susan Cantor had an inflated opinion of herself," Sherman recalls of her work on the documentary. "She didn't know a thing about journalism, much less television. And she expected everybody to be her servant."

While Sherman managed to steer clear of Cantor, his friend Tom Lennon didn't. Lennon, a film expert who had worked hard to become a solid reporter, had been in Brazil for more than a week assembling a segment on that country's debt problem when Cantor arrived to help out. Both Lennon and Sherman recall that Cantor had strongly implied a mastery of Portuguese, and Lennon was surprised to find she didn't speak the language. Still, when Cantor began bragging of her extensive Brazilian contacts, Lennon went along, hopeful of gaining an exclusive interview or two. Topping Cantor's list was a pair of well-known Brazilian professors.

"Everything with Susan was done with a whisper: 'I can get you with these guys. They never talk to the American media, but I think I can get them. I think they're going to give us a totally different perspective,'" Lennon recalls. "Always the whisper, and great promises. Then we get there [for the interview], and as we arrive, another television crew is moving their gear down, and best yet, it was another ABC crew. It was just so ludicrous, so pathetic, you couldn't believe it. Anybody could have talked to those guys."

Afterward, Lennon recalls trying to fob off minor duties on Cantor, anything to keep her out of the way. So he was stunned to hear Cantor, in conversations with their New York bosses, saying it was Lennon, not her, who was the gopher. "Her line," Bill Sherman recalls, "and this is an absolute quote, was: 'I've got everything under control. I've taken care of the story and the editorial content. Tom's taking care of some of the pictures.' Lennon did all the work, and she called superiors and said she had done it! Richard [Gerdeau] and I were just in hysterics. Lennon used to call and we just used to laugh about her, just laugh and laugh and laugh."

Privately, Lennon, who by his own estimate had arranged most of the interviews before Cantor arrived in Brazil, didn't think her claims were so funny. "It was insulting and a lie," Lennon recalled. "But it stung me where I was most vulnerable, because I had spent several years trying to shed that image." For months afterward colleagues used Cantor's line as a joking put-down: when Lennon would venture an opinion at a crowded news meeting, Sherman or Gerdeau would pipe up, "Wait a minute, Tom, you're just the picture guy."

The joking stopped when it came time to assign credits on the completed documentary. Lennon was assigned an associate producer credit, as expected. But Cantor prompted a minor uproar by obtaining a special designation. "Cantor went above me and got a 'reporter' credit, which was very unusual in those days," recalls Gerdeau, the program's director. "There was a big squall over the whole thing. On the one hand, I couldn't have cared less. On the other I was kind of annoyed, because it screwed Tom Lennon."

As much as she grated on coworkers, Cantor showed flashes of real talent. She helped assemble what Richard Gerdeau recalls as one of the debt documentary's best segments, the profile of an international loan by a bank group led by J.P. Morgan. For the segment, Cantor developed contacts at Morgan and obtained a copy of the loan agreement. A Morgan executive later wrote ABC a congratulatory note on how well the segment had come out.

The problem, of course, was that for every hard-won achievement, Cantor was gaining enemies. "By the end I loathed her," said Tom Lennon. "Sherman just wanted to murder her. Gerdeau was very alienated by her. You almost felt sorry for her. You had to have mercy on her. Where she should have had journalism experience she had ambition, just driving, driving, overreaching ambition. From a journalist's point of view, it was terrifying."

By the summer of 1983, after a year or so at "CloseUp," Cantor was in the market for a new job assignment. Her work on another documentary, this one on Mexico, had gone well, but not well enough to gain her important allies in the group. "She had rubbed a lot of people the wrong way," said Robert Ross. "It was time to move on."

But if her colleagues thought Susan Cantor was washed up, they had underestimated her resourcefulness. By the end of 1983 Cantor signed on as a personal assistant to the veteran correspondent Richard Threlkeld. "I heard that she was dangerous, from a number of different people," recalled Threlkeld's personal producer, Sally Holm. "But when Dick got into how much he wanted her, I had no evidence of my own, so of course I agreed."

Like others before her, Holm was soon sorry. "She made me nervous from the start because she smiled all the time, inappropriately," Holm recalls. Her first glimpse of Cantor's character came when the network president, Roone Arledge, dropped in on the two women as they reviewed film in an editing room, where Cantor remained a novice. Arledge complimented Holm on a recent piece, then hurried off without meeting Cantor. The moment he left, Holm recalled, Cantor exploded. "She literally went ballistic [because] I hadn't introduced her to Roone Arledge."

Cantor's new job entailed helping Threlkeld and Holm assemble the correspondent's segments, gathering videotape, arranging interviews, and brainstorming on how to approach the complex subjects Threlkeld tackled. She was a hard worker, well-organized and possessing a wealth of contacts, although Holm was never sure how well she actually knew the big names she called her friends. "She was an incredible name-dropper," Holm recalls. "She led us to believe her Rolodex had to be carried around on a dolly."

Not surprisingly, perhaps, Cantor made it clear she resented the job's menial tasks, and began spending more time on reporting chores. She and Holm repeatedly clashed when Holm suspected Cantor was pawning off work on other ABC assistants. "She would tell me she had tried to reach people when I knew she hadn't," Holm said. "She told me she had set things up and I knew she hadn't. On a number of occasions, I remember telling her to her face I thought she was lying to me. It got to the point where I wasn't sure if Susan knew what the truth was."

In the months to come, Holm's concerns about Susan Cantor grew, despite Threlkeld's admonition that Cantor wasn't so bad. Holm felt Threlkeld was blinded to Cantor's shortcomings, in part because, in Holm's words, "Susan did everything possible to kiss Dick's ass." Years later, Dick Threlkeld would retain an image of Susan Cantor strikingly different from many of his ABC colleagues. "Her work for me was sterling," he would say. "She was bright and intelligent. What more can I say?"

At Threlkeld's suggestion, Holm reconsidered her feelings, but only completed the exercise feeling more strongly about Cantor than ever. "She was an amateur," Holm said. "She had such a strong point of view [politically], she was so easily carried away by conspiracy theories. She was very pro-Castro. She was always pitching stories that were so pro-left. I'm not sure she was capable of looking at a story on its merits. Susan would look at a story and say, what point can I make with it—and what points."

As relations between the two women neared a crisis, Holm noticed Cantor cozying up to other producers, apparently in hopes of moving to a better job. Among those she targeted was Tom Yellin, who, after returning from a stretch working alongside Peter Jennings in London, had taken over as a senior producer on the evening news in September 1984. Yellin not only supervised the network's New York correspondents, he doubled as Jennings's personal producer. Most mornings a dozen or so people would crowd into an office and plan that night's broadcast. Yellin soon noticed a woman he didn't know loudly contributing opinions. It was Susan Cantor. "She's one of those people who make tremendous first impressions. You don't know *who* she is," Yellin said. "I could never get a straight answer out of anyone: who the hell *is* this woman?"

Before long he found out, as Cantor began seeking his advice on her career. She rarely missed an opportunity to corner Yellin for a hallway chat, and flattered him shamelessly. "You're probably the most talented producer at ABC," Cantor would say. "I have so much to learn from you. I really want to be a top-notch producer." Again and again she complained that she was overqualified for her job, that she wanted to do more, that she wanted to be just like Yellin. At first Yellin warmed to her. "She was making a career change," he recalls. "She was in her mid-thirties, starting at the bottom, and so you cut her a break."

The hot new issue that season was Nicaragua, and because Peter Jennings wanted to plunge into it, Yellin suggested a series of mini-seminars in which he and the anchorman could talk at length with experts from the State Department, the World Bank, and various think tanks. He put Cantor in charge of arranging them, and she came through, setting up several sessions for the two of them over the next few months. But Cantor was eager to do more for Jennings, and so in the spring of 1985 Yellin gave her the chance. Jennings was planning a weekend fact-finding trip to Nicaragua, and Yellin made Cantor the advance person. Her job was to arrange meetings with government officials and experts on the Contra situation for Jennings. "'You have to go there ahead of us,' I told her," Yellin recalls. "As soon as I said that, she flinched. The idea of spending three or four days in Nicaragua by herself clearly made her nervous. And that made me nervous."

But not half as nervous as an incident involving his wife, Anne Locksley, an aspiring novelist. When Yellin mentioned her attempts to get a first book published, Cantor cheerily suggested a meeting with her husband, Alan Kahn, an executive at Barnes & Noble, the bookstore chain. Yellin enthusiastically agreed, and dinner was arranged at a trendy Upper East Side eatery named Jams. Though the evening was filled with light humor and Manhattan chitchat, Anne Locksley was quietly troubled. Locksley had been an academic most of her life, and Cantor's recollections of her stunningly successful career at Yale didn't ring true. When the conversation turned to the case of a female professor who had recently sued Harvard for denying her tenure, Locksley mentioned that she found the woman highly talented. "Yes, when they asked me for my opinion, that's what I told them, too," Locksley recalls Cantor saying.

It was a throwaway line, but for some reason it set Anne Locksley off. She knew a thing or two about tenure procedures, and she couldn't think of any reason why Harvard would have called a Yale grad student about the case. "This was a baldly fraudulent kind of remark," she recalls. "I said, 'Well, why would they call you?' I challenged her twice on that. It just couldn't be true. So she said, 'Oh, well, they just called and asked me what I thought over the phone.' That was such a piece of shit. That was the first time I knew she was a fake."

But that exchange was nothing compared to the proposition, Locksley says, Cantor made during a trip to the powder room. The evening was drawing to a close, and the two women had been talking about the difficulties Locksley was having on her novel.

"When we got to the bathroom," Locksley recalls, "she turned to me and said, 'Look, let's just put it out on the table: if your husband promotes me to producer, my husband will get your book published.'" At first Anne Locksley was so startled she didn't know how to respond. "So I said to her, 'You've got to show Tom your stuff. You're going to Nicaragua and you've got the opportunity to show what you can do. If you do well, you'll get promoted. You don't need me.'" And then Locksley returned to the dinner table as quickly as possible, grabbed her husband, and went home. "The minute we walked into the apartment I turned to my husband and told him, 'Please, Tom, don't have anything more to do with her.'"

But the Nicaragua trip was already scheduled, and Yellin, despite his growing misgivings about Cantor, sent her to Managua to work with ABC's Central American correspondent, Peter Collins, laying the groundwork for Jennings's weekend trip. On the appointed Friday night, Jennings and Yellin flew to Miami, then chartered a plane to Managua, where they arrived at sunup Saturday. No sooner had the two walked off the plane than Cantor took Yellin aside.

"'I got to tell you something, this guy Peter Collins is an asshole,'" Yellin recalls Cantor saying. "'I don't know who he is. He could be a CIA agent. But he's bad news. I can't work with him.'" Across the way, Yellin saw Collins take Jennings aside. "'I got to tell you something, this woman doesn't know anything,'" Collins said. "'She's got her head up her ass. Get her out of here.'"

Yellin rolled his eyes: it was the last thing he needed on such a short trip. "I ask her what she's set up for Jennings, and it's basically nothing: some kind of professor that night, and one other," Yellin recalled. He was disappointed, and told her so; he suddenly had the uncomfortable feeling Susan Cantor had never even been to Nicaragua, or at least hadn't visited for a decade. But he didn't reveal his suspicions.

Instead, he and Jennings set off to a combat area near the Honduran border with Peter Collins, leaving Cantor in Managua to arrange additional interviews, if she could. "Jennings was allergic to her from the beginning," Yellin said. "She gave him the willies." Jennings later met with Cantor's two sources and found them somewhat useful, but by the end of the weekend, both he and Yellin realized that Cantor was, in Yellin's words, "a fish out of water," unsuited for field assignments.[*]

Waiting for their return flight Monday morning, the two newsmen decided to play a trick on Cantor, who they knew wasn't fond of flying. "Gee, I hope they fix the plane," Jennings said.

"You mean the door?" Yellin replied, playing along.

"That was a bit of a drag on the way down, having it come off and all."

"Yeah, hope it doesn't happen again."

---

[*]Peter Jennings confirms his leeriness of Cantor. "I was amazed by this woman," he recalls. "There was an anxiety about her that made me just plain nervous."

Yellin noticed Cantor was growing nervous; after a few more moments of teasing, she finally asked if the door could be fixed.

"No, Susan," Yellin finally said. "We're only joking."

Peter Jennings, normally a patient man, wanted nothing more to do with Cantor, and took a separate car to the airport. Yellin rode with Cantor. "Susan," he asked, bringing up her fear of planes, "so how do you fly?"

"I usually get drunk," he recalls her saying. "But I'm usually on a diet, so I don't get drunk. I take a Valium."

Once the plane was on the runway, Yellin and Jennings were forced to wait, exchanging glances, while Cantor returned to the terminal building to go to the bathroom. Upon her return, it was obvious to both men that she wasn't fit to fly. "She's terrified, absolutely terrified," Yellin recalls. To make things worse, the small Lear jet didn't have a toilet.

Yellin had had enough and ignored her, but Jennings, regaining his patience and anxious to return to New York, took Cantor by the shoulders and urged her to breathe deeply, to relax. Still, she remained so nervous that, once the Lear was aloft, Jennings and Yellin were obliged to remove a pair of seats, pull down some curtains, and construct a makeshift toilet for her. "And she basically sits there on the toilet the whole time, talking to the pilots" for the entire trip, Yellin recalled.

It was the last time Cantor worked closely with Tom Yellin. But she was destined to have far better luck with another ABC producer she wooed, a public television veteran named Charles Stuart, who in the fall of 1984 was heading ABC's "futures" unit, the group that supervised long-term feature projects. One day that fall Cantor stuck her head into Stuart's office and complained that a piece Dick Threlkeld was completing on the guerrilla war in El Salvador didn't include any interviews with the left-wing guerrilla leadership. Cantor thought it only fair that the Marxist opposition be represented on camera, and when Stuart agreed, she volunteered to fly to Toronto that weekend to interview a guerrilla leader in exile. She did so, and excerpts from the interview were inserted into Threlkeld's piece.

Charlie Stuart was impressed. An independent-minded investigative reporter distrustful of what he viewed as ABC's formal, "corporate" style of journalism, Stuart took an instant liking to Susan Cantor. He realized she wasn't popular with colleagues, but many of the best reporters he knew weren't popular in the newsroom. And if she was a bit of a conspiracy enthusiast, well, that side of Cantor appealed to Stuart. He found her sometimes bizarre ideas challenged him, forced him to rethink the way he viewed situations. In time the two grew close, especially after Stuart accepted Cantor's gracious offer to have her husband help get his wife's first novel published. And when Stuart was given the go-ahead to form a new investigative unit for ABC in 1985, he chose Cantor as one of his associate producers.

Charlie Stuart was the best thing to ever happen to Susan Cantor at ABC. In the months to come, theirs was a workplace marriage unlike any she had enjoyed before. Stuart thought Cantor showed real potential; she was a hard-charger, a relentless reporter when given the right assignment. And under his nurturing wing she began to flourish. He paired her with correspondent Lynn Sherr and the two produced what Stuart considered an excellent piece on Pentagon spy satellites aboard the space shuttle. Stuart was so pleased that he put Cantor in charge of a three-part series on espionage that centered on issues of technology transfer to the U.S.S.R. Cantor, working with correspondent John Martin, handled much of the reporting, worked on the script, and fell down only in the editing room, where she remained out of her depth.

Stuart didn't care. ABC was swarming with people who could edit tape. What the network needed, he felt, were more diehard reporters like Susan Cantor, people who were willing to go after the tough stories, no matter how difficult. To other members of the small investigative group, Stuart and Cantor appeared inseparable, always whispering behind closed doors about the latest rumors of Contra atrocities, working into the wee hours pursuing all manner of shadowy stories.

The problem, as every investigative journalist knows, is that few of these stories actually pan out, as a case involving Cantor illustrated in early 1986. That winter two stories dominated the headlines: the explosion of the space shuttle *Challenger*, and investigations into the high life of former Philippine strongman Ferdinand Marcos. Someone at ABC—a number of associates say it was Cantor—was given a box of documents indicating that Marcos might have stolen as much as $750 billion from the Philippine treasury. The documents were considered so sensational that a number of ABC correspondents and producers, including Cantor, were thrown onto the story.

Among those reluctantly pulled along was Bill Sherman, the newsman who had joked about Cantor's grocery shopping habits in 1983. As one of two producers overseeing ABC's coverage of the *Challenger* explosion, Sherman was less than thrilled to be shanghaied into a Marcos piece, especially when he heard that the recipient of the sensational documents was Cantor. Assigned to track down lead elements of the story, Sherman reached several sources who ridiculed it. Already suspicious of the documents' authenticity—he had noticed that key papers were in a different typeface than the rest—Sherman's antennae rose further when he phoned a gold broker and learned that the $750 billion Marcos was said to have stolen was more than all the gold held by every nation on the Pacific Rim.

"This story was so hot, we had dozens of people running after it all over the world, it was just huge," recalled Sherman. "People went nuts on something when you should've sat back, taken a look, and known there was nothing to it."

Instead, ABC formed a task force, impressively led by a vice president named David Burke. The group met twice a day in a large conference room off Burke's office, taking calls from people dispatched to the Philippines and Washington. His skepticism growing, Bill Sherman recalls sitting in meetings and watching in amazement as Cantor trumpeted the documents as a news story of the first order. "She had the ability to get everybody—I mean, everybody—crazy about things," recalled Sherman. "She got everybody wired up over something that was just nonsense."

For weeks ABC personnel chased the story, focusing on finding the documents' elusive signer, Ferdinand Marcos's personal secretary. Eventually the man was found living with a relative in southern California; after matching the man's signatures to those on the documents, it was determined the papers were, as the secretary insisted, fakery. The task force, and Susan Cantor's hot story, evaporated overnight.

Soon after the Marcos debacle, Cantor found herself in hot water at ABC, but not over her reporting work, which Charlie Stuart thought was steadily improving. Instead she was summoned to the office of Bill Lord, executive producer of ABC's "World News Tonight," who had been hearing complaints about Cantor's abrasive behavior toward coworkers, allegedly ordering people around in the editing room or demanding special attention in the library.

"What the hell is it about Susan Cantor?" Bill Lord asked Stuart afterward. "I like her. I trust her. What the hell do so many people have against her?"

"I don't know, Bill," Stuart replied. "She's getting good stuff for us. As long as she delivers—I think she's smart, she's resourceful—who cares if she angers people in the editing room? They're just jealous that I've made her a producer."

Charlie Stuart ended the conversation by promising he would talk again with Cantor about her behavior, and he did. "Susan, there's no reason to piss off all these people," he counseled her. "You're stepping on too many toes." It was a twist on a conversation Cantor and Stuart had had several times before. Day by day Stuart was growing less comfortable with ABC's staid journalism, and he had used his own disillusionment as an argument that perhaps Cantor wasn't suited for the network either. As much as he liked her, he realized that she still wasn't adjusting.

"Susan, you don't think like people at ABC News," Stuart had told her. "You don't fit in, and quite honestly, I think that's to your credit. This is not a place for you, and I don't think it's a place for me. You ought to think about getting out." They had both talked about leaving ABC, perhaps to set up an independent production company together.

This time Cantor promised to be more courteous, but in fact her fate was already sealed. Within weeks the problem of her behavior toward colleagues came up again, this time in a phone call one of Stuart's other assistants, a veteran associate producer named Eileen Russell, took from a congressional aide.

"Is Susan Cantor in?" the aide asked.

"No."

"Well, is Karen Burns in?" Burns was one of the unit's top correspondents.

No, Russell said. She introduced herself and asked whether she could help. "Well, I don't know what to do," the aide said. "I talk to Susan and she says I can't talk to anyone else at ABC but her. Now Karen has called me for a story." The man wanted to know if it was okay for him to talk to Burns, the correspondent, in addition to Cantor.

Eileen Russell was furious. She had never liked Cantor. To her, the aide's complaint sounded exactly like the kind of stunt she would pull. This kind of squabbling made the network look bad; furthermore, the aide was an important source, not someone to alienate. "Listen," Russell said, "this is bullshit. We all work together here. We're not separate entities."

The aide agreed, and went on to assert that Cantor had been bad-mouthing Burns behind her back. Russell got even angrier. If the investigative unit's boss, Bill Lord, found out about this, he would no doubt fire Cantor. Enough was enough: Russell strode into Charlie Stuart's office. "We've got a problem," she said, explaining the conversation. "Apparently Susan is bad-mouthing Karen in Washington. She has to go, Charlie. She has to go."

For Charlie Stuart the episode with the congressional aide was the final straw. He called Cantor into his office and broke it to her gently. "Use this as an opportunity to explore what you're best at," Stuart told her. "See what you really want to do." After their talk, Cantor reluctantly agreed to resign.

Afterward Cantor asked Eileen Russell to take an awkward walk with her on Central Park West. Apparently she blamed Russell for her resignation. "Well," Cantor began.

"Well, what?" Russell said.

"Well, what do you have to say?"

Russell thought a moment, then took a deep breath. "You have to grow up," she told Susan Cantor. "You're an adult. You can't go around destroying people's reputations."

Cantor denied bad-mouthing Karen Burns, but her protestations fell on deaf ears. "Are you an only child?" Russell asked.

"Yes."

"Well, you've got to get beyond that. Because it shows."

After Susan Cantor's resignation, nearly everyone at ABC lost track of her. Charlie Stuart was among the few to keep in touch. From time to time rumors floated back that she was writing a television screen-play, or that she was up for a reporting job at *The New York Times.* Months later, news of her hiring at American Express filtered back only gradually. Sketchy reports that she was working as a personal assistant to Jim Robinson, flying around the world in his corporate jet, were met with amazement and disbelief. More than one former colleague was sent scurrying for an American Express annual report to verify her new job.

"I was absolutely stunned," said Richard O'Regan.

"I was shocked," said Tom Yellin.

"Are you fucking serious?" said Bill Sherman.

But it was true. Susan Cantor's ambitions marched onward, now under the supervision of an inventive executive named Harry Freeman, who sat at the right hand of the chairman of American Express, James D. Robinson III. The only thing that could have surprised her former ABC colleagues more was to have learned exactly what it was American Express had hired Susan Cantor to do.

11

Welcome! Come in, come in."
Maya Jurt opened the door of her tidy little home on the outskirts of Geneva and shook Susan Cantor's hand as she stepped across the threshold. It was four o'clock on the afternoon of February 8, 1987, and Jurt—eyes bright, always willing to assist a fellow journalist—issued her visitor into a lively little kitchen looking out onto the Swiss pastureland. Jurt's young son, Gyan, the reason she worked from a home office, scampered by as the two women made their introductions.

"Tell me what I can do for you," Jurt offered. "If I can help, I will help."

So began one of the strangest source relationships Maya Jurt, one of Switzerland's leading journalists, would ever have. Jurt worked as a reporter for *Bilanz*, a monthly business magazine, but over the years had written for a number of Swiss papers, covering OPEC, North Africa, and a hodgepodge of economic issues. She could be abrasive and bluntly direct, but there were few journalists in Switzerland who could match her when it came to digging out tough stories, and her standards were higher than most. Her work had appeared in European publications like *Stern* in Germany, *The Guardian* in England, and *Euromoney*. In Geneva few were surprised that Maya Jurt had been the one to break the story linking Edmond Safra's private jet to the Iran-Contra scandal.

Arriving in Geneva in the first days of February 1987, just over a year before Safra was scheduled to reopen the doors of his Swiss bank, Susan Cantor had gotten Jurt's phone number from a woman named Irene Hirsch, a husky-voiced Argentine who covered the Swiss arm of the United Nations for newspapers in Madrid and Mexico City. Hirsch, in turn, had been urged to see Cantor by a mutual friend, an art dealer in Paris. Cantor had breezed into the press room at the UN, found Hirsch in her cubicle, and enjoyed an evening with the reporter at her home in one of Geneva's French suburbs.

"She told me she was a producer–vice president at ABC; I distinctly remember her saying vice president," Irene Hirsch would recall. "But she said she was on the way out at ABC to join American Express, which she said was more interesting. She said this project she was working on was the last thing she was doing for ABC. She was very vague about what it involved, but she was interested in Iran-Contra, that was clear. She was checking secret bank accounts to see where [Oliver North's] money was." While she never mentioned Safra, Cantor did indicate an interest in meeting Maya Jurt, and Hirsch happily passed on Jurt's telephone number.

As they took seats in the kitchen, Susan Cantor seemed to Maya Jurt an attractive professional woman not unlike herself, almost the same age, in fact. Jurt felt a degree of empathy for another woman reporter working alone, especially when she learned Cantor was working on the same frustrating investigation she was, the Iran-Contra scandal. Cantor repeated the story she had told Jurt on the phone, a story different from the one she had told Irene Hirsch: she was a former ABC News producer, now a free-lance writer, working on an article about Iran-Contra for *Time* magazine. (Jurt had written in her date book, "Susan/*Time*.") There was no mention of her real employer, American Express, or of her new boss, Harry Freeman.*

To Maya Jurt, who had spent a year in the United States in the 1970s, Cantor seemed the prototypical East Coast American liberal. She dropped all the right names, and often: the Christic Institute, Pierre Salinger of ABC, the Institute for Policy Studies, Seymour Hersh. Cantor invoked Hersh's name a lot, Jurt noticed. "You know Sy," she would say offhandedly.

Opening her files to a visitor was nothing new for Jurt. She always stood ready to help fellow journalists, or just about anyone else who came calling. Operatives for the vaunted detective Jules Kroll made Jurt's home an occasional stop on their European circuit, and her reporting often reaped the benefits of her eagerness to help out foreign guests.

---

*In a statement issued to *The Wall Street Journal* in 1990, Susan Cantor denied misrepresenting herself.

On the other hand, just two months earlier, having broken the story of Safra's jet, Jurt had turned over her research to a *New York Times* reporter, then watched in amazement as items from her file made the rounds of other reporters visiting Geneva. She knew this ought to make her mad, but for some reason the anger wasn't in her.

For Cantor's visit, Jurt did as usual, lugging down a series of files from her upstairs office to the kitchen table. There the two women pored over the scores of documents Jurt had obtained from the Geneva commercial registry, as well as her notes, written in flowing French on graph paper. In the two months since the Safra story in early December, Jurt had concentrated her reporting on Willard Zucker, the American lawyer who played a role in Oliver North's Swiss finances, and who had incorporated the shell company that owned Safra's private jet.

Among the scores of questions Jurt was pursuing was what, if any, role Safra played in the scandal. She had obtained the records to every company whose records Zucker had publicly filed in Geneva, as well as the records of every company several of Zucker's business associates had filed. Jurt had doggedly researched the names listed on each filing, but after dozens of calls had come up with nothing that shed any light on Iran-Contra or the part Safra might have played in it.

As they spoke, Maya Jurt's kitchen table slowly disappeared beneath a sprawl of papers and files. It was the typical minutiae of an investigative reporter—nine parts smoke to one part fire—but Cantor seemed interested in it all, especially anything to do with Safra. She had little to offer in return—she hadn't been working on the story long, she admitted—but did have some details on American weapons sales to Iran, shipment dates for TOW and Hawk missiles, leads a good reporter could track down. Cantor wondered aloud whether Safra's little jet might have carried weapons shipments to Iran, but at this point it was only speculation.

The two women sipped tea and worked late into the night, long after Jurt put her son to bed. As they talked, Cantor scribbled notes into a tiny pocket notebook. When a document caught her interest, Jurt stepped out into a storage room to photocopy it for her. It was a pleasant evening, the kind working journalists have all over the world. At its end Cantor, loaded down with documents, invited Jurt to visit her in New York, and the two women promised to stay in touch.

Maya Jurt didn't know it then, but elements of her research, mostly papers dealing with Willard Zucker shell companies, would later form the bulk of an anonymously written, seven-page report produced by attorneys for a French newspaper named *Minute* to lawyers representing Edmond Safra. Shown the report four years later, Jurt identified several appendices as documents she photocopied and gave to Cantor. "Yes, yes, I gave her all this," Jurt said. She even identified a single page of handwritten notes tucked into one of the appendices. "Oh, good Lord," she said. "That's my writing."

That winter Harry Freeman had sent Susan Cantor's résumé down to the forty-eighth-floor office of Walter Montgomery, the public relations chief who had left Kekst & Company years before. On it Freeman scribbled a note to the effect that he found Cantor an intriguing possibility for a spot on the headquarters p.r. staff, and he asked Montgomery to follow up with an interview of his own. A onetime Chinese history teacher at Brown, Montgomery, too, found Cantor's mix of network television and academic experience interesting, even more so after she delivered a solid interview and received a rousing recommendation from her old boss Richard Threlkeld.

The only problem was, American Express was in the midst of one of its periodic hiring freezes, and Montgomery, despite all his efforts, hadn't been able to hire anyone to bolster his sorely overworked staff. Susan Cantor's hiring shouldn't—and wouldn't—have gone through, except for the personal intervention of Harry Freeman. "If you like," Freeman told Montgomery, "why don't you go ahead and hire her."

And so the rules were bent, as they sometimes were, and Cantor was hired, at an initial salary of around $65,000. She was given an office on the north side of the public relations section on the forty-eighth floor, and Montgomery sat her down and talked through some simple assignments she might handle, nothing too financial or technical at first, since she had little business experience.

Walter Montgomery had hardly introduced Cantor to his other fourteen staffers before he took another call from Freeman, who broke the unusual news that he was looking for someone to travel to Geneva to do a little digging into Edmond Safra's affairs. Montgomery had seen the *New York Times* article about Safra's jet, and didn't have to be told what the digging involved.

"I'm checking with all my departments," Freeman said. "Is there anybody in yours capable of doing something like that?"

"I can't really think of anybody in the department who'd be good," Montgomery said. "I suppose you could argue, because of her investigative reporting background, Susan would be good."

No sooner had the words left Montgomery's mouth than Freeman leaped on them. "That's an interesting idea, a great idea," Freeman said. "Send her up."

Montgomery did so. Only later, after the full scope of Susan Cantor's work became known, would some in Walter Montgomery's department come to marvel at how quickly Freeman had selected Cantor. It was almost, they speculated, as if the whole thing had been planned from the start.

Within days of her summons to Harry Freeman's office, Susan Cantor disappeared on the first of a series of overseas trips, full details of which would never be divulged. Often during that spring and summer of 1987 her office lay empty, a fact that provoked resentment among Walter Montgomery's harried staff. At one point or another, almost every member of the department approached Montgomery to complain that Cantor wasn't pulling her weight, and to inquire where she was all the time. Only Montgomery knew, and he wouldn't say. "Look, she's off doing something for Harry," he told one aide, rolling his eyes. "I can't talk about it. I know you're not happy, but it's not like she's off on vacation or something."

What her office mates didn't know was that Cantor, under the personal supervision of Harry Freeman, had embarked on a special, top-secret, solo investigation of Edmond Safra. Freeman had laid it all out for Cantor in her visit to his office: the *New York Times* article, the strange story of Safra's jet, Willard Zucker. By all accounts Cantor, a political animal avidly following coverage of the spreading Iran-Contra scandal, ate it up.

"She was quite eager," Freeman recalled, though at least at first for entirely the wrong reason. "Her view was, 'Boy, we ought to really find out about all this stuff on Iran-Contra, because if it's true, we could get rid of President Reagan and Bush all at the same time.' I said, 'Come on, Susan, we're both Democrats, but American Express is not in the business of unseating Presidents of the United States. Cool it. Your job is to think about how to go about seeing whether or not Safra is involved in all this.'" These political references, Freeman recalled, were the only occasions he ever had reason to second-guess his selection of Cantor to spearhead the investigation he and Jim Robinson had in mind.

Whatever Cantor's motivations, Freeman and Robinson's were crystal clear. American Express needed dirt on Edmond Safra, and it needed it fast. If Cantor found something damaging enough, Freeman saw at least three possible uses for it. First and foremost, they could confront Safra with what they had found, and demand that he stop all efforts to solicit TDB employees and depositors. This, of course, was the corporate version of blackmail, but in Freeman's mind, a tough challenge called for an equally tough response.

Second, they could funnel damaging information to Swiss banking regulators in hopes of sabotaging Safra's new banking license. At Robinson's suggestion, Freeman says he alerted the bank's general counsel, John Junek, to their plans, and Junek signaled his willingness to use anything Freeman might find in their Swiss filings.

But it was the third option Freeman foresaw that went straight to Safra's Achilles' heel: the strategic leak of damaging information to journalists. From his earliest talks with Cantor, Freeman spoke of the press as a likely outlet for their findings, albeit one to be approached with great discretion. Feeding dirt to reporters was a risky endeavor, he always said, only to be used with the best information and the best journalists. Still, if American Express couldn't pressure Safra directly, Freeman felt there was no more reliable an investment for indirect pressure than the press. "It was clear that if we had factual stuff," he recalled, "we would take it to the most credible media possible."

Much later, in an internal memo to American Express attorneys, Freeman explained his mission against Safra this way: "My task was to develop some kind of counterattack, *both in the media and in the bank license procedure* [italics added]. According to Freeman, he and Jim Robinson never discussed which individual reporters they might approach. Between the two old friends, both well-schooled in sophisticated press strategies, he says it was simply assumed that the media was a natural outlet for anything they might find.

Thus briefed, Cantor leaped into her new assignment with tremendous energy. As her colleagues sulked, she spent most of the following weeks—her first weeks at American Express—traveling in Europe, where she struck a gold mine of information during the long evening with Maya Jurt. Though in those first days she busied herself chasing documents at various Swiss agencies, she was free to range across Europe in search of anything damaging on Safra. "I gave her great latitude," Freeman said. "I said, 'Go wherever you need to get what you're looking for. Follow the hottest lead.'"

Upon her return, Cantor insisted on briefing Freeman at length. "She would come to my office and sit down and she would have this stack of things," Freeman recalled. "She would start on about going to the Civil Aviation Authority [of Switzerland] and spending two weeks going through records. All this stuff about tail numbers on planes. I'm sitting there sinking in my chair, going, 'I don't really care.' I wanted to see hard evidence [of wrongdoing]. My question was, 'Can't you show me [evidence]?' She said, 'No, I have to take you through it.' She insisted on going through tremendous amounts of detail."

On any given day Freeman and Jim Robinson chatted often, five or ten times or more, and in the weeks to come Cantor's investigation became a regular topic of their caucuses. "In the area that I operated in, Robinson knew everything that was going on," Freeman says. "We frequently talked about [Cantor's investigation], sometimes two or three times a week. It was no secret." Robinson was interested enough in Cantor's probe that he, too, received briefings on her findings, both in one-to-one meetings with Cantor in his fifty-first-floor office and, as she began doing more chores for him in the months to come, during long flights on his private jet.

"Robinson had the same problem with her I did; after a while, she gets into such detail, you just sort of turn off," Freeman recalled. "When Susan [flew] with him—poor Jim—Susan probably sat there talking about tail numbers. Robinson sat there [thinking], 'How do I get this babe off my goddamn corporate jet? I want to sleep.'" Freeman acknowledges that his information on what Cantor told Robinson is limited. "I don't know what Susan told Jim. I wasn't there. But I know she told me she tried to brief him in as much detail as possible. I know he complained that she would talk an awful lot [to him]. He said [to me], 'My God, Susan Cantor, do I have to keep listening to her?' I suspect that he had more hours of briefing with her than I had....But I remember Jim said, 'Boy, I turn off pretty fast'" when Susan began her Safra briefings.

Robinson and Freeman weren't the only ones to receive earfuls about Safra from Susan Cantor that spring. Upon her return from Europe, for example, she telephoned Charlie Stuart at ABC and eagerly described her new investigation for American Express. Maybe, Cantor suggested, the network itself might be interested in delving into Safra. "She begins to blow in my ear, 'Hey Safra this, hey Safra that, hey Safra and McFarlane and a plane that,'" recalled Stuart. "It was the same kind of stuff like at ABC. 'Did you know this, isn't this interesting?' I said, 'Susan, if you can nail it down, I'd be interested.' But she couldn't nail it down. It was just the same old Susan I knew at ABC, always spreading gossip....She couldn't sort out what was real from what was unreal."

Cantor also described her investigation to an old source and neighbor on Central Park West, David Aaron, who was left with the impression she was probing Safra's activities not for American Express, but for a free-lance article. "I recall her talking about him, and saying unkind things," said Aaron, a novelist and a former assistant national security adviser during the Carter administration. "I remember her saying things along the lines of, 'His bank does dirty deals.'" Aaron, who knew little of Safra, was nevertheless intrigued by Cantor's work, since he wanted a character in his next novel to track down the movement of "dirty" money in Europe. He listened intently as Cantor described her recent excursion to Geneva, including a side trip by train to a second Swiss city where she said she reviewed more records on Safra.

Harry Freeman had outlined the possibilities for approaching "the most credible media possible," and as she gathered more material Cantor began doing just that. That spring, as she continued her research on Safra, she traveled to Washington and visited her old friend Sy Hersh at his office in the National Press Building. The former *Times* reporter, who had become a successful author after leaving the newspaper in 1979, remembered Cantor fondly from the coup in Chile, and listened as she attempted to interest him in another story, this one a hot new angle on the Iran-Contra scandal involving a shady Swiss banker named Edmond Safra.

"She came to me with all this stuff she had about Safra," Hersh recalled. "It had to do with stuff she had found in Geneva, a whole series of corporate exchanges, documents and transactions involving [Albert] Hakim. The thing with Willard Zucker. She was very interested in getting me into Iran-Contra. She was trying to make some connections on the basis of these Swiss documents.* She had all these grandiose ideas. She said, 'We can do it together.' I didn't see the story." Despite Sy Hersh's skepticism, Susan Cantor would keep at him about a Safra exposé for weeks.

Some of the "grandiose ideas" Cantor was pursuing that spring were laid out in a now-infamous 1986 lawsuit filed by a liberal public-law group, the Washington-based Christic Institute. The Christic "mystics," as a *Washington Post* editorialist dubbed the group, alleged in their suit that American foreign policy since 1959 had been shanghaied by a "secret team" of CIA agents and sundry spies, including Iran-Contra figures like Richard Secord. This "secret team," Christic's suit charged, had had a hand in everything from the Kennedy assassination to Watergate to the 1973 Chilean coup to secret assassination programs in Vietnam to Laotian opium traffic to—and here it dovetailed with Cantor's interest— Iran-Contra. Christic's grand conspiracy theory, which initially attracted the attention of many journalists, was ultimately discredited so thoroughly that a federal court not only threw out its suit, it fined the group $1.1 million for filing "frivolous" litigation, the largest such penalty in American judicial history.

What drew Cantor's attention was Christic's contention, deep into a forty-four-page affidavit by the group's cofounder, that Willard Zucker's company was among a plethora of firms used by the "secret team" of former CIA men to fund their Iran-Contra activities—a contention that, if proven, might conceivably tie another Zucker client, Edmond Safra, even closer to spy-world machinations.

"That was, to her, a very hot lead," recalls Maya Jurt, who reviewed Cantor's copy of the Christic affidavit during a second trip Cantor made to Geneva later that year. Jurt noticed factual errors in the Christic affidavit—Panama-based companies were identified as Swiss companies— that led her to have serious doubts about its accuracy. "I told her, 'No, no, this is all wrong,'" Jurt says. As she watched, Cantor bracketed the questionable paragraph, scribbled down the word "wrong" beside it, and

---

* Among the possible "connections" Cantor had made involved Sylvain Ferdman, the lawyer who was cited in the 1967 *Life* article as a Mafia courier, and whose name appeared on records of a Willard Zucker shell company having no links to Safra. Sy Hersh says he can't remember his talks with Cantor well enough to confirm this. He declines to discuss Cantor's "grandiose ideas" in detail. And though he says he retains materials Cantor provided him— "I've got boxes and boxes of stuff she gave me," Hersh says—he declines to make it available for review.

underlined it twice. Elsewhere Cantor had underlined or scribbled questions beside several sections dealing with Willard Zucker's firm.

In New York that spring, Cantor breezed around the forty-eighth floor of American Express headquarters openly excited about the prospect of Sy Hersh's tackling a major exposé of Safra's shady Iran-Contra ties. While she continued her briefings in Robinson and Freeman's upstairs offices, Cantor also began mentioning things to new friends in the p.r. department, including her boss Walter Montgomery. Coworkers, a handful of whom had caught on to the nature of her secret assignment, couldn't help but hear about her efforts to interest Sy Hersh in Safra: "I talked to Sy...I'm really pushing Sy...Sy says he's interested"—it went on and on.

More than one colleague cringed at Cantor's indiscretion. It was bad enough that one of their number was involved in something approximating a "dirty tricks" campaign, but Cantor was so obviously intoxicated by her introduction to corporate intrigue, she seemed intent on telling others about it. Office mates took to joking about her "war stories." Though no one knew exactly how she spent her time overseas, in the months to come Cantor told of altering her appearance during her European forays, at one point changing her hair color. To one colleague she claimed to have posed as a prostitute to get tips about Safra; another understood her to have disguised herself as someone's mistress to gain entrance to a cocktail party of some sort. Perhaps the most exciting moment Cantor described came when, during a trip to the French Riviera, she crept up to La Leopolda and snapped pictures she said she hoped to sell to *Paris Match* for a story on Safra.

No one could tell whether Cantor's stories were pure fantasy or based on kernels of truth. She often embroidered them with tales of her past. At times she spoke of being a member of "the underground" in New York during the 1960s, and of meeting the Panamanian strongman Manuel Noriega. In Latin America, she told one colleague, she liked to approach the masseuses of powerful figures she was investigating to find out what was really on their clients' minds.

Freeman soon realized that Cantor, in his words, "tended to glory in the Mata Hari image; she liked to be seen as mysterious." On her European trips she would phone his office in New York to check in, only to say little because, she said, she didn't trust the phones. On another occasion Freeman says she insisted on meeting at a midtown Manhattan hotel, intimating she thought his office might be bugged. "She liked to view this as a spy novel," Freeman recalled. "But as long as it didn't cause any trouble, I didn't care. I was willing to put up with eccentricities to get what I was after. I wanted results."

Between her trips for Freeman, Walter Montgomery attempted to interest Cantor in more traditional public relations assignments, but he met with little luck. Cantor was peripatetic, and colleagues complained that she was unable to focus on normal duties, especially when immersed in her secret work for Freeman. Her liberal harangues, meanwhile, put off several coworkers: on the subject of Third World debt, which caused American Express Bank to take a big write-off that June, Cantor was particularly outspoken, going on and on about how it represented a capitalist plot to exploit South America. "She always seemed to subscribe to the conspiracy theory of everything," recalls another colleague. "The weather, the traffic, no matter how simple a matter it might be, there was always a complicated answer that only Susan seemed to understand."

Far more worrisome to Cantor's colleagues were her problems briefing reporters. When she was allowed to field questions on a minor press release, one coworker complained to Walter Montgomery that Cantor was entirely too forthcoming, too glib, that she didn't seem to realize the limits of propriety in even the most basic discussions with a journalist. Montgomery was obliged to have other staffers sit in on Cantor's conversations to ensure she didn't say the wrong thing. "Just make sure she sticks to the text" of the press release, Montgomery told one staffer.

Cantor, meanwhile, kept at Sy Hersh about a Safra exposé but never managed to overcome his skepticism, even after relating stories about organized crime at Kings Lafayette, the Brooklyn bank Safra had purchased fifteen years before. When she persisted, Hersh suggested she take her ideas to a friend of his, Jeff Gerth, an investigative reporter in the Washington bureau of *The New York Times*. Gerth had done extensive work on Oliver North's money trail and had been among the first reporters to delve into Willard Zucker. "She was trying to get a journalist interested in her story," Hersh confirms. "I gave her to Jeff."

Gerth met with Cantor once or twice in mid-1987, and took copies of her materials on Willard Zucker, Albert Hakim, and Republic National Bank. Like Hersh, he knew Cantor worked for American Express, and wasn't exactly sure how that figured into what seemed like a personal investigation of the Iran-Contra affair. Gerth might have given Cantor more thought, but her materials were of little use to his reporting, and he ultimately discarded them, putting the incident out of his mind.

The *Times* bureau wasn't Cantor's last stop in Washington. Joseph P. Saba, a staff counsel on the House select committee investigating Iran-Contra, was surprised one day that spring to be handed a note telling him that someone was waiting to see him outside his office. Saba emerged to meet a smiling woman who introduced herself as Susan Cantor, a former journalist doing some free-lance investigating into Iran-Contra. Cantor, who held a bulky binder under her arm, emphasized to Saba that her current employer, whom she pointedly declined to name, knew nothing about what she was doing. She was just digging a little on her own, and had found some things she felt the committee might find interesting. "She said she was doing it for primarily journalistic reasons," Saba recalled.

Joe Saba, no stranger to zealots and conspiracy nuts, took Cantor's binder and saw that it contained a wealth of European news articles, some about Safra's plane, as well as a clutch of Willard Zucker's records from Geneva's commercial registry. Saba promised to look into it, and Cantor promised to stay in touch. All that summer she did just that, telephoning Saba often to pepper him with tips and bits of information and theories about Republic and Safra. "It was always, 'Here's what I've got, what do you think?'" Saba recalls. "And my answer was, 'Not much.'"[*]

Still, Saba kept up the relationship with Cantor, who introduced him to Sy Hersh, presumably in hopes of rekindling the reporter's interests in Safra. Saba, meanwhile, took the stories about Safra's plane, as well as questions about Zucker's use of Republic accounts, to Walter Weiner in New York, who helped Saba track down exactly what Zucker had been doing. After talking with Weiner, Saba reached the conclusion that neither Republic nor Safra had any significant or knowing role in Oliver

---

[*] Cantor, it should be noted, was far from the only person tracking down seemingly bizarre conspiracy theories in Washington that summer. The capital, in fact, was awash with them. *Newsweek*, in a 1991 cover story that traced the popularity of the so-called "October Surprise" theory to this period, termed the middle months of 1987 "high summer, so to speak, for conspiracy buffs." The reason, it suggested, was the fast-breaking Iran-Contra scandal, which, as *Newsweek* put it, "showed that the [Reagan] administration was eager to engage in covert action, and that it was ready to lie, destroy documents and cover up a range of covert activities that violated the law."

North's finances. "It was just one of hundreds of conspiracy theories we had to track down," Saba says, "and we decided there was nothing to it."

As for Susan Cantor, Joe Saba grew curious. Just who was she? Her explanation didn't make much sense: free-lance investigative journalism in her spare time for an unknowing employer? Saba was suspicious enough that he asked one of the committee's press aides to check out who Cantor really was. It only took a few phone calls to find out she worked for American Express. "We said, 'That was fine,'" Saba recalls. The committee's job was to get to the truth, using whatever sources possible. "Motive," Saba says, "wasn't something I was interested in."

All that summer Cantor continued to disappear regularly into Harry Freeman's fifty-first-floor office, keeping him up to date on her progress, or rather her lack of it.* She also continued to brief Jim Robinson, though no one has come forward to detail their private sessions. For all her digging, by that summer it was painfully clear that Cantor still hadn't found anything approaching a "smoking gun" on Safra's supposed criminality. It was during her courtship of Joe Saba that she and Freeman agreed she could use some assistance.

"Susan made a trip or two, came back and said, 'I need help badly,'" Freeman recalls. "She said, 'This is a big job; [I'm] going all over Switzerland checking records. This will take ten years...'" Clearly it was time for professional help. For guidance he turned to the man who had aided Bob Terrier on the TDB refugee issue, Paul Knight, American Express's security chief for Europe and the Middle East.

By the time Freeman called that spring, Knight already knew about the quiet little investigation of Safra. Susan Cantor had recently blown into his London office, asking for an update on the bank's Geneva investigations, seeking tips on Safra and dropping seemingly every name in sight, including Freeman's, Jim Robinson's—repeatedly—as well as that of Sy Hersh, whose name meant nothing to Knight. When Cantor stepped out to the bathroom, Knight, immensely skeptical that a woman

---

* For all the detail of Cantor's briefings—or perhaps because of it—Freeman claims his own memory of those briefings, and of Cantor's doings in general, is hazy at best. Of Sy Hersh, he says: "I think she mentioned to me approaching Sy Hersh. She would come back to me and talk an awful lot. I don't remember a lot of what she said."

Freeman on Jeff Gerth: "Gerth rings a bell...I don't remember anything else."

Freeman on Joe Saba and the Iran-Contra committees: "I know she went to Washington but I wasn't sure what she was doing. I remember once she said she wanted to talk to the committee, and I said, 'Susan, be careful.'"

of Cantor's breezy manner would be entrusted to such a sensitive mission by Jim Robinson, immediately called Freeman in New York. "Harry, this girl, who is she?" he asked.

"Anything she says to you, Paul, it's me talking," Freeman said. "You can have confidence in her."

By several accounts, Paul Knight was instantly leery of Cantor, and so when Freeman called soliciting help for her, Knight deftly dodged the bullet by suggesting they bring in outside help. For Knight the choice of investigators was obvious: Jules Kroll.

By the late 1980s Kroll, a smooth, heavy-lidded former assistant prosecutor, had established his firm, Kroll Associates, as the investigators of choice for top U.S. companies who needed some dirty laundry sorted. From his suite of wood-paneled offices on Manhattan's Third Avenue, Kroll and his band of former FBI men, lawyers, and investigative reporters made their reputations dishing dirt in the takeover battles of the 1970s and 1980s. In the thick of a heated proxy contest or tender offer, Kroll and his people could be counted on to root out a nasty divorce case or a padded résumé, anything embarrassing enough to give one corporate titan leverage over another. Over the years they had investigated everyone from Ivan Boesky to Saddam Hussein; the Texas raider Boone Pickens always complained that Kroll simply sold and resold his bulky file on him to every company he bid for. But there was no disputing Kroll's effectiveness; in at least one case, a hostile raid on Avon, his people reportedly unearthed tidbits humiliating enough to scare off an unwanted suitor altogether.

By the time Freeman sent Susan Cantor to sit down with Jules Kroll in mid-1987, the canny detective was well aware of the ill will between American Express and Safra. During the past few months he had been contacted by both sides; Ken Bialkin of American Express had inquired about his availability to investigate the TDB refugees, though nothing came of it. Later Robert Siegfried of Kekst had asked about his representing Safra, but again nothing happened.

Even before they met, Kroll's radar had picked up on Cantor's curious project; friends working among the government's Iran-Contra investigators had passed on gossip about her quiet relationship with Joe Saba. Then, in the late spring or early summer of 1987, Kroll took a phone call from his friend Paul Knight. Kroll knew Knight had been involved in efforts to pin down the TDB refugee issue in Geneva, though he hadn't followed the case closely. "They're doing some things out of New York, too, on this," Knight told Kroll, "and they could really use some help." Knight mentioned Susan Cantor's name and said she was working for Harry Freeman.

"You know who he is, don't you?"

"Sure." Kroll had never met Freeman, but knew him by reputation as Jim Robinson's right-hand man. That gave Knight's call the highest priority, and Kroll promised to look into the case personally. And he did, ushering Cantor into his corner office one day that summer and listening as she laid out details of her investigation. At that meeting, and in a later follow-up, Cantor's manner was brisk and energetic. She seemed always in a hurry, rushing off to one foreign capital or another. In her eyes Jules Kroll saw the fervor of the true believer. Cantor, it was clear, thought Edmond Safra was a criminal of the first order.

That summer Cantor remained focused on two things: Willard Zucker and Safra's jet. Kroll glanced through the documents she had accumulated and promised to look into the matter. Over the course of a month or so he hired a Swiss investigator to examine records in Geneva, and did some informal checking on Safra himself. But neither effort produced anything like the criminal evidence Cantor and Freeman wanted to find.* For all the rumors, Safra seemed clean; American Express's investigation, Kroll felt, was wrongheaded. After thinking it through, he returned to American Express to say so.

"I think you guys are barking up the wrong tree," Kroll told Freeman and Cantor during a meeting in Freeman's office. "I believe your enthusiasm for achieving a difficult objective is clouding your view." Freeman didn't argue, and didn't discuss the proposal further.† Once Kroll declined the assignment, it was as if a door had closed. Freeman thanked Kroll for his work, said he appreciated the advice, and ended the meeting after twenty minutes or so. The detective didn't bother to send a bill. But in the months to come he kept his ears open for anything new about American Express's little investigation. Somehow Jules Kroll knew it wasn't the last he would hear of it.

In the wake of her meetings with Kroll, Susan Cantor remained

---

* Among Kroll's friends was Peter Cohen, who told the detective that Safra wasn't involved in anything nefarious.

† Freeman says he doesn't remember any such meeting, nor the fact that Kroll did any work on the Safra investigation.

upbeat. Back at her office, she told at least one colleague she was making headway at amassing evidence against Safra. It was no secret what Susan Cantor intended to do once she had "enough": slip it to more journalists. "We're not ready to go to the press just yet," this former American Express executive recalls Cantor saying in mid-1987. "It's too risky."

Investigating Edmond Safra was by no means the only task Susan Cantor pursued at American Express that year. Harry Freeman drafted her to help on a number of the special projects run out of the chairman's office, where in the months to come she undertook an array of assignments in public relations and Latin American affairs, and where she would come into regular contact with the man whose name would always seem to be on her lips, Jim Robinson.

By 1987 Robinson, in his self-designated role as "corporate statesman," was increasingly involved in devising a solution to the problem of Third World nations indebted to the world banking system. American Express Bank had a huge problem with Third World debt, and if Robinson could somehow broker a solution, he would bring an avalanche of business to the company. Cantor became one of dozens of specialists assembled into an ad hoc group to brainstorm the project, which took its name from the international agency whose formation Robinson would unsuccessfully urge: the Institute for International Debt and Development, known as I2D2.

That year Jim Robinson traveled widely seeking ideas and backers for his plan. Cantor had been selected for the I2D2 team in part because of her contacts in Latin America, and once aboard, she, too, traveled extensively, helping to promote Robinson's plan to any number of Latin American businessmen and diplomats. Her best contacts, former colleagues say, were with two of Venezuela's most powerful families: the Cisneros clan, which owned television stations and supermarkets and was one of the largest Pepsi bottlers in the world; and the Mendozas, an old-line family with investments in agriculture, cement, and a number of other industries. According to Harry Freeman, Robinson considered Cantor his top marketer of I2D2 to Latin American opinion makers.

When Robinson himself flew to Latin America, Cantor sometimes accompanied him on the long flights aboard an American Express jet, acting as the chairman's "advance person" for trips to Venezuela, Mexico, and Argentina. Part of her job was preparing Robinson beforehand, helping to compile thick briefing books on the situation in each country he would visit. Once on the ground, she was an all-purpose aide, at one point, a former colleague remembers, securing a hangar from Mexico's minister of tourism for Robinson's jet. Cantor rarely tired of recounting these long trips with Robinson to friends and, later, to at least one journalist on the Safra beat, Maya Jurt.

At headquarters, Cantor became one of the few to achieve access to the chairman's office, where from time to time, she told friends, she sought Robinson's advice about her future at American Express. When Robinson or his aides convened meetings of the I2D2 team, Cantor was a voluble presence. "Her gestures were always quite exaggerated, she was always a little frayed, and practically speaking, she didn't have much time for those below her, and that was a lot of people," recalls a senior member of the I2D2 team. "She was very difficult for everyone to get along with."

Still, in the months to come only the vaguest hint of Cantor's other work, her secret project for Freeman, reached her new colleagues outside the p.r. department. "It became clear to me and to others working on the project that she was doing something more than working on this project, but no one knew what it was," recalls the I2D2 team member. "She was an enigma to me. A lot of people were traveling all over the world, talking to people who were then collaborating on other efforts to come up with solutions to the debt situation. Usually you would see some explanation of their trip, a memo, something. With her it was nothing. With her, it was just silence."

Cantor's work for Jim Robinson didn't stop at arranging overseas trips. Investment bankers in the Third World debt group at Shearson Lehman were surprised one day when she popped into their offices and announced that Robinson had appointed her to coordinate matters of debt policy among headquarters, Shearson, and American Express Bank. On the surface some sort of coordinator made sense: the Shearson group, which attempted overseas debt swaps and other complex transactions, was always feuding with Bob Smith's people on the best way to solve American Express Bank's own debt problems. "Everyone hated the bank," a former Shearson official recalls, "and the bank hated everyone."

But Jay Newman, the Shearson group's chief, was puzzled why Robinson had sent someone like Susan Cantor to mediate. While she had some contacts to offer in Venezuela and Mexico, Cantor didn't appear to know the first thing about international banking. "Who the fuck is she?" Newman asked after Cantor's initial appearance. "Who is this flaky woman?" No one knew.

In fact, as Newman came to know her, Susan Cantor spent less time "coordinating" policy than asking him to teach her the ins and outs of the business world, much as she had sought advice from Tom Yellin at ABC News on how to become a television producer. "Her schtick was always, 'I want to learn about business, I'm doing this for Jim, but I want to get serious,'" says a former member of the Shearson group. "She knew so little, absolutely nothing about business...it was amazing."

As time went by and Cantor became a regular visitor to Jay Newman's office, she might have become a pest, but she didn't. To Newman's crowd, Cantor was the best possible emissary Jim Robinson could have sent them; she was cute and funny and wore great clothes, not at all like the temperamental international bankers they usually dealt with. And best of all, they thought she was harmless.

Her liberal politics, though, placed her at odds with Newman's top aide, Keith Fogerty, who often visited New York from his base in London. A vocal conservative, Fogerty never tired of needling Cantor. "To her the Sandinistas are Jeffersonian Democrats," he joked. The two would get in long, loud arguments, with Fogerty dismissing Cantor's radical theories as "drivel." More than once he denounced her as an "educated slut" and openly ridiculed her degree from Yale. "Oh, Ph.D. except for the thesis," Fogerty said with obvious sarcasm. "Oh, come on, Susan, if I had a nickel for everyone with a Ph.D. but for a thesis, I'd be rich."

For all the ribbing, Cantor proved a good sport. And Newman's people were careful not to push the teasing too far; however ignorant she was of economics, Cantor's position as Jim Robinson's personal representative gave her clout far beyond that of other p.r. executives. "She always projected herself as representing Jim, that we wouldn't want to do something that pissed Jim off, that we were in line with his views," Keith Fogerty recalled. "It was constantly Jim this, Jim that." And neither Fogerty nor Newman had reason to doubt her. On at least one occasion Robinson called their offices from his car phone looking for Cantor.

In the p.r. department, meanwhile, Walter Montgomery continued trying to draw Cantor into more conventional work. After deciding she wasn't ready to talk to reporters about press releases, he happened upon a project that seemed perfect for an aggressive, quintessential New Yorker like Cantor. He made her publicity liaison for a major arts event American Express was sponsoring the following summer, the New York International Festival of the Arts. At meetings, festival officials were initially charmed by Cantor, who came across as witty, bright, and intellectually curious. But as pleasant as she could be, it quickly became apparent that Cantor didn't know the first thing about running a publicity campaign. Talk of press kits and advertising strategies either eluded or bored her, festival officials weren't quite sure.

"She never said she was a p.r. person, and she wasn't," recalled one colleague. "It was always unclear to us why she was on this project, when she was so clearly not qualified for it. There seemed to be something else she was working on. She was always kind of vague about who she was and what else she was doing. We knew she was taking trips with Jim Robinson. She was working for him, doing assignments for him, traveling around with him. She was always out of the country, gone for weeks at a time. We began wondering, 'What the hell is she doing?'"

The question of Cantor's travels arose again that fall when, after Walter Montgomery's resignation to join the p.r. firm headed by Jim Robinson's wife, Linda, the department's new No. 2, Matthew Stover, brought up the subject with its new No. 1, Lawrence Armour, a former spokesman for Dow Jones & Company, publishers of *The Wall Street Journal*. While studying his budgets, Stover was surprised to see the number of overseas trips Cantor was taking; her expenses alone threatened to throw the department's travel allowance over budget. Stover took Armour aside to ask what he should do. Without divulging details, Armour assured his aide he needn't worry about Cantor, that it was all being taken care of. Matt Stover did as he was told, and in all the months he worked alongside Cantor, he says he never did figure out what her secret project involved. "I was always told, 'You don't want to know,'" he says.

By the end of that summer of 1987 American Express's battle with Safra was nearing a climax. On August 31 the company formally filed its opposition to Safra Republic's new license with the Swiss bank board. At a Geneva criminal court, Bob Terrier and other TDB executives continued giving secret testimony to a Swiss judge on the missing computer files. Despite the skepticism of several of the company's top lawyers, many at

American Express felt confident the legal cases were strong, and might actually allow TDB to evade the looming challenge from Safra's return, then just six months away.

It was against this backdrop that Cantor returned to Geneva in the first days of September and checked into the opulent Hôtel Beau-Rivage, just across Lake Geneva from Safra's headquarters. Among the people she contacted was her friend Irene Hirsch at the UN, who agreed to come by her hotel room for lunch. Hirsch was surprised to find Cantor staying at such a high-profile downtown hotel, given the sensitive nature of her Iran-Contra investigations, but said nothing, not wanting to be rude.

As they chatted in her room, Cantor explained that, as she had mentioned that winter, she had indeed left ABC for American Express, but that she hadn't given up journalism altogether. Now, she said, she was pursuing a "top secret" story on Iran-Contra she hoped to have published in the *Washington Post*. The explanation struck Hirsch as odd: how was Cantor able to combine investigative newspaper work for the *Washington Post* with a job at American Express? Somehow, Hirsch decided, and she couldn't quite put her finger on it, there was more to Susan Cantor than met the eye.

Before leaving for lunch, Cantor apologized and said she had to make a call to her boss in New York. That, too, struck Hirsch as odd. "Aren't you in touch with the people at your local branch here in Geneva?" she asked.

"No, this is private," Cantor said. "I don't know the people here. My bosses are in New York." She even mentioned one of them: Harry Freeman.

Later, as the two women walked out through the lobby, Cantor left a message at the desk for Maya Jurt. "The impression I got was, she was extremely anxious to keep up the professional relationship with Maya Jurt," Hirsch recalled. "She seemed to think she had a lot of stuff coming from Maya Jurt." The two women walked out along the lake, ducking into a shopping arcade or two and enjoying a light lunch. Irene Hirsch returned to her cubicle at the UN afterward perplexed by Cantor; she realized that after two sessions together, she still had no idea what the woman was up to.

At least one other person had dealings with Cantor during her stay at the Beau-Rivage that September. Bob Terrier, the man running the investigation of the TDB refugees, was told by one of his superiors to prepare a list of ex-employees suspected of working for Safra. When the list was completed, Terrier was told, it was to be forwarded to a woman named Susan Cantor at the Beau-Rivage. For some reason Terrier felt uncomfortable about the request; something about it seemed fishy. Nervous, he typed the names out on an unmarked sheet of computer paper instead of American Express stationery, then slipped it into an unmarked envelope and had it messengered to the hotel. It was the only time Terrier had ever heard the name Susan Cantor. He never found out what Cantor did with the names.

Susan Cantor's taxi pulled into the narrow lane leading to Maya Jurt's home around six on the evening of September 1. Jurt was glad to see Cantor, for after building a file on Safra for the better part of a year, she had finally begun working on a major magazine piece on the mysterious banker. As they renewed their acquaintance, Cantor seemed eager to help. Her own piece in *Time* apparently hadn't worked out. Now, Cantor explained, she had obtained a grant and was working on a book on Iran-Contra. Just as during her first visit, there was no mention of her working for American Express.

The two women picked up where they left off seven months before. Over dinner they discussed Iran-Contra and Safra, again well into the night. But unlike her earlier visit, this time Cantor was the one brimming with news and rumors about Safra, much of it, she told Jurt, obtained from her sources on the Iran-Contra committees in Washington. She had so many stories Jurt couldn't keep them all straight. Some seemed promising, but most seemed the flimsiest of gossip, no doubt impossible to pin down. A few, involving strange CIA doings in Latin America, had little to do with Iran-Contra or anything else. Always though, Cantor came back to Safra.

However confusing they might be, Cantor's stories had a place in the article Maya Jurt planned. And Cantor was so willing to help that she encouraged Jurt to write out a series of questions—about Safra's plane, about rumors of arms deals—that she could carry to her Washington sources. Cantor was so eager, in fact, that around midnight she stepped to the telephone in Jurt's living room, dialed one of her American sources and relayed a few of Jurt's questions. No answers were immediately forthcoming, but Cantor promised it was only a matter of time before they would be.

Maya Jurt had to admit it; she was impressed. And like any good reporter, she was also curious about the identity of Cantor's sources, how reliable they were, and why they should be so willing to help a mere free-lancer like Cantor. When Cantor finally left after midnight, promising to send on more materials from her investigation, Jurt couldn't shake a troubled feeling. There was something about Susan Cantor that didn't quite fit. Who was she, really? She was always talking about her days as a student radical, about trips to Cuba. Was she for real? Could her stories be trusted?

Maya Jurt badly wanted to know. She found herself looking at her living room telephone. Suddenly she realized it had a "redial" button. The last number dialed on the phone had been Cantor's call to Washington. Jurt picked up the phone, pushed the redial button and heard the multi-toned sound of an international call going through.

A woman's voice answered.

"What number is this, please?" Jurt asked. The woman's voice repeated the number. Jurt jotted it down on a pad by the phone. "Thank you," she said.

The next morning Maya Jurt called her magazine's correspondent in the United States, gave him the number, and asked him to check it out. Later that day, the correspondent called back to say the number was for the office of Joseph Saba, a staff counsel on the House select committee investigating the Iran-Contra committee. Jurt had to hand it to Cantor: she indeed had good sources.

The next day, when Cantor phoned to arrange a follow-up dinner date, Jurt felt the need to tell her what she had done. Not surprisingly, Cantor got angry. "You shouldn't have done that," she said.

"But Susan, I had to," Jurt said. "You understand, I had to check your source out. I can't accept information blindly like this. I don't work that way. I know you hate what I did. But I had to do it."

Cantor calmed down after a moment. Yes, she said finally, she understood what Jurt had done. Any good journalist would have done the same.

The next morning, Jurt decided to take the initiative and telephoned Joe Saba in Washington. The lawyer was courteous and agreeable, eager to swap leads with anyone who might offer information on Oliver North's Swiss finances. When Jurt explained her interest in Safra's jet, Saba agreed to fax her some figures. At 12:28 that day Saba's message inched across Maya Jurt's home fax machine in Geneva, addressed, incorrectly, "To: Canter." Below, Saba listed five Zucker payments to a Swiss company that maintained a fleet of private jets, including Safra's. For Jurt the information was potentially quite useful.

In the weeks to come Maya Jurt spoke often with Saba, though she never amassed anything more than rumors about Safra's purported Iran-Contra connections. She also stayed in touch with Cantor, who had promised to send on more materials. On the morning of September 24 she faxed Jurt three pages, including two documents she had apparently gotten from Saba regarding various Willard Zucker payments. On a third page Cantor scribbled the names of six pilots who might have flown Safra's jet on Iran-Contra–related missions. The information was helpful, but as she looked at the fax, Maya Jurt's eyes were drawn to something far more illuminating.

There, at the top of each page, was a clearly printed fax telltale: "SEP 24 '87 08:24 AMEX CORP COMM ° NYC." Susan Cantor, Jurt saw, had used a fax machine in the corporate communications department of American Express's New York headquarters. Maya Jurt knew all about the feud between American Express and Safra. Suddenly a number of things that had troubled her about Cantor made sense: how a meagerly paid American free-lancer could afford to stay at Geneva's two-hundred-dollar-a-night Hôtel Beau-Rivage; most of all, why Cantor seemed so obsessed by Edmond Safra.

Feeling used and growier angrier by the minute, Jurt called Cantor in New York and confronted her. Years later she would vividly recall the conversation.

"I asked her point-blank, didn't she think it was very incompatible, what she was doing," Jurt recalled. "She said, 'Yes, it was very difficult.' She said she was just working for American Express part-time, because she needed the money. Oh, she was good. She was very smooth.

"I said, 'How can you do that? That's not right.'

"She said, 'I need the money. You can't expect me to give up being a journalist just because I need money. This allows me to travel, and I can profit from my travels by doing my own thing.'

"At the time," Jurt continues, "it actually made sense. I believed her." Still, Jurt felt used. When she hung up, she looked over the documents Cantor had given her. They were, no doubt, legitimate, as were the questions about Safra. When she thought about it, there was really no reason to view her work with Cantor as tainted. It didn't matter where the information came from, Jurt told herself, as long as it was accurate. She couldn't allow Cantor's motivations, however twisted, to get in the way of a good story.

And they didn't. Maya Jurt's piece was published in *Bilanz*'s November issue. It was a straightforward business profile, keyed to Safra's looming return to Geneva and noticeably light on Susan Cantor's suspicions of shady activity, though Jurt did include a sidebar detailing Republic's involvement in Oliver North's money trail and recapitulating the controversy over Safra's private jet.

However revealing, it was hardly the stirring indictment Susan Cantor and Harry Freeman were hoping for. In fact, after the better part of a year digging into Safra's background and business dealings, American Express had little to show for its efforts, or so it seemed. Something more, it was clear, would have to be done, and done fast, if Safra's planned reopening in March 1988 were to be stopped. If not, Freeman feared his inevitable attack on TDB could cripple the bank, and along with it the fragile financial health of American Express Bank itself. Left unspoken was the fact that such a scenario, coming after Safra's embarrassing departure three years before, would make Jim Robinson, the man whose reputation Freeman so zealously protected, look very, very foolish.

By that fall Freeman had already taken the next step in their investigation, telephoning the London security chief, Paul Knight, and asking for some additional guidance. It was a fateful call. Just days earlier, Knight told Freeman, he had received a strange tip about Safra's largest bank from one of his oldest informants, a special operative who had proven invaluable to American Express in any number of sensitive international situations over the years.

His name was Tony Greco.

12

A sharp sense of anticipation hung in the humid Florida air as Ray Sanchez and his boss pulled into the parking lot of a plush Miami Beach hotel. The drive over from the American Express offices in Coral Gables hadn't taken long. Inside, they were to meet a man known only by his odd code name, "Musashi," a moniker Sanchez would later learn to be the name of a Samurai warrior of Japanese antiquity. It was all a little dramatic, Sanchez felt, but if half the stories told about the man were true, "Musashi" had more than enough reason to guard his identity.

It was the spring of 1982, and Ramirio "Ray" Sanchez had been in his new job as a special agent in American Express's Miami security office since the beginning of the year. A Bay of Pigs trainee, the bald, Cuban-born Sanchez had left his position as a homicide detective with the Miami police department for what he hoped would be a less stressful job at American Express. His assignment was busting the sophisticated rings of South American counterfeiters and thieves who were making millions every year preying on American Express travelers cheques and charge cards.

The man Ray Sanchez and his boss, a Cuban woman named Marisa Gracia, were to meet that day, the one they called Musashi, was probably the closest thing American Express, or any other major corporation, had to a secret agent. By trade he was an informant, not only for American Express but over the years for a number of foreign and American agencies, including Scotland Yard, French and Spanish authorities, the DEA, the FBI, and, it was rumored, the CIA.

But Musashi was no run-of-the-mill snitch. Sanchez had heard the stories of his exploits throughout Europe, rubbing shoulders with Italian Mafiosi, South American assassins and Spanish fences, risking his life to help American Express establish fraud cases against some of the continent's more notorious criminals. More than that, Musashi was rumored to have been used by American Express's New York headquarters for all sorts of dirty jobs. Sanchez didn't ask more questions, and got the clear impression he wasn't supposed to. Musashi was too important to alienate. "They were treating him like one of the crown jewels," Sanchez would recall years later.

Given all he had heard, Ray Sanchez was more than a little surprised that day when he and his boss were ushered into Musashi's hotel room. Instead of a suave secret agent, Sanchez was introduced to a small, dark Italian in his early forties with an arrogant, almost surly disposition. Sanchez immediately disliked the man, whom he found thuggish, "a common criminal, a small-time hood," as he later described him to his wife.

The man they called Musashi had come to Miami to help American Express do battle against the South Americans, though Sanchez heard rumors he had left Europe with at least one police force in close pursuit. In his new guise Musashi was nominally to work for Sanchez. But in the weeks to come, the informant never visited the American Express offices, and Sanchez caught only occasional glimpses of him as he slid through and around Miami.

Just as well, Ray Sanchez felt. In their few meetings together, he quickly tired of Musashi's insolent attitude, especially the way he bragged of his contacts in the Mafia. Sanchez, in fact, thought so little of Musashi he began calling him what he was: "the informant." The tag never failed to irk his boss, Marisa Gracia, who insisted on using the job description preferred by their New York superiors. Don't call the man an informant, she repeatedly told Sanchez. It sounded too sleazy, too criminal. "Call him a consultant," she said.

It would be some time before Ray Sanchez would learn the American Express "consultant's" real name: Giuseppe Antonio Greco. But what little Sanchez knew—and what almost everyone else who encountered Tony Greco knew—stopped at the edges of his personal experience, leaving details of Greco's far-flung career shrouded in rumor and half-truths. Probably no one holds the entire story. But surely what little is known must constitute one of the stranger chapters in the history of American business.

To this day, Victor Raul Haya de la Torre is the closest thing to a legendary figure in the modern history of Peru. The mystical, almost messianic leader of a political party known as the American Popular Revolutionary Alliance, or APRA, Haya de la Torre dominated his country's politics for a half century. Upon his death at age eighty-four in 1979, *The New York Times* termed him "the elder statesman of Latin American democracy" and "a symbol in Peru and Latin America of the chronic struggle for power between democratic political movements and authoritarian military leaders."

Born to an aristocratic family in the northern city of Trujillo in 1895, Haya (pronounced *I*-ya), as he was known, rose to national attention as a student leader during the 1919 riots in Lima. Exiled in 1922, he wandered the world for eight years, lecturing at Harvard, studying at Oxford, meeting Leon Trotsky in the Soviet Union, and steeping himself in intellectual circles throughout Western Europe, Mexico, and Cuba. Returning home in 1930, he delivered a series of charismatic speeches that inflamed Peru's poor and earned him the lasting hatred of the country's powerful military. Violent riots in 1932 led the army to slaughter six thousand young Apristas and chase Haya into hiding, where he remained for years. But the Apristas remained a vibrant movement and, under Haya's leadership, came close to ruling the country after World War II.

His fame growing, Haya traveled and wrote widely, meeting world figures as varied as Bertrand Russell and Albert Einstein. After Aprista partisans were blamed for a series of bloody riots in October 1948, he drew world headlines for seeking refuge in the Colombian embassy in Lima, where he remained for five years, until Peruvian authorities, under intense international pressure, allowed him to leave for Mexico. Two years later the government collapsed and Haya returned to Lima, where he set to work preparing for his next run at the presidency in 1962.

In June 1959 Haya de la Torre, then sixty-four years old, left Peru to visit his beloved Europe on what amounted to a nine-month sabbatical in Rome. Though political opponents criticized him for living a life of Italian luxury, Haya in fact lived modestly, renting a small room in a boardinghouse on the Via Fratelli. During the day he wrote; as they had all his life, articles sprang from his typewriter by the dozens, to be published in newspapers across Latin America and Europe. In the evenings he attended courses at the nearby Dante Alighieri Center. Only when his classes ended each evening would he entertain visitors and well-wishers.

It was in Rome that the elderly Haya de la Torre, visionary leader of the mighty Peruvian Apristas, first crossed paths with the Italian youth named Antonio Greco. More than thirty years later, the story of their first meeting is still remembered by one of Haya's closest friends and Aprista allies, a seventy-five-year-old Peruvian senator named Armando Villanueva. "Haya was taking a course in order to improve his Italian, and on the way out of one of his classes—this version I know through Greco and Haya himself—he almost fainted," Villanueva recalled. "He leaned against one of the walls. A young man approached him and saw this old man in trouble and asked to help. Haya thanked him."

The young man was Antonio Greco, and the chance meeting would change the Italian's life. Little is known of Greco's early years. According to most records, he was born in the opening months of World War II, on December 16, 1939, in Calabria, the southernmost Italian province, opposite Sicily. He grew up in Rome, where his family to this day runs a number of small inns.

As Armando Villanueva tells it, young Greco helped Haya back to his room, and was surprised to find him living alone, with no domestic help. "Greco told Haya, 'You're living here on your own, I'm going to tell my sister to come and help you,'" the old Aprista recalled. "Greco took his sister to help Haya, and this is how the friendship started. The whole family came to know Haya. Some time later, this lady"—Greco's sister— "came to get married, and Haya was her husband's best man. I've seen pictures of the wedding."

Young Tony Greco, no doubt realizing the opportunities afforded by friendship with such a renowned figure, offered his services to Haya at every turn. If Haya needed to be driven somewhere, Greco volunteered to chauffeur him. If he needed a book, Greco scouted the stores until he found it. When it came time for Haya to return to Lima, the old politico showed his gratitude by inviting Greco's newlywed sister and brother-in-law to follow him to Peru. They accepted, settling in Lima and opening a pastry shop in a middle-class section known as San Isidro. "Everybody was saying the Italian family was here, the family that helped Haya," Villanueva recalled. "So we all went to this pastry shop to help them."

Soon after—several in Lima put the year at 1962—Tony Greco followed his sister to Peru. "He was a young man looking for something new, looking for his future, just as so many people are when they come to America," Villanueva recalled. What none of the Apristas seem to have known is that Greco may have had another reason to start over in Peru: the previous year, 1961, at the age of twenty-one, a court in Rome had convicted him of petty theft.°

Determining the nature of Tony Greco's relationship with Haya de la Torre in Peru during the 1960s depends on whom one asks. Older APRA leaders like Armando Villanueva suddenly lose all memory of the young Italian once he arrived in Lima. Younger Apristas, protective of Haya's memory, characterize Greco as their *jefe*'s valet or personal assistant, if they acknowledge the friendship at all. Others put into words what for years has only been hushed gossip in Peruvian political circles: Tony Greco, they say, was Haya de la Torre's young lover.

"Greco came here as Haya's young boyfriend," recalls Enrique Zileri Gibson, editor of a leading Peruvian news magazine, *Caretas*, who covered the Aprista leadership as a young reporter in the 1960s. "It was an extravagant situation. Greco never came with Haya to a meeting. But it was a household affair. Haya would sort of bring in his little friend. The only explanation he would have for him was this was his boyfriend. Many of the Apristas deplored this situation, found it very embarrassing. But Haya was a very strong leader, the oracle of the party."†

Whatever the exact nature of his relationship with Haya, the whis-

---

°Greco, while confirming his friendship with Haya, gives a different version of his immigration to Peru. In several rambling telephone interviews with the author in January 1992, he claimed that, as a student at "Rome Technical" in the late 1950s, he had been heavily involved in rocket research, "developing my own fuel and everything." After declining an American professor's offer of a scholarship at the University of Pennsylvania, he claims, he moved to Peru to pursue his research. His 1961 arrest on theft charges, he said, was a tangled affair involving a clandestine group of Peruvian generals meeting in Rome who asked him to arrange a burglary; he declines to give further details.

†Haya's homosexuality has generally been accepted by those who studied his life and times. "Not only his enemies but many a devoted Aprista had little doubt that Haya was indeed a homosexual," notes the Peruvian leader's American biographer, Frederick B. Pike, in his 1986 book, *The Politics of the Miraculous in Peru*. According to Pike, who terms Haya's homosexuality "probable," much of the military's enduring hostility toward Haya can be explained by tales of his homosexuality. Pike recalls discussing Haya with a macho military man in a Lima bar in 1962, and listening to the man swear that the army would never, ever report to a homosexual commander-in-chief.

pers followed Tony Greco wherever he went in Peru. What is clear is that Greco was a favorite of Haya's, and was often seen in his entourage. In small groups the two chatted in Italian. "Everyone knew Haya was very fond of him," recalled Hugo Otero, a young APRA militant in the mid-1960s who went on to become a presidential adviser in the 1980s. The two were close enough, Otero recalls, that members of Haya's inner circle were scandalized by Greco's familiar behavior toward their leader. "He called Haya by his first name, Victor Raul," Otero recalled. "He was very confident with Haya. This was not accepted by many. Remember, even the APRA secretary general called Haya 'jefe.' It created a bad atmosphere for him among those close to Haya. He got secret hatred from many."

The magazine editor, Enrique Zileri, remembers that "Greco was then a rather aggressive boyfriend. According to the stories that went around, he had a domineering attitude toward Haya. I know some people were concerned that he was a little rough."

But if older party leaders were wary of Greco, their younger counterparts seemed eager to court the favor of a man so close to Haya. Indeed, his special ties gave Greco entry into the most rarefied of Peruvian political circles. His outgoing personality helped; by some accounts, young Greco was a bit of a clown. He was glib and fun-loving and brash, and, while at least one Aprista remembers he could have used a stronger deodorant, he made friends easily, counting among them the sons of several party leaders as well as an Aprista journalist named Victor Tirado. "You have to understand, Haya's presence was very strong; Haya, for the Apristas, was like an Inca, a god," said Hugo Otero. "You can imagine the importance Greco achieved by being so close to Haya." It was an influence that would linger in Lima for nearly thirty years.

By early 1963 Greco's profile in Lima had grown so high that gossip surrounding his relationship with Haya became rife, an ominous portent given Peru's volatile political climate. The previous summer Haya had won a three-way race for the Peruvian presidency by the narrowest of margins. Almost immediately, rumors had swept Lima that the military was on the verge of intervening to prevent him from taking power. Haya began tense talks aimed at forming a coalition government, but it was too late. Just after two o'clock on the morning of July 18, 1962, a Peruvian army tank battered down the gates to the Government Palace as a four-man military junta seized control of the country. New elections were announced for mid-1963, and this time the army was determined that Haya de la Torre would not emerge victorious.

It was in the midst of Haya's unsuccessful campaign, on April 9, that the ruling military junta passed Supreme Resolution No. 2712, an executive order deporting twenty-three-year-old Antonio Greco from Peru. According to the order's published text, Greco was to be deported under laws permitting the expulsion of any foreigner who engaged in illicit acts or who posed a threat to the country's "peace and tranquility." Political insiders in Lima, however, knew the real reason was to humiliate Haya by highlighting rumors of his "special relationship" with the young Italian. Aprista leaders reportedly had warned Haya to distance himself from Greco, but if he did, it came too late to matter.

If Greco left Peru, he returned soon after. For a scruffy Italian from the streets of Rome, the opportunities provided by his powerful new friendships in Lima must have been attractive enough to risk further harassment from the military.* And indeed, during the years after the deportation order Greco seems to have prospered in Peru. In time he opened a restaurant in Lima's cosmopolitan Miraflores section. One old friend, an Aprista politico named Raoul Trujillo, recalled that it was named Tres Coronas, or "Three Crowns." On most nights, Greco could be seen hobnobbing with well-to-do guests, offering suggestions on the best selection of international cuisine. In time he moved from his home in San Isidro to a flat on Miraflores's main street, Diagonal, just across from the district's central park and a few blocks from the blue Pacific.

Often Greco invited Haya de la Torre to his restaurant for dinner, and former friends say Haya's occasional visits gave the place a certain cachet, especially among the Apristas. But again, Greco rubbed some the wrong way. "He really took advantage of Haya's friendship," recalls Hugo Otero. "He would boast of it, though he didn't have to. It was, 'Hey, Victor Raul' this, 'Hey, Victor Raul' that. He would offer journalists interviews with Haya. He really didn't know how to handle the attention Haya had given him. He went over the line."

By the fall of 1966 Greco's luck had run out. No two people agree on

---

*Greco confirmed his arrest. "I was kidnapped by the military," he says, "I was tortured, they kept me for three weeks. They wanted me to say I was working for the presidents of Venezuela, Chile and Bolivia to finance a revolution in Peru. The Italian embassy came in and got me released...I went from there to Chile. A year later the [Peruvian] congress passed a law for me to come back into Peru."

the exact circumstances that led Tony Greco to leave Peru, but it appears his "special friendship" with Haya played a role. According to Hugo Otero, rumors of trysts between the two, fanned by Aprista opponents, threatened to get out of hand, to the point that they could have jeopardized Haya's chances for the presidency in the upcoming 1968 elections.

"There were stories of sentimental links between Haya and Greco" is how Otero diplomatically puts it. "Political enemies would start them, and it was pushed by people within the party as well who were jealous of [Greco]. The time came when it was suggested to Victor Raul that it was necessary for Greco to leave the country. He had created many problems. There were problems with the restaurant, there were too many debts, many, many misunderstandings. After all that had happened, it was practically impossible for him to remain in this country."

That may have been the case. A Peruvian attorney who has researched Greco's legal history says that the official reason given for his 1966 deportation was passing bad checks. But another Aprista veteran, an acquaintance of Greco's since 1962, suggests a far more serious reason for the Italian to leave Peru. According to this politician, Greco was arrested by the military and interrogated about his relationship with Haya, apparently in hopes that he would provide information embarrassing to the Aprista leadership. But Greco, this friend says, admitted nothing, and was ultimately released and again deported, this time for good.

For whatever reason, people in Lima say Greco was ordered to leave Peru a second time in October 1966. According to one source, he was placed on a plane to Panama. Several of his friends from the 1960s say they never saw Greco again, despite the fact that members of his family continued to live in Lima well into the 1970s. To them, he had simply vanished.

Only a few would hear of his quiet return some twenty years later, when his old Aprista comrades had achieved top positions at the sprawling Government Palace in downtown Lima. Even fewer would learn of the intricate favors Haya de la Torre's "special friend" would manage to secure then, after so many years in the void.

After his departure from Peru, the story of Tony Greco's odd career descends into one of its dark periods, about which little is known. He landed for a time in Acapulco where, he would later boast to Peruvian friends, he seduced the daughter of a well-known Hollywood producer. But if he intended to woo American starlets, he ended up engaged to someone far less glamorous, a seventeen-year-old high school girl from Long Meadow, Massachusetts, named Diane Flax. According to her father, Jack, it was on the beach in Acapulco, during a family vacation, that young Diane Flax met and fell in love with the swarthy Tony Greco.

By early 1968 Greco had joined his bride-to-be in the United States. He entered the country at Laredo, Texas, in February 1968, listing his destination for immigration officials as the "St. Maritz [sic] Hotel, NYC." Among his first stops was Chicago, where that May he was issued a driver's license. Two months later, Greco and young Diane Flax were married by a rabbi in Stamford, Connecticut. On his marriage license Greco listed his occupation as "importer," the irony of which would soon become apparent. Afterward the newlyweds walked into the Valley Bank & Trust in downtown Springfield, Massachusetts, took out a loan to buy a brown 1967 El Camino, and hit the road—a road that would prove far bumpier than either could have expected.

Over the next three years Tony Greco would be arrested a half-dozen times for a variety of petty crimes, most of them linked to his involvement with roving gangs of Italian immigrants peddling counterfeit Rolex and Omega watches. That winter of 1968, for instance, he was arrested at a Ramada Inn outside New Orleans carrying ninety-six fake Omegas he had tried to sell at a nearby country club. After Greco claimed to have bought the watches from an Italian seaman in New York, a local attorney managed to get the charges dropped, but not before a Louisiana prosecutor put together a list of witnesses against Greco that traced the Italian's travels across America that fall of 1968. The manager of a Chicago-area golf club was set to tell the story of how Greco had attempted to sell him counterfeit Omega watches. An assistant pro at Houston's Eldorado Golf Club had a similar story. Customs agents from New York, Chicago, Houston, and New Orleans had all been set to detail their investigation.

Freed from custody, Greco took his wife, who divorced him soon after, and moved to south Florida, where they set up house in an apartment in a heavily Italian section of the Miami suburb of Hallandale.* To

---

*Greco says he came to the U.S. not as a poor immigrant to sell counterfeit watches, but to work for the CIA. "Yes, that was all for the government," he says of his arrests between 1968 and 1972, declining to give any details. In 1969 he and his wife sued federal officials in New Orleans to retrieve their impounded El Camino, but their attorney at the time says the couple dropped the litigation when Greco, suspicious of Louisiana authorities, refused to return to the state to give a deposition.

this day much of the counterfeit watch trade remains controlled by organized crime, and law enforcement officials would later speculate that by the time he reached Florida Greco had established his first contacts in the American arm of La Cosá Nostra, the Mafia.

At first, it seems, he was a hanger-on, a fast-talking mob courier who continued to make his living trundling counterfeit watches to hotels and country clubs. In April 1970, for example, police officers in Pompano Beach were called to the Sea Garden Motel, where they found Greco and another Italian with a mound of gold jewelry spread out on a clerk's desk. Flashing an expired peddler's license, the two were thrown into a patrol car and placed under arrest. On the ride to the station, Greco told the arresting officer that he could keep the jewelry if he set them free. When the officer asked him to repeat the offer, he did—and was promptly arrested again, this time for attempted bribery. Neither charge led to a conviction.

In time Greco found more serious pursuits. On December 9, 1971, three policemen in Miami Beach, accompanied by a pair of federal narcotics agents, crept up to room 508 of the fashionable Eden Roc hotel and rapped on the door. When a voice inside asked who it was, the officers said, "Houseman." Greco let them in without a fight. The federal agents, tipped by one of their drug informants to check out the slim Italian, proceeded to search the room. On the dresser they found a fifty-dollar First National City Bank traveler's check, with a clearly forged signature. The officers read Greco his rights, then, after nosing through a dresser, placed him under arrest. In a top drawer they had found a .25 caliber automatic pistol with a full clip. After taking Greco downtown, the officers charged him with carrying an unregistered firearm.

The contents of Greco's wallet were even more interesting. There were several fake immigration cards, all under different names; an immigration hold was placed on Greco, and an Agent DuPuis was summoned to question him about his legal status. Greco carried an obviously faked ID card listing him as a co-pilot for Linea Aerea Italiana; it was wrapped in cellophane and appeared handmade. Three days later Greco was released into the custody of immigration officers. The gun charge was dropped so that immigration could charge him with the more serious violation of possessing false immigration cards; bail was set at $100,000, and Greco was remanded to a Dade County jail. Three weeks later, while still in jail, he was indicted in a Miami federal court for carrying the faked immigration documents.

A trial date was set for that February, but again, Greco's luck won out. His attorney charged that the arresting officers had neither an arrest warrant nor a search warrant when they arrived at Greco's room wanting to question him. Moreover, Greco told the court, the agents had burst in, guns drawn, without identifying themselves. Two weeks before the trial was to start, a judge threw out the indictment. For at least the fourth time in as many years, Tony Greco was a free man.

That, at least, is the story told by court records. What actually happened is more complex, and leads to a bizarre, untold chapter of the U.S. government's fight against organized crime in the 1970s. One day in 1972, Dante "Dan" Avanti, a senior chief in the Internal Revenue Service's intelligence group, was called to the Department of Justice in Washington for a meeting with a group of attorneys and agents from the FBI, Customs, and Immigration. Sitting merrily among the assembled lawmen when he arrived was a slight Italian who introduced himself as Tony Greco.

Greco, Dan Avanti was told, had earned his freedom after an arrest in Miami by tantalizing immigration officials with tales of his contacts among New York's Mafia families. The immigration men had been interested enough to pass Greco on to Justice, which called in Avanti because of his experience with delicate undercover operations. For years Avanti's IRS men had been running a network of informants across the country that supplied tips to any number of law-enforcement agencies; one of its more creative operations was a travel agency that specialized in gambling junkets to Las Vegas and the Bahamas—and which gathered valuable information on big-time gamblers. Justice officials wanted Avanti's opinion of Greco's suitability for an operation they had in mind.

"He was a weasel," a long-retired Dan Avanti would recall twenty years later. "You could see it in the way he talked. He spoke in very broken English. I didn't want anything to do with him." Greco's English was so bad, in fact, that Avanti, one of the few federal agents that day who could speak fluent Italian, took him aside and spoke to him in his native tongue, a move that clearly surprised the would-be informant.

Avanti quizzed Greco, then thirty-two years old, about his qualifications as an informant, and Greco replied haughtily that he had been a Mafia courier for years, smuggling counterfeit watches, among other things. To Avanti he appeared genteel, a bit of a dandy. "He complained

that some of these things [he was being asked to do] were beneath his
dignity," the IRS man recalled. "I said, 'Do you know what they really
want to do? They want to put you right into Little Italy.'"

And they wanted Dan Avanti's IRS unit to oversee the operation—a
very special undercover operation, fueled by a fifty-thousand-dollar Justice Department grant. As Justice sketched the plan, Tony Greco was to
do what he had done in Peru, run a restaurant. Only this restaurant
would be on Mulberry Street, the main thoroughfare at the heart of
New York's Little Italy section; it would be secretly financed by the Justice Department, and the tips Greco would collect weren't coins but
information—on the Mafia. Tony Greco was to be the federal government's eyes and ears in the middle of Mob Central. And to Avanti's surprise, Greco was happy to do it, excited to do it.

At the Justice Department's insistence, Dan Avanti reluctantly
agreed to personally supervise the operation. He got Greco a Green
Card and instructed him to travel to New York and get a driver's license.
The IRS kept a "safe house" apartment in a building at 400 East Fifty-
sixth Street in Manhattan, and it was set aside for Greco's use. To top it
all off, according to former law-enforcement officials involved in the
operation, Greco was named the IRS's newest employee. "He actually
went on the payroll as a Schedule A IRS agent," confirms William Aronwald, then an attorney with a federal organized crime task force that
helped oversee the project.

Dan Avanti, meanwhile, scouted Mulberry Street for a restaurant to
buy, and managed to procure a lease on a luncheonette at 131 Mulberry,
on Little Italy's restaurant row next to the famed Umberto's Clam
House, where mobster Joey Gallo had been rubbed out the year before.
The IRS spotted Greco $20,000 or so to buy the place, and by early 1973
"Santa Lucia Restaurant," as Tony Greco's government-owned Italian
diner was renamed, was open for business.*

At first, everything went like clockwork. Greco formulated his own
cover, posing as an Italian pilot grounded after being caught smuggling.
He hired a cook to handle the routine chores, then sat back and watched

---

*New York City records indicate "Santa Lucia Restaurant" was incorporated on Valen-
tine's Day, 1973, by a Mott Street woman whom former federal agents say unknowingly served
as Greco's partner for a time. As of mid-1991, according to state records, Santa Lucia, though
long closed, remained an active corporation in the state of New York "under good standing."
In the fall of 1991 the site was an abandoned storefront strewn with garbage.

as customers poured into the new restaurant: neighborhood people, tourists and, to Dan Avanti's delight, more than a few mobsters. "I couldn't believe what was happening," Avanti recalled. "I said, 'Holy Christopher, this is great!'"

As his IRS handlers looked on approvingly, Greco used his mob contacts to begin putting together deals, fencing thousands of dollars in stolen securities, jewels, and stereo equipment and taking a commission. "Tony was a middleman," another IRS agent, James Delgado, recalled. "He was always in the middle of something. If there was a deal to be done—stolen securities, whatever—he would go to everyone in every family of the mob, trying to hustle a deal." To his handlers, Greco boasted of his independence from his mob contacts. "He once told me— and I'm trying to remember the exact words he used—'I will never get married to the mob,'" Jim Delgado recalled. "'I will always work between the mobs, because that is where the money is.'"

Once a week, Dan Avanti took the shuttle to New York and checked in at the New York Hilton on Fifty-third Street, where he would meet Greco. There, alone in a hotel room with a tape recorder, Avanti forced his newest snitch to talk, about Little Italy, about every mobster he met, about what he was learning of the structure of New York's Five Families. Reluctant at first, Greco slowly began filling tape after tape for Avanti, who would turn the tapes into weekly reports for his secretary to transcribe. "The tapes were fantastic, reel after reel of just great stuff," Avanti recalled.

But then the problems began. Spending his days chatting up the Mulberry Street crowd over tiny cups of espresso, Greco seemed to grow more interested in impressing his mob cronies than his IRS bosses. Nattily dressed in silk shirts, French cuffs, and tight bell-bottom pants— "real tight in the butt," Avanti says, "that was his style"—Greco affected the air of Mafia gentry, wearing an overcoat draped across his shoulders, European-style. The flow of information to his IRS handlers became increasingly erratic. And then he began to disappear.

After several instances of Greco vanishing for days on end, Avanti tracked him across the Canadian border to Montreal. Not knowing exactly what his informant was up to, and not trusting him one bit, Avanti tipped the Royal Canadian Mounted Police, who began tailing the Italian. The Mounties returned to Avanti with pictures of Greco in

Montreal, and in several of them he could be seen hobnobbing with known members of the Mafia's Canadian arm.

"I confronted him after he got back" from one trip, Avanti recalled years later. "He told me he had been asked to make a delivery up there, by a mob guy. He said it was completely legitimate." It turned out, Avanti learned, that Greco was running messages back and forth between New York and Canadian cells of La Cosa Nostra. "He was playing both sides against the middle—all informants do that," Avanti recalled. "I told him, 'Whatever you're doing, stop it now. You have to document everything you do with us.' I feared he was using our protection to run his own illegal operations on the side."

But something else had happened in Montreal. In one of the Mounties' pictures Greco could be seen with a girl. Her name was Joanne Orlando, and she was said to be a schoolteacher from Brooklyn. Greco had always played the ladies' man, never missing a chance to flatter even the plainest mob wives about their hair or dresses. But now, Greco confessed, he was in love. The IRS man didn't mind the romance a bit, especially when he learned that Joanne Orlando's family lived in a mob-riddled neighborhood in Brooklyn.

"He asked me how to court this girl," Avanti recalled. "I said, 'You have to ask the parents, these are first- or second-generation Italians. You have to be polite. But don't go sticking your nose into the wrong places.' I told him, 'Go easy, you're likely to come out of there with your head in your hands.'"

Falling in love may have complicated Greco's undercover life, but spending time in Brooklyn plugged him into a new network of contacts. "That's when things really got good, as far as his connections were concerned," Avanti recalled. As Greco tapped into mobsters in Brooklyn, the IRS men were flooded with tips. Avanti, though, wasn't taking any chances with his erratic young informant. He decided to put a full-time IRS man, Jim Delgado, into the restaurant to keep an eye on Greco. Santa Lucia was losing money fast, in part because Greco was buying its food at a local supermarket. "Who ever heard of a restaurant buying its food at the grocery store?" the former prosecutor, William Aronwald, recalls. "That's when we really began to suspect Greco had sold us a bill of goods" about his experience managing a restaurant. Among his other talents, Jim Delgado knew how to run a greasy spoon.

"It was a great place to make deals," Delgado recalled. "Every day you literally had two or three mob guys coming in; one guy says, 'I got $2 million in stolen paintings to move. Know anybody?' Next guy, he's got a trailer full of stolen electronic equipment. Know anybody? Another guy comes in with a vanload of stolen securities, bearer bonds and stuff. Know anybody? We could pick our deals."

And they did. The problem, though, was that Greco's deals tended to evaporate as soon as the IRS men got involved. The first transaction Greco and Delgado attempted, the sale of $40,000 in stolen diamonds, went awry when Delgado was called out of town at the last minute. He returned to find Greco had sold the diamonds, and had already spent the proceeds. The same thing happened with a load of machine guns they were to buy from a crew of New Jersey mobsters, and with $3 million in stolen artwork they were to buy from a Brooklyn Mafia family. "Tony was impossible to control," Delgado recalled.

In the months to come Greco's performance grew increasingly slap-dash. Time and again, Avanti would pressure Greco to give him information that might lead to an arrest, but each time the Italian got cold feet. Several times, for instance, Greco had secured an airplane for Mafia pals to fly cash to Florida where it could be laundered. The mob, of course, had no way of knowing the plane was owned by the IRS, or that the pilot was an IRS employee. But when Avanti pressed him to let the mobsters use the plane to ferry a shipment of stolen securities out of Boston, Greco balked. The crazy thing, Avanti recalled, was that the Mafia wanted to use the plane as badly as the IRS wanted them to use it; only Greco stood between the agents and a sure bust. And, as Avanti writhed in frustration, Greco won the day. There were no busts.

Nor were federal agents able to arrest a pair of customs agents suspected of taking bribes from Greco's Brooklyn mob friends. Greco had gotten Avanti's approval to visit relatives in Italy, and while there, had been asked by mob friends to smuggle a suitcase full of counterfeit watches into the United States. Crooked customs agents would ensure his safe passage into the country, Greco reported. But when Avanti told Greco he would need to be photographed going through customs in order to make a case against the agents, Greco demurred. He refused to have his picture taken, and he further refused to do anything that might lead to the arrest of the Mafia men handling the bribes. To Avanti's frustration, another promising case went down the drain.

The Italian trip was typical of how difficult Greco could be to control. While in Europe he telephoned Avanti and described contacts he had made with the Camorra, the vicious Mafia chieftains of Naples, second in importance only to their cousins in Sicily. Avanti warned Greco not to go any further, because the IRS was prohibited from managing informants overseas; Washington had already slapped his hand for bringing in the Mounties. But Greco went ahead anyway, taking an assignment to smuggle a shipment of stolen bearer bonds into Switzerland. On his return, Avanti would have strangled him except for the detailed information Greco brought on the payoffs made to ensure a quiet passage across the Swiss border.

As the months wore on, Dan Avanti began to wonder whether Greco was more trouble than he was worth. In September 1972, for instance, he had been arrested at the Pan Am counter at the Miami airport using a stolen airline ticket. A suspicious reservations agent called in police, who after matching ticket numbers against a list of stolen tickets led Greco off to jail. Court records in Miami don't indicate what happened after Greco's arrest, but presumably his federal handlers got the case dismissed. Ten years later a warrant for Greco's arrest on the charge would still be outstanding.

By late 1974 Avanti had had enough. They had ample evidence to end the Santa Lucia sting and press any number of criminal cases against Little Italy mobsters, provided Greco testified in court. But Greco refused, at which point Avanti decided to play hardball. "I told him he was either going to testify or I would have him deported," the IRS man recalled. But nothing could budge Greco. He simply wouldn't testify.

In the end, Tony Greco's time as a Little Italy restaurateur apparently didn't lead directly to a single criminal case. But according to Avanti, the tapes Greco made were a treasure trove of mob lore, and, when parceled out to the New York Organized Crime Task Force, the FBI, and the DEA, led agents to any number of investigations. "I don't share that assessment at all," counters William Aronwald, the former prosecutor. "It never paid any real dividends; it wasn't one of our better operations. It was unfortunately one of those pink elephants the government sometimes buys."

To ease himself out of the operation, Greco spread the word he would have to "lay low for a while" after having received a subpoena. Government attorneys supplied the paperwork, demanding Greco's presence before a federal grand jury in November 1974. When Greco didn't show, he was ordered in February 1975 to appear in court and explain why, or be cited for contempt. There is no indication Greco ever appeared—or any hint that the government threat was anything more than an official cover for his disappearance.

As for Greco, the last Jim Delgado heard of him, he was headed for the Caribbean after marrying his Brooklyn sweetheart. Federal records shed no light on his immediate fate; twenty years later, much of his file at the Immigration and Naturalization Service's New York office remains classified. Almost three years would pass before Tony Greco would again emerge from obscurity, this time in the unlikely role of a valued consultant to a budding global conglomerate named American Express.

As long as there have been travelers cheques, there has been travelers cheque fraud. Since 1891, when an aide to J. C. Fargo dreamed them up, the specter of theft and counterfeiting has plagued American Express executives. The key to the cheque's viability, after all, was American Express's guarantee that any lost or stolen cheques would be reimbursed, a promise that has long made the company vulnerable to fraud.

American Express's security arm, called the inspector's office, was formed to investigate stolen and counterfeit cheques in the 1920s; according to one company history, among the inspectors' early victories was helping to snag the mobster Bugs Moran. After the Salad Oil swindle of the 1960s, American Express strengthened its security forces with an influx of former policemen, many of them right off the streets of New York. The ex-cops were quick to pounce on pickpockets and the occasional stolen shipment, but as the 1970s dawned, American Express found itself under attack from new and increasingly sophisticated criminals worldwide. Cheques stolen in France would materialize the following week in Venezuela. Counterfeits from Montreal surfaced in the Caribbean. European counterfeits appeared in the Far East, and Chinese gangs brought stolen checks into the teeming Asian communities of Vancouver and San Francisco. Organized crime, cut off from many of its profit centers by zealous U.S. prosecutors, was also moving into the counterfeit business, and there were signs that the Sicilian and Neapolitan Mafias might be leading the way.

Something had to be done, and so in 1975 American Express hired an upright former FBI man named James McGrath to begin shaping a more aggressive approach to fighting crime. As McGrath surveyed the horizon from his office in lower Manhattan, he didn't like what he saw. Theft was worse than ever. Between 1977 and 1980, American Express paid off more than $50 million in fraudulently cashed travelers cheques. Pickpockets were the most common culprit, though larger thefts were growing in number.

In early 1978 a pair of South African businessmen walked into a Johannesburg post office, forged the signature of an American Express courier and walked off with two bags bulging with $2.2 million in negotiable travelers cheques. The loss wasn't even noticed until the pair was nabbed attempting to peddle the cheques in Switzerland. (Ironically, American Express ultimately made a profit on the theft; the thieves had used some of the checks to buy gold bullion, which by the time it was retrieved had appreciated in value.) Not all incidents had such a happy ending. The company recovered little of the $2.4 million in cheques stolen from an Ottawa post office on Easter Sunday, 1979. Years later, despite a number of arrests in the case, the stolen cheques were still surfacing as far away as Beirut.

The problem wasn't just theft: where travelers cheques were concerned, there were hundreds of ways for American Express to lose money. When fighting broke out in Lebanon in 1975, Palestinian employees at a number of Beirut banks passed out American Express travelers cheques to warring militias like Halloween candy. Despite warnings, company officials had waited too long to retrieve them. For years afterward, American Express security officials speculated that the $1.5 million in lost cheques had bought enough guns to arm every guerrilla in the country. Other cases were far more mundane. In 1977 a clerk at a San Fernando Valley savings and loan mistakenly gave a pair of local firemen $130,000 in checks instead of $13,000. Before American Express caught up with them, the two had fled to the Philippines and blown the money making a porno film.

As its corporate profile rose in the 1970s, American Express joined the ranks of U.S. businesses unfortunate enough to become targets of international terrorists. The year 1982 would be particularly bad, as a series of bombings damaged company offices in Rome, Paris, and Athens. In the summer of 1980 the threat of violence struck closer to home. A pipe bomb in a package addressed to Jim Robinson was left at an American Express office in lower Manhattan; attached was an extortion note, ostensibly from Puerto Rican terrorists, threatening Robinson and his family. The chairman, flanked by FBI agents, took two telephone calls from the extortionists, who promised detailed instructions where money should be left. Robinson, whose wife and children were immediately placed under twenty-four-hour protection, was so mad he insisted on delivering the money to the rendezvous point on a darkened Bronx street himself. Only strenuous objections from Jim McGrath and the FBI kept him behind a desk. After a federal agent made the drop, two local criminals with no terrorist connections were arrested.

Some incidents were no more than mischief, such as the occasion in 1978 when an American Express employee in Fort Lauderdale leaked Robinson's personal credit card number to a couple of cronies. According to former company officials, the two used the number to obtain an emergency replacement card, then used the card to run up charges estimated at more than $50,000. Jim McGrath's people caught the pair trying to rent an airplane for a trip to Las Vegas.

All these problems, of course, paled before the man who could ruin an American Express executive's sleep like no other: the counterfeiter. The company regularly saw crude counterfeit cheques, but none had ever done any serious damage. The real threat, Jim McGrath knew, was a counterfeit American Express card. Through the 1970s, no one had successfully copied the Card, but McGrath was convinced it was only a matter of time. He was right. In November 1980 Paris police busted a small counterfeiting operation that had managed to make three crude copies of the familiar green card.

McGrath's worst fears came true the following year. In early 1981 a police informant alerted authorities in Stockholm to a major counterfeiting operation. When Swedish police and American Express investigators swooped down on three houses in the Stockholm area, they were stunned to discover a ring of European criminals poised to distribute thirty-thousand fake American Express cards through a network of couriers and contacts spread across Europe and the Middle East. If the tip had come just two weeks later, Jim McGrath told his superiors, the company could have faced a loss of $25 million or more.

Under normal conditions, American Express might have continued battling criminals as it had for years. The company had long enjoyed warm relations with Scotland Yard, Italy's Guardia di Finanza, and agencies throughout Europe and North America, particularly Interpol. (From time to time company p.r. people would claim the company was "the only corporate member of Interpol," a falsehood that drove Jim McGrath crazy.) All not only shared information with American Express, but could be counted on to arrest criminals the company's investigators rooted out. But by the mid-1970s, this cooperation was waning, as police worldwide spent more time fighting drug traffickers. Cops simply didn't have as much time to spend on American Express anymore. Inside the company's security arm, the feeling grew that McGrath's people were on their own.

Most frustrating of all was the sense that American Express simply didn't know enough about the criminal world preying on its products. They knew a little—dribs and drabs coming in from the occasional police snitch, whenever a local cop thought to pass it on—but what they needed was a way to preempt criminals, bust them before they stole or counterfeited. "We're sitting here trying to make judgments in a room in New York and we don't know what's going on," McGrath complained. "We've got to find out what these people are doing out there. We need intelligence."

Everyone knew what that meant: informants. The notion made McGrath's boss, the corporate secretary Hob Miller, queasy. Over the years, American Express had paid snitches a time or two for tips on counterfeiters, but had shied away from their systematic use. "Hiring informants is a terribly risky undertaking," Miller recalled. "Informants by nature are not Wall Streeters, they're not corporate executives. They're crooks. Their lives are different. Their risks are different. By their very nature they are always double-dealing someone. Some of them require extensive amounts of hand-holding. They must be treated very, very gingerly." Shady characters were forever approaching the company asking for money in exchange for information. McGrath had learned the hard way that making those payments rarely secured useful tips; more than once the tipster vanished, the money used, McGrath had no doubt, to bankroll a counterfeiting ring.

From a practical standpoint, there was no one at American Express who had experience running an informant network. McGrath, though FBI-trained, was a lawyer. Miller had worked behind enemy lines for the OSS during World War II, but had no experience with snitches. The problem was solved by turning to a former federal narcotics agent named Paul Knight, who was hired in 1975 to take over the company's London-based European security operations.

An expatriate New Englander, Knight's career in the DEA—then the Bureau of Narcotics—had taken him from Beirut to Kabul to Rome to Washington, and finally to a top posting as the Paris-based senior agent in charge of Europe, Africa, and the Middle East. Knight was Harvard-trained and fluent in French and Italian, and his extracurricular passions included French wines, motorcycles, and Japanese martial arts, none of which helped him fit in with the beer-swilling ex-cops of the American Express security corps. Their reaction to Knight was predictable when, while attending a company security gathering in Arizona, he lay out by the pool in tiny French bikini briefs reading a book. "Who's that guy?" the security men joked. "Is he with us? Fuckin' Frenchie! Fuckin' Frog!"

However eclectic his tastes, Paul Knight would prove as effective a fraud fighter as anyone in American Express history, smoothly coordinating his investigations with police across Europe and the Middle East. With Hob Miller's go-ahead, Knight began assembling a network of European informants and spies who could give American Express its first glimpse into the world of criminals arrayed against it. Knight came up with the code name for his program: Kendo, referring to the Oriental art of ritual fencing with bamboo swords.

Hiring informants for Knight's Kendo network wasn't easy. Hob Miller and Jim McGrath were so skittish they insisted on reviewing each of the nominees in detail. The trio would talk through the pros and cons of each applicant, weighing his reliability, his inevitable criminal record and his likelihood of helping them break into a counterfeiting or theft ring. By design, little if anything was written down. Only a record of payments to each code-named informant was kept in detail, so that Miller could placate the company's auditors. (By 1982 the Kendo budget would grow to $250,000.)

The program got off to a slow start when Knight's first few snitches proved unable to come up with information leading to "recoveries" of stolen cheques. Looking for a more seasoned operative, he turned to friends at the DEA's London office and was given a new name: Tony Greco. This Greco, Knight was told, had done some solid undercover work for the agency in England and Italy, and could be trusted to follow orders. He was also said to be known by several other European and American agencies, including the FBI, the IRS, and, it was rumored, the

CIA. After their first meeting Knight's only reservation was Greco's spotty English.*

"He was not a nice man," Hob Miller recalled of his first briefing on Greco. "But he had an extraordinary range of, shall we say, acquaintances in the counterfeiting business, both in the U.S. and internationally, all kinds of criminal activities. The drug business. Fraud, passing paper, you name it." And, to Hob Miller's surprise, Greco came cheap. Initially, American Express paid him a few hundred dollars or so for a three- or four-day assignment. Later, when Greco was working nearly full time for the company, he would receive as much as $25,000 a year.

A quick learner, Greco took in Paul Knight's briefings on travelers cheque fraud and wasted no time plunging back into the underworld of thieves and counterfeiters where Knight hoped to make their cases. Under Knight's tutelage, he became what is known inside American Express as a "centralizer," that is, a fence for stolen and counterfeit travelers cheques. The best centralizers in Europe bought and sold millions of dollars in cheques a year, harvesting stolen cheques from "pickpockets," the street thieves who preyed on tourists across the continent, then cashing them through "negotiators," the wandering middlemen who put themselves at risk by cashing stolen cheques, usually with the help of false identification papers.

Working out of his home in the London borough of Redbridge, Greco always masqueraded as a Mafioso with strong contacts in Naples and Las Vegas; if a listener didn't believe him, he was known to demand a phone, place a long-distance call to Naples, and put the doubter on the line with someone who identified himself as Don So-and-So.† The stunt always worked. To cops and crooks alike, Greco's style was always the same: smiling, smooth, and nonconfrontational, he was a fountain of compliments

---

*Before reporting to American Express, Greco says he worked for the London office of the DEA in a pair of undercover operations, one involving the movement of narcotics out of Eastern Europe. But Italian records also indicate a person with Greco's name and birthdate was convicted of theft there in September 1976. Details of the conviction aren't publicly available, but Greco insists it was a "mixup" involving his use of a bank's letter of credit. According to a printout of Greco's Italian criminal record, his yearlong jail sentence and fine were pardoned as part of a general amnesty two years later.

†Greco's penchant for personal security was reflected in the high wall and gates he built in front of his London home, as well as a special secure phone system he installed. Neighbors complained to town officials that the new walls uglied up the neighborhood and brought an action to force Greco to tear them down. He won.

and an expert on every subject, even those he knew nothing about. In his own rough way, he had pretensions at being a gentleman, wearing a diamond pinky ring and criticizing anyone who cursed in front of a lady. It was an act that would prove extraordinarily successful, and because he spoke Italian, Spanish, French, and broken English, Greco was able to take it all over Western Europe, deep into the cesspool of thieves and counterfeiters Knight and his superiors were dying to infiltrate.

Thanks to Greco and other informants, they succeeded, constructing for the first time a picture of the European criminals arrayed against American Express. Many, the company found, were South Americans preying on tourists. By one internal estimate, more than two thousand South Americans, most based in Spain, made their living stealing American Express products, and their tentacles reached out across Latin America, the Caribbean, and into south Florida. "The South or Central American," a 1981 American Express internal report concluded, is "sometimes raised at a near-starvation level and accustomed to beg, borrow, and steal almost from infancy [and] has no acquired ethical or moral block against stealing. Stealing is in some cases encouraged, and training begins at an early age."

Prowling sports events and busy train terminals on the lookout for tourist prey, South American thieves worked in teams, harvesting wallets and purses by the dozens. The cheques they found were quickly extracted and mailed to the supervising centralizer, who passed them on to negotiators. The negotiators roamed Europe and South America, cashing the stolen cheques in lots of $20,000 to $30,000 at unwitting banks. Most negotiators received a third of the take; the best cleared $100,000 a year. Centralizers, who provided safe drop sights, false documents, and bail when necessary, could clear $1 million.

Greco's value was established early on, when he helped American Express solve one of the most frightening cheque heists in its history. One night in February 1979, a freighter named the *Atlantic Song* slipped its berth in Liverpool, England, and steered into the icy waters of the Irish Sea. Bound for the Port of Newark, New Jersey, its cavernous hold carried dozens of forty-foot cargo containers, stacked in rows one hundred feet high. Deep amid the stacks, their contents cloaked in the tightest security, were two large containers holding some $2 billion in blank American Express travelers cheques.

The cheques, printed at a pair of plants in the north of England, had arrived at the docks in a convoy of armored trucks, escorted by police-men and American Express security personnel in unmarked cars. Once on the docks, the containers had been placed under twenty-four-hour guard. By prior arrangement with the shipper, the two were to be placed deep in the *Atlantic Song's* hold, beneath at least three rows of contain-ers and flanked by as many on each side. No one, the company insisted, should be able to get near them.

The loading had gone smoothly. Then, within days of the *Atlantic Song's* departure from Liverpool, Paul Knight took a call from Greco, who passed on worrisome news. Underworld contacts were spreading the word that upwards of $1 million in blank American Express travelers cheques were available for sale on the streets of London. Greco didn't know where they had come from, but both men knew the cheques would disappear fast—if American Express didn't act faster.

This was fraud of the highest order, and Knight quickly relayed the news to Jim McGrath in New York. McGrath immediately assumed the cheques had been been stolen from London's Heathrow Airport, a long-time sore spot for the company. Every year crooked shippers and work-ers at Heathrow cost American Express thousands of dollars in stolen cheques, a loss Paul Knight's agents had managed to curb but had never eliminated.

But when company security men checked Heathrow, everything was in place. In fact, the only cheque shipment unaccounted for in all of Great Britain wasn't in Great Britain at all, but at sea, aboard the *Atlantic Song*, in mid-ocean steaming toward Newark. In New York, Jim McGrath had the ship radioed and asked the captain to climb down into the hold with a flashlight to check the American Express containers. When the captain radioed back, their worst fears were realized: a gaping, three-foot hole could be seen in one container. Exactly how much, if anything, remained inside was unclear.

McGrath's people panicked at the prospect of a $2 billion loss, which potentially dwarfed that from the Salad Oil scandal. "We can all start looking for another job if they're gone," McGrath said grimly. At head-quarters, Hob Miller was calling around for a helicopter to fly him out to the ship when cooler heads prevailed. Finally McGrath led a squad of FBI and Customs agents to an Italian restaurant near the Newark port, where on the night of March 1, 1979, they dined on pasta and awaited the ship's arrival at eleven o'clock.

When the *Atlantic Song* docked, McGrath's squad pounded aboard and hustled down darkened gangways into the hold. They found one of the two containers still intact, but there, just as the captain had reported, a hole yawned in the second. Someone, it appeared, had taken an ax to it. The ship's crew was detained while the remaining cheques were counted. All told, negotiable cheques totaling $850,000 had vanished—not $2 billion, but still a sizable loss. No sooner had they made the discovery than Tony Greco came through again. Even before Scotland Yard could mobilize to find the thieves, Greco fingered them, a motley group of British thugs, whom British police effortlessly picked up at a London-area Hilton Hotel. The cheques were recovered with minimal loss.

Relief swept the cadre of American Express executives who knew of the theft. Hob Miller, for one, thought Greco was a hero, and was fascinated by what he heard of his exploits. He was also curious: What kind of man was this informer? What made him tick? Later, on a trip to Paris, Miller heard that Greco was in town and asked Paul Knight to arrange an introduction. The meeting was set in a lounge at Miller's hotel, The Bristol, and there, American Express's No. 4 executive first spied the man who was fast becoming one of the company's most valuable intelligence assets. But as Miller walked into the lounge, a strange thing happened. He studied Greco's visage for a moment, then walked off without introducing himself. For some reason, he lost all desire to meet Tony Greco the moment he laid eyes on him. There was something menacing about the informant. "I didn't want to meet the man, I don't know why," Miller would say years later. "I didn't even want him to know who I was."

Not all Greco's operations went as smoothly as the *Atlantic Song* incident. In December 1979 he was arrested in Genoa, Italy, after two of his accomplices were picked up at the Genoa train station holding nearly $10,000 in stolen cheques. All Greco's protestations that he was actually working for American Express fell on deaf ears. Charged with handling stolen goods, he apparently served no jail time after his arrest, and wasn't convicted until three years later, when an Italian court ruled he had been "the organizer of the criminal activity" and sentenced him to three and a half years in prison; two years of that sentence were later set aside as part of a general amnesty. Greco stayed out of prison only by zealously avoiding Italy while his lawyers fought the charge. Court records indicate his sentence was ultimately set aside in 1990.

Shortly after the Genoa arrest, Greco ran into trouble again, this time in London. In February 1980, former company officials say, he was leading a joint American Express–Scotland Yard sting operation against a ring of South American cheque thieves over from the continent. The plan was for more than a dozen of the ring's negotiators to gather at the Piccadilly Hotel, then fan out across London to cash as many stolen cheques as possible. But on the appointed day, something went wrong. Apparently some crossed into the jurisdiction of the City of London and were arrested, prompting city police, to American Express's dismay, to descend on the hotel and arrest everyone in sight, including Greco.

A steaming Jim McGrath called to brief his boss Hob Miller, who was in Paris on other business. "I thought McGrath was going to have a hernia," Miller recalled. As London police made noises about arresting Paul Knight, who they believed had overseen the operation, McGrath quietly hustled Knight out of the country, leaving Hob Miller to take a 5:00 A.M. flight to London and attempt to get Greco out of jail—and, not incidentally, make sure American Express's name stayed out of the head-lines. Miller got half his mission accomplished: the British press never figured out it was a botched American Express sting operation, but Greco remained in jail. The London police, who didn't care about Greco's informant status, simply wouldn't release him, a fact that hardly mollified the outraged Italian or his frantic wife. "As I recall," Miller says, "he was pretty mad we couldn't get him out of jail."

Years later, as he recalled Greco's incarceration from an easy chair at his sprawling New Jersey home, a twinkle came to Hob Miller's eye. "We didn't mind him serving time in jail," Miller said, smiling. "All this enhanced his value to us. By doing time, by getting arrested, his impor-tance on the other side of society actually grew. It established his bona fides. Harvard Business degrees don't enable you to become a very good double agent, you know."

By and by Greco was freed, though the London police made clear he had better leave the country. After his release from custody he fled Great Britain, never to return, at least not officially. He was forced to relocate, this time to that famed den of thieves, the Mediterranean coast of Spain.

From his office in lower Manhattan, Jim McGrath was thrilled to hear Greco was shifting his base of operations to Spain, which since the death of Franco in 1975 was filling fast with criminals of all stripes, many of them South Americans whose schemes to steal American Express travelers cheques were spreading throughout Europe. Joining a tide of Italian criminals fleeing their country's attacks on the Mafia, Greco settled outside Barcelona, buying a villa shrouded with greenery in the beachside resort town of Castelldefels, six miles south of the city. For almost two years he managed to stay out of serious trouble, growing wealthy as an American Express–sponsored centralizer while feeding Paul Knight a steady flow of tips.

On a Thursday morning in late October 1981, one of Knight's top men sat down in an undisclosed location to begin a debriefing session with one of his Kendo program's best informants. The snitch, assigned the code name Alice, began talking every morning around nine-thirty and, with breaks only for coffee and meals, spoke straight through until midnight every day for a week. According to three former American Express security officials, Alice was none other than Tony Greco, and the twenty-eight-page report on his debriefing is a definitive snapshot of the criminal milieu Greco inhabited on the balmy Spanish coast. Even "his asides and anecdotes," Knight's man wrote, "provided an extraordinary pertinent insight into the modus operandi and personal characteristics of those criminals who appear to represent a substantial threat to American Express."

It was easy to see why Knight and his superiors loved Greco. His knowledge of Europe's network of centralizers, what Greco called "the community," was encyclopedic, and his eye for detail was keen. Greco's comments on a Barcelona centralizer named Ugo, as summarized by Knight's lieutenant, included these observations: "Has German shepherd dog, drives 850 FIAT, quiet dresser. Never seen wearing tie. Enjoys grilled meat...smokes Marlboro filters...Spanish wife approximately 33–36 years of age described as heavy in rump, dark hair which she dyes, very quiet..." From Greco's memory sprang details on dozens of European crooks, from Parisian centralizers to British gun-runners to Mafia cronies as far afield as Australia and Hong Kong. He seemed to know everything, down to their appetites in mistresses, massage parlors, cigars, jewelry and cars, even, where possible, their phone numbers. By the number for a Mafia fence in Genoa, Knight's man wrote in his report: "Ask for Franco."

The life of a centralizer—which remained Greco's cover—was a plush one as criminal endeavors go. Several of Greco's friends, he reported, were taking in an estimated $2 million a year or more from cheques alone—Greco's home was said to cost more than $500,000—and few limited themselves to a single endeavor; other European centralizers of Greco's acquaintance fenced stolen jewelry as well as passports, guns, cigarettes, and heroin. One was a contract killer. The most successful drove Rolls-Royce Corniches, Mercedes convertibles, and Jaguars, wore $40,000 diamond rings and Rolex watches and channeled their profits into bars and discos in Marbella and Málaga, in Milan and Marseilles and Paris and Naples. Many owned legitimate businesses they used as fronts, an insurance office in Nice, a scrap yard in London, restaurants on Barcelona's Diagonal Street. And all traveled widely, moving cheques back and forth among negotiators in Peru, Venezuela, Spain, France, and, in some cases, the Far East.

But the best thing about fencing travelers cheques was its safety, both from violence and, in many cases, criminal prosecution. A wide variety of shady types, from drug traffickers to terrorists to gun-runners, found it handy to finance their schemes with stolen travelers cheques, a fact that put the most active centralizers in a superb position to catch the tidbits of raw criminal intelligence police craved. Many, like Greco, were police informants: they correctly deduced that the authorities would overlook their petty offenses in exchange for information on narcotics, arms, and organized crime. Ugo, the Barcelona centralizer with the German shepherd, was on a Spanish police department's payroll, as was a woman who owned a fruit shop in the Rampon Neau district of Paris and who served as a bulletin board for the centralizing community.

Soon after moving to Spain, former associates say, Greco established ties with the Barcelona police department and, according to former American Express officials, also maintained relations with members of French police and customs as well as Scotland Yard. When not working with friends in law enforcement, Greco retained his old ties to the Neapolitan Mafia, the Camorra. Though he continued to avoid Italy, several associates say Greco stayed in contact with the Camorra family of Italian mobster Michele Zaza. In his debriefing he gave Paul Knight's man details on the lives of a half-dozen major Italian crime figures. "Well-known to informant," the report noted of several mob centralizers.

All this activity kept Greco busy, too busy, it seems, to realize that his comings and goings in Spain had attracted unwanted attention. As early as 1982, Greco's name surfaced in the investigations of several Barcelona journalists as a soldier in the Italian Mafia's infiltration of Spain. A reporter named Antonio Rubio, who later went to work for *Cambio 16*, a respected news magazine, suspected that Greco might be related to the renowned Sicilian Mafia don, Michele Greco. The dogged Rubio remained so curious he actually took to following Greco through the streets of Barcelona, and in 1984 he snapped a series of pictures of Greco visiting contacts at the Barcelona police department. Greco's name, however, never surfaced in press accounts at the time, and Rubio's pictures would lie in a file unnoticed for years.

Tony Greco's days beneath the Spanish sun came to an abrupt halt not long after his debriefing. Just three months later, in January 1982, he and two others were arrested in Castelldefels, probably at his home. Spanish police took Greco to a jail down the coast in the city of Valencia, away from his friends in the Barcelona police, and charged him with smuggling counterfeit U.S. currency—according to several sources, hundred-dollar bills. Records at the Italian Embassy in Madrid show that Spanish police found illegal weapons and false identification papers in his possession; other sources say he was also under investigation for smuggling guns and diamonds. A month after his arrest, records indicate Greco was transferred to a high-security prison in La Mancha province near Madrid. For undisclosed reasons, he was to be tried under Spain's stiff antiterrorism law, and a trial date was set. But there the paper trail abruptly ends. According to embassy records, Tony Greco simply disappeared.°

Which one of Greco's law-enforcement allies—American, British, French, or Spanish—sprang him from jail isn't known, but it was American Express that spirited him out of Spain to America. "We wanted him to come to the U.S., because he had some valuable contacts, particularly in organized crime," Hob Miller recalled. "I knew that he was hot for some reason in Europe, and there was an opportunity to get him to Miami, which we had discussed with him. And so we did it. I would think we even paid for his trip over."

°According to a former American Express security official familiar with Greco's career, his 1982 arrest in Spain was the result of a rivalry between French and Spanish police not unlike the one that landed him in a London jail two years before. As this executive tells the story, among those arrested with Greco was a murderer who was one of the most-wanted criminals in France; Greco had actually been working for French police to track the man down. However, according to this account, Spanish police resented the French authorities's incursions onto their turf and petulantly arrested and prosecuted Greco along with those he had been informing on.

Once Greco was free of his Spanish complications, American Express planned for him to spearhead an offensive against exactly the kind of South American thieves he had grown to know in Europe. Jim McGrath was so happy with the Kendo program he was laying plans to use snitches around the world. Already American Express had begun funneling money to a criminal high up in a Southeast Asian syndicate, who was responding with tips that allowed the company to fight the Chinese crime rings that had plagued the region for years. Latin America, the source of a full two-thirds of the world's counterfeit cheques, was the next logical battlefront. At a company security conference in Torino, Italy, in 1982, the region's security chief received approval to introduce informants to Latin America.

In early 1982 one of Paul Knight's lieutenants, a beefy Dutchman named Herman Von Rossom, crossed the Atlantic to lay the groundwork for the new program, which American Express code-named Salsa. Von Rossom had hoped to use his best Kendo informant, a smooth Italian criminal code-named Antoine, who had fled to Los Angeles after his cover was blown in an operation in Belgium. But Antoine didn't work out, making Greco the obvious leadoff man for the new Salsa program, which promised to be their riskiest effort to date. "Operating Salsa," Von Rossom noted in an internal memo, "could be extremely dangerous regarding the personal health of participants."

And so Tony Greco, free once more, found his way to a Miami Beach hotel, where he met his new handlers at American Express, the suspicious former cop named Ray Sanchez and his boss Marisa Gracia. By all accounts, Greco slid easily into the south Florida scene he had left a decade before. He and his second wife bought a Spanish-style ranch house just off the golf course in a neatly trimmed development of expensive homes called The Country Club of Miami; it was this house on Royal Birkdale Drive, long abandoned by Greco, that Joe Mullen would visit seven years later.

Once again Greco went into the jewelry business, this time in style, telling friends he worked with a company called Monique International, which had offices in Miami's wholesale jewelry center, the Seybold Building. According to former associates, Greco arranged to import a variety of jewelry, some of it legitimate, some of it counterfeit Rolex watches he shipped in from Italy via Panama, where he kept several bank accounts and safe deposit boxes. Greco sold a number of these watches to the new friends he made at American Express's security offices in Coral Gables.

Soon, just as he had in Europe, Greco had feet firmly planted on both sides of the law, using law-enforcement contacts as a hedge against his renewed ventures into the shadier sides of south Florida life. For the former, Greco turned to the FBI, in the person of special agent Alfred LaManna, an organized crime expert in the bureau's Miami office. American Express's security chief, Jim McGrath, gave LaManna a sparkling recommendation for Greco, and soon he was peddling tips to the FBI as well as American Express; LaManna, much to his ultimate embarrassment, would remain in contact with Greco for the next decade.

On the other side of the law, Greco, a man who had worn many hats—jeweler, centralizer, FBI and American Express informant—added another: accused drug smuggler. As Spanish police later pieced together the story, Greco in 1982 met Ramon Puentes, a Miami car dealer whose wealth came not from selling Corvettes or Jaguars but, police alleged, from the large shipments of cocaine he smuggled into Florida for his close friends in the famed Ochoa family of Colombia's Medellín cartel. Puentes's chief money launderer was a handsome young accountant named Indalecio "Andy" Iglesias, the Panamanian-born son of a traveling Cuban pharmacist who pursued his education at Miami's La Salle High School, in business courses at Miami-Dade Community College, and, during the 1980s, in the lofty circles of South American drug traffickers. The pair's narcotics ring, which smuggled an estimated thirty-six tons of cocaine into the United States during the early 1980s, often in the hidden compartments of Ramon Puentes's automobiles, was called La Empresa (The Company).

Andy Iglesias says he first met Tony Greco when the Italian dropped by La Empresa's headquarters at Auto World, a car dealership Puentes owned on south Miami's Dixie Highway. Iglesias was impressed by Greco's savvy and his criminal contacts, and soon the two were brainstorming ways to marry Greco's counterfeiting expertise to La Empresa's money-laundering needs. "Tony was a free lance—he did whatever he wanted," Iglesias recalled. "Tony's after anything he can make a buck on. He'll get into any kind of business where he could make money. He's a good businessman."

Rumors of the scheme Andy Iglesias says he and Tony Greco cooked up have circulated through south Florida law-enforcement circles for years, though to date they have never crystallized into criminal charges in the United States. Iglesias, in an interview from his current home in a Madrid jail cell, describes the plan as a complicated money-laundering scheme, spread over four countries. "It wasn't just a drug deal," he says. "It was a watches-and-money-and-drugs deal."

According to Iglesias, Greco was to receive twenty kilos of cocaine, valued at just over $1 million, from La Empresa's Colombian suppliers. In turn, Greco promised to move a large shipment of fake Rolex watches out of Italy and into Nice, France. From Nice the watches would be shipped to Panama, and from Panama into the United States, where they would be sold on the streets. The laundered proceeds would flow straight to La Empresa; if successful, the scheme could be tried again and again, using far larger drug shipments. "It was a beautiful deal," Iglesias recalls.

Preparations were exhaustive. Iglesias says he accompanied Greco to Panama, where he was surprised by the number of people the Italian knew and the bank accounts he held; to New York, where the two breakfasted at the St. Moritz Hotel, and where Greco seemed to know everyone from the doorman to the shoeshine boy; and finally to Nice, where the counterfeit Rolexes were to arrive on the first step of their journey to America. Iglesias and two associates contacted Greco in Nice by leaving messages at a tea shop, and after the shipment was secured they all drove to the Spanish border, where Greco stayed behind, explaining that he had certain "problems" in Spain; presumably he was still being sought after his arrest there. Iglesias went on to Greco's home in Castelldefels, where he says one of Greco's partners showed him a secret room the Italian had built behind a hidden wall panel. "His contacts," Inglesias recalls of Greco's associates in France and Spain, "were all Mafia as far as I could tell. I never met anyone who knew Tony that was legitimate."

Of course, some of his friends were legitimate, as Iglesias knew. Greco bragged often of his job as a "special investigator" for American Express. He even gave Iglesias Paul Knight's telephone number in London, and urged him to get in touch; conceivably Iglesias, too, might enjoy some easy corporate money. But though he knew Greco was working with American Express and the Barcelona police—"In Barcelona he was a god; he said the police loved him there"—Iglesias never suspected Greco was an FBI informant. "Never," he says.[*]

Greco, Iglesias says, took the cocaine and passed it on to friends to distribute; La Empresa then waited for its money from the sale of the Rolexes. Greco, meanwhile, remained busy juggling other projects, including several involving American Express's new Salsa informant program. In the wake of his travels to Panama and elsewhere, he passed on several tips to Ray Sanchez at American Express in Coral Gables: of a counterfeit cheque "factory" in Panama; of a major European centralizer arriving at the Miami airport; and, perhaps most intriguing of all, of a vital "embosser" used to make counterfeit American Express cards at a Miami electronics store.

Ray Sanchez hadn't liked Greco from the moment they met. And the more he chased his tips, the more irritated he became. The Panama "factory" never materialized. Customs officers at the Miami airport detained and strip-searched the "major European centralizer" but found nothing, and were forced to set him free. Worst of all, though no fault of Greco's, was the debacle over the Miami electronics store.

Greco's tip was considered serious enough that a senior investigator was brought down from headquarters in New York to look into it. Greco, Sanchez recalls, thought the man looked so much like an ex-cop that he refused to deal with him, nicknaming him "Shiny Shoes" for his police-style wardrobe. At American Express's request, Miami police put the store under surveillance, but were finding nothing when, Ray Sanchez alleges, one of his superiors suggested they secretly slip into the store and steal the embosser. In the wake of strenuous arguments over what option to take, the operation was canceled—the embosser was never found—though the suggestion of an American Express-sponsored burglary became an issue in a nasty lawsuit Sanchez and a colleague later brought against American Express over their subsequent dismissals.

Ray Sanchez remained suspicious of Greco. "He never gives us anything," Sanchez complained to his boss, Marisa Gracia. "He's lying all the time." Sanchez thought Greco was dealing in stolen cheques himself and padding his expense accounts, charges he said his superiors didn't want

[*]Greco, while offering no details, suggests his work with Iglesias was part of an unspecified law-enforcement investigation.

to hear about their prized informant. "Don't let Jim McGrath hear you say that," he says Gracia told him.

That fall of 1982 Ray Sanchez was busy pursuing the first of American Express's Salsa undercover stings, an investigation of Bogotá counterfeiters in conjunction with the Colombian police. But even had he been so inclined, Greco wasn't available to help. Late on the afternoon of October 6, 1982, he pulled his car out of a parking lot on Northwest Thirty-sixth Street in Miami and was nearly run down by a police car, which was forced to brake sharply to avoid an accident. In the process of ticketing Greco for failing to yield, Officer David Chirinsky ran a check of his driver's license and turned up an outstanding warrant from Greco's arrest at the Miami airport in 1972. Chirinsky placed Greco under arrest and took him to the Miami Springs police station, then to Dade County jail. Greco gave his address as the old IRS apartment on 56th Street in Manhattan, and his business address as 122 Mulberry Street in Little Italy, a funeral home down the street from his IRS-owned restaurant. Asked his occupation, Greco told the officers he was in the restaurant business. Three weeks later the case was dismissed; court records don't indicate why.

Despite the occasional brush with lawmen, Greco seemed to have it all in Miami: a new home, a family, shelter from bothersome European police, solid contacts on both sides of the law. But then something happened, and all at once he disappeared. Monique International's office at the Seybold Building closed. Court records in Miami show that the house on Royal Birkdale Drive was abandoned, its mortgage ignored, despite all attempts by the lender to track Greco down. "He left in forty-eight hours," Andy Iglesias says. "His wife, his kids, they simply vanished."

What had happened, Iglesias alleges, was this: somehow Greco's Rolexes-for-cocaine deal had come up $700,000 short, and La Empresa's powerful boss, Ramon Puentes, wanted his money—and badly. As rumors flew around Miami that a contract had been issued on Greco's life, Iglesias says he scoured the city for the missing Italian, so intent on reclaiming the missing drug money that he looked into the possibility of putting a lien on Greco's vacant home. Finally, after more than a month, Greco telephoned. "He was afraid for his life," recalls Iglesias, who says Greco probably wasn't in as much danger as he feared. "It didn't get to a point of putting a contract on this guy, [although] I wouldn't have been the one to give the order to kill him."

Greco had moved to New York, where real-estate records indicate he bought the house on Staten Island's Douglas Road in June 1983. Andy Iglesias, accompanied by two bodyguards, says he immediately hurried north to confront him over the missing $700,000. Greco, surrounded by four Italian bodyguards of his own, met him in a Little Italy restaurant before adjourning to dinner atop the World Trade Center. In an understandably tense meeting, Greco explained that the money was missing because many of the Rolexes had been stolen by one of his partners.

Against his better instincts, Iglesias found himself being swayed. "If you talk to Tony, he's so persuasive, he'll convince you to jump off a bridge," says Iglesias. "I don't know if you know how the drug business works, but many times you have to forgive something like that if you want to be in business with the guy. It all works out. Eventually we more or less ended up with a good relationship, even though I knew he had stolen the money."

Greco's move to New York signaled the twilight of his business relationship with Iglesias and, for entirely different reasons, with American Express. That year, 1983, budget cutbacks forced Jim McGrath to cut back his prized Kendo programs; the next year, after Hob Miller's retirement, he had to eliminate the use of informants altogether, not just Kendo and Salsa but also a top-secret plan for using snitches in the U.S. code-named Yankee. Along with lesser informants around the world, Greco was cut from the payroll and set adrift, though tales of his adventures were to keep his legend alive in the halls of American Express for years to come. "This guy could do anything, given the proper motivation," Hob Miller recalled. "He is the most skillful, crafty little son-of-a-bitch I've encountered in the consulting business. I wouldn't put anything past him."

Over the next three years Jim McGrath stayed in touch with Greco, taking time for a lunch or two every few months. Shuttling between his homes in Staten Island and Spain, Greco kept in far closer contact with Paul Knight, who gave his longtime operative's career close attention. It was with Knight's help, in fact, that Greco struck up a new relationship with a respected Washington-based security consultant named Philip Manuel. For Greco, it was the first step in the common transition from paid informer to the cushier job of private detective.

A Watergate-era Senate investigator, Phil Manuel ran a small, no-nonsense shop whose outsized prestige and Washington contacts could be measured by the photos and letters lining the walls of its Pennsylvania Avenue office suite: there hung a glossy photo of Manuel shaking hands with President Reagan, who named him to a presidential commission on organized crime, next to laudatory missives from the likes of Ted Kennedy, Ed Meese, Strom Thurmond, and George Bush. If Jules Kroll ran the ultimate supermarket of detective services, Manuel's agency was an exclusive boutique whose specialties included combating all manner of counterfeit goods: watches, liquor, electronics, perfumes, pharmaceuticals, anything and everything made in some Asian sweatshop and passed on to consumers as the real thing.

In the spring of 1984 executives at one of Manuel's oldest clients, the cosmetics maker Charles of the Ritz, were wringing their hands over an alarming number of fake bottles of Yves Saint Laurent perfume appearing on cosmetics shelves worldwide. The counterfeit, commonly a knockoff of the thirty-milliliter bottle of YSL's Opium brand spray, was of amazingly good quality, the perfume, plastic top, and packaging so close to genuine that company officials at first failed to realize they were fake. Charles of the Ritz executives understood that cracking down on the sleazy retailers peddling the fakes would do little good. What they wanted, and this was Manuel's challenge, was to follow the trail "upstream," that is, trace the phony perfume back through distribution channels to its source—the counterfeiters themselves—find their illicit manufacturing operation, and identify the scientific "brain" behind it.

That summer of 1984, as Manuel cast around for a suitable undercover agent to find and infiltrate the counterfeiting ring, he heard stories of Tony Greco's prowess at American Express. He contacted Paul Knight in London, and Knight arranged a rendezvous with Greco in Paris that July. What Manuel saw in that first meeting with Greco he liked: an operative with a history of criminal contacts no undercover policeman or FBI agent could fake, and blessed with that striking combination of cockiness, moxie, and charm born of years walking the thin line between the criminal and law-enforcement worlds. Manuel checked Greco's references with the FBI and the IRS and, despite his continuing "problems" in Italy, liked what he heard: Greco, each of his handlers said, was capable of first-class work if—and this was the "if" Manuel heard at every stop—he was closely monitored and controlled.

It was a warning Phil Manuel took to heart over the course of three years supervising Greco in a pair of complex European counterfeiting investigations. "I tried to keep close control over him, and I did; for the sake of a good operation, anyone who wants to be successful with him had better do it," Manuel observed. "Tony is very quick; his mind runs ahead of me, ahead of you, ahead of anyone's. He's always thinking down the road, planning his next manipulation. If you don't stay close to him, he'll get so far ahead of you that you'll be lost. He'll be running the operation then, not you. Then he'll be telling you what to do.

Under Phil Manuel's watchful eye Greco turned in a top-notch performance, smoking out the perfume counterfeiters in a labyrinthine sting operation lasting nearly two years. The first bottle of the fake Opium had surfaced at his old haunt, Miami's Seybold Building, and it was there that Greco picked up the scent. Posing as a front man for an investor group looking to put money into the scheme—but using his own name and criminal background—Greco followed the trail to Panama, where counterfeits of every stripe mingled easily with legitimate goods stored in the free-trade zone. Ingratiating himself with corrupt Panamanian distributors, Greco learned that the Opium knockoff was coming in from West Germany, a discovery that led him and Manuel into long months of investigative work in Europe.

Deftly stepping up each rung of the counterfeiting ladder, Greco—reporting regularly, sometimes in Italian, to Manuel in Washington—ultimately rose far enough not only to identify the financial masterminds behind the scheme, a group of corrupt businessmen in Saarbrücken, Germany, but also the location of their secret factory, at a warehouse in the remote jungles of the Asian island nation of Sri Lanka, as well as the ring's "brain," a former perfume-industry scientist in Paris. By 1986 it was over: the German businessmen arrested, the Sri Lanka factory shuttered, and Phil Manuel left to marvel at Greco's ability to maneuver in the criminal world.

Even as he worked Manuel's perfume case—for which he was paid between $100,000 and $150,000 a year—Greco busied himself with other money-making projects. "With Tony, he makes no bones about it, he has a number of things going on at any one time; you never know what he's doing," Manuel said. After somehow clearing the 1982 criminal charges in Spain—"probably by turning someone else in," Andy Iglesias speculates—Greco seems to have stepped up informant work with

European law-enforcement agencies, including the Barcelona police; according to two people in Europe, he was paid by Spanish intelligence in the mid-1980s for information about links between Spain's Basque terrorists and Italy's Red Brigades. According to another detective who worked with Greco, he kept up strong contacts with French customs.

It was during his work for Phil Manuel that Greco began reconnoitering his old haunts in Peru. After the late Haya de la Torre's APRA party finally ascended to power in 1985, he reestablished contacts with several friends in Lima, often pestering them with money-making ideas. Not all were glad to hear from him; Hugo Otero, Peru's ambassador to France at the time, recalls ducking dozens of Greco's telephone calls in the mid-1980s. The new regime's press secretary, Victor Tirado, the big Aprista who would later betray Greco to Safra, was startled one day in the summer of 1985 to hear from his old friend, who had arrived in Lima brimming with ideas to make money: buying and selling airplanes and setting up casinos or privately run prisons, among others. Peruvian friends noticed that Greco seemed to keep a low profile when in Lima, fearful that enemies in the military might notice his return.

But of course, that was the very place Tony Greco seemed most comfortable, in the shadows: no one, it appears—not American Express, not Phil Manuel, not the FBI, not his associates in the Mafia, narcotics or counterfeiting businesses—really knew all the angles Greco was working at any given time. He was a consummate big-money hustler, a streetwise jack-of-all-trades who through a beguiling combination of chutzpah and gutter charm managed to move in circles both high and low, cop and crook, American and European and Latin, wherever it took to make a buck.

"That was all Tony cared about, the money," said Irwin Robbins, a south Florida private detective who shared tips on perfume cases with Greco. "Tony always bragged that he made $500,000 one year, a million the next. Let me tell you, no investigator makes that kind of money. When he said that, I knew there had to be [other income]. He'd make money anywhere he could find it. He'd work either side [of the law]. Whoever pays."

The seemier aspects of his career not only didn't hinder Greco's work for American detective agencies; they were the reasons he attracted assignments. In 1987 he completed his second operation for Phil Manuel, slipping into Bulgaria to identify a liquor-counterfeiting operation. But by that September the Manuel agency's backlog of counterfeiting cases was spent, and while Manuel remained fond of Greco, he simply had no more work for him.

Once again Paul Knight came to the rescue. On Knight's recommendation, Greco picked up an assignment that fall from Jules Kroll, whose London office commissioned him to investigate a Spanish businessman as part of a routine due-diligence case. It didn't go well: Kroll's people weren't at all pleased with Greco's work, and urged their bosses in New York not to hire him again. Part of the problem, it seems, was that the case called for Greco to perform conventional detective work, a task for which Phil Manuel knew him to be almost totally unqualified. As a detective Greco was an undercover expert, an operative who learned things by befriending criminals, not investigating them. Worse, after so many years on the streets, Greco had a style singularly unsuited to traditional investigative work.

"He was a bully," recalls an American executive familiar with Greco's work for Kroll. "No one wanted to work with him. He was arrogant. A know-it-all. He liked to come across as a tough guy. He had this menacing quality that really put people off."

This, then, was the man Paul Knight suggested that Harry Freeman hire to investigate Edmond Safra. It was at best a dubious recommendation, but one on which Freeman never sought a second opinion. And so that fall Tony Greco—paid informant; fledgling private detective; consort of Mafiosi, assassins, and thieves; a man who in the previous decade had seen the inside of jail cells in at least four countries—joined forces with Freeman and a woman named Susan Cantor, giving American Express all the ingredients it needed for a debacle of truly stupendous proportions.

13

They met for the first time, the onetime campus radical and the smooth European snitch-cum-gumshoe, at a restaurant in Nice, France, in August 1987. Like so many others, the rendezvous between Tony Greco and Susan Cantor was arranged by Paul Knight, who never missed a chance to schedule a meeting in Nice, where he could enjoy restaurants famed for the best pizza in Europe. Greco, looking for work following his last case for Phil Manuel, had leaped at the idea for a new assignment investigating Safra.

Over lunch he and Cantor fell into intense conversation as Cantor laid out her progress and discussed the hazy tip Greco had earlier relayed to Knight, concerning a $40 million letter-of-credit scheme at Republic to defraud banks in Austria and Switzerland; it was the very allegation that would pop up in the Bern letter to Interpol five months later. Almost from the first words they exchanged that summer day in Nice, Greco and Cantor shared a tendency to broadcast their suspicions about Safra. As their discussion grew more intense, Knight noticed they abandoned all attempts at discretion, loudly discussing Safra's supposed crimes within earshot of other diners. When they persisted even after some of Greco's acquaintances joined their table, Knight rose and excused himself. This was something, he had the feeling, for which he wanted no responsibility. "The two of you," he said, "are on your own now."

That night Cantor joined Greco and one of his friends for a long dinner, and by the next morning the groundwork had been laid for one of the most unfortunate partnerships in American Express history. Soon after, Harry Freeman hired Greco as a consultant, sight unseen. Details of the Italian's work for American Express between August 1987 and May 1989 remain in the company's files. To this day, neither Greco nor Cantor nor any American Express official has spoken publicly about the company's "investigation" of Safra. But a portrait of the probe can be pieced together based on interviews with current and former American Express officials, including Harry Freeman and Bob Smith, as well as journalists and former government officials in the United States, France, Great Britain, Switzerland, Spain, Peru, Uruguay, and Argentina.

At the beginning, the pair was supervised by Freeman, who approved Greco's $750-a-day fee, plus expenses, a sum he wasn't at all happy with. "The guy was expensive," Freeman recalled, "and he wanted more." Via Cantor, Freeman promised the possibility of added compensation, perhaps a bonus, if the investigation went well. Later, as Greco began crisscrossing the world in pursuit of the dirt Freeman and Jim Robinson so badly wanted to find on Safra, it was Freeman who approved the detective's expense vouchers. He insists he never met Greco face-to-face. It was Cantor who personally supervised Greco. She handled his regular payments, often in increments of $15,000 or more. Over time the total payments grew so large, Freeman recalls, they threatened to throw his entire department over budget.

Freeman alerted Jim Robinson that he had hired a "consultant," and in the days and weeks to come, he says, Robinson's inquiries about Greco became a staple of their daily chats. "Jim certainly knew we had Greco," Freeman recalled. "We talked about it all the time. He'd say, you know, 'Is Greco working out?' And I'd say, 'Well, we're working hard, but we haven't found anything. I'm getting worried about it because we're spending a lot of money. But Susan thinks we're on the right track, and they're rolling.'"

At the risk of oversimplification, private investigators can be broken into two groups: those who have worked in law enforcement and rely on old police cronies for information, and those who generate leads by their own investigations. In practice, Tony Greco belonged squarely to the former group, a paid informer with long ties to law enforcement but little or no background in formal investigations himself. Not surprisingly, then, among the first stops Greco made on his new assignment for American Express was Washington, where in late September 1987, according to several people, he met with officials of the Federal Bureau of Investigation.

After returning to the United States in 1982, Greco had worked as an informer for the FBI's Miami office, and among those he contacted at the FBI that fall of 1987 was his Miami-based control agent, Alfred LaManna. LaManna, who later retired and joined the same detective outfit as Greco, the Washington-based Philip Manuel Resource Group, has declined comment on his talks with Greco that fall, but one of his friends insists that all LaManna did for Greco was refer him to FBI agents in Washington. Little is known of Greco's meeting with LaManna or other FBI agents except for this: while asking for any information the bureau might have on Safra, Greco—as the mysterious "Miami source"—is believed to have passed along tips of his own, including the rumor of the $40 million letter-of-credit scheme, and Cantor's scanty findings about Safra and Willard Zucker. *

Tips like Greco's flow into the FBI each year by the hundreds of thousands. Many languish in forgotten files, some are investigated and found to be groundless, and a few actually lead to criminal cases. That fall, almost certainly because of the mention of Zucker, the FBI channeled Greco's tips to the office of the Iran-Contra prosecutor, who later asked the legal attaché in Safra's home country, at the U.S. Embassy in Bern, Switzerland, to lodge an inquiry with Interpol's Vienna office for more information on Safra. That inquiry, in the "Bern letter," was made January 29, 1988.

It was a simple matter, purely routine, but Greco's dubious tips, once insinuated into the confidential flow of FBI intelligence, were to have profound repercussions for Safra. Months later Greco would again dip into that flow, somehow obtaining a copy of the Bern embassy's request to Interpol, and slip it to any number of people, including *Minute*'s Jean Roberto. By reprinting the letter, Roberto and others created the indelible—and misleading—impression that Safra and Republic were being seriously investigated by American authorities.

There is, in fact, no evidence that U.S. investigators made any concerted effort to follow up Greco's tips on Safra. A year later, in their October 1988 letter to Safra's attorneys, federal prosecutors said the

---

* Greco confirms his meeting with the FBI, but will offer no further details. "Any operation I start, before I say yes, I go to the authorities, people I know, people I've been working with for years," he asserts, "and I say we will work together and I need support and I pass information to them. I never in my life start an investigation in a country without asking authorization, without working with the authorities."

matter had been dropped; privately, they acknowledge it was never pursued. But despite that, and despite the fact that the tips had come from an operative working for Safra's adversary, the information remained in FBI files, and the sketchy Bern letter became the centerpiece document of the campaign against Safra.

The Bern letter wasn't the only repercussion to be felt from Greco's meeting with the FBI. Afterward he informed Cantor he had learned that the DEA had been looking into allegations of money laundering at Safra-controlled banks in Miami, Los Angeles, and New York since 1984—the very allegation Walter Weiner would later discover in the anonymous report received from *Minute*. The DEA refuses to publicly confirm or deny the existence of its investigations. But given the dates and locations, Greco was almost certainly referring to the joint DEA-IRS investigation into the marijuana-smuggling ring of champion powerboat racer Ben Kramer, which, according to the DEA's Miami office, had actually cleared Safra's little Florida bank of any wrongdoing.*

Briefed regularly by Cantor, Harry Freeman grew excited by Greco's findings, including odd rumors he reported of Safra's ties to the Swiss, French, and Israeli governments. Freeman developed a theory that Safra's banks were regularly placed at the disposal of foreign intelligence services. And while he says he doesn't specifically remember his reaction to Greco's tip about a federal investigation into Safra's banks, Freeman has no doubt how he would have reacted. "My reaction," he said, "would have been, 'Terrific, if they're investigating Safra, terrific, we've won the game.'"

The moves in Harry Freeman's exciting "game," of course, were to have the severest of consequences for Safra, as illustrated by the case of Greco's written reports. By November 1987 Greco had been on the job barely three months, but the pressure to stop Safra was mounting; Safra was scheduled to reopen in Switzerland in less than six months, and if his license was to be blocked, immediate action seemed crucial. At about that point Freeman suggested to Cantor that it might be wise for Greco to summarize his findings to date in a report that, at least theoretically, could serve as the basis for renewed complaints to the Swiss banking regulators pondering Safra's application. According to information later gathered by American Express lawyers, Greco asked for an additional

---

*See footnote, page 169.

$60,000 to undertake that task. Whether Freeman and Cantor agreed to pay that amount isn't known—Freeman says he can't recall—but Greco did in fact produce a report: the very same odd seven-page document he later gave to several people, including Jean Roberto of *Minute*, and which *Minute*'s lawyers handed over to Safra's attorneys.

Greco's report, then as now, was practically "gibberish," in Freeman's words, an amalgam of Cantor's Willard Zucker materials, details on Safra's private jet, a long passage from the 1967 *Life* magazine article, plus the contention that Republic had been under FBI investigation for racketeering for ten years, since 1978. Perhaps the only nugget of "usable" negative information was Greco's contention that Safra Bank of Miami had been under investigation since 1984 for laundering drug money, again an apparent reference to the Ben Kramer marijuana-smuggling probe. Citing "a confidential and reliable source"—probably one of his friends in law enforcement—Greco wrote that "this source was unable to say where this story stands at the present time."

By all accounts, both Cantor and Freeman thought Greco's report was worthless. "I got to the end of the first page and said, 'What is this?'" recalled Freeman, who termed the report "bizarre." He says he told Cantor: "'Why are we spending all this money for this incomprehensible report? Jesus, let's throw this one out.'" By one account, Cantor demanded a better effort, and Greco subsequently produced a second report, this one incorporating, among other things, the fifteen-year-old stories of Safra buying the mob-connected Brooklyn bank Kings Lafayette. That second version has never surfaced.

Another person who received the "gibberish" report from Greco that winter was one of the detective's friends, a Miami-area private eye named Irwin Robbins. Bald, his jawline cloaked in a salt-and-pepper beard, Robbins worked out of an unmarked office behind a lounge on a dusty side street in the suburb of Hollywood. His role in the Safra investigation wouldn't surface until three years later, after details of Greco's activities were first described in *The Wall Street Journal*. At that point Robbins approached Republic's Walter Weiner and offered information about Greco, though little of substance was ever forthcoming. According to Robbins, a licensed private investigator who says his specialty is overseas undercover probes of counterfeit and gray-market perfumes and cosmetics, Greco approached him in late 1987 and asked him to help investigate Safra. Robbins claims to have done some initial spadework, but says he stopped after Greco failed to come through with payments. After that, Robbins said, he did no further work on Safra.

If Cantor was frustrated by Greco's sloppy report, the detective apparently returned the ill will in spades. As the weeks went by, he began complaining regularly to Paul Knight about Cantor, whom he characterized as arrogant, overbearing, and insecure; her radical politics seemed to especially anger Greco, whom one longtime handler describes as "just to the right of Genghis Khan politically." Over time Greco's complaints grew more serious, causing Knight's own doubts about Cantor to deepen. "This is the most vicious, dangerous woman I've ever met," Greco told Knight one day. "She would betray anyone for her own interest in an instant."

Despite friction between the two operatives, Freeman and Cantor were both excited by the thrust of the information Greco was uncovering. Bit by bit, their probe was moving away from Iran-Contra matters to new, darker alleys, where Greco was unearthing delicious tidbits about Safra's supposed criminal empire. Investigations by the FBI and DEA, rumors of shady ties to several governments, Iran-Contra, Kings Lafayette—it slowly came together in a mind-set shared by Freeman and Cantor that Safra was, in Freeman's words, "a world-class criminal." Freeman passed on their suspicions to Jim Robinson, and in time Robinson, too, began referring to Safra as a "criminal of world-class proportions."

"We were finding this guy was much more involved in illegal activities than anybody dreamed," Freeman recalled. What they were finding, in fact, were mostly rumors and other sketchy tips Greco passed along. What they still lacked was a single piece of solid evidence that Safra was engaged in anything illegal. "The general view [Susan had]," Freeman recalled, "was, 'This guy is a pretty bad guy. I wish we could prove it. He's in bed with all these governments.' She was very frustrated. She said, 'I know this guy has done all these things. But I can't find [proof of] it.'"

Not everyone who knew Greco was as impressed by his findings. One senior member of American Express's security department, treated to a few earfuls of Greco's "tips" on Safra, found them to be nothing more than hollow conspiracy theories. "Everything to Tony was a conspiracy," this official said. "You know, Safra is Jewish, and Peter Cohen is

Jewish and my first wife was Jewish, and her name was...It was all a conspiracy to Tony." *

As the paranoia over Safra's reopening mounted that winter, Freeman and Cantor were eager to let others know of their suspicions. Freeman, after all, had never been interested in gossip for gossip's sake. "I only wanted information we could use against Safra," he emphasized. That winter, as they had in Cantor's earlier approaches to reporters, those two driving needs—exposing Safra's "shady" side and putting their information to work—coalesced once more, as morsels of Tony Greco's freshly dug dirt began circulating among journalists preparing stories on Safra's imminent reopening in Geneva.

Freeman's fingerprints in particular were all over the February 1988 cover story in *Euromoney* magazine, "Safra Seeks His Revenge." In several casual, off-the-record telephone conversations with his friend Neil Osborn, one of two London-based reporters who wrote the article, Freeman passed on any number of unflattering anecdotes about Safra as well as intimations of what might be termed Safra's darker side. Osborn freely incorporated Freeman's anonymous comments throughout the article, disguising him alternately as "an American executive" and a "source." Two of Freeman's anonymously told "snide little stories," as Osborn termed them, constituted the lengthy article's opening paragraphs.

Here are a couple of snide little stories about Edmond Safra—the kind that are giggled over in some quarters of American Express. Dear American Express, enjoy them while you can, because this is the year Safra means to beat the living daylights out of you.

Snide little story one: An American executive was plodding through Paris airport when he spotted Safra and his wife. The immensely wealthy couple were waiting patiently at the end of a long queue at the VAT refund counter. "A billionaire scrabbling up a few pennies," the executive observed with scorn.

---

*Greco doesn't appear to have pursued the American Express investigation full-time. In January of 1988, for instance, Jules Kroll reluctantly hired him again for an investigation during the midst of a major takeover contest. Kroll's client, New York-based Sterling Drug, had come under attack in the opening days of the year from the Swiss pharmaceutical giant Hoffman LaRoche. Sterling executives, scrambling to find any kind of dirt that might fend off their attackers, hired Kroll to investigate Roche and passed on rumors that Roche was moving cash illegally out of its operations in Peru and Bolivia.

Kroll had barely two weeks to investigate the charge and, with few contacts in either country, turned to Greco, who had bragged of having excellent contacts in Peru. According to people familiar with his work for Kroll, Greco reported back that he might be able to authenticate the charges. The contest ended, however, before he pursued them.

Snide little story two: Some time after American Express bought Safra's Geneva-based Trade Development Bank in 1983, the Lebanese banker was invited to fly from Geneva to New York for a meeting in an American Express jet. The fleet at that time included a Gulfsteam II and a slightly more modern Gulfstream III. When he heard that Gulfstream II was scheduled to pick him up, Safra lost his cool. "He thought he had been insulted and screamed for the Gulfstream III," reported one source, adding: "He comes across like the chief villain in a James Bond film."

These tales may paint a totally inaccurate picture. On the other side there are dozens of senior financial figures who testify that Safra, 56, is an admirable man—hard-working, shy, calm, generous and, in a gruff way, charming. But Safra must know what's said behind his back in some American Express circles.

Neil Osborn summarized more of Freeman's off-the-record remarks in a section on Safra headed "A Cultivator of Shadowy Relationships." "Safra's detractors," Osborn wrote, "like to mutter about his alleged relationships with unsavory governments—although they can never quite pinpoint the governments or what they think Safra gets out of them. They point to a scrap of information from Irangate. Republic accounts were used for payments to the air leasing company that hired the plane Oliver North [sic] used to fly to Tehran. Republic uses the same leasing company."

Even as Freeman leaked details of their investigation to a friend in the financial press, the month of January 1988 brought two events that propelled American Express's investigation along its increasingly aggressive course. First the Swiss bank board signaled its willingness to grant Safra's license. In New York, Freeman felt the decision could be overturned, but only if they moved quickly. Then, near the height of anti-Safra paranoia, Freeman received what must have been stunning news, a disclosure in the Italian magazine *L'Espresso* that a 1957 U.S. report implicated Safra in the morphine trade. Though Freeman now downplays its significance, others suggest the article captivated him, for it jibed perfectly with the picture emerging in his mind of Safra as a kind of fiendish "James Bond villain." Greco may have been dispatched to Rome to follow up the report, but if so he brought back little of use.

By some accounts, the Italian article emboldened Freeman, who predicted to executives in the upper reaches of the American Express Tower that they might still head off Safra's imminent return that March. A background in narcotics, after all, was hardly the kind of past Swiss regulators sought for their famed private bankers. "This is under control," one colleague recalls Freeman saying that winter. "Don't worry, we'll stop Edmond." It was at this point that Freeman took Bob Smith to dinner at Pearl's, briefed him on the *L'Espresso* article and Cantor's investigation, and vowed that Safra wouldn't get his license. Smith, who was equally determined to stop Safra, was so tickled he shared the secret with his No. 2, Bob Savage. "He's not going to get his license," he promised. Smith recalls, "I was so excited I nearly fell out of my shoes."

Cantor, attempting to authenticate the article, called Paul Knight, who had long, strong contacts in Italian law enforcement, and asked him to track down the government report mentioning Safra. But after promising to help, Knight phoned Cantor several days later and said he couldn't find any trace of such a report. It was a lie: Knight, after giving the matter some thought, had simply decided he wanted nothing more to do with Cantor, and had done nothing.

In light of the failure to verify *L'Espresso*'s allegation, the question remained: what to do with the article? It's not clear whether American Express ever brought it to the attention of Swiss regulators; Freeman doesn't believe it was. But at the height of tensions that winter, it was slipped to someone, a journalist—one Jacques Bertrand, at *La Dépêche du Midi*, in Toulouse. Tony Greco made the contact with Bertrand, who maintains he had never before met Greco and never understood why the detective had singled him out. Bertrand suggests he was contacted because of his "national reputation" for investigative work. That seems doubtful; neither Bertrand nor his newspaper had any national reputation to brag about. Greco may have received the reporter's name from a friend in the Barcelona police department.

Who if anyone authorized Greco's approach to Jacques Bertrand remains unclear. Freeman denies knowing anything about the *La Dépêche* incident, though he would have had little grounds to object, having spoken himself about Safra to *Euromoney*'s Neil Osborn. According to a person whose information has proven accurate on other matters, it was Cantor who asked Greco to interest a reporter in following up the *L'Espresso* article. Greco, this person says, demanded an astounding $500,000 to do so, a sum he never received. However, after several more talks with Cantor, Greco may have operated under the belief that he would be paid additional money if he were successful in generating news coverage of Safra's "criminal ties." Later, after the first *La Dépêche* article appeared, this person says, Greco told Cantor the information had been passed to the newspaper by a friend of his in the Barcelona police.*

In fact, according to Jacques Bertrand, it was Greco himself who visited Toulouse several weeks before the first *La Dépêche* story on Safra appeared that March. They met in a bar. Using his real name, Greco deliberately kept his identity vague, describing himself as an operative for a U.S. government agency that investigated the movement of drug money through large international banks. He handed Bertrand a fat dossier on Safra and Republic and began spinning the first of many tales of Safra's exploits in the criminal world.

As Greco spoke, Bertrand leafed through the file and found the *L'Espresso* article, as well as news items about Kings Lafayette's mob connections and plenty of Cantor's information about Willard Zucker and Iran-Contra. An avid conspiracy theorist himself, Jacques Bertrand perked up when Greco mentioned that Safra had done favors for the CIA. The French reporter surmised that his mysterious visitor, for whatever reason, was working at the CIA's behest to "give up," or sever, Safra from the intelligence world. To Bertrand it was clear Greco was out to smear Safra; he just thought it was some kind of convoluted CIA plot. "Yes, I understood that very quickly," Bertrand recalled with a knowing eye. "I know the CIA's way of doing things."

It was all interesting enough that Bertrand decided to print some of it; he did no additional reporting and never attempted to reach a Safra spokesman for comment. His article appeared March 11. By one account, Tony Greco forwarded a copy of the story to Cantor, who gave it to Harry Freeman, who had it translated from the French. (Freeman, while insisting he doesn't remember the incident, says it "could have" happened this way.) Afterward Jacques Bertrand received a congratulatory phone call from Greco. "He was very pleased," the old French reporter recalled. "He said he might have more information for me later."

Despite all their efforts, the team of Harry Freeman, Susan Cantor, and Tony Greco uncovered nothing to dissuade Swiss regulators from allowing Edmond Safra to reopen his doors for business, as he did in Geneva on March 1. The fight to stop Safra had ended in failure; by all rights,

---

*The faxing of the fateful *Life* magazine article—probably sent from Cantor to Greco—can also be traced to this period; its "telltale" was dated February 25, 1988.

American Express's investigation should have ended there. It didn't. Safra Republic's Swiss start-up, however, coincided with a four-month lull in the American Express–influenced stories about Safra; the next would not appear until July. In those four intervening months Cantor and her investigation would undergo major changes—changes whose causes would later be hotly debated.

One was a major career move for Cantor herself, courtesy of Jim Robinson. One day that spring Bob Smith was surprised to pick up his phone at American Express Bank to hear the chairman of American Express suggest they have a conversation about Cantor's future; Smith recalls that he recognized her name as that of the woman doing investigative work for Freeman. Robinson said he had an idea for Smith, though an "idea" from Jim Robinson was tantamount to a direct order: American Express Bank was to hire Susan Cantor.

"Why don't you give her a call?" Robinson suggested, as Smith recalls the conversation. "She's about finished up with her assignment in corporate. She knows a lot of people in Latin America and could probably help in fighting Safra." When Jim Robinson spoke, Bob Smith moved—and fast. He pondered positions in the bank where Cantor might fit in, but after meeting her, realized she would need months of training before she could operate as a banker. Susan Cantor was many things, but she was not an international financier, and Smith could only marvel at Robinson's thinking.

Later, many of those involved would question the reasons behind Cantor's transfer to American Express Bank. One reason, no doubt, was that she wanted it: Cantor made no secret of the fact that she desired a line position, a job that would give her real responsibility in the business world. She had talked with Jay Newman at Shearson about the possibility, and told a number of people she had made the same pitch during face-to-face talks with Jim Robinson.

Still, there may have been more to it. When the full scope of Cantor's actions later became known, Bob Smith theorized that he had been cleverly set up by Jim Robinson and Harry Freeman, who wanted to distance themselves from the evolving covert campaign against Safra. Smith claims Cantor later told him as much. "They wanted to get rid of her in the worst way," Smith said. "So they put her under me. It was all part of the plan to move the operation to the bank, away from headquarters. They couldn't take the chance they might be found out."

Harry Freeman denies this, insisting the transfer was all Cantor's idea. He does say he wasn't sorry to see her go. "She was [getting to be] sort of a pest," he said. "She would call me all the time, wanting to see me ... She didn't have her heart in public relations. It took a disproportionate amount of time getting her to work on things. She loved the important stuff but wasn't really interested in the routine stuff."

Whatever the reasons for the move, it didn't signal an end to Cantor's investigation of Safra. Nor did she stop work with Jim Robinson; while at the bank, colleagues say, Cantor continued traveling with Robinson on private projects as well as new-business excursions to Latin America. Her transfer, however, did serve to blur the lines of authority above her: while on paper she now reported to Smith, in practice she continued to consult regularly with Freeman, particularly about Safra matters, though Freeman goes to great lengths to play down his subsequent involvement with Cantor. "I saw Susan occasionally," he says. "She would come and see me sometimes, because she knew I was interested [in Safra]...[But] my interest level dropped, from three on a scale of ten, to .01."

It is here, in the question of who supervised Cantor after her transfer, that accounts of American Express's investigation grow contentious. At times, Harry Freeman tries to blame everything that happened afterward on Bob Smith; Smith, for his part, vehemently places responsibility on Freeman. Though it is possible to discern the outlines of what likely happened where their versions overlap, the two men agree on little. Freeman, for instance, insists Smith and other top executives had known about Cantor's investigation from the beginning; he says he and Smith discussed Cantor's work regularly before her transfer that spring. Smith, however, in assertions backed up by several top executives at the time, insists he knew nothing of Cantor until he and Freeman dined at Pearl's, around February 1988. Smith's version seems the more probable: Freeman is unable to recall any specific conversation the two had prior to Cantor's move, and several other executives vigorously dispute Freeman's assertion that Cantor's investigation was discussed at meetings of senior management.

What is clear is that, around the time Cantor transferred to the bank, Freeman and Smith had begun conferring about the Safra investigation. That spring, in fact, after Safra's reopening, Cantor and Greco's probe hung in limbo for several weeks as Freeman, among others, tried to determine what, if any, direction it should take. Though Safra Republic was open for business in Geneva, Freeman held out the hope that its license could still be revoked if they could link Safra to criminal activity; at the very least, he felt, the beginning of the long-anticipated onslaught on TDB's deposit base justified keeping the investigation active.

"'What to do now' was the question," Freeman recalls. "Both before and after Safra reopened, Bob Smith and I continually discussed what to do. The main subject was, 'Do we stop or do we continue?' There was a consensus between Smith and myself: there seemed to be some pretty good evidence out there, and perhaps it was worth going after."

Together, Freeman says, he and Smith decided to go forward with the investigation; Freeman says he notified Jim Robinson of their intentions. "But that was very brief and occasional," he insists. "I would tell Jim, 'Oh, we're moving along.' And he would say, 'Oh, be careful.' I said, 'Well, Smith and I think there's a possibility of finding some good stuff yet.'"

Bob Smith's account puts far less emphasis on his own role in the investigation. He agreed to hire Cantor at Jim Robinson's behest, he says, with the understanding that she would continue to report to Freeman on her Safra diggings. "I told Susan, I told Harry, 'I don't want to know what you're doing,'" Smith insists. "I don't want anything to do with it."

But Smith did get drawn into Cantor's work, as he readily admits. Early on, Smith says, Cantor brought him the first of a series of payment vouchers made out to Tony Greco.

"What's this for?" Smith recalls asking.

"He's a consultant. Someone we're using."

"Who is he?"

"He was recommended by security," Cantor explained. "He used to work for the company."

"Fine," Smith said. He says he added: "You're sure we're not doing anything wrong here? This is all on the up and up?" Smith would later remember asking Cantor this question a half-dozen times in coming months.

"No, nothing," Cantor said each time. "Everything is on the up and up. You have nothing to worry about."

To Smith's way of thinking, ignoring details of Cantor's work shielded him from responsibility. He told himself and a handful of his subordinates it was a headquarters project, a Harry Freeman project. The bank wasn't involved. "Obviously I knew she was up to something, I was signing Greco's vouchers," Smith recalled. "But I did it because I assumed it was Robinson's project. Susan worked for Harry, and Harry was Jim's best friend, his right-hand man. I assumed Jim knew everything that was going on."

Smith insists he never discussed Cantor's work with Robinson, though it is clear Harry Freeman continued to. In fact, it was to the chairman's office that Freeman went sometime in mid-1988—no one would remember the exact date—when he and Cantor received a scare of such intensity they were forced to reassess the entire idea of investigating Safra.

"I'll never forget this," Freeman said. Cantor had just returned from a trip to Brazil—presumably on I2D2 or bank matters—when she rushed into Freeman's office. "She came in and said, 'Are you aware that Safra had his wife's first husband murdered?'" Freeman recalled. "I said, 'No, what are you talking about?'"

Cantor, as Freeman tells the story, proceeded to unravel a tortured tale of how Safra had fallen in love with his wife-to-be Lily, and was obliged to hire a contract killer to murder her husband so that he could marry Lily himself.

"I said, 'Susan, why didn't they prosecute?'"

"She said, 'You've got to be kidding. He was too powerful to prosecute.'

"I said, 'Tell me this again?' I mean, you don't hear this kind of stuff every day.

"She said, 'It's common knowledge! It's common knowledge! Everyone in Brazil knows about it.'"

As outlandish as the rumor might sound, in the wake of all the stories they had heard about Safra's criminal activities Freeman was both stunned and worried. "If it's true," he told Cantor, "I'm a little worried about your security, and for that matter, my security. If the guy has a propensity to put out contracts, this has assumed a little different dimension." Freeman hustled into Jim Robinson's corner suite, where he briefed the chairman on Cantor's breathless story. If Safra was in the habit of employing contract killers, Freeman was not only concerned about his own safety, he was worried about Robinson's.

Robinson's reaction was predictable. "[He] said, 'You gotta be fucking kidding,'" Freeman recalls.

"I said, 'No, I'm not kidding. Susan says it's common knowledge.' I said, 'This is kind of scary.'

"Jim said, 'You're right, maybe we ought to drop this thing.'

"I said, 'No, we're getting closer and closer to finding something.'

"[He said], 'Well, tell Susan to be terribly, terribly careful.'"

In the days to come Freeman and Robinson spoke several times more about Safra's putative Brazilian murder contract, and eventually worried themselves to the point that Robinson made an extraordinary suggestion: maybe they should go to someone outside the company, someone independent, and brief him on the company's investigation. "That way, if anyone gets [hurt]," Robinson told Freeman with a straight face, "at least someone will know."

The suggestion both excited and frightened Freeman. "This was a fascinating conversation," he recalled. "I don't think I've ever been in a situation like this in my life. I said, 'Well who?'"

"What about Lloyd Cutler?" Robinson suggested. Cutler was among the most respected lawyers in Washington, and Robinson thought highly of him.

"I said, 'Well, okay, I'll call [Cutler] up and let's see him,'" Freeman recalled. But the more he thought about it, the sillier he felt they would look. He could just imagine himself describing the situation to Cutler: "Uh, Lloyd, Jim and I wanted to tell you, if we get murdered, we want you to know who to look at," Freeman remembered thinking. "He'd have sat there bug-eyed."

Ultimately, Freeman took Robinson up on his suggestion, and sat down with his personal attorney in Washington and explained how he and Cantor had been investigating Safra for the last year. He also urged Cantor to scale back her activities if she were worried about her security. "I said, 'Look, Susan, getting killed is not part of your job description here,'" he recalls.

In the end, of course, Freeman and Cantor both survived their brush with death, leaving them with nothing more than one more reason to hate Edmond Safra.

Wild rumors swept the bank's executive suite as Susan Cantor set up her office on the twenty-third floor of American Express headquarters, on the bank's executive floor. "Who is this woman?" colleagues asked as they popped their heads into one another's offices. "Is it true she works for Jim Robinson?"

Her new coworkers noted that Cantor kept to herself, traveled overseas often and, when in her office, liked to keep the door shut. She seemed to be involved in something strange and top secret, a number of bank executives decided, but exactly what, no one knew. There were hints and suggestions, no doubt spawned by Cantor's conspiratorial leanings and her travels to Latin America on behalf of Robinson, that she had contact with the FBI and the CIA, and a few coworkers actually suspected she might be working to somehow help the Reagan White House fund the Nicaraguan Contra fighters.

The man Cantor initially reported to, Bob Budenbender, the bank's chief financial officer, pondered her career as a journalist and came to the conclusion she was secretly writing a book about American Express. "Be careful what you say around her," Budenbender cautioned colleagues. "She's out to win a Pulitzer Prize."

Others found different reasons to be wary of Cantor; a few tagged her as a headquarters spy on bank operations. "She was a foreign agent" is how José Muzaurieta, a Cuban who was one of the bank's top Latin American experts, put it. Muzaurieta, who would work alongside Cantor on a number of Latin American assignments, was as confused by her presence at the bank as anyone. She wasn't a banker; what was she doing at a bank? "She was a really big deal, because of Jim Robinson," recalled Muzaurieta, who like many in the bank's male-dominated hierarchy harbored his own sexist speculation about Cantor's unexplained rise. "Everyone thought she was sleeping with somebody," he recalled, "but no one could figure out who."

Bob Budenbender set up a series of training sessions for Cantor to attend, beginner's briefings on letters of credit and foreign exchange. But she proved a lackluster student, and Budenbender was irritated at her frequent, unexplained disappearances, which Cantor explained only by saying she was off on overseas errands for Jim Robinson. Budenbender had no choice but to go along when the chairman's name was invoked, but as Cantor missed more and more training sessions, he went to Bob Smith and pleaded to be told what Cantor was really up to. He was surprised when Smith wouldn't tell him. "Don't worry about it,"

Smith assured him. "We have nothing to do with it. It's a corporate project. We're covered."

But before long, Bob Smith says he, too, grew exasperated by his
inability to keep track of Cantor's travels. Whenever he or Budenbender
needed her, he says, "She was always with Freeman. She had lunches
with Freeman. She was always off with him...or on some Robinson
project."

Over time Smith found Cantor's behavior so puzzling—her secrecy,
her Latin American contacts—that he began to wonder whether she was
really working for American Express at all. Smith and his wife, Miriam,
shared a long ride with Cantor aboard one of the company's private jets
to Mexico City later that year, and as they talked, Miriam Smith was
struck by all the people Cantor seemed to know; she dropped names
faster than they could count. "What a piece of work she is," Mrs. Smith
told her husband when Cantor stepped into the little jet's bathroom.
"Where'd you get her?"

When Cantor rejoined them, Bob Smith tried out a hunch. "Susan,
tell me," he said, "were you ever in the CIA?"

"No," Cantor replied with a big smile. "Oh, no."

Once settled in at the bank, Cantor faced the question of what direction to take their Safra investigation. Among other things, she was sitting
on great piles of supposed evidence that, for lack of an outlet, might
never be revealed. "I got the impression she was sort of lost on this Safra
thing," says a former American Express executive who spoke with Cantor in Harry Freeman's office that summer. "I don't think she really knew
what she wanted to do."

In early summer—one participant puts the date in June—Cantor
took a step toward resolving the question, telephoning the London security chief, Paul Knight, and asking him to attend a strategy meeting she
intended to hold in New York. Knight called his boss Jim McGrath in
New York and told him of Cantor's request. McGrath already knew that
Knight had put Cantor and Freeman in touch with Tony Greco.

"What's the meeting for?" McGrath asked.

"Well, she wants to have a strategy meeting where we're going to
talk about this project," Knight said. "That's all I know." McGrath
promised to look into the situation and get back to him. Later McGrath

took the matter up the ladder to his boss, American Express's second-ranking attorney, the bearded Larry Ricciardi. "Look, they want Knight to come over here for this thing," McGrath told Ricciardi. "I don't understand. What's this all about?"

Larry Ricciardi didn't know, either. But whatever it was, it made no sense for Knight to come all the way from London. "If they want a meeting, *you* can go," Ricciardi said.

"I don't even know who this woman is, do you?"

"I don't know who she is, or what she wants," Ricciardi said. "Have her call me."

Ricciardi wasn't surprised, then, when Susan Cantor telephoned shortly after. She introduced herself, but pointedly didn't say what her project entailed. However, she immediately made it clear it was a top priority. "I was asked to do this by Mr. Robinson," Cantor said. "This is his show."

"Who are you investigating?"

"I'm not sure I can say."

Ricciardi pressed, and after a few moments, Cantor relented. "Edmond Safra," she said.

"Hold on," Ricciardi said, his suspicions aroused. "Susan, my people are very busy. I don't use them for these kinds of things."

"This is very important," Cantor said. "I work for Harry Freeman. This is for Jim Robinson. This is his show."

It was exactly the wrong thing to say to Larry Ricciardi. Pulling rank was one of the easiest ways to get Ricciardi's dander up. He was tight with American Express's No. 2 executive, Lou Gerstner, and had little to fear from Jim Robinson. Worse, the mention of Freeman's name immediately set off alarm bells in Ricciardi's mind. He and his friend the general counsel Gary Beller had been leery of Freeman's projects for too long. If this was a Freeman idea, he wanted nothing to do with it.

"You tell Jim Robinson to call me if he wants to use Paul Knight," Ricciardi said.

Ricciardi had almost forgotten the exchange when, not long after, he took a second call from Cantor. She had something on her mind, she said, and asked to come by his office for a talk. When she arrived, her attitude was conciliatory, her bearing apologetic.

"I'm new here," she said. "I'm trying to fit in." Clearly Cantor realized she had alienated Ricciardi. And she was smart enough to know that

American Express's number two attorney was someone best used as an ally, not an enemy.

"Susan," Ricciardi said, "you can't enter an organization like American Express and behave as though you're running it and expect people to cooperate with you. Things don't work that way around here." Ricciardi spent fifteen minutes kindly briefing Cantor on how to get things done at American Express.

Afterward Ricciardi, still vaguely troubled, phoned Freeman and asked for a meeting about Cantor's mysterious Safra project. He didn't understand what the two were doing, but it made him nervous. He asked the security chief, Jim McGrath, to be there as well, and McGrath was the first to Freeman's office. The two had known each other as nodding acquaintances for years. "This is your meeting," Freeman said, as if to say he had no agenda.

"No, no, I was just told to be here," McGrath said. They began talking about the presidential election that fall. McGrath knew Freeman was an ardent Democrat, and assumed he was hopeful of a post in any Dukakis administration.

The two had been talking for several minutes when Ricciardi and Cantor walked in together. The lawyer took a seat while Cantor stood to one side. She began explaining her project in the vaguest terms. Safra, she noted, had a "lot of problems" they had managed to uncover. She claimed he was being investigated by a number of law-enforcement agencies. "The question is, what do we do now?" one participant remembers Cantor asking. "Do we contact someone in the U.S. government about this?"

For several minutes Ricciardi and McGrath tried to pry out of Cantor exactly what her project entailed. Both men found her evasive. Behind his desk, Freeman was noticeably quiet. He would later claim he wasn't really paying attention to what Cantor was saying.

"Listen, Harry," Ricciardi said. "I don't know what you're doing, but I won't let you use any of my people. You'd better be very careful here. If I were you, I would stop whatever it is immediately."

Jim McGrath agreed. Cantor was clearly up to something, and neither man, each well schooled in bureaucratic "cover-your-ass" procedures, wanted to be pulled into it.

"Well, Paul Knight used to be in law enforcement," Cantor offered. "He might be able to do something."

Ricciardi was shaking his head. "If you need anything like that, Jim can handle people in Washington."

As the meeting wound down, McGrath rose and left, leaving Ricciardi behind for some parting words with Freeman. Later McGrath telephoned the lawyer for a debriefing. "Look, I don't know who this woman is," McGrath said, "but she wasn't making any sense at all in there. That was really bizarre."

"She's dangerous, I'll tell you," Ricciardi replied. "I don't want any of your people involved in this, whatever it is. If you get any more calls from her, you tell me. Because I'll tell [Gary] Beller about it."

For weeks afterward the incident nagged at Larry Ricciardi. He didn't know what Cantor and Freeman were up to, but he had a hunch it might get them all in trouble. He shared his concerns with Beller, the general counsel, and with his immediate superior, Aldo Papone, head of American Express's main TRS division. "Just be careful, Gary," he told Beller. "Someday this woman is going to write a book." Beller apparently harbored his own private concerns. More than one company official had observed that American Express's general counsel felt powerless to rein in Harry Freeman. "You know Harry," Beller told one executive with a sigh. "He's uncontrollable."

Even as American Express's two top lawyers commiserated about Freeman's projects, the riskiest endeavor of Freeman's career was beginning to spin dangerously out of control. Neither lawyer knew it, but as later events would indicate, Susan Cantor had finally chosen a path of action, and it involved Tony Greco's picking up exactly where he had left off the winter before: talking to journalists.

Only later, much later, would American Express officials have reason to examine how that decision was made. The one person who knew for certain, Cantor, would insist she received the go-ahead from Harry Freeman, a contention Freeman would be hard-pressed to deny. Long afterward, Freeman recalled, "I asked her about that. She said, 'Well, I asked you, Was it okay for Greco to hand something to someone, and you said okay.' I said, 'Susan, I don't remember that'...I just don't recall...It may have been that Susan thought I had approved something. It also may have been that she had taken that and ran with that. It could have happened."

Was Cantor given direct orders by Freeman or Robinson or Bob Smith to pass materials to the press that summer? Or did she merely proceed because she believed it to be part and parcel of her duties? The distinction is almost beside the point. From the beginning, everything Cantor and Freeman had done together—brainstorming approaches to the press, Cantor's soliciting Sy Hersh and Jeff Gerth and Maya Jurt, Freeman's chatting up *Euromoney's* Neil Osborn, Greco meeting with Jacques Bertrand of *La Dépêche*—was oriented toward spreading their findings about Safra. From that morning in December 1986 when they first gaped at a *New York Times* article in the chairman's corner office, Freeman and Robinson hadn't sought dirt on Safra for their own files, but for the files of others. They wanted something to stop Safra. They wanted something they could use.

And in the summer of 1988, from her new office on the executive floor at American Express Bank, Susan Cantor and her "consultant" Tony Greco continued giving it to them.

Whether by accident or design, American Express was poised to enter a strange new world, the world of international disinformation. It is a realm populated by all manner of conspiracy theories and wild stories, of American "ethnic bombs" designed to kill only black Africans, of shadowy American industrialists trafficking in the body parts of infants, of CIA plots to spread the AIDS virus, spike the punch at Jonestown, and assassinate everyone from Swedish prime minister Olaf Palme to Indian leader Indira Gandhi. The stops on this intercontinental rumor mill constitute the true dregs of world journalism, obscure radical journals, little-known Marxist-oriented newspapers, and an array of Third World magazines and television and radio stations where fact, rumor, and propaganda are shaken and stirred into an unrecognizable blend of fact-based fiction that serves as news in many of the world's developing countries to this day.

The primary exploiter of these outlets, the American government charged for years, was the Soviet Union. The Soviets, both the U.S. State Department and Russian defectors insist, maintained an extensive bureaucracy devoted to feeding anti-American news stories to the international press that went far beyond traditional propaganda. Entire scholarly journals are devoted to the tracking of Soviet disinformation, be it tales of "ethnic bombs" or American plots to spread AIDS to the Third World, through willing newspapers and journals in places like Ghana, Namibia, and India.

Some might attribute this process to bribery or corruption. But while money can buy news columns in many countries, especially in Latin America—in Mexico City bought-and-paid-for news items run under italics headlines known as *gasetillas*—it is a sad fact of life that outside the major media outlets of the United States and Western Europe the quality of much of what passes for journalism is dreadfully low. In some Third World countries, newspapers come and go like full moons. Meagerly paid reporters hop from job to job like migrant workers. Fact-checking is an all-too-rare luxury. Reprinting items from foreign newspapers without permission or verification is the rule rather than the exception. The proliferation of international news wires, not all of them entirely reliable, only exacerbates the problem.

Once a shred of rumor or fiction is published in such an environment, it is almost impossible to stamp out. In the rare instance when a publication agrees to correct an egregiously false news item, readers often overlook the correction, as do other news outlets that might have republished the erroneous piece. And for every newspaper or magazine that prints a correction, a dozen won't. Thus stories literally take on lives of their own. A "hot" story is passed along from journalist to journalist, newspaper to newspaper, sometimes via unreliable news wires, sometimes by word of mouth, sometimes by more unorthodox means. In 1989 alone, the AIDS-as-American-lab-virus story, a Soviet-inspired canard that received wide credence in areas of the Third World, surfaced in a Brazilian magazine and a Brazilian newspaper; on West German television; in Panamanian and Yugoslavian newspapers; in the Turkish newspaper *Sabah*; and in the Peruvian newspaper *Hoy*.

Perhaps the definitive case study of this phenomenon is the infamous "baby parts" story, which spread throughout the world in the late 1980s, often with the help of Soviet and Communist-allied publications. In its most basic form, the oft-repeated report charged that Latin American slum children were being bought and sold to be used for organ transplants by wealthy Americans. The articles grew so pervasive that the U.S. Information Agency, which has tracked Soviet disinformation for years, ordered a study in an attempt to trace them.

The baby-parts rumor, the agency found, began with a January 1987 article in a newspaper in Honduras. The item quoted a senior Honduran health official fretting about organized trafficking of organs taken from small children. When published, the official immediately recanted the story, saying he was merely passing along local gossip, but it was too late. The Honduran story was quickly picked up by papers in Guatemala and Panama, which attracted the notice of Soviet journalists, who reprinted the stories in *Pravda*. The *Pravda* story, in turn, beamed around the world by the news agency Tass, was reprinted in both Communist-backed and mainstream newspapers across the Third World, from Nicaragua to India.

Once begun, the baby-parts stories were simply unstoppable. Asked for comment by one newspaper, a United Nations official attacked them as "fictitious rumors." But no one was listening; the story had evolved overnight into one of those folk tales repeated so often it was taken as fact. After reading the stories, for instance, a provincial judge in Paraguay complained to a reporter from the Reuters news agency that missing children in his country would probably end up as organ donors in the United States; in the resulting Reuters story the judge's comment was portrayed as a serious avenue of inquiry rather than an offhand remark. Alerted to the mix-up, Reuters was unable to correct the misimpression before the story shot around the world once more, appearing in France, West Germany, Switzerland, Austria, Belgium, Portugal, Italy, Norway, Canada, New Zealand, Argentina, and Brazil. By then, of course, any effort to stop the flow of stories was hopeless. To this day, the baby-parts story periodically sweeps one country or another, most recently hitting Mexico in 1990.

This, then, was the impressionable world press Edmond Safra faced in 1988 and 1989, but with an insidious difference. Unlike tales of ethnic bombs and baby brokers, which are alarming enough by themselves to draw an editor's attention, the misinformation about Safra didn't actually take on a "life of its own" for some time. Instead, the evidence shows, it was actively promoted and distributed for months by people working for American Express who knew exactly what they were doing, who sought to create the very brand of press hysteria that spread stories of baby parts and CIA plots.

To a striking degree, in fact, the American Express campaign against Safra resembles a classic Soviet-backed disinformation effort. An American Express operative, like the Soviets, planted fabricated and badly slanted articles, some containing kernels of truth, in obscure Third World and fringe publications. Like the Soviets, American Express's operative passed on anonymous reports and forged news items whose veracity would never be challenged by the journalists who incorporated them into still more articles. Later, much as the Soviets published outrageously false books about the CIA—one Soviet primer includes an entire chapter on how the U.S. government masterminded the Jonestown massacre—equally obscure books would surface incorporating American Express's "planted" articles about Safra.

By the time American Express's operatives halted their efforts to spread stories, this process would waft misleading articles on Edmond Safra to a dozen or more countries, including France, Switzerland, Great Britain, Peru, Uruguay, Argentina, Panama, Turkey, Lebanon, and, inevitably, the United States.

In their own minds, most of the journalists and free-lance hacks who publish this handed-down disinformation probably don't believe they're passing on lies, and neither, one suspects, did Susan Cantor and Tony Greco. By most accounts Cantor, like Freeman, had developed a strong belief that Edmond Safra was a criminal of "world-class proportions"; no doubt to her thinking his illegal activities cried out to be exposed. The plan, it appears, was for Greco to pick up where he had left off in Toulouse that winter, passing on dossiers on Safra to journalists.

And so, in the summer of 1988, Tony Greco once again began approaching reporters. But unlike Cantor's contacts with Sy Hersh and *The New York Times*, or Freeman's chats with *Euromoney*, Greco scrambled through the gutters of journalism. Unlike Cantor's friends—seasoned skeptics who took a tip and did their own digging and confirming—Greco's contacts would prove to be low-rung foreign reporters who took his dubious stories about Safra's criminal activities as gospel, and who did little if any corroborative reporting of their own. Thus, due largely to the practices of journalists he approached, the stories Greco discussed with reporters would take on the more decisive character of "plants" rather than "tips."

One of Greco's first steps came that summer in Peru. He flew to Lima and looked up his old friend Victor Tirado—the same Victor Tirado who would later betray him to Safra. At the time, Tirado was working in a senior position at the communications ministry and was soon to join the staff of the Peruvian embassy in Washington. Details of the pair's collaboration remain sketchy, but the basic outline is clear. As he had with Jacques Bertrand in Toulouse, Greco briefed Tirado on

Safra and said he was interested in placing articles about the banker's criminal activities in South American newspapers. He specifically mentioned an interest in Brazil and Chile.

Victor Tirado could certainly help in Peru, and he did. His closest ties to newspapers remained at the Aprista-controlled *Hoy*, where he had been a columnist and editor and still wrote from time to time. One defender of Tirado's suggests that all the Peruvian did was refer Greco to an editor friend at *Hoy*. But there is persuasive evidence that Victor Tirado gave American Express's "consultant" far more help than that.

Hoy's managing editor at the time was another of Tirado's old friends, Pablo Truel. The two men had worked together at various Lima papers over the years. It was Truel who, when confronted by the Safra detective Matthew Wolinsky, claimed to have received *Hoy*'s article on Safra from the hands of its author, Pedro Cardozo, "the former mayor of the La Victoria section of Lima."

Confronted with evidence to the contrary, Truel changes his story. "Pedro Cardozo didn't write the article," Truel acknowledges in an interview. "This article was brought to *Hoy* by Señor Tirado. Tirado was the one who used the pseudonym of Pedro Cardozo. There was a Cardozo we both knew who worked in journalism many years ago in Lima. He had nothing to do with this. He is no longer alive."

Events that led to the *Hoy* article's second life, its reprinting in Mexico City's *Uno Mas Uno* on July 9—also seem to have taken place in Peru. According to officials at the Anti-Defamation League in New York, which briefly investigated the matter at Safra's request, *Hoy*'s "Pedro Cardozo" article was transmitted to Mexico City by the Lima office of the Cuban news wire Prensa Latina. Several *Hoy* editors were friends with correspondents at Prensa Latina, which was known for dispensing political favors to leading Apristas. Any one of a number of journalists at *Hoy*, including Tirado, was in a position to plant an article on the Cuban wire. *Hoy*'s former editor Luis Guerrero fingered the president's friend Francisco Landa, who had contacts at *Uno Mas Uno*, but Landa denies any involvement. So do other top *Hoy* editors. Exactly which of Greco's Peruvian friends was responsible remains a mystery.

By early August, Greco had returned to France. There he spoke again with Jacques Bertrand and handed over more materials on Safra. Among the new items Bertrand received were the articles Greco had planted in Peru and Mexico City as well as photos of Safra's villa, La

Leopolda, perhaps the same pictures Cantor told of having taken. By then Greco had also given Bertrand a copy of the 1967 article from *Life* magazine, but the reporter, who couldn't speak English and didn't have a translator, never bothered to read it. Nor did he notice the American Express fax telltales atop several of its pages. Bertrand's second article appeared August 13.

The first phone call from Tony Greco came to Jean Roberto's desk at *Minute's* Paris offices that same month, August 1988. It was a call that would change the French reporter's life. For unlike Jacques Bertrand, whose relationship with Greco was more or less ephemeral, Greco would become one of the most useful—and most dangerous—anonymous sources Roberto had ever encountered. Over the course of their ensuing collaboration the French reporter would come to respect and even protect Greco, showing him a loyalty surpassing that of many reporter-source relationships.

The only account of their work together is Roberto's, and because he, like so many journalists, worked alone, little of what he has said can be independently corroborated. His files, however, reviewed by the author and later by lawyers representing Edmond Safra, contain numerous items, including photos of a smiling Tony Greco, that tend to confirm major elements of his story.°

Roberto returned Greco's initial call and accepted his invitation to visit him at his luxurious four-star hotel, The Intercontinental, just off the Rue de Rivoli, where an elegantly dressed harpist serenaded a lobby lined with Persian rugs, elegant French antiques, and white-coated butlers. There Greco, projecting a mysterious air, introduced himself simply as "a detective," and hinted broadly that he worked for the FBI or the CIA. He deflected Roberto's other questions about his identity.

As the two sat and chatted, Greco began weaving a story of high international intrigue that would have entranced any reporter, particularly one as scoop-hungry as Jean Roberto would prove to be. It was then

---

°Roberto has given two, slightly differing versions of how he came to meet Greco. During an interview with the author, he recalled that Greco telephoned *Minute* out of the blue in mid-August 1988, and was referred to him as the newspaper's senior reporter. The message Roberto received was that an anonymous source had called, offering information on a prominent banker involved in laundering drug money. In a later interview, Roberto told Safra's attorneys that Greco had gotten his name from another French reporter and called him directly. The two versions don't necessarily contradict themselves.

that Roberto heard Edmond Safra's name for the first time. The reporter's hurriedly written, nearly illegible notes from that meeting recount Greco's stories of Safra in detail.

"He's a clever man originally from the Lebanon," Roberto wrote. "The CIA used Safra in the Contra affair. The CIA knew Safra in Brazil, where he was a big gold dealer. Some of Safra's friends were arms smugglers, including Edwin Wilson and Khashoggi."

Roberto grew excited. To him, this mysterious detective's story sounded like a tremendous scoop. But there were other agendas at work that made Greco even more valuable to the French reporter. Unlike most U.S. journalists, who would have sought independent confirmation of Greco's stories, *Minute*'s brand of gossipy journalism required Roberto to do little such digging. He could run Greco's stories exactly as they spilled from the detective's lips. As Greco continued, Roberto's notes reflected his story line, which closely paralleled the stories already printed in *Hoy* and *Uno Mas Uno*: how Safra had made a fortune smuggling arms during the Vietnam War; how Safra had used a Mafia lawyer named "Khel"—presumably a misidentification of Ted Kheel—to open doors for him in New York; how "Khel" had recommended buying a mob-dominated bank, Kings Lafayette.

"One suspects," Roberto scribbled into his notebook as Greco continued, "Safra banks launder drug money. And that information comes from the DEA." Much of that drug money, Greco said, came from Panama, Brazil, and South America. Among those who regularly squirreled away millions at Safra banks, the detective said, was General Antonio Noriega, then at the height of his power. "There had been investigations" of Safra banks, Roberto wrote, "but they were all stopped because of Safra's influence." Now though, Greco said knowingly, the DEA was again investigating Safra's empire. An arrest, he hinted, was coming soon.

Jean Roberto met again with Greco the following week at the Intercontinental. By the end of their second meeting, the detective had shown Roberto copies of the articles in *La Dépêche*, *Hoy* and *Uno Mas Uno*, and had handed him a copy of the Bern letter, which to Roberto authenticated Greco's tales of U.S. investigations into Safra's affairs. Greco encouraged the reporter to write a story, and indeed, Roberto was ready. He was only worried that Safra might sue.

"Safra won't say a word," Greco predicted, as Roberto remembers the conversation. After all, he pointed out, Safra hadn't sued *La Dépêche*, had he? "It proves he's guilty," Greco said.

Before publishing his first article, "Millionaire of the White Stuff," Jean Roberto says he telephoned Greco's other reporter friend, Jacques Bertrand in Toulouse, and asked if Greco could be trusted. Bertrand, who thought Greco was a CIA agent, nonetheless replied emphatically that he could, and that Greco had documents to back up his claims. Neither reporter seemed to care that he didn't have the first clue who Tony Greco really was.

Jean Roberto's first two stories in *Minute* ran August 31, 1988, and, just as Greco had promised, Safra didn't sue. Roberto was thrilled. Greco returned to Paris several times in the coming weeks, each time summoning Roberto to the Intercontinental for more discussions about the wealthy Jewish money launderer, Edmond Safra. At first Roberto had no way to contact Greco, and was forced to eagerly await his telephone calls and sudden appearances. In a pinch, he would leave messages at the hotel. Later Greco gave him telephone numbers where he could be reached in Staten Island, Washington, and Spain.

Each time they met, Greco arrived with new, colorful stories about Safra and his criminal banks: Safra and Noriega, Safra and the story of the bank manager found dead in an Ecuadoran harbor, Safra cowering in his villa on the French Riviera, living in fear of Colombian hit men. Greco characterized Safra as a key player in the Iran-Contra scandal, and lavished detail on Roberto about his dealings with Willard Zucker.

All these tales Roberto scribbled down, many of them to resurface shortly after in the pages of *Minute*. Roberto insists he made cursory efforts at independent reporting and indeed, his notebooks contain the phone numbers of reporters at *The Wall Street Journal* and *The New York Times* who had written about money laundering. (The *Times* reporter, ironically, was Jeff Gerth, who a year before had met with Cantor.) But Roberto never spoke with anyone remotely connected to the American authorities, a fact that wouldn't stop him from publishing Tony Greco's increasingly lurid stories about Edmond Safra.

American Express's "investigation" of Safra had been under way for nearly eighteen months when Tony Greco sharply escalated his efforts to "brief" journalists that summer in Peru and France. The questions left in the wake of his actions are the ones asked in so many far larger American scandals, from Watergate to Iran-Contra: Who knew what? And when did they know it?

Concrete answers are especially hard to find in the case of American Express, since neither Cantor, Greco, nor Jim Robinson has publicly discussed events, nor has any lawsuit or subpoena succeeded in prying open the company's files. Other than the author's, the only formal investigation of these events has been carried out by the audit committee of American Express's board and the company's own lawyers, who in 1989 interviewed Robinson, Freeman, Greco, Cantor, Bob Smith, and others and produced an internal report on their findings. That report has never been released.

But various people who have read it have briefed the author and others on its contents. In sum, the report indicates that no one involved in American Express's investigation of Edmond Safra has admitted doing anything unethical. When confronted, Freeman and Greco tend to blame Cantor, whom they portrayed as out of control; Cantor, in turn, insists she was only taking orders from Freeman. For the most part, no one pointed a finger of accusation at Bob Smith. Nor were serious accusations leveled at Jim Robinson—but more on Robinson later.

Based, then, on admittedly incomplete evidence, two conclusions can be reached:

1) *That summer Cantor and Greco were acting on implicit rather than explicit orders from Freeman and Robinson.* There is scant evidence that either Freeman or Robinson specifically knew in advance of, much less directed, Greco's approaches to the press that summer. Both men have denied it, and no one—neither Bob Smith nor Susan Cantor nor anyone else—has come forward with evidence to contradict their denials. The very nature of Greco's contacts would seem to discount the idea: if Robinson and Freeman were personally directing him, is it likely Greco would be hitting up personal friends like Victor Tirado and cold-calling obscure French journalists?

What actually happened seems to have been more complicated. The most likely possibility, in fact, suggests that the answer to the question of who supervised Cantor and Greco that summer is that no one supervised them at all. This scenario, which assumes that Smith and Freeman are both telling at least what they perceive to be the truth, is essentially this: that Cantor fell briefly into a supervisory vacuum, in which neither Smith nor Freeman sought full details of what she was doing.

It may be no coincidence that the most aggressive phase of American Express's "counterattack" occurred immediately after Cantor's transfer to American Express Bank, at a time when she barely knew her new boss, Bob Smith, and was newly removed, at least physically, from her old boss, Harry Freeman. It is entirely possible that in the permissive, "don't-bother-me-with-details" environment that flourished among staffers in Jim Robinson's retinue, Cantor and Greco, taking their cue from the history of press contacts Freeman had forged, marched forward without anyone peering intently over their shoulders. The two, after all, were acting exactly as they had from the beginning, freely contacting reporters with no interference from Freeman or anyone else.

At the time, both Freeman and Smith had reasons to distance themselves from Susan Cantor. By most accounts, Freeman, like Paul Knight, Jim McGrath, and others, had been around Cantor long enough to brighten at the prospect of her transfer to the bank. Smith, in turn, was more than willing to go after Safra as long as Freeman took responsibility for the dirty work. "Don't worry, we're covered," as he told Bob Budenbender. "It's a corporate project."

In retrospect, it had all the makings of a classic bureaucratic vacuum, both men able to rationalize that Cantor was reporting to the other and neither willing to take full responsibility for her actions. Neither man was stupid; both acknowledge, in so many words, that they knew Cantor's investigation was a ticking bomb. But in their efforts to pass it off on each other, the bomb seems to have dropped between them—and gone off.

2) *Both Harry Freeman and Bob Smith came to suspect Cantor and Greco were behind the articles, but did nothing to expose it and little to prevent it from happening further.* While it's possible that neither Freeman nor Smith gave advance approval for Greco's approaches to journalists that summer, it stretches belief to suggest the two remained ignorant of American Express's involvement in the articles after they began to appear. And indeed, both Freeman and Smith acknowledge that, at various times, they came to have suspicions about what Cantor and Greco were doing.

Bob Smith says he first became suspicious early that fall, when one of his wealthy Brazilian depositors showed him an article about Safra from a Latin American paper; presumably it was Peru's *Hoy* or Mexico City's *Uno Mas Uno*. When the Brazilian asked pointedly whether American Express had had anything to do with the piece, Smith denied any-thing of the sort. Privately, though, Smith says he immediately suspected Susan Cantor.

But rather than confront her himself, Smith says he telephoned Freeman and brought up the Latin American article. "Is something going on?" he recalls asking. "Are you guys doing anything?"

"No, Bob," replied Freeman, denying any knowledge of the article. But, Smith asserts, Freeman suggested it might be best for everyone if Cantor's opportunities for mischief were curtailed. As Smith recalls it: "He said to me something like, 'Her work for me is almost over. We ought to keep this woman real busy.'" Freeman insists he doesn't recall the exchange, but says Smith's scenario is "possible...I probably said to Smith something along the line of, she could be good at developing pri-vate banking business, but you've got to keep her busy, because if you don't, she's still driving on this Safra business. I said, 'The more bank stuff you throw at her, the better off we're going to be, for a lot of rea-sons.'"

If these recollections are accurate, both men seem to have made a choice all too common in corporate scandals, what might be called the Ostrich Option. Both suspected wrongdoing, but neither was eager to expose it—almost certainly, one suspects, because to do so might have led to the discovery of something for which they might be blamed. The easiest option was to ignore what had happened, and quietly make sure it didn't happen again. "Yes, I suspected something was going on," Bob Smith acknowledges today. "No, I didn't go out and expose it. Did I want to? No, why should I? Why get the company in trouble when I thought the problem was corrected?"

Smith's way to "correct" the problem was to maintain closer tabs on Cantor. To keep her out of mischief, he says, he transferred her that fall into a rigorous training program in the bank's foreign exchange depart-ment. "We started to really crank up the workload on her. We said, 'Okay, you can't just fly off to Venezuela if you feel like it. You've got to tell us why you're going.' From that point in time, she was pretty much in control."

But though Smith suspected the truth and buried it, it is Harry Freeman who must bear the greatest share of responsibility for Cantor and Greco's actions. It was Freeman who created and nurtured their investigation, and it was to him, by most accounts, that Cantor continued to look for guidance. If Freeman didn't know what Cantor and Greco were doing, it was because he didn't want to know. Though in frustration he has sought to shift the blame to Smith—"This was Bob Smith's operation now," he said halfheartedly at one point—Freeman acknowledges there is scant evidence to back up his assertion. Though he rails at others, including Jim Robinson, in the end Harry Freeman reluctantly shoulders the blame.

"What I can be tagged with is excessive delegation and lack of appropriately detailed supervision of a very sensitive operation," he said in an interview. "I really should have paid much more attention to what I was being told and perhaps asked more penetrating questions...If I made a mistake, and I think I did, it's that I didn't realize how sensitive this was."

Certainly this was not Harry Freeman's only mistake. For if this scenario bears some resemblance to what actually happened—if he and Bob Smith chose to "bury" Cantor rather than explicitly confront her and end the investigation—their plan had one glaring fault. No one thought to stop Tony Greco.

Even as Cantor sank beneath an avalanche of financial arcana that fall of 1988, Greco continued his meetings with Jean Roberto of *Minute*. The French reporter, angered over the subsequent description of his activities in *The Wall Street Journal*, refused to further discuss his work with Greco for this book; when asked to confirm details of the following passage, which is based on his debriefing by Safra lawyers, he angrily denied several assertions and refused to discuss others.

Despite that, it is clear Roberto remained spellbound by his new source. Whatever doubts he might have had about Greco were dispelled by an incident that October. In their talks Greco had frequently mentioned Safra's banks in the same breath as another bank whose infamy wouldn't splash onto the international scene for another three years: BCCI. In the vaults of both institutions, Greco asserted, lay the stolen millions of the Panamanian strongman, Antonio Noriega. Both banks, he said, were on the verge of being indicted by U.S. authorities.

Roberto had been scribbling down Greco's stories for over a month when, in early October, Greco told him an indictment of BCCI was imminent. Roberto, more focused on Safra, did nothing with the tip. And so, a week or so later, on October 11, he was stunned to read wire service stories that BCCI and nine of its officers had been indicted by a

Florida grand jury in what American authorities called the first case in history in which an entire banking institution was charged with drug-related offenses.

"See, you could have written it first," Greco teased Roberto after word of the indictments broke. The BCCI case was front-page international news, and became the subject of public hearings before the Senate Foreign Relations Subcommittee. In Paris, Roberto drank in the BCCI reports with equal parts regret and jubilation, angry that he had missed a massive scoop, but thrilled to be privy to a source with such valuable information. Greco had been right about everything: the drug money, the indictment, the Noriega millions. To Roberto, it lent inordinate weight to Greco's claim that Safra and Republic were next on the Americans' hit list.

Buoyed by the BCCI story, Roberto brushed aside concerns about Safra's lawsuits and weighed in with his strongest story yet the week of October 26—the long article that directly accused Safra and his banks of laundering millions of dollars for drug traffickers. Roberto felt confident he was one step ahead of an American grand jury. Once his article was published, he sat back and waited for news of the indictment to break.

It was during this period, probably in November, Roberto told Safra lawyers, that he accepted Greco's invitation to visit his villa on the Spanish coast south of Barcelona. Greco enticed the reporter with a promise he could witness a rare event: a major drug bust, scheduled to take place right there in his seaside home. The detective explained that he had been working undercover to help break a major international narcotics ring. The very day Roberto was due in Barcelona, he claimed, Spanish authorities were planning to arrest the conspirators. Roberto, he promised, could see it all.

But when Roberto arrived in Spain, there was no drug bust. There were policemen, one anyway. At his villa Greco introduced the French reporter to a man he said was the former police chief of Barcelona. The two shook hands, but Roberto spoke little Spanish, and couldn't participate in the conversations the man had with Greco.

The failed "drug bust," Roberto would later recall, was the first time his confidence in Greco wavered. As if he sensed the reporter's concern, the detective seemed to go out of his way to impress Roberto with his status. Greco, Roberto told Safra attorneys, showed him what appeared to be a photograph of himself posing beside, of all people, the Ayatollah

Khomeini. Gesturing to the photo, Greco bragged that his contacts among Iranians living in Spain had helped free the American hostages from Teheran in 1981.

To Roberto the photograph was impressive, but it did little to solve his central worry. Back in Paris, Safra had been filing lawsuits against *Minute* almost every week since mid-October, and Roberto's editors were growing nervous about the veracity of his stories. They were pressing him for proof of Safra's guilt, and Roberto had begun to press Greco as well. The detective had been free with anecdotes about Safra, but with the exception of the Bern letter he had been stingy with supporting documents.

In Spain, Greco handed him a thick file of papers he indicated would prove everything he had said. Among other things, the French reporter saw it contained the strange "Meyer Lansky" chart Greco had never before allowed him to keep. Greco had mentioned that his assertions about Safra's ties to gangsters were established in a *Life* magazine article, and Roberto asked for a copy of that as well. According to Roberto, Greco didn't have one handy, but said he had given a copy to Jacques Bertrand at *La Dépêche*. When Roberto contacted Bertrand, the Toulouse reporter agreed to mail him Greco's *Life* article. Roberto didn't notice the fax telltale lurking at the top of the *Life* article's pages, and even if he had, he probably wouldn't have cared.

Tony Greco had promised Jean Roberto that top executives at Republic National Bank would soon be indicted for money laundering, and that December they were. But it wasn't officials of Edmond Safra's Republic National Bank of New York that the American authorities indicted, it was another bank with almost the same name, Republic National Bank of Miami.*

On December 2 Republic of Miami's former president was indicted for dealings with a renowned south Florida money launderer. Federal agents had long been suspicious of the Miami bank, which called itself Florida's largest Hispanic-owned banking institution, and their investiga-

---

*Over the years press coverage of the Miami bank's troubles so irritated Safra that he had offered to buy rights to the Republic of Miami name, to no avail. On one occasion, Robert Siegfried was forced to issue press statements denying links between the two banks. In any case, Safra's name wasn't mentioned in any of the stories about Republic of Miami's problems that winter.

tions of Republic would continue for months afterward. Greco was probably quite familiar with the workings of Republic of Miami, for the Florida money launderer indicted along with its president that day was none other than his old pal Andy Iglesias.

In mid-December Greco did a curious thing: he faxed Roberto a copy of an American news wire story on the Republic of Miami indictments. The French reporter did nothing with the piece, probably because of his own legal problems. Still, Greco's faxing of the story to Roberto raises questions about the lengths to which he was willing to go to smear Safra. Was Greco simply mixed up? Did he not realize the two banks were unconnected? Or had he grown so intent on smearing Safra he was willing to intentionally mislead a reporter as to which Republic Bank had been indicted?

Greco's own explanation, made in a rare comment to the author about the Safra investigation, suggests he may have confused Republic of New York with Republic of Miami, an admission that, if true, might explain many of the bizarre stories he spread about Safra. "I cannot tell if [Republic of Miami] was related with Republic National Bank of Safra," Greco said. "I don't know. I just sent it to Roberto because I thought he might be interested. I can't recall why I sent it. I sent Roberto a lot of material."*

By December 1988 American Express's special "investigation" of Edmond Safra was almost two years old and beginning to show signs of running out of steam. In New York, Bob Smith was trying to keep Cantor occupied with banking minutiae and staying notified on her whereabouts. There were hints that Freeman too had soured on Cantor. When she passed through London, colleagues noticed that Freeman wasn't returning her calls as quickly as he once had, when he returned them at all. More than one person familiar with Cantor's work believed Freeman was attempting to distance himself from the "secret weapon" he had taken into the American Express fold.

* It is tempting to suggest that at least some of the stories Greco passed to reporters about Republic of New York were actually tales he had heard about Republic of Miami, perhaps from Andy Iglesias. But while Iglesias acknowledges hearing stories similar to those Greco transmitted, he insists he did not relate them to Greco, nor were the stories necessarily about Republic of Miami. For instance, of the vivid tale of the Republic bank manager found dead in an Ecuadoran harbor, Iglesias says: "I've heard that story, yes. But it's about [still] another Republic Bank, in Panama. It went out of business several years ago."

From the picture of their activities that later emerged, it appeared that the American Express operatives mustered enough energy for one final project, a complex affair in a faraway country, which would create more negative publicity for Edmond Safra than the besieged billionaire had experienced in a lifetime. And best of all, if everything went right, there wouldn't be the slightest hint that Susan Cantor, Tony Greco, or anyone affiliated with American Express was ever remotely involved.

14

All through 1988 Susan Cantor had remained in touch with Jay Newman and the other members of Shearson Lehman's Third World debt group. That fall their occasional chats took a new turn. It began during a typical conversation. Cantor, eager to be taken seriously as a banker, was talking about all the people she knew in Brazil, Venezuela, Peru and other Latin American locales when Newman stopped her.

Peru?

Yes, Cantor assured him, she knew someone who had close ties to the administration of President Alan García. Her friend was an American Express consultant, in fact, and had handled a number of sensitive jobs for the company over the years.

Peru was of special interest to Jay Newman that winter, and to every banker in the field of international debt. As part of a plan to revive his country's economy, President García had announced his intention to repay its mountainous debt on no terms but its own, which amounted to ten percent of its export earnings, a trickle for world banks. An assignment to straighten out Peru's debt quagmire would be a real plum, and Newman was immediately interested in Cantor's consultant friend. "Bring him in," he encouraged her.

But nothing was that easy. The "consultant," Cantor said, would want to be paid by the hour, a concept as alien to Jay Newman's international bankers as pro bono work. Hourly wages were for maids. Middlemen, Newman explained, worked on a percentage. "He doesn't work that way," Cantor countered, and later returned to reemphasize her point. Her man worked by the hour, or not at all.

"What the fuck?" Newman said. "That's not the way this business works, Susan. We get paid if we produce. He gets paid if he produces."

The matter was left there for a time, as Cantor disappeared again and Newman and his troops scattered on a variety of assignments. When next Cantor brought up the subject of Peru, Newman insisted on talking directly to her "consultant." But like so many middlemen, Cantor was reluctant to hand over her source. She insisted on handling all communications between Newman's people and the mysterious American Express consultant.

Finally, after more fruitless back and forth, Newman had enough. "Susan, either I talk to him, or we forget about it," he told her. "This is just too complicated."

And so a conference call was arranged, Newman and Cantor and the consultant, whose name, of course, was Tony Greco. They went back and forth for what seemed like hours, Greco insisting on being paid by the hour, Newman refusing to pay any other way than by percentage. His aide Keith Fogerty was brought in and had talks with Greco. Eventually, a compromise was struck. Newman and Shearson agreed to advance Greco an all-expense-paid trip to Peru, plus a bonus they would work out later. If Greco's work resulted in an assignment for Shearson Lehman, then they would talk more about compensation.

Jay Newman was satisfied. And despite the hassle, as time went by he found himself growing excited about Greco's trip to Lima. Here, it seemed, was a rare chance for Shearson to pry into one of the toughest niches of the international debt game. For days Newman and his team waited for word, until finally Susan Cantor phoned and said Greco had come through. They had established contact with Carlos Morales, Peru's presidential press secretary, a man who could really get things done.

Members of Peru's foreign press corps first noticed Carlos Morales in the mid-1980s as the man who stood on the tarmac at Lima's Jorge Chavez International Airport and greeted Alan García when the young president returned home from trips abroad. As public affairs chief at the state airline, Aero Peru, Morales was a García favorite. He was loyal to the Aprista movement, smooth and European-styled, exactly the kind of Peruvian García favored for his inner circle.

In November 1988 Morales was named Alan García's presidential press secretary. Jaded press veterans found Morales a pleasant if uninspired palace spokesman. He had little experience with foreign journalists, and sometimes seemed at a loss to answer their questions. At the first meeting he arranged between President García and members of the Foreign Press Association, Morales handed out Aero Peru flight bags brimming with Aero Peru tourist guides, pads and pencils, and cassettes of Peruvian music—all of which sealed his reputation as a mediocre press contact, but the first man a foreign correspondent called when he lost his airline tickets.

Peru's presidential palace rises from the grimy streets of downtown Lima across from the broad, flat Plaza de Armas, where stern-faced army sentries in crisp uniforms stare down passersby. Behind its high spiked gates, Carlos Morales's offices lay across the hall from those of Hugo Otero, the senior adviser who had made Greco's acquaintance in the 1960s. It was there, in early December 1988, that Morales says he received his first visit from Greco, who had been introduced to him by Greco's friend Victor Tirado.[*] The reason for the call, Morales says, was Shearson's proposal to solve Peru's debt problem.

"Greco was constantly phoning and trying to get a meeting with me," Morales recalled. "He must have called a thousand times." Only when he reluctantly agreed to an appointment, Morales says, did others at the palace tell him of Greco's past. "When Greco arrived in my office, everyone started making jokes about gays and all that," Morales said. "I asked, 'Who the hell is this man?' They told me the whole story of his background, that he was very, very close friends with Haya."

Carlos Morales insists his meeting with Greco covered only the proposal the detective had brought from American Express and Shearson for the restructuring of Peru's debt. "He said he was bringing a very important message from an American organization that wanted to help Peru," Morales said, "that he had previously tried to get in touch with other people in the government, but had been put off. We talked specifically only about Shearson Lehman Hutton and American Express."

At Greco's suggestion, Carlos Morales says he telephoned the New York office of Susan Cantor, who confirmed both Greco's representation of American Express and the outlines of Shearson's interests. A meeting

---

[*] This despite the fact he had denied knowing Greco to the Safra detective, Matthew Wolinsky. "I remember the existence of some person with that name, from twenty years ago, connected with the government," Morales had said.

was arranged in Lima; the Shearson bankers were to come to Peru to make their proposals in person. Morales confirmed the appointment via fax with Cantor on December 12. "Based on the coordination with Mr. Antonio Greco in Lima," he wrote Cantor, "it would be a pleasure to meet with you in our capital city on Friday the 16th of December at 10:00 A.M. There we shall have a meeting with the minister of economy and finance of our country...."

That meeting never occurred, after Shearson's Jay Newman refused to fly all the way to Lima without an indication that the Peruvians were serious about doing business. Not to be deterred, Greco and Cantor arranged a second meeting, this one in New York. This time Carlos Morales accepted their invitation to visit American Express headquarters in lower Manhattan. According to Morales and other people involved in those meetings, his flight was scheduled to arrive at Kennedy airport late on Wednesday, January 18, 1989.

In the days immediately prior to his trip to New York, and while in contact with both Tony Greco and Susan Cantor, Carlos Morales did a strange thing. In separate conversations, two former Peruvian government press aides say he asked them to undertake an unusual task: delivering dossiers on Edmond Safra's criminal activities to Lima's international press.

It was an unusual request, but Morales selected messengers he could trust. One was William Betalleluz, a big, doughy former newspaperman who sometimes handled press inquiries for President García's wife. Foreign reporters knew Betalleluz as one of García's motley crew of media handlers, an immense man who scurried about checking microphones at presidential press conferences. "I used to tell Fatso Betalleluz he was the president's dog to bark at journalists," a Spanish correspondent, Francisco Figueroa, recalled. "But he was a nice guy, not too intelligent, but nice."

The second man Carlos Morales briefed was his replacement as Aero Peru's public relations chief, a sly, soft-featured thirty-year-old named Freddy Chirinos. Chirinos, though at his new post barely two months, was a veteran p.r. man, well known among the Peruvian press corps as an errand boy for the APRA leadership.

"One day Señor Morales showed me some clippings from foreign newspapers where they mentioned Señor Safra and Republic Bank, and

[said] they were involved in something related to money laundering," Freddy Chirinos recalled in an interview. "Señor Morales well knew the kind of job I did and the excellent contacts I had with journalists. So he asked me if these newspaper clippings could be of any interest to the foreign press. Assuming that these clippings were true, I told him, yes, they would be of interest. He asked me if I had any contacts—all of this was informal, just between friends—to whom I could give the information on Señor Safra."

Freddy Chirinos suggested two names, a reporter with EFE, the Spanish news service, and a Peruvian correspondent with the Associated Press. When Morales asked for the name of another person who could discreetly approach the journalists on his behalf, Chirinos came up with another name: Marcos Roncagliolo, a former editor at the Lima newspaper *El Nacional*. A jovial extrovert, Roncagliolo was a longtime Peruvian newsman who had traveled widely with Alan García and by his own admission adored him.

At Chirinos's request, Marcos Roncagliolo eagerly signed on with the Aprista plan. "Freddy is a friend, he asked me to do this as a favor to a friend," Roncagliolo recalled. "He didn't tell me a lot about why we were going to spread these stories. But he said they were looking for this information to be broadcast through the cables of the foreign press agencies. It was to be a covert operation. The idea was for the press to do our dirty work, so as to hurt Safra's image....I thought it was a harmless operation. None of us really knew what we were doing. Nobody really knew the dynamite we had in our hands." There was another, more pressing reason for Roncagliolo to go along with the plan: he was unemployed and needed money. "We talked about price *if* the effort was successful," Roncagliolo said. "I was a fool. If I had realized how important this all was, I would have charged a lot of money."

On Tuesday morning, January 17, the day before he was to meet Tony Greco at New York's Kennedy airport, Carlos Morales sent his three operatives to fan out through Lima's dusty streets to pay visits to a half-dozen members of the foreign press. Each man carried a thick folder stuffed with Jean Roberto's *Minute* articles, as well as articles on Safra from Swiss and U.S. publications. There were items on money laundering from *The Wall Street Journal* and other publications. Also included was a copy of the Bern letter, its U.S. Embassy logo prominently displayed.

The core of the dossier, the text that held its disparate elements together, was the so-called four-page intelligence document later described to the Safra detective, Matthew Wolinsky. Located in a Lima journalist's files, this document turned out to be nothing more than the Spanish-language text of the article Victor Tirado had planted the previous summer in *Hoy*, and which had been republished in Mexico City's *Uno Mas Uno*. Long, complicated to the point of being incomprehensible, it contained all the standard elements of the American Express disinformation effort: Safra the CIA man, Safra the drug lord, Safra and Iran-Contra, Safra and Willard Zucker.

Dossier in hand, Marcos Roncagliolo's first stop that day was the townhouse office of the Spanish news agency EFE, tucked away on a side street in the shadow of the modern glass-and-concrete headquarters of the state oil company, Petro Peru. Around noon Roncagliolo stepped into the small, dark lobby decorated with a portrait of Spain's King Juan Carlos, then walked down a short flight of steps into the narrow little newsroom, lined with clattering teletype machines and glowing green computer screens. There he handed a copy of the Safra file to an old friend, a slight, mild-mannered Peruvian reporter named Miguel Paredes. Paredes had worked for several news operations during his career, including eighteen years as a reporter at the Reuters news service in Lima. He greeted Roncagliolo warmly; the two had known each other since the 1960s.

"Marcos asked me to do him this favor, to issue a dispatch about something that was very important," Miguel Paredes recalled. "He asked me to understand, that he was unemployed and needed to do this to make some money. I told him to leave the documents with me and I'd make the dispatch. I told him to come back the next day to get the copy."

Roncagliolo left EFE's office in high spirits, confident Paredes would complete the first step of his unusual mission. "We were friends," Roncagliolo recalled by way of explanation. "No one asks why a friend asks a favor. It was a favor from one professional to another. He said he would do the job, without asking about money."

It was a promise Miguel Paredes couldn't keep. Flipping through the Safra dossier, he instantly realized how damaging its publication would be to Edmond Safra, a man he had never heard of. When his boss, EFE's aggressive young bureau chief Francisco Figueroa, arrived later that day, Paredes explained his predicament. At thirty-six, "Paco" Figueroa was already a veteran foreign correspondent, having headed

EFE bureaus in Portugal, Paraguay, and Brazil before coming to Lima two years earlier. A dashing figure in Polo shirts and sockless Italian loafers, Figueroa listened intently as Paredes related the conversation with Marcos Roncagliolo. He didn't have to hear much of the tale to realize the government men were up to no good. *"Eso guema, devuelvelo,"* Figueroa told Paredes. "That's too hot. Give it back." EFE, he said, wasn't interested.

But Miguel Paredes had made a promise to a friend. When Roncagliolo telephoned to see how things were going, he stalled, unsure of what to do. "[Miguel] started cheating me," Roncagliolo recalled. "He started telling me that he had problems with his satellite, that he had stomach problems. He had a million different excuses why he couldn't print the information."

As Miguel Paredes pondered his next move, similar scenes were playing out at news offices across Lima. Several blocks away, Alberto Ku King welcomed the portly William Betalleluz through a black wrought-iron gate into his garden office on General Cordova Street. Ku King, the half-Chinese, half-Peruvian correspondent for the Italian news agency ANSA, didn't know Betalleluz well, but assumed he acted as a messenger from the palace. Betalleluz seemed furtive, and the newsman was instantly curious about what he was up to.

Standing in Ku King's office, Betalleluz handed the reporter the thick folder of documents and articles describing Safra. Like so many other journalists that day, Ku King had never heard of Safra, a man who seemed to have no obvious link to Peru or the Aprista leadership. When Ku King wondered why he or other correspondents should care about this Safra character, Betalleluz suggested, with a wink and a nod, that the banker had grown quite close to a number of Peruvian politicians, including Alan García's rival, the former finance minister Luis Alva Castro. Ku King didn't miss the hint. Betalleluz promised that he could deliver photographs of Safra and these politicians. Ku King, though, never saw any pictures.

Then Betalleluz made his mistake. If Ku King could get an article about Safra published on his agency's wires, Betalleluz said, he was prepared to pay him a sum of money, roughly four hundred dollars. Ku King was genuinely offended by the offer; his colleagues in Lima's press corps, many of them Americans, hadn't elected him chairman of the Foreign Press Association for nothing. When Betalleluz left, having elicited Ku

King's promise to consider the offer, Ku King began to get angry. The more he thought about the conversation, the angrier he got.

The next morning Ku King took a call from the worried EFE reporter, Miguel Paredes. Both men agreed something untoward was going on. They decided to call Ku King's friend at the U.S. Embassy, Chuck Loveridge, to see whether the dossier's DEA "report" was genuine. Loveridge, the embassy's public affairs officer, came directly over. From a cursory glance he judged the report an amateurish attempt at disinformation. Later he took Ku King's file to the embassy and confirmed it: the report was a fake.

No sooner had Miguel Paredes returned to his EFE office that afternoon than he received a visit from the two anxious Aprista messengers, Marcos Roncagliolo and Freddy Chirinos. "Paredes came out of the newsroom very scared and said this information was burning, that it was too hot," Roncagliolo recalled. "He said he could lose his job. And he could lose his head, too. He said he had investigated this and felt that I was in the hands of bad men. That's when I began to get scared. I began to get worried."

Things hadn't gone well for Roncagliolo. He had also struck out in an attempt to get an old friend at Agence France-Presse to print the Safra materials. "We tried four times at French press," he said. "But the Paris office rejected it. They wanted more information. They didn't just want assumptions. They wanted true facts. They wanted names, figures."

Freddy Chirinos, meanwhile, had run into similar troubles getting a jowly old Associated Press reporter named Luis Podesta to print the Safra materials. Over lunch Chirinos had handed Podesta the dossier, hinting that, as an executive at Aero Peru, he was in a position to bestow certain favors if the Safra materials should find their way onto the AP wires. "He sort of conveyed the idea that if I wanted, I could travel abroad for free, just take some tickets and go," Podesta recalled. But when the reporter requested additional information on Safra, Chirinos had to admit they had nothing more. "That's when Podesta started doubting," Roncagliolo recalled. "I began to have my doubts as well." An honorable man, Luis Podesta tossed the dossier into a wastebasket.

But Marcos Roncagliolo, still eager for a big payday, would not be deterred. "I tried every means to have this information published by the agencies," but had gotten nowhere, he recalled. It was at that point, in a conversation with Freddy Chirinos, that Roncagliolo first suggested forgery. "It was my idea," he admits. "I tried to do it, and I did it. On a typewriter."

The document Roncagliolo anonymously produced—a forged Associated Press dispatch about Edmond Safra's supposed drug ties—wouldn't come to light for nearly two years, when in early 1991 Safra lawyers discovered it among a group of files turned over to them by Jean Roberto in Paris. Correct in form to the last detail, it read:

AP068/432-88

DEA INVESTIGA OPERACIONES ILEGALES DE BANCO USA EN SUDAMERICA
[DEA Investigates Illegal Operations of USA Bank in South America]

LIMA, Jan. 17 (AP)—In a reserved report by the DEA revealed in Lima, police sources warned against the possible relations the Republic National Bank of New York might have established with banking institutions in Peru, Argentina, Brazil and Venezuela, with the purpose of laundering narco-dollars.

The Republic National Bank, owned by the Lebanese banker Edmond J. Safra, a naturalized Brazilian, is one of the new banks with the largest expansion in the U.S.A. This prosperity results from its role of intermediary in the illegal acquisition of arms. Its responsibility has been clearly demonstrated in the loss of the US$40 million which were to help provide arms for Nicaraguan Contras.

It has been understood that Republic National Bank and Edmond Safra oriented their activities to obtain dollars from the increasing narco-traffic business in Peru, Argentina, Brazil, and Venezuela.

For the DEA, Republic National Bank and Safra are trying to control the whole itinerary of laundered dollars that land in banks in Miami, Los Angeles, New York, Luxembourg, France, and Switzerland. The dollars from this illegal business can thus enter legally the international financial circuit, leaving important incomes for the agents compromised in the operations.

Based on the DEA report, Interpol has advised the banking institutions of the four South American countries concerned to be watchful of all operations with the Republic National Bank and its subsidiaries controlled by the Lebanese citizen Edmond J. Safra.

AP/11:35 AM.
JMP.RAZ-068/43

Confronted with the forged document in an interview with the author, Marcos Roncagliolo beams with pride. He points to the small print at the end of the dispatch, the telex operator's initials and the time, eleven-thirty-five. "See, the time is key," he says. "Only the operators know about that. We knew everything. It was a perfect operation. Perfect. I knew the whole style. It's like a false hundred-dollar bill. Beautiful. It was a well-intentioned attempt at forgery." He pauses, then smiles. "I was a fool."

If Roncagliolo was satisfied, his partner Freddy Chirinos was positively buoyant. "He said it was perfect," Roncagliolo recalled, "just what we needed."

It was at this point that the Aprista pressmen grew frightened. Alberto Ku King, acting as chairman of the Foreign Press Association, told William Betalleluz in a strained phone call that, not only wasn't he going to print the Safra materials, he was seriously considering an article detailing the palace's disinformation campaign. Chirinos and Roncagliolo, meanwhile, began hearing rumors that Betalleluz was out offering money to anyone in town to print the Safra dossiers. "I found out about what Betalleluz was doing, and that's when I got really scared," said Roncagliolo. "There was a general panic. We decided to abort the mission. People decided to abandon ship. I realized I had made a terrible mistake."*

The only problem was that evidence of their operation remained in the hands of at least six journalists. Led by Roncagliolo, the Aprista operatives scrambled to retrieve the dossiers, in some cases offering money for its return. They were successful in a few cases—EFE's Miguel Paredes returned the documents—"but we lost most of them," Roncagliolo acknowledges. Among others, the Aprista editor visited Alberto Ku King, but Ku King said he no longer had the materials. "Ku King said he knew there was a plot," Roncagliolo recalled, "that the word was out."

As if to placate Ku King, Roncagliolo assured him that the government would soon provide him with new, undisputed proof of Safra's guilt in the form of news reports to be published in Argentina and Venezuela. Ku King got the clear impression the Peruvian government was taking a hand in getting the articles published. Months later, Roncagliolo would

* Freddy Chirinos claims he actually confronted his boss Carlos Morales over the rumor that Betalleluz was paying to have the articles published. "I was upset. I said, 'How could you send us to do something like this when someone else is out there offering money?'" Chirinos said. The claim seems disingenuous. According to Marcos Roncagliolo, the two had talked about offering money to journalists from the outset. "When all this started," Roncagliolo said, "there was all this talk of big money being involved. I never knew where the money was coming from. We tried to make up a black bag, you know, full of money. In Latin America, you can do whatever you want, make up any story, if you have enough money. We were going to offer it to people. But it never came off."

claim to have heard some such talk, but insisted he had no direct knowledge of the Apristas' successfully planting Safra articles in other countries.

The entire sordid episode should have ended there, the Apristas sent scurrying for cover, the Safra dossiers tossed into file cabinets and wastebaskets. No new stories about Safra had appeared in Lima papers. As far as Alberto Ku King and the other foreign journalists were concerned—and they later conveyed this to the Safra detective Matthew Wolinsky—there was no harm done. No stories had gotten out.

They were wrong. The same morning the other dossiers were delivered, William Betalleluz had visited the offices of the Cuban national news service, Prensa Latina, which seven months before had transmitted an article on Safra to a newspaper in Mexico City. Not for two years would the document that resulted from Betalleluz's morning visit find its way into Edmond Safra's hands. It was a news story, dated that same day, January 17, 1989. "DEA Pursues a Fraud of $40 Million," the headline read. The accompanying eight paragraphs of text hammered home the theme Tony Greco had been peddling for nearly a year.

LIMA, Jan. 17 (PL)—The Drug Enforcement Agency (DEA), the US agency responsible for pursuing narco-trafficking, is running after a man who seems to have embezzled US$40 million from the United States government in the Iran-Contra affair.

In its wish to capture the banker Edmond Safra, identified as a Jewish Lebanese of Brazilian nationality, the DEA circulated a detailed report in which it revealed another chapter of the scandal by the illegal financing of the Nicaragua Contra-revolution, also called Irangate.

With the risk of being confronted with the Central Intelligence Agency (CIA), which the DEA accuses of benefiting from Safra's services, or maybe with the intention of cleaning its image by chasing a presumed protagonist of its illegal activities, the DEA warns against all business with Safra, designated as a dangerous man.

Who in reality is Edmond Safra? Where does he live, to whom is he connected, where has he invested his money, who are his friends and associates? These are questions that could find an answer—either true or false—with the future disclosure of a new scandal in Argentina, Venezuela, or Brazil....

Prensa Latina wasn't William Betalleluz's last stop that morning. At the offices of a little-known Rome-based news wire named Inter Press

Service, known as IPS, he handed his dossier to its bureau chief, Abraham Lama. Months later, a long IPS dispatch on Safra would also surface:

Latin America:
Investigation of Plan by Narcotraffickers
to Dominate Latin American Banking

LIMA, Jan. 17 (IPS)—A North American financial group linked to arms and drugs traffickers intends to capture control of Latin American banking flows and its immediate targets are banks in Argentina, Brazil, and Venezuela, according to information received by Peruvian authorities.

The document provided by the DEA to the Interior and Economics & Finance Ministries of Peru identifies at the center of the "Mafia-like" organization Edmond Safra, a Brazilian of Lebanese origin, who made a fortune as an intermediary of the CIA in arms trafficking and now begins activities in large-scale drug-money laundering....

Later, the validity of both the IPS and Prensa Latina dispatches would be called into question. Officials at both agencies have denied that either article was transmitted on their wires; IPS's Abraham Lama, in an interview, strenuously denies writing any article on Safra. Lending weight to these denials was the fact that no newspaper could be found that had reprinted either dispatch at the time. Marcos Roncagliolo, for one, denies forging either dispatch. One possibility is that the stories were typewritten by paid-off IPS or Prensa Latena employees in Lima, handed to the Aprista couriers, and simply never transmitted, a scheme that would have cheated the Peruvians but, because the stories were never actually transmitted, eliminated the risk of being caught. To this day, the exact origin of the two dispatches remains a mystery.

Still, as press manipulation goes, it was not a bad day's work for the Aprista messengers: six journalists approached, three stories produced, at least one of them forged. And not the slightest hint of involvement by anyone or anything associated with a faraway company named American Express.

A day after his aides visited a half-dozen foreign press agencies in Lima, Carlos Morales and another Peruvian official arrived at New York's

Kennedy airport, where they were met by Tony Greco. Greco ushered the two Peruvians into a waiting limousine and whisked them downtown to the Vista Hotel, just across from Shearson headquarters in the World Financial Center, where they freshened up.

That night Jay Newman was waiting as the Peruvian delegation, escorted by Greco, stepped from the mahogany-paneled elevator onto the lush carpet of Shearson's investment-banking offices. Newman was introduced for the first time to the slim, well-dressed Morales. But it wasn't the dapper Morales who left an indelible impression on Jay Newman's bankers. It was Tony Greco. Escorting Morales into a conference room, Newman was introduced to the detective, and was startled. Greco was squat, straining at the seams of his well-tailored Italian suit, like a barrel of black powder on the verge of exploding. *Powerful*, Newman thought more than once. The image that stayed with him was of the reputed Mafia boss John Gotti: sharp, well-dressed, dangerous, powerful. Tony Greco had an inescapably threatening physical presence, thoroughly out of place in the hushed dark-wood halls of Shearson Lehman Hutton.

"So, Tony, what exactly is it that you do?" Keith Fogerty, Newman's aide, ventured.

"Actually," Greco said, "I'm a private detective."

In the conference room, Morales and Greco listened patiently to Shearson's presentation. Susan Cantor showed up and sat by in a corner. The session appeared to go well, and the next day Newman's team picked up where it left off, adding layer upon layer of detail to its plan to settle Peru's debt problems. Talks continued through the day Thursday. At one point, Peru's finance minister, in Manhattan on other business, stopped by to check in on the discussions; when he left, Morales and his aide rolled their eyes in obvious contempt for the minister's intellectual faculties.

By Thursday evening prospects for an agreement looked bright, and Newman arranged for everyone to attend an elaborate dinner at the haute midtown Manhattan restaurant Le Bernardin. Laughter dominated a thoroughly charming evening: Greco, for all his tough-guy appearances, turned out to be quite the wit, telling self-deprecating jokes about how little he knew about international debt. Newman and his men could only marvel at how a private detective had brought Shearson together with senior officials of a major Latin American country. The next day Shearson and the Peruvians would agree on the draft of a formal proposal that Carlos Morales would take back to Lima for Alan García; with any luck, it would lead to a multimillion dollar assignment for the Wall Streeters.

That night, bottles of expensive French wine flowed freely, and everyone seemed to have a delightful time. Just days after a trio of Peruvian government operatives distributed dossiers on Edmond Safra to reporters in far-off South America, Carlos Morales, Tony Greco, Susan Cantor and a handful of unsuspecting investment bankers exchanged toasts and best wishes well into the night. Everyone, it seemed, had plenty to celebrate.*

What actually happened during that strange January of 1989?

From all appearances, the dissemination of dossiers on Edmond Safra was carried out not by American Express, but by the Peruvian government. Also evident is that the Peruvians received the dossier from the one person in the world actively passing it around, Tony Greco, a private detective under contract to American Express. The question is: why would the Peruvians cooperate in the scheme?

One possibility, of course, is money. American Express, via Greco, could have paid Carlos Morales to distribute the anti-Safra materials. Two of Morales's Peruvian bagmen say they heard repeatedly of the "big money" behind their visits to Lima's foreign journalists. If money was paid, it can be assumed that neither American Express nor the Peruvian government would admit such an arrangement. Barring a legal investigation, one can safely say the question of secret payments won't easily be resolved.

The question of money aside, the Peruvians' motivation was clear. Over the years the Apristas have shown a tendency to engage in some wonderfully Byzantine political intrigues. For them, the plan to smear Safra, using Greco's materials, may simply have represented a convergence of interests. Carlos Morales and his aides could hope to strike a stiff blow by later linking Safra to their rival, Luis Alva Castro. If, during the process, the scheme also helped Tony Greco and his employer

*The dates of the Peruvian delegation's visit to Shearson, January 18–21, 1989, are based on the recollection of three of the meeting's participants. In addition, Carlos Morales, in a telephone interview, says Shearson's completed letter to Alan García was dated Friday, January 20.

American Express, so much the better. Everyone would be happier.

For his part, Carlos Morales denies any involvement in passing out information about Safra. When confronted with his aides' stories, he weaves a strange tale of receiving an unmarked manila envelope full of Safra-related clippings in the mail. He acknowledges discussing the envelope with Freddy Chirinos and journalists who also received it anonymously, but insists he asked no one to pass it around. When pressed, he accuses Victor Tirado of being behind the scheme; given the help Tirado had earlier supplied Greco, it's entirely possible he did so again, perhaps somehow persuading Morales to go along with the plan. Neither Tirado nor Morales will say any more.

Whatever the case, it appears Tony Greco got more out of the arrangement than his Peruvian friends. As Marcos Roncagliolo understood it, the key to the government's plan was getting the Safra materials sent out on a foreign news wire, which could then be picked up in Peru, a twist that would make the news appear all the more authoritative. "We had to get it published by a foreign agency here in Peru," Roncagliolo said. "It had to be Peru. We didn't care about getting things published in Europe, unless it was reprinted in Peru. The intention was to hurt Alva Castro, and in that event it was a total failure."

Greco, though, got exactly what he must have wanted. The three articles "planted" in Peru—Prensa Latina, IPS, and the forged AP dispatch—would later surface, in one guise or another, as far away as France, Switzerland, Argentina, Uruguay, and the United States. After their creation in Lima, Greco appears to have moved fast. According to *Minute*'s Jean Roberto, the detective faxed copies of all three articles to him in Paris within days of their appearance in Peru. (A fax telltale on Roberto's copies reads "JAN 23 '89," the Monday after Greco and Cantor met with Carlos Morales in New York.) Presumably one of the Peruvians relayed the articles to Greco, since there is no indication that the detective was personally involved in their distribution during the week of January 17.

Roberto, in turn, passed on many of the tainted materials, including the three new Peruvian dispatches, the Bern letter, Greco's "gibberish" report, and the *Hoy* article, to the Swiss reporter Jean-Claude Buffle at *L'Hebdo* magazine. "Thanks for the documents. They will be most helpful in the investigation of Edmond Safra," Buffle wrote Roberto, adding: "One last thing—in the memo that you gave to me that comes from your

American source—many different enclosures are mentioned. Do you have them and could you send them to me?"

Buffle's article was published in *L'Hebdo* several months later, in May 1989. Though largely factual, it did rely on tainted materials for some of its key section about Safra's supposed criminal links. Buffle cited the Bern letter, whose confidential "Miami source" was in fact Tony Greco; the *Hoy* article, which Greco planted via Victor Tirado; and the January 17 dispatches out of Lima, which can all be linked to Greco.

But the trail of disinformation didn't end there. Buffle, in turn, shared the tainted materials with at least two Swiss colleagues, the television journalists Yves Lasseur of *Le Temps Présent*, who was preparing a documentary on Swiss money laundering, and Philippe Mottaz, who had been among the reporters to break the story of Republic's ties to Shakarchi Trading. That spring Buffle and his two friends swapped a wealth of leads and information as they pursued separate stories on Safra and money laundering. "There were rumors galore about Safra," Mottaz recalled. "All these things were circulating around among a small group of us."

Yves Lasseur's primary interest was money laundering in general, and though he kept Safra's p.r. man Robert Siegfried busy answering questions for weeks, he ultimately failed to include anything new about Safra in his documentary. Philippe Mottaz, however, was deeply intrigued by the materials he received, including the Peruvian articles from *Hoy*, IPS, and Prensa Latina as well as an abbreviated version of the "gibberish" report Greco had given Jean Roberto. Mottaz spent much of May and June 1989 peppering Siegfried with questions about Safra, many of them arising from his reading of American Express–inspired disinformation.

Luckily for Mottaz, he was a more thorough reporter than most. In late May 1989 he met with a trio of DEA officials in Washington and asked, among other things, about the supposed DEA alert on Safra to South American banks. "We advised you that DEA did not issue any such 'alert' or 'warning,'" the agency's deputy chief counsel, Robert T. Richardson, later wrote Mottaz to confirm their conversation. Mottaz proved so dogged he actually attempted to confirm the reports during a trip to Peru, but, unable to do so, he eventually gave up. His subsequent reports on Safra, while spurred by the tainted material he had read, steered well clear of it and hewed closely to information from the DEA report on Shakarchi Trading and other official sources.

Ripples from Jean-Claude Buffle's reporting in *L'Hebdo* would continue for more than a year. Nine months later, Buffle's passages on Safra were summarized in a widely read February 1990 book by a Swiss sociologist and politician named Jean Ziegler. Ziegler's book, *La Suisse lave plus blanc* ("Switzerland Washes Whiter"), a treatise on money laundering, cited *L'Hebdo* as its source for a two-page discussion of Safra and what it termed "the possible implication of Safra in the laundering of intercontinental rings of drug traffickers." In a footnote, Ziegler suggested readers wanting to learn more consult articles in *L'Espresso* of Italy and *Hoy* of Peru.

Safra sued. In a case that drew publicity across Europe, he sent Georges Kiejman into a Paris court, and Kiejman again emerged victorious, securing a judgment against Ziegler and his publisher for 150,000 French francs plus a promise to edit the charges against Safra from forthcoming copies of the book. "These allegations indisputably cast a slur on the honour and reputation of M. Edmond Safra," the French court ruled. "The moral and professional damage caused to M. Safra is quite substantial since this time it emanates not from a journal normally associated with scandals but from a man with a legitimate reputation for integrity, a university professor, member of parliament, and author of a great many works in the field of sociology."

Swiss writers weren't the only ones to be taken in by the strange stories emanating from Peru. Another tentacle of the scheme ensnared a Spanish newspaper reporter named Victor Ducrot. Shortly after the Safra dossiers were distributed in Lima in January 1989, Ducrot, a Latin American correspondent for a Madrid-based paper named *Gaceta de los Negocias*, visited Lima on assignment. During the course of his reporting, he says he interviewed an aide to Carlos Morales. "I talked to him two or three times in Lima," Ducrot recalled. At one point, according to Ducrot, Morales's aide "asked to go off the record," then handed Ducrot a copy of several articles about Safra and suggested a story on the banker. By then the Aprista dossier had been updated with the articles from Prensa Latina, IPS, and the forged dispatch from Associated Press.

Returning to his office in Buenos Aires, the unsuspecting Ducrot did what any good reporter would do: he filed the Safra materials away, "saving string" for a story on money laundering, and began collecting whatever he could find on Safra. In the months to come, he mentioned Safra's name to friends in South America and Europe, but found few knew of him. If someone was curious, Ducrot would unselfishly photocopy materials from the dossier and hand them out. He insists he never authored a story on Safra himself, but like the carrier of some contagious journalistic disease, Ducrot infected a number of other reporters with the bogus stories.

Among those who received Safra materials from Victor Ducrot were his close friends Alberto and Louise Dufuy of *Noticiero*, the small Spanish-language newsletter in Geneva. *Noticiero's* February 1989 article on Safra, "The Swiss Drug Connection," is almost a word-for-word reproduction of the January 17 Prensa Latina dispatch out of Lima. In a letter to one of Safra's Swiss attorneys the following spring, Alberto Dufuy had asserted exactly that, that the article was simply a reprint from Prensa Latina. But Dufuy couldn't produce a copy of any Cuban article, and until the Prensa Latina dispatch surfaced two years later, Safra's people didn't believe him.

Much to Safra's dismay, Victor Ducrot would maintain an interest in money laundering long after the spring of 1989, and long after Safra's lawyers and investigators believed they had ended the American Express campaign. Later that year, Ducrot mentioned Safra to a spokesman for the Argentine government named José Luis Ponsico. Ponsico worked for the country's drug-fighting vice president Eduardo Duhalde, and was a frequent source of narcotics-related stories for Argentine journalists. Ponsico had never heard of Safra, but accepted copies of the tainted IPS and Associated Press articles from Ducrot and promised to study them.

Ponsico, in turn, passed along copies of the articles to an Argentine reporter named Ramon Vasquez, who wrote for a Buenos Aires scandal sheet named *El Informador.* Vasquez's resulting story was printed a full nine months after the Safra dossiers were handed out in Peru, on October 20, 1989, under the headline, "Information from the DEA in the Hands of Duhalde: An Investigation of Drug Traffickers' Plan to Control Latin American Bank." The story, reminiscent of so many American Express–inspired pieces, was a long rewrite of the IPS dispatch, with a quote from the forged AP story thrown in for good measure. It suggested that Vice President Duhalde's investigators were actively pursuing a probe of Safra's banks, when in fact they were doing no such thing.

But Victor Ducrot didn't stop there. He also shared stories from his

Safra file with another friend, an Argentine political refugee named Juan Gasparini who had fled to Geneva after being imprisoned and tortured by the Argentine military in the 1970s. There Gasparini had made the rounds of Swiss journalistic circles, and became friendly with a number of reporters, including Susan Cantor's two acquaintances, Maya Jurt and Irene Hirsch.

In June 1990 Gasparini, who was also friends with the Swiss politician Jean Ziegler and had collected Jean-Claude Buffle's articles, published a book in Buenos Aires that incorporated several passages about Safra's supposed criminal activities from a number of tainted sources, most notably *Hoy*. The book itself, *El Crimen de Graiver* ("The Murder of Graiver"), dealt with an infamous Argentine financier, David Graiver, who died in a mysterious plane crash in the 1970s. Safra's attorneys seriously considered suing Gasparini, but eventually gave up, deciding a lawsuit would only draw more publicity to the little-read book.[*]

The three dispatches out of Lima—IPS, AP, and Prensa Latina—also served as the basis for passages about Safra in a second book published that summer of 1990, in Montevideo, Uruguay. *El Enjuague Uruguayo* ("The Uruguayan Wash"), written by a prominent local journalist named Samuel Blixen, dealt with the topic of Uruguayan money laundering, and includes an entire chapter on Safra's supposed illegal activities, "The Accounts of the Restless Mr. Safra."

It's all there: Safra and Iran-Contra, Safra and Oliver North's phantom $40 million, Safra and DEA alerts to South American banks. Reached by phone in Uruguay, Blixen confirmed his use of the tainted dispatches, but insists he acquired them when they were transmitted via news wires. But since at least one, and perhaps all three, of the articles were forged, it is likely Blixen received them from another journalist, probably Juan Gasparini, who has also written for Blixen's paper. Gasparini, however, denies any contact with Blixen.

• • •

* Ducrot, who says he now works for the Spanish newspaper *El Sol*, described his role in the Safra affair in two 1991 telephone conversations with the author. Later, after learning that Safra had sued several journalists over the stories, he attempted to back away from his earlier assertions. "I didn't give these things to my friend Mr. Dufuy—well, I don't remember, maybe I did," Ducrot said in an early 1992 interview with the author. "Listen, I don't want to be involved. I did nothing important here." Of Juan Gasparini, he said: "I know Mr. Gasparini well, but I didn't give him any information." Reminded of his earlier statements, he says: "Well, oh, maybe I did."

By no means was all the searing press coverage Safra suffered during that frantic first half of 1989 planted or even influenced by American Express. Reports of Shakarchi Trading's accounts at Republic formed the core of Swiss coverage for much of that spring, and little of that journalism appears to have been "infected" by American Express. In fact, one way to analyze the firestorm of publicity Safra endured is by isolating what might be called the "Greco strain" of American Express disinformation from the "Shakarchi strain" of "legitimate" rumors.

Safra's involvement in the Shakarchi stories can be traced to a single DEA report, written January 3, 1989; the report described Shakarchi's alleged links to several Middle Eastern money launderers and in the process included a brief profile of Republic as one of Shakarchi's banks. In March 1989 that report was leaked to three reporters in Washington: Knut Royce of *New York Newsday*, Peter Samuel of the *New York City Tribune,* and Philippe Mottaz, the Swiss television correspondent.

There is no indication that the leak of the DEA report was connected in any way to American Express or its dispute with Safra. All three journalists who received it, while refusing to name their source, describe the person who leaked the report as a high-ranking government official. Each of the three reporters was working on a story—Mottaz and Royce on the Polar Cap money-laundering investigation, Samuel on a "Bulgarian connection" to heroin trafficking—in which Shakarchi was thought to have played a role. The leak of the report, with its passing mention of Safra, may simply have been a way for U.S. officials to "brief" a few reporters on their suspicions on Shakarchi, and perhaps add momentum to their investigation. That the leak occurred in the wake of an American Express-inspired media campaign seems to have been pure coincidence.

It's safe to say the American Express-inspired stories about Safra's drug links, however, had an indelible effect on those journalists pursuing the more mundane stories of Republic's links to Shakarchi, both in the United States and Switzerland. Reporters like Philippe Mottaz and Jean-Claude Buffle saw the DEA report, which quickly made the rounds of reporters on the Safra beat, as confirmation of much of what they were reading in the dispatches out of Peru and France and no doubt gave a harder edge to their stories about Safra. Some, like Mottaz, kept their reporting to the firmer ground of Shakarchi's relationship to Safra. But others, from Geneva to Uruguay, weren't as thorough, and were drawn into the maw of American Express disinformation.

The question of Shakarchi's implication in money laundering, meanwhile, has never been satisfactorily answered. For all the damning information in the DEA report, neither the company nor any of its principals have ever been charged with any wrongdoing.

The only piece of clearly American Express–influenced journalism to wash up on U.S. shores was the May 1989 article in a Fort Lauderdale, Florida, newspaper by an obscure syndicated columnist named Cody Shearer. The Washington-based Shearer was a free-lance journalist and former congressional aide whose column was distributed to perhaps fifteen or twenty newspapers by the North American Syndicate, a division of the Hearst publishing empire that also handles columnists like Carl Rowan, Lewis Grizzard, and Heloise.

Shearer's column on Safra and the murdered Glenn Souham, which sent Safra aides into spasms of damage control, was attributed to "members of French intelligence." That may be. But a closer reading of Shearer's article suggests that a more likely source for his information was Jean Roberto's pieces in *Minute*. In fact, the resemblance between Shearer's May 1989 article and Roberto's August 1988 articles is so striking that a line-by-line analysis suggests the columnist relied heavily on the French paper for his facts, even his turns of phrase.

For all the similarities, Shearer insists he never read the *Minute* articles, and two of his former editors say they never had any problem with his reporting over the years. Still, after Safra's complaints, Shearer's North American Syndicate retracted the offending column. The syndicate's executive editor, Tom Pritchard, explains that the only sources Shearer offered to authenticate his column were European newspapers whose names he has forgotten. "He was able to convince us that it had come from European newspapers...he quoted some to me," Pritchard recalls. "The secret sources, the intelligence sources [he mentioned], we didn't think were strong enough."

A retraction was ordered only after syndicate officials learned the "European articles," presumably *Minute*, had been retracted themselves, a discovery Tom Pritchard calls, without a trace of irony, "the horror of journalism."

Weeks had passed since the meeting between Carlos Morales and the Shearson bankers in New York, and Jay Newman was growing pessimistic about the prospects of a deal with the Peruvians. Morales had seemed certain they could work something out, but if so, Shearson should have had a response by now. With each passing day prospects of success grew dimmer.

Irritated, Newman had tried to take his anger out on Greco, who had sent a large bill for his services. "Fuck this guy," Newman told his aide, Keith Fogerty. "I don't want to pay him anything." Newman told Susan Cantor, who repeatedly insisted that Greco be paid promptly, that he was incensed that Greco was charging Shearson for the limousine he had used to escort Morales around Manhattan. "Susan, come on," he said. "This is not reasonable. Why did he need a limo?" But Cantor was insistent. Newman got the clear message that higher-ups at American Express wouldn't be happy if Greco was offended. Finally he told Fogerty to deal with the question of Greco's reimbursement.

One night, Fogerty sat down in his London flat and telephoned Greco in Staten Island. For an hour the two wrangled over the fee Greco would receive for bringing the Peruvian delegation to New York. Greco held out for $40,000, but Fogerty wanted to pay far less. Eventually they agreed that Greco would receive $15,000 or $20,000— no one would remember the exact sum—for his services. Even as they haggled, there was something else on Fogerty's mind. Both Jim Robinson and the Peruvian president, Alan García, were scheduled to be in Caracas, Venezuela, shortly for the inauguration of that country's president, Carlos Andres Perez. There had been some talk that Robinson and García might meet. If the two could sit down and discuss things, Fogerty felt sure they could cut a deal for Shearson to represent the Peruvian government.

"Tell you what, Tony," Fogerty proposed. "Take the money we agreed on for the meeting in New York, and I'll give you five thousand more to make sure Robinson and García meet."

It was probably the easiest five grand Tony Greco ever made.

Five thousand dollars, though, was minuscule compared to the ballooning checks Tony Greco was extracting from American Express via Cantor. By early 1989 Greco's payments on the Safra project were approaching $500,000 for a year and a half of work. Bob Smith had been approving the detective's vouchers since the previous spring. The bank's chief financial officer, Bob Budenbender, also approved at least one payment of $30,000 in Smith's absence, despite Cantor's unwillingness to explain who Greco was or what he was doing.

A half-million dollars, however, wasn't enough for Greco; he wanted more. The suggestion of paying the detective some kind of bonus was floated again that winter, apparently first by Cantor, who mentioned it to Smith. Smith, in a characteristic attempt to distance himself from scandal after the fact, recalls telling Cantor to discuss it with Freeman; Freeman recalls that he discussed the bonus with Smith himself.

Whatever the case, Freeman agreed that a bonus was in order, but the reasoning he would give was puzzling. "I had the sense that firing this guy might be a little risky," he said. Greco, Freeman notes, was in a position to know exactly which side of the ethical line American Express had been walking. "You want a soft landing for this guy," he said. "As time went on, I became suspicious without ever having anything to be suspicious about. In my mind, I thought it best if it were an amicable parting. That was a very major consideration in my mind...I mean, the guy had us over a barrel. We didn't know a lot about him, but he knew a lot about us."

Freeman's explanation stops just short of admitting he knew Greco had crossed an ethical line. Why, in fact, was the bonus paid? In the most conspiratorial hypothesis—if each of Greco's approaches was, in fact, orchestrated by Freeman or Robinson—the obvious reason was for a job well done. But if Freeman's version is accepted, then his explanation is a diplomatic way of calling Greco's bonus what it probably was: hush money.

And when American Express wanted someone to keep quiet, it could be very persuasive. The bonus Freeman and Smith approved for Greco that winter was an astounding $300,000, bringing the detective's total payments on the Safra investigation to nearly $1 million. (By several accounts, the final dollar figure later compiled by American Express attorneys was $937,000.) The bank's general counsel, John Junek, was directed to draw up a contract, and Greco received the bonus in two payments of $150,000 each.°

° Junek, for one, seems to have been determined to make sure American Express got its money's worth out of Tony Greco. When Bob Smith's Connecticut home was ransacked by burglars that February, Smith came to Junek to ask whether the lawyer knew anyone in law enforcement who might be able to track down his wife's lost jewelry. Junek, Smith recalls, suggested Greco. And apparently Greco was instructed to look into the case. A police detective in Fairfield, Connecticut, who investigated Smith's burglary, vaguely recalls "some guy American Express security sent up here to nose around. He didn't know what he was doing."

Before approving Greco's payment, Freeman says he discussed it with Jim Robinson. "I had the same kinds of conversations about this with Robinson [as with Smith]," Freeman said. "I said [to him], 'Greco wants additional compensation; he wants a hell of a lot of money, and Smith and I are talking about it.' Jim would say, 'Well, what's his base rate? What do you think?'

"I said, 'Well, it's the same old problem, you've got a guy working on sensitive stuff; you don't want to just cut him off....He's working his tail off for us.'

"Jim said, 'Okay, take care of it.'...He just shrugged his shoulders and said, 'Take care of it.'"

By the time Tony Greco received his bonus, the American Express probe appears to have been winding down. By early 1989 Cantor had tapered off her investigative work to concentrate on banking, where several colleagues acknowledge she was beginning to show real promise; her contacts in Venezuela and Mexico are said to have opened a number of doors for the bank. Even so, Cantor maintained a keen interest in Safra. Through friends at Shearson she had met *The Wall Street Journal*'s international banking reporter, Peter Truell. That winter Truell was surprised when, during one of their occasional chats on banking matters, the conversation took a surprising turn. "She asked me about Safra and the drug trade: did I know anything about it?" Truell recalls. "It came right out of the blue. [She said] she had been hearing stuff. I thought it was silly. I ignored it."

By all indications, Susan Cantor ignored little when it came to the Safras. After the death of Lily's son and grandson in Brazil that February, Bob Smith says she hurried into his office with a juicy rumor. "She came in and told me they'd been rubbed out," Smith recalls. "I told her, 'You're crazy.'"

As Edmond Safra's detectives nosed through Peru and Europe that spring, word of his anger reached the top floors of American Express Tower, where it set off curious maneuvers by many of those in a position to know the truth behind Safra's troubles, most notably Jim Robinson and Harry Freeman. On March 12, two months after three Peruvian messengers made their strange rounds in Lima, an unknowing Safra sat in his Fifth Avenue apartment and complained to Robinson about the articles he was seeing. Ten days or so later Robinson telephoned Safra and told him he had checked with Freeman and Smith—he mentioned them by name—and found no efforts by any American Express employees to besmirch Safra's reputation.

"[Robinson] did come to us," Smith recalls. "He said, 'You better check your people, Edmond is bitching.' I said, 'He's always bitching.' I talked to [Bob] Savage, I talked to Budenbender, I talked to Susan. Everyone said nothing, it's bullshit. Susan said, 'No, I haven't done anything, there's nothing going on.' She ranted and raved. She assured me she had done nothing wrong, had never done anything wrong...I went back to Robinson, and said, 'Not here.'"

Jim Robinson also discussed Safra's complaints with Freeman, who denied any knowledge of the stories. "As far as I know," Freeman says he told Robinson, "our activities are over." But Freeman told Robinson other things as well, as he described in an odd memo he sent to Bob Smith. On April 12, a month to the day after Robinson and Safra met, Freeman sent one of his little typewritten notes to Smith. It read, in part: "I spoke rather directly and sharply with JDR3 [Robinson] re talking with Susan Cantor about certain activities, tell [sic] him he was nuts to obtain any information regardless of its inherent interesting nature and regardless of whether the stuff they discussed were activities of a current nature or a year or two ago. As a matter of fact the [less] said by anyone the better. I am a little worried that SC [Cantor] may have a propensity to talk to gain recognition for her services."

Freeman's memo bears the unmistakable scent of a cover-up. But the memo, like the man himself, is maddeningly ambiguous on the subject of what Jim Robinson knew, and when he knew it. Did Freeman actually tell Robinson, as the memo implies, not to ask Cantor about the Safra investigation? That was how Bob Smith read it. "It just confirmed the feeling I had that Harry knew what was going on, he didn't want me to know, and he didn't want Jim to know," Smith recalled. Surprisingly, Freeman had no explanation for the memo. "I was worried about her being flamboyant," he noted of Cantor, a comment that suggests Jim Robinson was incapable of discerning the truth on his own. "I sensed the situation was getting serious," Freeman said a moment later, changing tack, "and the less Robinson knows from now on, the better."

That Freeman thought the situation was "serious" clearly doesn't jibe with his continuing pleas of ignorance—nor with Jim Robinson's. If Freeman's memo is accepted on its face, it raises a troubling question where

Robinson is concerned: would any responsible chief executive heed advice that he was "nuts to obtain any information" about an employee, in this case Susan Cantor, involved in such a sensitive, top-secret investigation? To any prudent listener, such a warning should have set off alarm bells and perhaps triggered an internal investigation. There is no evidence that any such investigation took place at that time. To this day, Robinson has maintained he knew nothing of contacts between Cantor or Greco and the press. Based on Freeman's memo, it is clear that Robinson remained ignorant only by intentionally doing so, by closing his eyes to a warning so blatant it was tantamount to a confession.

There is at least one other possible, and far more Machiavellian, interpretation of Freeman's memo. Could it represent a canny attempt by Freeman, a man perhaps anticipating an investigation into his activities, to lay a paper trail exonerating his boss, Jim Robinson? By telling Smith of his "warning" to Robinson, the clear subtext of the memo is that Robinson hadn't known what Cantor was doing. There are obvious problems with this reasoning: if Freeman were only attempting to exonerate his boss, why would he also make incriminating statements like "the [less] said the better"? Freeman, for one, dismisses the notion as ridiculous.

Whatever the case, it wasn't Jim Robinson's last involvement with Cantor in those critical weeks. According to an account confirmed by Bob Smith, it was during the company's annual bonus reviews that Robinson suggested to him that Cantor be included in a special "capital appreciation" bonus plan set aside for top executives, including the top fifteen or so executives at American Express Bank. The bonus plan, involving a lucrative three-year investment, had paid Smith $1.3 million the previous year, and would have provided hundreds of thousands of dollars for Cantor. Smith says he took Robinson's suggestion to his No. 2, Bob Savage.

"I went to Savage and said, 'Why don't we put Cantor in,'" Smith recalls. "Savage says, 'That's crazy.' He says, 'I don't think she should be in there. She's not senior enough. If Robinson wants her to be in there, why doesn't he do something with her [regular] bonus?' And so we did."

After Bob Savage's opposition, Smith says, Robinson personally authorized an increase in Cantor's normal bonus—from $150,000 to $200,000. The whole episode struck him as strange. "It was a little uncommon for [Robinson] to come back and say, 'You should put this woman into this plan,'" Smith says. "Because he knew as well as I did that she didn't fit in that plan. She didn't deserve it." Even the increase in her bonus seemed excessive to Smith. "He increased it by fifty grand, which was a third, a little bit high, I thought."

For once Harry Freeman agrees with Smith. "Jim was involved in a decision he shouldn't be involved in," says Freeman, who professes to know nothing about Cantor's bonus arrangements. "With a vice president, you don't usually involve the chairman. It's not a chairman-level decision. She must have asked him. I didn't."

That Jim Robinson would take the occasion in his famously crowded schedule to personally intervene in Susan Cantor's bonus deliberations suggests a degree of familiarity with her work beyond anything he or American Express spokesmen have been willing to admit. That aside, the obvious question remains: why did Robinson do it? Surely he would say it was Cantor's work at the bank, dealing with wealthy Latin American clients. That may be. But given Harry Freeman's concern—that Cantor "may have a propensity to talk"—a suspicious mind would be led to the conclusion that a more likely reason for Robinson's unusual largesse was a desire to keep Cantor, like Greco, calm, quiet, and happy.

It was in the midst of all this behind-the-scenes activity that Cantor and Greco first learned of Safra's investigation into their activities. The two probably heard of the developing probe from Jean Roberto in late March or early April 1989, after the French reporter received his first visit from the dizzy Australian "free-lancer" named Sandra Sutherland. Greco certainly knew by late April, when, after receiving his own visit from Sutherland, Jacques Bertrand of *La Dépêche* telephoned Greco from Toulouse and briefed him on his lunch with the sickly woman.

"[Greco] reacted immediately, and said, 'Of course she must be working for Safra,'" Bertrand recalled. As he recounts the story, a mischievous smile crosses the old Frenchman's face. "[Greco] was very curious about her," he says, "but as I didn't sleep with her, there was only so much I could say."[*]

It was at that point that Greco and Cantor's damage-control efforts swung into action. That same night, after Bertrand's call to Greco, the

---

[*] "The first day [Sutherland and Palladino] were involved in investigating me, I knew," Greco confirmed in a January 1992 interview. "I knew everything that was happening, when she was in Paris, in Toulouse, in Rome, in Switzerland."

first of two anonymous phone calls was delivered to Sutherland's Geneva hotel room by a deep-voiced man who wished to speak Italian: presumably this was Greco, identifying his two pursuers and making sure they were in Geneva.

The next day, the Swiss reporter Maya Jurt received a worried call from Cantor, a call she would remember vividly months later. "Cantor called me and said, 'There are two people, maybe three, coming to Geneva,'" Jurt recalls. "'One of them is a woman. She's an Australian, her name is Sandra Sutherland. And the guy she's with is Palladino. I think they're Safra people, and they're trying to get all the journalists who wrote about Safra in trouble.'"

It was the first time Maya Jurt had heard Sutherland's name. She remembers: "I said, 'Well, that's interesting, Susan, I'll certainly want to see her. Maybe I'll have them by for lunch.'

"[Cantor] said, 'No, don't!'

"I said, 'Susan, I'll see who I want. No one orders me who to talk to.' She got very excited. She tried not to sound excited, but it was clear she was. I said, 'Why shouldn't I talk to them?'

"She said, 'Because we believe they're CIA. It's believed they're either Safra people or CIA.' She stressed CIA. That made me laugh. I would love to have had CIA people in my home."

The very next day, just as Cantor had warned, Jurt received her first call from Sutherland. Later, after grilling her during a long lunch, Jurt found the Australian "free-lancer" a physical and mental wreck, almost too fatigued to carry on a coherent conversation. Jurt didn't believe for a minute Sutherland was an operative for Safra, much less a spy. "She's not CIA," Jurt told Cantor in a later conversation. "She's completely lost, completely neurotic."

Nine days later, on May 7, an irritable Tony Greco, consumed with curiosity about Sutherland's activities, arrived in Paris and stormed out of a Chinese dinner with Sutherland's translator, Sophie Hardy. Seventeen days after that, on May 24, Safra detectives secretly photographed Greco having lunch with Cantor at the fashionable New York restaurant Bouley.

By then the long drama was almost over. There was only time for one final act.

15

Babysitters don't make allowances for stakeouts.

Which explained why, on the morning of Saturday, May 27, Joe Mullen's daughter Bonnie sat with her five-year-old daughter in a convertible parked on Central Park West, watching Susan Cantor's building from a discreet distance. Her husband was supposed to have come pick up the fidgety little girl, but hadn't been able to make it. Cantor hadn't shown her face all morning, but Bonnie Mullen already was imagining what it would be like tailing her through the streets of Manhattan towing a five-year-old.

By and by she was relieved to see her white-haired father, Joe, puffing around the bend, sweating from his morning jog in the park. When his granddaughter Lizzie saw Mullen trudge up to the car, she burst out the door and sprang into his arms, brimming with news of her first stakeout. "Poppy! Poppy!" she cried. "I know what the woman looks like, and she hasn't come out."

The Mullen agency's stakeouts of Tony Greco and Susan Cantor were continuing in the warm afterglow of its success at linking the pair three days before. Surveillance teams had been outside Greco's home in Staten Island and Cantor's building on Central Park West that following day, but neither had been spotted. Greco hadn't appeared for a second day as well, prompting some concern among Mullen's people. But Susan Cantor had obliged, emerging from the front doorway of her Central Park West building a few minutes before eight Friday morning, strolling to a nearby parking garage, then driving downtown to American Express in a Mercedes.

Now, on Saturday morning, after Joe Mullen spirited off his granddaughter, Bonnie Mullen watched as Cantor left her building shortly before noon with her husband, who was carrying a garment bag. When the couple ducked into a taxi, she scribbled down the license-plate number, then eased her father's Dodge convertible into traffic to follow. Minutes later, Bonnie Mullen watched as Cantor's husband stepped out at the corner of Sixty-eighth Street and Madison and walked into a Giorgio Armani boutique. The cab, with Cantor still inside, cruised ten blocks north and double-parked as Cantor scurried inside an apartment building.

Twenty minutes later she reemerged, and a cab drove her to a store on Lexington Avenue, before she rejoined her husband at Armani. After twenty minutes the couple shuttled to Bloomingdale's. Bonnie Mullen scrambled out of her car to follow, but gave up after making sure Cantor and her husband were only shopping.

Tailing Susan Cantor through Bloomingdale's wasn't exactly high intrigue, but it was a routine the Mullen detectives would come to know well in coming weeks. Now confident their prey was squarely in his sights, Stanley Arkin gave the go-ahead to begin surveillance of American Express headquarters the following Monday, May 29. He emphasized to Joe Mullen the importance of keeping track of Cantor's comings and goings there.

Mullen's son Tommy drew the American Express duty most often. Many days he parked his black Maxima near one of Manhattan's ubiquitous Sabrett hot-dog stands, and before long had struck up a friendship with the vendor. When the man needed to run off for change or a restroom break, Mullen began volunteering to watch his stand. "Take your time, no hurry," Mullen would say. In his absence the detective could dish up five or ten hot dogs for American Express's hungry office workers, and found he was pretty good at it. For his trouble the vendor gave Mullen free franks and soft drinks. "Thanks for keeping such a good eye on the building," he said with a wry smile.

From time to time American Express security men would force Mullen to move his car, but only once did one of the guards question him. Thinking fast, Mullen said he owned a string of hot-dog stands, and was just checking up on the one in front of American Express. He feared exposure only once and ironically it wasn't from the company's security men. The detective was sitting in his car one evening waiting to follow Cantor home when a long black limousine pulled up alongside. A number of men jumped out so forcefully that one of the limo's doors banged into Mullen's car.

"What the hell?" the young investigator yelped. He turned just in time to see none other than Gerald Ford, the former President who served as an adviser to American Express's board of directors, emerging from the limo. Mullen's first instinct was to reach for the camera on his passenger seat, but as he did, his quick movement caught the attention of Ford's bodyguards—Secret Service men, Mullen assumed. Two of them peered intently into Mullen's car as he tried to look as innocent as possible.

Amazingly, news that Tony Greco had finally been tied to American Express failed to set off fireworks inside the Safra camp. Walter Weiner was pleased, but wanted more, much more. He wanted the whole episode laid directly on Jim Robinson's doorstep. Weiner knew Cantor had been tracked to a high floor at American Express headquarters, but how high?

"Can we get it to Jim?" he asked Arkin repeatedly. "Stanley, we've got to get this to Jim." Weiner was worried that without laying the smear campaign at the chairman's doorstep, their chances of frightening American Express into ending it weren't good. Arkin could only assure Weiner the detectives were hard at work, and that if a direct link to Robinson could be found, they would find it.

In Geneva, Safra's spirits too failed to lift, largely because of the continuing threat of hostile press. At least two Swiss journalists, including Philippe Mottaz, had stories in the works on money laundering in which, they made clear, Safra and Republic played some kind of role. Safra was so worried he had personally taken over supervision of the detailed replies Robert Siegfried was drafting to dozens of questions the Swiss journalists had lodged.

The identification of Susan Cantor did, however, serve to heighten the debate among Safra's aides about the best way to confront American Express. A direct appeal clearly hadn't worked, and Safra was leaning against filing a lawsuit that could drag on for months, maybe years, consuming more time, stirring up more controversy and allowing more opportunities for American Express mischief. What they needed was to end this quickly, cleanly, and quietly. Somehow there had to be a way to let Robinson's people know of their findings without revealing all Safra knew. Gershon Kekst had been toying with the idea of planting some kind of news story of their own for weeks, but so far hadn't found a way to do it cleanly. Then, during one of their endless meetings in Safra's penthouse office, Stanley Arkin broached a new idea.

For weeks Arkin had been mulling the possibility that what American Express and Tony Greco were doing constituted criminal fraud. Smearing a competitor to take his business, Arkin felt, amounted to a crime, and he had directed one of his associates to research the issue, not because he thought Safra would actually bring criminal charges, but because in the inevitable showdown to come he would need lots of ammunition to fire Jim Robinson's way. To a media creature like Arkin, disinformation was a fascinating legal issue. He wrote a monthly column on business crime in the *New York Law Journal*, and had already thought of discussing the matter in his forthcoming column that June. What if, Arkin asked the group in Safra's office, he illustrated his column with the real-life example of Edmond Safra and American Express?

Weiner's first reaction was horror. Arkin clearly loved the idea; it appealed to his sense of drama. But Weiner knew Safra would cringe at the publicity such a move would bring. He politely told Arkin he didn't think it advisable. "Fine," Arkin said, clearly annoyed. "I'll make it an apocryphal article."

"I still don't think it's such a great idea," Weiner ventured.

At that point Arkin got a trifle smug.

"Let me remind you, Walter, that it's my article," he said. "I'm not asking for your permission. I don't have to mention anyone's name. Therefore I can write anything I want." The meeting ended like so many others, with nothing decided, but later Weiner gave in to Arkin's strong feeling that his column was the right venue to fire their warning shot at American Express. To himself Weiner thought it was a waste of time.

The following Sunday afternoon Arkin sat down in a sunlit alcove of his Upper East Side apartment and wrote the column out in longhand on a yellow legal pad. One of his associates had already done the legal research; all Arkin had to do was pen the beginning and throw in some pithy remarks and the article would be ready to go. When he was done, Arkin had to admit he was pleased. He sent his final draft to Weiner's office for review the following week.

Weiner read the proposed column over the Memorial Day weekend while relaxing at his weekend home in a grove of pines near East Hampton. He was impressed; Arkin had pulled off the idea far more smoothly than he had thought possible. He called the lawyer and said so. Arkin was only worried about one phrase. He had described the chief executive in their apochryphal example as having a "Boy Scout" reputation. "You think that's too strong an identification of Robinson?" he asked.

"No," Weiner said. "I think it's fine." Privately he loved it.

No one but Arkin seemed to think the column had much chance of catching Jim Robinson's attention. Safra himself didn't even bother to read it. By the following week Arkin had submitted the article and all was set for publication. Everything seemed to be going according to plan. On the eve of their long-awaited shot across Robinson's bow, the only worrisome development came from the streets of New York, where the stakeout teams returned with bad news. Both Tony Greco and Susan Cantor had vanished.

Maya Jurt was surprised to hear Cantor's voice on the phone. The two women hadn't seen each other in almost two years, despite their occasional phone conversations. She was in Paris, Cantor said, and wanted to come to Geneva for a day to visit. Jurt tried to dissuade her, especially when Cantor mentioned she was pregnant and having problems keeping the baby. "I told her not to come," Jurt recalled. "It made no sense. She shouldn't be doing something like this if she was having health problems."

But Cantor insisted. On Sunday, June 4, Jurt hopped into her red Volvo and drove down to the train station in downtown Geneva to meet her. She was shocked by what she saw. "Susan looked awful," Jurt recalled. "She looked ten years older, very thin and drawn, just ravaged." Jurt drove her to the house and fixed a light lunch.

Cantor hadn't explained her visit, but Jurt was fairly certain it had to do with Sandra Sutherland's appearance in Geneva six weeks before. No doubt Cantor wanted to know whether her cover had been blown. And so Jurt was surprised when the Sutherland episode didn't come up during more than two hours of conversation. Instead the two women talked about private matters, about Cantor's health and Jurt's work and the problems Cantor was having remodeling a room in her Central Park West apartment. Only once did Cantor bring up Edmond Safra, to ask Jurt whether she planned to use some Mexican and French articles she had sent on.

"Look, forget it, Susan," the Swiss reporter said in her brusque style. "I can't use that stuff. It's not conclusive. It's just a bunch of newspaper articles. I'm not going to copy out of other newspapers."

Cantor, clearly fatigued, didn't argue, and soon it was time to catch her train back to Paris. It was the last time Maya Jurt would see her curious friend. After she had disappeared into the station, Jurt watched the trains pull away, wondering what would become of Susan Cantor.

Stanley Arkin's column was published the following Thursday, June 8. Beneath the headline "Disinformation: Competition by Mail Fraud," Arkin argued that the American business world was being undermined "by dirty tricks, reminiscent of Watergate." He then sketched out a hypothetical example to illustrate his point:

Apocryphally, I have the image of the chairman of a huge multinational corporation, sitting comfortably in his Manhattan offices with two of his closest advisers. On the agenda, aside from expanding the number of stock options he is to receive together with other and new perquisites, is the subject of how to deal effectively with a competitor that is making substantial inroads on the multinational tourist ship business. After going through all of the expectable and lawful means of resisting competition and enhancing market share, one of the participants comes up with a wholly new approach. "We have just the way to sink their ships," she says. "We'll leak it that their boats are unsafe, they are constantly being used to transport drugs and thus frequently subject to search by the Coast Guard and FBI during cruises, and that, moreover, there is a government investigation into whether that company is in fact Mafia-controlled. All enough, I am sure you will agree, to diminish passenger loyalty, and, likely to drive customers away from them and, perhaps, to us."

The chairman, being a canny fellow (someone who cherishes his Boy Scout image), says something innocuous like "Look into it," and tells her to report to one of his top deputies. She, just by chance, has a friend who is a former fringe member of the intelligence community and an effective Jack-of-all-dirty-trades. It does not take long, and in various unimportant or even fringe publications, of which there are countless numbers, stories began to appear suggesting that shipping company No. 2 is unsafe, a subject of federal investigation and a conveyor of narcotics. Company No. 2 is now compelled to devote extraordinary amounts of time, energy and money to prevent the outflow of customers— efforts, together with occasional successful defamation suits, that have so far been successful. But company No. 1 and its cast of dirty tricksters, operating with the acquiescence of the chairman, are a persistent lot. Thus, after an intensive investigation, company No. 2 now decides to go to the appropriate authorities and/or pursue further litigation....

Those behind the disinformation have, in fact, committed crimes—specifically, mail or wire fraud....

The article went on at length, detailing legal case after legal case that might tend to support the criminality of such deeds. Arkin was pleased. Now he sat back and waited for something to happen. Exactly what, he had no idea.

That weekend Tommy Mullen was sitting in his usual spot on Central Park West when he glimpsed Susan Cantor and her husband piling out of a taxi in front of their apartment building. Apparently they were returning from their vacation, or wherever they had gone. Through binoculars he could see they were wearing blue jeans and matching red-and-white Mickey Mouse T-shirts. Even through binoculars, he could also see that Cantor looked very tired.

For most of the following week Joe Mullen kept people on Cantor as she shuttled back and forth to work. Just as before, they reported back that she seemed a typical career woman, getting to work early, staying late, spending time with her husband. There was no hint she suspected she was being followed, although Tommy and Bonnie Mullen survived a close call Friday evening, June 16.

That night the two were following Cantor's Mercedes on the Upper West Side near her apartment. Cantor appeared to be looking for a parking space. Bonnie Mullen had just pulled her car to the curb and was calling her father on a portable phone when, out of the blue, Cantor's Mercedes pulled up directly beside her. Stunned, Bonnie quickly sat on the phone.

"Are you leaving?" Cantor asked.

It took a second for the question to register: she wanted their parking space.

"Nah, we just got here," Tommy Mullen said hurriedly from the passenger seat. "If you wait thirty minutes or so, we'll give it to you."

Cantor moved her car on, as the two Mullens took a very deep breath.

For a full week after Arkin's column, no one heard anything from American Express. Weiner wasn't surprised; he hadn't expected anything anyway. Gershon Kekst sent a copy of the article to an editor at *The Wall Street Journal*, hoping it would pique his curiosity; it didn't. Arkin told himself he would find some other way to get Jim Robinson's attention.

None of Safra's men knew it at the time, but from all indications no one at American Express had, in fact, noticed the article, at least not at first. But someone else had, someone who had been quietly watching the case from the periphery for two long years: Jules Kroll. From his corner office above Third Avenue, the canny detective hadn't forgotten about Susan Cantor and her avid interest in spreading word of Safra's supposed criminal activities. Having hired Tony Greco for two overseas assignments, Kroll also caught the occasional rumor of his work on behalf of American Express. Few people in the world could sniff out a dirty-tricks campaign like Jules Kroll.

When one of Arkin's friends pointed out the lawyer's curious column, Kroll didn't need to be told what Arkin was up to. The article bothered him, but not for any obvious reason. For years, as head of one of the world's top detective agencies, Kroll had fought to make corporate leaders recognize his trade as a legitimate part of their world, and he detested the occasional controversies that portrayed corporate investigations as dirty, sleazy work. It was bad for the industry. And what was bad for the industry was bad for Kroll's bottom line.

From the look of Arkin's column, it was clear American Express and Safra were headed for an Armageddon-style confrontation, a showdown nasty enough, perhaps, to do irreparable damage to the investigative field. Kroll knew almost everyone involved: Gershon Kekst, Robert Siegfried, Arkin, Ken Bialkin, Paul Knight, Peter Cohen at Shearson. There had to be a way, he told himself, that he could use what he knew to prevent the inevitable blowup.

It was a delicate situation. After mulling things over for several days, Kroll finally called Peter Cohen, and set an appointment to go downtown to lay out his concerns. After the two friends had talked it through, Cohen thanked Kroll and promised to look into the matter.

Several nights later, Tommy Mullen and his sister Bonnie were sitting outside American Express headquarters when they were stunned to see a familiar face striding up to the building's entrance. "What the hell?" Tommy Mullen blurted.

Tony Greco was wearing a brown suit and a white shirt, but disappeared inside American Express before either of the Mullens could get a better look. In a flash they called their father uptown. "You wouldn't believe who's down here," Tommy told his father.

Something was going on. They already knew Greco was back in town. Having vanished for the better part of a week, he had reemerged earlier that day in Staten Island. Mike Kohut had followed Greco's white Lincoln across the Verrazano Bridge to Brooklyn, where he had visited a woman they believed to be his mother-in-law. No one, though, had seen Greco heading for Manhattan.

The two Mullens were waiting outside American Express at ten o'clock that night when Greco and Susan Cantor walked out of the building together and slipped into Greco's car. With the two detectives following at a discreet distance, Greco drove uptown toward Central Park, where he pulled up across from Cantor's apartment building. Alerted, Joe Mullen slipped out of his midtown apartment to help watch the two American Express operatives as they sat in Greco's darkened car at the curb, talking. The three Mullens kept watch for nearly forty-five minutes, until Cantor finally stepped out of the car and walked into her building.

"God," Joe Mullen said. "What I'd have given to be a fly on the wall during that conversation."

Even as signs of activity stirred at American Express, Walter Weiner was busy orchestrating a rendezvous of a far different kind in Geneva. The *Minute* reporter, Jean Roberto, had managed to contact Republic through a Swiss intermediary and had requested a meeting. His newspaper was again up for sale, Roberto passed word, and the purpose of his approach was to see whether he might broker *Minute's* sale to Republic. Safra had no intention of buying *Minute*, but Weiner, thinking Roberto probably had something else in mind, ignored the advice of his ever-cautious Swiss lawyers and arranged a meeting at a lakeside restaurant in downtown Geneva.

The American attorney, Peter Mansbach, was flown in to meet with Roberto, who appeared nervous and unkempt as he kept a one o'clock lunch appointment that Wednesday, June 21. The two men, accompanied by a Swiss translator, took seats at an outdoor table and Roberto, exactly as they had suspected, immediately said he was not in a position to broker a sale of *Minute*.

Mansbach didn't care. He had only one thing on his mind. "Could you identify your sources of information?" he asked.

Yes, Roberto said after some hemming and hawing, leaving Mansbach with the clear impression that money might loosen his tongue. It was just the response Mansbach had expected. For the moment he ignored the suggestion and pressed for more on Roberto's source.

"Does the name Tony Greco mean anything to you?"

Roberto replied in French. "He's met Tony Greco," the translator said, "but he won't say anything else."

"Is Tony Greco the source?"

Roberto spoke again. "He won't say one way or another," the translator replied.

Mansbach pulled out a copy of the *Life* article with the American Express telltale and handed it to Roberto. The reporter said he recognized it but added that he had no idea how the telltale got on it. American Express, he said, had nothing to do with his articles. Roberto seemed increasingly nervous. The restaurant was growing crowded. He raised the issue of compensation.

"You want money?" Mansbach asked. "Tell us how you can be helpful."

Roberto seemed to think for a moment, then mentioned that other reporters were working on Safra stories and that they sometimes "cleared" these articles through him. He could stop these stories from appearing, Roberto said. Mansbach thought the idea sounded suspiciously like blackmail.

"Does Tony Greco work for American Express?" he asked again.

"No," Roberto said. "You people believe it's American Express, but it is not. There are important investigations going on in the U.S., by the government. These investigations will not let go."

"What investigations?"

"The FBI."

Mansbach could see this was going nowhere. "How else can you help me?"

Roberto repeated that he could stop any further stories, especially those appearing in Switzerland. Then he returned one final time to the question of money. A group of *Minute* employees, he said, was attempting to buy the newspaper for themselves. "I need one million dollars,"

Roberto said. "The newspaper requires one to one and a half million dollars. As soon as possible. We can buy it for that much."

Peter Mansbach had had enough. "What you've given me is worth shit," he told the reporter. "It's not worth a penny to me. You know what I want. I want your source. If you want money from us, give us your source."

And with that, Mansbach got up and left. In the weeks to come Roberto telephoned several times more, but no more meetings were immediately forthcoming. Of everything Roberto told him, Mansbach had grown excited only by the detailed description he had offered of an Australian free-lancer named Sandra Sutherland. The lawyer, who knew nothing of Safra's quiet use of detectives, hustled back to Walter Weiner and excitedly described the strange woman, convinced it was really Susan Cantor.

Weiner could only laugh. "Peter," he said, "you've just described one of our own operatives."*

Tommy Mullen was sitting outside Cantor's building on Central Park West a week later when he saw him: a big man, maybe six foot one, 210, short gray hair, in his early fifties. He was dressed casually, loitering on the sidewalk near the building's entrance. Mullen watched as the man paced up and down, glancing occasionally in his direction. One word flashed across Mullen's mind: *cop.*

More likely, Mullen thought, pondering the man's age, ex-cop. Sensing trouble, Mullen got out of his car and walked to the corner pay phone. He saw the man staring at him. Mullen stared back. After a moment, he dialed his service and checked for messages, pretending he was in an argument with his fiancée. All the while he kept glancing over at the man on the sidewalk.

Replacing the phone, Mullen returned to his car. He watched as the gray-haired man walked past and turned his back. Mullen was certain the man had just written down his license-plate number. Irritated, he gunned the Maxima's engine, pulled away from the curb, and drove

---

*This version of the Mansbach-Roberto meeting is based exclusively on Mansbach's recollection; Roberto insists he can't recall any such meeting in Geneva and denies soliciting money from Safra.

around the corner. Finding a second parking spot, he slipped on a pair of sunglasses, pulled on a sweater, and walked back toward Cantor's building. He peered around the corner. The man was still there. Returning to his car, Tommy Mullen picked up the mobile phone and called and briefed his father. "I'll bet you anything he's an American Express security guy," the younger Mullen said.

If their instincts were correct, both men knew it meant they had been spotted. Tommy Mullen decided to test his hunch by driving over to the parking garage Cantor frequented. If they were wrong, he could still pick her up when she came to get her car. Mullen hadn't been sitting in his new position long when he saw the gray-haired man come into view. Again he called his father. "The same guy's over here," he said. "I think we're made."

"Get out of there," Joe Mullen grumbled.

Quickly the elder Mullen alerted Stanley Arkin, who to his surprise, didn't seem to mind the new development a bit.

"Not at all," he told Mullen.

"Stanley, we have an American Express security guy here. He knows we're tailing her."

"So what?" Arkin said.

"That's okay?"

"Sure."

It was, in fact, almost Arkin's last hope to get Jim Robinson's attention. There hadn't been a word out of American Express since his column two weeks before. Arkin knew it wouldn't be long before someone at American Express put two and two together and realized what a tail on Susan Cantor must mean. He passed the news on to Walter Weiner, but otherwise let things lie, hoping to stoke the fire he was building under Robinson's seat.

The next evening, as Tommy Mullen followed Cantor's Mercedes up the West Side Highway, he noticed something different about her driving. Cantor seemed to be fiddling with her rearview mirror more than normal. She would slow down and accelerate for no apparent reason, erratically weaving through traffic. At stop lights, she actually turned her entire body around and stared out the car's rear window. It didn't take a genius to see that Susan Cantor suspected she was being followed. Mullen stayed well back, keeping the Mercedes in sight with a pair of binoculars.

The following morning, June 29, Cantor left for work at seven-thirty. There was no sign of American Express security. Mullen was behind her as she drove south toward Wall Street. He had changed cars in the hopes of avoiding notice. But if anything, Cantor's driving was even more erratic than the day before. Stop, start, fiddle with the mirror. It took forever to get downtown. Eventually Mullen drove on and waited for her at American Express. He was certain that if she hadn't seen him, she at least suspected she was being followed.

That was it. That afternoon at four-thirty Joe Mullen called and yanked his son off surveillance duties at American Express. He and Arkin had agreed it was finally time to call it quits. The stakeouts were over. With any luck, Arkin told himself, they had sent Jim Robinson a message.

And he was right. They had.

The deadline for responding to many of Philippe Mottaz's questions had come and gone, but Safra insisted on more time to review their replies, micro-managing every word. Friday afternoon, June 30, the day after the Mullen agency ended its stakeouts, he and Weiner were still poring over the replies in his office when the phone rang. Safra picked it up. It was his secretary.

"Jim Robinson?" he said.

Weiner saw Safra's eyes flare. He motioned for Weiner to pick up an extension. "Put him on," Safra said.

A beat.

"Hello, Edmond?"

"Hello, Jim." Very civil. It was early in New York, a few minutes before eight.

"Edmond, how dare your people follow our people!" Robinson blurted. He was as angry as Safra had ever heard him. Apparently Susan Cantor had indeed picked up her tail. "This has got to stop," Robinson went on. "They're being harassed." He mentioned detectives. "It's just not right. You have to put a stop to this."

When Robinson finished, Safra was silent. This was the moment he had been waiting an eternity for.

"Jim," Edmond Safra finally said, "we've got you. Don't tell me about following your people. We've got mountains of evidence of exactly what your people have been doing. I have all the proof right here in my pocket." Safra's voice rose as he spoke. "Before you hurt me again, Jim, believe me, I will hurt you far worse. I tell you, I have to protect my family, my blood! You want my blood? If you are looking for my blood, you are going to lose much more blood than I! We are going to start a major lawsuit, Jim, a major lawsuit! We've got you!"

This, clearly, was not what Robinson had expected.

"Well, uh, Edmond," he said, "I think I'd better talk to my people and call you back." The conversation was over in minutes.

"You were magnificent," Weiner said as they replaced their receivers. "Absolutely perfect. You couldn't have done better." Safra had bluffed only a little, conveying the impression that a lawsuit was to be filed any day. He couldn't believe Robinson's gall, calling about detectives when he knew full well his people had been defaming him for months.

"What chutzpah!" Safra exclaimed. "What balls he has, that son of a bitch!"

And that was how it ended, with a single, sharp bang and the ghost of a whimper.

Unknown to Safra, Stanley Arkin's column had already had its intended effect, though it took a circuitous route to bring it to Jim Robinson's attention. Alerted by Peter Cohen about his conversation with Jules Kroll, the general counsel Gary Beller had first touched base with Kroll, then wasted no time bringing in outside attorneys. Beller tracked down Ken Bialkin in Jerusalem and read him Arkin's column. Neither man was particularly worried that Safra would file criminal charges; just the fact that Arkin was making threats was cause for genuine alarm.

If there was any truth to Arkin's column, Gary Beller knew enough to identify the most likely culprit as Harry Freeman. When Beller confronted him with Arkin's column, Freeman was surprisingly sanguine. "I said, 'So what?'" Freeman recalls. "'We haven't done anything. He's not going to sue us. Don't worry about it.'" But Beller was worried, very worried—"scared shitless," in Freeman's words.

By the time Jim Robinson made his call to Geneva, Gary Beller had already summoned another outside attorney, a former federal prosecutor named John Martin, and asked him to see whether there was any substance to Arkin's thinly veiled threats. Among the first things Martin found when Harry Freeman turned over his files was a cache of scathingly critical articles about Edmond Safra.

Arkin left a Manhattan courtroom that Friday exhausted, wanting nothing but a little rest over the court's five-day July 4 recess. He had been in court defending a figure in the infamous Yuppie Five insider-trading ring since the middle of May and, for all the success of his law journal column, hadn't actually been giving the Safra case his full attention for weeks. But Safra was a difficult client to say no to. Hours after Weiner phoned with news of Jim Robinson's call, Arkin found himself on a flight to the south of France. He was coming, the lawyer told Weiner, but only if he got a day or two to relax on the beach.

The next morning a chauffeured Mercedes picked Arkin up at Monte Carlo's Hôtel de Paris and spirited him through the gates of La Leopolda, where an exuberant Weiner bounded out to meet him. The two men walked around by the pool, where Arkin saw Edmond and Lily and a small army of grandchildren frolicking around the water. As he and Weiner shared a bottle of wine over lunch in a room off the pool, Arkin could only reflect that this was a fine way to work. Afterward he slipped on a swimsuit and joined a bare-chested Safra by the pool, where the two men talked architecture, French wines, and the history of La Leopolda before coming around to what they sought in the impending talks with American Express.

What Safra wanted was simple. He wanted Jim Robinson to apologize for what his people had done, and he wanted him to do it publicly. Beyond that, they would push for damages of some kind in an effort to underscore the campaign's severity, and they would seek every piece of information they could find on what Cantor and Greco had done. Safra was preoccupied with the idea that there were reporters out there hovering over their typewriters readying new attacks on him, and he wanted American Express to detail every last journalist its people had spoken to in order to prevent those stories from seeing the light of day.

From all appearances, they would get what they sought. After their initial conversation, Jim Robinson had all but disappeared; instead he had designated Peter Cohen to handle most of the communications with Weiner and Safra. Both sides were playing things close to the vest, but in telephone conversations that stretched through that weekend, Cohen gave the clear indication that American Express felt some kind of apology was in order.

That night, after slipping back to his hotel to change into evening clothes, Arkin found himself standing on a veranda at La Leopolda with Edmond's brother Joseph, who was visiting from Brazil. The sun hadn't yet set, and Arkin, like another Safra lawyer so many months before, couldn't help but marvel at the beauty of the setting, the gardens cascading down the hillside below, the grand estates of Cap Ferrat and the sea beyond.

The setting was the last thing on Joseph Safra's mind. To Arkin it was clear Edmond's brother took the attacks by American Express every bit as personally as his sibling. He wanted to make sure Arkin understood the importance the family attached to defending its name. "This must be resolved quickly," he told Arkin. "Whatever you must do, do it. You solve this case, and you'll be amply rewarded."

At dinner Arkin was tickled to see that Safra's other guest was Sandy Weill, the former American Express president who, Arkin knew, was one of the lawyer Ken Bialkin's closest friends. Weill was blissfully ignorant of the weekend's other agenda and, over a banquet of veal and a fine Château Petrus, watched in wonder as Weiner and Safra shuttled back and forth from the table to Safra's office, where they continued the talks with Peter Cohen. Arkin could see that Weill was curious about his presence, but the lawyer resisted his attempts to find out what he was doing at the estate.

"Oh, Edmond and I are just friends," Arkin smirked, loving every minute of it. News of his being at Safra's side, Arkin hoped, would send one more message to Jim Robinson of the gravity with which his client regarded the defamation campaign. Afterward Safra led the group into a living room, where they sipped brandy and shared fine Cuban cigars. When Weill finally left, Arkin turned to Weiner and grinned. "How long do you think it'll take before he calls Kenny?" he wondered. "Eight minutes? Four?"

Monday Safra and his entourage scrambled aboard Republic's private jet for an early flight to Geneva. Arkin was less than pleased to lose his planned vacation on the beach, which Weiner dismissed with a shrug. "We'll make it up to you," he promised. The strategy sessions they planned for Geneva, however, never got off the ground. Philippe Mottaz struck again that evening, suggesting on Swiss television that Republic might be the focus of a DEA money-laundering investigation. A second reporter aired a short profile of Safra, all of which sent Weiner and other aides into frantic damage-control efforts that consumed all the next day.

By Wednesday Arkin was back in New York, where he spent the day in court before hustling off to the Grill Room at the Four Seasons for a dinner appointment with John Martin, the attorney American Express had brought in to investigate Safra's complaints. The mood was tentative, as both men maneuvered to ascertain the cards the other held. American Express, it was clear, wanted to find out just how much Safra knew about its little smear campaign. "Can you give us anything, anything at all?" Martin wondered at one point.

"I can give you one name," Arkin offered.

"What's that."

"Tony Greco." From the look on John Martin's face, Arkin could tell it was all he had to say.

Afterward things moved swiftly. Over the next two weeks Arkin met almost daily with the two American Express lawyers, Martin and Bialkin, roughing out the outlines of a formal American Express apology to Safra. To his credit, Jim Robinson hadn't attempted to deny what Cantor and Greco had done. Rather, he decided to come clean, make a fast and thorough apology, and hope the whole matter would blow over in the late-summer media doldrums. The fact was, his people had been caught red-handed, and in a drawn-out fight American Express had as much to lose—maybe more—as Safra.

In talks between their attorneys, however, Robinson steadfastly refused to give in to Safra's demands for a detailed accounting of every journalist Cantor and Greco had spoken to. No matter how much Arkin pushed, Robinson for some reason wouldn't budge. The most nettlesome question of all—whether American Express would pay a cash settlement—was handled quickly, in a single phone call between Safra and Robinson. The two agreed that American Express would pay $8 million to four different charities to be nominated by Safra; Safra himself, as incorrectly reported in numerous press accounts—including one in *The Wall Street Journal* by the author—never received a dime of settlement money from American Express, not even to cover an estimated $4 million in fees run up by his lawyers and investigators.

By the end of July the negotiations were complete. A public announcement was prepared, and American Express had readied its spin-control experts to contain the public relations damage. A press release was issued on Friday afternoon, July 28, the favored timing of so many pieces of negative corporate news, the better to bury it in little-read weekend papers. The highlight was an exchange of letters between Robinson and Safra. Robinson wrote,

Dear Edmond,

Information has come to my attention that certain persons acting on behalf of American Express began an unauthorized and shameful effort to use the media to malign you and Republic National Bank of New York. I recently saw media stories which appeared in various parts of the world following this effort, and I regard them as untrue and defamatory.

The entire matter saddens me personally. This effort was totally contrary to the standards of conduct of American Express as well as common standards of decency and ethics. While I believe in vigorous competition, there is no room in our organization for actions which could cause unjustified harm to a competitor. Therefore, I want to apologize to you and your organization.

I have taken the actions necessary to assure that this effort has been terminated and that, in the future, no one affiliated with American Express will be a party to such behavior against you or your banks. I have informed key officers of American Express that this conduct will neither be condoned nor accepted here and must never be revived in any form.

You have a well deserved excellent personal and professional reputation, and you and Republic National Bank of New York are highly regarded throughout the world. I respect your professional abilities as well as the very substantial past records of Republic National Bank of New York and its management. This has been reinforced to me by our experience with Trade Development Bank. Your reputation as a preeminent banker has been achieved with enormous effort over a lifetime, and so I appreciate even more how painful it must have been for you to endure these baseless attacks.

As a gesture of our respect for you and of our apologies and to start off a new chapter between our institutions, American Express will, at your request, contribute $1 million each to the following charities of your choice: United Way of America, Anti-Defamation League of B'nai B'rith, Hôpital Cantonal de Genève and the International Red Cross....

With great respect and the highest regards, personally and professionally,

Sincerely,

Jim Robinson

Dear Jim [Safra responded],

I very much appreciate your letter of today's date and the spirit in which it was written. I believe you had no personal involvement in or knowledge of the false rumors and innuendos about me and Republic National Bank of New York. I am grateful that you have uncovered and have brought to a halt these irresponsible and unauthorized acts of certain people acting on behalf of American Express and that you have agreed to take appropriate action to prevent any continuation or recurrence.

You are a person of decency and honor.

Sincerely,

Edmond Safra

The initial pr ss coverage, first in Saturday's daily papers, listed *Minute, Hoy,* and several other of the press accounts. But there was no mention of Cantor or Greco or Freeman or exactly what the unnamed "persons acting on behalf of American Express" had done to influence the stories. That weekend the company's best spin doctor was Jim Robinson himself, who, while candidly admitting the company's mistake, downplayed the announcement in "background" interviews with major business publications.

Still, there was no blunting the power of the more thorough articles when they hit Monday, and matters only grew worse when reporters discovered that American Express was lying about the amount of the settlement. While Robinson had agreed to pay Safra's charities $8 million over two years, his letter only seemed to mention $4 million, an impression confirmed by company spokesmen under pressure from lawyers trying to diminish the likelihood of shareholder lawsuits. The company's top p.r. man, Larry Armour, later insisted it was a harmless misunderstanding, but in fact it was anything but. As his boss at the time, Harry Freeman, recalls: "Larry Armour, who's an honest guy, came to me and said,

'I've been asked to put this out and it's just not true; within hours, we're going to be chastised as liars.' I said, 'Larry, you can either put it out or resign.'" According to Freeman, Armour put it out rather than lose his job.

The clumsy subterfuge only intensified the pressure inside American Express to find a scapegoat. Freeman would never forget the moment he walked into a meeting of lawyers in Robinson's office to discover, purely by the cold stares he received, that he was to be the one. The realization stunned him; the lawyers wanted his head. The following Tuesday night he took the call he half-expected from an emotional Jim Robinson. "Harry, I think you're going to have to take a leave of absence," Robinson began, apparently fighting back tears. "I think this investigation is growing more serious."

Robinson choked up before he could finish. His wife, Linda, came on the line. "Jim can't talk anymore," she said. "This investigation is getting pretty serious. You're going to have to take a leave of absence until this thing is cleared up. Jim is so broken up he can't talk about it."

Freeman talked over matters with his wife and his personal lawyers. He was disgusted. Yes, he felt he bore some responsibility for what had happened, but all of it? Why weren't the lawyers hounding Smith or Robinson? Of course he knew the answer to that. He also knew what he owed Robinson, and what he owed American Express. He decided there was only one thing to do.

Two days later Harry Freeman fell on his sword, announcing his retirement, to take effect no later than year's end. "Mistakes were made on my watch," he wrote in a letter to Robinson, "and accordingly I believe my decision to retire, while painful, is appropriate. I want to apologize for this unfortunate episode to you, the Board and all my colleagues at American Express."

Robinson announced his old friend's decision in a memo to the company's 100,000 employees. "Harry," Robinson wrote, "is a unique executive with the capacity to think strategically, deliver innovative approaches to complex problems and lead change....One of Harry's great strengths has been his ability to assemble and motivate highly creative people, empowering them to perform as an extraordinary corporate support staff....Harry is much loved throughout our organization, and like others, I will miss his wisdom and great sense of humor."

All across Wall Street Freeman's decision was greeted as a brave act from a loyal soldier. "This is a very sad event, because Harry is a world-class professional in his area. He's in a class by himself as a public affairs guy," opined Kenneth Roman, chairman of American Express's major advertising agency and the man who briefly replaced Freeman. "It's hard to speculate on what happened. He has excellent judgment and high integrity. He makes things happen. But you can't make everything happen perfectly."

Immediately after announcing his retirement Freeman and his family disappeared on a three-week African vacation. Upon his return he was surprised to find himself the object of a strange esteem, respect for a man who had taken a bullet for his general. By year's end he had opened an office in Washington, hanging out a shingle as a business consultant, and busied himself heading a coalition of U.S. businesses active at the GATT talks in Geneva. That fall Freeman bravely told a number of friends he thought his reputation had actually been enhanced by the whole episode. Not for months would his feelings begin to change.

Whether it was an Exxon supertanker spewing oil onto the beaches of Alaska, E.F. Hutton wringing its hands over a massive check-kiting conspiracy, or one of the countless defense contractors grilled on "60 Minutes," American companies embroiled in dirty little scandals have invariably surrounded themselves with a crew of savvy damage-control experts: public relations representatives to "spin" press coverage, Washington lobbyists to argue their points on Capitol Hill, and highly paid New York lawyers to fight the inevitable class-action lawsuits from shareholders.

During the 1980s corporate America added a new weapon to its damage-control arsenal, the well-publicized internal investigation. The idea, of course, was to show the public—as well as shareholders, inquisitive prosecutors, and even congressmen—that the company's executives were cleaning their own laundry, before someone did it for them. The blue-chip "independent investigators" who oversaw these probes were brought in from outside, though they were almost always attorneys paid by the company and thus, many critics charged, firmly under the company's control. It was a position so open to compromise that some lawyers disdained the very idea of company-sponsored probes. The problem, as Arthur Liman put it, was, "You're put in the position of maintaining independence in circumstances where your credibility is subject to suspicion because you're being paid by the company."

It was no coincidence, critics felt, that these company-sponsored investigations inevitably cleared senior managers of wrongdoing. E.F. Hutton, for instance, hired former attorney general Griffin Bell to head its 1985 probe of check-kiting allegations; no one was exactly stunned when Bell, whom Hutton paid more than $800,000, or roughly $1,700 an hour, cleared top managers of criminal liability and blamed instead a handful of their mid-level subordinates. It was a pattern repeated at company after company. For lawyers the business was so profitable that at least one firm, New York's Milbank, Tweed, Hadley & McCloy, established an entire department for the purpose of conducting corporate investigations.

In the wake of the Safra settlement, American Express, too, went this route, bringing in not one but three outside law firms, a crew of accountants, and a committee of board members to sort through what had happened. The directors most involved in the probe, insiders say, were the committee's chairman, Charles Duncan, the former energy secretary, and Vernon Jordan, the Washington attorney and former civil rights leader who, Harry Freeman complained, seemed less interested in getting at the truth than shielding Jim Robinson from embarrassing disclosures.

Much of the real work was handled by the lawyers, led by Ken Bialkin and the newcomer, John Martin. Directors themselves, it is said, interviewed only four people: Harry Freeman, Jim Robinson, Bob Smith, and Susan Cantor. The lawyers interviewed others, including Bob Budenbender, Jim McGrath, Larry Ricciardi, and Paul Knight. According to one source, one of John Martin's associates traveled to Paris to interview Tony Greco. The detective's payment vouchers were assembled and totaled, and the committee was briefed on Robinson's involvement in the bonuses paid to both Greco and Cantor.

It's impossible to tell how vigorous the committee's investigation really was. Its report has never been released. Neither the company nor any of the directors or lawyers who worked on the probe have discussed it publicly. But there is reason to believe that American Express's investigation was less than comprehensive. There is no indication that anyone at American Express spoke with journalists approached by Greco or

Cantor—not Jean Roberto, not Maya Jurt, not Jacques Bertrand—or made any serious efforts to discern the extent of their journalistic contacts; before being told by the author, company attorneys didn't even know Cantor had represented herself to European journalists as working for *Time* and the *Washington Post*. There is no indication that anyone at American Express went to Peru to investigate what happened there. Nor does anyone appear to have seriously investigated the extent to which Greco may have poisoned FBI files with tips about Safra.

Arthur Liman, the New York attorney who counts American Express among his clients, acknowledged in a February 1992 interview with the author that the company's internal investigation was limited by design. "As I understood what John [Martin] was trying to do, it was not the kind of investigation that you've conducted as a journalist—how did this operation work—he was trying to make assessments as to managerial responsibility for it," Liman said. "The things that were important to him were contacts [between Cantor and Greco] and either Harry or Jim, people like that."

Several people interviewed as part of the probe, meanwhile, say the questions they answered hardly amounted to a grilling. "My session with Bialkin couldn't have lasted more than fifteen minutes, and with the board, no more than a half hour," recalls Bob Smith. "I wasn't too surprised: from day one Robinson and Bialkin had told me this was Harry's problem, not mine."

Freeman, who would be surprised by the committee's report for reasons of his own, was mystified by the lawyers' seeming lack of interest in his activities. No one, he claims, even asked him to explain the April 12 memo he had written about his discussions with Robinson. "The sessions I had with the lawyers were extremely brief, and extremely general," Freeman recalled. "I was always wondering why they weren't asking me more probing questions."

The thoroughness of the committee's work is doubly important because some of the matters it investigated could have criminal implications. First and foremost are the repeated suggestions—by Victor Tirado, among others—that Greco paid sums of money to have articles published. While no proof of such payments has been made public, there may well be evidence in American Express's files, as an August 1989 internal memo from Freeman to Ken Bialkin suggests.

"You've told me," Freeman wrote, summarizing their conversations to date, "that there were sufficient materials developed by John Martin to suggest that there was more than a remote possibility of either false or misleading information being supplied to the media about Safra and *possible payments to the media* [italics added], the net of which is that we would have protracted litigation with uncertain outcome should Safra choose to sue."

Freeman's memo, written just days before his retirement was announced, suggests that the possibility of improper payments was strong enough that it played a role in Robinson's decision to capitulate to Safra. Putting aside the obvious ethical question, would such payments be illegal? Answer: only if made to government officials, say attorneys familiar with the Foreign Corrupt Practices Act. Thus, while American Express could brush aside any money slipped to a reporter, payments made to officials of the Peruvian government—who, after all, did Greco some tremendous "favors"—could fall outside the law. And of course, if such payments were illegal, American Express might also face legal complications for failing to turn over any evidence to the proper authorities.

One of the thorniest questions the committee faced was whether to take legal action against those involved, in hopes of recouping the $8 million American Express was to pay Safra's charities. The committee ultimately judged a suit not to be in the shareholders' best interest, citing among other factors the bad publicity it would bring. In any suit, it concluded, Freeman would simply insist he had relied on what Cantor told him of her activities; Cantor, if sued, would claim she was following Freeman's instructions. Why the board didn't sue both of them is unclear.

In fact, the only punitive action American Express seems to have taken following the Safra settlement was to cut—one American Express executive says eliminate—Susan Cantor's bonus for the year. "Susan became a member of the lepers' colony," one colleague recalled. "People didn't want to be seen with her. You didn't go into her office for fear you'd get a call from Gary Beller." Still, Cantor, after a lengthy maternity leave, kept her lucrative job at the bank, almost certainly, colleagues felt, because of senior management's fear that if fired she would tell all.

To no one's surprise, the committee's report cleared Jim Robinson of any wrongdoing. Neither Smith, Freeman, nor Cantor asserted that the chairman had any direct knowledge of Greco's work with journalists. Still, Freeman, who was able to read the report only after repeated requests, said he was surprised by the lack of focus on Robinson's role. The report, he said, "was basically an accusatory document of me. There's no mention of Jim Robinson in it, which I thought was bizarre. There's no mention of Smith."

At calmer moments Freeman admitted he wasn't so surprised. An able corporate gamesman himself, he came to view the company's investigation as exactly that, a game. "What happened was a game common in Corporate America called 'Protect the CEO,'" Freeman said. "It was designed to protect the corporation, the chairman, and lay the blame on me. It was a big mistake." He faults company lawyers for this rather than Robinson, though he believes the chairman of American Express should share the responsibility for an investigation he himself initiated. "There were two failures of oversight," Freeman says of Robinson. "Mine and his. Me overseeing Susan. And Jim overseeing me."

Freeman, in fact, suggests that Robinson was in a far better position to deduce any wrongdoing on Cantor's part than he. "After she joined the bank, she spent much more time with Robinson; they were always in South America together, because she was in business development," Freeman says. "Susan has a huge propensity to talk about what she's doing. By the nature of her personality. She's a very talkative person. She was also very worried that she may not get ahead in the company because few people knew what she was doing. She was always telling people what she did...And Jim, it should be pointed out, is very interested in this kind of stuff, this detective stuff. He found it fascinating. He was always open ears. Robinson loved to sit down and listen to all this stuff. I didn't think this was the greatest idea in the world, let me tell you. [But] he and Susan talked about Safra all the time.

"Knowing her, knowing Robinson, there's no question, she filled his ears with all kinds of information on these trips aboard the plane. I know Jim. He felt very strongly about Safra. It's a one hundred percent probability that she briefed Jim, in detail, about what she was doing."

Other former insiders, including Bob Smith, who believes he was "set up" by Robinson, agree that the chairman must have known far more about Cantor's work than he has admitted. "There are three alternatives," Bob Smith said. "Jim didn't know about it, Jim knew everything about it, or Gary Beller told Jim about it" after being warned by Larry

Ricciardi. "In my opinion, the last is what happened. Beller went to Robinson, and from what I know of Beller, he must have told Robinson. Beller is too much the organization man—cross all the *t*'s, dot all the *i*'s—not to have told Robinson. Robinson must have known. Nothing else is possible. If you ever put one of these guys on the stand, you'd know for sure. It's the only way you'd know, though."

Another former top American Express man agrees with Smith's scenario. "Beller was warned repeatedly about what Freeman and Cantor were up to," this executive said. "I have to believe Beller went to Jim and said, 'Knock it off.' I have to believe that. Nothing else makes any sense."

Still, it remains possible that no one mustered the courage to alert Jim Robinson to the full extent of the company's actions against Safra. If so, it wouldn't be the first time in recent American Express history that controversy has arisen over what subordinates did or didn't tell Robinson, who since the resignation of Roger Morley in 1979 has harbored a reputation for dealing harshly with errant subordinates while surviving such contretemps himself. When American Express's vaunted earnings record was shattered in 1983 after the explosion of unexpected losses at Fireman's Fund, Robinson claimed he had been "blind-sided" by the unit's managers, who he said hadn't told him of the mounting problems, much less of the accounting sleight of hand that had stoked the unit's profits; Fireman's Fund executives claimed they had been warning Robinson for months. In the end, it was Fireman's Fund management, not Robinson, who took the blame—and lost their jobs.

A strikingly similar scenario was repeated in the fall of 1991 when Robinson again stunned the investment community by unveiling major losses in the new Optima Card. Once again the company brought in outside lawyers and announced that it was launching an internal investigation into whether mid-level managers at Optima's Jacksonville, Florida, operations center had quietly covered up runaway defaults among card holders. When the probe was completed, senior management in New York was again judged to be blameless, a number of Optima executives resigned, and securities analysts were left shaking their heads at Robinson's inability to recognize internal problems before they blew up in his face. "My understanding," one analyst told *The Wall Street Journal*, "is that senior management has little tolerance for bad news, and this is the latest in a series of incidents where operating managers tried to forestall the inevitable."

The same questions are raised, though far more pointedly, by Robinson's performance in the Safra episode, which unlike the scandals at Fireman's Fund's far-off headquarters in California or Optima's Florida operations center took place right under the chairman's nose, among his personal staff. In the end, one reaches the conclusion that Greco's approaches to the press probably weren't personally directed by Robinson. They resulted from something far more frightening: three overzealous personalities—Freeman, Cantor, and Greco—handed all the resources of a $25 billion conglomerate, allowed to run amok on an ill-conceived "investigation," and armed with an attitude so aggressive it bordered on malice.

Jim Robinson must bear a good deal of responsibility for this, an investigation he initiated and monitored, however closely. It was Robinson, after all, who received briefings from Cantor and Freeman on its progress, who knew and often inquired about Greco's findings, who authorized Freeman to conduct "background" talks with reporters about Safra's shortcomings, who personally oversaw bonuses for both Greco and Cantor—but who nevertheless claimed total ignorance that the two were passing on their "findings" to reporters. Either Jim Robinson knew and approved of what his aides were doing, or he knew he didn't want to know. It's hard to say which is worse.

Epilogue

The Monday after news of American Express's settlement with Edmond Safra broke in late July 1989, I returned to my desk at *The Wall Street Journal* after a six-month leave of absence. Neck-deep in finishing my first book, *Barbarians at the Gate*, written with my *Journal* colleague John Helyar, I all but ignored the strange story that had interrupted the newsroom's summer slumber. I had never met Harry Freeman, and didn't especially care when he resigned.

After a flurry of articles, the controversy over what American Express had done died down. Only one publication, *New York* magazine, published a feature-length analysis of the case, and its reporting, though typically solid, was unable to penetrate the cloak of silence that had immediately fallen over events; neither Susan Cantor nor Tony Greco was identified by any publication, nor was there any hint of how the articles on Safra had been planted.*

My editor, Byron E. Calame, first broached the idea of an in-depth investigation of the case that fall. I demurred, preferring to develop my

---

* The first journalist, as far as I know, to hear either Greco's or Cantor's name in connection with the Safra case was Daniel Hertzberg of *The Wall Street Journal*, a Pulitzer Prize winner who, having been elevated to senior editor, passed Greco's name to me in early August 1989. Among the first journalists to delve deeply into the case was Kurt Eichenwald of *The New York Times*. Eichenwald, I'm told, pursued the story for several months, unearthed a good deal of information about Cantor and Greco, but, for whatever reason, was unable to persuade his editors to print what he had found.

An entire year passed before Greco's and Cantor's names surfaced publicly, in a passing reference buried deep into a novella-length article about American Express by writer Connie Bruck in *The New Yorker*. Bruck's article was to have an ironic footnote. Shortly after it appeared I heard a rumor that Bruck had been a college chum of Cantor's at Barnard. When I asked a mutual friend to telephone Bruck and ask about this, she denied it, until it was pointed out that Cantor in those days had gone by her maiden name. When Bruck made the connection, I could hear her scream of recognition ten feet away.

own ideas. Again and again over the next six months he urged me to look into what had happened at American Express. Each time I begged off. I knew a few of the people involved in the case and had gotten cold-shouldered when I asked about the chances of unearthing the full story. Finally, in June 1990, almost a year after the announcement, Calame came to me with an offer: he and the *Journal's* top two editors, Norman Pearlstine and Paul Steiger, had persuaded a person knowledgeable about the Safra affair to discuss it. It was an offer I literally couldn't refuse.

My *Wall Street Journal* story was ultimately published in September 1990, following a four-month investigation, and despite a determined effort by American Express spokesmen and attorneys to squelch my interest. The company had retained Arthur Liman, and Liman threat-ened me with a libel suit if the *Journal* published anything linking Jim Robinson to the scandal. Harry Freeman likewise hired a big-name libel lawyer who made similar threats. "This," Liman suggested, referring to my investigation of Robinson's role in the case, "is a textbook case of what libel is all about."

After the article's appearance American Express didn't sue the *Jour-nal*, but by the following spring several stockholders had sued American Express, charging Robinson, Freeman, Cantor, and the board of direc-tors with "gross mismanagement" in connection with the Safra investiga-tion. Their attorneys made clear the suspicions they would attempt to prove: "We believe the campaign couldn't have been done without the consent and approval of Jim Robinson," charged the leading shareholder lawyer, Richard Greenfield.

Robinson commissioned Liman to fight the suits and, it was widely believed, make sure that no discovery proceedings would succeed in unlocking American Express files on the affair. Liman opened talks with a number of the shareholder attorneys, leaving several with the impres-sion that if they dropped the litigation American Express would consider paying a large settlement. To date, Liman has managed to tie up the suits, which, more than a year after their filing, have yet to progress to discovery.

By the time the suits were filed, I had begun research for this book. Unlike my first such project, *Barbarians*, in which many people wished to share their impressions, this one proved a far more difficult, and at times distasteful, endeavor. American Express stonewalled me at every turn, attempted to silence people who were speaking to me, and generally did everything it could to make getting at the truth as difficult as possible. Somewhat as she had Safra, Susan Cantor reportedly bad-mouthed me to mutual acquaintances; I could only laugh when one of them relayed her comment that I had taken $1 million from Safra in a Swiss bank account. Harry Freeman broke two years of public silence on the matter to talk with me, but his memory lapses proved frequent. Bob Smith repeatedly changed his story to admit greater involvement as I returned to him with new evidence. After nearly two years, I believe I have gotten as close to the truth concerning Bob Smith's involvement as I ever will.

Early on, a number of ironies became apparent. The first was how unnecessary the American Express campaign against Safra had been. Within months of Safra Republic's opening in Geneva in March 1988, Bob Smith concluded that Safra was not stealing back his former TDB depositors anywhere near the extent American Express had so vividly feared. Not only did American Express Bank not lose a significant number of deposits to Safra that year, its deposit base actually grew. By year's end Smith realized that the danger posed by Safra had been hugely, and foolishly, overestimated.

As I delved deeper, some sources seemed awed by the scope of the effort against Safra, which included articles in more than a dozen countries on three continents. But as I followed Cantor and Greco's trail through France, Switzerland, and Peru, what I found surprising about the "campaign" was that it wasn't much of a campaign at all. By my count—and I can't claim to know every journalist to whom the American Express operatives spoke—Greco passed stories on Safra to a grand total of five people (not counting the FBI) over the course of an assignment lasting nearly two years. Cantor can be linked to perhaps five more over a period of two and a half years.

Just as surprising was how much negative publicity those few contacts were able to generate. The stories Greco influenced, passed from journalist to journalist around the world, can be traced to articles published in France, Switzerland, the United States, Mexico, Peru,

Argentina, and Uruguay.* Almost single-handedly, though helped by the Shakarchi Trading scandal in Switzerland, he managed to create a cloud of criminality around Safra that far surpassed the whispered suspicions that had trailed him over the years.

Much to Safra's dismay, that cloud has proven remarkably durable, as evidenced by articles about his supposed criminal ties that continue to this day. They appear every few months now—in February 1990 it was an Arab-language newspaper in London, in February 1991 West German television—forcing Safra's aides to scramble to gain retractions. Not even Walter Weiner, the most militant of Safra's aides, believes American Express or Greco is planting the continuing items. Rather, Weiner and others realize the discredited American Express stories remain in journalists' files the world over, lying dormant until a reporter unfamiliar with American Express's campaign comes upon them and incorporates them into a story. A November 1990 incident in Buenos Aires was typical. When a Republic employee was found dead in a city park, an apparent suicide, the respected newspaper *Clarin* reported that police were investigating whether the death might be linked to published allegations of Republic's involvement in money laundering. Citing an article in the tabloid *Cronica*, the newspaper rehashed all the old allegations of a DEA warning about Republic. Only after Safra's lawyers loudly complained did *Clarin* publish a retraction.

Sometimes the stories come in waves, one article begetting another as Safra lawyers race from place to place to stamp them out like pesky grass fires. One such wave began in April 1990, when three Guatemalan newspapers reported that during a crackdown on illegal exchange houses, police searched two American banks suspected of laundering drug money. One of the two banks was identified inaccurately as Republic National Bank of New York. How the mix-up occurred was never explained, but the

---

*The only major news items that remain unexplained are those that appeared in Argentina in the spring of 1989, when two radio stations, a television outlet, and a major newspaper all carried stories of a DEA warning on Safra's banks. The newspaper story was uncredited, and officials at all four outlets are at a loss to remember, much less explain, the stories on Safra. At least two journalists with interests in Safra, Juan Gasparini and the Spanish reporter Victor Ducrot, have contacts in the Buenos Aires press, but both deny any knowledge of the stories. One possible link between the four accounts was the three major Argentine news wires, but officials at each of the three deny carrying any stories on Safra.

The Argentine accounts were carried just six weeks after Safra dossiers were circulated in Peru, but despite the similarities in fact, no link between the two outbreaks can be proven. As for Tony Greco, his American Express Card receipts indicate he was in Lima at the end of February, immediately prior to the Argentine stories, but they contain no suggestions that he made any stops in Buenos Aires.

reports were clearly false: Republic, as Guatemalan government officials later acknowledged, had no office or operations in Guatemala.

Before the facts could be straightened out, the stories were reprinted in a Panamanian paper. Three days later they were rebroadcast by the French news service, Agence France-Presse, whose dispatch was picked up and amplified by a paper in Antwerp. "The Banker, Safra, Named in Money Laundering Affair," the Belgian paper's headline read. The story was also carried by *Le Soir* of Brussels, which mentioned the settlement with American Express as well as stories in Italy's *L'Espresso*, *L'Hebdo,* and the book published by the Swiss politician Jean Ziegler. "In the final analysis, is there any connection between Edmond Safra's bank and any laundering network?" *Le Soir* asked. "The Guatemalan authorities claim, without a shadow of doubt, that there is."

The coverage ended only when a Safra lawyer, Alan Levine, hustled to Guatemala City and persuaded the government minister who had misidentified Republic to issue a statement saying he had been mistaken. Eventually both Belgian papers and the French news wire printed retractions.

Suspicions about Safra also remain alive among a group of international journalists who have chosen to downplay American Express's role in spreading the rumors. When the BCCI banking scandal broke in the summer of 1991, Safra and his aides held their breaths, convinced that one of these writers would attempt to link Republic to it. Almost inevitably, a flurry of reports suggesting vague ties between Safra and BCCI appeared, first in Barcelona, then in Montevideo, Uruguay, before being picked up by a Buenos Aires radio station. Weiner swung into action, quickly ascertaining that all the articles had been written by the Argentine expatriate Juan Gasparini.*

---

*One of the allegations against Safra that is all but impossible for a journalist to prove or disprove is his supposed involvement with the CIA. While no evidence has surfaced to back up the vague charge, it is by no means farfetched. Intelligence agencies are forever sniffing around big international banks looking for information. Given Safra's zest for information-gathering, as well as his relationships to Israeli officials, it's not inconceivable that he might harbor back-channel relationships with the CIA or other Western intelligence agencies.

For its part, American Express is in no position to criticize any intelligence ties Safra might or might not have. More than one of its own executives are rumored to have CIA ties. Bob Smith, for one, freely admits contact with the agency. "The CIA came in and interviewed me," he told me one day over lunch at a Manhattan oyster bar. "They said, 'You travel a lot, you see a lot, if you have anything interesting, will you call us?' I said, 'Sure.'" Smith insists he never had occasion to follow up on his pledge.

Nor are American Express's hands spotlessly clean when it comes to matters of money laundering. In April 1989 the company's senior executive in France was arrested at Paris's Charles de Gaulle Airport and indicted on charges of laundering money for an international cocaine-smuggling ring.

By mid-1991 Safra had had enough. Not only were the continuing stories a major distraction; after two years of stewing he had grown obsessed with the man he believed had personally authorized the campaign against him, yet had never been brought to justice: Jim Robinson. The only one as determined as Safra to expose Robinson was Weiner, who continued to spend much of his time supervising detectives in investigations of Greco and the continuing articles. The two wanted nothing less than Robinson's resignation and public humiliation. That summer, as preparations began for Safra's fourth and final libel proceeding, against the Swiss magazine *L'Hebdo*, they decided to make their move.*

More trouble with Edmond Safra was the last thing Jim Robinson needed in 1991. Though the American Express board had reportedly warned him against any further missteps following the settlement with Safra, no one had seriously expected him to be ousted, largely because he remained in firm control of his board, which was largely populated by old friends like the former RJR Nabisco chief Ross Johnson.

Over the intervening two years, however, speculation about Robinson's future had steadily increased as American Express was shaken by one disaster after another. In early 1990 Shearson, for instance, was rocked by huge losses, forcing Robinson into a costly bailout that prompted American Express to post a quarterly loss of $620 million, the largest in its history; Peter Cohen was forced to resign and, deeply embittered, he hired the nettlesome Stanley Arkin to negotiate his severance package. At the same time, Robinson formally recognized the failure to incorporate TDB into the American Express family by selling it to a Swiss company for $1 billion, rejecting a similar bid by Safra. American Express p.r. people hailed the price as nearly twice TDB's 1983 price tag, but Safra's people were convinced American Express had somehow used accounting magic to inflate its profit.

By the fall of 1991 a nationwide recession had begun to take its toll on the company's core operations, cutting profits in the charge-card businesses that many onlookers had thought were immune to economic

---

*Safra's woes do not extend to his banks. In Geneva, Safra Republic reached $6 billion in deposits in 1991. In New York, Republic, eschewing such 1980s-style vogues as LBOs and bridge loans, entered the 1990s as perhaps the single strongest major American bank; a Salomon Brothers research report calls its overall performance "second to none."

woes. Meanwhile, merchants in Boston launched a public revolt against the high rates American Express charged them, prompting new waves of stinging publicity. Then came the flash flood of red ink at Optima, once the brightest star on American Express's horizon. Optima's losses caused the company's main TRS division to post the first loss in its history.

As American Express stock slid, Wall Street analysts for the first time began openly questioning Robinson's ability to run the company. After the Optima debacle, *Business Week* wrote of "a yawning credibility gap" in American Express's executive suite. Among themselves, reporters began speaking of a Robinson "death watch," speculating how long the chairman could hold onto his job. Robinson and his wife Linda lowered their social profile, keeping their heads down against the threat of more unfavorable publicity.*

Safra quietly resurfaced that July, his first feelers reaching out via Weiner to Henry Kissinger, who sat on the American Express board, and who encouraged them to call Robinson. Safra followed up with an August 1 letter to Robinson, in which he asked for help in gathering information about Greco and Cantor's activities that could be used in the *L'Hebdo* trial; among other things, Safra's lawyers were searching for something to tie American Express to the three Lima wire reports the magazine had written of. But that explanation masked Safra's underlying agenda, which was to flush out embarrassing details that would increase the pressure on Robinson to resign.

The settlement "should have been the end of a sordid chapter," Safra wrote Robinson, his anger thinly concealed. "Perhaps you think it was. But I regret to tell you that, two years later, I must continue to deal with the widespread consequences of that defamation campaign." Audaciously asking Robinson to disclose information from American Express's files, Safra wrote: "Please understand now the need to take this further step to help end the terrible damage the Amex campaign continues to inflict."

Several days later Robinson replied with a gracious note, suggesting

---

*There are indications that the view of Safra as a master criminal remains alive and well within certain quarters of American Express. In July 1991, company spokesman Larry Armour informed me of speculation that an upcoming magazine piece on Safra would, by breaking news about illegalities inside Safra's banks, "blow the lid off this whole thing." When the piece appeared, it contained nothing approaching such a bombshell. In fact the writer, Diane Goldner, noted that two American Express associates had suggested she call both Jean-Claude Buffle and another reporter suspicious of Safra, probably Philippe Mottaz.

Safra contact Arthur Liman for the help he sought. And for a week or two, in meetings and correspondence with Safra's lawyer Alan Levine, Liman was cordial and agreeable, actually offering to make available Cantor and Freeman as well as to share new information on their activities. But within weeks the dialogue collapsed in a series of minor squabbles and foot-dragging. Asked to sign an affidavit affirming his description of some of Greco's activities, for instance, Liman refused, saying the document was inaccurate but repeatedly declining to say how.

Then, on October 8, as Safra and his aides continued to debate what to do about American Express, a new crisis in Brazil diverted their attentions. A little-known legislator named Aldo Rebelo, a member of the Communist Party of Brazil, stood up in the country's chamber of deputies and suddenly denounced Safra as a drug trafficker. His evidence: passages on Safra deleted from a Brazilian translation of the Swiss politician Jean Ziegler's book on money laundering. Unaware that the sections on Safra had been ordered cut by a French court, Rebelo called for an investigation of Safra and how he had managed to alter Ziegler's work.

Weiner was immediately dispatched to Brazil, where he picked up suggestions that more was afoot than a single misinformed congressman. The expatriate Argentine journalist Juan Gasparini, an admirer of both Ziegler and L'Hebdo's Jean-Claude Buffle, had reportedly been seen in Brazil and was said to have met with Rebelo. Weiner's operatives, meanwhile, tailed the congressman on a trip to neighboring Uruguay, where he met with another member of the "Safra-as-druglord" school, the journalist Samuel Blixen. Weiner came to the conclusion that L'Hebdo journalists, working with Gasparini and Blixen, were behind Rebelo's call for an investigation. Weiner believed Buffle was attempting to provoke an official probe that could be cited as evidence of Safra's guilt in the upcoming trial.

Despite an intense campaign by Joseph Safra's people to educate legislators about his brother's problems with the press, Congressman Rebelo would not be swayed. On November 8, a week before the L'Hebdo trial, he again denounced Safra's drug ties, quoting both Buffle and Blixen. In the end, however, the Safras won out. A week later, the investigations committee of the Brazilian congress, having studied Safra's arguments, announced it would launch no investigation.

Even as he awaited the outcome of the fracas in Brazil, Safra shuffled through a desultory drizzle to join two dozen spectators crammed into a tiny hearing chamber deep within Geneva's hulking, two-hundred-year-old courthouse to attend the *L'Hebdo* trial. He was in a foul mood, not only because of the gauntlet of flashing cameras and television crews he was forced to run, but because American Express had failed to come through with anything usable against *L'Hebdo*.

Sitting beside his lawyers, Safra watched balefully as Buffle, an intense Swiss, presented his evidence. Addressing the panel of three judges himself, the reporter began by dramatically producing a set of binders that, he said, held "the fruits of fourteen months of international investigative work" in six countries. His evidence, Buffle announced, was more than "ample" to prove Edmond Safra's crimes. "Everyone with a big name in money laundering," he charged, "uses Safra's banks."

In the unstructured style of the Swiss courts, Safra's black-robed lawyer, a dashing figure with flowing silver hair named Marc Bonnant, quickly leaped forward and engaged Buffle and his two attorneys in a spirited four-hour debate. Interrupting the reporter at every opportunity, Bonnant took relish in trumping several of his key arguments. When Buffle told of a Republic account in Luxembourg seized as evidence against Colombian drug baron Pablo Escobar, Bonnant unfurled an American judge's order explaining that it had been a mistake, that the account had nothing to do with Escobar or drug money at all. When Buffle charged that Republic's Uruguayan branch had been used by the Medellín cartel in a money-laundering case, Bonnant introduced evidence that it had been Republic that had exposed the scheme to the DEA in the first place.

The trial's emotional climax came when Buffle, under Bonnant's intense questioning, acknowledged using the three dispatches that had emanated from Peru on January 17, 1989. First Bonnant maneuvered the reporter into saying that yes, he had relied on the IPS story.

"It is...a fake!" Bonnant announced with a dramatic flourish.

The stunned courtroom was still murmuring when Bonnant brought out the Associated Press article to which Buffle had also referred. Yes, Buffle acknowledged, he had read and referred to it as well.

"It is...a fake!" Bonnant proclaimed once more.

Buffle's two lawyers were sweating noticeably by the time Bonnant took out the third dispatch, from Prensa Latina, and announced, as everyone now expected, "It too is a fake!"

Soon Buffle seemed to be backtracking to more defensible ground. Yes, he told the judges, he had taken materials from *Minute* despite warnings from Safra's Swiss lawyers that its stories were false. No, he said, he couldn't prove that Safra was personally involved in money laundering. No, he couldn't prove that Safra knew of any wrongdoing. "But Mr. Safra should have known," he insisted. "Their verification procedures are rather loose."

Safra's witnesses took the stand the next morning. The long-retired American narcotics agent who had written the 1957 letter was brought in to say the whole episode was a case of mistaken identity that he deeply regretted. The executive director of the IPS newswire in Rome testified that the dispatch from Lima had never been transmitted by his agency, and was by all indications a forgery. An American banking consultant Republic had hired, Charles Morley, testified to the strength of the bank's controls against drug money. Shown the DEA report on Shakarchi Trading that mentioned Safra and Republic, Morley shrugged it off as next to meaningless, a routine survey of intelligence taken from DEA files that may or may not have proven accurate. "These DEA files, I should point out, even contain the name of our Vice President, Dan Quayle," Morley quipped.

At day's end a hush fell over the courtroom as Safra's final witness, his friend the Nobel laureate and Holocaust historian Elie Wiesel, stepped into the courtroom. News of Wiesel's scheduled appearance had made headlines in Geneva that week. Outside, a chill, drizzly Swiss twilight was slowly passing into night as the famed writer sat before the judges.

It was the first hour of the Jewish Sabbath, Wiesel noted. "I should have respected the Sabbath," he said, "but to save the life of a man, it is permitted to transgress. And the honor of Edmond Safra, that is his life." As reporters scribbled furiously into their notepads, Wiesel described the day he had met Safra in Poland, "at a place called Auschwitz, where we walked together on the ground of death," in a demonstration where thousands paid tribute to those who had perished at the Nazi death camp. They had cried together that day, Wiesel said, as they walked beneath the leaden Polish skies. Later, on a visit to Cannes, he had dined with the Safras, where they spoke once more of their persecutions as Jews. "Again we cried," he said. "It was the beginning of an important friendship. For me Edmond is like the brother I never had."

Elie Wiesel's voice was the only sound in the courtroom as he described his reactions upon reading the stinging press about his friend. "When I read in certain journals what Edmond Safra is accused of, I wanted to cry, because these are terrible accusations, the worst of accusations. I am sworn in here, and I say that it is impossible that this man whom I have chosen as a friend to be the man described in these articles.... What has been said is inconceivable to me. That's not the friend I know. That's not the friend that's part of my inner landscape."

Wiesel concluded by speaking simply of the ordeal Safra had endured. "I saw him suffering," Wiesel said. "Every time we spoke, I saw him keep quiet, and his silence was a sad sound. After all, what remains of a man after his death? Not his money. It is his name, his reputation, his honor."

There was a long moment of silence as Elie Wiesel finished. The three judges sat at rapt attention, as did the assembled reporters and spectators. At his lawyers' table, Edmond Safra's heavy, tortoise-like eyes stared forward, expressionless.

Few were surprised when the verdict, issued several weeks later, was a ringing victory for Safra. The Swiss judges found Buffle to have acted "irresponsibly and incautiously," fined him five-thousand Swiss francs and, because state prosecutors had joined in Safra's complaint, gave him a suspended ten-day prison sentence. *L'Hebdo* was ordered to print notice of the judgment in fifteen newspapers. Though the verdict prompted an outburst from the Geneva Press Association, which warned that it would curtail investigative journalism, some Swiss newspapers seemed to retreat from their previously unconditional support of *L'Hebdo's* reporting. "Edmond Safra's honor has been saved," wrote one.

But Safra refused to end his campaign against those he believed had wronged him. Even before the *L'Hebdo* verdict was announced, he launched his harshest attack yet against Jim Robinson. In a December 2 letter to the embattled American Express chairman—but pointedly carbon-copied to all Robinson's directors—Safra dropped all pretense of diplomacy, openly suggesting that American Express's internal investigation of the affair had been "a cover-up," imploring the board to reexamine its findings, and charging that the defamation campaign had never, in effect, ended. "Your withholding of information [for the trial] is an unforgivable manifestation of a continuing effort to cause harm to me, my family and my banks," he wrote. "It is clear by what is going on that the despicable effects of the American Express campaign have not been stopped."

Then, in the form of several questions, Safra made a thinly veiled threat to reopen the case, perhaps to examine the possibility that Greco had slipped misleading information on his activities into government files. In addition to the FBI's Bern letter, Safra had come to suspect that the detective might also have poisoned files in France, Switzerland, Italy and perhaps Argentina.

Did [the] special committee [Safra wrote] limit its "investigation" in 1989 to establishing reporting lines (as your counsel recently informed ours) rather than conducting a thorough inquiry into the nature and extent of the campaign, the activities employed, and any possible individual or corporate responsibilities— civil or criminal?

If that "investigation" was so limited, could it be regarded as an attempt to whitewash or cover-up?

Who might be protected by a cover-up or whitewash?...

Were there actually two campaigns—the one involving the media, publicly referred to by the July 1989 letter, and another (information about which came only recently to our attention) to corrupt and falsify official records of several governments, in some cases using forged documents?

And finally, are you and American Express better off, in the long run, to remove any shroud of secrecy or to keep facts from the public? Only by making all the information available will the truth come out so that I can defend myself and my institutions from continuing attacks.

You say the matter is closed. Closed? For whom? Certainly not for us! And if not for us, it cannot be closed for American Express....

Safra's letter succeeded in finally ruffling Jim Robinson's feathers. In his December 16 reply, Robinson assailed the suggestion of a cover-up as "outrageous" and added: "Your other allegations are equally preposterous." American Express, he insisted, could not be held accountable for continuing articles it didn't directly plant. "American Express does not control the international press," Robinson wrote.

And there the matter lay, as Safra pondered whether to sue Robinson over the second "campaign"—the possible poisoning of government files—or perhaps take the case to a U.S. Attorney to seek prosecution. Walter Weiner, meanwhile, continued to pursue stealthier avenues.

Through mutual friends he had begun floating messages, alternately threatening and conciliatory, to Susan Cantor in a long-shot hope that Cantor might crack and provide evidence of Robinson's culpability.

His efforts were fruitless. American Express, in fact, has managed to keep Cantor under tight wraps for almost three years now. She refused to cooperate with my reporting for this book and, after the *Journal* article was published, attacked it as "malicious" in a brief phone conversation. She remains an executive at American Express Bank, although associates say she often stays out of the office for long periods and is shunned by some.

"My impression is, she's been put on ice at the bank," Harry Freeman told me in September 1991. "[She's been told] if she talks to anyone in the media, she can pack her bags. She's told me that. I told her, 'Susan, you have two choices, if you want to stay at the bank and make a lot of money, you follow instructions. Or you leave and write a book. You can't have it both ways.'" Since his resignation, Freeman insists, he and Cantor have spoken little about their days probing Safra. "I talk with her," he says. "[All she says is], 'What should I do? What should I do? My life is ruined. My life is ruined. My life is over. What should I do?'"*

Like Cantor, a number of those caught up in the Safra affair have not fared well in its wake. In the spring of 1989, months before the scandal broke, Bob Smith resigned from American Express under pressure after company auditors questioned a number of his expenses, including a bank check he had used—and repaid—to buy an antique car. Smith retired to a home on Lake Winnipesaukee, New Hampshire, and was replaced by his longtime No. 2, Bob Savage, who himself was replaced in 1991. Many of the executives who crossed paths with Cantor have also left the company. Paul Knight retired in September 1991 and settled in Chapel Hill, North Carolina. Jim McGrath, who works as a security consultant, and Hob Miller, who is retired, live in suburban New Jersey. Bob Terrier heads a large Swiss trading company. Larry Ricciardi accepted a job as general counsel for RJR Nabisco in New York, where he reports to Lou Gerstner, who left American Express in 1989 to take the helm at RJR.

---

*Susan Cantor's lone communication with the author in the last fifteen months was a February 6, 1992, letter from her lawyers, which advised that "Ms. Cantor has instructed us to vigorously pursue all of her legal remedies in the event your book damages her in any way at all."

Among those in the Safra camp, Tom Sheer found work as an executive for W. R. Grace in Boca Raton, Florida. Sandra Sutherland recovered from her mysterious malady, which was diagnosed as an intestinal yeast infection, and continues detective work alongside her husband Jack Palladino and their operatives Matthew Wolinsky and Jennifer Taylor. Stanley Arkin still represents Safra and a string of other high-profile clients, most recently including Alan Fiers, a CIA man implicated in the Iran-Contra scandal. Gershon Kekst and Robert Siegfried continue their work as Wall Street spin doctors.

Of those outsiders caught up in events, Jean Roberto of *Minute* was last seen writing for a Parisian real-estate newsletter. Maya Jurt took a yearlong sabbatical before recently returning to reporting. Sy Hersh's most recent book, *The Samson Option*, an examination of the Israeli nuclear program, was published in 1991 to critical acclaim. Philippe Mottaz remains the Washington bureau chief for a Swiss television network, where he maintains an avid interest in Edmond Safra. Peter Samuel lost his job when the *New York City Tribune* folded; today he attempts to free-lance articles on environmental issues while servicing vending machines in suburban Maryland. Cody Shearer, whose column was dropped by North American Syndicate, was recently cited in *Newsweek* as one of two journalists to have interviewed a prison inmate who claimed to have sold drugs to Vice President Dan Quayle.

Victor Tirado, meanwhile, claims to have lost out on a job at the Organization of American States after the story of his "honorarium" was first reported in *The Wall Street Journal*. "I'm penniless," he complained to me in October 1991. "I'm walking the streets. I live [in Maryland] with my daughter, who cleans houses." Tirado said he lives in fear of retribution from Tony Greco. "He has taken me down to Little Italy before; I see how he kisses the old guys there, just like in the movies," Tirado says. "He knows the Mafia very well. These people put contracts out on people. Believe me, I'm scared."

By the fall of 1991, however, Greco was in no position to do harm to Victor Tirado, or anyone else. That April a squad of Spanish policemen crept through the streets of a resort town south of Barcelona, where they surrounded a small villa surrounded by greenery. As they approached, a man emerged from the front door with a packed suitcase and presented the surprised policemen with his wrists for handcuffing. "It's about time," Tony Greco said. "I was waiting for you."

• • •

I had been pondering the best way to approach Greco for months when in June 1991 I heard the rumor: a former American Express executive called to say Greco had been arrested in Spain, and was at that moment locked in a prison outside Madrid. A normally dependable source checked out the story and reported that the man being held was a different Greco. I had almost forgotten the matter when the American Express man called back to add more details: Greco's wife, Joanne, was said to be frantically telephoning old handlers like Paul Knight, Phil Manuel, and the ex-FBI agent, Alfred LaManna to pressure Spanish authorities into releasing her husband.

By August, through the yeoman efforts of Jim Sutton, a well-connected law-enforcement expert at the University of Chicago, I confirmed that Greco was in fact being held at a prison near Guadalajara, northeast of Madrid. Sutton graciously dispatched a Spanish associate to the prison for me. I heard that both Walter Weiner and one of the class-action lawyers suing American Express had also sent emissaries in hopes of debriefing Greco.

Spanish authorities refused to say why the detective was being held. Not until September did news filter back that the matter related to his old friend, the Florida money launderer Andy Iglesias. This was interesting news, for by the summer of 1991 Iglesias was at the center of a major international scandal. Arrested in Madrid that spring, he had landed in a Spanish jail, where he tantalized authorities by promising to name names in exchange for leniency. And the names Andy Iglesias named, in an interview with the Spanish magazine *Cambio 16*, were stunning: the in-laws of the president of Argentina, Carlos Menem. Members of Menem's family, Iglesias charged, had helped him and others smuggle drug profits belonging to Colombia's Medellín Cartel into Uruguayan banks. The allegations received coverage around the world and briefly threatened to bring down the Argentine government.

They also threatened to bring down Greco, for among the other stories Iglesias told Spanish police was the alleged watches-for-cocaine deal he had attempted with the Italian in 1983. He also claimed that Greco had bought cocaine from Ramon Puentes for European distribution as late as 1986.

But Greco's problems weren't limited to Andy Iglesias. A Spanish drug dealer under arrest in a related case had also named him as a conduit for Colombian cocaine finding its way into Spain; the trafficker's charges had been reported in June 1990 in a Spanish magazine I had seen in Peru. As if that weren't bad enough, a new book published in Madrid on the Italian Mafia's activities in Spain named Greco as an associate of the Neapolitan Mafia, terming him "a low-level Mafioso who worked mostly on the Mediterranean coast of Spain between Barcelona and Valencia."

When I arrived in Madrid in the fall of 1991 in a vain attempt to see him, Greco's situation seemed dire. A Spanish judge refused to allow visitors other than family and lawyers, although Safra detectives lurking around the prison noticed a beautiful dark-haired woman who paid him regular visits. Greco was said to be held in solitary confinement, probably because he had been identified in the Spanish press as a police informant following his arrest. By all accounts his wife's efforts to free him were making little headway. She had hired a Washington attorney, who was filing Freedom of Information Act requests with U.S. law-enforcement agencies to gather proof that Greco was a valued informant. "I don't think anybody—the FBI, anybody—is willing to help him now," Irwin Robbins, the Florida detective, told me. "I think he gave 'em a couple bad tips. Some of 'em had to do with Safra. They sort of hate wild-goose chases. It leaves a bad taste in their mouths."

Then, a week before Christmas, drug-related charges were announced against more than thirty targets in the Menem investigation, including the Argentine president's sister-in-law, her former husband and, in a footnote overlooked by the world press, a little-known Italian named Giuseppe Antonio Greco. Greco's subsequent release on bail set off a scramble among those who wanted to hear his version of the Safra investigation. He was said to be disenchanted with American Express, and Walter Weiner, for one, was certain he was poised to hand over a "smoking gun" on Robinson. I had kept up my own efforts to contact him, passing a list of questions through his Washington attorney; I later heard that Greco used this list, which included references to his work for the IRS and other agencies, to argue for bail.

Still, I was surprised one Sunday afternoon in January to find a message on my office answering machine from a Mr. Greco. When I telephoned the Barcelona-area number he had left, I heard the heavily accented voice of the man whose life I had spent eighteen months researching. Greco was polite, apologizing for the reception on his cellular phone. "I'm out in the garden, by the tennis court," he explained.

After agreeing to see me in Barcelona—he knew all about my research—Greco proclaimed his innocence of all charges the Spanish courts had levied against him. "All this is a fake charge," he said. "I have evidence that Mr. Iglesias is lying. The truth will come out, believe me."

But neither I nor Walter Weiner was the first to reach Greco. A lawyer believed to be working for Melvyn I. Weiss, one of the New York attorneys pursuing litigation against American Express, had that pleasure, meeting Greco on January 20 in Barcelona. Weiner was said to have arrived in Spain at almost the same time; Greco had instructed me to call a day later. No one, however, came away pleased. By one account, Greco teased the shareholder lawyer with promises of major revelations. "Believe me, I can give you what you want," Greco reportedly said.

The problem, it soon became apparent, was that Tony Greco gave nothing away free. The asking price for his "revelations," he is said to have hinted, began at $1 million. Both the shareholder lawyer and Weiner returned to New York in defeat. Several days later I got through to Greco, who apologized but said he wouldn't be able to meet with me. Clearly I wouldn't pay money, much less $1 million, for his story, and Greco was canny enough to realize he would never get anything from Safra or the shareholder attorneys if he poured out his story to me gratis. "It is not important what people read about me," he said. "For me the best defense is to just be quiet. It is not to attack. I cannot defend myself."

He did, however, agree to talk about his pre-Safra career, rambling on for more than an hour about unspecified work he had performed for the CIA, about meeting the pope, about investigating international figures like Michele Sindona, about detective work he had done for everyone from IBM to the World Bank. And though he resisted all my attempts to solicit his story of the investigation, his anger toward Safra was apparent.

"Mr. Safra is the one who put me in prison for eight months," Greco insisted. "He wants to screw me every way he can. Why? I didn't try to hurt him. I was hired to investigate him. It was nothing personal." While working for American Express, Greco claimed, Safra's men had offered him money to end his investigation. "They tried to buy me," he said. "Somebody came to me and said, 'Is two million dollars enough for you to stop?' But I told him, no money can buy [me]." Greco, however, offered no more evidence to back up this claim than any other he made about Safra.

Over the course of several conversations Greco remained courteous and calm, which made his remarks during our final conversation all the more unsettling. Recently, he said, he had begun a new investigation—of me. "I know a lot of things about you," he said matter-of-factly. "I have a picture of you in front of me now. I know what you look like. If you make suggestions about me in your book that are a lie, then I will have to respond, with information about you. I know about things you did when you went to college, about people you had sex with, about things you like sexually, about things you did when you first went to work. I will have to publish these things."

An ending to Tony Greco's long, twisted story has yet to be written, but a number of his former handlers fear it won't be a happy one. He has been publicly identified as a police informant not only by *The Wall Street Journal* but by several Spanish publications. In January 1992 Sandra Sutherland called me from San Francisco to pass on a tip she had received from a New Jersey private detective: New York's Genovese crime family, it was said, had issued a contract on Greco's life. No explanation for the rumor was forthcoming, but given Greco's history of Mob associations and his status as a publicly identified informant, it's not hard to imagine one.

But if Tony Greco lives today in fear, he apparently shows no signs of it. Because publicity over the Safra affair has all but forced him out of the investigative field, he is said to be opening a restaurant in Barcelona, where, while awaiting trial on Spanish drug charges, he can regale visitors to this summer's Olympics with tales of foreign intrigue and a peculiar man named Edmond Safra.

What lessons, if any, can be drawn from the story of American Express and Edmond Safra? One might as well ask what lessons are to be drawn from the Hatfields and McCoys. The American Express–Safra feud was born of a clash in corporate cultures that both sides could have foreseen. Nine years later it has mushroomed into a pointless test of wills that will end only with the downfall of Safra or Robinson, if then. On the facts alone, the case is about as significant as two bullies grappling on a cement playground.

More notable is the tactic American Express operatives employed, the media smear campaign. Such campaigns, whether run in the corporate, political, or religious worlds, are by themselves nothing new. Statesmen and military leaders since Sun Tzu have used deception and lies to deceive their opponents. The Nixon White House spread false reports on Democratic rivals in the early 1970s. Even the televangelist Jimmy Swaggart allegedly circulated rumors about a rival's alleged sexual escapades that ended the man's career. In the business world, the basic act of a smear campaign—bad-mouthing an adversary—is as rooted in practice as every widget salesman's daily pitch: "I can do it better than the other guy."

How common are full-fledged, premeditated corporate smear campaigns? Probably not too common, though they're far from unknown. Perhaps the most publicized such affair in recent years involved two families of warring Sephardic Jews, the Nakashes and the Marcianos, owners, respectively, of Jordache and Guess jeans. For most of the 1980s the two archrivals exchanged fusillades of lawsuits, maneuvered small armies of lawyers and private detectives—including Stanley Arkin, Jules Kroll, and Palladino & Sutherland—and even took turns siccing journalists, prosecutors, the IRS, and congressional committees on each other. For sheer vitriol, it was the nastiest corporate fight of the decade.

At a lower level, one suspects such tactics are increasingly common. Today, private detectives like Kroll and Palladino are routinely hired in every major corporate lawsuit, takeover contest, and proxy fight. Supervised by lawyers like Arkin, they are euphemistically referred to as "litigation support," and their main purpose is to dig up dirt on the client's adversary. That dirt, much as that sought by Jim Robinson and Harry Freeman, is rarely intended for internal consumption. First and foremost, it is for blackmail—scaring off the adversary. If that doesn't work, the dirt find its way into legal briefs or news columns.

This process is often accompanied by a certain amount of glee by the participants. I remember one major corporate raider several years ago slapping down a legal document on the table before me in his Fifth Avenue office. "Kroll's people found that for me in a little country courthouse in Virginia," he said with obvious relish. I saw that the document referred to a divorce case in which the raider's opponent, the chief executive of the company he had targeted, had been named a corespondent. "Can you believe that?" the raider said. "Guy was porking his secretary! I can't wait to see his face when we throw that in front of him."

"Dirt" dug by corporate detectives, of course, is only one brand of information regularly offered to journalists. What Harry Freeman and Susan Cantor and Tony Greco did, in fact, was simply an egregious example of something that goes on in the American press every day. Rare is the week that goes by—the day, sometimes even the hour—that an individual journalist doesn't receive a tip from a confidential source. And every source, whether it's a talky congressional aide, a Wall Street short seller, a private detective, a disgruntled former executive, or a Susan Cantor peddling rumors on a competitor, has a motive for telling his story.

In that light, journalists are often asked how they avoid being used. The answer is they don't. The journalist's job is not to ascertain the source's motive, though it's good to be aware of it, but to confirm the truth of the story that's being offered. If Woodward and Bernstein, for instance, were handed evidence of Nixon's guilt, it simply wouldn't matter whether it came from a political rival, a private eye, or a government prosecutor. All that mattered was whether it was the truth.

What made the American Express effort possible were international reporters willing to print even the most scurrilous rumors without basic attempts at confirmation. Sadly, the state of world journalism isn't likely to improve anytime soon. The better question might be this: could such a campaign have succeeded in the United States? One would like to believe it couldn't. Certainly top journalists like Sy Hersh and Jeff Gerth, when confronted by the American Express whisper campaign, knew enough to avoid it. But by no means all U.S. journalists are as scrupulous as Hersh and Gerth. What if American Express had gone to the *National Enquirer* instead of *Minute*? Would other, more respected publications have taken notice and reprinted the charges? It's difficult to say they wouldn't, given the progress of allegations against the Democratic presidential contender Bill Clinton that began in a supermarket tabloid.

These are ruminations, of course, that neither Jim Robinson nor Edmond Safra, consumed with their own challenges, have probably given much thought to. In the late winter of 1992 pressure was building weekly on Robinson; a February cover story in *Institutional Investor* noted that many on Wall Street were "howling" for his resignation. Visitors to his office spoke of how tired and haggard Robinson looked, how the drumbeat of corporate embarrassments and negative reviews seemed to be finally taking a toll on the chairman's traditionally seamless façade.

Watching with satisfaction from Geneva and midtown Manhattan, Safra and Weiner weren't inclined to idly await news of Robinson's fate. Instead they busied themselves plotting their next strike, perhaps a new, harsher letter to the American Express board. In the angry rhetoric that coursed through their strategy sessions, it was possible to glimpse ironic similarities to the paranoia about Safra that enveloped American Express headquarters in the mid-1980s. The vendetta, it seems, has now swung full bore. Now it is Safra who schemes and plots revenge; now it is Safra who looks for ways to humiliate and topple Robinson. Witnessing it all, one can only hope that Safra and his aides have learned a cautionary lesson from the tale of American Express and the perils of corporate zeal.

Acknowledgments

This book would not have been possible without the encouragement and help of my colleagues at *The Wall Street Journal.*

For the opportunity to report and write it I owe thanks to Norman Pearlstine, Paul Steiger and Byron E. Calame, the *Journal's* three top editors, who each urged me to pursue the original story and later offered regular encouragement on the book.

On so many occasions *Journal* reporters and editors put aside their own important work to throw me a badly needed hand: thanks especially to Tim Carrington in London; Matt Moffett in Mexico City; Phil Revzin and Christy Hobart in Paris; Carlta Vitzthum in Madrid; Jonathan Cavanaugh and family in Lima; Tom Kamm in Rio de Janeiro; Peter Truell in Washington; and Jim Stewart, Dan Hertzberg, Jeff Trachtenberg, Mike Connor, Steve Adler, George Anders, Elyse Tanouye, and Bruce Levy in New York. Thanks, too, to Roger Ricklefs and Roger Lowenstein, whose language skills helped save hours of international telephone calls.

A number of interpreters and researchers were of great assistance, especially Miriam Ramos, as able a translator and guide as one is likely to find in Lima; Carolina Keller in Buenos Aires; Carmen Ferreira in Rio; Maria Luisa Santos in Madrid; and André Marling in Geneva. Also, Jim Sutton at the University of Chicago unselfishly volunteered to do me great favors in navigating the labyrinth of Spanish law enforcement.

Several fellow journalists were also of considerable help. Chris Byron at *New York* magazine, Sam Dillon of the *Miami Herald*, and Susan Feeney at the *Dallas Morning News* offered valuable tips, as did Jonathan Kwitny and Mike Smith. Jeff Leen at the *Miami Herald* was a patient guide through south Florida law-enforcement circles. Manuel Cerdan at *Cambio 16* in Madrid unlocked a number of doors. And for all her help I can never adequately thank Maya Jurt in Geneva; her patience, integrity, and professionalism were invaluable.

I sometimes think medals should be cast for those long-suffering friends who read an author's unfinished manuscripts. I'm grateful for the advice and guidance offered by my *Journal* colleague Steve Swartz, and by John Helyar, whose partnership I sorely missed. In these litigious times lawyers are often a journalist's best friend, and Dick Tofel was certainly one of mine, saving me from myself on numerous occasions.

For all his counsel, and for his keen sixth sense of the publishing world, I am indebted to my agent, Andrew Wylie, and to his colleagues Deborah Karl, Sarah Chalfant, and Bridget Love. At HarperCollins, Rick Kot was once again a good-humored and patient editor. Thanks also to Sheila Gillooly, Jim Fox, and especially Bill Shinker, who believed in the project from the beginning. Most of all, as always, I must reserve the final and deepest thanks for my wife, Marla Burrough, my first reader, editor, and muse, who lived through it all and kept her faith, even when mine wavered.

Notes on Sources

R oughly eighty-five to ninety percent of the information contained in this book comes from interviews conducted by the author, as well as various documents gathered over the course of the last two years. Where possible I have always attempted to conduct interviews "on the record," but a number of individuals, for various reasons, including personal security and fear of retaliation by American Express, insisted on anonymity. Four investigators who have worked undercover—two in private practice, two at the IRS—also asked that their names be changed: the altered names in the text are James Delgado, Dan Avanti, Matthew Wolinsky, and Jennifer Taylor.

Close readers of the 1990 *Wall Street Journal* article that served as the basis for *Vendetta* will notice a handful of factual differences in this more detailed account. In the *Journal* article, for instance, I reported the recollections of two former American Express security officials that Tony Greco had been an informant of Paul Knight's at the DEA; that proved to be incorrect. Knight met Greco only after leaving the DEA in 1975. Perhaps the most significant change is in the description of the events of May 24, 1989, the day Stanley Arkin's detectives succeeded in linking Greco to Cantor. The fuller version herein was made possible by interviewing several sources not previously available.

In compiling a list of published sources, I have intentionally excluded articles such as *Minute*'s that I believe to contain American Express–inspired disinformation. In the end I felt that publishing a complete bibliography, which would contain a number of essentially misleading articles, was not only a disservice to the truth, but might hinder Edmond Safra's campaign to clear his name.

As for more reliable books and articles, I found a number of published accounts of American Express, Safra, and other subjects helpful, including:

"The Gilded Lily," *Women's Wear Daily*, August 6, 1988, and *Women's Wear* publisher John Fairchild's book, *Chic Savages* (Simon & Schuster, 1989). The description of Safra's party in Chapter 1 was taken from these two items and from recollections of several participants.

Aleppo Chronicles, by Joseph A. D. Sutton (Thayer-Jacoby, 1988), and *Magic Carpet: Aleppo-in-Flatbush*, by Joseph A. D. Sutton (Thayer-Jacoby, 1979). These books contain excellent descriptions of Jewish life in old Aleppo.

The Other Jews: The Sephardim Today, by Daniel J. Elazar (Basic Books, 1989). A helpful source for describing Sephardic customs and communities.

"The Secret World of Edmond Safra," *Institutional Investor*, May 1979. Cary Reich's excellent article remains perhaps the definitive profile of Safra. I have borrowed from it liberally.

American Express: The Unofficial History of the People Who Built the Great Financial Empire, by Peter Z. Grossman (Crown Publishers, 1987). I am heavily indebted to Grossman's outstanding corporate history for passages on American Express's past.

Two of the best articles on Jim Robinson remain "Do You Know Me? An Intimate Profile of Jim Robinson, CEO of American Express," *Business Week*, January 25, 1988, and "Undoing the Eighties," *The New Yorker*, July 23, 1990.

A number of articles described relations between Safra and American Express. These include:

"American Express Still Trying to Integrate Safra's TDB," *The Wall Street Journal*, December 1, 1983.

"The Mystery Man American Express Is Banking On," *Fortune*, December 12, 1983.

"Inside the Safra–American Express Divorce," *Institutional Investor*, April 1985.

"American Express Thrives on Diversity," *Los Angeles Times*, June 30, 1985

"AEB Adapts to Life Without Safra," *Euromoney*, July 1985.

"Financier Safra Targets Europe for Expansion," *The Wall Street Journal*, August 26, 1985.

"Safra Seeks His Revenge," *Euromoney*, February 1988 (cover story).

The description of the "baby parts" rumor in Chapter 13 was taken from two articles:

"Rumor of Baby Parts for Sale in U.S. Hits Mexico," *Sacramento Bee*, September 25, 1990, and "Nailing Disinformation: The Slum-Child Tale," *Washington Post*, August 26, 1988.

The only other feature-length analysis of the Safra affair published in the United States was "Bank Shot," *New York*, September 18, 1989.

Corporations' growing use of internal inquiries is described in "Firms Faulted for 'Independent' Inquiries," *The Wall Street Journal*, June 14, 1989.

The history of Swiss banking is described in *Safety in Numbers: The Mysterious World of Swiss Banking* by Nicholas Faith (Hamish Hamilton, 1982) and in *Those Swiss Money Men* by Ray Vicker (Scribner, 1973).

Index